# THE

# KOREA

## GUIDEBOOK

### *1990 Edition*

A Comprehensive Guide
to the
Republic of Korea

KYUNG CHO CHUNG, principal author, is an educator, linguist, writer, and world traveler. Educated at Waseda University in Tokyo, Seoul National University, Columbia University, and New York University, he has made Korea his special field of research and has returned to Korea numerous times. In his writings, Dr. Chung has consistently called for dialogues between North and South Korea in order to achieve eventual reunification of divided Korea. He is the author of KOREA TOMORROW; NEW KOREA: and KOREA: THE THIRD REPUBLIC (all published by Macmillan); and articles on "Korean Unification" in *The New York Times* and "Seoul" in the *Encyclopedia Americana*. Dr. Chung has received Outstanding Achievement and Distinguished Service awards; has been honored with Doctor of Literature and Doctor of Law degrees; and is listed in WHO'S WHO IN ASIA, WHO'S WHO IN AMERICA, and WHO'S WHO IN THE WORLD.

PHYLLIS G. HAFFNER has degrees in International Affairs from Mount Holyoke College, Oxford University (where she was a Fulbright Scholar), and the Fletcher School of Law and Diplomacy. She has taught political science, economics, and international politics for many years. Her specialty in Soviet-American relations led to an interest in Korea as more than just a pivot of great-power conflict. In addition, as a teacher of yoga, she has deeply researched Eastern philosophy and culture. An experienced world traveler, Ms. Haffner recently has made two trips to Korea.

FREDRIC M. KAPLAN is founder and publisher of Eurasia Press. A specialist on contemporary Asia, he is co-author of the annual CHINA GUIDEBOOK, ENCYCLOPEDIA OF CHINA TODAY (M.E. Sharpe and Eurasia Press, 1989) and the JAL GUIDE TO THE PEOPLE'S REPUBLIC OF CHINA, and is a former member of the National Board of Directors of US-China Peoples Friendship Association. Mr. Kaplan is director of the China Book Club and Far East Book Society and president of China Passage, Inc., which organizes specialized and "adventure" tours to China and Asia. During the past decade, Mr. Kaplan has visited Asia on over 80 occasions, including several sojourns in Korea.

# THE
# KOREA
# GUIDEBOOK

*1990 Edition*

Kyung Cho Chung
Phyllis G. Haffner/Fredric M. Kaplan

PERENNIAL LIBRARY

HARPER & ROW, PUBLISHERS, INC.
New York

EURASIA PRESS
Teaneck, New Jersey

Dedicated
to those who rendered great service
in the cause of
international understanding and reunification of
Korea

---

Third Edition (1989), 1989
**FOURTH EDITION (1989), 1990**
First Printing

\*

Typography by V&M Computer Graphics, Inc., Genesis Typography, Inc.,
and Logic Communications, Inc. Text set in Goudy Old Style.
Cartography by David J. Hildebrand, Genesis Typography, Inc.
Korean typography by Visual House International.
Color and black & white photographs supplied by
Korea National Tourism Corporation, Seoul, Korea.

\*

Produced by Eurasia Press, 168 State Street, Teaneck, NJ 07666-3516

---

Library of Congress Catalog Card Number 89-659506

ISBN 0-06-096456-1

90  91  92  93  10  9  8  7  6  5  4  3  2  1

# CONTENTS

# 6
## CONTENTS

# 7
## CONTENTS

## V ■ DOING BUSINESS WITH KOREA

## DOING BUSINESS IN KOREA: A SPECIAL REPORT
### By Trenholme J. Griffin / 178

# 8
## CONTENTS

# 9
## CONTENTS

## PERSONAL STRATEGIES FOR BUSINESS SUCCESS IN KOREA
### By S.H. Jang / 237

## TEN COMMANDMENTS FOR DOING BUSINESS IN KOREA / 243

## VI ■ FOR TRAVELERS WITH SPECIAL INTERESTS

## VII ■ THE KOREA TOUR: CITIES AND SITES

# 11
## CONTENTS

## 12
### CONTENTS

## CONTENTS

## VIII ■ APPENDIX

## KOREAN LANGUAGE GUIDE

## TOURIST DIRECTORY

# LIST OF MAPS

# PREFACE

Korea is rapidly becoming a major world tourist destination, and it is drawing an increasing number of tourists from around the globe.

It is nearly 30 years since my *Korea Tomorrow* was published, almost 20 years since the appearance of my *New Korea*, and about 10 years since the publication of my *Korea: The Third Republic*. In these books, while presenting a comprehensive survey of Korea's history, culture, economy, and political structures, I also drew a picture of the Korean people—their aspirations, their hopes, their desire to perpetuate liberty and to achieve economic progress and the reunification of their country.

The Korean question is no longer merely an historical and political puzzle, a military or economic conundrum. The phrase, indeed, must be changed to the plural: "questions about Korea." How has the Republic of Korea managed to achieve so startling an economic recovery? What is the country like now? Who are the Koreans? From what background and cultural tradition do they spring? How do they live today? What are the prospects for the restoration of the historical unity of this divided nation?

Why not go to Korea to see for yourself? Are you thinking of a pleasant journey, of combining a pleasure with a business trip to Korea, or of an exciting trip to the site of the 24th Olympics in Seoul? If so, congratulations! You will enjoy relaxing fun, attentive service, and complete comfort while you are in Korea, one of the most vibrant countries in the world.

In the following pages of *The Korea Guidebook*, you can take a fresh look at the country and its people. See what Korea has to offer—a fresh image yet to be presented to the world audience. Eye-opening, stimulating—that's Korea today. Discover one of the world's modern economic miracles while sightseeing in one of the world's oldest civilizations. This timely book provides concise, detailed answers to your questions about Korea; it is simultaneously a comprehensive introduction to many aspects of the country and a practical source of information so that you can make the most of your time and money on an exciting and enjoyable trip to the Land of the Morning Calm. Bon Voyage!

*Kyung Cho Chung*

Carmel, California
December 10, 1989

16

# ACKNOWLEDGMENTS

16

This guidebook has benefited from the encouragement and cooperation of more persons than I can list here.

First, I wish to acknowledge my collaborators, Mr. Fredric M. Kaplan and Ms. Phyllis G. Haffner, for their valuable advice and editorial assistance in the preparation of this guidebook. Important updating and revisions were provided by the Seoul staff of *Travel Trade Journal*.

Among friends and colleagues who gave encouragement to the project, I want to thank Dr. Sang Hyup Kim, chairman of the Korean Red Cross Association and former prime minister, Republic of Korea (ROK), for urging me to write this book.

For their kind assistance and generous cooperation, I am particularly grateful to President Roh Taewoo, ROK; Dr. Il Kwon Chung, former prime minister, ROK; President Choong Kun Cho (KAL); Chairman Pyong Do Min (KCTC); Chairman Sang Hong Kim (Samyang Group); President Dae Don Ha, Vice-President Zohng-chill Kim, Mr. Yang Hee Lee, and Mr. Kwang Hee Lee (Korean National Tourism Corporation — KNTC); Vice-President Sang Ho Cho (Seoul Olympic Organizing Committee); Dr. Jon Carter Covell, writer; Mr. Edward B. Adams, author; Dr. Kuk Bom Shin, chief secretary to the president for Education, Cultural Affairs, and Public Information; Dr. Seung Kook Lew, president, Academy of Korean Studies; Ms. Sue Ja Bae, manager, Korea Branch, Royal Asiatic Society; Mr. Kwang Sook Kim, Cultural Affairs director, International Cultural Society of Korea; President Hern Soo Ryu and Director In Ho Kim, Samhwa Printing Company; Mr. Toshiji Isaka, managing director, Hotel Lotte; Mr. William R. MacHarrie, U.S. Government; Attorney Hong Kwan Kim (Seoul); and Attorney Paul F. Douglass (Washington, DC).

At Eurasia Press, invaluable assistance in preparation of the Third Edition was received from Oscar Bernal, Editorial Coordinator; Debra E. Soled, Managing Editor; and Jenny Gibbs, copyeditor. We are indebted also for research assistance provided by Mr. Kim Soon Min.

Factual materials in *The Korea Guidebook* were derived from the *New York Times*, London *Times*, *Time*, *Newsweek*, *Far Eastern Economic Review Yearbook*, the *All-Asia Guide*, *Asian Survey*, *Korea Annual*, *Korea Herald*, *Business Korea*, and *Korea Times*; the United Nations, United States government, and Republic of Korea publications—especially materials produced by the Korea National Tourism Corporation (KNTC), Korea Overseas Information Service, and the Seoul Olympic Organizing Committee.

The bibliography cites the sources of material referred to in the text and is also a useful list "for further reading."

K.C.C.

# INTRODUCTION

**M**any years ago there was a flourishing Asian kingdom called by its people *Chosun* (also spelled Choson), which means, literally, "Land of the Morning Calm." Europeans knew this kingdom as Korea, a name derived from the Koryo Kingdom (918–1392). The name Chosun suggests an exotic, peaceful Shangri-la, far from the turbulent stream of civilization. This lovely country, with its Blue Diamond Mountains and picturesque temples, was in fact quite remote and relatively quiet.

Known as the "Hermit Kingdom," Korea was isolated from outside influence for many centuries. But in modern times the struggle for supremacy over Korea, waged by China, Japan, and Russia, resulted in two wars: the Sino-Japanese War of 1894–95 and the Russo-Japanese War of 1904–05. These wars culminated in the Japanese military occupation of Korea in 1905, which was followed by outright annexation in 1910, when Korea lost her national independence. Until it surrendered to the Allied forces on August 14, 1945, Japan had exercised complete dominion over the social, economic, and political life of the Korean people.

Korea had expected to regain her independence in 1918, when Woodrow Wilson's Fourteen Points gave promise of self-determination for small nations. Twenty-five years later, on December 1, 1943, the Cairo Declaration that "in due course Korea shall become free and independent" was made by the wartime leaders of the United States, the United Kingdom, and China; this was affirmed at Potsdam on July 26, 1945; and was subscribed to by the Soviet Union on August 8, 1945, when it declared war on Japan. Immediately after its liberation on August 15, 1945, Korea loomed large as a potential trouble spot in the Far East.

For purposes of the military operations of the occupying powers, Korea was divided north and south of latitude 38 into Soviet and American areas, respectively. The line of demarcation was intended to be temporary, and only to fix responsibility between the United States and the Soviet Union for implementing the terms of the Japanese surrender. What turned into the prolonged division of the country has resulted in unhappy consequences for the Korean people. Postwar political confusion in the rival occupation zones produced critical problems impossible to resolve. Upon their liberation from the Japanese, the Korean people had great hopes for complete independence. Great efforts were made to eliminate the arbitrary division of the country. The problem was taken up at international conferences, but a satisfactory agreement could not be reached. Few nations have suffered so much from foreign influence as has unhappy Korea, squeezed into partition by conflicting great-power interests.

The division along the 38th parallel created two states out of areas which had been closely integrated and interdependent. Two governments adopting divergent ideologies claimed sovereignty over the entire country. These governments followed the policies of their respective sponsors and became dependent on them for aid and protection. Long a victim of Japanese domination, Korea became a battleground where the smoldering antagonisms between the Soviet-sponsored regime to the north and the American-supported Republic of Korea (ROK) burst into open military conflict. Now, more than 30 years after the armistice that concluded that war, Korea is far from being a united nation. But the Republic of Korea is a thriving country, a veritable economic miracle. Its hardworking and fun-loving people eagerly hosted the 24th Olympic Games.

The Koreans have always been hospitable people. Aided by the international prestige of having hosted the 24th Olympiad with a $3 billion-investment, they are again reaching out to the world. Some 10,000 Koreans volunteered their services during the Olympics and, in effect, virtually every Korean served as a tour guide. Now, following the successful staging of the Olympics, Korea has become an acknowledged gold-medal winner in a world-class effort. Once again the Korean people are poised to welcome their new-found friends from around the globe.

K.C.C.

# Chapter I
# KOREA
# AT A GLANCE

**KOREAN PENINSULA
Provincial Boundaries**

DMZ

Kangwon do

Kyungki do

Chungchon
Pukdo

Chungchon
Namdo

Kyongsang
Pukdo

Chulla
Pukdo

Kyongsang
Namdo

Chulla
Namdo

# KOREA'S PEOPLE

A nation's future lies in the character and traditions of its people. Koreans are the descendants of a Mongoloid race and tend to be taller and more robust than most other Orientals. They have ruddy complexions and hazel eyes and are readily distinguishable from their Chinese and Japanese neighbors. Forged of a long tradition, Koreans are a homogeneous people, speaking one language and adhering to a single culture—a blending of Confucianism, Buddhism, Shamanism, and Western ideas—rich in dance, music, and the arts. They are extroverted, active, and fun-loving and noted for their qualities of diligence, perseverance, patriotism, and social cohesion. They are generous, friendly, hospitable, and individualistic, with a strong sense of humor. Filial piety toward parents and ancestors, love and modesty toward family, and respect for others are virtues revered by all Koreans.

"Land of Courtesy in the East" (Tongbang Yei-Ji-Kuk) and "White-Clothing People" (Paekui Minjok)—these appelations reflect the politeness of the Koreans and the white clothing they often wore. Their peace-loving nature is evidenced in such ordinary greetings as Hello: "May you come in peace"; Goodbye: "May you go in peace"; and Good night: "May you sleep in peace."

When Koreans meet, the junior bows lower than the senior or superior. Given names in Korea are not used as readily as they are in the West. The most common Korean surnames are Kim and Lee; and the total number of family names is fewer than three hundred. The family name (usually single word) comes first, followed by the given name (usually double word), for example, Chung Kyungcho.

## POPULATION

The population of South Korea is homogeneous; with the exception of U.S. armed forces (41,000 in 1988), approximately 50,000 Chinese, and a small but growing number of foreign businesses and missionary residents, all the inhabitants are Koreans. Korea has a total population of 70 million—an estimated 42 million in the South and an estimated 30 million in the North. Korea's most abundant resource is a growing working-age population, with 60 percent under the age of 25 years.

Korea ranks eleventh among the nations of the world in population size, and fourth in terms of density per square mile. The

most densely populated areas are the coastlines and the adjacent plains. The population used to be chiefly rural, but now with increased urbanization the farm population accounts for only 28 percent of the total. Approximately 40 percent of these live in small villages adjacent to their fields.

Cities have grown remarkably in the South. This urbanization is characterized by the dominance of Seoul over the life of the nation. Nearly 25 percent of the population lives in the capital city, which is the center of government, industry, education, and culture. Nearly 56 percent of the population of South Korea is centered in the nation's 36 cities and the four metropolitan areas of Seoul, Pusan, Taegu, and Inchon. Impressive gains in rural development and the designation of industrial estates outside of the capital area, however, have helped to balance the attractiveness of Seoul; the numerous satellite towns being built on its outskirts are enforcing this trend.

**Growth Rates.** Since the Korean War, the population has been increasing at the rate of 1.75 percent per year. The proportion of women to men, 103 to 100, places the total excess of females over males at nearly one-third of a million. Not surprisingly, this proportion of women to men increased during the course of the Korean War. Programs for more adequate diet and improved facilities for medical care, sanitation, and hospitalization caused the population to increase rapidly. In recent years, however, owing to a successful family planning program, increased urbanization, a higher standard of living, and a trend toward later marriages, the rate of population growth has been declining.

The increase in population has necessitated a corresponding increase in the number of Koreans emigrating to foreign countries. At least one-tenth of all Koreans are now living in other countries. More than 100,000 Koreans are living in the United States, half a million in Japan, half a million in China (mostly in northeast China, formerly Manchuria), and a quarter of a million in the Soviet Union (southeastern Siberia).

**Minority Groups.** Approximately 50,000 Chinese live in Korea; some 70 percent of this group are males engaged in small business enterprises and laborers who came to Korea to work. They remain segregated in their own neighborhoods, with their own schools, clubs, and social diversions. Many have established successful trading companies for trade between Korea and China. Since the liberation from Japan in 1945, the number of missionary residents from the U.S., England, France, and Canada has increased. There has also been an increase in the number of Japanese and Western businessmen and technicians in South Korea, and the number of Americans there has been increasing significantly since the Korean War. Every year, more than two million foreign tourists visit South Korea. Meanwhile, the number of Chinese and Russian residents has increased in North Korea.

Historical experience and the rigors of modern life have made Koreans highly competitive and disciplined; they rank near the top in national productivity ratings. The "new order," a gradual fusion of Western civilization and traditional heritage, has created one of the world's most rapidly progressing nations. With the old and the new existing side by side and with a renewed confidence and pride, an increasingly successful harmonizing of the best traditional and modern values is meeting the needs of today's Koreans.

## URBAN LIFESTYLES

Urban life is characterized by an exuberance born of the rapid progress and change the country is experiencing; the meeting of the modern and the traditional, the search for methods of achieving economic development, the renaissance of the arts, and the vibrance of people competing, playing, and going about their daily lives.

*Village rooftop tiling*

In Seoul, the capital city, men and women in traditional dress mix with those in the latest Western styles. Royal palaces nestle among bustling luxury hotels and tall office buildings. Ancient gates are reminders of bygone eras. Large markets, small shops, and department stores supply everything from the most sophisticated electronic gadgets to the most mundane daily necessities. Night clubs and theaters provide a variety of entertainment, and restaurants serve food that ranges from the ordinary to the exotic. Automobiles, most of them Korean-made, are everywhere, and the downtown area is congested with traffic. Rows of high-rise apartments house workers who have streamed into the capital to work in the factories and the growing middle class of managers, entrepreneurs, and other professionals.

With the impact of Western culture, much of Korea's traditional way of life is on the wane. However, many aspects of the Korean social character—such as the respect for one's elders, the significant family role of the eldest son, and the trust between friends—are still preserved in time-honored fashion. Even the home, despite the presence of air-conditioning, television sets, and other amenities, retains a traditional Korean ambience. Heavy tiled roofs curved upward at the corners are still the rule, and most modern homes are equipped with an electric or steam version of the centuries-old *ondol*—under-the-floor brick flues carrying heat from the kitchen stove throughout the house. Korean living is still relatively relaxed and low-key, with mobile cushions and mats being preferred to Western-style furniture.

Korean men and women are not so conservative in fashion. But even in the cities many older Korean women still prefer to wear the traditional costume of a long, full skirt and a short jacket, instead of the trendy Western apparel favored by most younger women. Young men are partial to Western business suits, but many elderly gentlemen still don traditional male garments—a vest, pantaloons, and a natty white straw hat with a black band.

By far the greatest change has taken place among people in the cities, where the dynamic elements of the society are found. Traditionally home-bound, young Korean men and women are now beginning to assert their independence. While most industry is concentrated in the urban centers, and manufacturing and foreign trade, which are centered there, are the most vigorous sectors of the Korean economy, a great improvement in living conditions is evident throughout the land, albeit to a lesser extent in rural areas.

## RURAL LIFESTYLES

Korea's farmers have in general supported changes that have led to higher incomes and living standards. The New Community Movement (*Saemaul Undong*) was launched in 1971 to improve economic conditions in rural Korea as well as to achieve a balanced development of agriculture and industry. It has promoted agricultural modernization—mechanization, scientific farming—and the elevation of cultural and social standards of the rural population. National consciousness and a spirit of diligence, self-help, and mutual cooperation have been fostered among the people.

The New Community Movement has contributed to cooperative attitudes and sound management of rural community life, including maintaining order, helping less-privileged neighbors, clearing villages, saving energy, and encouraging friendship with neighboring communities. This movement has made significant progress in eliminating rural poverty and in improving the economic well-being of the rural people. In fact, the income of the average rural household has surpassed that of the average blue-collar family. The New Community Movement model has been introduced to many developing nations throughout the world.

Like farmers and fishermen everywhere, those in Korea follow a seasonal pattern of preparation, planting, cultivation, and harvesting, but their methods have become highly mechanized, freeing

*Harvesting rice*

them to participate in home and community improvement projects as well as to enjoy the benefits of a more productive and enriched rural life.

# KOREA'S GEOGRAPHY

Owing to its geographical location, Korea is one of the world's most strategic areas. Bordered by Soviet Siberia on the north, China to the west, and Japan by water to the east, it has been both a bridge and a buffer between these powerful neighbors. This location places Korea in a pivotal position with regard to East Asian affairs and presents problems to those powers wanting to control its policies. The land is rich in mineral resources; the surrounding seas abound with a variety of fish; the climate is temperate. The rural landscape is beautiful with its blooming orchards and green, rice-planted fields.

Korea consists of a long, S-shaped peninsula projecting about 600 miles southeastward from the continent of Asia and includes about 200 islands, the largest of which is Cheju off the east coast. The entire country, including the offshore islands, covers a land area of 85,256 square miles and thus is slightly smaller than Great Britain. South Korea (38,031 square miles) and North Korea (45,768 square miles) are separated by a 2.5-mile-wide demilitarized zone (487 square miles), which divides the country at roughly the 38th parallel. It is 600 miles in length from west to east and 1.35 miles wide at its narrowest point. The coastline is about 6,000 miles long.

The peninsula is washed on the east by the Eastern Sea (Sea of Japan), on the west by the Yellow Sea, and on the south by the Strait of Korea. To the north it is separated from Manchuria and Siberia by the Yalu River (Aplok-kang) and the Tuman River, both of which have their headwaters at and flow in opposite directions from Whitehead Mountain (Paektu-san).

The east coast of Korea is steep and rock-bound and the deep water has a tidal rise and fall of one to two feet. The indented coastline posseses few good natural harbors other than Wonsan and Chungjin, where the tidal rise and fall ranges from 20 to 36 feet. At Chinnampo and Inchon there is a maximum difference of 29 feet between low and high tides, after the Bay of Fundy the greatest tidal movement in the world. Kunsan and Mokpo are the best natural harbors on the west coast; the low south coast has a variation of 20 or more feet in the tidal rise and fall, and the

_Mt. Sorak san_

islands and inlets along the shore help to form several other good harbors, notably Pusan.

**Physical Features.** Korea is a transition area between the con-tinental forms of Manchuria and north China and the island forms of Japan. It has widely diverse landscapes and an unusual richness and variety of plant growth. The peninsula is notable for its great age, being composed mainly of Archean rock. Physiographically, the country is mountainous. The Taeback (Ever White) mountain range lies in the northern part of the peninsula, with a maximum elevation of 9,000 feet. Lying near the eastern coast, the Taeback Mountains form the backbone and watershed of the peninsula. Although few are very high, their profusion is an impressive sight. The southwest comprises excellent farmland and is considered the granary of Korea.

Around and between Korea's mountain ranges lie discrete low-lands formed by river valleys and sea terraces. Large tracts of lowland lie near the seashores. In the mountain areas, low plains are found almost exclusively in central and southern Korea. These are expanded river valleys or nearly closed intermountain valleys. The largest lowlands are in the western part of the country, along the shore of the Yellow Sea. Some of the lowlands, such as that of the Taedong River (Pyongyang) and that of the Han River (Seoul) have comparatively even or slightly undulating surfaces. The lowlands comprise the most extensively cultivated areas in Korea.

## SEAS AND RIVERS

The Eastern Sea is deep, accommodating large ships all along Korea's east coast. The warm waters of the Japan Current flow along Korea's eastern shore and forestall freezing temperatures dur-ing the winter. The coast is mountainous and fairly regular, and its waters are rich with fish, sea animals, and sea plants of many varieties. The Korean Strait connects the Eastern Sea with the East China and Yellow Seas. It is approximately 34 miles wide and, while not as deep as the Eastern Sea, it can accommodate large ocean-going vessels. The shoreline of the strait is rugged, forming many peninsulas, capes, gulfs, and bays.

The Yellow Sea is shallow off the coast, and its floor abounds with sandbanks which hamper sea traffic. Wide areas of the coast and the lower reaches of the rivers, to about 30 miles above their deltas, are flooded with salt water. High tides provide an important

*Chonjiyon Waterfall, Sogwipo, Cheju Island*

potential source of energy. The sea is subject to seasonal changes of currents, and its waters sometimes freeze along the shores of northern and central Korea. The western seaboard, like the southern, is rugged, with many bays and gulfs.

Korea has many rivers. In the mountains, streams of varying size rush swiftly and noisily over steeply sloping stony beds which are strewn with boulders and cliff splinters, forming numerous rapids and waterfalls. At lower altitudes, some flow more gently through fertile plains, and several are navigable in their lower reaches. Rivers of the western and southern slopes of the mountain country in the Yalu River region have many rapids and tumultuous currents which produce an abundance of hydroenergy: large, modern power plants and primitive rice milling technologies exist side by side.

The terrain of western Korea is marked by large, meandering rivers and rich alluvial plains. Most important of these rivers are the Yalu, the Taedong, and the Han, all of which flow into the Yellow Sea Basin. The Yalu River (491 miles long and averaging 175 yards wide) rises on the southern slopes of Paektu Mountain, flows in a southwesterly direction along the border of Manchuria, and empties into the West Korean Gulf at the port of Yongampo. The Yalu is a significant source of hydroelectric power. The

Taedong River (247 miles long and averaging 329 yards wide) plays an important role in navigation. It rises in the southern slopes of the Yalu mountain country and, after absorbing a number of mountain tributaries, enters the plain as a wide and full-watered river. The Han River (292 miles long) originates on the western slopes of the Taeback Mountains and crosses almost the entire peninsula; it is navigable for more than 180 miles upstream from its mouth.

The only river of significance on Korea's east coast is the Tuman (324 miles along and averaging 329 yards wide), which originates on the eastern slopes of Whitehead Mountain. It flows through a deep and narrow valley between the mountains of North Korea and eastern Manchuria into the Eastern Sea at the border of the Soviet Union. The largest river on Korea's southern shore is the Nakdong (326 miles long); it flows down the southwestern slope of the Taeback Mountains, through a deep valley in the mountains of eastern Korea, and into the Korean Strait in the southeastern part of the peninsula.

## CLIMATE

The climate of Korea is more continental than oceanic, although the country is bounded by the sea on three sides. The continental climate is more pronounced in the north, while the ocean's influence is more apparent in the south. Two crops ripen each year in South Korea. Korea's climate is greatly affected by its many mountains. The east coast is warmer than the west coast because it is sheltered by mountains from the immediate impact of the winter winds. The climate is considered healthful, comparing favorably with that of the East Coast of the United States.

The temperate Korean climate is characterized by extremes of cold and heat; the phenomenon of frequent short bursts of mild weather are commonly described as "three cold and four warm." The coldest month is January; the hottest months are July and August. The average temperature in summer is 70° F., and in winter, 33° F., occasionally dropping to zero. Characteristic seasonal contrasts are shown by the extremes at Seoul, where the highest temperature is over 100° F. and the lowest is 10° F. These extremes are greater in the north and in the interior than in the south or along the coast. Both spring and autumn are short but delightful seasons.

Average annual rainfall is about 40 inches. There is little precipitation except during the rainy season, which comes in July and August. Sunlight is strong and abundant, and because the air is very dry, evaporation is great. The direction of the prevailing winds remains virtually constant, that is, northwesterly in winter and southerly in summer. Korea is fortunate in being outside the track of typhoons.

The winter monsoon does not cause a sharp drop in temperature because the air warms as it passes over the Yellow Sea. During January the winds of the winter monsoon reach their greatest force; in February and March the weather grows warmer everywhere, and the air becomes more moist. Spring is a time of sunny weather, alternating winds, and slight precipitation. In April the average monthly temperature rises to 50° F. in the north and to 54° F. in the south. May is Korea's sunniest and most pleasant month.

Summer comes in June. By that time the country is in the grip of the summer monsoon, but the winds are still quite moderate. In July the monsoon increases sharply, and the entire country is dominated by strong sea winds, which bring cloudy weather. July is especially cloudy and rainy, and hot weather prevails throughout the country. The temperature may reach 104° F., but the average holds at 68° to 70° F. In August the average temperature is 70° to 72°F. and the humidity and precipitation decrease somewhat. In September winds start blowing from a northerly direction, humidity decreases, and clear, cloudless days usher in the dry weather. This is an important season of the year for the country's economy, for this is the time when most crops are harvested.

During October the days remain sunny and dry, and crops are still being harvested and threshed. It is one of the most delightful and healthful months of the entire year. A mantle of snow covers the north by the end of December.

In short, Korea is truly a land of all seasons, each one distinct, each with its own flavor. In the spring a year is born, and the timeless cycle begins with a golden field of flowers on Cheju Island and a delicate veil of cherry blossoms that envelops the countryside from late March through May. Lush green is the color of summer in Korea—beckoning all to the great outdoors. Summer is the season when vacationers seek out the beaches, the mountains, the temples, the resorts—to escape the city heat and enjoy informal days of leisure and relaxation.

Autumn skies are blue, and the air is invigorating. The mountains are alive with brilliant yellows and vivid reds. It is the season of harvest and festival—symbolic of culmination and fulfillment.

Winter in Korea is the season of serenity after the long harvest. It is appreciated as a time to ruminate on the past year, a time of anticipation of the new year to come.

**Fauna and Flora.** The Korean tiger, traditional symbol of the nation's character, has disappeared with the encroachment of modern civilization on its native habitats, but water deer, wildcats, and wolves still roam the mountainous areas. Also, because Korea is situated along the main migration route for birds that breed in Manchuria and Siberia and winter in Japan, Southeast Asia, and Australia, some 400 bird species have been recorded. Most common are the crow, magpie, jay, heron, crane, oriole, lark, sparrow, robin, pheasant, and quail. The country also is visited annually by migratory species such as geese, ducks, teals, swans, and white egrets. Predatory fowl include the rare and large Steller's sea eagle and the white-tailed sea eagle. Domestic animals include cats, dogs, horses, oxen, sheep, and common farm animals.

Trees common to Korea include the pine, maple, oak, larch, spruce, elm, willow, juniper, alder, birch, and poplar, as well as such fruit-bearing species as the apple, pear, peach, persimmon, orange, and tangerine in the south. Nut trees include the walnut, chestnut, pine, and gingko. Vine fruits and numerous other temperate and subtropical flowering shrubs and plants also are cultivated and grow wild in all parts of the country.

One of the scenic wonders of the world, and the pride of Korea, is the famous Diamond Mountains (Kumkang-san) in the northeastern part of the country (in North Korea). This spectacular aggregation has some 12,000 peaks; the highest one, the Piro Pong, is about 6,000 feet high. The circumference of the range is about 50 miles. There are clusters of countless rocky peaks in fantastic shapes, with primeval forest vegetation below and numerous ravines and canyons through which crystal-clear waters flow amid high, grotesquely shaped rocks forming many beautiful waterfalls. In the days before Korea's unhappy division, the Diamond Mountains were a favorite attraction for tourists. They remain a symbol of the hope of the Korean people, and many tourists, that happier days will return when the country is reunited.

Koreans call their homeland *Kumsu Kangsan*, which means beautiful landscape. Koreans call the rose of Sharon, which is the national flower of Korea, *Mukung-hwa* (Everlasting Flower). As a whole, the moderate and balanced climate of Korea is unsurpassed in the Orient. For this reason, the country has been called "Land of the Morning Calm." And today, favored with beautiful natural scenery and relatively mild weather, Korea is aptly called the "Switzerland of Asia."

# KOREA'S HISTORY

**K**orea traces its origins back more than 5,000 years. Present-day Korea is a reflection of its geographical location and past heritage. Thrusting southward from the Chinese mainland, the Korean peninsula lies only 120 miles west of the islands of Japan. Because of Korea's buffer position in East Asia, it has also served as a bridge between China and Japan.

Situated at a crossroads of civilization, Korea has frequently been a battleground for major powers in their struggle for domination. Major powers have long understood that a strong military power in control of the Korean peninsula would have a strategic advantage over neighboring states. Thus, the Korean people have experienced invasion, intervention, foreign military occupation, foreign rule, war on their soil between alien armed forces, and internal struggle stimulated and kept alive politically by foreign influence.

## CHRONOLOGY OF
## KOREAN DYNASTIES AND REPUBLICS

**Ancient Korea Period—Han Korea**       2333 B.C.–313 A.D.

**Three Kingdoms Period**       37 B.C.–935 A.D.
     Koguryo (North)/37 B.C.–935 A.D.
     Paekje (Southwest)/18 B.C.–660 A.D.
     Silla (Southeast)/57 B.C.–935 A.D.

**Silla Kingdom—Unified Korea**       675

**Koryo Kingdom—Name of Korea**       935–1392
     Founder—General Wang-Gun; state religion—Buddhism
     Mongol invasion/1231–1368

**Choson (Yi) Dynasty—Choson/Land of the Morning Calm**    1392–1910
     Founder—General Yi Songgye; state religion—Confucianism
     Japanese invasion/1592–1598
     US-Korea Treaty/1882
     Sino-Japanese War/1894; Russo-Japanese War/1895

**Japanese Colony Period**       1910–45

## DIVIDED KOREA

**Divided Korea (One people—two nations)**　　　　　　**1945**
　　South Korea—Republic of Korea (ROK)
　　North Korea—Democratic People's Republic of Korea (DPROK)

### NORTH KOREA

**Russian Military Government Period**　　　　　　**1945–48**

**"Democratic People's Republic of Korea": Kim Ilsung**　　**1948**

### SOUTH KOREA

**American Military Government Period**　　　　　　**1945–48**

**First Republic of Korea**　　　　　　**1948–60**
　　President—Syngman Rhee
　　Korean War/1950–53
　　Korean students' revolution/April 19, 1960—downfall of Rhee
　　caretaker government

**Second Republic**　　　　　　**1960–61**
　　Prime Minister—Chang Myon
　　Military Coup/May 16, 1961—resignation of Chang
　　Military Government/1961–63; Head—General Park Chunghee

**Third Republic**　　　　　　**1963–79**
　　President—Park Chunghee
　　President Park assassinated by Korea CIA Chief/October 29, 1979,
　　caretaker government

**Fourth Republic**　　　　　　**1979–80**
　　President—Choi Kyuha

**Fifth Republic**　　　　　　**1980–88**
　　President—Chun Doohwan
　　Democratic Justice Party; Reunification Democratic Party

**Sixth Republic**　　　　　　**1988–93**
　　President—Roh Taewoo
　　Democratic Justice Party (ruling party)

---

During the transition from the old kingdoms to the present divided Korea, three forces have dominated Korean politics: nationalism, factionalism, and reliance upon allies. Throughout the vicissitudes of a long and unhappy history, the Korean people have maintained an unquenchable desire for self-determination and national identity as an independent nation. Korean political development has been greatly influenced by its neighbors—China, Japan, and the Soviet Union—and by the United States. A divided Korea is now enmeshed in world politics on the international frontier between East and West.

### ANCIENT KOREA (2333 B.C.-313 A.D.)

In the 25 centuries before the birth of Christ, the Korean peninsula was inhabited by various tribes and immigrants from the Mongolian plateau and the northeastern Asian continent. Many archaeological remains have shown that waves of migration began to reach the Korean peninsula during the Mesolithic era. Unable to move further southward, and bound by a common fate within the confines of a narrow peninsula, the various peoples of the Tungusic branch of the Ural-Altaic group blended to produce a homogenous culture and political legacy.

Tangun, the legendary first great ruler of Choson and held up as the guiding genius of Korean national spirit, established his capital at Pyongyang in the northern portion of the peninsula in 2333 B.C. This earliest form of government was theocratic, making no distinction between government and religion. Another great ruler of Choson was the Chinese scholar Kija, who migrated to Pyongyang in the third century B.C. The rule of the Kija dynasty ended in 194 B.C., when power was seized by Weiman, who also came to Pyongyang from China. In 108 B.C. the Chinese Han dynasty extended its power over the northern portion of the Korean peninsula, and Pyongyang became the capital of Lolang Commandery for the next 400 years. The spread of Chinese civilization through Lolang had an immense influence on the native people. The concept of a central administrative authority was adopted into the society of the early Korean people and evolved into centralized monarchies between the first and fourth centuries A.D.

### THREE KINGDOMS (37 B.C.-675 A.D.)

In the southern portion of the peninsula, the Han tribes formed their own central power structures. They were divided into three federations called the Three Hans—the Ma Han, the Chin Han, and the Pyon Han. In 57 B.C., Chin Han and Pyon Han merged to form the Kingdom of Silla. In 18 B.C., Ma Han developed into the Kingdom of Paekje. In 37 B.C., a people known as the Koguryo migrated from southern Manchuria to form a third kingdom in the north. Thus began the period of the Three Kingdoms, which is well documented from about the time of Christ.

The Kingdom of Koguryo built a strong military state and destroyed Lolang in 313 A.D., ruling at Pyongyang until 668 A.D. The administrative positions in Pyongyang were occupied by nobles and warriors directly serving the king of Koguryo. In 372 A.D.,

Buddhism reached Koguryo from China, and the Buddhist concept of obtaining happiness through the protection of the nation was quickly adopted. Confucianism was introduced to Koguryo at about the same time and was spread by means of Chinese-style colleges designed to teach the Chinese classics and the Confucian canon to the sons of the nobility.

The Kingdom of Pækje (18 B.C.?–660 A.D.) succeeded in subjugating all of the tribal states in the western part of the peninsula, but it lacked popular support and effective organization. Both the central and the regional administrative positions were held by sons of the king or members of the royal family. Consequently, Pækje, though heavily populated, was forced to ally with Silla to protect itself from Koguryo's southward thrusts into the agriculturally rich southland. Silla, not wanting Koguryo to take the lands of Pækje, united with the Chinese Tang dynasty and in turn conquered Pækje in 660 A.D., despite attempts by Japan to help the latter.

By borrowing Chinese political institutions, the Kingdom of Silla (57 B.C.–935 A.D.) gradually developed the tribal system

*The Emille Bell (771 A.D.), Kyongju Museum*

of the southern part of the peninsula into a more autocratic and bureaucratic form of government. The three-fold function of government as postulated in the Confucian theory of statecraft—to increase the people, to enrich them, and to enlighten them—became the norm. The theory of monarchy based on the virtue of the ruler was strengthened by making the distinction between the ruler and the ruled permanent. In 668 A.D., Silla again allied with the Tang empire and overthrew the Kingdom of Koguryo in the north. Thus, with Silla's hegemony extending over the entire peninsula, Korea was, for the first time in history, unified as a single nation.

## UNIFIED KOREA (675–935)

The Kingdom of Silla succeeded in driving out the Tang armies and bringing about a political union of the country, an amalgamation of all the tribes in the peninsula, which provided a basis for the development of the Korean people as a distinct nation.

After achieving unification, Silla enjoyed a period of sustained, undisturbed peace and turned from military exploits to cultural development. Silla was a kingdom in which a small aristocratic class, based on blood relationships with the king's family in Kyongju, ruled a large number of subject people.

Culturally, the Silla era was the golden age of Buddhism in Korea. A prolonged period of peace, combined with the wealth and leisure of the aristocracy, stimulated cultural achievement. The study of Chinese classical literature and Confucianism also prospered in unified Silla, leading to the establishment of the first national university in the capital. But aristocratic Silla gradually fell victim to an internal power struggle and subsequent corruption among the leaders in the nobility. The ruling class grew utterly decadent and completely ignored the welfare of the common people. A lack of discipline among government officials and the failure of crops contributed to revolts in areas remote from the capital. The dissidents grew in number and strength owing mainly to the fact that Silla's power was concentrated in the extreme southeastern part of the peninsula. Dissident elements eventually united under General Wang Kon and in 918 founded the Koryo Kingdom. In 935, the king of Silla surrendered peacefully and Korea, which had again seemed on the brink of dissolving into contending groups, remained unified as the new, vigorous Kingdom of Koryo.

## THE KINGDOM OF KORYO (935–1392)

Koryo consolidated its power by completely subjugating dissidents in the southwestern provinces and stationing a strong defensive force along the northern boundary to repel invaders. Because its capital, Songdo (Kaesung), was located in the central part of the peninsula, Koryo was in a much better strategic position than Silla in dealing with the defense of the northern frontier. The administrative system was completely restructured and farmlands were nationalized. Each farmer was given a plot of land to cultivate during his lifetime. Various social security measures were introduced, and educational facilities were greatly expanded. For its first 200 years Koryo enjoyed political stability and cultural development. The name Koryo, a shortened form of Koguryo, was itself later to evolve into the name Korea.

The founders of Koryo built strong kinship-based institutions and curbed the power of the aristocracy and local strongmen by disbanding all private armies not in the service of the state. The kings of Koryo maintained control over landholding and taxation, enforced a hostage system, and excluded the military from important positions in the central government. The governmental structure continued along the lines of the Tang Chinese system, and its officials were selected through the Confucian-oriented examination system. This merit system attracted aspirants from the previously excluded lower class and gave them the opportunity to master the Confucian canon and the Chinese classics.

At the center of the government was the Privy Council, the highest organ of the Koryo Kingdom, which assisted the king. With increasing political stability, an aristocracy of government officials evolved. Since persons aspiring to a military career were excluded from all important positions in the central government to prevent them from monopolizing governmental powers, the Koryo bureaucracy was divided into a civilian wing and a military wing. The ranking officials of these two wings formed the upper classes in Koryo society. The two wings were called *yangban* (two noble groups) to distinguish the military and civilian groups from the commoner class.

The Kingdom of Koryo officially adopted Buddhism and Buddhist thought in government in the early eleventh century, and Buddhism flourished as the national religion. Many eminent Buddhist priests were given positions as royal tutors and consultants to the state. The institution of Buddhism acquired tremendous political power with tax-exempt lands and patronage from the kings. Deci-

*Kyongbokkung Palace tower (1348 A.D.), great Koryo dynasty monument*

sions of state were influenced by monks and priests, and Buddhism attained such power that the king became a Buddhist monk in order to reign.

An outstanding cultural relic of the Kingdom of Koryo, and a significant landmark in the history of Buddhism, are the 81,258 wooden printing plates of the Tripitaka, a Buddhist scripture. Koryo's exquisite celadon ware is world-renowned for its delicacy and great beauty. Great works of architecture such as temples and stone pagodas were Buddhist-inspired.

Koryo's political stability and flourishing culture were disrupted by the gradual ascendancy of aristocrats who gained the innermost circle of the governing elite through intermarriage with the royal line. The nobility precipitated incessant court intrigue and inter-necine warfare through shifting matrimonial alliances. The political chaos at the court led to the seizure of power by the military in 1170. A group of army generals, who were dissatisfied with the system of civilian supremacy and the political prejudice against the military, launched a bloody military coup against the government, killing most ranking civilian officials. With Koryo ruled by generals and the court split among military cliques seeking to obtain the

*Chondungsa Temple (14th century), Kanghwado Island*

ruling monarch as their puppet, there was a continuous struggle for power. The government found itself defenseless against the series of foreign invasions that were to follow.

In 1231, Mongol hordes invaded Koryo by crossing the Yalu River and divided the peninsula into military districts. The invasions continued intermittently for nearly 40 years, and great suffering was inflicted upon the Korean populace. In 1270, an armistice was concluded under which the Mongolians recognized the Koryo monarchy and Koryo, in turn, became virtually a vassal state of the Great Khan. Mongolian national institutions and customs were adopted and the Koryo people were mercilessly taxed to help the Khan prepare for the attempted invasions of Japan in 1274 and 1281.

In 1368, the Kingdom of Koryo regained its freedom from Mongol domination, but the last king of this decaying dynasty was controlled by a scheming Buddhist monk who goaded him into attacking the new Ming empire of China. The king ordered his general, Yi Songgye, to lead the army to the Yalu River and from there to invade Manchuria. However, backed by a pro-Ming faction, General Yi instead succeeded in toppling the Koryo, which was on the verge of collapse owing to factional feuds and corruption. In 1392, General Yi ascended to the throne and moved his capital from Songdo to Hanyang (Seoul). The ancient name of Choson was adopted for the new kingdom, the last Korean dynasty.

## THE CHOSON DYNASTY (1392–1910)

Reflecting the reaction against the Koryo, General Yi Songgye replaced Buddhism with Confucianism, making it the moral foundation of Choson (also known as Yi) feudal society for the ensuing 500 years. Confucianism formed the basis of government and education as well as of the daily life of the Korean people. During the first 100 years of its rule, Choson was a kingdom administered by civilians who faithfully followed the Confucian principles. Scholars became prominent in government, and the valuable books they wrote have exerted a considerable influence on contemporary Korean society.

The early Choson period saw much progress in governmental administration. In the latter years, powerful administrative positions revolved around the king. Personal grudges and emotional enmities were carried down from one generation to the next, and Confucianism, which emphasized obligations to the family line, did nothing to ameliorate this. Instead, it taught that sons and

*Tomb of the great King Sejong (1419–50), inventor of rain gauge and "Hangul" alphabet, Yongnung*

grandsons should share in the quarrels of their forefathers and avenge their wrongs.

In the Choson dynasty the king ruled with the assistance of the "two noble groups," the *yangban*, most of whom formed a privileged upper class. In 1576, the royal court split into two aristocratic parties known as the East and West parties. With the inception of these two parties came centuries of intrigue and dissension that gradually sapped the strength of the government, and the social development and cultural growth of the early years was followed by foreign invasions. In 1592, the Japanese, under General Hideyoshi Toyotomi, invaded Korea as part of an ambitious plan to conquer mainland China. On land, the Koreans proved generally helpless against the Japanese army, but at sea, Korean admiral Yi Sunshin smashed the Japanese invading fleet with his tortoise-shaped warships, the world's first ironclad naval ships. In 1627, the Manchus invaded Korea and made Korea a vassal state of the Chinese Qing (Ch'ing) dynasty.

**Influences from the West.** In 1777, Catholicism was introduced into Korea from China. Since the practice of Christianity rejected certain Confucian ethics, the government violently opposed this alien religion by persecuting its adherents, among whom were many scholars. The new Western learning fell victim to the traditional forces and political factions, thereby leading the Choson dynasty down a path of decline. Despite an all-out national endeavor to consolidate the government, political and social chaos crept into the declining Choson dynasty as foreign powers vied for hegemony on the strategic Korean peninsula.

In the last quarter of the nineteenth century, factional warfare centered on the controversy over Westernization. The court remained divided by factionalism, which had come to characterize Choson politics, and the pressure of power politics thwarted any constructive effort at reform from within. The two principal rivals for the control of the court were Queen Min and the king's father, Taewon-gun. Because the government was corrupt and factions often sought support from other nations to gain control, Korea was vulnerable to Western influence.

Taewon-gun had adopted a closed-door policy, refusing commerce with the Western world. This caused Korea, known for centuries as the "hermit kingdom," to remain isolated from international entanglements. But in 1871, American naval units seized the forts on Kanghwa Island, and in 1876, Japan forced a treaty with Korea. This paved the way for the signing of similar treaties with the United States, Great Britain, Germany, Russia, and France. Korea had become a pawn of the contending powers.

In an effort to expedite Korea's modernization, the Choson government sent a group of young politicians to Japan and China with the primary purpose of bringing back to Korea knowledge of advanced institutions. It also revised the administrative structure and appointed a Japanese officer to train the Korean army. These measures resulted in a clash between the pro-Chinese conservative forces and the pro-Japanese progressive circle. A coup d'etat took place in 1884 under the leadership of the progressives, but failed after three days. Then the Tonghak Rebellion (1894) swept across the entire southern part of Korea, touching off a full-scale war between China and Japan in 1894-95.

The Japanese forces defeated the Chinese army, and an ambitious Japan further secured her influence on the Korean peninsula. (In 1898, a Japanese minister was a collaborator in the plot to murder Queen Min.) Czarist Russia, in search of ice-free ports in the Far East, extended its influence over the Korean Peninsula by obtaining several concessions from the Choson government. In 1897, the name "Choson" was changed to "Empire of the Great Han," and the Choson king was called the Reformation Emperor. But the Korean government was scarcely able to maintain itself in the vortex of foreign struggles. In 1905, Japan defeated Russia, its chief Western rival for influence in Korea, and on November

*Chojijin Fortress site, early battle place between Western and Choson forces.*

15, 1905, Japan forced Korea to accept the "Protectorate Treaty" on terms prearranged by the Japanese with the support of the United States and Britain. This treaty, which regulated Japan's control over Korea's administrative functions and foreign relations, enabled Japan to seize the paramount political, military, and economic interests in Korea. In 1910, Japan finally and entirely annexed Korea. For the first time in Korea's long history, the Korean people lost all of their national sovereignty and independence to an alien nation.

## JAPANESE COLONY (1910–1945)

Korean politics, education, business, and press were vigorously suppressed under the Japanese governor-general. The structure of the colonial government was pyramidal. At the apex of the Japanese tyranny stood the governor-general, a general or admiral who exercised nearly absolute power over administration, justice, and public safety. Japanese colonial policy called for a virtual monopoly by Japanese of higher administrative positions; Koreans were appointed only to the lower positions in the government. Japanese became the official language of the government and the courts, and the Japanese national religion, Shintoism, was favored. Through the use of spies, secret police, and the army, the Japanese governors-general were able to exercise a tight rein over political activities and to curb quickly and ruthlessly any signs of nationalistic unrest. Korea under the Japanese military government was a police state.

Korea was reshaped to provide for the needs of the Japanese economy, and it became the "rice bowl" of Japan. Natural resources necessary to complement, but not to compete with, Japanese production were developed, usually under Japanese ownership and management. Industry, transportation, and communication were built up to promote the Japanese exploitation of Korea and to support the Japanese war machine. The Korean economy was controlled by Japanese government ownership of banks, railroads, communications, and rural cooperatives. The Oriental Development Company was one of the powerful quasi-official corporations set up by the Japanese for the economic exploitation of Korea. Thus Japan dominated not only the political but also the economic life of the Korean people, transforming Korea into a Japanese colony.

**The Korean Independence Movement.** On the day Japanese rule began, the Korean independence movement also began, and it never ceased to exist as an organized movement and as a dominant spiritual force in the lives of the Korean people. While ruthless Japanese oppression stirred up strong anti-Japanese sentiments among the Koreans, U.S. president Woodrow Wilson's enunciation of "national self-determination" for oppressed peoples throughout the world encouraged the Koreans in their quest for national independence. On March 1, 1919, 33 patriotic Korean leaders demanded Korean independence, and over two million Koreans participated in peaceful independence demonstrations, which spread to every part of the country. The Japanese police arrested the leaders and ruthlessly suppressed the independence movement, crushing Korea's hope for regaining national freedom by means of appeals to the outside world.

A large number of Korean leaders fled to China and there, in Shanghai, established the provisional government of the Republic of Korea, assuming overall command of all resistance movements both at home and abroad. The devoted leaders-in-exile expanded their organized movement in Manchuria, North China, Siberia, and the United States. They also strengthened the Korean independence army that was taking shape in China. At home, the resistance movement was carried on by every segment of the Korean community, with intellectuals and students particularly active. While preparing for war in Manchuria and China, Japan toughened its colonial policy against the independence movement and intensified the military oppression of the Korean people.

When Japan started its offensive war against China in 1937, Korea was transformed into a "continental logistical base." Furthermore, Japan attempted to tap Korea's manpower for its war effort by instituting a "voluntary enlistment" system for Koreans. This system was changed to conscription in 1942, in the name of "assimilating" the Korean people into the Japanese race. The Japanese implemented the assimilation by force, to such extreme lengths as to prohibit the Koreans from speaking their own language, to force them to worship at Shinto shrines, and to change Korean names to Japanese names. Japan's colonial policy inhibited the training of Koreans in political, economic, and scientific fields and did nothing to help Korea escape from political turmoil and economic poverty.

The Japanese colonial government in Korea developed in several stages. During the decade of 1910-1920, the Japanese created the administrative machinery of control and set the pattern for colonial exploitation; in the decade of 1930-1940, the Japanese overlords built up their colony to feed their growing war machine by accelerating the rate of economic exploitation and political suppression. During the war years, Korea was turned into a virtual armed camp. The imposition of Japanese on the political life of the Korean people did not, however, radically change the basic heritage that had characterized Korea from ancient times. The Korean tendency toward factionalism allowed the Japanese colonial officials to utilize the divide-and-rule method, but Korean nationalism was strengthened by the impact of the West. The reservoir of Korean patriotism built up under the Japanese domination was ready to be tapped at the moment of liberation.

A glimmer of hope for international guarantees of Korean independence, which had faded in 1919, reappeared in the Atlantic Charter during World War II. On December 1, 1943, at the Cairo Conference, President Franklin D. Roosevelt, Prime Minister Winston Churchill, and Generalissimo Chiang Kai-shek jointly declared that "we are mindful of the enslavement of the people of Korea and are determined that in due course Korea shall become free and independent." Accordingly, Korea was set free from the status of a Japanese colony, and a bright future of freedom and independence seemed assured to the Korean people.

## KOREAN LIBERATION AND PARTITION (1945)

Korea was liberated from 35 years of Japanese domination on August 15, 1945, when Japan surrendered to the Allied forces. However, the northern part of the Korean peninsula was occupied by the Soviet army and the southern part by the United States army, with the 38th parallel serving as an arbitrary military demarcation line hastily drawn under a wartime secret agreement. This artificial division between the industrial North and the agricultural South soon hardened all phases of Korean life into two separate patterns. As Korean political problems became linked with the deteriorating relations between the United States and the Soviet Union, the Koreans of each side became alienated from each other despite the fundamental homogeneity of the Korean people. The liberation of Korea by the Allied forces did not fulfill the hopes of the Korean people for an immediate restoration of their national independence.

At the time of liberation, South Korea was a classic case of an underdeveloped country. Since all political activity had been suppressed for many years, there was no organized political authority in Korea immediately after the end of Japanese rule. In the midst of the resulting confusion there was intense political activity, and numerous political organizations came into being; from these, three groups emerged: the extreme rightists, the centrists, and the extreme leftists. An "interim government" failed to establish effective control over the chaotic situation because its leaders split into two rival rightist and leftist factions.

The leftists then formed a self-styled People's Republic of Korea, a coalition government with Dr. Syngman Rhee, who was in the United States at the time, as the figurehead president, but with leftist leaders in most of the key posts. The rightists under the conservative nationalist Kim Songsu rejected the People's Republic and formed the Korean Democratic Party. The Korean Democratic Party supported the provisional government in China, which was composed of exiled nationalist leaders of the Korean independence movement and headed by Kim Ku. By the time the American occupation forces landed in South Korea in mid-September 1945, the rightists and leftists were deadlocked.

Dr. Rhee's Society for the Rapid Realization of Independence, formed to launch a united nationalists' front to achieve independence for the country, tried to negotiate a merger with the other two rightist parties—the Korean Democratic Party of Kim Songsu and the Korean Independence Party of Kim Ku—but failed to achieve unity. The leftist parties were less clearly defined, and many moderates were associated with them off and on. The extreme left, originally the Korean Communist Party, changed its name to the South Korean Labor Party in 1946. Organized in 1925, the Korean Communist Party had been unable to establish a foothold in Korea owing to Japanese suppression and disruptive intraparty factionalism. In 1928, it was expelled from and dissolved by the Comintern and was not revived until 1945. In 1946, the Korean People's Republic organized by the leftists was dissolved by the United States military government.

## THE UNITED STATES MILITARY GOVERNMENT
### (1945–1948)

Shortly after the arrival in South Korea of U.S. armed forces from Okinawa on September 8, 1945, Lieutenant General John R. Hodge took over authority from Japanese Governor-General Abe and established the U.S. military government. The American military government did not recognize any Korean political authority and temporarily retained the existing Japanese administration to facilitate the occupation, thereby provoking intense dissatisfaction among Koreans. As the United States moved indecisively toward the institution of at least a semblance of self-government in South Korea, Koreans were placed in charge of government administration with Americans in advisory capacities. This "interpreter's government" (persons with a knowledge of English seemed to be preferred for higher positions) was gradually replaced by the interim government.

Despite a difficult language barrier and insufficient knowledge about Korea, the U.S. military government had an outstanding record in South Korea in regard to the educational system, the judiciary, and public safety. Administrative structures were established in the executive, the judiciary, and the legislative branches, and these branches assumed normal governmental responsibilities. The American occupation policy developed administrative responsibility in the Korean bureaucracy, established a semilegislative assembly to share the burden of policy-making, and suppressed the threat of a Communist revolution in South Korea. The major tasks facing the U.S. military government were to rehabilitate the Korean economy, which was suffering from the aftermath of the Pacific War, and to establish a democratic leadership.

The U.S. military government, replacing the Japanese colonial administration as the governing body in South Korea, was beset by a series of internal political and economic confusions. Because of what many Koreans described as the "vagueness" of U.S. policy in Korea and the "unfamiliarity" of American officials with Korean conditions, the military government's efforts to prepare for eventual Korean self-government were not fully appreciated by the Korean people. Nevertheless, the U.S. military government was favorably received by the conservative rightist forces.

**The Moscow Conference and Its Aftermath.** Although Korea's independence was repeatedly discussed in wartime meetings among the Allied powers, no detailed plan was formulated until the Moscow Foreign Ministers' Conference, held on December 27, 1945, by the United States, the United Kingdom, and the Soviet Union. The conference agreed that Korea would be placed under a five-year trusteeship by the big three Allied powers plus China to prepare Korea for full independence. The plan was a complete surprise to Koreans and violent demonstrations against it were staged throughout South Korea. Despite stiff opposition, U.S. and Soviet occupation authorities implemented the Moscow Agreement and formed an American-Soviet Joint Commission on Korea at Seoul in January 1946. The commission was charged with making necessary preparations for a provisional government in consultation with the political parties and social organizations in Korea. Repeatedly the commission was deadlocked in its selection of the political parties it was to consult. The second Joint Commission likewise failed to agree on which political parties should be consulted before establishing a Korean provisional government. Consequently, the two occupation forces failed to integrate the two zones for the unification of Korea.

During the American-Soviet Joint Commission sessions, the political situation in South Korea became further complicated. While the leftists stepped up their campaigns against the military government, three rightist leaders—Syngman Rhee, Kim Ku, and Kim Kyusik—disagreed among themselves. Kim Kyusik led the moderates in the nationalist camp to seek a national coalition with the leftists. Syngman Rhee and Kim Ku, on the other hand, opposed the trusteeship, and Dr. Rhee urged immediate independence and the establishment of a separate government in South Korea. In May 1947, the U.S. military government set up a South Korean interim government, with a legislative assembly comprising a coalition of 90 rightists and "middle-of-the-roaders." The final veto right was reserved for the U.S. occupation authorities, and American officials continued in their advisory capacities.

In September 1947, the United Nations General Assembly resolved that a provisional government should be formed by the Korean people themselves, and it created a special commission to expedite the establishment of such a government. A dissident group of nationalists, led by Kim Ku and Kim Kyusik, meanwhile was attempting to explore with the Communists the possibility of forming a coalition government. They visited Pyongyang in April and met there with Kim Ilsung, the Communist leader of North Korea. Their plan failed, and Kim Ku was subsequently assassinated in Seoul. In the chaotic wake of liberation, terrorism and assassination accounted for the loss of many political leaders.

The Soviet Union not only refused to discuss the establishment of a Korean government with the United Nations commission (the United Nations Temporary Korean Commission), but also refused to permit the U.N. commission to enter North Korea. Finally, the commission recommended that national elections be held in South Korea, and following acceptance of this recommendation by the U.N. General Assembly, national elections were held to form the National Assembly and to formulate a Constitution for the new nation. The single-house National Assembly convened its first session on May 31, 1948, adopted the new Constitution, and on July 24, 1948, elected Dr. Syngman Rhee as the Republic's first president.

### THE FIRST REPUBLIC (1948–1960)

On August 15, 1948, the anniversary of V-J day, and following three years of American military occupation, General Douglas MacArthur proclaimed in Seoul the passing of the Korean government from American to Korean hands. The first president of the First Republic, Dr. Syngman Rhee, accepted the authority of the new government in South Korea as the only "lawful government in Korea."

Three weeks later, on September 10, 1948, under Soviet sponsorship, the "Democratic People's Republic of Korea" was formed in North Korea, with Kim Ilsung as premier. The establishment of two separate governments, each recognized by its guardian protagonist, precluded any further direct jurisdiction either by the United States or by the Soviet Union. The two independent regimes faithfully mirrored the points of conflict of the two sponsoring

*MacArthur Statue, Free Park, Inchon*

great powers. Korea seemingly had no hope of regaining its unity peacefully while the stalemate continued and the Cold War intensified. Korea became a country divided into two parts under the rule of mutually antagonistic regimes. Each of the rival governments claimed sole right to jurisdiction over the entire nation, and the use of force was often threatened.

The withdrawal of the United States forces from South Korea and the dissolution of the American military government were completed in June 1949, but provisions were made for the continuation of American economic and military aid. The new Republic, without American aid, would have faced a North Korean army estimated at 150,000 men, trained and equipped by the Soviet Union. An enlistment program was initiated, and an American military advisory group comprising 500 officers and men assisted in training the army of the Republic of Korea (ROK).

**The Korean War.** On June 25, 1950, Korea ceased to be the "Land of the Morning Calm." The outbreak of hostilities between the North and the South brought international war in its wake. The United Nations immediately created a force to assist the ROK, branded the North Korean attack a breach of the peace, and called for a cessation of hostilities. The ROK army, together with forces from fifteen U.N. members, including the United States, commanded by General Douglas MacArthur, launched a counterattack and forced the North Korean army to retreat, pursuing it to the Yalu River on Korea's northern border with Manchuria. In November 1950, Chinese Communist troops entered the Korean War, forcing the U.N. troops southward, but the U.N. forces counterattacked anew and pushed the Communist troops into general retreat along the thirty-eighth parallel. The Soviet delegate to the United Nations proposed a cease-fire, and an armistice agreement was signed on July 27, 1953, over President Rhee's objection.

On October 1, 1953, a mutual security treaty was signed by the United States and the Republic of Korea to defend South Korean territory. In July 1954, a political conference for Korean unification was convened in Geneva, to which the U.N. member nations that had participated in the Korean War on behalf of the Republic of Korea were invited along with the Soviet Union, Communist China, and North Korea. The Geneva conference demonstrated a widespread desire for Korean unification, but no agreement was reached by the attending powers. The United Nations Commission was in turn superseded by the United Nations Commission for the Unification and Rehabilitation of Korea, whose limited operations have been confined to observing political events in South Korea and reporting to the General Assembly once a year, without making any real headway toward Korean unification. Since 1953, there have been numerous but fruitless meetings between the armistice commissions of both sides in vain attempts to bring about a settlement of the Korean issue.

During the bitter war years, the government of Syngman Rhee became increasingly dictatorial. Dr. Rhee's first step toward the imposition of one-man rule began with the formation of a dominant parliamentary group called the Liberal Party. In order to impose his will on the legislature, martial law was proclaimed—ostensibly to curb Communist guerrilla activities—and 50 assemblymen were arrested on vague charges of conspiracy. When the remainder of the legislators still opposed his proposed constitutional amendment and boycotted Assembly meetings in protest, they were arrested, forcibly taken to the Assembly hall, and under the threatening clubs of the police were compelled to pass the constitutional amendment. By force of such police-state methods, Dr. Rhee was reelected in 1952 and claimed his first mandate through popular vote.

President Rhee, advancing in age, became increasingly intolerant of criticism, and many political opponents were imprisoned. Looking ahead to a third term, Rhee's Liberal Party proposed a second constitutional amendment that would permit an indefinite number of terms in office. Again, his Liberal Party was unable to muster sufficient votes to pass the amendment, even though they openly purchased the votes of 34 legislators. When the issue came to a vote in November 1954, the amendment failed to secure the 136 votes required for passage, but the next day Rhee ordered the amendment passed, based on a new method of tabulating votes whereby, two-thirds of 203 being 135.3, the fraction .3 was to be counted as a unit, i.e., one full vote. As a consequence, Rhee lost most of his remaining popularity, even among the conservative rural population.

In September 1955, the embittered and frustrated opposition forces countered by forming a new conservative party called the Democratic Party. Popular opposition to Rhee was reflected in the May 1956 presidential elections when, although elected to a third term, he received only 55 percent of the vote. Moreover, his running mate, Yi Kipoong, was defeated by Chang Myon, the Democratic Party's vice-presidential candidate.

Uncertain about his chances of election to a fourth term in March 1960, President Rhee and his Liberal Party supporters proposed still another constitutional amendment. The new amendment would permit the election of the president by the National Assembly rather than by popular vote. In August 1959, when it became apparent that the constitutional amendment was unattainable, Rhee introduced the National Security Law, which would permit the suppression of the opposition by indicting them as Communists or subversives. Confronted with vigorous opposition in the Assembly chamber, the Liberals ordered 300 policemen to remove all uncooperative opposition members and lock them up in the basement of the Assembly building. Thus unopposed, the Liberals passed some 25 bills, including the controversial new National Security Law and the Local Autonomy Law. The new laws gave Rhee's government complete control of all political activity down to the very lowest levels.

Democratic rallies were prohibited throughout the nation, and instructions sent to every police chief by the home minister, Choe Inkyu, specified the exact plurality by which Rhee and Yi Kipoong were to be elected. Hundreds of thousands of premarked ballots accompanied the instructions, and these were dutifully stuffed into the ballot boxes on election day. The result was a foregone conclusion, and Rhee and Yi were "elected" by a majority, exactly as the home minister had directed. In protest, the Democratic Party declared the election illegal.

**The Fall of Rhee.** The Korean people did not accept the rigged election complacently. On April 19, 1960, led by massive student demonstrations and infuriated by the indiscriminate killing of student demonstrators by the police, the entire country rose up against Rhee's dictatorial administration. The April student uprising not only forced Rhee to resign and leave the country, it also drove Yi and his entire family to suicide. Although the last official act of President Rhee before his resignation was to declare a state of martial law, the military adopted an attitude of sympathetic neutrality toward the students. The martial law commander maintained order until the discredited National Assembly hastily convened and appointed an interim government headed by Huh Chung, then foreign minister.

The caretaker government prosecuted former cabinet ministers on charges of election fraud. The legislature also passed an amendment to the Constitution which made the prime minister responsible to the lower house of the national legislature and the chief executive of the government, and changed the office of the president to the largely ceremonial post of chief of state. The legislature then resigned to make way for a new national election. Owing to the Koreans' unfortunate experience of excessive one-man rule under Rhee, the caretaker government stripped the office of the president of its vast powers and entrusted most executive power to a prime minister and cabinet wholly dependent on what promised to be a parliament of many parties.

In the election of July 29, 1960, the Democratic Party was predictably victorious. Yun Posun, leader of the Old Guard faction of the party, and Dr. Chang Myon, head of its New Faction, were elected president and prime minister by the National Assembly. In the election, which was conducted honestly, the Democratic Party won a majority of seats in both the House of Representatives and the House of Councillors.

## THE SECOND REPUBLIC (1960–61)

The government formed by the New Faction of the Democratic Party on August 23, 1960, marked the beginning of the Second Republic. Chang Myon's administration restored all constitutional rights, but it disappointed the people by becoming embroiled in factional feuding over patronage and power. The ruling Democrats were again torn in two by the Old Guard faction of President Yun Posun and the New Faction of Prime Minister Chang Myon.

The executive branch of Chang's government was weak.

Cabinet members changed constantly, and corruption and nepotism soon riddled his administration. The economic situation continued to deteriorate, and unemployment rose steadily. The government sought to alleviate the tension by diverting defense expenditures to relief needs, but a projected reduction of the armed forces by 100,000 men did not materialize, owing to opposition from the military. Under Chang, South Koreans practiced popular politics on a large scale and with more vigor and intelligence than ever before. Their participation was marked by the growing exercise of individual free will and the absence of blind worship of a national hero, but they also abused some of the new freedoms and opened the doors of South Korea for subversive organizations, political confusion, and social disorder.

The failures and problems of the new government were dramatized by the press, further compounding Chang's difficulties. The number of newspapers and periodicals increased immensely, and many reporters employed by these papers tried their hand at blackmail. The weakness of the Chang government became obvious, and public dissatisfaction grew. The administration was unable to secure the cooperation of its huge majority in the legislature and to control the increasing waves of daily violent demonstrations. There was mounting popular suspicion that the new regime had already betrayed the spirit of the April 19 revolution.

Organized by the newly formed league of Pan-National University Students for National Unification, a student movement for the neutral reunification of Korea rapidly spread through schools and colleges. The South Korean students affiliated with the league wanted to hold negotiations between students of South and North Korea as a preliminary step for unifying Korea, and they proceeded with a plan to hold such negotiations at Panmunjom, the site of the signing of the armistice. Until the military stepped in to stop the students from carrying out their plan, the atmosphere was ominous, filled with intimations of another crisis.

Owing to underdeveloped party traditions and a multiplicity of party factions, the government of the Second Republic brought only instability to South Korea. With insufficient outlets for their energies and talents, the young people of the South were becoming increasingly restive. Because of meager scholarship funds, opportunities in civilian universities for talented children of lower-income families were very limited. Their only chance for higher education was generally via military schools. Thus a number of bright young officers from poor families, filled with resentment against privileged civilians and incompetent politicians, were emerging from these military schools. Advances in military technology and increasing experience in military administration since the liberation made the young officers increasingly confident of their superior power over unruly civilian elements and ready to step forward in times of crisis.

The ROK army had developed into a very strong organization, and its leaders gradually became interested in being masters rather than instruments of the civilian government. As in many underdeveloped nations, the military represented a popular cross-section of people with above-average education, trained to respect honesty and discipline and motivated by nationalism. Most of the Korean military leaders, having been trained under American auspices, had better civic, technological, and administrative training than many politicians. These officers came to be the intellectual vanguard of South Korea. Since civilian party government had failed completely, the military, with a strong, independent-minded leadership, emerged in a position of strength in South Korea. On May 16, 1961, a group of combat-seasoned junior officers, mainly from the 8th Military Class of 1948–49, successfully overthrew Chang's government in a coup d'état.

## THE MILITARY COUP AND MILITARY GOVERNMENT (1961–63)

The military coup of May 1961—conceived as early as February 1961 by a group of army officers led by Major General Park Chunghee and Lieutenant Colonel Kim Chongpil—was aimed at eliminating the alleged incompetence, corruption, and chaos which had plagued the liberal but faction-ridden Second Republic. The victorious officers immediately formed a Military Revolutionary Committee, proclaimed martial law, dissolved the national assembly and local councils, suspended party politics, and took over the executive, legislative, and judicial functions of government. On May 19, the Military Revolutionary Committee was renamed the Supreme Council for National Reconstruction of Korea. The young nationalist officers were influenced substantially by the Japanese modernization experience. Their First Five-Year Plan concentrated on three basic areas: electric power as a basis for heavy industry, public works development as a quick alleviation of hardship, and agriculture as a means of achieving food self-sufficiency. The military government's first priority was to obtain public approval, via national referendum, of major constitutional amendments. Second, it sought to make intensive preparations for the restoration of civilian government in 1963, which had been promised on August 12, 1961, by General Park, chairman of the Supreme Council.

As the period progressed, living conditions worsened and the divisive effects of factionalism became evident. Against this background, on February 27, 1963, General Park candidly admitted partial failure of the revolutionary military government and declared that he would not participate in any civilian government. There was a minor crisis in March 1963 when General Park, in a sudden reversal of his earlier position, proposed four more years of military rule in South Korea. Later, he modified his position in the face of mounting foreign and domestic pressure. The antagonism and bitterness that had served to involve the army in politics now had come to pervade and weaken it as a cohesive political organization.

Within the civilian side, the bitter conflicts which emerged in the course of negotiations for the organization of a single opposition party dealt a fatal blow to opposition politicians. Their partisan struggles in the face of their common political enemy, the soldier-politicians, cost the civilian politicians much support and sympathy among the people.

In the presidential election of October 15, 1963, General Park Chunghee of the Democratic Republican Party won by a narrow margin over Yun Posun of the Civil Rule Party. On December 17, 1963, the National Assembly formally convened and a new cabinet was formed. This marked the founding of the Third Republic.

## THE THIRD REPUBLIC (1963–1979)

The transition to the Third Republic occurred under a new leadership that was to a great extent military. The military coup leaders worked actively to establish a political party, known as the Democratic Republican Party (1963–1980), in preparation for the return of politics to the civilians, but former politicians were prohibited from engaging in organizational activities. The presidential and National Assembly elections of 1967 and 1971 were closely contested. Park won the 1967 election with about a 10 percent margin against Yun. In the 1971 election, Park narrowly defeated the New Democratic Party candidate, Kim Daejung. During that campaign, President Park promised that if he were elected for one more term, he would never again ask the people to vote for him.

Although there were numerous student demonstrations against the Park regime, particularly in 1965 when it restored diplomatic relations with Japan and in 1966 when it decided to send 45,000 combat troops to support the government of South Vietnam, the government managed to control the students without producing any casualties in their confrontations with the police.

President Park soon took additional measures to tighten his control over the country. The constitution of 1972 allowed him to succeed himself indefinitely, to appoint one-third of the National Assembly members, and to exercise emergency powers at will. The president was to be chosen by the 2,000 locally elected deputies of the supposedly nonpartisan National Conference for Unification, who were to cast their votes without debate. Students and intellectuals conducted a national campaign to revise the constitution in 1973, and in January 1974, as it gathered momentum, the president issued his first emergency decree outlawing all such campaigns. Succeeding emergency measures imposed further restrictions on political activities by other segments of society, but the harshest and most comprehensive restrictions were imposed by Emergency Measure No. 9. Issued in May 1975, this decree made it a crime to engage in opposition activities.

Kim Daejung went abroad after the election and remained there after the president declared martial law. He traveled between Japan and the United States, conducting anti-Park activities. Having concentrated all power around himself, President Park suppressed his opponents—to the extent that agents of the Korean Central Intelligence Agency (KCIA) abducted Kim from a hotel in Tokyo in August 1973, precipitating a major crisis in Japanese-Korean relations.

In August 1974, President Park narrowly avoided an assassination attempt by a Korean youth whose stray bullets killed the president's wife instead. Park became a more reclusive figure and began to rely more and more on his chief bodyguard, Cha Jichul of the Presidential Security Force. Cha became the second most powerful person in the regime.

**The Yushin Constitution.** When the United States sought rapprochement with the People's Republic of China in 1972, South Korea faced a new international security situation. In order to give President Park additional power to meet potential crises with speed, the Yushin (Revitalizing Reforms) Constitution was approved in a nationwide plebiscite. It gave extraordinary power to the president to enact emergency measures, and granted limited freedoms of speech and publication. The methods used by Park's lobbyists to gain support for these authoritarian measures in the United States Congress drew increasing attention and ultimately resulted in exposure by the U.S. press of the embarrassing "Koreagate" affair (including alleged attempts at interference with Congress) in 1977.

On the positive side, President Park led the nation onto a course of remarkable development. This period was highlighted by rapid economic advance, normalization of relations with Japan, and active expansion of diplomatic relations throughout the world. Korea successfully weathered the 1974 oil crisis, and the economy continued to grow. The New Community Movement brought increasing prosperity to both rural and urban areas. By 1976, things were looking quite hopeful for developing Korea; but dangers lurked just under the surface of events.

Trouble erupted in 1978 after President Park ran for a six-year fourth term. Widespread opposition to Park and the Yushin Constitution was growing. President Park's failure to groom a successor and to prepare the political ground accordingly aggravated the difficulty of transition. When university students in Pusan poured into the streets and clashed with police, the government declared martial law in the city. When students in Masan launched a demonstration, the army was made responsible for public order.

On October 26, 1979, the nation's most powerful figures, President Park, Cha Jichul, and KCIA Director Kim Jaekyu, met in a KCIA safehouse restaurant to discuss the Pusan situation. During the sharply divided discussion, Kim shot and killed first Cha and then Park, and other KCIA agents under orders from Kim killed four bodyguards, ending President Park's 18-year rule of the country.

## THE FOURTH REPUBLIC (1979–1980)

Following the assassination of President Park, Prime Minister Choi Kyuha became acting president, and martial law was declared. After being elected president by the National Conference for Unification (an electoral college as well as a forum for unification policy), Choi called for an early revision of the constitution and for the election of a new government. The caretaker government of President Choi was handicapped in dealing with the daunting political problems. The task of charting a new political course required a fresh mandate based on broad popular participation, but the Choi regime had no popular mandate in the eyes of the people. The constitution had been so tailored to support Park's authoritarian and self-perpetuating rule that without him it could not provide the equilibrium needed for continuity.

The ruling Democratic Republican Party elected Kim Chongpil, one of Park's most trusted lieutenants since 1961, to succeed the late president as the party leader, making him a front-runner for presidential succession. Kim disavowed presidential ambitions for the time being, stating his belief that a constitutional revision should be carried out through bipartisan cooperation with the opposition New Democratic Party.

Kim Daejung's return to political life had a predictable result—the reinvigoration of the political arena and an intense rivalry among the "three Kims": Kim Daejung, Kim Chongpil, and Kim Youngsam (the leader of the New Democratic Party). One of the Kims would have become the next president if the politics of transition had been allowed to run their course without military intervention. But that was not to be.

Repercussions of the Park assassination had by no means died away, and South Korea faced serious political, economic, and social problems. At this juncture, General Chun Doohwan, a man with leadership ability and a new vision for the future, emerged to carry out many reform measures, hoping to restore law and order and people's confidence in the government. In December, a group of junior generals under General Chun staged a coup against senior generals suspected of complicity in Park's assassination. Forty senior generals were forced to retire. The coup marked the beginning of the rise to power of a new generation of military officers, most of whom were post-1955 graduates of the Korean Military Academy.

**Martial Law.** Under Martial Law Decree No. 10, the junta banned all forms of political activity and labor strikes, imposed censorship, ordered universities and colleges closed, and prohibited criticism of former presidents or of the present one. Kim Chongpil, together with Lee Hurak and Pak Chongkyu (the former head of the Presidential Security Force) and seven other leaders of the Park era, was arrested on charges of corruption. Kim Daejung was arrested on charges of sedition, and Kim Youngsam was placed under house arrest. The National Assembly was closed as were the headquarters of the majority and minority parties. This removed from Chun's path the last of the "three Kims" who had been the leading candidates for the presidency.

Students grew restless and worried. Sometimes regarded as a major political force "without guns" (the other being the military "with guns"), university students continued to regard themselves as the political conscience of the nation—pure, spontaneous, and uncorrupted, in the tradition of the righteous student uprisings of the past. Defiance against perceived unjust authority, foreign or indigenous, had become part of the historical consciousness of the

Korean student movement. Student activism, again turned political, was expressed in demands for an immediate lifting of martial
law, speedy democratization under a new constitution, and removal
of Chun from both the Defense Security Command and the KCIA,
of which he had become acting director. But the military suppressed
the student movement.

The military takeover became overt and systematic when a
25-member Special Committee for National Security Measures was
formed; a majority of its members were military officers. A powerful,
military-dominated standing committee was chaired by Chun, who
became the most powerful man in the country.

Militant student demands for liberalization and for the ouster
of the generals from the political arena escalated steadily in the
spring of 1980. The Choi government issued stern warnings against
the student disturbances, but these were tempered by conciliatory
gestures. The generals viewed the unfolding situation with alarm,
aware that from spring into summer is the traditional season of
student discontent. In May 1980, Korean students again observed
this national custom, with intensive demonstrations against the
military coup. Demonstrations unleashed in Kwangju were violent
enough to indicate serious trouble ahead.

**The May 18 Demonstrations.** Military crackdowns touched off
student demonstrations on May 18 in Kwangju, which was a regional stronghold of Kim Daejung. News of the brutal treatment of
the students by paratroopers of the Special Forces spread quickly
throughout the city, provoking other students and townspeople to
join the demonstrators. The nine days of bloody civil uprising,
which were ended by a predawn army assault backed by tanks,
resulted in several hundred casualties. The Kwangju incident had
a chilling effect on the population.

In retrospect, the turbulent student-military confrontation in
Kwangju was a catalyst, giving the stability-and-order-conscious
generals a rationale for direct intervention in politics. Led by then
Lieutenant General Chun Doohwan, a group of military officers
cleaned out perceived sources of sociopolitical disruption. The resulting purges in the key sectors of society meant the rise of a new
generation of political actors, new ground rules for politics, and
new institutional devices to link the grass roots to the government—all under the new constitutional framework laid down by
the military in October 1980 to establish the political structure of
the Fifth Republic. General Chun stressed the need for a new
generation of leaders in South Korea, asserting that the country

required military leadership and control. To pave the way for his formal installation, General Chun was promoted to full general and received the endorsement for the presidency of the chiefs of staff and ranking commanders of the armed forces.

## THE FIFTH REPUBLIC (1981–88)

General Chun Doo Hwan, as the rising figure in the military elite, became president in succession to Choi Kyuha, who was a civilian without a power base. Choi resigned the presidency on August 16, 1980, although without bringing the Fourth Republic to an end. General Chun retired from the army and was elected president by the National Conference for Unification. A newly amended constitution, limiting the president to one seven-year term, among other liberalizing provisions, was adopted by a national referendum.

On March 3, 1981, President Chun inaugurated his term of office. The administration was streamlined and laws and regulations were simplified or eliminated. The 36-year-old curfew from midnight to 4 a.m. was lifted, and international travel restrictions were eased to permit Koreans to study, work, and travel abroad.

Inflation slowed to an annual rate of less than five percent, and the government's economic stimulus package featured drastic cuts in interest rates and taxes. The Fifth Five-Year Economic Development Plan (1982-86) projected the real GNP to grow at an average annual rate of 7.6 percent.

**President Chun and the Unification Issue.** Detente between the two superpowers, the United States and the Soviet Union, changed the mood in the international community and brought many changes in Korea. North and South Korea began a series of dialogues. The Red Cross has sought to help in reuniting families separated by the division of Korea as a humanitarian service preliminary to political reunification. But the critical reality of inter-Korean confrontation remains. Efforts continue on both sides to reconcile differences and reduce inter-Korean tensions, but so far to little avail—partly because of ingrained mutual distrust and suspicion and partly because of the linkage of the two Koreas with the converging but conflicting interests of the major powers relative to the Korean peninsula: the United States, the Soviet Union, China, and Japan. Normalization of relations between Korea and the major European and Asian Communist powers is a foreign policy goal for Korea in the late 1980s.

In 1985, President Chun renewed his proposal for a meeting with North Korea's Kim Ilsung at any time, and without conditions, to open a dialogue on the peaceful reunification of the peninsula.

He also proposed that work begin immediately to draft a constitution for a unified Korea and to negotiate a Provisional Agreement on Basic Relations between the South and the North to govern the relationship between them while the work on the constitution goes forward. The agreement would preserve the existing political and social systems of each party to the negotiations as well as their international agreements and national security arrangements. North Korea has made lukewarm responses to these initiatives. The United States and some 100 other nations endorsed this approach.

Within his administration, President Chun appointed to important positions both military men and civilians who had supported him in his rise to power, among them, Roh Taewoo, appointed president of the Democratic Justice party, as well as to the chairmanship (later advisor) of the Seoul Olympic Organizing Committee.

**Democratization and Reform.** Despite impressive economic gains in the mid-1980s, the Chun administration became increasingly mired in domestic unrest. Students and other opposition groups grew more vocal and militant in their criticism of the government's slow pace of democratization. In April 1987, President Chun announced that the process of free political debate leading up to an open election for the presidency in 1988 would be frozen. Instead, the government would revert to the indirect electoral college system of selection.

Chun's announcement inflamed the opposition, which accused the government of short-circuiting the goal of an openly elected president. The country became polarized over the issue, with antigovernment demonstrations growing in size and intensity.

Roh Taewoo, President Chun's chosen successor and leader of the government's Democratic Justice Party since February 1985, was formally nominated by his party for the presidency on June 10, 1987. Roh's nomination was viewed by the opposition as a further step by ruling powers to perpetuate their grip on the government. Demonstrators in Seoul and other cities intensified their protests.

On June 29, 1987, in a political gesture as dramatic as any that had taken place in Korea in recent memory, Roh Taewoo announced that he would personally press the government to adopt wide-reaching political reforms, including the release of political prisoners and the holding of free and open elections before the year's end. The entire country seemed swept up in the new political debate and fervor touched off by Roh's pledge of democratization, and before the summer's end, the Chung government agreed to hold an open presidential election.

## THE 1987 PRESIDENTIAL ELECTIONS

On December 15, 1987, the Republic of Korea held its first direct presidential election in 16 years. The principal candidates were Roh Taewoo, from the ruling Democratic Justice Party; Kim Daejung, the formerly imprisoned leader of the Peace and Democracy Party (who had participated in the previous direct election of 1971, having been narrowly defeated by the incumbent Park Chunghee); and Kim Youngsam, from the moderate opposition Reunification Democratic Party. The election, held amidst relative calm, produced an impressive 89.2% voter turnout (23.1 million votes cast). Roh Taewoo was declared victor with 36% of the votes cast. Although Roh was able to emerge only as a minority leader, his margin of victory was nonetheless greater than predicted.

## THE SIXTH REPUBLIC (1988–1992)

Korea's new president, Roh Taewoo, was inaugurated on February 25, 1988. But his first months in office were marked by continued unrest and lingering suspicion that he had won the post unfairly. Among supporters of the opposition candidates, the prevailing view was that the election had been rigged and that Roh was cut from the same cloth as Chun Doohwan. President Roh's initial choice of cabinet members, retaining several from the previous regime, did little to change that perception. At first, even abroad, there was some question as to his staying power.

But, in sharp contrast to Chun, Roh cultivated an image as a man of the people, insisting on putting aside the imperial trappings of office, and developing a more collegial governing style than his predecessors. He has shown that he is not simply another general and intends to preside over a civilian, not military, government. Among the major tasks of his first year has been weeding out corruption left over from the Chun administration, even to the point of putting Chun's own brother on trial and sentencing him without special treatment. The former president has not been immune from prosecution; in late November 1988 Chun publicly apologized to the nation for the abuses of power under his administration, and promised to return his wealth acquired during that period. At the same time, Roh has walked the thin line between slow political liberalization and keeping social peace in peparation for the international audience attending the Olympic Games. While middle class support for democratization of the political process and rapprochement with North Korea is strong, toleration of student demonstrations has waned. Roh has committed himself to the difficult task of working within the framework of a democratic system, yet he must decisively take hold of the tractious domestic situation in order to govern. Making his job harder are the student dissidents who have continued to incite disturbances, such as the call in May 1988 for joint sponsorship of the Olympics by both North and South Korea, when such a proposal was patently unrealistic by this late date.

Parliamentary elections in April 1988 did not bring a majority to Roh and the DJP. But the opposition, which garnered substantial support, was again unable to present a united front. Voting showed a marked tendency to align on a regional basis and the parties consistently failed in efforts at coalition. Whether by clear mandate or by default, the reins of government are in Roh's hands.

Roh's next crucial political test came in early 1989 when opposition leaders demanded that he call for a "mid-term appraisal" in a national referendum, as he had promised to do in a pre-election vow designed to show his responsiveness to the voters. Roh, amidst demonstrations by students and attacks by opposition leaders, steadfastly refused to comply, stating that it would serve no useful purpose at this time.

**New Dialogues.** On the international scene, Roh has begun to open the Republic of Korea to new dialogues, most notably with North Korea, China, and the Eastern bloc. While economic relations with the United States remain problematic due to the growing Korean trade surplus, and among Koreans there is a desire to lessen the US presence on the Korean peninsula, the relationship is still considered vital. South Korea has reconsidered its place in the world and decided that it is ready to join the ranks of the industrialized countries, including reevaluating its status vis-à-vis its powerful protector. While Roh agreed to the US demand that Korea take on a greater proportion of the cost of maintaining American troops on its soil (currently 5.4% of GNP), he also pressed Korean insistence on acquiring an increased share of defense technology as a result of the US presence.

Relations with North Korea have not yet taken off and efforts at dialogue have shown uncertain success to date. Concessions to the North's proposals are feared as North Korean propaganda victories. But both of North Korea's great allies, the Soviet Union and China, have an interest in lessened tensions in the region and support rapprochement between North and South Korea. China and South

Korea have developed substantial indirect trade (some US$1 billion in 1988), and in 1989 the Republic of Korea finalized trade relations and established reciprocal trade offices with Russia and several other Eastern European nations. Diplomatic relations were even established with Hungary at the Embassy level. Korean-Russian joint ventures in hotels and in the development of Siberia's vast natural resources are at the forefront of a new relationship. Aeroflot is even planning service to Seoul. Relations between China and Korea has expanded to the point that direct trade is now possible and Korean factories have been constructed in China. Korean tourism was also starting to include China as a destination. Even direct charter flights from Seoul to Shanghai were being scheduled. The backlash of the student uprising in Beijing put some of these projects on hold, however.

Finally, despite wage hikes, union strikes, and the appreciation of the Korean *won* against most of the world's currencies, Korea's economy remains healthy, as one of Asia's "Little Tigers."

**The XXIV Summer Olympiad.** Held in Seoul, the Olympiad was the most successful in Olympic history. Security was air-tight as thousands of athletes, coaches, and officials from a record 160 countries participated. The participation of Olympic teams from China, Russia, and Eastern Europe not only meant that it was the first virtually boycott-free Olympics in a dozen years, but that the threat of terrorist activity from the North would not be tolerated. The Seoul Olympics were also financially quite profitable.

The Olympics were a proud moment for all Koreans whose appearance in the international spotlight was a revelation to literally billions of people around the world. The unprecedented coverage of Korea in the worldwide media was the public acknowledgement of the nation's coming of age. After hosting the world, Korea announced that it was also ready to take several big steps in its own progressive democracy. One of the most popular among the Korean population was the gradual lifting of overseas travel restrictions. Now after years of pent-up desire to see the world, Koreans are traveling abroad in record numbers. In 1987 only 13,000 Korean tourists traveled abroad. In 1988 during the gradual lifting of the restrictions, those figures grew tenfold to 130,000. Totals for 1989 are expected to reach 1.5 million.

# KOREA'S CULTURE

Throughout their long history the Korean people have not only endured but have produced artistic, scientific, and literary achievements of great distinction; and all the while they have maintained their distinct cultural identity, despite the pressures and influences of mightier neighbors. Even today as Korea is becoming one of the most dynamic economies in the world, the people of Korea remain fiercely proud of their long, rich, and distinguished cultural tradition.

The arts of Korea, which served for centuries as a link between Chinese and Japanese cultures, have long been overlooked, although those of China and Japan are world renowned. Korea is a country blending change with tradition that has grown out of a long history to form a rich cultural heritage which, like Korean food, has a special flavor all its own. Korean artists have expressed a vitality and unique outlook blending the exuberant spirituality of Shamanism, the naturalism of Taoism, the devotion of Buddhism, and the disciplined harmony of Confucianism with a particularly Korean love of life.

Because many priceless relics and techniques were lost over time and through the ravages of war, the government has now taken steps to protect the nation's cultural remains to ensure the preservation of historic relics and treasures. Early artworks, antiques, and ancient buildings, as well as "intangible treasures" such as traditional dance, music, drama, and individual performers and craftmen, have been designated as culture treasures.

During the Three Kingdoms period, Koguryo produced monumental cave tomb murals in the Pyongyang area and other uniquely inspired works of art. The most common cultural remnants of the Paekje civilization are colorful and intricate picture tiles and comma-shaped jade jewelry. Silla created exquisite pieces of jewelry in gold and jade. The artistic development of Korean needlework art and bell-making are recognized throughout the world as achievements of Korea's priceless cultural legacy, as are the typical Korean architectural designs that are found on gates and pagodas as well as in palaces and temples.

**Sculpture and Architecture.** Historically, Buddhism during the Silla and Koryo periods dominated the cultural life of the Korean people. Sculpture and architecture were the predominant art forms and cultural landmarks, and they are a major attraction for overseas visitors. Korean architecture has four formative factors: religion,

*Traditional Mask Dance*

Korea's natural landscape, available materials, and for the most part, an aesthetic preference for simplicity. The best-known example of secular architecture during the golden age of Silla is the Pulguk-sa (Pulguk Temple) in Kyongju, including the stone observatory—a bottle-shaped structure which is the oldest existing example in Asia. During the Choson (Yi) dynasty, a tremendous amount of building took place in Seoul, the capital city of its kings; magnificent palaces (Kyongbok, Changdok, Changgyong, Toksu, and Kyonghui palaces) and royal gardens still exist downtown and are a major tourist attraction, and their breathtaking classical architecture provides a colorful guide to the 500 years of the Choson dynasty.

Seoul was once surrounded by a 10-mile wall with nine city gates, five of which still remain. Seoul's magnificent South Gate, one of the finest examples of Korean classical architecture and a landmark on Seoul's main thoroughfare, presents a majestic sight for travelers from overseas. With its characteristic gently sloping roof lines and sturdy, undecorated pillars, Korean architectural style is infused by a harmony with nature.

**Buddhist Influences.** Korean Buddhist temples, built around religious objects and integrated into the surrounding landscape, have become an integral part of Korean culture. Devotion and striving toward physical beauty, technical refinement, and grandeur are evident in the sculpting of stone images and temple monuments. Halls enshrine various sculptural Buddhist images made of stone or gilt-bronze, and pagodas with their carved images fill out the main temple compound. The Buddhist grotto called Sokkuram behind Pulguk-sa in Kyongju is the most outstanding stone sculpture found anywhere in Asia. Probably the most significant of all the gilt-bronze and gold artifacts are the contemplative Maitreya figures on display at the National Museum in Seoul.

**The Koryo Period.** No discussion of Korean culture would be complete without mentioning the "secret green-colored kingfisher" celadon ware that is now highly praised by collectors around the world. The Koryo is noted for its subtle blue-green celadon ceramics. With unrivaled quality, Koreans achieved remarkably original techniques in glaze and inlay. These delicate vessels, incised with white and black chrysanthemums, cranes, clouds, and other favorite symbolic themes, are world renowned. In contrast to the refined, feminine elegance of Koryo pottery, Choson (Yi) dynasty ceramics have a straightforward, solid masculinity and are typical of Korean aesthetics: swiftly accomplished in an assured manner, yet with a casual appearance. In their creative and artistic handling of pot decorations, Choson potters were guided by the tradition of Korean ceramics and instinctive ability. They developed a ceramic art heritage that is one of Korea's unique accomplishments.

**The Choson (Yi) Period.** Choson dynasty artisans achieved a multitude of patterns in woodcrafts and furniture suitable for the Confucian Korean home. Lacquerware with mother-of-pearl, brass, or wrought iron as well as high contrast wood was used. Antique furniture is recognized as a folk art and is rapidly becoming a collector's item.

**Painting.** The Choson dynasty is also recognized for its painting, since an accomplished Confucian scholar had to excel in three skills: poetry, calligraphy, and painting. The paintings are almost monochromatic, relying for effect on shading and a few subdued touches of color, thus conveying an impression of serenity and oneness with nature and a quiet dignity—a trait that prevails throughout the history of Korean art.

Korean painting had four purposes: religious, memorial, record-keeping, and household. Anonymous works were created to take their place in the lives of the people without conscious labels. With the ascendancy of Buddhism in the Silla and the Koryo, however, painting took on a largely religious character: portraits of great religious patriarchs, for example.

Confucianism had a profound influence during the Choson (Yi) dynasty, and even today the Korean way of doing things is largely Confucian. Traditional concepts of human relations, including a respect for age, strong loyalties, proper decorum, and generosity among friends, are still at the heart of today's society.

Since Confucianism dominated the cultural and social life of the Korean people, calligraphy and poetry were predominant. One who wrote good poetry in an excellent calligraphic style enhanced his chances for promotion. The style of painting associated with the Chinese scholarly class came to be a favorite with the *yangban* (noble) aristocracy, and calligraphy became a driving force in the academic world.

While there was Chinese influence in techniques and the selection of themes such as flowers, birds, animals, and landscapes, indigenous technical and stylistic developments were evident in portrait painting of great scholars and statesmen and in genre painting, which sought to capture the common folk of Korea at play and work in their daily lives. An exceptional collection of Korean painting can be seen at the National Museum in Seoul.

The recent "5,000 Years of Korean Art" exhibitions in the United States and England, although displaying only a fraction of Korea's vast repository of art, have given the Western world a rare glimpse of the richness, tradition, and diversity of one of the most important artistic traditions in Asia. In museums throughout Korea, the visitor can clearly recognize the directness of Korean art, mixing fantasy and reality with a reverence for religion as well as nature, that distinguishes the Korean tradition.

**Inventions, Printing, and Publishing.** Korean inventions and innovations include the oldest observatory in Asia; a comprehensive history book in 543; movable metal printing type in 1234; the spinning wheel in 1376; an observation balloon in the sixteenth century; and the world's first iron-clad battleship, which helped defeat the Japanese navy in the war of 1592-98. In addition, in 1448, a unique Korean phonetic alphabet was developed, which linguistically is considered one of the most perfect in the world.

The art of printing and publishing books is among the oldest of Korean achievements. One of the great cultural legacies of Korea is the world's oldest and most comprehensive collection of Buddhist sutras known to exist, called the *Tripitaka Koreana*; it comprises 81,258 large wooden printing plates and took 16 years to complete. The *Tripitaka Koreana* is not only a Korean national treasure but is also a treasure of civilization.

In 1442 King Sejong of the Yi instructed that a bronze instrument be made for measuring precipitation. Thus, Korea has the oldest and most continuous record of rainfall in the world. A suspension bridge was built over the Imjin River 100 years before this type of bridge was seen in the West.

In the fifteenth century a 112-volume encyclopedia was compiled by Korean scholars, 300 years before the French Encyclopedist movement. These volumes contain virtually all known facts about ancient Korea; a copy of this historic work is in the Library of Congress in Washington.

*Tripitaka Koreana: 300,000 pages of Buddhist scripture on wooden blocks*

*Drum dance festival*

**Music and Dance.** Both traditional and Western music are popular in Korea today. Traditional music is divided into majestic court music and lively folk music. Korean operas, singing dramas, folk music, and dance in rites, games and festivals are performed, along with modern music, dance, and ballet. Mask dance-dramas are comic love stories and satires that depict the depravity of aristocratic classes. Western music, first introduced by Christian missionaries, enjoys a major role in the cultural scene of today.

**Contemporary Cultural Institutions.** Korea's leading cultural institutions include the National Museum, with many provincial branches, the National Folk Museum, and the National Classical Music Institute. The Sejong Cultural Center in the heart of Seoul has a huge main hall capable of seating 4,000 and a stage that can accommodate up to 500 performers. The National Theater is situated at the foot of Nam-san and the Seoul Arts Center complexes consist of six halls in Socho-dong, in the Southern section of Seoul. Operas, ballets, choruses, dances, and dramas are frequently staged at its two halls, one accommodating 1,500 and the other 350. Paintings—Western and Oriental—are actively acquired in Korea, and the National Museum of Modern Art houses a fine collection.

With an increasingly educated population, the cultural level of the Koreans has risen. While promoting the revival of the traditional culture, the Koreans have also developed a modern culture. The number of public and private museums and libraries, cultural societies, centers for performing arts, and theaters has been steadily increasing with the promotion of cultural events in Korea.

Besides Korea's cultural relics vividly displayed in numerous national municipal and private museums, the annual ceremonial music, and the classical dance, two distinct types of music and dance are performed in Korea today: traditional and Western. Korea boasts a lively cultural scene, especially in Seoul and Pusan, that blends traditional culture with major influences from the West. Classic Korean dramas as well as productions of Broadway shows are available, and the visitor can see a classical Korean concert of elegant court music or just as easily attend a Beethoven symphony. Traditional music and dance performances are given at the "Seoul Nori Madang," an open-air theater for tourists near the Seoul Sports Complex.

Classical court music, court dances, folk dances, and satirical mask dramas provide entertainment alongside Western movies, symphonies, and nightclubs. The Palace Orchestra, founded 500 years ago, still performs, while Western music, both classical and popular, also plays to appreciative audiences.

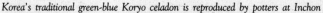

*Korea's traditional green-blue Koryo celadon is reproduced by potters at Inchon*

## LANGUAGE AND LITERATURE

The Korean language has its own alphabet written in syllables, each syllable forming a separate character, divisible into component parts. The language has retained its distinct grammatical structure while borrowing from the Western languages many words for the purposes of embellishment and precision. Korean has developed systematically, with many honorific forms for courteous expression, reflecting an engrained Confucian humility. The sounds of the Korean language have retained vestiges of vowel harmony, a characteristic of Altaic languages, which are mild and soft, with little accent in pronunciation. Chinese characters, the use of which predates the development of the Korean alphabet, were given Korean pronunciation while retaining their basic meaning. The use of Chinese characters in Korea is comparable to the use of Latin in the West.

The Korean alphabet is considered one of the simplest and most efficient phonetic writing systems in the world. The language makes extensive use of postpositions, conjugations, euphonic changes, and graduated address. In 1446, King Sejong directed a committee of Korean scholars to simplify and systematize the native language. As a result, *Hangul*, a phonetic alphabet consisting of 11 vowels (10 are now used) and 17 consonants (14 are now used), came into being in December 1443. The new alphabet was officially promulgated in October 1446. It was much easier to learn than Chinese characters (which do not contain a precise phonetic system). One of the important benefits of *Hangul* was the translation of the classical Chinese canon into Korean. The new alphabet was intended by King Sejong to bring education within the reach of everyone.

The syntax of Korean is similar to Japanese: (1) the sentence order is always subject, object, verb; (2) particles are used after substantives to indicate their function; (3) nouns usually, and verbs always, have neither number nor gender; (4) modifying words, phrases, and clauses are placed before the words they modify; (5) verbs are conjugated by adding auxiliary suffixes to the stem, and tenses are made by infixing to the stem. Because the *Hangul* script is phonetically and syntactically simple, one can quickly learn to read and write it.

A writing form simple enough to be easily mastered, yet precise enough to indicate exact meanings, is one of the greatest of all civilizing influences. *Hangul* was used to write simple tales and songs. The Bible was translated into *Hangul* by missionaries, and the alphabet came into wider use when the first newspapers began to be printed at the turn of the century. Most newspapers are printed in a mixture of *Hangul* and Chinese characters. The Korean written language is a combination of the newer phonetic *Hangul* (24 alphabet letters) and the old Chinese root ideographic characters (about 3,000) with Korean pronunciation. Since the liberation from Japan, North Korea has eliminated the use of Chinese characters.

By means of the written or printed word, civilizations of the past are preserved for succeeding generations. The printed word carries to every segment of society the knowledge that opens the doors of the mind and unlocks the power of the will. Today, the *Hangul* alphabet is the gateway to education and a symbol of hope for the future, for it provides the means to achieving mass literacy, and in fact, illiteracy in Korea has virtually disappeared.

**Korean Literature.** Korea has produced some excellent literature relating, principally, to religious ceremony. Poetry, the genre of all who aspired to the classical in literature, is found chiseled on granite rocks at waterfalls, in mountain passes, or at particularly beautiful scenic spots, as well as on the pillars of houses. The great Chinese classical canons, including the records of the teachings of Confucius, were translated into Korean using the new Korean alphabet. Korean compositions, like the Chinese, dealt with morals and ethics; Chinese historians called Korea "the land of scholars and gentlemen."

Before the twentieth century, nearly all Korean literature was written in the Chinese language. The first known work in Chinese by a Korean was "Song of Orioles," a poem by King Yuri (19 B.C.-18 A.D.). In the sixth century, a scholar named Sul Chong invented the *yidu* form of writing to translate Chinese characters into the Korean vernacular, and the first native Korean poetry or folk verse (*hyangga*) was recorded in this style. The poets developed Buddhist, legendary, and nature themes in their verses.

With the development of a writing system, most early prose literature was concerned with the recording of historical and religious events. These included important sources of ancient Korean history such as the *History of the Three Kingdoms (Samguk sagi)* by Kim Pusik and the *Historical Relics of the Three Kingdoms (Samguk yusa)* by the great monk Ilyon. One of the greatest contributions to literature was the *Scriptures of Great Deeds (Taejanggyong)* in the Koryo period. This work, also known as the *Tripitaka Koreana*, consists of 81,258 wooden blocks engraved with the text of Buddha's teachings and achievements. This is the most complete and best preserved of all the Buddhist scriptures, and as mentioned earlier, it can be seen at the haein Temple near Taegu.

With the invention of the first movable metal-type printing press in 1234 (some two centuries before Gutenberg), the Choson dynasty produced numerous scholarly books on philosophy, history, governmental codes and regulations, personal etiquette, and musicology, as well as an encyclopedia.

The growth of a vernacular, truly Korean verse had to await the creation of the *Hangul* alphabet. The most popular Korean poetic form, the *sijo*, was written in *Hangul*. Chinese characters predominated until the end of the nineteenth century, but *Hangul* has been used almost exclusively by Korean writers since the turn of the century.

Modern Korean writers are reviving national traditions, reevaluating their own classical literature, and steeping themselves in world literature. Many romantic and naturalistic novels and poems have been written. An outstanding contemporary author is Yi Kwangsu, who wrote *Mujong* (*The Heartless*), *Sarang* (*The Love*), and *Huk* (*The Soil*). Recent Korean literature combines traditional Oriental perceptions with Western pragmatism. The strong influence of English culture is revealed in the writings of Kang Younghill: *Ch'odong* (*The Grass Roof*), a poetic autobiography, and *East Goes West*.

The prodigious output of Korean authors today is improving with the influence of Western thought and literary works. The International P.E.N. Congress has been held in Seoul and is expected to return to Korea in the near future.

## THE SOCIAL ORDER

Korea's rich cultural past is reflected in palaces and temples throughout the country; in *Tanchong*, Korea's resplendent roof art; and in the poetry-inspiring ponds filled with lily pads. As it is with *um* and *yang* (Korean for the Chinese *yin* and *yang*), red complements green, black complements white. Happiness is accompanied by sadness, birth by death. The life cycle and the color wheel keep spinning.

**Traditional Structure and Values.** Traditionally, Korea was divided into four rigid classes—the nobility, the middle class, the commoners, and the outcasts. Social relations were governed from the time of the Choson (Yi) dynasty by the Confucian system of

*Children's Sebae—bowing to elders on New Year's Day*

ethics, which emphasized hierarchical social relationships, filial piety, and patriotism. The extended family was the basis of social and economic life. A classical Confucian education was necessary for advancement in government and was reserved for the nobility.

Japanese colonialism, the division of the country, the Korean War, the industrial revolution, and the invasion of Western values have all combined to transform the traditional social system. While social class is based on education, occupation, and wealth, these are no longer hereditary or restricted to the old nobility. There is an increasingly large middle class of professionals, mid-level industrial managers, small businessmen, and skilled workers, with relatively small upper and lower classes. Social mobility is great, especially among those who can benefit from the economic successes of industrial development.

In Korea, family ties are still strong, and filial piety and patriotism are resurgent values. The nuclear family has largely supplanted the extended, three-generation home, especially in the cities, and large numbers of well educated women are assuming a much more active social role. Urbanization and rapid economic development have brought great changes in the social structure and philosophic outlook of the Korean people: with new confidence and pride, they are experiencing the present in the light of traditional values.

For generations, Koreans revered the traditional customs. Society was based on the five Confucian laws, which governed relationships among men: between father and son, Faith; between king and courtier, Righteousness; between husband and wife, Deference; between old and young, Degree; and between friends, Friendship. Allied to these were the five virtues: Love, Righteousness, Ceremony, Knowledge, and Trust. These five laws and five virtues were the ideal of Korean society.

The family is the traditional social unit of Korean society and the determining factor of a Korean's life. The man as head of the family is greatly respected. Although many Koreans do not adhere to the old customs today, some husbands still do not appear in public with their wives. However, Korean women are fast becoming Westernized, and modern Korean women are radically different from those of the past, not only permitting themselves to be seen in public, but also participating in social activities and occupying professional positions.

**External Influences.** Images of dynamic and progressive neighboring nations and of the United States are influential in South Korea, especially among the students. Their relations with foreigners are cordial and cooperative. Eager to go to America, to read American books, and to meet American people, they look positively upon Western and Japanese education and Western culture; they pragmatically weigh American and Japanese policies and actions by their intentions and results rather than on ideological or historical grounds. Progressive in spirit, the students reject any attempts to encourage authoritarian government or to discourage their burning desire for the reunification of the South and the North.

There are many aspects of Korean behavior that may confuse visitors from abroad until they learn something of the traditional heritage and culture of Korea, which is still so much a part of present-day life. Korean culture developed from Chinese, Indian, Japanese, Confucian, and Buddhist traditions, just as Western culture developed from Greek, Latin, Roman, Jewish, and Christian traditions.

True, with the rapid impact of Western culture and American influence, much of Korea's traditional way of life is changing. Although English may be spoken, forks used with ease, and modern technology practiced, many aspects of Korea's 5,000 years of culture and customs still exist, and the old ways are still strong in social interactions. While there is a strong tendency toward Westernization on the one hand, there is a strong will toward preservation of traditions and cultural treasures on the other.

**Entrees to Korean Society.** The easiest way to learn Korean culture is to get to know Koreans. Learning the Korean language— carrying on friendly conversations, even with a few expressions— will definitely help speed the learning process. In shopping trips alone, visitors will not only gain confidence and a feeling of achievement, but a whole new world will open up for them. Joining in the activities of Korean people is enjoyable and educational and thus will make one's visit more rewarding.

The Confucian ethic and tradition placed great value on the scholar, with the farmer next, then the entrepreneur or engineer, with the merchant and the soldier very low in the hierarchy. Confucianism is based on a system of personal relationships, which carefully defines an ethic—one that the Korean people have lived by—based on the five hierarchical relationships: king-subject, husband-wife, father-son, elder brother-younger brother, and between friends.

For thousands of years, Koreans have also lived in the context of the family unit: one is one's father's son, great-grandfather's descendant, and also son's father. One's success, or one's birth, is a gift from the family to be repaid and continued. The Korean is not "I" so much as a part of "we." Devotion to the family continues to be the strongest value for every individual. A contributing factor to family closeness is an absence of alternatives; family members support each other. Filial piety, the respect of children for their parents, is another important social value. From this develops the respect of the young for the old. In general, age is more important than social class.

Adulthood was traditionally established for a man upon his becoming the father of a son, which ensured the continuity of the family. Most of the family property was passed to the eldest son, as was the responsibility of caring for the fortunes of the family and concern for one's ancestors. He was responsible for maintaining the clan name books, which listed all the relatives and ancestors back to the originator of the clan name.

One custom that can help one understand Korea is the use of the dynasty name instead of dates. Dynasties are the historical framework identifying cultural periods of major family or clan rule.

Koreans will give a positive answer because they do not want to offend the others. In general, independent decision-making is rare, and business ritual is endless. Bewildered Koreans, trying to make sense of their Western friends, look askance as Westerners try to do business before establishing a proper social relationship, or refuse with a brusque negative some request for a favor. In the final stage of adjustment, the visitors accept the customs of Korea as just another way of living within a new environment without feelings of anxiety, and actually begin to enjoy Korea.

# THE KOREAN GOVERNMENT

*Trenholme J. Griffin*

The Korean government is organized under a constitution which took effect in 1988, creating the Sixth Republic of Korea. The Korean Constitution, like its predecessors, generally provides for a presidential system of government with a relatively small degree of authority given to the legislative and judicial branches. Some aspects of a parliamentary system have been incorporated into the constitution, so Korea's institutions are substantially different from a United States-style of government. What is most striking about the Korean system of government is the tremendous power given to the president and the executive branch.

## THE EXECUTIVE BRANCH

The president of Korea functions not only as head of the executive branch in domestic affairs, but also as the head of state in foreign relations. The president also has the express constitutional duty of pursuing the peaceful unification of the country. He is the chairman of the cabinet (sometimes referred to as the state council), as well as commander-in-chief of the armed forces. The president has the power to appoint or dismiss the prime minister and cabinet ministers, heads of government agencies and offices, ambassadors, provincial governors, mayors and many other senior public officials. He has the power to conclude treaties, accredit or dispatch diplomatic envoys, and declare war or conclude peace, as well as to grant amnesty or commutation of criminal sentences and restore civil rights to convicted felons.

The president administers the government through the following officials, ministries, boards, offices, and agencies (among others):

## GOVERNMENT AND POLITICS

Prime Minister
Economic Planning Board
Ministry of Foreign Affairs
Ministry of Home Affairs
Ministry of Finance
Ministry of Justice
Ministry of National Defense
Ministry of Education
Ministry of Sports
Ministry of Agriculture, Forestry, and Fisheries
Ministry of Trade and Industry
Ministry of Energy and Resources
Office of Legislation
Office of Patriots and Veterans
Ministry of Construction
Ministry of Health and Social Affairs
Ministry of Labor Affairs
Ministry of Transportation
Ministry of Communications
Ministry of Culture and Information
Ministry of Government
Ministry of Science and Technology
Ministry of National Unification
Ministry of Agency for National Security Planning

Of the above government organizations a smaller number are particularly important to foreign business. These organizations are identified and described in greater detail below:

**The Economic Planning Board (EPB).** The EPB is responsible for overall plans for the development of the economy, formulation and implementation of the government budget, mobilization of resources, investment, research and development, and economic cooperation with foreign countries and international organizations. The minister of the EPB is concurrently deputy prime minister, and coordinates among the ministries with control over matters pertaining to economy and finance. The EPB has bureaus of Economic Planning, Price Policy, Project Evaluation, Post Evaluation and Coordination, Economic Research and Statistics, a Budget Office, and a Fair Trade Office. The Fair Trade Office is particularly important to foreigners, since this is the office which must approve many types of agreements with Korean businesses.

**The Ministry of Trade and Industry (MTI).** The MTI is responsible for commerce, foreign trade, industry, and trademarks and patents and establishing standards for manufactured products. This ministry is also responsible for cases of unfair competition. It is also concerned with import and export regulations. The MTI has bureaus of Trade and Commerce, International Trade Promotion, Small and Medium Industry, Basic Industry, Electronics and Electrical Appliance Industry, Machinery Industry, and Textile Consumer Goods Industry. The Office of Industrial Advancement Administration and the Office of Patents are under the control and supervision of the MTI.

**The Ministry of Finance (MOF).** The Ministry of Finance is responsible for the government's financial affairs, including legislation, currency, national bonds, accounts, taxation, customs, foreign exchange, and control of state-owned and vested properties. This ministry controls and supervises the Office of Monopoly, Office of National Tax Administration, and Office of Customs Administration. The ministry has bureaus of Treasury, Finance, Securities and Insurance, International Finance, Customs, and National Tax Assessment. It also directs and supervises private banks in which the government is the largest stockholder and the special banks established by the government.

**The Ministry of Labor Affairs (MOL).** The MOL is responsible for managing and coordinating matters related to the standardization of working conditions, occupation stability, job training, insurance, and social welfare for workers, and labor disputes. The ministry has bureaus of Planning and Management, Labor Cooperation, Occupational Stability, and Job and Labor Insurance. Under the control of the MOL are the offices of Local Labor Administration, Rehabilitation, National Labor Science Research, the National Job Training Center, and the Central Labor Commission.

Korea is administratively divided into five special cities and nine provinces. The provinces are further divided into county (*gun*), city (*si*), township (*eub*), and village (*myon*).

## THE NATIONAL ASSEMBLY

The National Assembly is a unicameral legislature composed of 299 members. Of the total number of legislators, 224 seats are filled through direct elections at the district level and the 75 remaining seats are assigned on the basis of proportional representation by political parties. The National Assembly has the power to enact legislation, approve foreign treaties and approve the national budget. The legislature also has power to conduct investigations into government activities. This will be an important factor in the years to come as opposition parties attempt to uncover irregularities under previous regimes. The role of the National Assembly in

GOVERNMENT AND POLITICS

government is limited by the fact that most legislation is drafted by the executive branch. Also limiting the power of the legislature is the fact that members of the National Assembly nearly always vote along party lines. Traditionally, the National Assembly has served more as a forum for debate on national issues than as a source of government policy.

The current breakdown of political party power in the National Assembly is as follows:

| | | |
|---|---:|---|
| Democratic Justice Party | 125 | (42%) |
| Party for Peace and Democracy | 70 | (23%) |
| New Democratic Republican Party | 35 | (12%) |
| Reunification Democratic Party | 59 | (20%) |
| Independent | 10 | ( 3%) |

## THE JUDICIARY

The highest tribunal of the nation, the Supreme Court, examines and makes final decisions on appeals of the decisions of appellate courts in civil and criminal cases; its decisions are final and indisputable, forming judicial precedents. The chief justice is appointed by the president to a single five-year term with the consent of the National Assembly, and justices of the Supreme Court are appointed by the president upon the recommendation of the chief justice. The Constitution empowers the chief justice to appoint judges of all lower courts. The role of the Supreme Court is strengthened by allowing it to appoint judges and justices, as well as to establish special Supreme Court departments for such matters as public administration, taxes, labor, and military affairs. Korean courts do not take an active role in establishing policy. For example, the Korean courts have never directly overturned a presidential decree or executive order.

There are three appellate courts in Korea (in Seoul, Taegu, and Kwangju); they hear appeals against verdicts by district courts in civil and criminal cases. They hold their own trials to pass decisions for or against lower court verdicts and may also pass decisions on administrative litigation filed by individuals or organizations against government decisions, orders, or actions. District courts are established in major cities and exercise jurisdiction over all civil and criminal cases filed in the first instance. The family court hears matrimonial problems and examines cases involving juveniles; its sessions are closed to the public in order to protect the privacy of individuals.

# KOREAN POLITICS

The political scene in the Republic of Korea in recent years has been both turbulent and unpredictable. Much of this can be traced to the relatively recent transformation of Korea from a feudal or colonial state to a democracy. With no democratic tradition upon which to draw and with a history of an autocratic style of government, the development of South Korea into a genuine democracy has been slow, uneven, and sometimes painful. Making matters more difficult for those Koreans working to build a democratic system is the fact that the economy of South Korea has developed at an incredible pace which the political system has not come close to matching. The increasingly affluent Korean electorate feels they are entitled to a genuine voice in how they are governed. This explains much of the political problems which have beset the Republic of Korea in the mid-1980s.

## POLITICAL PARTIES AND LEADERS

Compounding the problems impeding the progress of democracy in Korea is the fact that political parties are more coalitions of individuals seeking government power than groups advocating a slate of issues. As will be explained, every political party bases its strength in a particular region of Korea, which exacerbates the problem of building a truly democratic system of government. The four major political parties in present-day Korea cannot be accurately described without simultaneous consideration of their leaders. They are:

**The Democratic Justice Party (DJP) and Roh Tae Woo.** The DJP is the most powerful and best organized of Korea's political parties. The DJP was formed on January 15, 1981, by former Korean President Chun Doohwan and a group of military officers and civilians following the coup which gave the military control of the government. After the election of Roh Taewoo to a five-year term as the president of the Republic of Korea in 1987, the DJP has been undergoing a rapid and extensive transformation as party members linked with former President Chun and the military have been removed from party and government leadership positions. The power of the DJP lies primarily in the immense power of the Korean president and its internal discipline and organization.

President Roh Taewoo is a retired general and a native of North Kyongsang Province. Roh, like many leaders of the DJP, is a graduate of the prestigious Kyongbuk High School in Taegu. Presidents Roh and Chun were classmates at the Korea Military Academy (11th Class), and were senior officers in the South Korean military forces in the Vietnam War. Since assuming the presidency in 1987, Roh has worked hard to portray himself as an "ordinary man." Roh has rejected many of the imperial trappings of office enjoyed by his predecessor. He refuses to be called "Your Excellency," and no longer uses a throne-like chair in meetings. He is more candid and friendly in appearance than Chun. He also has a legitimate claim to the office, having received the most votes (36,070) in the 1987 presidential election.

Roh moved to appoint a number of more moderate officials in his first cabinet. Some former cabinet members, including the Minister of Trade and Industry and the Economic Planning Board, were retained, which resulted in criticism by the opposition. Other moves by Roh include an increasing emphasis on regional development (particularly in the Cholla provinces), and an increasing trade with communist countries. Roh has also promised to hold a vote of confidence on his performance as president after the Olympic Games are held in September 1988.

**The Party for Peace and Democracy (PPD) and Kim Daejung.** The PPD and its leader are clearly the most radical of Korea's major opposition figures and parties. The backers of Kim Daejung and the PPD are largely students and residents of the economically less-developed Cholla provinces. The populist policies of the PPD reflect Kim Daejung's idealism and common origins. His political views are roughly equivalent those of a Social Democrat in Europe or a Liberal Democrat in the United States. While Kim Daejung only finished third in the 1987 presidential elections, the PPD emerged from the April 1988 National Assembly elections as the largest opposition party in the legislature. Kim Daejung is an excellent public speaker, but his political and economic agenda is often criticized as being unrealistic. Recently, he has tried to temper his radical image in an effort to appear more statesmanlike. Kim Daejung has participated in politics as an opposition figure for many years. During his 30-year political career he has been jailed, exiled, kidnapped, and sentenced to death.

**The Reunification Democratic Party (RDP) and Kim Youngsam.** This party and its leader have suffered a number of setbacks since a historic agreement between political parties in Korea was reached in 1987 which led to the adoption of a new constitution. The first setback occurred when Kim Youngsam was unable to convince Kim Daejung to merge the PPD into his RDP and thus create a unified opposition capable of electing Kim Daejung in the 1987 presidential election. These efforts to merge the two parties failed, and despite the fact that the opposition collectively obtained four million more votes than the DJP, Roh Taewoo was elected President with only 36.6% of the vote. Later, in National Assembly elections held in April 1988, Kim Youngsam's party obtained only 59 seats to Kim Daejung's 70 seats despite the fact that his party obtained more popular votes.

Kim Youngsam is more of a pragmatist and is less politically radical than Kim Daejung. His views are roughly equivalent to those of a Christian Democrat in Europe or a mainstream Democrat in the United States. His reputation as an excellent political strategist and deal-maker was tarnished by Kim Daejung's "one legislator per district" political strategy which allowed the PPD to capitalize on its strength in the Cholla provinces and win more National Assembly seats than any other opposition party. The support of the RDP extends *more widely* beyond its principal power base (the Pusan area) than does support of the PPD. Kim Youngsam's support comes largely from younger and middle-class Koreans who are relatively more dispersed around Korea.

**The New Korea Democratic Party (NKDP) and Kim Jongpil.** The NKDP is headed by Kim Jongpil, a conservative ex-general who was prime minister and heir apparent to President Park Chunghee prior to his assassination. While Kim Jongpil heads an "opposition" party in the sense that its goal is to replace the DJP, the party platform of the NKDP is far to the right in the political spectrum relative to the PPD and the RDP. In fact, his views may be more conservative than those of the DJP. Little government policy would change if the NKDP gained power, only the individuals holding power. The strength of the NKDP lies primarily in regionalism, since his support is based in the Chungchong provinces and in some sections of Kyonggi Province.

## POLITICAL PRESSURE GROUPS

South Korean political party conventions are held annually in Seoul. Despite the strong disciplinary powers available to the party leadership in South Korea, party members are prone to shifting their loyalties whenever they are offered an opportunity for advancement. This occurs because political loyalties are to individuals rather than platforms. Since members of the National Assembly enjoy power and influence and have a strong desire to increase their position, party leaders have been able to manipulate and control the Assembly members without much difficulty. Also, substantial campaign funds are needed to ensure success in elections.

Political patronage in Korea is limited to positions at the top which are occupied by the inner circle of the party in power. There are no patronage positions in the middle echelons of government since they are occupied by members of the national civil service. In the National Assembly, a seniority rule does not operate in assignments to important committees and their chairmanships, so the Korean parties reward those members who have proved themselves capable and faithful in their service to the party. All decisions of the Korean parties are theoretically made through committees and the annual convention, but in practice decisions are frequently made by the leader of the party, or by a small informal group within the party.

Korean parties are organizations of politicians rather than organizations of ordinary citizens, so they do not have strong grassroots support. They have not developed into "policy" parties and lack long-term overall goals. As "personality-centered" parties, they tend to function on the basis of personality and relationships, rather than on the basis of abstract political principles. Personal relationships are in turn conditioned by the matrix of birthplace, family connections, and school ties. No political party is free from the frequently divisive influence of these personalized social relationships.

Korean political parties are influenced by numerous pressure groups: the army, intellectuals, students, foreign governments, businessmen, or unions. Small movements, social organizations, and research institutes sporadically exert limited influence over political parties, but they have failed to achieve organizational autonomy as pressure groups.

Politically articulate persons in South Korea include professionals, students, journalists, military officers, businesspeople, and government functionaries, but the most outspoken groups of the population are the army and the students. After the student uprising in April 1960, student participation in numerous politically-inspired demonstrations and activities became a fixture of South Korean life. Although the politically active elements appeared to represent only a relatively small number of students, they have become a significant pressure group. Rather more idealistic than practical in their political aspirations, the students are intensely

## GOVERNMENT AND POLITICS

nationalistic and extremely sensitive to any signs of foreign domination or interference in Korea's internal affairs. They favor elected civilian leadership and desire the early reunification of North and South Korea. Both the students and the army tend to regard themselves as the moral watchdogs of government, political parties, and society. The Democratic Justice Party has traditionally derived an important part of its strength from the armed forces, which has traditionally constituted the most powerful pressure group.

Korea's intellectuals are composed of academicians, university professors, doctors, journalists, and persons within the fields of artistic and literary endeavor. This pressure group has been more exposed than others to Western democratic ideas. Many intellectuals have tended to assume a consistently critical position of the military-based leadership, and their ideas enjoy wide dissemination as a result of their influence on students and through the press, publishing, and the popular arts.

Since Korea requires economic and military assistance from its allies, Korean politicians at times seem more sensitive to external than internal pressures. Consequently, support from trade partners is an important driving force for Korean parties. Winning the confidence of a friendly ally is often achieved through individual contacts with foreign envoys in Seoul, not by the action of a group. This results in the strengthening of a person's political base, which furthers factional strife within the party; ultimately, such attempts to enhance the political strength of particular party leaders subjects a party to both direct and indirect foreign intervention. Because Korean parties are quite dependent on the influence of foreign forces, the relationship between the parties and representatives of friendly allies is delicate.

As events of 1987 have demonstrated, the politics of modernization have begun to lead Korea away from one-man rule, corruption, demagoguery, election fraud, excesses in adversary politics, and lack of dialogue among competing political actors. The development of an orderly, yet vigorous multiparty system appears to be one of the significant outcomes of the 1987 and 1988 elections. Roh Taewoo's promises of reconciliation, reform, and liberalization in domestic matters seem to have begun a general process of change in the general atmosphere of Korean life. While the responsiveness of Roh Taewoo's announced program to popular needs and the desire for a united country have been credibly demonstrated, popular expectations keep gradually rising as a result of the remarkable economic and political developments of recent years.

# KOREAN UNIFICATION AND RELATIONS WITH NORTH KOREA

The first contact in the quarter-century history of national division between the South and the North was made in 1971. Red Cross officials from the two sides began to meet in August 1971 on the issue of reuniting separated families. In a joint communiqué released on July 4, 1972, the two sides promised cooperative efforts to achieve peaceful reunification. No meaningful communications between the two sides occurred until talks which were designed to lead to a South-North Prime Ministers Conference took place beginning in February 1980. Repeated overtures by South Korea were rebuffed repeatedly by the North. A major setback to peace and democracy occurred on October 9, 1983, when North Korea staged a terrorist attack on a presidential delegation to Rangoon, Burma, in which 17 government officials (including four cabinet ministers) were killed. Brief periods of diplomatic contact occurred during 1983 and 1984, including talks to form a single team to participate in the Olympic Games. The only tangible result occurred when aid shipments were sent by North Korea to victims of flooding in South Korea. Major economic talks began in May of 1985 which eventually led to an exchange of citizens and performing arts troupes. In January 1986, the North Koreans broke off the talks.

With its rapidly developing culture and expanding economic strength, the Republic of Korea confidently looks forward to achieving the historic mission to peacefully reunify their divided country and establish a modern democratic society in Korea. Without peace and stability, South Korea's continued progress will be threatened. Having created a stable system internally, the Chun government looked outward to nations to establish mutually beneficial relations and to promote economic cooperation, regardless of conflicting ideologies. In accordance with its "open door" policy, South Korea is working to improve relations with Russia and China as well.

The Republic of Korea has proposed that Korean reunification be achieved step-by-step and peacefully. As the Republic of Korea advances economically, the basis for future reunification will become even stronger. South Korea's economy makes North Korea's pale by comparison. This will place increasing pressure on the North to make concessions on reunification issues.

**The Reunification Issue Today.** Much of the reunification fever that gripped the South during 1989 was the result of a government authorized visit to North Korea by Chung, Ju-yung, the Founder and Chairman of Hyundai Group, one of Korea's largest international conglomerates. The purpose of Mr. Chung's visit was to explore the possibility of economic cooperation between the North and South, especially in the development of a special "tourist zone" that would encompass the fabled Kumgang Mountains in the North and Mt. Sorak National Park in the South. This special zone would create a tourist flow that would enable citizens from both the North and South to mix and intermingle. Unfortunately, little has resulted from Chung's visit.

Following Chung's visit to North Korea, the dissident Reverend Moon Ik-hwan made an unauthorized visit to Pyongyang, where he met with North Korean dictator Kim Il-sung. The reverend was prosecuted by the Korean government for failing to gain their prior authorization. Supporters, including radical students throughout Korea, demonstrated on his behalf. Later in the year, it was revealed that a dissident lawmaker from an opposition party had also traveled illegally to North Korea and met privately with Kim Il-sung. He was also prosecuted amidst heavy demonstrations.

North Korea's attempts to force its way into the role as co-host of the 1988 Seoul Olympics resulted in the construction of an enormous stadium in Pyongyang. As a means of "saving face" in regards to their Olympic rebuff, and as a ploy to gain a measure of international respectability, North Korea hosted the 1989 World Youth Festival. Although primarily a propaganda vehicle for socialist countries, the World Youth Festival often attracts considerable participants from various democratic and non-aligned nations around the world. North Korea urged students in the South to attend, even though their government forbade their attendance. The North even offered free passage through Panmunjom, the armistice village that connects the two halves of Korea for very infrequent official contacts. Radical students, incensed by the poor progress of reunification and the loss of an opportunity to visit their counterparts in the North, staged a number of demonstrations and symbolic marches to Panmunjom. Most Western nations boycotted the festival.

As a result of South Korean diplomacy and its economic growth, the Republic of Korea is rapidlly approaching the status of a middle political and economic power with considerable world influence. In recognition of this, Seoul has been chosen as the meeting site of such major international organizations as: the World Bank, the International Monetary Fund, the Inter-Parliamentary Union in 1985; the Asian Games in 1986; the Summer Olympic Games in 1988; and the Rotary Club World Congress in 1989.

# KOREA'S ECONOMY

*Trenholme J. Griffin*

## ECONOMIC HISTORY

The progress which South Korea has made economically since the early 1960s is often referred to in the media as a "miracle." While clearly an overstatement, the development of South Korea's economy during this period is truly remarkable. To understand the magnitude of this incredible economic transformation, it is necessary to examine the state of Korea's economy at the end of the Korean War in 1953. The Japanese occupation which began in 1910 and continued until the end of World War II, the subsequent division of the peninsula by the Allied Forces, and the destruction which occurred during the Korean War left the Korean economy in ruins. Partition of the nation left nearly all power-generating capacity and approximately 60% of heavy industry in territory controlled by communist North Korea. The Korean War also created enormous social dislocation as approximately 220,000 Korean military personnel and 380,000 civilians were killed in the war. The capital city of Seoul was left in ruins as it changed hands four times during the hostilities. Few buildings were left standing in Seoul when the armistice was signed in 1953. During the war, the impoverished nation had been stripped of nearly all its wood and trees by Koreans struggling to keep warm during the bitterly cold winters.

Economic development immediately after the Korean War was also hampered by the fact that the newly-created government of the Republic of Korea was struggling to establish democracy simultaneously with placing the nation's economy on the road to recovery. President Syngman Rhee was a skilled politician but he was not an economist. The Rhee government often manipulated the economy to achieve political objectives. The Korean economy was extremely dependent upon foreign aid, most of which was needed in order to feed the nation's citizens. The shortage economy of Korea in the 1950s was a ripe setting for corruption and political favoritism, and numerous irregularities produced a number of scandals.

Problems with the economy and political corruption first led to a 1960 student rebellion which toppled the Rhee government. When it became clear that the new government formed after the rebellion would be equally ineffective, a group of Korean army officers led by Park Chunghee seized control in a military coup. It is at this point that most economic historians set the benchmark for measuring Korea's recent economic development. Per capital income in Korea in 1962 was the equivalent of US$82 and the nation's total exports amounted to only US$43 million.

Blackening Korea's future economic prospects was the fact that the nation has no natural resources. Korea has no domestic petroleum resources, very few metal ore deposits, relatively small amounts of anthracite coal, and mountainous terrain which is mostly unsuitable for agriculture or animal husbandry. In effect, people (and the value they add to imported raw materials) are the nation's only resource. The value of this resource is substantial. The people of Korea are hard-working (they have the longest average working week in the world), highly literate, and educated (the literacy rate is over 97%), and highly motivated. They want to succeed and advance their economy, and are willing to work to achieve these objectives.

When Park Chunghee and his fellow officers took control of the South Korean economy in the early 1960s, they knew a major change in economic policy was necessary. Over considerable opposition from economic nationalists, a decision was made to base South Korea's economic strategy on increasing exports. This increase in exports was achieved by creating a variety of incentives and benefits for those companies which exported goods. These benefits included tax incentives, generous wastage allowances, special financing, interest rate subsidies, and advantageous depreciation. Substantial investments were made in the production of the necessary raw materials and intermediate goods. Because the nation's domestic savings rate was insufficient to support the investments necessary to build a modern economy, substantial amounts were borrowed by the government on international financial markets. These loans would eventually exceed US$45 billion. The foreign exchange which was obtained from these loans, as well as all foreign exchange earned from exports, was allocated to companies which exported goods. Korean companies were thus motivated to shift gears to export activities.

The government did not choose to rely on the "invisible hand" of economic competition to produce economic growth. Instead, the government took an active role in managing the direction of the economy. While decisions made by the government were not always correct, they were largely successful. Some industries succeeded despite a lack of government support and others failed in spite of receiving it. General government policies toward business were set out in a series of Five-Year Economic Plans. Each plan contained targets for increases in key economic indicators, as well as a list of major infrastructure projects to be completed by both the public and private sectors.

The major aspects and performance of the Korean economy during each of these Five-Year Economic Plans were as follows:

**First Five-Year Plan (1962–1966).** The focus of this plan was on building a foundation for increasing the nation's industrial base. Major emphasis was placed on increasing energy production. Increases in electricity-generation capacity were of particular importance. However, the key strategy of this and all future plans was to increase the level of Korean exports. When viewed as a whole, the first plan was a major success. The economy grew at an annual rate of 8.5%, which substantially exceeded the plan's targets. Exports, primarily produced by light industry, grew to nearly US$250 million in the last year of the five-year period.

**Second Five-Year Plan (1967–1971).** Experience gained during the first plan was used to create a much more sophisticated economic road map for the second five years. More emphasis was placed on developing heavy industry as well as on increasing agricultural production. It was thought that light industry would benefit from the intermediate products of heavy industry through backward linkages. The second plan was also very successful. Actual growth in South Korea's gross national product on an annual basis during this period was 9.7%. The export drive also moved ahead as exports increased by over 300% over the five years of the plan. Moves to increase agricultural production were fruitful, but total output was not sufficient to meet demand. Imports of agricultural goods will always be necessary because of South Korea's population density and lack of arable land. South Korea is a huge importer of corn and wheat, but it is self-sufficient in rice and barley.

**Third Five-Year Plan (1972–1976).** South Korea's economic planners continued to emphasize heavy industry during the third plan. In addition, government officials began to place more emphasis on social factors such as increasing rural development and evening the distribution of wealth. Korea's economy continued to grow during the third five years. Exports rose to US$7.8 billion and average annual growth in gross national product increased to 10.1%. On the negative side, imports outstripped exports. As a result, increased foreign borrowing by the South Korean government was necessary.

**Fourth Five-Year Plan (1977–1981).** This plan was only partially successful, since world economic events (such as the OPEC-induced oil shock) and domestic problems (poor harvests because of unfavorable weather) battered the economy. The assassination of President Park created both political and economic instability. In addition, previous government emphasis on heavy industry had left the economy dangerously imbalanced. The parts and components sector was extremely weak, making the nation dependent upon Japanese suppliers. The most positive development was that annual GNP growth during the fourth plan continued at an average annual rate of 5.5%. Exports rose to US$20.8 billion during the last year of the plan.

**Fifth Five-Year Plan (1982–1986).** This plan was the first to add the words "social development" to the title. This was done to demonstrate a government commitment to increased expenditures on social welfare and infrastructure projects. The fifth plan was also the first to recognize that the government's role in directing the economy had to be reduced because the economy was increasing so rapidly in size and complexity. Average GNP growth was 7.6% during the five-year period, and exports rose to US$33.9 billion in 1986. South Korea achieved two important firsts in 1986. The nation had a current account surplus of US$4.6 billion, and domestic savings surpassed gross investment for the first time. This means that South Korea can now move toward becoming a creditor rather than a debtor nation.

**Sixth Five-Year Plan (1987–1991).** This is the plan under which the economy is currently operating. For the first time, economic planners placed more emphasis on stability than on growth. The government planned to take all steps necessary to control inflation and increase income distribution. Despite the emphasis on stability, the rate of GNP growth exceeded 12% in 1987. Per capita income increased to US$2,826 in 1987 (up from US$82 in 1961), and exports rose to record levels. The nation's total GNP in 1987 was US$118.6 billion. The overall domestic savings rate rose to an incredible 36.7%. This compares with a savings rate of less than 4% in the United States. The manufacturing sector led the economy to record levels showing growth of 16.4% in 1987. Exports in 1987 were worth a record US$47.1 billion.

## ECONOMIC OUTLOOK

No economy in the world is growing as rapidly as South Korea's. In 1987, the country saw increases in nearly every important economic indicator including exports, employment, savings, and investment. Although some slowing of the economy can be expected in the future due to the rising value of the *won* relative to major currencies, rising labor costs, increased raw material costs, and increased protectionism abroad, Korea should continue to significantly outperform the economies of other newly industrializing countries as well as those of developed countries.

The major economic problems which Korea must face in the future are:

(1) US$10-billion trade surplus with the United States in 1987;

(2) overdependence on the United States market (over 40%);

(3) US$5-billion trade deficit with Japan;

(4) higher wages;

(5) rising raw materials costs;

(6) appreciating value of the Korean *won* (9% in 1987; as much as 20% in 1988);

(7) increased protectionism in foreign markets.

These problems will be difficult to overcome, but Korea has a recent track record which suggests success will be achieved.

The Korean Development Institute has issued the following projections for yearly growth of the Korean economy:

| | |
|---|---|
| 1986–1991 | 8.6% |
| 1992–2000 | 6.8% |
| 2001–2018 | 5.8% |

Growth at this level would put per capita gross national product at US$5,000 by 1992. If achieved, the targets would mean a per capita GNP of US$10,000. South Korea would as a result be considered a developed nation.

## FOREIGN INVESTMENT

One measure of the health of the South Korean economy is the level of foreign investment. Foreign investment increased by over 300% to US$1,060 in 1987, according to the Korean Ministry of Finance. Investments by foreigners are again expected to exceed US$1 billion in 1988. Japan was responsible for 47% of all foreign investments in South Korea in 1988. The United States had a 21% share and Europe a 20% share in 1987. Government figures for foreign investment show a rise from US$189 million in 1982, to US$269 million in 1983, to US$442 million in 1984, to US$532 million in 1985, to US$354 million in 1986. Investments by American companies are typically very large and are usually made by very substantial companies. As a rule, Japanese investments are smaller in amount but more numerous.

## KEY INDUSTRIAL SECTORS

Because South Korea's economy is resource poor, the manufacturing sector has always been given primary attention by the government's economic planners. The manufacturing sector of the Korean economy has developed in distinct stages. The first stage (1961–1972) was dominated by light industries such as textiles and footwear. The second stage (1972–1980) was marked by a distinct emphasis on developing heavy industry. Companies in areas such as shipbuilding, refining, and steelmaking received many government benefits during that period. The move toward heavy industry was so strong that it produced severe problems in 1980 due to structural imbalances. It was at this point that the government began to move the economy into a third stage. Technology- and capital-intensive industries such as electronics, automobiles, and machinery are the principal industrial categories which are being targeted for development and rapid growth in this third stage.

Korea today has a mix of industrial sectors which make up its economy. The major sectors are:

**Electronics.** The electronics industry has recently surpassed the textiles as South Korea's leading industry. The industry began its move to prominence in the 1970s as a result of the government's enactment of the Electronics Industry Promotion Law. Production in the electronics sector increased from US$138 million in 1971 to US$17 billion in 1987. In recent years, the major products in this industry have been televisions, video-cassette recorders, microwave ovens, and personal computers. Growth has also been strong in the industrial electronics sector. Exports of electronic products from Korea are projected to reach US$25 billion by 1992.

**Textiles.** This industry has played an extremely significant role in the development of the South Korean economy. Until recently, this sector was the leading employer and the leading exporter. Total exports of textiles were US$11.7 billion in 1987. However, in the years to come, South Korean textile producers will be facing an uncertain future as higher wages and the cost of raw materials, as well as increased protectionism in developed countries and increased competition from developing countries, make South Korean textiles less attractive to foreign buyers. South Korean textile companies are beginning to move production facilities overseas to low-wage countries (such as Thailand) in anticipation of the "sunset" of this industry in Korea.

**Footwear.** The South Korean footwear industry has been a significant part of the economy for over 20 years. Most footwear exported from South Korea takes the form of leather-upper athletic shoes. Factories established by South Korean companies, such as H.S. Corp., Kukje, Samwha Co., and Tae Hwa Corp. have made South Korea one of the world's largest producers of footwear. The Republic of Korea shipped footwear with a value of approximately US$2.8 billion in 1987, an increase of over 30% over 1986. Experts predict that footwear exports in 1988 may reach US$3 billion. This industry has been given "sunset" status by economic planners.

**Automobiles.** The automobile industry has experienced incredible growth since exports to the United States and other countries began in 1986. In 1987 alone, automobiles valued at US$2.7 billion were exported. The major automobile exporters are Hyundai (in which Mitsubishi has a minority interest), Daewoo (a joint venture with General Motors), and Kia (in which Ford and Mazda have a minority interest). The principal problems facing this industry are a lack of domestic subcontractors and labor unrest which has significantly interrupted production. Each of the "big three" automakers has made very large capacity investments in the past year, which should result in greater production in the late 1980s and early 1990s. One or two large business groups are expected to enter the automobile assembly business in Korea.

**Machinery.** The South Korean government has targeted this industry for development largely because more than 50% of domestic demand is met by Japanese suppliers. To decrease this dependence, research and development expenditures have increased dramatically. Much of this industry's problems can be traced to prior focus on increasing capacity rather than on increasing technical standards. Another problem has been the inability of domestic companies in the industry (which are mostly small- and medium-sized companies) to secure capital. In 1987, South Korea met 65% of its domestic demand for machinery. Export sales of machinery were US$9.3 billion in 1987.

**Iron and Steel.** This industry was initially established to meet domestic demand. As production capacity increased, exports then became important in the late 1970s. Beginning in 1986, domestic demand began to rise so quickly that significantly less steel was available for export. In the future, domestic markets will drive the industry. The major steel producer in Korea is the Pohang Iron and Steel Company ("POSCO"), which is currently government-owned but will be gradually privatized. POSCO is now the second largest steel company (in terms of production) in the world. Annual capacity at POSCO's Kwang Yang Bay facility is now 14.5 million metric tons. Construction on more iron and steel production facilities has already begun.

**Shipbuilding.** This very important Korean industry has been faced with hard times recently due to a worldwide recession caused by overcapacity and the rising cost of labor and materials. Nevertheless, new orders given to Korean shipbuilders amounted to 3.4 million gross tons in 1987. The major Korean shipbuilders are Hyundai, Samsung, Daewoo, and Korea Shipbuilding and Engineering. The government has needed to give this industry tremendous amounts of financial assistance to keep the shipbuilders financially healthy. Korean companies will work to increase the domestic content of ships built in their shipyards and to produce more specialty-type ships in order to maintain profitability in this industry.

**Petrochemicals and Refining.** This industry is struggling to meet booming domestic demand for petrochemicals. Profitability is excellent due to strong demand. Shortages exist in a number of important sectors and will continue until the increased capacity which is now under construction comes on line. Total production of petrochemical products was 2.2 million tons in 1987. The major petrochemical producers are Yukong, Lucky, Honam, and Samsung. Many of them produce refined goods under technology licenses and through joint ventures. Most of this important industry is located in the cities of Ulsan and Yeochon. The continued health of this industry is largely dependent upon international oil prices since South Korea imports 100% of its petroleum. Over 80% of South Korea's energy needs are met by imports. Prices are closely monitored by government authorities.

**Construction.** The South Korean construction industry began domestically with the need to build major highways, plants, and roads after the Korean War. In the 1970s, the Middle Eastern construction boom changed the South Korean construction industry's focus to overseas projects. In 1978, gross earnings of the overseas South Korean construction industry as a whole rose to US$15 billion. In the 1980s, the Middle Eastern market had faded, resulting in only US$2 billion in new orders. Making matters worse is the fact that payments on old projects in the Middle-East are seriously delinquent. Future growth in the domestic construction market is expected to allow the construction industry to recover its financial health.

## THE CONGLOMERATES

The economy in the Republic of Korea is dominated by a small number of industrial conglomerates known as *chaebol*. *Chaebol* are, as a rule, owned and controlled by one family. They produce a wide range of goods which are sold on both domestic and international markets. The largest five *chaebol* account for over 20% of all sales of manufactured goods. The ten largest *chaebol* have a 30% share of manufacturing sales. Most commentators are referring to the largest 30 to 50 business groups when they use the term *chaebol*. The Korean government is working to reduce the influence of the chaebol to increase the stability of the economy and to increase the distribution of wealth. Loans to large companies are being reduced by banks pursuant to government directives. *Chaebol* are also being pressured to sell shares to the public to raise capital, thus diluting the control of the founding family and exposing the firm's finances to public scrutiny.

# Chapter II
# PLANNING A TRIP TO KOREA

## Time Zone Conversion

The following chart shows time difference between Seoul and other major cities.

| Area | Time | | | | | | | |
|------|------|------|------|------|------|------|------|------|
| Rio de Janeiro<br>São Paulo | 13 | 16 | 19 | 22 | 1 | 4 | 7 | 10 |
| New York<br>Montreal<br>Bogota<br>Toronto | 11 | 14 | 17 | 20 | 23 | 2 | 5 | 8 |
| Chicago<br>Houston | 10 | 13 | 16 | 19 | 22 | 1 | 4 | 7 |
| Vancouver<br>Seattle<br>San Francisco<br>Los Angeles | 8 | 11 | 14 | 17 | 20 | 23 | 2 | 5 |
| Sydney<br>Melbourne | 2 | 5 | 8 | 11 | 14 | 17 | 20 | 23 |
| SEOUL<br>Tokyo | 1 | 4 | 7 | 10 | 13 | 16 | 19 | 22 |
| Taipei<br>Manila<br>Hong Kong<br>Kuala Lumpur<br>Singapore | 0<br>24 | 3 | 6 | 9 | 12 | 15 | 18 | 21 |
| Bangkok<br>Jakarta | 23 | 2 | 5 | 8 | 11 | 14 | 17 | 20 |
| New Delhi<br>Calcutta | 21 | 24 | 3 | 6 | 9 | 12 | 15 | 18 |
| Tehran<br>Kuwait<br>Jeddah | 19 | 22 | 1 | 4 | 7 | 10 | 13 | 16 |
| Hamburg<br>Rome<br>Paris<br>Amsterdam | 17 | 20 | 23 | 2 | 5 | 8 | 11 | 14 |
| London<br>Madrid | 16 | 19 | 22 | 1 | 4 | 7 | 10 | 13 |

*The dark colored boxes indicate the previous day.*

# KOREA'S TRAVEL POLICY

**K**orea has seen a remarkable increase in both international and domestic tourism in recent years. Economic development and the improvement of the people's living standards as well as expansion of transportation networks have contributed greatly to the growth in volume of domestic tourism and also invited increasing international tourism. The government has been assisting tourism, both domestic and international, by constructing facilities and infrastructure for travelers. In addition, the Korea National Tourism Corporation (KNTC) stages national campaigns to increase public awareness of the importance of tourism to Korea's international position and its economy, and to encourage the conservation of resources and maintenance of a clean environment in resort areas. Having joined the upper ranks of Asian nations through the improvement of facilities and services, Korea is now conducting a policy of harmonious side-by-side development of international and domestic tourism.

Enhanced understanding of Korea in international society has produced a positive impact on Korean tourism. The total number of foreign visitors to Korea in 1987 exceeded 1.874 million (including Korean overseas residents returning for visits). This trend has continued to grow at an annual rate of 12.9 percent, allowing for the balanced development of facilities throughout Korea. Koreans have recognized the importance of tourism, not only as a means of communication among peoples, but also as an industry for earning foreign exchange and increasing employment. This is reflected in decisions to hold large-scale international events in Korea, such as the International Monetary Fund/International Bank for Reconstruction and Development meeting in 1985, the Asian Games in 1986, the International P.E.N. Congress meeting in 1988, the Summer Olympic Games in 1988, and the World Convention of Rotary International in 1989.

Korea has rapidly upgraded tourist facilities with provisions for better services for foreign visitors, especially through staff training in languages and cuisine, in addition to building new hotels, sports complexes, and resorts. Twenty percent of visitors now come on business, and Korea has already developed a strong conference market. Quality pre- and post-conference tours, as well as attractive shopping programs, are offered in conjunction with the meetings. As awareness of Korea and Korean culture increases abroad, tourism is becoming so popular that 70 percent of travelers now come solely on vacation. The other 10 percent are officials and professionals.

*Springtime on Mt. Soraksan*

The number of outbound Korean residents has reached 510,000 per year. Major destinations are Asia (60 percent), the Americas (30 percent), and Europe (10 percent). Countries visited by the greatest numbers of Korean residents are Japan (40 percent), the United States (25 percent), and Saudi Arabia (5 percent, because of Korean export leader business ventures there). The purpose of the majority of visits is culture, sports, and education.

**Arrivals by Nationality.** Among foreign visitors, arrivals from Japan top the list with 48 percent; the United States is next with 18 percent; followed by overseas Koreans (13 percent), the Republic of China (Taiwan), the United Kingdom, West Germany, France, and Australia. Tourism from the United States increased by 14.7 percent from 1986 to 1987.

**Earnings.** Total earnings from tourism have risen to nearly $800 million, comprising 10 percent of invisible trade receipts and contributing significantly to the balance of payments. The average per capita expenditure of foreign tourists rose to $1,250 in 1987.

**Popular Destinations.** As the nation's capital and largest urban center, Seoul, with deluxe hotels and beautiful old palaces for sightseeing, attracts 80 percent of foreign tourists. Other destinations are the port of Pusan, 30 percent; Folk Village (near Seoul),

15 percent; Kyongju (ancient city of the Silla Kingdom), 20 percent; Panmunjom (where the Korean War armistice was signed), 10 percent; Cheju Island (semitropical resort island southwest of the peninsula), 10 percent; the Kongju-Puyo area (historic site of the Paekje Kingdom), five percent; Mount Sorak and the East Coast, five percent; and Hallyo Waterway Marine Park, five percent.

**Duration of Stay.** Overseas visitors stayed an average of eight days; for tourists the average was five days. As might be expected, travelers from Europe and America stay longer than Pacific basin visitors: the U.S., 13 days; France, 12 days; West Germany, 9 days; Canada, 8 days; United Kingdom, 15 days; Australia, 12 days; Japan, 6 days; Taiwan, 5 days.

**Patterns of Domestic Travel.** Among Korean travelers, one-day and weekend tours account for the majority of trips; the most popular overnight accommodation is the inn; 80 percent go by bus or train. The Seoul metropolitan area and Mt. Sorak are the most popular destinations; summer is the busiest season of holiday travel.

## KOREAN DIPLOMATIC MISSIONS ABROAD

Korean diplomatic missions deal not only with governmental relations but also with private travel requests. They issue visas and assist in travel arrangements for commercial visitors. The Republic of Korea Embassy in Washington, D.C., plays an important role in evaluating travel and trade proposals and developing commercial relationships. Consular offices also issue visas and assist with business relationships.

## DIRECTORY OF MAJOR KOREAN EMBASSIES ABROAD

ARGENTINA: Av. del Libertador 2257, Cap. Fed., 1425 Buenos Aires
AUSTRALIA: 113 Empire Circuit, Yarralumla, Canberra, A. C. T. 2600
AUSTRIA: Kelsenstrasse 2, 1030, Vienna
BELGIUM: Avenue Hamoir 3, 1180 Brussels
BRAZIL: Sen-Avenida das Nacoes, Lote 14, 70436, Brasilia-DF
CANADA: 151 Slater Street, Fifth floor, Ottawa, Ontario, K1P 5H3
DENMARK: Dronningens Tvaergade 8, 1302 Copenhagen
FRANCE: 125 rue de Grenelle, 75007, Paris
FEDERAL REPUBLIC OF GERMANY: Adenauerallee 124, 5300 Bonn 1
ITALY: Via Barnaba Oriani, 30, 00197, Rome
JAPAN: 2-5, Minami-Azabu, 1-chome, Minato-ku, Tokyo

MEXICO: Lope de Armendáriz no. 110, Col. Lomas de Chapultepec, 11000 Mexico City
NORWAY: Bjorn Farmanns gt. 1, Skillebekk, 0271 Oslo 2
SPAIN: Miguel Angel 23, 28010, Madrid
SWITZERLAND: Kacheggweg 38, 3006, Bern
TAIWAN: 345 Chung Hsiao East Road, Section 4, Taipei, 10515
UNITED KINGDOM: 4 Palace Gate, London W8 5NF
UNITED STATES OF AMERICA: 2370 Massachusetts Avenue, N.W., Washington, D.C., 20008

## KOREAN CONSULATE-GENERAL OFFICES IN THE U.S.

CHICAGO: 500 North Michigan Avenue, Chicago, IL 60611;
 tel: (312) 822-9485
HONOLULU: 2756 Pali Highway, Honolulu, HI 96817;
 tel: (808) 595-6274
HOUSTON: 1990 Post Oak Blvd., Ste. 745, Houston, TX 77056;
 tel: (713) 961-0186/0798
LOS ANGELES: 5455 Wilshire Blvd., Los Angeles, CA 90036;
 tel: (213) 931-1332
NEW YORK: 460 Park Avenue, New York, NY 10022;
 tel: (212) 752-1700
SAN FRANCISCO: 3500 Clay Street, San Francisco, CA 94118;
 tel: (415) 921-2251

# KOREA NATIONAL TOURISM CORPORATION (DEPARTMENT OF TRANSPORTATION)

Under the guidance of the Korea National Tourism Corporation (KNTC), Korea is constantly instituting more effective measures to develop markets and improve service to satisfy tourist needs, and it is actively preparing for ever-increasing large-scale events. The KNTC functions on both the domestic and international levels. Domestically, it authorizes all plans and promotions, training and travel-assistance programs, and undertakes the construction of resort areas. Internationally, the KNTC undertakes all promotions, including sponsoring seminars with travel agents from various world markets, participating in major tourism exhibitions and conventions, advertising in many different media, and distributing guide materials. By the mid-1980s, annual target figures of 1.5 million international tourist arrivals and US$800 million in international tourist earnings were met owing to the KNTC efforts.

With a number of offices around the world, the KNTC has increased tourism from the European market, especially from Great Britain and Germany, and from the Asian market, especially Japan, through close cooperation and joint promotional programs with major airline companies, cruise operators, travel agents, and hotels. To convene various types of international events successfully, the KNTC has intensified cooperation with the World Travel Organization, the Pacific Area Travel Association, the American Society of Travel Agencies, and other organizations, created favorable conditions for holding international conferences in Korea, conducted the Hospitality Campaign for Overseas Visitors, guided the training of employees in the travel trade, and established excellent shopping tour programs. The KNTC also developed the advertising and media publicity campaigns for the 1988 Summer Olympic Games in Seoul.

**New Hotels.** As Korea approached the Olympic Games, the government concentrated on developing adequate hotel facilities for the expected influx of visitors from abroad. Construction of seven new hotels with a total of nearly 2,500 rooms proceeded during 1988, the largest of thesse are the Sophie Hotel with 520 rooms, the New Giant Hotel with 500 rooms, and a new Lotte World Hotel. Other hotels being built are the Hannam Tourist, the Hwarang Tourist, the Ramada Renaissance, the Capital Hotel, the Universe Tourist, the New World Tourist, the the Sun and Clover.

**Designation of Tourist Resorts.** When a place is designated as a resort area it becomes eligible for development as a tourist center, while at the same time the protection of natural resources is taken into account. More than 100 tourist resorts are listed throughout the country and the government has recently upgraded more than 20 to international-class standards. The area of these resorts accounts for two percent of the total national territory, and they include lakes, islands, beaches, hot springs, parks, temples, forests, caverns, streams, waterfalls, castles, historic sites, and scenic spots.

**American Family Reunion Program.** In commemoration of the centennial of diplomatic relations between Korea and the United States, the KNTC, in cooperation with U.S. Armed Forces in Korea, initiated a reunion program for the families of the U.S. service personnel, enabling them to visit Korea on a five-day program. This contributes to diversification of the travel market and introduces Korea to families visiting loved ones stationed in Korea.

KOREA NATIONAL TOURIST CORPORATION

**KNTC Offices.** The KNTC main office in Seoul is located at 10 Tadong (757-0086); the Tourist Information Center (757-6030) provides tour information and source materials free of charge; reservations and ticketing for sightseeing, accommodations, and transportation; exhibitions of photos, maps, and indigenous products of each province; and presentations of films and slide-shows on Korea. The following KNTC overseas offices will give special assistance and send free resource materials to ensure that travelers enjoy their trip to Korea.

## DIRECTORY OF MAJOR KNTC OVERSEAS OFFICES

CHICAGO: 230 North Michigan Ave., Ste. 1500, Chicago, IL 60601; tel: 312-346-6660

FRANKFURT: Wiesenhütten Platz 26, 6000, Frankfurt am Main, West Germany; tel: 069-233226

HONOLULU: 1188 Bishop St., Century Sq., PH 1, Honolulu, HI 96813; tel: 808-521-8066

HONG KONG: Rm. 506, Bank of America Tower, 12 Harcourt Rd., tel: 5-238065

LONDON: 1 Hanover Square, London, W1R 9RD, United Kingdom; tel: 01-409-2100

LOS ANGELES: 510 West Sixth Street, Ste. 323, Los Angeles, CA 90014; tel: 213-623-1226

NEW YORK: 460 Park Ave., Ste. 400, New York, NY 10022; tel: 212-688-7543

PARIS: 33 Avenue du Maine, B.P. 169, Paris, 75755, France; tel. 01-45-38-71-23

SEATTLE: % Erhig and Associates, 4th & Vine Building, Seattle, WA 98121; tel: 206-441-6666

SINGAPORE: 24 Raffles Place, #20-03 Clifford Ctr., Singapore 0104; tel: 533-0441

SYDNEY: Ste. 2101, Tower Blg., Australia Square, George St., Sydney 2000, Australia; tel: 27-4132

TOKYO: Rm. 124 Sanshim Blg. 4-1 1-chome, Yuraku-cho, Chiyoda-ku Tokyo, Japan; tel: 03-580-3941

# KOREA TRAVEL OPTIONS: GROUP TOURS AND INDEPENDENT TRAVEL

In the mid-1980s, almost 40 percent of total foreign visitors to Korea arrived as members of group tours arranged through international travel agencies. Group travel, including packaged sightseeing, dining, and hotel arrangements, makes the most efficient use of Korean travel facilities and of the tourist's time and money. There is no doubt that tour groups see more of Korea and at a lower cost than is possible on an unplanned individual trip through the country. Members of group tours arrive with the assurance of a hotel room, transportation, dining arrangements, and a bilingual sightseeing program.

In spite of the advantages of group tours, there are, of course, always some travelers who, for a variety of reasons—time constraints, itinerary requirements, professional interests, or personal inclination—find group travel impractical and prefer to travel independently. Although costs are higher and more time must be spent in advance planning, individual travel is a viable option in Korea today. In fact, it opens many opportunities for exploration, discovery, and enjoyment of personal contact with Korean people.

# CHOOSING A GROUP TOUR TO KOREA

Travelers seeking to visit Korea as tourists can purchase space on a tour through travel agents anywhere in the world. It is not unusual for group tour participants to save more than 50 percent of the cost they would pay were they to follow the same itinerary on their own. They also are spared all logistical difficulties: hotel space is prebooked; sightseeing programs, intercity transfers, and meals are prearranged; guides and interpreters are provided. Groups usually consist of 10 to 50 people and follow a fixed itinerary that includes three to six cities; many include stopovers in Tokyo, Hong Kong, or other Asian cities. Costs of tours vary considerably; travelers should be alert to differences in places of interest included, quality of lodgings, meals provided, and trans-Pacific routings used, as well as their preference as to time of year, length of stay, and theme (if any) of the tour.

*Court flower dance*

Standard itineraries range from five to 13 days in Korea and usually encompass Seoul as well as two to four other cities or resort areas; a recent innovation is the "regional tour," which skips Seoul. For the great majority of visitors arriving and leaving via Kimpo International Airport, Seoul is the logical first and last stop. Other points of entry are Pusan and Cheju Island. Most moderately priced tours include Seoul, Kyongju, and Cheju Island; the longer ones include Mt. Sorak National Park, Taegu, and/or Pusan.

### SAMPLE ITINERARY
### STANDARD KOREA TOUR (13 DAYS–11 DAYS IN KOREA)

Day 1—Depart San Francisco/Los Angeles/New York for Seoul; cross international date line

Day 2–12—Arrive Seoul (4 days)–Panmunjom (1 day)–Kyongju (2 days)–Pusan (2 days)–Cheju Island (2 days)

Day 13—Depart Seoul for San Francisco/Los Angeles/New York

# TOURING KOREA ON YOUR OWN

### PLANNING AN INDEPENDENT KOREA TRIP

The individual visitor to Korea can, with prior research and planning, enjoy contemporary city life, see beautiful scenery and historical relics, and pursue special interests. In Seoul and other cities, most of the major historical sites are in the downtown, old-city areas and are accessible by walking. Many of the most noteworthy temples, however, are in the mountains. Resorts have been established in places of special interest. Those whose interest is Korean culture will want to visit Seoul and Kyongju, where classical architecture survives and many other relics of "old Korea" can be seen. Seoul and Kyongju have been designated as international cultural centers for foreign visitors in view of their rich cultural assets, and the government has designated Cheju Island as an international resort area because of its exotic natural resources.

A typical itinerary for the tourist spending two weeks in Korea is: Seoul and vicinity, including Panmunjom and Mt. Sorak (4–5 days); bus trip to Taejon, Taegu, Kyongju, and Pusan (4–5 days); cruise the Hallyo Waterway (1 day); trip to Kongju and Puyo area and return to Seoul (3–4 days); for Cheju Island, add 2 days.

**Special-Interest or Professional Tours.** Tours in Korea for those with a particular interest, profession, or specialty can be arranged so that part of their time in Korea is spent in meetings with professional counterparts and visiting institutions or other appropriate sites.

**Tours for the Adventurous.** Active modes of tourism, including camping, trekking, mountain climbing, wilderness exploration, golfing, skiing, and water sports are becoming increasingly popular. Retaining the group format and costs, these programs offer extraordinary access to the Korean countryside.

It is possible to travel in Korea for as little as $20 per day, all costs included, by arranging to use youth hostels (*yogwan*), seeking special intercity travel rates, doing a lot of walking, and so on. A more realistic average for free-lance travel in Korea would be $50 per day and up, including room, meals, and transportation. An average of $100 or more per day adds up quickly with deluxe accommodations and meals and long-distance intercity travel. Of course, longer stays tend to become less expensive per diem, as do trips by two people sharing one hotel room. Many hotels in Korea are priced at $40 to $70 per night; traditional inns can average less than $15. Three meals per day in hotel dining rooms total about $30. Banquet-type meals with entertainment naturally cost much more. Travel between major cities by train costs $20 to $50; bus fares are somewhat less. Within cities it is easy to get around by public bus or by taxi at quite reasonable fares, as well as on foot.

## KOREA TOUR COSTS

Tour operators, travel agencies, and airlines sponsoring tours to Korea provide listings of their trips for the upcoming year upon request; these include dates and points of departure, a detailed breakdown of itineraries, and prices. Care should be taken to determine what is included in the package and tour policy regarding revision of air fares.

**Group Land Costs.** The cost of a group tour includes all land costs in Korea—hotel accommodations, three meals daily, tour escorts, and all surface and air transportation within Korea. For the mid-1980s, land costs varied considerably—from a low of about $700 for seven days in Korea ($100 per day) to as much as $3,000 for 15 days ($200 per day). Many tours now use the newly available deluxe hotels, which doubles the cost of accommodations.

**Single-Occupancy Supplements.** Hotel accommodations are allocated on a double-occupancy basis; single rooms are available at a surcharge of about $30 per day. Single occupancy should be requested immediately upon arrival in each city and the surcharge paid directly; singles cannot always be guaranteed in advance.

**Costs for Individual Travel.** Individual tour itineraries are of three types: "full-day deluxe" packages with hotel, all meals, private guide, and car, $150–$300 per day per person; "half-day deluxe," with hotel, all meals, and escorted sightseeing, $80–$150; and "mini deluxe," including hotel and breakfast but without escorted sightseeing, $50–$80.

**Intercity Travel.** Intercity bus or rail fares must be added to the prices given above; these usually are $20 to $50 depending on distance and type of travel.

## AIR FARES

**Group Inclusive Tour Fares (GIT).** Most air fares quoted by tour sponsors are based on the GIT economy fare, which requires that a minimum of 10 persons travel together for at least 14 days and for not more than 35 days; the group must remain intact until the last stopover point in Asia. Passengers are allowed individual stopovers on the route home at no extra cost, providing they do not travel beyond the final group destination in Asia or beyond the 35-day limit. GIT fares from the U.S. West Coast range from $950 to $1,200 for a standard flight from Los Angeles or San Francisco–Tokyo–Seoul–return; flights from the East Coast are about $300 more.

**Budget Fares.** Major airlines with direct trans-Pacific routes to Korea (Korean Air, Japan Air Lines, Northwest Orient, United Airlines) offer a variety of low-cost budget fares for groups; these have more restrictions than GIT fares: stopovers are not permitted, reservations are only accepted from seven to 21 days prior to departure, and cancellations are subject to a 50 percent penalty. Budget fares are also available to individuals, but with even greater restrictions. The fare from San Francisco to Seoul and return is $800–$950.

**Individual Inclusive Tour Fares (IIT).** Individuals traveling in Korea with a group, but requiring separate travel either before or after the tour, should inform their travel agent in advance; the agent can arrange an IIT fare, which is higher than GIT, but less than separately purchased tickets.

**Economy Fares.** Individual travelers can take advantage of economy fares offered by most airlines; these carry few restrictions and usually are valid for up to one year. San Francisco or Los Angeles to Seoul and return costs $1,200 (KAL).

## WHEN TO GO

The word Korea (or Koryo) means high and clear and is symbolic of the country's towering mountains, clear blue skies, and rushing streams—which have earned Korea the nickname "Switzerland of Asia." Like the United States, Korea has a temperate climate with four distinct seasons; being relatively small, the extremes are not great, but winters are milder in the south. Spring and autumn are very pleasant, with many days of sunshine, and are the most popular times for visiting Korea. Summers are hot and humid: July is the wettest month, and August is the hottest. Knowledgeable travelers have made September and October the peak season. Discounts and other incentives are offered for "off" season travel—November through March.

## HOLIDAYS AND SEASONAL EVENTS

Korea has 13 official public holidays; these are occasions for family gatherings and outings. The government has formal public displays for Independence Day, Buddha's Birthday, and Armed Forces Day. Business travelers will want to avoid the national holidays, as enterprises and government offices are closed. New Year's Day is officially celebrated on January 1, but many people still enjoy a three-day celebration of the traditional New Year, which comes in January or February, according to cycles of the Chinese lunar calendar. The 13 official holidays are:

| January 1 | New Year |
| January* | Folklore Day |
| March 1 | Independence Day |
| April 5 | Arbor Day |
| April* | Buddha's Birthday |
| May 5 | Children's Day |
| June 6 | Memorial Day |
| July 17 | Constitution Day |
| August 15 | Liberation Day |
| August* | Thanksgiving Day |
| October 1 | Armed Forces Day |
| October 3 | National Foundation Day |
| October 9 | *Hangul* Day |
| December 25 | Christmas Day |

* Date varies, according to the lunar calendar.

## SPECIAL EVENTS

The two English-language newspapers, the *Korea Times* and the *Korea Herald*, print lists of current movies and plays, stage shows, public concerts, special seminars, sports events, and church services. The exact dates of many annual events vary because they follow the lunar calendar. Below are holidays, celebrations, and other events that visitors may enjoy.

## ANNUAL EVENTS

Festivals are an important feature of Korean life; many are of a religious nature, and others commemorate national events of ancient and modern times. Often they are filled with pageantry, merrymaking, and colorful rites. Although Korea officially follows the Western Gregorian calendar, many of its holidays originated centuries ago, and their dates are based on the ancient Oriental lunar calendar. The Lunar New Year occurs in late January or early February by the Gregorian calendar. The old festivals are celebrated in the traditional way in the countryside; in Seoul, some urbanites follow old customs out of habit or nostalgia, while others simply use the free day for family activities.

*Solnal (January 1-3).* The first three days of the Gregorian New Year are recognized officially, but many Koreans still observe the traditional Lunar New Year about a month later.

*Ku-jung (Lunar New Year).* The whole family dons their best clothes, and members of the younger generation bow to their parents and grandparents as a reaffirmation of family ties.

*March 1, Samiljol (Independence Movement Day).* Independence Day honors the 1919 Independence Movement against Japanese colonial rule. The Proclamation of Independence signed by 33 patriots in 1919 is read at Pagoda Park in Seoul.

*March 10, Labor Day.* Although Labor Day is not a government holiday, banks and business establishments are closed, and many enjoy a day off.

*Hansik (105th day after center of winter day, sometime in early April).* Koreans prepare wine, fruit, cakes, and vegetables for ceremonies at the graves of their ancestors.

*April 5, Arbor Day.* Trees and shrubs are planted by children and adults all over the countryside as part of Korea's reforestation program.

*May (first Sunday), Chongmyo Ritual.* Ceremonies with special music and dances honoring ancestors, at Chongmyo Shrine.

*Sokchon Ceremony (early May and in the fall).* Sokchon rites honor the great sage Confucius in ceremonies at Songkyunkwan University campus in Myongnyundong; the exact dates are set by the lunar calendar.

*Buddha's Birthday (April or May).* Buddha's birthday is a national holiday, celebrated on the eighth day of the fourth lunar month. That evening, thousands of lanterns illuminate the city. People hang paper lanterns on specially strung strands of wire in temple courtyards, and a lantern parade winds through the city, finishing at Chogye Temple downtown. Crowds gather there and at other temples all over Seoul. Toson Temple is spectacular, aglow under its blue tile roof in a setting of green trees. Pongwon Temple, behind Ewha Woman's University, holds performances of liturgical Buddhist dances in the evening. The strings of candlelit lanterns illuminating the hillside slope behind Pongun Temple (directly across from the Korea Exhibition Center [KOEX]) cast a lovely shimmering glow over the whole area.

*May 5, Children's Day.* Originally celebrated as "Boys' Day" in Korea, this national holiday in spring has become popular as a time for families to take their children on excursions.

*May 8, Parents' Day.* Sons and daughters pay respects and show love to both their parents.

*Tano Day (5th day of 5th lunar month, late June).* Tano is one of the three great celebration days of the lunar year, together with

New Year and Chusok. Summer food is offered at the household shrine of the ancestors. It is also known as "swing day" since girls dressed in their prettiest clothes often enter swinging competitions.

*June 6, Memorial Day.* On this legal holiday the nation pays tribute to the war dead. Memorial services are held at the National Cemetary in Seoul.

*June 15, Farmers' Day.* This is not a legal holiday, but farmers are honored throughout the country with colorful folk dances performed to the accompaniment of traditional music played on centuries-old instruments.

*August 15, Liberation Day.* This national holiday commemorates Japan's acceptance of Allied surrender terms in 1945, thereby freeing Korea from 36 years of Japanese domination. Military parades and ceremonies are held throughout the country. The observances also mark the formal proclamation of the Republic of Korea in 1948.

*Chusok (15th day of 8th lunar month, latter part of September or early October).* Chusok is one of the great national holidays, the Korean Thanksgiving Day. It has traditionally been set aside as a day for paying respect to ancestors, when people in beautiful traditional dress place newly harvested foods and wines at family tombs. Song and dance continue until the harvest moon appears brightly shining above the horizon.

*October 1, Armed Forces Day.* Colorful military parades and aerial acrobatic shows mark this national holiday. Honor guard ceremonies are held around the reviewing plaza on Yoido, an island in the Han River.

*October 3, National Foundation Day.* Also called Tangun Day, this holiday commemorates the day when the legendary founder of the Korean nation, Tangun, established his Kingdom of Chosun in 2333 B.C.

*October 9, Hangul Day (Korean Alphabet Day).* This national holiday celebrates the anniversary of the promulgation of *Hangul*, the written language of Korea, by King Sejong in 1448.

*December 25, Christmas Day.* Christmas is observed as a national holiday as it is in the West. The Catholic Cathedral in Myong-dong is noted for its beautiful Christmas masses; other churches also have lovely services.

The visitor who is in Korea at the time of one of these festivals will enjoy a panorama of processionals and performances of traditional music, drama, and martial arts, and will have an opportunity to gain insight into traditional Korean culture.

## RELIGIOUS SERVICES

The following churches hold English-language services: the Anglican Cathedral next to Toksu Palace; the Lutheran Church and Center in Hannam-dong; Seoul Union Church (Protestant) in the Grand Ball Room at the Chosun Hotel; the Yongkak Presbyterian Church near Paik Hospital; the World Mission Center at the Yoi-do Full Gospel Central Church; the Church of Jesus Christ of Latter-day Saints at South Post Chapel on the U.S. Army base; Seoul International Baptist Church on Yoi-do; the Seventh Day Adventist Church at Seoul Sanitarium Hospital in Tongdaemun-ku; the Roman Catholic Franciscan Chapel near the MBC Building on Sinmunno Avenue; Jewish services on the U.S. 8th Army South Post; the Islam Mosque in Itaewon; Buddhist services at Chogye-sa; Greek Orthodox services at St. Nicholas Orthodox Church in Ahyon-dong; and Christian Science services at Miju Apartments in Pil-dong.

## SPORTS

The Korean people love all kinds of sports, individual and team, both as spectators and as participants. Popular Western sports include baseball, soccer, basketball, volleyball, boxing, tennis, and table tennis. The traditional Korean martial arts of *taekwondo* and *ssirum* are also widely enjoyed, and traditional folk games still survive. During the National Folk Arts Contest at the end of October, provinces vie for honors. Particularly colorful is *kosamnori*, a group game recalling ancient battles. On the international level, Korean men and women have become highly competitive in a number of sports. Seoul frequently hosts national and international sports events. In 1988, of course, Korea successfully hosted the 24th Olympic Games.

For the visitor to Seoul, the following are some of the more accessible sports.

*Swimming.* Outdoor public pools are crowded, but for indoor swimming the Taenung Olympic-size pool is excellent. Major hotels have indoor and/or outdoor swimming pools.

*Fishing.* Fishing is now a major leisure activity among Koreans, and Korea is a virtual paradise for sport fishermen. Surrounded on three sides by the sea, surf fishing is popular. Because Korea is surrounded on three sides by the sea, surf fishing is popular. Inland, myriad streams, ponds, and lakes provide excellent freshwater fishing.

*Golf.* There are 20 golf courses in and around Seoul, and the sport is gaining in popularity as leisure time increases. The courses are private, but it is relatively easy for foreign visitors to play as guests, especially during the week.

*Tennis.* Tennis has been growing faster than any other sport in Korea, and Seoul has many courts, public and private, including several indoor courts. Try the Seoul Union Club (753-2871).

*Skiing.* Five major ski resort areas are easily reached from Seoul. Yongpyeong Resort (Dragon Valley) (548-2251), Yong-in (744-2001), Chonmasan (744-6020), Alps (546-6962), and Bears' Town (546-7210). All offer good skiing, comfortable accommodations, and plenty of night life.

*Climbing.* Seoul is close to precipitous peaks that challenge the skills and equipment of the avid climber. Insubong near Paegundae is considered the most difficult. There are many established trails through less difficult terrain, and hiking groups offer group trips in the Seoul region.

*Martial Arts.* Korea's *taekwondo* and *yudo* are similar to Japanese karate and judo. The World Taekwondo Association as well as the National Taekwondo Association are headquartered in

*Taekwondo demonstration*

Seoul; they hold regular exhibitions at Kukkiwon, the main *tae-kwondo* gymnasium (567-3024). Seoul Yudo College is devoted to teaching and developing the art of *yudo*. Both martial arts are also taught in many small practice halls throughout the city.

*Other sports.* Facilities for hunting, waterskiing, wind surfing, and even ice sailing can be found in and around Seoul.

## THE SEOUL OLYMPICS

The 24th Olympic Games, anxiously awaited as South Korea's rise to prominence on the world stage, will be remembered as much for its high drama in sports competition as for peripheral events surrounding the Games. A record 160 countries participated in the Games; nearly 10,000 athletes competed in 23 official sports, three demonstration sports, and one exhibition sport (bowling). Korea's performance placed it sixth in total medals at 33, and fourth in gold medals, behind the Soviet Union, East Germany, and the United States. Compared to the previous Summer Games in Los Angeles,

Korean athletes earned twice the number of medals. Traditional rivalries between East and West surfaced in the gymnastic, diving, and team sport events for the first time since 1976 (owing to the boycotts of 1980 and 1984).

Moments of individual triumph and personal defeat went hand in hand: the artistry, strength, and competitive edge of the US diver, Greg Louganis, marked this Olympiad as surely as did the fall from grace of the Canadian runner, Ben Johnson, over his suspected use of illegal steroids. Of the 250,000 foreigners expected to attend, actual estimates were closer to 150,000, of which about 30,000 came from the US. For Korea, media coverage of the Games was a mixed blessing, showing off the country's prosperity but also laying bare the raw emotions of its sports community and the Korean public. What remains, however, aside from the honor of having hosted the Games, are several fine arenas, hotels, and transport facilities which can be used for future international events.

*Chamshil Gymnasium*

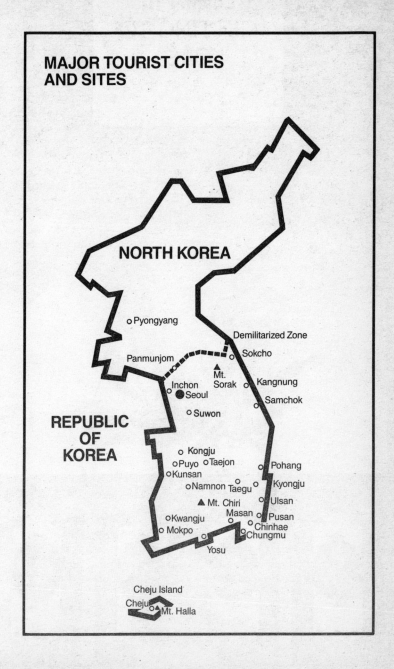

**MAJOR TOURIST CITIES AND SITES**

NORTH KOREA

Pyongyang

Demilitarized Zone

Panmunjom

Sokcho

Mt. Sorak

Inchon

Kangnung

Seoul

Samchok

Suwon

**REPUBLIC OF KOREA**

Kongju

Puyo

Taejon

Pohang

Kunsan

Kyongju

Namnon

Taegu

Mt. Chiri

Ulsan

Masan

Pusan

Kwangju

Chinhae

Mokpo

Chungmu

Yosu

Cheju Island

Cheju

Mt. Halla

# Chapter III
# GETTING TO KOREA

# VISA APPLICATION FOR KOREA

제7호서식

## 대 한 민 국
### REPUBLIC OF KOREA

## 사 증 발 급 신 청 서
### APPLICATION FOR VISA

APPLICATION NO._____

DATE_____

PASSPORT CLASSIFICATION
DIPLOMATIC ( )
SPECIAL ( )
REGULAR ( )

1. NAME_____ (SEX ) 2. NATIONALITY_____
       LAST   FIRST   MIDDLE
3. PLACE OF BIRTH_____ DATE OF BIRTH_____
4. PRESENT ADDRESS_____ PHONE NO._____
5. PERMANENT ADDRESS_____
6. SPOUSE'S NAME & NATIONALITY_____
7. OCCUPATON & TITLE(EXPLAIN FULLY)_____
8. PURPOSE OF ENTRY (EXPLAIN FULLY)_____
_____
_____

9. PASSPORT NO._____ ISSUED BY_____ ON_____ VALID TILL_____
10. PREVIOUS VISIT, IF ANY_____ DESIRED LENGTH OF STAY_____
11. PORT OF EMBARKATION_____ MEANS OF TRANSPORTATION_____
12. PORT OF ENTRY (KOREA)_____ EXPECTED DATE OF ENTRY_____
13. ADDRESS IN KOREA_____ PHONE NO._____
14. THREE REFERENCES IN KOREA (FOR ENTRY VISA ONLY)

| NAME | ADDRESS |
|---|---|
|  |  |
|  |  |
|  |  |

5. IMMEDIATE MEMBERS OF FAMILY, IF ACCOMPANIED

| NAME | SEX | AGE | RELATION | NATIONALITY |
|---|---|---|---|---|
|  |  |  |  |  |
|  |  |  |  |  |
|  |  |  |  |  |

6cm/6cm
PHOTO

I declare that the statements made in this application are true and correct to the best of my knowledge and belief, that I will observe the provisions of the Law on Control of Exit and Entry of the Republic of Korea, and that I will not engage in any activities irrelevant to the purpose of entry stated herein.

____DATE____ ____SIGNATURE OF APPLICANT____

SPACES BELOW FOR OFFICIAL USE ONLY

# VISA PROCEDURES FOR
# KOREA TRAVEL

E ntry into Korea is simple. Travelers are required only to present a valid passport when applying for a visa. Transit visitors with onward reservations are allowed a 15-day stay without a visa. Usually it is possible to add a stopover in Korea when purchasing tickets to Tokyo or Hong Kong with no added cost.

**Transit without Visa.** An overseas visitor holding a ticket with a confirmed reservation for the next destination can land in transit for general tourism by getting a landing permit from the immigration inspector at the port of entry. If the stay exceeds 15 days then a visa must be obtained at a Korean embassy or consulate.

**Passport or Travel Document.** An overseas visitor entering Korea must have a valid passport, except in the following circumstances: Stateless persons or visitors from a country whose government is not recognized by the Republic of Korea may be issued a Travel Document for Aliens by a Korean embassy or consulate abroad in lieu of a passport; uniformed U.S. Army personnel falling under the Status of Forces Agreement (SOFA) are not required to obtain a passport; a *Laissez-passer* issued by the UN is officially recognized as a valid passport.

**Visa Applications.** An overseas visitor planning to travel to Korea must obtain a visa from a Korean embassy or consulate. The traveler who has a reentry permit can enter the country within the period of the permit. Those making direct arrangements can obtain a visa application form from a Korean consular office. The Korean embassy usually returns the passport with a visa stamp in less than a week. Transit visitors who plan to be in Korea longer than 15 days must obtain a visa in the same manner.

**Visa Exemptions.** Nationals of countries that have visa exemption agreements with the Republic of Korea, insofar as their purpose is tourism and not engaging in any activity for remuneration, may enter Korea without a visa for the periods indicated: for 90 days— Austria, Chile, Greece, Mexico, and Switzerland; for 60 days— most European nations; for 30 days—France and Finland.

**Special-Interest Visa.** To obtain a visa for special-interest or professional (including business) visits, travelers must have an official invitation to visit Korea. The invitation may be in the form of a letter or telex.

**Tour Group Visas.** Those traveling to Korea as part of a tour group do not need to obtain individual visas. Visas are granted to tours on a group basis; the group's escort will have a "visaed manifest" listing the names and nationalities of all tour members. The tour organizer supplies tour members with a visa application form in advance of departure and submits the completed forms to the Korean embassy to obtain the group visa.

## PROCEDURES FOR EXTENDED STAYS IN KOREA

**Korean Immigration Offices.** For help in any matter pertaining to visas or length of stay in Korea, the traveler should contact the Main Office in Seoul (776-8984) or the Kimpo Airport District Office (066-7611) of the Korean Immigration Bureau.

**Residence Certificate.** For most overseas visitors who intend to stay in Korea for more than 60 days, a residence certificate is required and can be obtained at the District Immigration Office before the expiration of 60 days after arrival in Korea. There are some exceptions to this rule, however.

**Change of Status of Entry.** An alien who desires to engage in a new activity falling under a different entry status must apply at the Residence Control Division of the Immigration Bureau for a change of entry status.

**Extension of Visa.** Tourist transit and 30-day visa holders who desire to extend their stay must apply at the District Immigration Office for an extension before the expiration of their authorized period of stay. Sixty-day visa holders who desire to remain longer must apply to the residence Control Division of the Immigration Bureau before the expiration of their 60-day stay; upon receiving approval of the extension, the visitor must apply at the District Immigration Office for a residence certificate. The certificate is surrendered upon departure.

## PROCEDURES FOR DEPARTURES FROM KOREA

**Permanent Departure.** An overseas visitor who has stayed in Korea on a transit, 30-day, or 60-day entry visa requires no additional documentation for departing; a resident visitor must surrender his residence certificate to the Immigration Office at the port of departure. The airport tax is ₩5,000 per person.

**Temporary Departure.** A resident alien who desires to leave Korea and return during the period of his/her authorized stay must apply at the District Immigration Office for a reentry permit.

# INTERNATIONAL ROUTINGS TO KOREA

Visitors arriving by airlines through Kimpo International Airport account for 85 percent of the total; Kimhae and Cheju international airports account for 10 percent; arrivals by ship through Pusan, Inchon, and other ports account for five percent.

**Airlines.** Korea is located within 24-hour flying time from any part of the world. Major international airlines depart from many cities in the United States and Europe daily; some fly directly to Seoul, and others connect with Korea-bound flights at international airports in the Far East. There are over 400 flights weekly by international airlines connecting Korea with Japan, Hong Kong, Taiwan, and Thailand. The flight from Tokyo to Seoul takes two hours; Korean Air and Japan Air Lines also connect Osaka, Nagoya, Fukuoka, Kumamoto, and Niigata with Pusan, Seoul, and Cheju Island. From Hong Kong, passengers can fly directly to Seoul in three hours via Cathay Pacific Airways and Korean Air, while many airlines link Taipei and Seoul. All-Nippon Airways (ANA) inaugurated service in 1988 between Tokyo and Seoul; connecting cities served include Los Angeles, Washington, DC, Sydney, Hong Kong, and Dalian. Japan Air System also flies between Japan and Korea. In late 1989, both Garuda and QUANTAS will begin passenger service to Seoul.

From the United States, three US airlines fly to Korea: Northwest, Delta, and United. Northwest has daily nonstop flights from Los Angeles and three nonstop flights a week from Seattle. Northwest (NW) offers connections from most major US cities which stop in Tokyo en route to Seoul. NW also offers nonstop service between Detroit and Seoul. In 1988, Delta increased its nonstop service from Portland to Seoul from three times weekly to daily flights. During peak season, United also flies from Seattle three times a week; their year-round daily direct flights depart from San Francisco. Daily flights also depart from New York, Chicago, Honolulu, and Washington, DC; all flights fly to Tokyo for their connections to Seoul. United flies Boeing 747 SPs and L-1011s on its flight to Korea. The flight to Soeul from the West Coast takes less than 12 hours.

Connections from Europe include British Airways, which now

offers direct service from London to Seoul once a week via the North Pole route. Lufthansa flies from Frankfurt to Seoul by way of Hong Kong. Among the other airlines which depart from European cities are KLM, Air France, Swissair, Dan Air, and Alitalia.

Korean Air has air routes between Seoul and destinations in the United States, Europe, and the Middle East. Their nonstop flights from the US depart from Honolulu and Los Angeles daily; direct flights from New York operate via Anchorage. Soon Korea will have a second airline offering international service. Asiana Airlines (formerly Seoul Air International), which initiated domestic service in late 1988, will introduce flights to Tokyo, Osaka, and Fukuoka starting at the end of 1989. In 1991, Boeing 747 service will be extended to Los Angeles, New York, and Honolulu, with other cities in East Asia and Europe under consideration.

*Logo for Asiana, Korea's newest airline*

In addition to the commencement of new routes, travel to Korea has been assisted by the recent opening of air space over China, shortening travel time in some cases by up to 1½ hours. Korea was also given the right to begin operating a few charter flights direct to Shanghai in the spring of 1989, with hope that they could soon go straight to Beijing as well. This was a sensitive matter, however, as North Korea objected. Now, with the aftermath of the student massacre, the ROK government has discouraged tourism to China again, at least temporarily. Aeroflot is also trying to begin flight service. Earlier this year Russia opened a trade office in Seoul. The interest shown by Aeroflot also means that flights originating from Korea may have a better chance to fly over Russian airspace enroute to Europe, saving both time and money.

Seoul is included in the round-the-world air schedule approved by the International Air Transport Association; this permits any passenger on a round-the-world ticket to visit Korea at no additional charge. At present, a total of 18 non-Korean airlines fly to Korea.

Korea has three international airports: Kimpo at Seoul, Kimhae at Pusan, and Cheju Island. The new Kimpo International Air Terminal in Seoul is fully equipped with the most up-to-date flight control equipment and other aviation support facilities. The terminal handles eight million passengers and .5 million tons of cargo annually. Its parking lots accommodate 2,400 vehicles. Information counters are located in the new terminal building: these include the General Information Desk operated by the Korea National Tourism Corporation and the Korea Tourist Association, Rent-A-Car Service, Walker Hill Airport Bus Service, Korea Hotel Association, Korean Air, and USO Information counters. In addition, a new airport check-in facility was opened this year at the new Korea World Trade Center in KOEX (Korea Exhibition Center) in Kangnam. It is called the City Air Terminal. The airport is 30 minutes from downtown Seoul and the Olympic complex.

## International airlines
## maintaining regular flight service

| | | | |
|---|---|---|---|
| Air France | (02) 753-2574 | Lufthansa German | |
| All Nippon Airways (ANA) | | Airlines | (02) 777-9655 |
| Asiana Airlines | (02) 771-71 | Malaysian Airline | |
| Cathay Pacific | | System | (02) 777-7761 |
| Airways | (02) 779-0321 | Northwest Orient | |
| China Airlines | (02) 755-1523 | Airlines | (02) 734-7800 |
| Delta Airlines | (02) 753-8087 | Saudi Arabian | |
| Japan Air Lines | (02) 757-1711 | Airlines | (02) 755-5621 |
| Pusan | (051) 44-1215 | Singapore Airlines | (02) 755-1226 |
| Japan Air System (JD) | | Swiss Air | |
| KLM Royal Dutch | | Thai Airways | |
| Airlines | (02) 753-1093 | International | (02) 779-2621 |
| Korean Air | (02) 755-2221 | United Airlines | (02) 757-1691 |
| Pusan | (051) 44-0131 | | |
| Cheju | (064) 22-6111 | | |

## Other airlines with resident offices

| | | | |
|---|---|---|---|
| Air-India | (02) 778-0064 | Philippine Airlines | (02) 725-1401 |
| Alitalia Airlines | (02) 779-1676 | Qantas Airways | (02) 777-6871 |
| American | | Pan Am World | |
| Airlines Inc. | (02) 755-3314 | Airlines | (02) 777-2993 |
| British Airways | (02) 777-6871 | Sabena Belgian | |
| Canadian Pacific | | Airlines | (02) 778-0394 |
| Airlines | (02) 753-8271 | Scandinavian | |
| Continental Airlines | (02) 778-0394 | Airlines System | (02) 725-5123 |
| Eastern Airlines | (02) 777-9786 | Swiss Air Transport | (02) 757-8901 |
| Finnair | (02) 734-7100 | Trans World | |
| Garuda International | | Airlines | (02) 777-4864 |
| Airlines | (02) 777-8251 | Varig Brazilian | |
| Gulf Air | (02) 779-1676 | Airlines | (02) 779-3877 |
| Kuwait Airlines | (02) 753-0041 | | |

### Airlines with off-line offices

| | | | |
|---|---|---|---|
| El Al Israel Airlines | (02) 755-1345 | Royal Jordanian | |
| Iberia Airlines | (02) 739-0941 | Airlines | (02) 774-1010 |
| Lan Chile Airlines | | | |

**Ferries.** The Pukwan (Pusan-Shimonoseki) Ferry provides service between Pusan, Korea, and Shimonoseki, Japan, three times weekly; its capacity is 952 passengers. Kukché Ferry offers twice-weekly connections between Pusan and Osaka, Japan. Temporary entry is allowed for private cars of visitors to Korea. The initial stay of 15 days can be extended for one 15-day period.

**Cruise Ships.** World cruise lines now feature shore excursions in Korea (Pusan) as highlights of their global voyages. Operators include Asia Cruises of the Royal Cruise and Royal Viking Lines.

# PACKING FOR A TRIP TO KOREA

**K**orea has four distinct seasons; lightweight clothing is appropriate for late spring, summer, and early fall; warm clothing is needed in late fall, winter, and early spring. Since Korea has many Western commodities and makes excellent suits, dresses, shirts, and blouses, the traveler can pack a minimum of things. Wash-and-wear clothing is convenient for touring. The major hotels have excellent laundry, pressing, and dry-cleaning services, including one-day service. A light raincoat is good for any time of year. Walking shoes are a must, with a dressier pair for dinners or special occasions. Bring regularly used prescription medicines and vitamins and basic first-aid remedies. Women may wish to bring sanitary supplies, although some Western products are available in Seoul. Film for cameras is available, but imported film is more expensive; therefore bringing your own film is advisable. Although there are a few 45-minute film developers, time considerations usually do not permit developing film in Korea. In addition, one-day service for Ektachrome slides is now offered at a few outlets in Seoul. Western spirits, wine, and cigarettes can be purchased in Seoul, but prices are higher than in New York or London, except for items in duty-free shops. There are no restrictions on bringing in Western magazines, books and maps; but firearms, "street" drugs, pornography, and inflammatory literature are all absolutely prohibited.

# Chapter IV
# TRAVELING IN KOREA

# GETTING ALONG IN KOREA

*GUIDELINES FOR BEHAVIOR AND DECORUM*

**General Conduct.** Whether traveling as an individual or in an escorted group, the visitor should try to relax and "go with the flow" of the tour as much as possible. Being courteous and patient will enhance one's enjoyment of the trip. Good Western manners are generally acceptable in Korea, but a certain restraint is advisable. Koreans, like other Asians, do not appreciate an overly outgoing style, and they generally limit direct physical contact to a courteous handshake. However, as one gets to know Koreans better, a greater familiarity becomes possible. Public displays of affection among members of visiting groups tend to be regarded as unseemly. Since Koreans themselves are reluctant to confront others with unpleasantness, the respectful visitor will attempt to maintain a pleasant demeanor, not showing anger or hostility in public toward either Koreans or fellow group members. Individuals should not be criticized or chastized openly; complaints about arrangements should be made first in private with an escort or interpreter.

Koreans expect guests to behave as representatives of their own countries, and they are respectful of cultural and national differences. Visitors should feel free to speak openly about differing religious beliefs, social customs, or political and economic systems, but disagreements should not be allowed to degenerate into indiscreet remarks that are disrespectful of Korean society or its leaders. The Western "let's get to the point" approach strikes Koreans as rude; even the busiest businessman takes time for the formalities of a proper introduction, or to serve a special cup of tea. There is no such thing as a "Dutch treat" among Koreans; the visitor should be prepared to be either host or guest. It is impolite in Korea to talk too much during a meal; real appreciation of the food and service is important.

In short, harmony is the byword in Korea. Koreans go out of their way to be conscious of others' feelings, and a similar awareness on the part of visitors will ensure the development of positive relationships.

**Punctuality and Protocol.** Punctuality is expected for all social occasions and business appointments. All planned activities should be attended, for great effort will have gone into making the arrangements and trying to please the visitors. Delegations visiting an institution or arriving at a negotiating session should be cognizant

Pyebaek *nuptial ceremony—paying respect to the families*

of protocol requirements. The leader or senior member of the party should enter first, since the Koreans will have lined up the hosts in protocol order. It is appropriate to introduce group members individually after the Koreans have made their introductions, noting anyone who may have special expertise in the subject at hand.

**Tipping.** Tipping is prohibited in Korea; a service charge is included in the hotel or restaurant bill, so tipping is not necessary. A smile, a slight bow, and a word of thanks in English or Korean will express gratitude appropriately.

**Meeting Koreans.** Tourists who approach people on the street in Korea will find the Koreans warm and friendly, ever willing to assist an overseas guest or just to exchange a little conversation. Students are especially eager to meet visitors and practice language skills. When entering a Korean home, shoes are removed; Koreans sit, eat, and sleep on the floor, so shoes are not worn into the living areas. Traditionally, Korean women stand when a man enters the room, but visitors may choose not to conform to this custom.

**Communicating with the Koreans.** English and other foreign languages are now widely taught over radio and television as well as in schools and universities in Korea. In larger cities, it is quite common for Korean students to approach visitors in a friendly attempt to develop their foreign language skills. These conversations often develop into good-humored discussions about different lifestyles and invariably offer some insights into life in Korea.

**Korean Names.** A basic feature of Korean names is that the family name (usually one syllable) precedes the given name (usually two syllables). Thus, Chung Kyung Cho should be addressed as Mr. Chung; the given name is used only by family members or close friends. Koreans take pride in the origin of their family name and ancestry, and the women retain their maiden name even after marriage. Changing Korean names to English spelling produces considerable diversity: thus, the popular Korean name of Lee might also be written as Yi, Li, or Rhee.

# KOREAN CUSTOMS PROCEDURES

**K**orea has simplified procedures for short-term foreign visitors. An oral declaration is normally sufficient for hand baggage, but a written declaration is required if the baggage contains any of the following articles: jewelry, articles made of precious metals, watches, cameras, furs, firearms, knives and swords, and other valuable foreign-made items. Such articles are itemized on the Customs Declarations Form; a copy of the completed form is given to the visitor for presentation when leaving the country.

**Non-Dutiable Items.** Nonresidents may bring in:
1. 400 cigarettes, 50 cigars, 250 grams of pipe tobacco, 100 grams of powder tobacco, 100 grams of brick tobacco, or a mixture of those items within 500 g.
2. Two bottles of alcoholic beverages, which are subject to being opened.
3. Two ounces total of perfume and/or eau-de-cologne.
4. Duties are levied if more than 10 pieces of the same article are brought in.
5. Other articles with a purchase price of up to $125 are eligible for duty exemption.

**Dutiable Items.** The following items require payment of duty: household effects, autos, motorcycles, boats, pianos, organs, video-tape recorders, video cameras, movie cameras and projectors (16mm or larger), air conditioners, hunting weapons, and textile fabrics (not more than 12 sq. yd. may be brought in).

## Additional Information

1. Articles for reexport: Articles brought in as baggage to be exported again within a six-month period are not dutiable; after six months, excise duty must be paid.
2. Passengers whose unaccompanied baggage will arrive by a later flight must make a customs declaration and obtain a clearance record of unaccompanied baggage at time of entry.
3. Bulky items such as washing machines, refrigerators, etc., cannot be checked as personal effects, but must be shipped as cargo.
4. Prohibited: any kind of narcotics, obscene or inhumane pictures, films, subversive publications, firearms or other weapons, and articles for espionage or intelligence activity.
5. A green channel without customs inspection for travelers carrying less than $440 worth of merchandise is being introduced. The green gate may also be used by passengers carrying packages weighing less than 44 pounds and carrying less than $3,000 in cash.

## Currency Imports and Exports

1. Foreign currencies valued at more than $5,000 must be declared on the "Foreign Exchange Record."
2. Unused local currency can be reconverted into U.S. dollars or Japanese yen up to the equivalent of $100.
3. When accompanied by a receipt for foreign currency conversion, unused local currency can be reconverted once within the amount originally exchanged at foreign exchange banks.

## Four Cardinal Rules

1. Declare all items required on the Customs Declaration Form. Personal possessions taken into Korea must be taken out again. Time will be saved by having them readily available for inspection if requested.
2. Do not attempt to bring in any contraband or other illegal items.
3. Save all currency-exchange vouchers and receipts for major purchases. The currency-exchange vouchers will be needed to reconvert unused currency; Korean currency is not to be taken out of Korea. The receipts for purchases may be required by customs upon leaving Korea.
4. Items categorized as "cultual relics" may not be taken out of Korea without evidence that they have been officially approved for export; proof consists of a wax seal or an export certificate from the Ministry of Culture and Public Information.

**Vaccinations.** Immunization against smallpox and cholera is required for travelers arriving from areas infected with these diseases. Children under one year old and people whose age or health prevents such immunizations are exempt upon presentation of a doctor's certificate to that effect.

**Pets.** Cats and dogs must be left in quarantine for 10 days for observation (to check for possible diseases) before being released to their owners. All animals must be declared upon arrival to animal-quarantine officials at the port of entry, with a certificate of quarantine of the country from which the traveler has come.

**Other Animals.** All wild animals are prohibited except by special permission from the Ministry of Agriculture and Fisheries.

**Plants.** Plants and parts of plants must be declared upon arrival to plant-quarantine officials, with plant-quarantine certificates from the home country.

## MONEY IN KOREA

**Korean Currency.** The official unit of currency of the Republic of Korea is the *won*, which is indicated by ₩ in print, but often written as a simple W preceding the amount, as W10,000. The *won* comes in 500, 1,000, 5,000, and 10,000 denomination notes, and in 1, 5, 10, 50, 100, and 500 *won* coins.

**Foreign Currency.** Foreign currencies and traveler's checks can be converted into *won* at currency exchange counters at airports, foreign exchange banks, and major tourist hotels. The exchange rates are subject to fluctuations; as of late 1988, equivalents were about 698.90 *won* per one US dollar and 5.39 *won* per one Japanese yen. *Won* cannot be purchased outside Korea. Banking hours are 9:30 a.m. to 4:30 p.m. Monday through Friday, and 9:30 a.m. to 1:30 p.m. on Saturday.

**Reexchange of Won.** Unused local currency may be reconverted into foreign currency within the amount originally exchanged if a proper exchange receipt is shown. Up to US$100 may be reconverted without a receipt.

**Travelers' Checks and Credit Cards.** Traveler's checks can be cashed at banks and major tourist hotels. Hotels, department stores, some shops, and some restaurants accept American Express, Visa, MasterCard, or Diners Club credit cards.

**Letters of Credit and Bank Accounts.** Overseas businessmen can arrange a letter of credit payable through the Bank of Korea or Korea Foreign Exchange Bank. This can be done through most large international banks for a service fee. Frequent travelers to Korea, especially for business, may want to open an account with the Bank of Korea or Korea Foreign Exchange Bank.

# HEALTH

The traveler leaving for an extended trip should always consult a physician and carry medical records and a supply of regularly needed prescription drugs. In the event of an emergency, excellent medical services are available to visitors at hospitals and local clinics in Korean cities. Korean physicians are well-trained as are nurses and medical technicians. Modern hospitals offer comfortable accommodations and most of the sophisticated diagnostic equipment found in the West.

The most common maladies afflicting travelers in Korea are respiratory problems such as head colds, bronchitis, and sore throats, and diarrhea or constipation. It is wise to carry remedies recommended by one's own physician, but it is easy to obtain standard antibiotics and medication in Korea if needed. Major hotels have house doctors and nurses, and hotel pharmacies dispense Korean-made drugs, which are considered safe, many having been manufactured under licensing and technical supervision arrangements with major international firms.

Should an ambulance be needed, the hotel desk will call one. Recommended hospitals in Seoul are Seoul National University Hospital (7601-0114), Severance Hospital (392-0161), Korea National Medical Center (265-9131), Ewha Woman's University Hospital (762-5061), and St. Mary's Hospital (789-1114).

In general, sanitary conditions are good throughout Korea. Hotel rooms are supplied with drinking water, ice is made from purified water, and local beverages are safe. Restaurants take into account the sensitivity of overseas guests' stomachs, and Korean cuisine provides the built-in safeguards of fresh seasonal ingredients cooked quickly at high temperatures. Tour guides are extremely solicitous about health problems: at the first sign of illness they will recommend seeing a doctor and help the visitor make necessary arrangements.

# DOMESTIC TRAVEL CONNECTIONS IN KOREA

**M**ost overseas visitors travel between major cities of Korea by express bus or train because of their frequency and air-conditioned comfort; also, bus terminals and railway stations are conveniently located in downtown areas. Air service between major Korean cities is increasingly available and popular, especially among business travelers.

**KAL Domestic Flight Services.** Korean Air exclusively serves eight domestic routes, with an array of jet aircraft, but mainly Boeing 707s. There are some 50 to 70 flights per week linking Seoul–Pusan and Seoul–Cheju Island; five to 10 flights per week link the capital with Taegu, Sokcho, Kwangju, Taejon, Chinju, Ulsan, Masan, and Yosu. Since Korea is a peninsula, the duration of flights is around one hour to reach any of these destinations, and the fare is under $50 for adults and children over twelve years of age. Passengers using shuttle tickets or a season ticket must reconfirm within 24 hours before departure. Packages up to 15 kg are transported free of charge. For KAL information: KAL, 41-3 Sosomun-dong, Seoul; tel. 756-2000.

## By Air

Korean Air exclusively services domestic routes.

| From Seoul | Frequency per day | Duration | Fare |
|---|---|---|---|
| Pusan | 26 | 50 min. | ₩25,900 |
| Cheju | 8 | 55 min. | 33,100 |
| Taegu | 3 | 40 min. | 19,300 |
| Sokcho | 2 | 50 min. | 17,500 |
| Kwangju | 3 | 50 min. | 20,200 |
| Chinju | 2 | 70 min. | 26,600 |
| Yōsu | 4 | 70 min. | 26,200 |
| Ulsan | 5 | 50 min. | 23,300 |

| From Cheju | Frequency per day | Duration | Fare |
|---|---|---|---|
| Seoul | 8 | 60 min. | ₩33,100 |
| Pusan | 6 | 40 min. | 21,000 |
| Taegu | 1 | 50 min. | 26,100 |
| Kwangju | 3 | 35 min. | 12,800 |
| Chinju | 1 | 45 min. | 18,800 |
| Yōsu | 1 | 45 min. | 15,000 |

| From Pusan | Frequency per day | Duration | Fare |
|---|---|---|---|
| Seoul | 26 | 50 min. | ₩25,900 |
| Cheju | 6 | 40 min. | 21,000 |

| From Ulsan | Frequency per day | Duration | Fare |
|---|---|---|---|
| Seoul | 5 | 50 min. | ₩23,300 |

# AIRPORT TRANSFER INFORMATION
## Seoul, Pusan, Cheju

**Kimpo Airport—Downtown Seoul**

| Kimpo Int'l Airport | 35 min. by airport bus No. 601 ₩500<br>35 min. by city express bus No. 63 ₩350<br>35 min. by city express bus No. 68 ₩350<br>30 min. by taxi ₩2,700 or by hotel bus<br>30 min. by call taxi ₩5,000<br>50 min. by city local bus No. 41 ₩120 | City Hall |
|---|---|---|
| | 35 min. by city express bus No. 68 ₩350<br>40 min. by airport bus No. 601 ₩500<br>30 min. by taxi ₩2,700 | Seoul Station |
| | 50 min. by city local bus No. 105 ₩120<br>50 min. by airport bus No. 600 ₩500<br>30 min. by taxi ₩3,000 | Express Bus Terminal |
| | 70 min. by airport bus No. 600 ₩500<br>50 min. by taxi ₩5,000 | Seoul Sports Complex |

**Kimhae Airport—Pusan or Kyongju**

| Kimhae Int'l Airport | 1 hr. by airport bus ₩320<br>50 min. by taxi | Downtown Pusan |
|---|---|---|
| | 2 hrs. by airport bus ₩2,100 | Pomun Lake Resort |
| | 1 hr. 40 min. by airport bus ₩1,940 | Downtown Kyongju |

**Cheju Airport—Downtown Cheju or Chungmun**

| Cheju Int'l Airport | 10 min. by taxi or hotel bus<br>20 min. by airport bus ₩1,000 | Downtown Cheju |
|---|---|---|
| | 40 min. by taxi or hotel bus ₩10,000 | Chungmun Resort |

DOMESTIC TRAVEL

KAL reservations offices: Seoul (02) 756-2000; Pusan (051) 44-0131; Cheju (064) 22-6111; Kwangju (062) 232-0551; Taegu (053) 423-4231; Yosu (0662) 3-2111; Sokcho (0392) 33-0331; Chinju (0591) 53-3906; Ulsan (0522) 75-8222.

**Rail Services.** Korea has an excellent railway network, connecting all the major cities. Korean trains run on time and are reliable; good meals are served in the dining cars between Seoul and Pusan. Deluxe new express trains, called "New Community" or *Saemaul-ho*, have air-conditioning and toilets between cars that have lights indicating when occupied. Vendors supply food and drinks en route, and dining car menus include hamburger and steak. The daily "Blue Train" between Seoul and Pusan is speedy and offers two classes of service: First Class and Special. First Class features seating comfort and plenty of leg room. The Blue Train is well-heated in winter and air-conditioned in summer. English-speaking hostesses are available to answer questions. Minimum baggage should be carried on this high-speed train, as no baggage cars are available and stops are very brief. Railway routes are: Seoul–Pusan (via Taejon, Taegu), 4 hours and 50 minutes; Seoul–Mokpo (via Taejon, Nonsan, Iri, Chongub, Kwangju), 5 hours and 45 minutes; Seoul–Chonju (via Taejon, Iri), 3 hours and 30 minutes; and Seoul–Kyongju (via Taejon, Taegu), 4 hours and 40 minutes. Besides providing excellent transportation, the Korean National Railroad acts as a mobile tour service through the countryside. For information: Korean National Railroad, 168 2-ka Pongrae-dong; tel. 392-0078.

**Long-Distance Bus Services.** Korea has a modern, long-distance highway system and an excellent intercity express bus service. Ten express bus companies operate a fleet of 900 buses connecting all the major cities in Korea. Advance ticketing is available at the Kangnam Bus Terminal in Seoul and at Express Bus Terminals throughout the country. Fares range from US$3 to $10, travel times from two to five hours. For information in Seoul, call 598-4151.

**Shuttle Bus Services.** The airport express bus runs between Kimpo Airport and major hotels in Seoul: it stops at the Seoul Garden Hotel, the Koreana Hotel, the KAL City Terminal, the Plaza Hotel, the Hyatt Hotel, the Shilla Hotel, and the Sheraton Walker Hill Hotel. Buses leave from Kimpo Airport every 10 minutes from 5:30 a.m. to 9:30 p.m., for downtown Seoul and the Sheraton Walker Hill by turns. The bus starts from the Sheraton Walker Hill every 10 minutes from 6:30 a.m. to 10:30 p.m.

Another line operates from Kimpo Airport to Chamsil, stopping at the Palace Hotel, the Express Bus Terminal, the Riverside Hotel, the Nam Seoul Hotel, the Korea Exhibition Center, and the Seoul Sports Complex. These buses depart from Kimpo every 10 minutes from 5:30 a.m. to 10:30 p.m., and the fare is less than $1. For shuttle bus information: 535-4151.

A shuttle bus operates from Kimhae Airport to the Kyongju Pomun Lake Resort, via Pusan and the Kyongju Railroad Station, leaving every two hours between 12 noon and 6:00 p.m. The full trip takes about two hours and costs $3. For information: 261-0439.

**Coastal Passenger Ship Services.** Boat travel, to enjoy coastal and offshore island scenery, is one of the most pleasant ways to travel around Korea. A little extra leisure time is, of course, required. The boats are modern, clean, comfortable, and inexpensive. Tickets can be purchased at travel agencies or at the docks. Frequent ferry services are Pusan–Cheju (11 hours; fare $20–$40; Seoul 730-7788); Mokpo–Cheju (five hours; fare $15–$30; Mokpo 2-9391); and Pusan–Chungmu (two hours; fare $8; Pusan 44-3851).

## GETTING AROUND IN KOREAN CITIES

**Taxis.** There are four types of taxis on Korean city streets. Regular taxis, usually yellow or green, charge a basic fee of ₩600 for the first two kilometers and ₩50 for each additional 400 meters; but for taxis that drive at less than 15 kilometers per hour, a surcharge at 50 *won* per each 95 seconds is added to the basic fare. Call-taxis, usually beige, can be summoned by telephone; their charge is ₩1,000 for two kilometers and ₩100 for each additional 400 meters. Taxi drivers do not expect to be tipped, although it is customary to do so if they assist with luggage. A 20 percent surcharge is added from midnight to 4 a.m., and up to 100 percent may be added for return trips. Some regular taxi pick-up points are covered. Many hotels now operate hotel taxis, charging rates of $8 per hour or $80 for a 10-hour day; a special four-hour tour of Seoul and vicinity is available at $45. For information: 414-0151/9. Finally, there is a fourth type of taxi. This one costs ₩800 from the start and increases by increments of ₩100. These are slightly larger than the ₩600 pony sedan taxis, and they are usually white with a blue stripe around them. Taxi drivers are also becoming quite obnoxious, refusing to take passengers places they do not wish to drive to, trying to charge excessive fares and trying to either not use the meter (thereby charging an excessive imaginary rate) or they do not turn off the meter from the previous passenger.

**Rent-a-Cars.** Rental cars are available for visitors who wish to drive in Korea. Rates of $30 to $50 for 12 hours, or $50 to $60 for 24 hours, include insurance. For information, call Hertz in Seoul: 585-0801. Caution must be exercised by tourists driving in Korea: children often play in the streets, and elderly people are accustomed to walking on country roads. On the superhighways, maximum speed is 55 mph; and it is important to know the exit desired so as to obtain a ticket at the entry toll gate.

**Local Buses.** Local buses are the most common means of transportation; they are plentiful, frequent, usually reliable, and often overcrowded. Buses serve all areas of the city and its suburbs and cost only ₩200 regardless of distance; there is no transfer system. Since no English markings or schedules are available, the visitor who wants to experience the bus system should ride with a Korean friend, or at least get careful written directions. Other passengers will often be able to assist.

**Subways.** The Seoul subway was opened in 1974 and now serves the city with well over 200 kilometers of track, enabling commuters to reach any point within the 45 kilometer radius of the capital city within an hour. Subway trains run at five-minute intervals during rush hours; at 7.5-minute intervals the rest of the day. Stations and ticket windows are marked in English as well as Korean. Cars usually are not crowded. Stations can be differentiated from pedestrian underpasses by their curved roof lines. The equipment is spotlessly maintained, and the ride is rapid, smooth, and quiet. Four subway lines now serve the city, in addition to lines of the Korean National Railroad. Line 1 runs from Seoul Railway Station in the heart of the city to Chongnyangni Station; it becomes an above-ground electric line at either end and connects Seoul and Suwon, Inchon, and Songbuk. Line 2 is a circular route, 48.8 kilometers long, extending to both sides of the Han River. Lines 3 and 4 criss-cross the city, more or less southwest to northeast and northwest to east, respectively. Subways are gradually replacing buses as the main means of city transportation and are expected to be of immense importance in transporting masses of visitors to the 1988 Olympic Games. Fares in Seoul are based on two zones: Zone 1—₩200; Zone 2—₩300.

**Bicycles.** Bicycles can be rented in Korean cities and provide an excellent way to see the smaller cities, towns, and the countryside. Seoul traffic is so heavy that bike-riding is hazardous; if attempted, the visitor should expect to walk the bike in many areas, as residents do.

**Police Assistance.** Korean police officers maintain a stern demeanor but are very accommodating toward visitors, providing directions, assistance with missing property, and other help. Officers in the larger cities have new dark blue uniforms; they are college graduates, and some speak English.

## URBAN SIGHTSEEING TOURS

Information on city tours can be obtained at Korea National Tourism Corporation (KNTC) offices in many cities, at hotel tour counters, and at travel agencies. A city tour often is a good way to see the main points of interest at a minimum cost of time and money. However, since many Korean cities have a large number of historic sites in a compact area, it is possible to do most sightseeing on foot. Many prefer a combination: inner-city walking tours and bus tours to outlying areas, or a bus tour for a general overview and returning to special points of interest on foot. Certified tour guides who speak English can be hired for approximately $40 for a half day; $60 for a full day. The KNTC also has a registry of Volunteer Guides who are ready to offer assistance to visitors (Telephone: 757-6030). Five major Seoul travel agencies offering Seoul, Seoul-vicinity, and intercity tours are Global Tours, Ltd. (777-9921), Hajin Travel Service (777-0041), Korea Travel Bureau (585-1191), Seoul Travel Service (754-6831), and Lotte Travel Service, Ltd. (733-010).

# HOTEL ACCOMMODATIONS

**M**ost travelers arrange hotel accommodations in advance through tour agencies or host organizations. Korea's recent surge of new hotel building ensures that the overseas visitor will have a wide selection among hotels of deluxe and first-class international standards. The most reliable in terms of comfort, amenities, and service are the more than one dozen deluxe hotels completed in the 1980s under joint-venture agreements with foreign interests, mainly U.S. and Japanese. Their management and service staffs are Western-trained and therefore adhere more closely to international standards than do their wholly Korean-owned counterparts. Although the joint-venture hotels are relatively expensive, they have the advantage of accepting direct bookings from outside Korea.

Korea has more than 150 hotels with 25,000 rooms; total accommodations were increased to over 300 hotels with 35,000 rooms by 1988, and the number of rooms is expected to increase to 51,400 by 1992. The first major event to test the current capacity in Seoul was the International Monetary Fund/International Board of Governors meeting in October 1985, the largest conference yet held at one Korean hotel, with 3,500 dignitaries and delegates and a total of 7,000 participants in various meetings. The city of Seoul hosted approximately 170,000 visitors for the 1986 Asian Games and hosted about the same number for the 1988 Olympics. During 1989 the International Rotary Congress was held in Seoul. It is the third largest event in the world after the Asian Games and the Olympics. New large, deluxe hotels are also being built in other cities and tourist sites in anticipation of such major events and of a continuing growth of international tourism in Korea.

The categories of super-deluxe, deluxe, and first class account for over 200 hotels and 25,000 rooms, with the remainder in the second and third class categories. The table below lists the deluxe hotels in Seoul with their telephone numbers. Reservations should be made in advance. Pusan, Kyongju, and Cheju Island have new deluxe hotels comparable to those in Seoul.

## DELUXE HOTELS IN SEOUL

Ambassador (275-1101)
Hotel Capital (792-1122
Hyatt Regency (798-0061)
Inter-Continental Seoul (555-5656)
King Sejong (776-1811)
Koreana (720-9911)
Lotte (771-10)
Lotte World (419-7000)
Nam Seoul Washington (555-7111/9)
New World Hotel (557-0111)
President (753-3131)
Ramada Renaissance (555-0501)
Riverside (543-1001)

Riviera Seoul (541-3111)
Seoul Garden (717-9441)
Seoul Hilton (753-7788)
Seoul Olympia (353-5121)
Seoul Palace (532-0101)
Seoul Plaza (771-22)
Seoul Royal (756-1112)
Sheraton Walker Hill (453-0121)
Shilla (233-3131)
Swiss Grand Hotel (356-5656)
Tower Hotel (236-2121)
Westin Chosun (771-05)

*Sheraton Walker Hill Hotel*

---

In addition to the deluxe hotels, where rates range from $60 to $160, there are first-, second-, and third-class Western-style hotels with rates from $30 to $90 for single rooms, and Korean-style inns or *yogwan* which charge $10 to $25. For information about *yogwan*, call 783-9866/7 in Seoul. Ten youth hostels, especially but not exclusively designed for school excursions from abroad, cost $4 to $10; for information call 266-2896. It is official policy in Korea to maintain costs of hotel accommodations for tourists at levels comparable to prices elsewhere in the world.

## HOTEL RESERVATIONS IN KOREA

Korea's newer international hotels offer direct-booking service from outside of Korea through international hotel reservation networks to which all travel agents have access. Tourists traveling during the peak seasons (April-May and September-October) to Seoul, Kyongju, or Cheju may experience difficulty in obtaining a room at the hotel of their choice, particularly if it is deluxe or first-class and in a central location. The hotels that accept direct bookings often can be of assistance in securing onward reservations.

## HOTEL SERVICES

The better hotels offer the range of services that tourists have
come to expect, including one or more bars and cocktail lounges;
restaurants with several cuisines; barber shops and beauty salons;
saunas; recreational facilities such as tennis courts, swimming pools,
and game rooms; souvenir shops and boutiques, laundry, pressing,
and dry-cleaning services that are quick and excellent; room service
(often just drinks and snacks); banquet halls; and equipment rentals
in resort areas. Most of the large hotels have postal, banking,
telegraph, and telex facilities on the premises; several have more
elaborate business corners providing facsimile and secretarial services. Arrangements for taxis, wake-up calls, and restaurant reservations can be made at the main desk or service desk. Storage
space is available at most Korean hotels for anything from a small
suitcase to a large trunk.

## HOTEL ROOM AMENITIES

The standard hotel room in Korea is simple, functional, clean,
and comfortable; furnishings usually are: twin beds, a desk, a chest
of drawers, and an easy chair. Deluxe accommodations are more
elaborate, and include television sets.

**Electricity.** The electric current in Korea is 100 volts and is
generally safe for Western appliances rated for 110–120 volts. Major
hotels in Seoul have both 100- and 220-volt outlets in each room.
For visitors with VCRs, Korea follows the NCST standards for TV
broadcasting (i.e., compatible with TV in the U.S.).

## CONVENTION FACILITIES

As Korea became the site of international conferences in the 1970s,
a shortage of capacity occurred. Government and industry have
responded by building several deluxe hotels and expanding existing
facilities to accommodate an ever larger number of conference and
convention attendees. Convention halls and hotels with capacity
for large-scale meetings and expositions in the Seoul metropolitan
area include the Sejong Cultural Center, the Inter-Continental Hotel,
KOEX/Korea World Trade Center, the National Theater, the Hotel
Lotte, the Sheraton Walker Hill Hotel, the Hyatt Hotel, the Seoul
Hilton, and the "DLI 63" Building. In Kyongju, the Tourism Center
is available.

HOTEL ACCOMMODATIONS

## YOGWAN

*Yogwan*, or traditional Korean-style inns, are found in major cities and in the smaller towns throughout the countryside. For those who wish to learn more about the country, their home-like atmosphere is appealing. Of course, some of the amenities of the luxury hotel are missing, but they have a comfort of their own. *Yogwan* feature heated floor (*ondol*) rooms, and the bedding brought out at night consists of a mattress (*yo*), a hard pillow (*pyogal*), and a quilt (*ibul*). Shoes are removed in the hall. In many *yogwan*, Korean-style meals are served with minimum advance notice.

## YOUTH HOSTELS

Youth hostels are a familiar and welcome institution for students world-wide. Ten hostels located throughout the country now are available to members. Visitors can join any hostel for a fee of $5 for high school students, $6 for college students, $22 for adults, or $30 for an entire family. Maximum economy, with maximum space and privacy, is provided by bunkrooms for six to eight people; double and twin rooms also are offered. The government has a positive policy of promoting study in Korea by students from overseas, and is particularly proud of the number of Japanese students coming to Korea to study. Korea's rich range of cultural and historical assets invites cultural and historical research tours as part of any Asian studies program.

Two of the largest youth hostels are the Bando Youth Hostel (02-567-3111/9) in Seoul, with 144 rooms accommodating up to 774 persons, and the Sin-dongyang Youth Hostel in Kyongju, with 104 rooms for up to 488 persons. The subway to the Bando is the green line, #2, at the Yoksam stop.

## TOURIST CENTERS

Having recognized that accommodations tended to be concentrated in Seoul, the Korean government has actively built new hotels and upgraded existing hotels in other cities; and it has created, in coordination with local resort area development plans, several major tourist resort complexes. Modern deluxe facilities have opened for visitors in Pusan, Kyongju, Cheju Island, Mt. Sorak National Park, and other areas.

# POSTAL SERVICE AND TELECOMMUNICATIONS

**K**orea maintains good mail and telecommunications links with the outside world. Telex, photo-telegraphic facilities, and cable services are available at all of the major hotels.

**International Mail.** Travelers should be aware that it takes many weeks for mail to reach Korea by sea; letters and cards with airmail postage usually arrive in six to seven days. If speed is essential, a telephone call or cable is recommended. The hotel desk will accept international mail, or it can be taken to the International Post Office, which is open from 9 a.m. to 6 p.m. Cost of an airmail letter or postcard to North America is ₩440 and ₩350, respectively; to Europe, ₩440 and ₩380; an aerogram is ₩350; and printed matter is ₩250 to America, ₩250 to Europe. Parcels sent abroad must go through the International Post Office. At the foot of the hill below the IPO, a packing office will crate and wrap items and afix customs-declaration stickers. Major hotels have a packing and wrapping service. Small packages can be mailed quite reasonably.

**Domestic Mail.** Stamps can be purchased in major hotels, certain shops, and post offices. Stamped materials may be posted at all hotels or dropped in postal boxes conveniently located around the city. Letters are delivered to local addresses, but packages must be picked up at public post offices. Deliveries are made within one day in Seoul, two or three days to provincial cities. The domestic postal rate is ₩80 per 50 grams for letters, ₩470 per 50 grams for registered letters, and ₩700 per two kilograms for packages.

## *TELEPHONE*

**Public Telephones.** Local calls can be made from red or green phones in most buildings and public phone booths all over the city for two 10-won coins; the connection automatically breaks off after three minutes. Coinboxes take only 100-won and 10-won coins; pips in the middle of the call indicate that time is up; to continue speaking put coins in the slot immediately. Unused money is returned when the receiver is hung up.

**Long-Distance Direct-Dial Telephones.** A direct dialing system links Seoul and major provincial cities. The code number is dialed first, then the individual telephone number. Long-distance direct calls can be made through yellow public pay phones available at major hotels and post offices. Area code numbers for direct-dial destinations are: Seoul—02, Inchon—032, Taejon—042, Chongju—0431, Pohang—0562, Kyongju—0561, Taegu—053, Pusan—051, Ulsan—0522, Masan—0551, Iri—0653, Chonju—0652, Kwangju—062, Mokpo—0631, Yosu—0662, Sogwipo/Cheju—064.

**International Telephones.** There are two sets of numbers, 1035 and 1037, for different geographical areas, as follows:

1035: U.S., Canada, France, Germany, Italy, Spain, Hong Kong, Singapore, Taiwan, Philippines, Australia
1037: Other countries
1030: Overseas Information Service (in Seoul); 117 from other areas.

The minimum charges for operator-assisted calls are ₩6,180 to the US and ₩4,890 to the United Kingdom. Direct-dial calls to the US start at ₩1,960; to the United Kingdom, ₩1,550.

## TELEGRAM SERVICE

**International Telegrams.** There are two ways of sending overseas telegrams. One is to deliver the message in English by dialing 115; informing the telegraph office of the sender's name and phone number, the type of telegram to be sent, and the name and address to which it will be delivered; and then giving the content of the message. The other is to visit a telegraph office of the Korea International Telecommunication Office (KIT) near the Capitol Building and present the message in written form. Types of telegrams are ORD (ordinary), LT (letter telegram), URGENT (urgent telegram); delivery times are 12 hours, 24 hours, and six hours, respectively. International telegram rates vary according to the type of telegram and its destination.

**Domestic Telegrams.** The visitor can have telegrams delivered via telephone by calling 115 from the hotel. Charges for ordinary romanized telegrams are ₩550 for the first 20 words and ₩80 for each additional five words; rates for urgent telegrams are double the ordinary rates.

**Telex.** Telex services are available at major hotels at their businessmen's service offices, which are open during normal business hours.

## INCOMING CORRESPONDENCE

Mail from North America or Europe takes 6–10 days to be delivered in Korea. If exact daily itineraries and hotels are known in advance, mail can be addressed to visitors in care of the hotels. Every effort is made to deliver cables promptly. For business travelers spending some time in one place, it is practical to register a cable address. Incoming telephone calls are connected by an overseas operator. Callers should instruct the operator to contact the visitor's hotel in order to locate the individual being sought before placing the call.

## TIME AROUND THE WORLD

Seoul time is standard throughout Korea. When it is 12 noon in Seoul, the standard time in the following cities is:

Amsterdam (3 AM)       Hong Kong (11 AM)       Paris (4 AM)
Bangkok (10 AM)        Honolulu (5 PM)*        Rome (4 AM)
Cairo (5 AM)           London (3 AM)           San Francisco (7 PM)*
Chicago (9 PM)*        Los Angeles (7 PM)*     Sydney (1 PM)
Dallas (9 PM)*         Montreal (10 PM)*       Tokyo (12 noon)
Frankfurt (3 AM)       New York (10 PM)*       Zurich (4 AM)
*The preceding day.

## KOREAN WEIGHTS AND MEASURES

Most of Korea's international trade is conducted in the metric system, but the following Korean weights and measures are still used in domestic transactions.

1 *kun* = 1.32 pounds
  = 0.6 kilogram
1 *ton* = 0.492 ton
  = metric ton
1 *ja* = 0.33 meter;  1 *pyong*
  = 30 sq. *ja*
1 *li* = 0.4 kilometer
  = 0.24 mile
1 *kan* = 180 centimeters

1 *chi* = 1/10 of 1 *ma*
  = 9.14 centimeters
1 *ma* = 10 *chi*
  = 91.44 centimeters
1 *hop* = 1/10 of 1 *toe*
  = 0.18 liters
1 *toe* = 10 *hop* = 1.8 liters
1 *mal* = 10 *toe* = 18 liters

# FOOD IN KOREA

One of the great adventures in Korea is to enjoy the food and experience Korean-style service. Recently, a variety of unique Korean dishes, called the "royal" or "court" cuisine, have become popular among international gourmets. The visitor will find Korean foods less oily than Chinese cuisine and not as bland as Japanese dishes. Korean food is often spicy hot, but also includes tasty milder dishes.

**Hotel Dining.** All of Seoul's deluxe hotels have excellent restaurants offering Continental, Chinese, and Japanese cuisines of the highest quality; several have pure Korean restaurants; others include Korean fare in their buffet or cafe restaurants. The deluxe hotels are the best places for Western cuisine; the Hotel Lotte and the Shilla Hotel have outstanding Korean restaurants.

Generally, tour groups and visiting delegations take their prepaid meals at their hotels (except for lunches on all-day excursions and banquets). Individual tourists find it is convenient to take most meals at their hotels too, where they can choose from a wide range of Western foods and other selections. Many hotels offer buffets for breakfast, lunch, and dinner. Hotel dining rooms tend to observe longer hours than restaurants.

**Restaurants.** Although it entails additional expense, eating at a high-quality local restaurant is recommended for atmosphere, authenticity, and variety of offerings. Most elegant is a banquet-style meal served in a private dining room. It is also interesting to try an ordinary meal in a popular restaurant. The traditional Korean place setting includes a small plate, a pair of chopsticks resting on a holder (but forks and knives always can be requested), a soup spoon, and two glasses—one for beer or soft drinks and a wine glass for toasts. Dishes are served according to a prescribed palate-stimulating sequence, starting with appetizers and continuing through 10 or more courses in a banquet-style meal. A well-balanced menu contains the five basic tastes of Korean cuisine: sour, hot, bitter, sweet, and salty. Dishes alternate between crisp and tender, dry and saucy, spicy and mild. Soup is usually served before the main course. Dessert is generally fresh fruit and some Korean pastries. The Korean rule for feeding overseas guests seems to be to serve as many dishes as possible; this can be too much for the average appetite, but it is polite to eat, or at least taste, a bit of each dish—pacing oneself through the many courses.

## THE CUISINE OF KOREA

The traditional Korean meal includes a soup, fish or meat, rice, several vegetable side dishes (*panchan*), and one or more varieties of *kimchi* (pickled cabbage). Seafood, fresh from the seas surrounding the Korean peninsula, is abundant and popular, but the most characteristic Korean dishes contain beef. However, vegetables predominate, even more than beef, in the diet of the Korean people, and most dishes are mixtures of meat and vegetables. In Korean cookery, soy sauce and bean paste are regarded as essential ingredients and both are used as a base for soups and as flavoring for side dishes.

*Pulgogi* (marinated beef slices grilled over charcoal) and *kalbi* (roasted short ribs) are the best-known meat dishes of Korea. The best known vegetable dish is *kimchi*, a fermented pickle usually made of cabbage, but also made of radish, turnip, or cucumber, and seasoned with red hot pepper. Fresh vegetables are lightly cooked and seasoned with red and black pepper, garlic, ginger root, sesame-seed oil, and soy sauce. Soups containing seaweed, meat, or fish are always served. Side dishes include bean sprouts, seaweed, *toraji* (bellflower root), *kosari* (young fern frond), *meruchi* (small minnow-like fish), and one or more types of *kimchi*.

A complete Korean meal includes selections from five categories of foods. The first category is rice; there are many rice dishes, including: white rice (*huin-pap*), glutinous rice (*chal-pap*), rice with red beans (*pat-pap*), rice with various beans (*kong-bap*), rice with vegetables (*chaeso-bap*), and rice with chestnuts (*pam-bap*). The second category is soup (*tchigae*), which is of two basic kinds: clear broth or a bean paste soup; both are made with meat and vegetables and may be seasoned with red pepper (*kochujang tchigae*) or soy sauce (*kanjang tchigae*). The third category covers the flesh, fowl, or fish portion of the meal and may be prepared in several ways: steaming with vegetables and seasonings (*tchim*), roasting or barbecuing (*kui*), deep frying (*twigim*), or frying in egg batter (*chon*). The fourth category is the *panchan* or side dishes: various boiled vegetables such as beans, bean sprouts, bluebell root, fern, and a beef, fish, or vegetable *chorim*—cooked in water or soy sauce until the liquid disappears. The fifth category of a Korean meal consists of *kimchi*; one or several types may be served.

Korean foods are cut into small pieces, for only chopsticks and spoons are used. Brass or stainless steel dishes, rice bowls, soup bowls, and other utensils are used because they hold heat and keep the food warm. Wood and charcoal as well as electricity are used

*Drying red peppers*

for cooking and heating. Considerable time is required to prepare Korean food, but the results are worth the effort. Both for quick cooking and for easy eating, vegetables, seafoods, and meats are cut into julienne strips, which create a confetti-like burst of color in the finished dish. Cooking techniques include charcoal grilling, sautéing, braising, deep-frying, and steaming. Seasonings are robust; Korean foods are laced with red pepper, garlic, and onions along with fragrant toasted sesame seeds, sesame oil, sweet soy sauce, rice vinegar, and fresh ginger root. The cinnabar-colored red pepper, *kochu*, is the base of a thick spicy soybean paste called *kochu chang*, which adds both a certain sweetness and a characteristic rosy color.

Ginseng is a Korean favorite because of its healthful properties; it is believed to retard old age, cure illness, and perk up the nervous system. It is made into tea and sweets and is used in cooking. A popular chicken soup made with ginseng contains a whole stuffed chicken with rice, dates, chestnuts, pine nuts and ginger.

Fresh and dried seaweeds are prized, too, for their beneficial qualities. A rich source of nutrients is phorphyra. *Kim* (laver) is a rich black sea algae pressed into thin sheets and used in making sushi. It is toasted, cut into squares, and used as an edible wrapping for scoops of hot steamed rice. To use chopsticks in wrapping the leaf of seaweed around the rice is a demonstration of real dexterity.

Today, meals are served on a large round table for all members of the family, but if an elderly father-in-law should be present he is given a separate table. Guests and host sit together at the same table. The place setting consists of plate, spoon, and chopsticks. The food is brought in and served on plates and a variety of small dishes.

At an elegant Korean dinner, the first course is *kujolpan*, similar to a French hors d'oeuvre tray. Cooked meat and vegetables are arranged on a large platter in a wheel of contrasting colors. In the center is a mound of thin pancakes. The guest picks up a pancake with chopsticks, selects some of the meat and vegetables, places them on the pancake, rolls it up, and eats it. A connoisseur's main course is *sinsollo* (Angel's Brazier), a regal casserole of meat, fish, egg, vegetables, and bean cake, with pine and gingko nuts, over which beef broth has been poured. This cooks and bubbles in a brass bowl suspended over a brazier filled with blazing charcoal. A gourmet meal includes over 15 dishes, prepared in the time-consuming style of a court banquet. Simpler fare is the *han jongshik* (Korean formal fixed meal) served in a small inn or restaurant and consisting of broiled beef or fried fish, cooked rice, a small bowl of soup, and five to eight different side dishes of seasoned vegetables, including *kimchi* for each person.

The favorite dessert is fruit in season, and occasionally cooked dried persimmons, date balls rolled in pine nuts, or chestnut balls dipped in honey.

**Beverages.** Koreans commonly use a rice or barley tea, although Korea today imports some leaf teas. The rice tea is made by browning a little boiled rice, then adding water and bringing to a boil. Dark-roasted barley boiled briefly in water also makes a satisfying brew.

The traditional alcoholic beverages in Korea are *takju, yakju*, and *soju. Takju* is a wine made of inexpensive stock such as corn, barley, or potatoes, and is rather on the raw side. *Yakju* is a rice wine, higher in alcoholic content than *takju* and a little smoother, also somewhat more expensive. *Soju*, made from grain or potatoes, is the strongest native liquor, although it looks as pure as water. Korean beer also is available and goes well with any Korean meal; it tastes as good as any Asian beer.

Soft drinks have delicate flavors: teas of ginseng, ginger, or cinnamon; *ssanghwangtang* tea containing fruits, dates, chestnuts, other nuts, and honey water; and fruit juices are popular.

## POPULAR KOREAN DISHES

*Pulgogi* — world-famous Korean barbecued beefsteak, marinated in soy sauce with sesame oil, garlic, onion, sugar, and pepper, and broiled over charcoal

*Chapchae* — mixed vegetables and shredded beef with soybean noodles, quickly stir-fried

*Kalbichim* — short ribs of beef in a rich stew with turnips, chestnuts, and mushrooms

*Ttokkuk* — sliced rice cakes boiled in beef soup stock; a New Year's dish found in restaurants in the wintertime

*Naengmyon* — a favorite summer food made with buckwheat noodles placed in a cold broth to which vinegar and mustard have been added, decorated on top with slices of beef, pear, cucumber, and boiled egg

*Pindaettok* — a favorite snack served with wine, made of green onions and strips of pork in a bean pancake

*Pulgalbi* — spareribs of beef or pork prepared in the same manner as *pulgogi*

*Kalbi-tang* — spareribs served in a mild soup

*Sollong-tang* — stew meat and vegetables in a beef-broth soup

*Yukkae-jang* — a very spicy soup of chopped beef and vegetables

*Chongol* — meat, vegetables, and noodles cooked together at the table

*Pibim-bap* — a delicious mixture of rice, egg, meat, various vegetables, and beans, served with a spicy red pepper paste called *kochujang*.

*Onmyon* — noodles served hot in a spicy soup

*Kuksu* — noodles made from wheat and served in a broth

*Taegu-tang* — an extremely spicy soup of codfish, onions, and other vegetables, typical of Taegu cuisine

*Rosu-kui* — thin slices of beef cooked in water and dipped into a sauce of soy sauce and sesame oil

*Mandu-guk* — soup with meat-filled dumplings

## KOREAN PANCHAN (SIDE DISHES)

*Kimchi* — pickled cabbage, or other vegetable, with red hot pepper (the further south one goes in Korea, the hotter the *kimchi* becomes)

*Tubu* — bean curd, served separately in several ways or as a component of a main dish

*Shigumchi* — a vegetable similar to spinach, topped with sesame seeds

*Kim* — strips of green laver (dried seaweed) fried in sesame oil and lightly salted

*Kongnamul* — bean sprouts, especially of soy beans

*Kong* — any one of a variety of beans

*Toraji* — Chinese bellflower root boiled and spiced

*Yonppuri* — root of lotus served in a sweet sauce

*Myolchi* — tiny anchovies served in a sweet sauce

*Tchigae* — a hot, spicy stew of fish or meat and vegetables, often served after the main course

*Kanjang* — soy sauce

*Kochujang* — hot sauce

## A KOREAN DINNER PARTY

Koreans like to entertain their overseas guests by treating them to a Korean dinner at one of the many excellent traditional restaurants. The shared recreation of dining and drinking with Koreans at a Korean-style restaurant or *kisaeng* house provides the best opportunity for an overseas traveler or businessman to get a feel for Korean culture and to engage in successful business relations. One drinking custom involves, as a gesture of respect and friendship, one party giving his wine cup to the other, conveying it politely with both hands. The companion receives the cup with both hands and holds it thus while it is filled to the brim, then drinks the wine. After emptying the cup, he uses both hands to return it to the host, then returns the favor by filling it for the host. A more extravagant version of this custom, using a stemmed glass, is sometimes encountered at *kisaeng* parties (served by traditionally-trained female escorts). So continues the evening.

The *kisaeng* are highly trained young female entertainers who play musical instruments, sing, dance, compose poetry, write calligraphy with brush and ink, and play in a band with Korean drums (*jangku*); some today might play an electric guitar or perform a go-go dance. They amuse the guests who sit around the table after eating their traditional-style feast. Like anywhere else, a dinner with drinking, singing, and dancing not only removes inhibitions, but facilitates cultural, social, and business interaction. Sharing these simple pleasures dissolves the language barrier and makes overseas visitors feel welcome. So participating in the *kisaeng* tradition for a few hours must be considered among the prime delights of Korea and can provide a life-time memory for the traveler.

*Korean restaurant repast*

# CULTURE AND RECREATION
# FOR THE KOREA TRAVELER

## THE PERFORMING ARTS

Koreans are an artistic people and are fond of expressing their
innate nature in drama, music, and dance. Overseas visitors usually
enjoy a variety of performances during their stay. Tickets may be
an extra-cost option, but they are worth it, for no trip to Korea
is complete without a sampling of Korea's rich cultural heritage in
the performing arts.

**Theater.** Although plays have been second to movies in popularity among most Koreans, the theater is enjoying a resurgence.
Many new works promote social themes; both these and classical
historical dramas are well-attended. Western plays and operas are
increasingly popular. As part of the influx of Western drama,
directors from the United States and Europe are invited to teach
new technology in props, lighting, and sound, and new techniques
of acting. Revivals of traditional love stories tend to delight both
Korean and foreign audiences; although a high degree of stylization
characterizes the presentations, the freshness and enthusiasm of the

## CULTURE AND RECREATION

*Folklore performance at Seoul Nori-madang, near Olympic Complex*

performers are contagious. Overseas visitors will not understand everything, but they cannot fail to be entertained.

Entertainers in Korean theaters and *kisaeng* houses are professionals who are not only highly skilled in the dance, music, and drama they perform, but also are deeply versed in the centuries-old cultural traditions of which they are a part. Today, two distinct music and dance cultures are practiced in Korea, and the government is encouraging young students in both the traditional Korean arts and in Western music, dance, and drama.

**Music.** To the Western ear, Korean music is apt to sound "out of tune," for it is not based on the "tempered scale" of the Western tonal system. Korean musicians have devoted themselves to the development of melody and rhythm, conceived as one melody flowing on without interruption, with rhythmic innovation. Traditional music is divided into three forms: court, religious, and folk music. Court music, reflecting Confucian influence, is slow, steady, dignified, restrained. Religious ritual music is mainly Buddhist-inspired, with chanting melodies and drum dances. Folk music is vivacious, emotional, and inventive. In ancient times, rituals to heavenly deities held before the planting and after the harvest united labor and the arts, farmers and priests, in a common cycle of endeavor. This harmony is part of the basic character of Korean artistic culture.

CULTURE AND RECREATION

The people's proclivity for music and dance has carried over into the twentieth century. Western music was introduced into Korea in the late nineteenth century by Christian missionaries, mainly through hymnals. As Western thought and learning spread, schools were established where Western music was included as a major part of the curriculum. Today, large symphony orchestras, chamber music groups, opera companies, and talented instrumental and vocal soloists are found everywhere in Korea. Many young Koreans have won international fame in recent years in Europe and America as pianists, violinists, cellists, and conductors.

**Dance.** Korean traditional dance, like music, is divided into court, religious, and folk dance. Royal court dance reflects Confucian austerity; movements are slow, elegant and majestic, sedate and restrained. The Korean court dancer remains the epitome of beauty, grace, modesty, and poise in her exquisite costume and tiny flower crown. Religious dance reflects shaman, Buddhist, and Confucian influences. Ritual (*mudang-kut*) dances contain a spiritual inner beauty aside from the outward aesthetic features, in contrast to Western ballet, which seeks overt beauty of form through rigidly controlled elaboration of technique. In folk dance, there is improvisational freedom, manifesting joy pouring forth from within. Graceful uplifting shoulder movements and slow rising and sinking movements of the knees are characteristic of these emotive dances.

**Mask Dance-Drama.** The mask dance-drama is one of the major forms of traditional folk art in Korea today. Originally it was a Buddhist morality play, much like the mystery cycles of medieval Europe. It was performed continuously through the mid-Yi Dynasty period, until the mask players were banished from the royal court by the neo-Confucians. Thereafter they dispersed to various regions of the countryside and the mask dance became a comic satire depicting the depravity of the aristocratic classes, the Buddhist clergy, and the triangular family relationships prevalent in society.

Side by side with traditional dance, Western ballet, modern, and creative dance are important in the Korean cultural scene of today.

**Drama.** Western-style drama made its debut in Korea at the turn of the century and has played an increasingly active role on the cultural scene. Today, Western-style drama is an integral part of stage, screen, radio, and television presentations, and works range from Shakespeare to the most modern American and European playwrights.

**National Classical Music Institute.** The government established this national institute to preserve the precious cultural heritage of Korea for posterity. Today regular performances of court music and dance are presented by the Institute and associated organizations at the National Theater, the Sejong Cultural Center, and other theaters.

**Cultural Festivals.** In addition to the many theater presentations of the traditional arts, many communities have annual cultural festivals that showcase art forms traditional in their region.

**Reservations and Tickets.** The performing arts are more reasonably priced in Korea than in the West, but tickets are often scarce; therefore, it is advisable to make ticket reservations at the hotel desk immediately upon arrival.

## FILM

Korean film-making began after the liberation. During the 1980s, films have been winning audiences through increasingly realistic characterizations, innocent romance, social satire, and humor. Film stars are very popular, and virtually every bookstore has photos and film magazines on sale. With government assistance, and newly imported modern equipment, Korean films have begun to come of age. Given the theatrical aspect of the Korean temperament, many film and television players of great merit are emerging. Most films shown to tourists are English-narrated documentaries on Korea's modern accomplishments or travelogues on interesting historical places for sightseeing. However, overseas visitors are welcome to join Korean crowds seeing current popular films.

## NIGHTLIFE

Korea's nightlife has returned to its normally active (if not to say frenetic) levels since the curfew was lifted. Many night spots stay open until 2 a.m. on weekdays and 4 a.m. on weekends. From midnight to 4 a.m., taxi fares increase by 20 percent. Major hotels have nightclubs with a band and usually two floor shows. There is a cover charge of about $5 at such clubs, and sometimes a minimum drink fee per table. The company of a hostess costs around

$20 for the evening, plus a tip of $10 to $20; some nightclubs put a hostess fee on the bill automatically, even if not requested.

Outstanding among Seoul nightspots is the Kayakum Theater Restaurant at the Sheraton Walker Hill Hotel. There guests can enjoy a delicious dinner plus excellent floor shows of traditional and modern Korean entertainment and from time to time a show straight from Las Vegas. The Walker Hill also has a casino, open 24 hours every day, several bars, and a disco.

At the Korea House, a traditional-style mansion, visitors can enjoy reasonably priced Korean food of court cuisine quality and performances of Korean folk dances every evening at 8:30. Reservations must be made two days in advance (tel. 266-9101).

There are many beer halls and bars throughout the city. There is no cover charge, and if the place has hostesses, the customary tip for a stay of two hours is $10. Snack plates cost about $4. Both bottled and draft beer are available.

The cream of Korean nightlife is still the famous *kisaeng* houses, where parties of guests dine royally and enjoy entertainment by the redoubtable *kisaeng* girls, who sing, dance, and play musical instruments. The Western visitor invited by a Korean friend to participate in this memorable experience-of-a-lifetime is indeed fortunate. Expenses can run to $200 and more per person, including the royal-banquet food, Western liquor, graceful service, shows, and dancing. (See the entertainment section in the Seoul part of this guidebook.)

## SPORTS

Spectator and player sports are very popular in Korea. Baseball, volleyball, and judo count the most participants; also attracting many are basketball, table tennis, swimming, soccer, tennis, archery, shooting, skating, skiing, boxing, wrestling, golf, judo (called *yudo* in Korea), and the native sports of *ssirum* and *taekwondo*. The government has taken a strong interest in fostering sports, both to promote physical fitness and to enhance national prestige by improved performance at international events. An 18-acre training site with the latest equipment and facilities for various athletic games has been set up on the outskirts of Seoul. The National Sports Promotion Foundation is charged with the responsibility for raising and administering funds for athletic activities. The Ministry of Sports coordinates government support for various sports programs. Attention is focused now on preparations for the Olympic Games.

## KOREAN GAMES

**Yut.** This old-style New Year's game employs a playing board with "Start" and "Home"; four sticks, with one side rounded and the other flat, function like dice; they are thrown into the air and tallied according to which side is up. Players or teams take turns and move their counters according to the fall of the sticks.

**Paduk.** This Korean game is called *go* in Japan. Two players face each other across a board drawn in squares; one has white counters and the other black; action takes place on the intersection of the lines. Rules are simple but strategies complex, as each tries to "surround" the enemy's pieces and render them helpless. It is a "lifetime preoccupation" for many, and there are championships, televised tournaments, and publications that analyze master moves and hypothetical games.

**Changgi.** In this variation on an ancient prototype of chess, players attempt to use the queen and other battle pieces to keep the king immobilized and protected. Each player has 16 pieces of seven types, and the game usually ends in checkmate, like European chess.

**Seesaw.** A girls' game, played on lunar New Year's Day; the seesaw is set on a low stone or bag filled with rice straw; the players stand, jump in the air, and come down hard. It is said to have begun to give girls a glimpse of the world beyond their walled gardens back when women were never permitted outside the home.

**Swinging.** Also originally for girls, swinging takes place standing up, and is associated with the New Year's, *Tano*, and *Chusok* holidays.

**Kite Flying.** Traditionally kites are flown in early spring, during the first month of the lunar calendar. Kite flying is often competitive, even to the point of one gluing powdered glass to his string so that it cuts another's in mid-air. At the end of the month, boys release their kites to bear away any bad luck.

## THE MEDIA IN KOREA

**Television and Radio.** Television sets, now mass-produced in Korea, are becoming less expensive; most city residents own or have access to one. Weekday daytime programming is mainly educational. News broadcasts rarely resort to sensational stories about accidents or murders; the emphasis tends to be on positive aspects

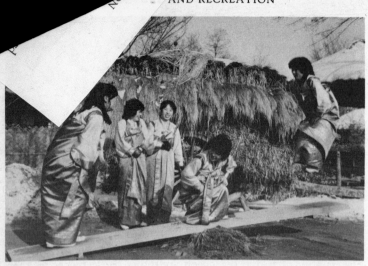

*Korean girls' see-saw*

of society. Much attention is given to the international scene, especially to news from the United States and Japan, but covering other countries as well. Evening broadcasting features films—often foreign films with Korean dubbed in—sports events, and acrobatic displays or shows of performing arts. Commercials are common in national programming.

Most large tourist hotels have installed TV sets in their guest rooms; many offer free closed-circuit programming consisting of imported TV series and films, mostly in English.

The Korean Broadcasting System (KBS) has a network of 21 local radio stations (supplemented by 41 relay stations) and two national television networks (MBC and TBC). There also are 31 private radio stations and 10 television networks being heard and viewed by the Korean owners of 12 million radios and five million TV sets. For overseas service, Radio Korea broadcasts 24 hours a day in Korean, Japanese, Chinese, and other languages. Having a number of private commercial and educational radio and television companies, usually owned by newspapers, is considered favorable to the development of pluralistic democratic institutions.

**Newspapers.** Foreign-language periodicals are not difficult to find in Korea. *Time* and *Newsweek* and a selection of other Western periodicals and newspapers, including the *Asian Wall Street Journal*, are available at newsstands in city hotels. Two English-language

dailies are published in Korea: the *Korea Herald* and
*Times*. Today there are 37 daily newspapers in Korea, of w
seven are national, with a circulation of 500,000 each: *Dong-A
Ilbo, Chosun Ilbo, Hankuk Ilbo, Kyunghyang Shinmoon, Joong-Ang
Ilbo*, and *Seoul Sinmun*. In addition, there are 114 weekly journals,
720 monthly magazines, and 18 juvenile periodicals; these include
the English-language weekly *Newsreview* and the monthly *Business
Korea*.

## CULTURAL SOCIETIES

**Royal Asiatic Society (RAS).** The RAS is Korea's most active
cultural society for those interested in tours, publications, and
outstanding lectures. The Korea Branch of the Royal Asiatic Society was founded in 1900 by a group of foreigners living in Seoul
who were interested in learning about the history and culture of
Korea. Affiliated with the prestigious RAS of London, it offers a
great variety of privileges and opportunities for overseas visitors
and foreign businesspeople. The RAS has the largest and most
complete selection of English books on Korea for sale. Semimonthly
meetings are held on Wednesday evenings; diversified programs
are presented, without admission charge. During the spring and
fall, RAS tours conducted by knowledgeable leaders are weekend
highlights. Members receive discounts; those who maintain mem-
bership after leaving Korea can do so at reduced rates, continuing
to receive publications and other benefits. The address is 136-46
Yunji-dong (tel. 763-9483).

**International Cultural Society of Korea (ICSK).** This non-
profit private organization offers cultural programs and services to
all foreigners in order to promote mutual understanding and
friendship. ICSK organizes seminars and symposiums on cultural
topics in conjunction with foreign institutions. The address: 526
5-ga Namdaemun-ro (tel. 753-6465).

# SHOPPING

Since Korea has begun to be known as a shopper's paradise,
renowned for outstanding bargains, some visitors are coming
just to shop. The overseas traveler will find everything from
personal computers and up-to-date fashions to unique traditional
handicraft items and antique art objects.

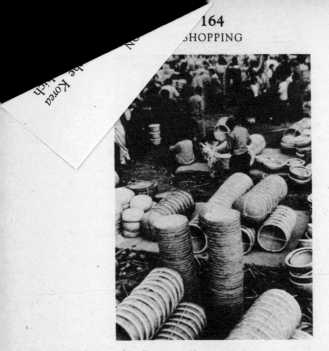

*Bamboo products market, Tamyang, Chonnam Province*

Seoul offers a great variety of shopping experiences: arcades, department stores, duty-free shops, specialized shopping districts, and outdoor markets. In the myriad arcades are shops selling all kinds of Korean consumer products: jewelry, amber and topaz stones, men's and women's clothing, electronic goods, leather goods, silk fabric and clothing, art and antiques, brassware, records and tapes, ginseng, and even computer software. Department stores offer similar selections at only slightly higher prices and with dependable quality and extra services. Itaewon, adjacent to U.S. Army headquarters in Yongsan, is the most international area in Seoul and the best place for real bargains in tailored clothes, sportswear, jogging shoes, eel skin products, and brassware. Insa-dong, or Mary's Alley, is the best-known district for antiques and art objects, such as old Korean chests, paintings and calligraphy, pottery, and other treasures. Myong-dong is not only the high fashion shopping area, but also the nation's busiest district. Even those who just change planes at Kimpo Airport can enjoy shopping at the duty-free shops in the transit area, which offer Korean dolls, silks, jewelry, and an assortment of imported perfumes, liquors, and luxury items.

American Express, VISA, MasterCard, Diners Club, 
Carte Blanche cards can be used in the tourist hotels, departm
stores, and high-quality shops in Korea. In smaller shops and public
markets, only the *won* is accepted. Most shops are open on Sunday,
and many close as late as 10 p.m. The major department stores
in downtown Seoul are the Lotte (tel. 771-25), the Midopa (tel.
754-2222), Hyundai (547-2233), and the Shinsegae (754-1234).

The tourist hotels all have convenient gift shops, but the dedicated shopper will want to explore the major shopping areas,
which in most cities are near the hotels. The visitor will find that
basic items are inexpensive and that bargains can be found on
such Korean specialties as silks, handicrafts, jewelry, and ginseng.
Korean antiques can be purchased with a government license, a
special customs declaration form issued at the time of purchase.
National Treasures cannot be exported. Most large stores will ship
items purchased from them, but the cost for large items is high.
Small items can be sent from the Seoul Main International Post
Office. Since surface mail often takes two months, various
categories of airmail should be investigated. *(For detailed advice on
shopping in Seoul, see Seoul chapter, below.)*

# Chapter V
# DOING BUSINESS WITH KOREA

# KOREA'S MAJOR TRADING COMPANIES

**Daewoo Corp.** 541 5-ga Namdaemun-ro, Chung-gu, Seoul (771-91) *Cbl:* DAEWOO SEOUL *Tx:* DAEWOO K23341/5
*Main Line:* trading, machinery, shipbuilding, plant projects, construction, chemicals, textiles, finance, energy & resources development, heavy construction equipment.

**Hyosung Corp.** 17-7 4-ga Namdaemun-ro, Chung-gu, Seoul (771-11) *Cbl:* HYOSTAR SEOUL *Tx:* HYOSTAR K23121/5
*Main Line:* tire & steel products, electric & electronic products, chemicals, general machinery, plants & industrial machinery, yarn & fabric, garments, tire cord fabric, leather products, agricultural & marine products, lumber & wooden products, vessels & yachts, wet battery, construction materials.

**Hyundai Corp.** 140-2 Kye-dong, Chongno-gu, Seoul (741-2111) *Cbl:* HDSANGSA SEOUL *Tx:* HDCORP K23175/7
*Main Line:* shipbuilding, automobiles, electrical & mechanical engineering, general contracting, shipping and ship repair services, industrial plants, offshore facilities, machinery, engines, rolling stock, electrical equipment, financing, metals.

**Korea Trading Int'l Inc.** 10-1 2-ga Hoehyon-dong, Chung-gu, Seoul (755-9261) *Cbl:* KOTII SEOUL *Tx:* KOTII K27434
*Main Line:* agricultural & marine products, textile goods, yarn & textile raw materials, machinery.

**Kukje-ICC Corp.** 191 5-ga Hangang-ro, Yongsan-gu, Seoul (797-7111) *Cbl:* KUKJECO SEOUL *Tx:* KUKJECO K27251
*Main Line:* machinery, electronics, footwear, textiles & garments, sporting & leisure goods.

**Lucky-Goldstar Int'l Corp.** 20 Yoido-dong, Youngdungpo-ku, Seoul (757-1234) *Cbl:* LUCKYSL *Tx:* K24235
*Main Line:* steel & iron products, nonferrous metals, energy, machinery, electric & electronic products, telecommunications cables, chemicals, foodstuffs, building materials, textile products, military supplies.

**Samsung Co., Ltd.** 250 2-ga Taepyong-ro, Chung-gu, Seoul (751-02002/6) *Cbl:* STARS SEOUL *Tx:* STARS K23657
*Main Line:* machinery, chemicals, textiles, garments, plywood, energy, general commodities, foodstuffs, steel products & metals, plant & overseas projects, special supplies, electric & electronic products.

**Ssangyong Corp.** 24-1 2-ga Jeo-dong, Jung-gu, Seoul (274-2781) *Cbl:* TWINDRA SEOUL *Tx:* TWINDRA K24270
*Main Line:* cement & building materials, construction equipment, iron & steel products, vessels & vehicles, machinery & industrial equipment, electric & electronic supplies, minerals military supplies, textile & garments, chemical products, foodstuffs, general merchandise.

**Sunkyong Ltd.** 5-3 2-ga Namdaemun-ro, Chung-gu, Seoul (758-2114) *Cbl:* SUNKYONG SEOUL *Tx:* SNKYONG K24851
*Main Line:* textiles, fibres, construction, chemicals, machinery, metals, electronics, plywood, shipping, tourism, hotels.

# KOREA'S NEW BUSINESS CLIMATE

The world economic center of gravity is shifting from the Atlantic to the Pacific. By the year 2000, the Asian-Pacific region, led by South Korea and other nations, may well begin to dominate both traditional manufacturing and high technology industries.

The Republic of Korea, once dependent upon American aid, has become the seventh largest trading partner of the United States, a good example of how American aid bears fruit. At present, the United States is Korea's largest single trading partner, taking 38.7 percent of Korea's exports and supplying 21.6 percent of total foreign imports. Thus, Korea's foreign trade is heavily dependent on business with the United States.

Doing business with Korea is not difficult or complex. Every Korean trading company has an English-language specialist, and much experience has been acquired in overcoming obstacles to communication in both human and technical terms.

South Korea, lacking in natural resources, imports mainly raw materials and high-tech capital goods. The major imports are crude oil, machinery, electric appliances, ships, iron, textiles, organic compounds, grains, coke, and timber; importing also includes the procurement of military hardware. The United States is second on the list of Korea's suppliers (about $8.8 billion), behind Japan (about $13.6 billion). The Republic of Korea currently is spending $7.2 billion (6 percent of GNP) annually on defense, especially for state-of-the-art weaponry, naval ships, and aircraft and was to purchase a total of $8 billion in U.S. arms between 1985 and 1989.

South Korea's 10 major export items are electric goods (color TV sets), steel and iron products, machinery, ships, synthetic resin (second in the world in tonnage), cement, footwear, automobiles, and plywood. The United States is Korea's major customer ($18.3 billion per year), followed by Japan ($8.43 billion per year). In 1986, Korea sold $7.1 billion more to the U.S. marketplace than it bought; for 1987, the surplus was $10 billion.

## KOREA'S FOREIGN TRADE STRUCTURE

The long-run objective of the government is to make South Korea as industrialized as Japan, and to do so as rapidly as possible. As a direct result, the standard of living of all its citizens and a broadening of the participation in the benefits of industrialization

KOREA'S NEW BUSINESS CLIMATE

*Seoul's striking new 'DLI 63' Building*

---

have been greatly improved over the last three decades. Leadership is a major factor in economic development in South Korea. Recent administrations have stimulated the country's export industry and enforced their brand of political stability toward the goal of economic growth.

The Korean government remains the undisputed formulator of economic policy and the ultimate arbiter of who receives the benefits of economic growth, although freewheeling businessmen pursue economic profits in both domestic and international markets. There are many important state-run enterprises, and some prices are under strict regulation. The trade system is a mixture of free enterprise and government control.

While the president has the final say on all policy, the prime minister and deputy prime minister are quite influential. The executive branch of the Korean government predominates, and economic decision-making is highly centralized; the deputy prime minister is concurrently chief of the Economic Planning Board, the most powerful economic agency in South Korea. At the national level, cabinet ministers have portfolios in commerce and industry, finance, energy and resources, science and technology, construction, agriculture and fisheries, and transportation and labor. They have subordinate units at various levels of local administration.

The government successfully relied on its ability to implement and formulate policy in directing the course of the country's ecomy. Leaders in the 1980s have also fostered institutions specializing in international marketing and others designed to promote technological innovation in the push to make Korea an industrialized nation. Its chief tools are the national budget, the regulation of markets and corporate behavior, the supply of credit, and even the establishment of state-run enterprises. Because the economy had grown so large and complex that government bureaucrats were unable to respond quickly to economic opportunity, recent administrations have liberalized the economic system by encouraging free markets and lessening government control.

**The Private Trade Sector.** Most of the nation's foreign trade is conducted by the private sector, and a system of government support for exports and imports linked to trading privileges sometimes virtually amounts to firm-by-firm regulations. The administration of the complex machinery is by and large objective and nonpartisan, but the official and political connections of the family firms do bring potential benefits.

The economy in South Korea is essentially characterized by private enterprise, and the government is an important partner in the growing ranks of Korean businessmen, even as the government itself spearheads many types of industrial activity. The typical business is a closely held, family-run enterprise. Although the market has recently grown to over 5,000 firms, not many firms, besides well-known conglomerates and business groups, are listed on the nation's stock exchange. Some businesses have debts equivalent to several times their equity, and firms rely on their own assets and the availability of loan funds to finance day-to-day operations and growth.

South Korea enjoyed a trade surplus of US$12 billion in 1988, resulting from the beneficial effects of the current favorable external trade milieu, falling oil prices, a strong Japanese yen, and lower international interest rates. Korean trade missions go to the United States to buy more American commodities; others go to the European Common Market to introduce sophisticated Korean products to European markets. American non-life insurance firms and foreign-made cigarettes are allowed to enter the Korean market, and also, since July 1, 1987, foreign copyright and product patents have been protected.

South Korea's conglomerates have four main business lobbying groups (Federation of Korean Industries, Korean Chamber of Commerce and Industry, Korean Federation of Small Business, and Korean Foreign Trade Association) that represent business in the councils of government; many private enterprises depend on the government for approval of major loans and projects, tax breaks, and financial bailouts when all else fails.

South Korea's foreign trade policy has been shaped by the nation's basic economic requirements. Official government measures have thus favored essential imports of raw materials and capital goods needed to produce items for both export and domestic consumption, restricted nonessential imports, promoted exports and diversification of export products, and also encouraged foreign investment in South Korea.

**The Government Role in Foreign Trade.** The government's direct participation in foreign trade is limited to imports made by the government's central buying agency and to imports of agricultural products under government-to-government concessional purchase arrangements; these sectors of the foreign trade operations are monopolized by the government. Most of South Korea's export-import trade is privately owned and operated by Korean nationals, but there is substantial foreign investment and export firms have increased in importance. Such firms export commodities valued at over 20 percent of the nation's total exports. Japanese firms have set up plants in South Korea supplying both the Japanese domestic market and traditional customers in the United States. Many American firms have participated in joint ventures with Korean partners because of the absence of legal restraints on foreign investment.

Korean industry has altered the country's landscape, drawing millions of laborers to urban manufacturing centers. Most industry is located in the urban areas of the northwest and southeast; heavier industry is generally in the south. Although the port of Inchon provides a convenient outlet for production, more than half of the nation's 30 new industrial estates are outside of the Seoul-Inchon area because the government disperses industry, partly to relieve the larger cities of population pressures, and partly to equalize income between regions. The southeastern port of Pusan is even more important to international trade, and the region near Pusan as a whole provides nearly half of all factory employment. An elaborate system of export incentives has grown by accretion over a decade. Additionally, the government has designated some 150 factories and 2 free trade areas for bonded processing of imported materials and finished goods, largely for export, and almost 70 bonded warehouses for the storage of imported materials. The Masan Free Export Zone, a free trade area, was established near Pusan at the southern end of Korea; and Iri, about halfway down the west coast of the peninsula from Seoul, was opened as a second free trade zone.

The South Korean government maintains branches of the Korea Trade Promotion Corporation and the Korea Exchange Bank in all of the nation's major markets and suppliers, including large cities in the West. The Korea Exchange Bank conducts all of the international banking and foreign exchange business of the central bank and has offices in all major financial centers. Foreign exchange is controlled by the Ministry of Finance, the Korea Exchange Bank, the Bank of Korea, and the branch offices of foreign banks in South Korea.

**Debt and Resource Management.** In the 1970s and early 1980s, Korea experienced a ballooning of its foreign debt. At that time it was the largest debtor in Asia and the fourth largest in the world with over $45 billion in 1986. Since then, the debt has steadily been reduced every year, decreasing to $35.5 billion in 1987 and projected to decline further to $30 billion by the end of 1988. Economists predict that Korea will be a net creditor by 1992. To that end, the following efforts are being made to reduce the foreign debt: (1) maintaining the debt-service ratio within the 12 percent level; (2) keeping the outstanding external debt within 50 percent of the GNP; (3) attracting other forms of long-term borrowing, including direct foreign investment; and (4) improving debt structure with increased shares of borrowing from international development banks and other financial institutions.

The rapid growth of the resource-poor Korean economy needs to secure adequate supplies of resources. To cope with the uncertainties surrounding world resources markets, foreign exchange reserves are maintained at a level of $11 billion, and stockpiles of crude oil raised to a 90-day supply level; moreover, rice reserves have been kept to a 100-day supply level since 1986.

For an uninterrupted supply of oil and other strategic materials, including foreign exchange earnings, the greatest possible use of domestic vessels is being encouraged for overseas marine transportation. Shipbuilding capacity was expanded to six million G/T in 1986, which also meant increasing annual steel production at the Pohang steel mills.

## KOREA'S NEW BUSINESS CLIMATE

Since energy has been one of the major bottlenecks to industrial growth in South Korea, the government has given top priority both to induce investments in energy-saving industries and to encourage investments for energy conservation. High priority in overall investment policies is still being given to investments in technology and manpower development, as well as to energy conservation.

The great strengths of Korea's economy are its educated and industrious work force, its scrupulously orchestrated planning, its domestic harmony, and the country's diverse and vigorous exports ($47.28 billion in 1987). Furthermore, the stepping stones of Korean economic ascent have been its diversification from light industry to advanced high technology, with joint ventures as the basis of the next stage of industrial growth.

In keeping with rapid economic growth, employment rose to about 18 million in 1988, and sharp rises in domestic saving and investments have fueled the high growth of the nation's economy in the past quarter century. Since the country's debt service ratio is at a manageable level and its exports continue to rise, the nation continues to enjoy good credit standing on the international financial market. Furthermore, the Korean Institute for Industrial Economics and Technology endeavors to meet the rapidly expanding demand for scientific, technical, and industrial manpower to boost the exports of more sophisticated and better quality products produced with greater efficiency.

South Korea is keeping the door open to normalization with North Korea, the People's Republic of China, and the Soviet Union. That North Korea offered flood relief to South Korea and assisted in reuniting families separated by the division between the North and the South are hopeful signs of accommodation. Therefore, free-enterprise Korea can be expected to change gradually. Although Korea's external debt will be about $20 billion in 1989, owing to its booming trade, it expects to become a creditor rather than a debtor nation before the mid-1990s.

Korea's new liberalization policy dramatically reverses previous practice by opening new markets to foreign goods, encouraging private ventures, and cutting red tape for foreign investments.

Indeed, the Republic of Korea's approach to economic growth—development led by industrialization and industrialization led by exports—has proved to be very compatible with the tempo of economic development in the industrialized nations, particularly the United States and Japan. South Korea could achieve one of the world's outstanding records of economic growth by the end of this century. In view of its past economic performance and future growth potential, it is predicted that by the year 2000, Korea will emerge as the 10th largest trading nation in the world.

## FOREIGN TRADE PRIORITIES

South Korea's foreign economic relations continue to be dominated by the United States and Japan. These nations are Korea's major export markets and suppliers and also the prime sources of private foreign investment, commercial loans, economic assistance in both grants and loans, and imported technology. Foreign trading and financial transactions are of fundamental importance to the economy and are closely interwoven with economic performance. The Korean economy tends to fluctuate with the swings in economic conditions in the industrial nations of the Western world owing to South Korea's close links to those countries. Recently the Foreign Trade Transaction Law has allowed trade with all Eastern bloc nations under government-required certificates.

The Republic of Korea, given the nearby example of Japan as a successful model, has a twofold economic strategy to achieve politically acceptable rates of trading growth: the development of a substantial manufacturing capacity for export items using imported materials and the replacement of imported goods by domestic products. Almost all of South Korea's exports consist of manufactured goods, and its most costly imports are crude petroleum, cereals, logs, and sophisticated technology—especially oil among the crucial raw materials.

**Energy Policy.** Korea's foreign exchange spending for the importation of petroleum has been expanded drastically. Since the share of imported energy consumption has been growing every year, the government has recently promoted the construction of atomic power, coal power, and hydroelectric power plants, discontinuing the establishment of new petroleum-fuel power plants. Meanwhile, Korea and Indonesia have agreed to jointly develop petroleum resources in East Java.

To reduce its overwhelming dependence on petroleum as a source of industrial energy, the government has a long-range nuclear energy program of major proportions, with plans to build a total of 13 nuclear power stations by 1991 with U.S., French and Canadian firms; these plants will provide 40 percent of South Korea's electricity.

Recently, Korea Electric Company, the state-run power corporation, has become involved in a joint uranium mining project in the Western African nation of Gabon with a French partner. The most important development in the country's power industry is its increasing reliance on nuclear power to reduce oil-burning power plants, thus decreasing oil imports and South Korea's balance of trade deficit. Korea's spending for petroleum imports has expanded to over $6 billion, representing about 14.7% of the country's total imports and about 5 percent of its GNP.

**Trade Diplomacy.** The Republic of Korea has held a series of governmental and nongovernmental conferences with the United States, Japan, European nations, Southeast Asian nations, Taiwan, and other nations in an effort to promote closer trade and economic cooperation. Furthermore, Korea has taken an active part in a number of conferences organized by international banking and economic institutions such as the International Monetary Fund, the United Nations Industrial Development Organization, the International Bank of Reconstruction and Development, the Asian Development Bank, the African Development Bank, the International Development Association, the Economic and Social Commission for Asia, and the General Agreement on Tariffs and Trade.

Economic cooperation between Korea and the United States has been increased through exchanges of trade and sales missions and private-level economic cooperation meetings in Seoul, Washington, New York, and Los Angeles. Recently, Korea has invited many economic and trade missions from Europe to visit Korea. The annual Korea-Japan talks (governmental and nongovernmental) exchanged a wide range of views on the removal of Japanese nontariff barriers on Korea goods, plant exports, technology transfer from Japan to Korea, and joint penetration into third countries for resources development.

**The Role of Electronics.** The Korean electronics industry has an annual growth rate of over 30 percent, whereas that of all Korean industry was around 18 percent in 1986, but declined to about 12% in 1988; its high technology industry has made an enormous contribution to national development, especially owing to its export orientation, its employment creating effects, and its backward and forward linkages to other parts of South Korea's economy. The quantitative and qualitative expansion of the Korean economy has been diverse, ranging from textiles to steel, shipbuilding and automotiles to electronics. A well-educated, but low cost work force, brisk foreign investment and joint ventures, and an increasing demand for consumer electronic products from larger purchasers in the United States and Europe are the main factors in the rapid growth of that industry. This has made Korea one of the 10 largest electronics exporting nations in the world. The broad range of consumer products include TV sets, VCRs, and audio equipment; industrial equipment, such as computers and data processing equipment; and components, including electronic tubes, discrete semiconductors, and integrated circuits.

South Korea's fishing industry has contributed both to the nation's export earnings and to the welfare of domestic consumers. The nation's deep-sea fleet is the sixth largest in the world, operating 750 vessels from 25 overseas bases and selling over $350 million-worth of fish to foreign markets. With plywood still an important export industry, South Korea imports over 80 percent of its timber, mostly from Malaysia and Indonesia. The textile industry, one of the oldest manufacturing businesses in Korea, is still a major exchange earner.

Since art and learning have traditionally served a moral and educational function in Korea as important transmitters of the values of the people, the publishing industry has greatly advanced and modern printing facilities have been developed: Kyobo Corporation and Dong-A Printing Company have already begun to trade in publishing and printing with the United States and Japan.

**U.S./Korea Trade Ties.** One of the benefactors of Korean economic prosperity is the United States. The Republic of Korea appears ready to increase its import of American raw materials, high-technology products, and luxury consumer goods for affluent Koreans. South Korea, as the fourth largest customer in the world for American grain traders (such as Cargill and Continental), imported over $1.5 billion worth of American agricultural products in 1986. Westinghouse has sold six nuclear power plants to Korea and Bechtel has built four.

General Electric, General Dynamics, Lockheed, Rockwell, Hughes, and Teledyne are profiting in sales of U.S. arms to South Korea. The Korean Lucky-Goldstar Group has already linked up with 40 foreign companies, including AT&T, Dow Corning, Honeywell, and NEC (Japan). A Daewoo/General Motors joint venture produces automobiles on a large scale: Ford works with the Korean Kia Industry Company; and Chrysler has made production arrangements with the Samsung Group—whose Samsung H-P is 55 percent owned by Hewlett-Packard. Hyundai Motor Company (15% owned by Japan's Mitsubishi) is successfully shipping cars to the Canadian and U.S. markets; and Mazda has arranged a production deal with Korea's Kia.

Foreign economic transactions, besides the flow of goods into and out of the country, include foreign exchange earned through tourism; payments and receipts from foreign investments: loans from private foreign banks; receipts of foreign exchange from spending by U.S. armed forces stationed in South Korea; and loans from international organizations and governments; as well as payments for freight, merchandise insurance, and transportation. The growth of tourism is largely attributable to the increase in the number of Japanese and American tourists, who are expected to be the dominant source of foreign exchange earnings from invisible transactions.

Transfer payments have been a significant part of the nation's international transactions. The large number of Koreans working abroad, particularly on overseas construction projects, and residents living abroad have sent funds to South Korea totaling more than $150 million, with some fluctuations from year to year.

# DOING BUSINESS IN KOREA:
# A SPECIAL REPORT

*Trenholme J. Griffin*

## THE ROLE OF THE GOVERNMENT IN FOREIGN TRADE AND FOREIGN INVESTMENT

It is nearly impossible to overemphasize the role of the government in the South Korean economy. The involvement of government bureaucrats in business affairs in South Korea is pervasive and ongoing. Nearly all major business changes and transactions require the approval of the government or a government-affiliated agency or corporation. The role of the government is so great that the words "government-directed" must be placed before "free market" in describing the economy of Korea. As a rule, government bureaucrats are very paternalistic toward Korean businessmen and often refuse to approve deals or terms fully desired by the South Korean side. Korean businessmen are generally quick to respond to government directives or "administrative guidance" even though they do not have the force of law. They will do this in many cases since they realize that they must obtain approvals on an ongoing basis. Significant efforts are made to maintain good relations with government officials for that reason.

The origin of the government-business relationship in Korea can be traced to neo-Confucian tenets which hold that the government must be benevolent in dealing with citizens and that citizens should follow government directives without question. Korean businessmen as a rule have a high regard for the opinions of government officials.

## SECURING ENTREE TO THE KOREA MARKET

Potential importers and exporters must first be invited to visit Korea. To obtain an invitation, buyers or sellers prepare a business proposal and submit it to an appropriate Korean company or business institution. Information and assistance can be obtained from US commercial attachés abroad, the US Commerce Department, and trade organizations in Korea such as the Korea Trade Promotion Corporation, the Korean Foreign Trade Association, the World Trade Center of Korea, the Federation of Korean Industries, the American Chamber of Commerce, the Korean Chamber of Commerce and Industry, the Korean Stock Exchange, the Korea Exchange Bank, and the Export-Import Bank of Korea.

**The Invitation.** The first step in establishing direct contact with a Korean importer or exporter is to locate the appropriate company. The Korea Trade Promotion Corporation (KOTRA) has 85 offices throughout the world and publishes a *Directory of Trade of Korea Today* (CPO Box 6494, Seoul; tel.: 779-1345) and *Korea Trade & Business* (monthly) about Korean products and industry. For certain commodities, the industrial end-user corporation or government agency handling their commercial transactions for a particular commodity, service, or technology may be identified. The next step is to refine the proposal and forward it to the appropriate company or office in Korea. Usually, foreign firms or individuals regarded as sound prospects will receive an invitation to visit Korea to engage in negotiations.

**The Business Proposal.** The initial proposal should be straightforward, technically explicit, and sufficiently specific to permit a comprehensive evaluation by the Korean company or agency. Importers hould state their exact requirements, and both importers and exporters should give detailed information about their company's history, product lines, and sales volume. Additional data such as financial reports are useful, but large firms should avoid confusing the issue with descriptions of divisions and product lines not relevanty to items or services to be traded.

**Korean Translations.** Translation of the proposal into Korean is a polite gesture which can save time and demonstrate goodwill. Nevertheless, translation of the proposal and cover letter into Korean is not essential. Most Korean companies maintain English-language translation specialists.

**Korean Visas.** Once an invitation has been received, the visitor must apply for a visa at a Korean embassy or consulate. A notarized letter from the sponsoring organization, evidence of financial responsibility, and indication of the duration of the visit are necessary for the visa application.

# FLOW CHART FOR FOREIGN INVESTMENT

| Preparation of Joint Venture Agreement | • Notarization of a notary public or a confirmation from a Korean Consulate or embassy |
| --- | --- |
| Application for Foreign Investment Approval | • Documents submitted to the Minister of Finance (or to the Governor of the Bank of Korea for automatic approval project applications) include project plan, joint venture agreement, power of attorney (if needed), certificate of nationality, and a detailed list of capital to be invested (if known at the time of application) |
| Approval of the Foreign Investment | • Automatic approval (10 days) given by the Governor of the Bank of Korea<br>• Screened approval (30-60 days) given by the Minister of Finance after an examination of the project, which includes consultations with institutions concerned (new investments for over US$3 million and capital increases for over US$5 million are reviewed by the Foreign Capital Project Review Committee). |
| Introduction of the Foreign Capital | • Application for detailed review and confirmation of imported capital goods should be submitted to the relevant ministry for the introduction of capital goods<br>• Report of capital introduction submitted to the Minister of Finance (to the Governor of the Bank of Korea for automatic approval projects) |
| Incorporation | • Actual investment of capital (cash, capital goods)<br>• Newly established company<br>• Capital is actually invested and the new company is established |
| Registration of the Foreign Invested Company | • Company should be registered with the Minister of Finance (or the Governor of the Bank of Korea for automatic approval projects) after payment of the subject matter to be invested.<br>• Post-investment management (approval of changes in scope of business, increase in business activity, reinvestment of dividends, disposal of invested capital, withdrawal of invested capital, remittance of dividends, receipt of additional taxes, etc.) |

Source: *Korea Traders Association*

# BUSINESS REPRESENTATION IN KOREA

Once a trading or investment relationship has been established in Korea, it is sometimes advisable for a foreign business representative to remain in Seoul to deal with any problems and to continue contact with Korean companies. Foreign business personnel are arriving in Seoul in ever-increasing numbers. Expenses tend to be lower than the world average, and the business person is likely to receive more personal attention from individuals, companies, and agencies. The capital city of Seoul, where most foreigners stay, is a fully modern metropolis with many deluxe Western hotels, English-speaking personnel in shops, bars, and restaurants, and excellent entertainment. At the same time, it is the repository of more than 600 years of Korean culture from the Choson Dynasty. The foreign business representative who resides in Korea will find that Koreans have learned hospitality from childhood, with a tradition that compels them to be solicitous of the feelings and comfort of others.

## PERSONAL INCOME TAXATION

Foreigners who are classified as "residents" under South Korean tax law are subject to tax on their worldwide income in the same manner as Korean nationals. However, individuals who are classified as a "nonresident" are only subject to tax on Korean-source income.

The Republic of Korea has a unitary system of individual income taxation under which gross income from all sources is aggregated and subject to taxation at progressive rates. Deductions and personal exemptions from taxable income are allowed for residents under certain conditions. Surcharges (for both defense and residence taxes) are added to the income tax in computing the total tax liability. Furthermore, a 10% penalty for any failure to file returns and the failure to pay taxes can be assessed. In the case of a nonresident foreigner having Korean-source income, he must obtain a Certification for Tax Due from the commissioner of regional taxation office or the director of district taxation office prior to remitting his income overseas.

Foreigners from a country which has entered into a tax treaty with the Republic of Korea may benefit from certain provisions of the treaty. Korea has tax treaties with 26 countries as of January 1, 1988. In general, a "resident" taxpayer is any individual who (1) has a domicile in Korea, (2) has had a place of residence in Korea for more than one year, (3) has an occupation which would require him to reside in Korea for more than one year, or (4) has his family in Korea and is thus deemed to reside in Korea for more than one year in view of his occupation or assets held in Korea.

The following types of income are considered taxable:

**Global Income.** This includes earned income (wage and salary), interest, dividends, real estate (rental), business income and other income.

**Earned Income.** This income is the remuneration received or accrued for services rendered. There are two different types of earned income. One is known as "Class A" and the other "Class B." The former is employment income received or accrued from a domestic employer. The latter is employment income received or accrued from a foreign agency or UN Forces (excluding US armed forces) in Korea or foreign corporations outside Korea. Other types of includable income are retirement income, capital gains, and forestry income. The following types of income are tax exempt: (1) wages received by foreigners serving with a foreign government or UN, and organizations thereof; (2) wages received by foreigners sent to Korea under a bilateral agreement between governments; (3) wages received by either foreigners engaged by a foreign invested enterprise (FIE) or foreigners furnishing services under the Foreign Capital Inducement Law within five years from the registration date of FIE or the approval date of technical inducement agreement; and (4) wages received by foreign technicians employed by Korean companies satisfying certain requirements.

Resident foreigners who have taxable income must file an annual tax return with the relevant district taxation office between May 1 and May 31 of the following year. They also must pay the tax due at any qualified bank or post offices. A foreigner who has only Class A earned income is not subject to tax return requirement. Instead, he will be subject to payroll withholding tax by either employer or payer on a monthly basis. An earner of Class B income may choose one of the following methods of voluntary declaring and withholding tax: (1) declare and pay tax annually during May of the following year; or (2) join a taxpayers' association and pay income tax monthly, which entitles him to a tax credit of 20% of such tax paid monthly.

The following types of income derived only from Korean sources are taxable: interest, dividends, real estate income, business income, personal service income (including wages and salary), royalties, gains from the transfer of securities, and other income specifically

# KOREA'S TAX SYSTEM

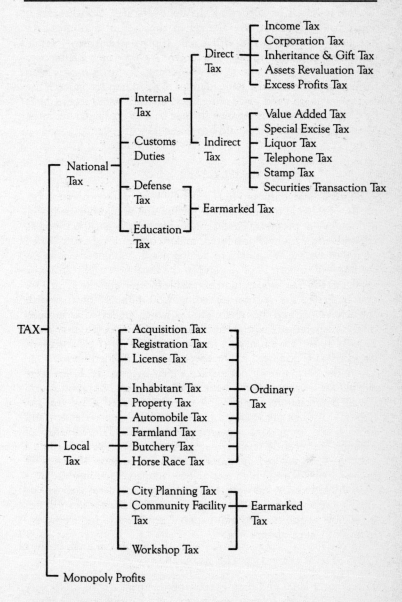

Source: *Ministry of Finance*

noted in the Income Tax Law.

Two methods of calculating the tax owing (i.e., global taxation and separate taxation) are applied in the case of a nonresident foreigner. An alien having either a fixed place of business (permanent establishment) or real estate income within Korea is subject to tax on an aggregated base of taxable income and thus must file an income tax return in the same manner as a resident foreigner. If the taxpayer has no fixed place of business or real estate income, he is liable to pay tax on his separate income base at graduated tax rates. Most of this income tax would be withheld by the paying individual or entity.

## CORPORATION TAX

A South Korean corporation is generally subject to corporation tax on its worldwide income (after applying any applicable credits or deductions) at progressive rates ranging from 20% to 30% (or 33%, applicable in case of a non-listed, major corporation having issued capital exceeding ₩5 billion or having net shareholders' equity exceeding ₩10 billion as of the end of the fiscal year). The 20% rate applies to the first ₩50 million of taxable income and the 30 or 33% rate applies to the portion exceeding ₩50 million. Together with the defense tax and the inhabitant tax which are levied as surtaxes on the corporation tax, the effective corporation tax rate may reach as high as 39.75% of taxable income (43.725%, if the company is classified as a nonlisted major corporation as defined above).

In the past, foreign companies which invested in Korea were eligible for a variety of tax benefits including tax exemptions and special depreciation. The possible benefits included a five-year tax holiday, customs tax exemptions, advantageous depreciation, and income tax exemptions for certain expatriates. The Ministry of Finance has recently severely curtailed these benefits for all but a few types of favored investments. Under current Ministry of Finance policies, only high technology companies involved in areas such as electronics, software, biotechnology, and aerospace will be eligible for tax favors. In a few years, even these categories will not be eligible as the need to grant special privileges to induce investments will have disappeared.

## BANKING AND FINANCE

Korea has a large and rapidly growing financial sector. Until very recently, the Korean government kept tight control over the financial sector to achieve a number of policy goals. This resulted to a large extent in the rapid development of many key industries and impressive economic growth. However, these controls tended to retard the development of the financial markets themselves both in terms of size and sophistication in relation to the overall strength of the economy. The Korean government has recognized this fact and is moving to both "privatize" and "internationalize" its financial institutions. These steps are being taken to increase efficiency through competition and because the size of the nation's financial market is outstripping the government's ability to regulate and control its operation.

**Government Institutions.** The financial sector in Korea is regulated by the Ministry of Finance and a number of related government-controlled entities. One of these entities is the Monetary Board which establishes monetary and credit policies. The country's commercial banking system is controlled by the Bank of Korea which has been the nation's central bank since 1950. The Bank of Korea is responsible for issuing the nation's currency as well as regulating and supervising all other banks in Korea. The central bank is also responsible for the lending and borrowing of the government and is a major lender to domestic financial institutions.

In addition to the central bank, the Korean government has created a number of special banking institutions — including the Korea Exchange Bank, the Small and Medium Industry Bank, the Citizens National Bank, the National Agricultural Cooperatives Federation, the Central Federation of Fisheries Cooperatives, the Korea Housing Bank, the Korean Development Bank, the Export-Import Bank of Korea, and the Korea Long-Term Credit Bank — to further the government's policy goals.

**The "City" Banks.** The principal commercial banks in Korea are known as "city" banks. The five city banks are the Bank of Seoul, Korea First Bank, Commercial Bank of Korea, Hanil Bank, and Cho Heung Bank. Two so-called "joint venture city banks" are also in operation. They are the Shinhan Bank and the Kor-Am Bank. Despite their names, each of the city banks has a nationwide branch network and numerous overseas offices.

The city banks are run by managers selected by the Korean government even though the government sold their shares to the public as part of the financial deregulation program. As a result, they follow government policy guidelines rather than seeking to maximize profits. The city banks loan huge amounts to Korea's large companies and are often required to participate in government-organized financial restructurings which has created high levels of bad loans. City banks in effect have full government financial support despite their weak financial condition.

Every large Korean company has a bank which acts as its "prime" bank. This prime bank must approve any loans made by secondary banks. In effect, this allows the prime bank to indirectly regulate a company's financial affairs. The prime bank will step in if the company's finances deteriorates.

Korea also has a variety of other financial institutions. Some of these institutions are:

**Regional Banks.** These ten privately-owned commercial banks operate solely in one of Korea's provinces or special cities. Each regional bank is allowed to open one office in Seoul. Regional banks generally raise a larger percentage of their assets from depositors and more often make loans to small- and medium-sized companies.

**Foreign Bank Branches and Representative Offices.** Over 50 foreign banks have established a presence in Korea. Branches are allowed to engage in far more activities than representative offices. Foreign bank branch operations have traditionally involved arranging loan syndications and were quite profitable. Funds were raised by foreign banks through a "swap" mechanism with the Korean government and loaned at a profitable margin. Recently, with Korea's excess liquidity, high domestic savings rates, and reduced foreign debt, foreign banks have had to look to new areas such as foreign exchange services and capital markets activities rather than syndicated lending for profits.

**Merchant Banks.** The Korean government has allowed the formation of six merchant banks which offer a range of financial services to customers. Merchant banks are involved in offering short-term *won* financing, short- and medium-term foreign currency loans, leasing, and capital markets transactions.

**Short-Term Finance Companies, Investment and Trust Companies, Credit Units, and Mutual Credit Associations.** These financial institutions were created to increase the domestic capital base and to serve the needs of individual and corporate borrowers. These organizations often drew deposits which would otherwise have been invested in the illegal "curb" private money market in which interest rates were very much above levels permitted by the government.

# THE KOREAN FINANCIAL SECTOR

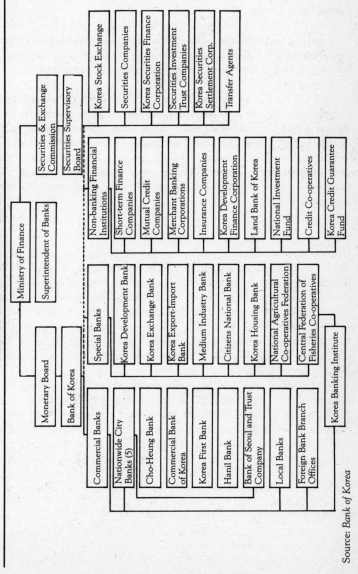

Source: *Bank of Korea*

**Insurance Companies.** Korea has both life insurance and property and casualty insurance companies. In general, profitability in these sectors has been low because of a lack of sophistication and government curbs on investments. Recently, US companies have entered this market.

**Leasing Companies.** Eight specialized leasing institutions have been formed to provide a range of leasing packages to businesses in Korea. Each is a joint venture with a foreign company.

**Securities Firms.** Korea has nearly 30 firms which are engaged in selling securities and providing other services related to the capital markets. These firms have offices both in Korea and abroad. A number of foreign securities companies have established representative offices in anticipation of the opening of the stock market to foreign investors. These offices conduct research and assist in the management of international investment trusts allowed by the government.

## THE STOCK MARKET

Even though the stock market in South Korea has made great strides and produced record profits in recent years, it is not well-developed when compared to the market standards of advanced industrial countries. To its credit, the South Korean government has taken steps to encourage the development of the nation's equity market. As of January 1, 1988, 389 companies were listed on the Korean Stock Exchange; market capitalization was in excess of the equivalent of US$37 billion. Average daily trading volume exceeded ₩70 billion in 1987.

The principal index of the performance of the Korean Stock Exchange is the Composite Stock Price Index (CSPI) which was at 525.11 at the end of 1987. This represented a rise of 98% in value over the CSPI at the end of the previous year. This increase was not a one-time phenomenon as stock prices on the Korean Stock Exchange rose by 330% over the five-year period ending on the last day in December 1987. A lack of investment opportunities and high domestic liquidity should propel the stock market even higher in years to come.

At the present time, foreigners who do not reside in South Korea are not allowed to directly purchase shares in Korean companies listed on public securities exchanges. The only way for nonresident foreigners to purchase such shares is to purchase units in one of the international investment trusts authorized by the Korean government. The most convenient way for foreigners to invest is to purchase units in either the Korea Fund, a US$100 million closed-end investment fund listed on the New York Stock Exchange or the Korea-Euro Fund, a US$60 million closed-end investment fund listed in London. The performance of both funds since their inception has been excellent. US$150,000 invested in the Korea Fund at its inception was worth well over US$1 million in June 1988. Because of the scarcity of investment alternatives, both of these closed-end funds trade at a significant premium over net-asset value. This premium will substantially decline or be eliminated when direct purchases of Korean securities by foreigners is allowed.

One other way for foreign investors to obtain shares in Korean companies is to purchase bonds which are convertible into shares. These convertible bond issues have been issued by major Korean companies since implementing regulations were promulgated in 1985. These bonds have appreciated substantially in value since they were issued. The issuers to date have been Samsung Electronics, Daewoo Heavy Industries, Yukong, and Gold Star.

## LABOR

The Korean labor force is well-educated, hard-working, and diligent. South Korea is fortunate in this respect since its people are the nation's most significant resource. Over 97% of South Koreans are literate. Over 90% of the country's children are educated until age 18, and over 30% attend a university. In fact, Korean workers may be over-educated given the level of development in the economy. Recent publicity concerning strikes and wage increases have tended to obscure the fact that Korea's labor force is one of the most cost-competitive and well-trained in the world. Even with recent increases in wage levels (which ranged from 15 to 20% on an annual basis during 1987 and 1988), Korean labor is still very competitive. Korean workers work an average of 54.5 hours a week, which is the longest industrial workweek in the world. This translates to over 2,500 hours per year, 25% more than Japan. It might however be noted that many foreign businessmen feel that Korean workers are not always productive during the workday and that overstaffing is common in Korean companies. Wage increases over the next several years should range from 15 to 20%.

Union activity can be expected to increase in Korea in the years to come, but labor disputes will only act to slow rather than stop an otherwise booming economy. One problem with resolving labor

## FINANCIAL INSTITUTIONS IN KOREA

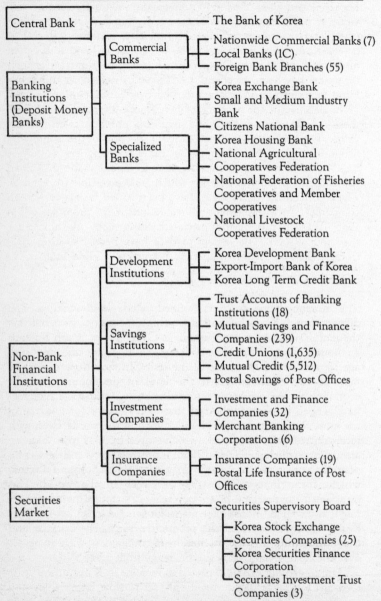

Central Bank ——— The Bank of Korea

Banking Institutions (Deposit Money Banks)

Commercial Banks
- Nationwide Commercial Banks (7)
- Local Banks (1C)
- Foreign Bank Branches (55)

Specialized Banks
- Korea Exchange Bank
- Small and Medium Industry Bank
- Citizens National Bank
- Korea Housing Bank
- National Agricultural Cooperatives Federation
- National Federation of Fisheries Cooperatives and Member Cooperatives
- National Livestock Cooperatives Federation

Non-Bank Financial Institutions

Development Institutions
- Korea Development Bank
- Export-Import Bank of Korea
- Korea Long Term Credit Bank

Savings Institutions
- Trust Accounts of Banking Institutions (18)
- Mutual Savings and Finance Companies (239)
- Credit Unions (1,635)
- Mutual Credit (5,512)
- Postal Savings of Post Offices

Investment Companies
- Investment and Finance Companies (32)
- Merchant Banking Corporations (6)

Insurance Companies
- Insurance Companies (19)
- Postal Life Insurance of Post Offices

Securities Market ——— Securities Supervisory Board
- Korea Stock Exchange
- Securities Companies (25)
- Korea Securities Finance Corporation
- Securities Investment Trust Companies (3)

*Note: Figures in parentheses represent the number of institutions as of the end of 1985.*
Source: *Bank of Korea.*

disputes in Korea is the fact that neither management nor labor has had significant experience in resolving labor management conflicts, which can (and have) lead to an inability to produce a labor agreement. This lack of experience explains recent bizarre behavior such as kidnappings of union leaders and the holding of executives as hostages. A factor increasing the incidence of labor disputes is the fact that the Korean government tends to remove itself as an arbiter of disputes so as to avoid criticism from both sides.

## FOREIGN-EXCHANGE CONTROLS AND EXCHANGE RATES

Any transaction involving a transfer of currency or creating a credit relationship between a resident and a nonresident of the Republic of Korea requires approval of the Korean government under the Foreign Exchange and Control Law and Regulations. Domestic corporations and Korean branch offices of foreign corporations are classified as "residents" for foreign-exchange control purposes. A foreign individual will be deemed to be a resident of the Republic of Korea for foreign-exchange control purposes if he works at a place of business in South Korea, engages in business in South Korea, or maintains a domicile or residence in South Korea for six months or more. In general, two types of approvals are required for foreign-exchange transactions under the Foreign-Exchange Control Law: (1) approval of the underlying agreement, and (2) approval of specific payments made under authority of the underlying agreement.

In most cases, if approval of the underlying agreement is not obtained in advance, authorization for specific payments will not be given. Foreign exchange controls should be liberalized gradually in years to come.

The rate at which foreign currency can be converted into Korean *won* is controlled by the Bank of Korea. This exchange rate is determined based upon a trade-weighted basket of foreign currencies. Traditionally, the exchange rate has been closely linked to the value of the US dollar to reflect the large proportion of total trade between the two countries. Beginning in 1987, the Korean *won*, in a trend just the reverse of major world currencies, began to appreciate (rather than depreciate) in relation to the value of the US dollar. This appreciation in the value of the Korean *won* is expected to continue until at least the mid-1990s.

## INTELLECTUAL PROPERTY PROTECTION

**Patents.** Most types of patents may be obtained in South Korea by foreign individuals and companies. Under Korean law, the term of a patent right is 15 years from the date of publication (or if the patent is not published, then 15 years from the date of registration). The term can expire earlier in the event of nonpayment of annuities, abandonment of the right, invalidation, or cancellation. Inventions or devices which do not fall within the definition of "invention" under the patent law, may be eligible for registration and protection under Korea's Utility Model Act. Similarly, a unique design may be protected under the Design Act. The term of a utility model right is ten years from publication (or from registration if it is not published), and eight years from registration in the case of a design right.

**Trademarks.** South Korea has adopted a "registration" system which allows foreigners and Koreans to register a trademark. Prior use is not a prerequisite for registration in Korea, but if a trademark is not used within one year after registration it may be subject to cancellation. A trademark application must designate the goods it is intended to be applied to and must specify with which of the 53 available categories it is to be registered.

**Copyright.** Under Korea's Copyright Act which came into effect on July 1, 1987, copyright protection is available for works in which thoughts or sentiments are expressed in a creative way and fall within the literary, scientific, or artistic fields. As a result, news reports, government publications, or other merely informational printed material—including slogans and catchwords which are in common use—are not entitled to copyright protection.

**Computer Programs.** South Korea protects computer software under the Computer Program Protection Act. A computer program is defined as a manifestation of a series of commands and directions used either directly or indirectly in a computer or other information processing machine, in order to achieve a specific result. Thus, the language used to write programs, rules, and solutions are not protected. The term of a computer program copyright is 50 years from the date of creation. The law provides for the establishment of a Registry of Programs which allows the author, within a year of creation, to record the following: (1) the name or title of the program; (2) the name, domicile, and nationality of the author; (3) the date of creation; and (4) an outline of the computer program. If, at the time of registration, a reproduction of the computer program is deposited with the Ministry of Science and Technology, it will be deemed to have been created on the date of registration.

# THE SPECIAL ECONOMIC ZONES

*INDUSTRIAL ESTATES AND COMPLEXES*

The South Korean government has decided to encourage construction of industrial estates and complexes to strengthen the foundation of export industries and thereby contribute to the expansion of exports and industrial development. As the scale of industrial estates has become larger, their character has diversified. These estates include: the Gumi Industrial Estate (the largest in Korea, an electronics industry estate); a petrochemical industrial complex in Ulsan; an iron and steel-related industrial complex in Pohang; a machinery industrial complex in Changwon; a chemical industrial complex in Yechon; and 11 complexes in Taegu, Taejon, Kwangju, Sungnam, and elsewhere, all constructed by local authorities. The number of tenant firms in the major industrial estates has reached more than 1,500, and the compounded effect has been reflected in great increases in exports and employment as well as foreign investment activity owing to the availability of suitable land and facilities.

**Ulsan Industrial Estate.** Ulsan, a coastal industrial estate, is conveniently located near Pusan harbor, the second largest port in South Korea, with 18,181,900 sq.m. of land plus a harbor with berthing capacity for 40,000-ton vessels and 1,440,000 tons of stevedoring capability. The Ulsan Industrial Estate with more than 16 large-scale factories, has become the center of such heavy industry as oil refining, petrochemicals, fertilizer, aluminum smelting, shipbuilding, and automobiles.

**Pohang Industrial Estate.** Pohang is also a coastal industrial estate located near Pusan harbor with an area of 11,702.5 sq.m. plus a berthing capacity for 80,000-ton vessels and stevedoring capability for 1,548,000 tons and 100,000 tons of industrial water daily.

**Gumi Industrial Estate.** Adjacent to the Seoul-Pusan Highway, with the nearby Hakdong River supplying enough water for industrial use, it encompasses 10,528,900 sq.m. This large-scale integrated industrial estate is composed of electronic plants and other industries of over 80 companies. The estate has contributed greatly to the development of industrial export electronics products. In accordance with the Law on Tax Exemption, privileges for exemptions from various taxes are given to tenant firms.

## FREE EXPORT ZONES

The free export zones were established by the Korean government in an effort to promote exports, improve technical skills, and increase employment by introducing foreign capital. The entire zone is bonded so that enterprises may import necessary raw materials tax-free for re-export and so they can enjoy further preferential treatment. The Masan Free Export Zone is an area of 942,000 sq.m. with more than 150 firms; standardized factories of 69,400 sq.m. of total floor space have been built, thereby accelerating the inducement for foreign enterprises to become involved. Another large free export zone is located in Iri, which links up with Kunsan Harbor to increase the transportation capacity of this complex for exports and imports.

# SELLING TO KOREA

In order for a foreign company to import, stock, and sell products in Korea, at least the following two licenses are required: a trader's license and an offer agent license. Without a trader's license, a foreign company cannot import products in its own name or engage in a wholesale business (whereby products are imported through a proxy importer on the Korean office's behalf and the Korean office in turn sells them to customers in Korea).

## TRADER'S LICENSE

Lacking a trader's license, an importer or exporter must hire a licensed local importer or exporter to conduct all import or export transactions and must pay service charges. These charges generally range from 1% to 3% of the price of the goods involved). In order to be eligible for import or export business licenses, local companies must (1) have a certain amount of paid-in capital; (2) receive a certain level of export letter(s) of credit amounting to US$50,000; and (3) meet certain other requirements. These standards are subject to regular changes, so listing the precise amounts is not useful here. At the end of every year, the trader's license must be renewed. Companies will be required to provide proof of a minimum yearly export performance in either of the past two years, in order to obtain a renewal of the license. The export requirement is a major problem for foreign companies which only import goods.

## OFFER-AGENT LICENSE

The Korean Foreign Trade Law also requires, with certain exceptions, that an offer sheet issued by a licensed local offer- agent be
submitted when the importer applies for an import license.

A local offer agent is normally paid a commission by the foreign
seller in each transaction when the foreign seller issues an offer
sheet, and the customary commission charged by licensed offer
agents may become a substantial burden unless this service is provided by the distributor. The authority of an offer agent appointed
by the foreign seller may vary along a wide range depending upon
the authorization specifically given by the seller. In some cases, the
agent may be given certain powers over the terms of the offer in addition to the authority to negotiate and solicit orders. Alternatively,
his authority may be limited to simply conveying to the buyer the
seller's offers under the agent's name as a means to technically
satisfy the requirement of the Foreign Trade Law.

Thus, if the distributor has an offer agent license, the distribution agreement may cover the offer issuance services without requiring additional compensation. If the distributor does not have such
a license, you may wish to require that it obtain one as a condition
precedent to the distribution agreement, or provide that the distributor is responsible for all payments for the offer agent's services.

The conditions under which an import license will be available
for a certain category of goods depends on the periodic notice for
export and import ("Periodic Notice"). The Periodic Notices are
issued by the Ministry of Trade and Industry (MTI) under the
Foreign Trade Law, and they divide goods into three categories:
1) automatic approval items; 2) import-restricted items; and
3) import-banned items.

Apart from the importation procedures, separate approval must
be obtained from a foreign exchange bank or the Bank of Korea
regarding the terms of payment if the terms do not conform to a
standard settlement method prescribed in the Foreign Exchange
Control Law and Regulation. Payment through a letter of credit
opened by a bank under on-sight settlement terms is a common
standard settlement procedure. On the other hand, deferred payment and payment in installments, for example, are non-standard
and require separate approval.

Under the Fair Trade Law, any import agreement or import
agency agreement between a foreign exporter and a Korean importer having a term of one year or more must be submitted to the
Korean Fair Trade Office for its approval within 30 days after execu-

tion. Such an agreement must be reviewed by the Fair Trade Office even if the specified term is for less than one year, if the agreement is subject to automatic extension for a period of one year or more.

The Fair Trade Office has issued guidelines which describe "unjust collaborative acts and unfair business practices" in an international distribution agreement. Under these guidelines, agreements which impose "on the distributor unreasonably restrictive condition which are not generally acceptable in view of international contract practices" will not be approved. This broad prohibition gives the Fair Trade Office wide discretion in disapproving agreements.

## IMPORTS FROM US BY COMMODITY

| Ranking | Description | 1986 | 1987 | % change |
|---------|-------------|------|------|----------|
| 1 | Electric machinery and equipment | 948 | 1,175 | 23.9 |
| 2 | Machinery and mechanical appliances | 784 | 1,254 | 60.1 |
| 3 | Raw hides and skins | 550 | 721 | 31.0 |
| 4 | Organic chemicals | 435 | 565 | 29.9 |
| 5 | Cereals | 399 | 609 | 52.9 |
| 6 | Iron and steel | 362 | 380 | 5.0 |
| 7 | Aircraft and parts thereof | 357 | 290 | −18.7 |
| 8 | Mineral fuels | 298 | 389 | 30.4 |
| 9 | All kinds of instruments and apparatus | 279 | 350 | 28.1 |
| 10 | Paper-making material | 239 | 373 | 55.9 |
| | Total | 6,545 | 8,758 | 33.8 |

Source: *KOTRA* (US$ Million)

## CUSTOMS TAX

Customs tax is imposed upon the importation of goods into Korea. The customs tax rates depend upon the Customs Cooperation Council Nomenclature (CCCN) of the goods to be imported and generally apply to the C.I.F. price of the goods. In addition to the customs tax, when importing foreign goods, importers must also pay taxes such as value-added tax (VAT), special consumption tax, any temporarily imposed importation tax, and defense surtax.

## PAYMENTS AND FINANCING

The potential exporter to Korea who accompanies the business proposal with a carefully devised financial package tailored to the needs of the budget-conscious Koreans will have an advantage over competitors. The three main variables to consider in designing the package are currency, maturity, and interest rates. The most common finance mechanism used to pay for foreign imports continues to be letters of credit (L/Cs). Current information can be obtained from the bank or other sources listed in this chapter.

Korea's import procedures differ according to the item to be imported and the terms of payment. The following procedures are required in the case of importing foods by commercial Letter of Credit. The importer must apply for and obtain an Import License (I/L) from an authorized foreign exchange bank. In the case of automatic approval items, the importer is simply required to fill out an application for an Import License and submit it together with a contract or firm offer sheet to a foreign exchange bank, and then it will be licensed without any specific formality. In the case of import-restricted items, the importer is asked to obtain a recommendation for the import from the relevant association and then to apply to a foreign exchange bank for the Import License. The documents required when applying for a license to import are: (1) four sets of the license to import application; (2) four copies of the firm offer or import contract; (3) a letter of recommendation from the association concerned in the case of restricted items; (4) a certificate of deposit for the imports; and (5) other documents as required.

After receiving the import recommendations from the relevant association the importer must obtain an Import License within 30 days. But with the opening of a L/C or the obtaining of an I/L, the importer will usually advise the foreign supplier of the fact by cable, telex, or letter so that the supplier can ship the goods within the designated period.

## SHIPPING DOCUMENTS

The importer is notified of the arrival of shipping documents by the opening bank. After the shipment is made, the foreign supplier will send the draft accompanied by the original shipping documents to the L/C opening bank, and the L/C opening bank will in turn deliver the documents to the importer in exchange for payment of the draft. Upon arrival of the import cargo, the cargo will be stored in a bonded warehouse and kept in the custody of the customs house.

No special regulations govern the preparation of bills of lading for shipments to Korea. To facilitate prompt customs clearance, shipping marks, numbers, and other particulars on a "bill of lading" must be exactly identical to those of the actual shipment, the applicable invoice, and the firm offer. A "commercial invoice" must be prepared by the supplier at the point of shipment and bear the full signature of the supplier. To facilitate prompt customs clearance, the supplier must furnish a certificate of origin along with duly signed commercial invoices to the consignee immediately following shipment. "Air cargo shipments" are subject to the same regulations that govern ocean freight shipments. All air cargo shipments must be accompanied by airway bills together with the consular invoices and certificate of origin. Commodities shipped by "postal flight or mail to Korea" are subject to all the regulations governing cargo shipped by ocean freight, including the requirement for quarantine and other special certificates.

Upon the delivery of livestock to Korea, the supplier sends current "quarantine certificates" issued by appropriate government agencies in the country of origin; then the application must be filed with the National Veterinary Quarantine Station for a Korean quarantine certificate before customs clearance can be secured.

## BONDED WAREHOUSES

Foreign goods imported into Korea must be discharged into a bonded area. These are classified as designated bonded areas operated by the customs house and licensed bonded areas operated by private companies under the supervision of the customs house. A bonded storage place, bonded warehouse, bonded factory, bonded exhibition place, bonded construction site, or bonded sales place may be the designated storage and licensed bonded area for customs inspection. The maximum permitted period of storage in a bonded area is two years, although this can be extended for an additional year. Foreign exporters may freely carry out sales activities in Korea due to the delivery terms of the ex-bonded warehouse. Foreign suppliers may utilize this type of sales promotion if marketability is assured and a reliable agent is located in Korea. Foreign goods can be re-exported or re-patriated at the request of the consigner of consignee. Bonded warehouses are located at every port of entry where a customs house is located, and storage charges are set at a reasonable rate by the customs house.

## CUSTOMS CLEARANCE

Having obtained a Delivery Order (D/O) from the shipping company or shipping agent in exchange for the applicable Bill of Lading (B/L), the importer will then carry out customs clearance procedures — directly for a few items or through a customs broker. Upon receipt of the declaration, the customs house appraises the import cargo and levies an import duty according to the tariff schedule. The documents for customs clearance are (1) the letter of import license; (2) one copy of the invoice; (3) a packing list; (4) a copy of the B/L; (5) the certificate of origin; and (6) other documents as deemed necessary by the head of a customs house. The importer will obtain an import approval from the customs house and then will receive delivery of the cargo at the bonded warehouse after payment of the duty.

## IMPORTS ON CREDIT

To maximize turnover, many importers are importing their goods on credit, i.e., on terms of Documents against Payment (D/P) and on Documents against Acceptance (D/A), or Letter of Credit payable against Usance Drafts. In the event that the local importer does not comply with his responsibility of payment within the maturity period designated in the contract and import license, the importer will be penalized pursuant to the Foreign Trade Law. The period of deferment will be designated between the foreign exporter and the local importer pursuant to the Foreign Exchange Control Act, and the importer must obtain the approval of a foreign exchange bank, the Bank of Korea, or the Ministry of Trade and Industry. For such imports, payment of a reasonable rate of interest is allowed by the authority. For the importation of plants, vessels, large equipment or facilities, grain, etc., the local importer can import on deferred payment terms.

## GOVERNMENT PURCHASES

The Office of Supply of the Republic of Korea (OSROK) is the government agency in charge of purchasing foreign and local supplies requested by government organizations and corporations. OSROK purchases all such supplies by open tender, except in rare cases of urgent or special purchases. The tender notice appears publicly in daily newspapers usually less than 40 days prior to closing tender, and the detailed Invitations for Bids (IFB) are provided to potential bidders upon request. Bidders are required to apply for registration for bidding with OSROK prior to the tender and must also deposit a bid bond in the form of cash, underwriter's bond, bank check, or Letter of Guarantee (L/G) pursuant to the General Provisions for Bidding and Contract, and IFB. After the public opening of bids, OSROK awards the contract on the basis of the lowest price, subject to quality and other terms and conditions specified in the IFB. The bid bond will be released after the award is made. The successful bidder must deposit a Performance Bond within a designated period after the contract is awarded and then must comply with all the terms and conditions stipulated in the contract. The performance bond will be forfeited unconditionally if the successful bidder fails to comply with such terms and conditions.

## SAMPLE AND EXHIBITION GOODS

Samples of no commercial value can be sent to Korea by airmail, air freight, or parcel post. In some cases, the sample may need to be defaced to destroy commercial value. Samples of commercial value may also be delivered to the receiver against payment of import duty at a specially designated sample rate. Foreign goods to be imported for the purpose of exhibitions sponsored or authorized by the government are exempted from import duty, subject to the condition that the goods will be repatriated after the exhibition is closed. The sample goods may be noted in the passport of the individual bringing them to Korea. The goods must be re-exported when the individual leaves Korea.

# KOREA'S TRADE WITH MAJOR PARTNERS

| | Year | US | | European Economic Community | | Japan | |
|---|---|---|---|---|---|---|---|
| | | Amount | % of Total | Amount | % of Total | Amount | % of Total |
| **Exports** | 1981 | 5,611 | 30.0 | 2,686 | 12.8 | 3,444 | 16.4 |
| | 1982 | 6,119 | 28.3 | 2,826 | 13.1 | 3,314 | 15.3 |
| | 1983 | 8,128 | 33.6 | 3,025 | 12.5 | 3,358 | 13.9 |
| | 1984 | 10,479 | 35.8 | 3,217 | 11.0 | 4,602 | 15.7 |
| | 1985 | 10,754 | 35.5 | 3,160 | 10.4 | 4,543 | 15.0 |
| | 1986 | 13,880 | 40.0 | 4,305 | 12.4 | 5,426 | 15.6 |
| | 1987 | 18,311 | 38.7 | 6,597 | 14.0 | 8,437 | 17.8 |
| **Imports** | 1981 | 6,050 | 23.2 | 1,925 | 7.4 | 6,374 | 24.4 |
| | 1982 | 5,956 | 24.6 | 1,732 | 7.1 | 5,305 | 21.9 |
| | 1983 | 6,273 | 24.0 | 2,151 | 8.2 | 6,238 | 23.8 |
| | 1984 | 6,875 | 22.4 | 2,713 | 8.9 | 7,640 | 24.9 |
| | 1985 | 6,489 | 20.8 | 2,991 | 9.6 | 7,560 | 24.3 |
| | 1986 | 6,545 | 21.0 | 3,215 | 10.2 | 10,869 | 34.4 |
| | 1987 | 8,758 | 21.4 | 4,613 | 11.2 | 13,657 | 33.3 |

(US$ Million)

Source: KOTRA

# BUYING FROM KOREA

Buying goods from Korea is considerably easier than importing since the government has worked since 1960 to increase the level of Korean exports. All efforts are made to make the export process as smooth as possible for foreign companies.

## DELIVERY

One of the most common causes of disputes in international commerce is the delay in delivery of products and consequent losses to the buyer. In the past decade, Korean exporters have become more attentive to timing, and fast deliveries are increasingly common.

## PAYMENTS

Where payment is to be made in cash on delivery, the standard payment clause in Korean export contracts calls for the foreign importer to open a confirmed L/C payable at a major bank in Seoul. Typical clauses may require that the L/C allow for transshipments and partial shipments, that the L/C must reach the seller at a specified date before the shipment date, and that it must remain valid for a certain number of days after expiration of the shipment period.

## EXPORT SHARES OF KOREA'S TEN LARGEST EXPORT CATEGORIES IN 1970, 1981, and 1986 (%)

|  | 1970 | 1981 | 1986 |
|---|---|---|---|
| Textiles | 40.8 | 29.5 | 25.2 |
| Electronics | 3.5 | 10.6 | 19.1 |
| Steel Products | 1.6 | 10.5 | 7.2 |
| Footwear | 2.1 | 5.0 | 6.1 |
| Ships | 0.0 | 6.7 | 5.2 |
| Automobiles and Parts | 0.0 | 2.6 | 4.8 |
| Machinery | 1.1 | 2.7 | 3.0 |
| Synthetic Resins | 1.3 | 2.9 | 2.7 |
| Toys and Dolls | 0.1 | 1.6 | 2.1 |
| Metal Products | 1.5 | 2.7 | 1.8 |
| Sub-total | 52.0 | 74.8 | 77.2 |

Source: *Korea Traders Association, Export Statistics, various issues.*

## EXPORT POLICY

Most of Korea's export transactions are made under irrevocable L/Cs, either in the form of usance drafts or at-sight drafts. Exports on D/A and D/P terms are permissable. Additionally, certain strategic items such as vessels are exported on deferred payment terms. Except in the case of plant exports and exports on deferred payment terms under which the collection period exceeds one year, issuing an export approval in the form of an "Export License" (E/L) is delegated to the heads of foreign exchange banks by MTI. To export an automotive approval item, an exporter applies for authorization to a foreign exchange bank; to export an export-restricted item, the exporter must obtain a recommendation from the association and then apply to a foreign exchange bank for export approval. If the terms of payment are non-ordinary special terms, the exporter must obtain an E/L from the Bank of Korea. Application documents include: (1) four sets of the application for export approval; (2) an original and duplicate of the L/C or export contract; (3) a letter of recommendation from the trade association concerned in the case of restricted items; and (4) other documents as required.

All export commodities, except those that are exempt from inspection, must be inspected for quality by the inspection agency prior to receiving customs clearance. The exporter has to install the export commodities in a bonded area prior to submitting documents to the head of a customs house. The customs house inspects export commodities against invoices and export approval certificates. If all is found in order, the customs house issues an export authorization for customs clearance. The required documents are: (1) five copies of the application for export declaration; (2) one copy of the E/L; (3) one copy of the invoice; (4) one copy of the packing list; and (5) other documents as required.

After obtaining an export authorization from the customs house, the exporter arranges with a shipping company for a vessel and also obtains marine insurance from an insurance company. The exporter will then have the export commodities loaded on board by the forwarder. The final stage of the export process is the collection of the export proceeds through a foreign exchange bank. After the shipment of the export commodities, the exporter issues a bill of exchange to collect the export proceeds. In addition to the bill of exchange, the exporter has to submit the shipping document, L/C, and other documents as required to the foreign exchange bank. Total export proceeds have to be collected within a period fixed by the export-approved bank within one year of shipment.

## PLANT EXPORT AND BONDED PROCESSING

With the achievement of recent rapid industrial growth on the basis of local experience and technical advancement, Korea is emphasizing the export not only of chemical and heavy industry products, but of whole plants. Korean industries have already exported paper-mills, automobile tire plants, portland cement plants, soda ash plants, textile plants, nail plants, synthetic resin plants, and other plants, all of which have shown excellent operational results overseas. With the encouragement of the Korean government, Korean companies are now negotiating with foreign governments and private companies for the export of steel plants, oil refinery plants, chemical plants, etc. Korean companies are also offering overseas customers engineering and construction services.

Manufacturers in Korea may operate a bonded processing factory when permission is obtained from the Customs Authority. They are permitted to import raw materials duty-free at bonded processing factories. A foreign businessman who wants to have products processed in a Korean bonded processing factory has to apply for the raw materials required at his own expense and pay processing charges and expenses. If the business is not a long-term undertaking, this method of processing is more convenient and less risky than operating a factory at one's own expense in Korea.

## LOCATING PARTNERS AND AGENTS

The American Chamber of Commerce, the British Chamber of Commerce, the German Chamber of Commerce, foreign businessmen, consulting firms, law firms, accounting firms, and domestic and foreign banks, as well as the Korea Trading Promotion Corporation (KOTRA) and their overseas branches, can provide advice and assistance to foreign businessmen in locating partners and agents. Foreign businessmen should consult with a number of businessmen, banks and other trade organizations and foreign chambers of commerce for an assessment of prospective partners. The choice of a Korean business participant is the single largest determinant of success in doing business in Korea (see US Connections for Trade with Korea, below).

# INVESTING AND LICENSING IN KOREA

## ALTERNATIVE BUSINESS STRUCTURES FOR A FOREIGN COMPANY

The alternative forms of business presence available to a foreign company which desires to establish a presence in Korea are as follows: (i) a liaison or branch office, and (ii) a corporation incorporated under Korean law, operated either as a joint venture with one or more Korean partners or as a wholly-owned subsidiary. A short discussion of each of these alternatives follows:

**Liaison and Branch Offices.** A liaison office is the lowest profile that a foreign corporation can establish in Korea since it will not be subject to Korean corporate taxes as long as it engages only in limited activities. All expenses of this office must be paid from abroad since the office may not generate any operating income. The liaison office may only conduct activities on behalf of the corporate entity of which it is a part. Generally, these activities are limited to (1) purchasing goods; (2) storing or displaying goods not for sale; (3) advertising, public relations, collecting information, and conducting research; and (4) other preliminary and auxiliary activities. Since a liaison office need not be registered with the tax office or the court, it technically has no legal existence, which can be inconvenient for the local representative. Government officials will pay surprise visits to liaison offices to ensure that taxable activities are not conducted.

The branch office is the form of business most utilized by foreign companies. A foreign company may open a branch office in Korea by reporting to the Bank of Korea and registering the office with the court. However, if the branch office wishes to repatriate or remit its earnings or profits in the form of foreign exchange overseas, it must be specifically authorized to do so by the Bank of Korea pursuant to the Foreign Exchange Control Act. Registered branches are allowed to conduct business for profit only in the manner approved by the Bank of Korea. Branches cannot own shares in Korean companies, cannot manufacture, and are prohibited from performing financial services. Special laws and procedures apply to finance, insurance, and securities companies interested in setting up operations. In these instances, prior authorization for establishing the branch must be obtained from the Ministry of Finance.

**Subsidiary or Joint Venture.** In order for a foreign company to form a subsidiary or invest in a joint venture with a Korean company pursuant to the Foreign Capital Inducement Law (FCIL), an application for foreign investment must be submitted for review and approval to the Ministry of Finance (MOF). The MOF will refer the application to the relevant ministry or ministries. The MOF will also refer the application to the Fair Trade Office in the case of a joint venture for comments and recommendations. The Fair Trade Office will then determine whether the reported agreements contain any unjust or unfair provisions which are regarded to be in violation of the Monopoly Regulation and Fair Trade Law. If the Fair Trade Office discovers any such provisions, they will recommend that the MOF either require deletion or modification of the provisions or disapprove the agreement. In this regard, the Economic Planning Board has issued a guideline which identifies certain unjust contractual provisions and unfair business practices in international agreements pursuant to the Fair Trade Law. The "relevant ministry" will review the application to ensure that it is in the interest of Korea and does not harm the domestic industry.

## FOREIGN INVESTMENT 1987

| Country | 1986 | | 1987 | | Increase Rate (% Change) |
|---|---|---|---|---|---|
| | Cases | Amount | Cases | Amount | |
| U.S. | 49 | 125 | 93 | 225 | 180 |
| Japan | 109 | 138 | 207 | 494 | 360 |
| Europe | 26 | 63 | 40 | 210 | 330 |
| Other | 21 | 28 | 33 | 131 | 470 |
| Total | 205 | 354 | 373 | 1,060 | 300 |

| Industry | 1986 | | 1987 | | Increase Rate (% Change) |
|---|---|---|---|---|---|
| | Cases | Amount | Cases | Amount | |
| Electric & Electronics | 36 | 67 | 79 | 208 | 310 |
| Machinery | 50 | 91 | 79 | 208 | 230 |
| Chemicals | 29 | 31 | 45 | 153 | 490 |
| Tourist Hotels | 4 | 62 | 8 | 249 | 340 |
| Other | 86 | 103 | 162 | 142 | 138 |
| Total | 205 | 354 | 373 | 1,060 | 300 |

Source: *Korea Foreign Traders Association*                     (Unit $1 Million)

# FOREIGN CAPITAL INDUCEMENT ACT

Under the revisions to the FCIL which became effective in 1984, foreign investment is permitted in all industries unless they fall within a Korean Standard Industrial Classification category which is on the "Negative List" of categories specifically prohibited or restricted with respect to foreign investment. As of the end of 1987, 211 of 999 industrial categories appear on the Negative List. Most types of manufacturing categories are permissable. Service industries and industries deemed vital to national defense dominate the Negative List. If an industry is open to foreign investment, then the foreign investor may apply for permission to acquire up to 100% of the equity of the foreign-invested enterprise which will result from this investment. In practice, the MOF has exercised some discretion in the proportion of the equity a foreign investor will be permitted to acquire. Foreign investment which results in the transfer of needed technology to Korea, or results in increased exports is much more likely to be approved in subsidiary rather than joint venture form.

**Expedited Approvals.** Under the revised FCIL, any project which satisfies certain conditions is eligible for an expedited approval procedure without referral to the relevant ministries or special government agencies charged with reviewing the application. The minimum foreign investment amount under the current FCIL guidelines is US$100,000. The minimum is lowered to US$50,000 when the foreign investor transfers advanced technology or enters into a joint venture with a small- or medium-sized Korean company. The Automatic Approval System was implemented in 1984 to simplify foreign investment approval procedures. Under this system, projects which fulfill specific conditions can be approved within ten days. The scope of projects eligible to receive automatic approval was later expanded to include projects with invested amounts up to US$3 million from the previous US$1 million. Furthermore, the authority to handle automatic approval projects was delegated to the Bank of Korea to simplify foreign investment procedures.

Post-investment controls were also relaxed. Once an approval of the investment by the government is obtained, the entire investment amount (as approved) must be invested in Korea within 24 months of the approval date. The FCIL guarantees the remittance of: (1) dividends; (2) proceeds of any sale of shares of the joint venture or subsidiary provided that a report of the sale has been confirmed by the MOF; and (3) liquidation proceeds. Any remittance of other fees and expenses must be separately approved under the FCIL (e.g., royalties under a technology license), or under the Foreign Exchange Control Law. In order to obtain government approval of a sale of shares by the foreign shareholder to a Korean shareholder, the shares must be appraised by the Korea Appraisal Board or one of several securities firms designated by the government. The government is unlikely to approve remittance of an amount in excess of the value of the shares as appraised.

**Stock Corporations.** The type of corporate business organization recognized in the Korean Commercial Code and most commonly used by foreign investors is the stock corporation. The legal framework and regulations governing incorporated business entities are similar to those found in the United States, Germany, and Japan. To establish a stock corporation, articles of incorporation must be prepared. Seven or more promoters are required for incorporation, none of whom need be Korean nationals. Under Korean law, their status as "promoters" lasts only until a board of directors assumes control of the company. Shares in the company may be issued as common or preferred. The consideration paid for the shares can be in cash or in kind (including industrial property rights or technology).

An application for incorporation and registration of the company must be submitted to a district court with the following documents:

1. Articles of incorporation;
2. Application form for subscription of shares;
3. Certificate of payment for shares on deposit in bank;
4. Documents detailing terms of issuance of shares;
5. Request of directors' and auditor's investigation;
6. Investment license issued by the Ministry of Finance;
7. Minutes of the board of directors' or shareholders' meeting to elect a representative director;
8. Minutes of the inaugural general meeting with the promoters;
9. Report on elections of directors and auditor;
10. Certificate of power of attorney, if registration is done by proxy; and
11. Document certifying actual subscription of shares.

After registration and payment of registration tax (equivalent to 2% of paid-in capital), the company may commence operations. It can enter into contracts, acquire rights and obligations, possess intangible property (such as patents and copyrights), own real estate, establish commercial credit, and undertake business transactions.

Within 30 days after the business commences, the company must apply to the district tax office for a business license. This license must be certified by government authorities twice a year.

A number of tax and other incentives have traditionally been available for foreign investors. These incentives are gradually being reduced as the need for incentives is diminishing. Most of the current incentives relate to investments involving high technology, so-called small and medium industry and certain special economic zones. The available tax concessions include special depreciation allowances and tax credits. Exemptions from value-added taxes and customs duties may also be available.

## LICENSING IN KOREA

The number of technology licenses from foreign firms to Korea has increased dramatically in recent years. Over 500 such technology licenses were reported to the Korean government in 1987 alone. Under the FCIL, a license agreement with a term of one year or longer which involves a transfer of technology to Korea must be reported to the "relevant ministry." The relevant ministry must approve this application before the Korean licensee may lawfully make any payments to the foreign licensor. Prior to granting this acceptance, the ministry will forward the license agreement to the Fair Trade Office for review and comment. The Fair Trade Office will comment on provisions of the license agreement which are objectionable under the Fair Trade Law.

The areas of concern to the Fair Trade Office include restrictions on exports, the ability to use the technology after termination of the license, rights to improvements in the technology developed by the licensee, and the resolution of disputes. In this regard, the EPB has issued a guideline which identifies certain unfair business practices. This guideline can be obtained from the EPB.

The relevant ministry will examine in detail the terms of the license and may require changes in the length of the license, the royalty rate, or other provisions. Compensation for technology or other technical assistance to be provided under the license agreement may include an initial disclosure fee, a running royalty, per diem fees for employees of the licensor, and the reimbursement of expenses incurred by such employees. Acceptable amounts or rates for compensation methods will vary depending upon the technology and services to be provided. The Korean government nearly always requires that the parties use its standard definition of "net sales" as the basis for the calculation of running royalties. Generally,

## KOREA'S BALANCE OF PAYMENTS

|  | 1986 | 1987 |
|---|---|---|
| 1. Current balance | 4,617 | 9,783 |
| • Trade balance | 4,206 | 7,652 |
| Exports | 33,913 | 46,185 |
| (Increase rate) | (28.3) | (36.2) |
| Imports | 29,707 | 38,533 |
| (Increase rate) | (12.3) | (29.7) |
| • Invisible trade balance | −628 | 947 |
| Credit | 8,051 | 10,120 |
| (Overseas construction) | (635) | (1,003) |
| (Travel) | (1,548) | (2,297) |
| Debit | 8,679 | 9,173 |
| (Investment income) | (4,020) | (3,555) |
| (Travel) | (613) | (704) |
| Unrequited transfers (net) | 1,039 | 1,184 |
| 2. Capital balance | −2,374 | −5,842 |
| Long-term capital | −1,982 | −5,844 |
| Short-term capital | −392 | 2 |
| 3. Errors & omissions | −543 | 1,316 |
| 4. Overall balance | 1,700 | 5,257 |
| 5. Financial account | −1,700 | −5,257 |
| Liabilities | −1,473 | −4,009 |
| Assets-increase | −227 | −1,248 |

Source: *KOTRA*                                    (US$ Million)

the maximum term of a technology inducement agreement is ten years and the maximum royalty rate is 10% of the net sales. In practice, however, the term and royalty rate which may be acceptable to the government are usually less than the above maximum and may be substantially lower, depending on the type of technology involved. Most royalties paid to foreign licensors are 5% of less.

## ACCOUNTING STANDARDS

Korean companies are required to prepare financial statements for shareholders (i.e., a balance sheet, an income statement and a retained earnings proposal). The company's statutory auditor must attest to the financial statements prescribed by the Commercial Code. The statutory auditor is an officer of the company who need not be a certified public accountant. His legal duty is to examine the statements prior to the general meeting of stockholders and to monitor the performance of company directors in carrying out their duties. The statutory auditor, unlike an independent auditor, generally does not verify the existence of assets and liabilities by physical examination, reference to authoritative documents, confirmation by third parties, or the like.

The External Audit Law of Stock Corporations specifies that independent audits by certified public accountants be conducted for companies registered with the Securities and Exchange Commission, capitalized above ₩500 million, or with assets in excess of ₩3 billion.

There are numerous aspects of Korean financial statements that may seem unusual to those unfamiliar with certain aspects of Korean commercial practice. A Korean company's figures for trade notes receivable and payable, for example, are generally higher than for a non-Korean company. This reflects the fact that the usual form of commercial payment in Korea is the promissory note, which is generally settled in cash in 90 or 120 days.

**Settlement of Commercial Disputes.** Since Korea is a member of the International Commercial Arbitration Association, any commercial disagreements can be handled by the local association or in Korean court. Korea is not a litigious society, and because Korean business practice emphasizes compromise, relatively few cases actually reach court. The Korean Commercial Arbitration Board was established to handle commercial disputes arising from business transactions in Korea or abroad. It provides services for the settlement of commercial disputes under the Arbitration Law of Korea, such as arbitration, conciliation, mediation, and consultation, as well as offering authorized recommendations for overseas remittance of agreed claims, fees, and commissions.

# GENERAL BUSINESS INFORMATION

## THE KOREA WORLD TRADE CENTER

A Korean World Trade Center has been constructed on a 200,000 sq. m. site in the Yongdong area, south of Seoul's Han River, which houses facilities totaling 560,000 sq. m. in floor space. This facility displays quality products to the public from around the world year round. The core facility of the center is the exhibition complex which accommodates both special events and permanent exhibitions and which will host approximately 40 international trade fairs and exhibitions annually. The complex consists of a four-story main building and three-story annex that together house three football stadium-sized exhibition halls and a trade mart for product showcases and permanent exhibition booths. The exhibition complex is managed by the Korea Exhibition Center Ltd. (KOEX) in cooperation with the Korea Trade Promotion Corporation (KOTRA).

The trade mart contains 800 permanent exhibition booths and 600 product showcases representing the main exports of Korea. The complex has conference halls, trade counseling offices, a post office, a bank, and other exhibition and general trade support facilities, as well as catering and dining facilities. In addition, business visitors have easy access to trade and exhibition information through a modern, computerized information service.

The 52-story trade tower accommodates the business activities of traders from around the world and serves as a dynamic symbol of Korea's trade. Along with business services such as telex, facsimile, and an electronic mailbox system, transportation services, insurance, and banking are also available in the building, which is occupied by such trade related organizations as KFTA, KOTRA, the export unions, and 250 small businesses. The tower has a trade club, international conference rooms with multi-visual systems and simultaneous translation facilities, and an observation tower lounge.

The complex embraces the Hotel Inter-Continental with 714 rooms, including 208 office suites, a 7,260-sq.m. main banquet hall, and leisure and sports facilities such as a health club, swimming pool, and racquetball courts. The office suites are designed to incorporate all the conveniences of both a deluxe hotel room and a fully-equipped office with first-class services and accommodations.

Complete, modern, and fully equipped convention and conference facilities for smoother communications and information exchange characterize the Korea World Trade Center. From a convention center to the wide range of room sizes in the trade tower, hotel, and the expansive Olympia Hall in the exhibition complex, the center is Korea's premier meeting and convention site.

Furthermore, the center has the city air terminal, which offers passengers using international flights the convenience of an immigration control office, quarantine station, customs house, and travel agency, as well as convenient transportation to and from the airport, making it possible for busy businessman and tourists alike to minimize the time required for dealing with immigration procedures.

*Korea World Trade Center*

# PRINCIPAL KOREA TRADE CONTACTS

## THE KOREA TRADE PROMOTION CORPORATION

The Korea Trade Promotion Corporation (KOTRA) surveys and explores overseas markets, promotes export industries and fosters new export industries, operates trade centers and participates in trade fairs, and issues publications regarding exports. KOTRA has set up permanent offices in many countries of the Americas, Europe and Asia. The nine US offices are: 600 New Hampshire Avenue NW, Washington, DC 20037 (tel: (202) 333-2041); 460 Park Avenue, New York, NY 10022 (tel: (212) 826-0900); 111 East Wacker Driver, Chicago, IL 60601 (tel: (312) 644-4323); 2050 Stemmons Freeway, Dallas, TX 75278 (tel: (214) 748-9341); 2 Canal Street, New Orleans, LA 70130 (tel:(504) 662-8351); 1150 South Olive Street, Los Angeles, CA 90015 (tel: (213) 748-5331); 2 Embarcadero Center, San Francisco, CA 94111 (tel: (415) 391-2637); 900 4th Avenue, Seattle, WA 98164 (tel: (206) 623-3558).

## OTHER KOREA TRADE ORGANIZATIONS

**The Federation of Korean Industries (FKI)** (124-1 Yoido dong, Seoul; tel: 783-0821) is a private, non-profit organization of Korea's leading business and industrial associations.

**Korean Federation of Small Business** (Yoido, P.O. Box 1030; tel: 785-0010) is the counterpart of the FKI for small businessmen.

**Korean Foreign Trade Association (KFTA)** (tel: 771-0041) is the organization and owner of the World Trade Center of Korea and a nonprofit government controlled organization of all licensed traders in Korea.

**Korea Chamber of Commerce and Industry (KCCI)** (45 4-ka Namdaemun-ro, Seoul; tel: 757-0757) is a national federation of leading Korean businessmen devoted to the development of commerce and industry, the promotion and protection of the interests of those engaged in business, and the strengthening of international economic relations.

**The Foreign Investment Information Center** (tel: 757-0757) answers any questions on foreign investments in Korea.

**The Economic Planning Board (EPB)** (82-1 Sejong-ro, Seoul; tel: 772-5221). A unit of this important government board provides information on Korean trading businesses.

**The Ministry of Trade and Industry (MTI)** (77-6 Sejong-ro, Seoul; tel: 722-2671). A special office of this ministry has been established to assist with Korean trade and investment issues.

**The Korea Exchange Bank (KOEB)** was established by the government to help finance foreign trade and to handle foreign transactions. The government has also instituted a system to fiance imports of raw materials for processing and re-export and commodities urgently needed for domestic use. KOEB publishes the Monthly Review in English for businessmen. It has over 30 branches throughout the world. The home office: 181 Ulchi-ro, Seoul; tel: 771-0046. Branches in the US are: 460 Park Avenue, New York, NY 10022; tel: (212) 838-4929; 33 North Dearborn Street, Chicago, IL 60602; tel: (312) 372-7890; One Houston Center, Houston, TX 77010; tel: (713) 759-1192; 624 South Grand Avenue, Los Angeles, CA 90017; tel: (213) 683-0830; 600 University Street, Seattle, WA 98101; tel: (206) 622-7821.

## US CONNECTIONS FOR TRADE WITH KOREA

**The US Embassy in Korea, Commercial Office** (82 Sejong-ro, Seoul; tel: 722-2601). The US Commercial Attaché can assist American businessmen with trade problems or inquiries about the Korean market.

**The American Chamber of Commerce in Korea (AMCHAM)** (Chosun Hotel, 3rd Floor; tel: 753-6471). A private, non-profit association of business executives from the US, Korea, and other countries concerned with trade and investment issues. AMCHAM lobbies the Korean government and briefs visiting businessmen as well as organizing seminars.

**The US Department of Commerce, Korea Desk,** Office of Pacific Basin Affairs, International Trade Administration (14th Street and Constitution Avenue, Rm. 2308, Washington, DC 20230; tel: (202) 377-4957).

# BUSINESS TRAVEL IN KOREA

Since major Korean companies have head offices in Seoul, many business transactions in Korea do not require visiting more than the one city. Should circumstances require additional domestic travel, business visitors should be prepared to make their own connections to other cities as well as any additional arrangements for the return flight home. For ticketing within Korea for both domestic and international connections, transactions can be conducted at any travel agency and at all international airlines operating in Korea that maintain offices in Seoul. Several daily flights are available between Seoul and major Korean cities. It is possible to hire a car as well as a driver to travel within Korea.

Costs for individual travel in Korea are still reasonable compared to many other countries. In general, Seoul is the most expensive city in Korea. However, the standard of accommodation and cuisine is much higher. The following itemization indicates what a business person might expect to spend during one day in the Korean capital.

## A BUSINESS DAY IN SEOUL

| Item | Cost |
| --- | --- |
| Hotel Lotte (single room) | US$140.00 |
| Lunch at hotel | 10.00 |
| Taxis | 25.00 |
| Laundry & dry cleaning | 15.00 |
| Telex/telephone to US/Europe | 20.00 |
| Dinner at restaurant | 20.00 |
| Guide (half-day) | 40.00 |
| TOTAL | $270.00 |

A budget of US$250 per day for basic living expenses in Korea is now about average. For a ten-day business trip to Korea originating in the United States or Europe, the prospective traveler should contemplate a total outlay in the range of US$3,500, including airfare, but excluding expenses for entertainment, liquor, incidentals, gifts, or extensive travel by taxi.

# TRADE FAIRS AND EXHIBITIONS

A year-round foreign trade center is being developed in Seoul which continues (despite government efforts to achieve the contrary) to expand its role as the major focal point of Korean industry and trade. Several hundred foreign businesses have set up representative offices in Seoul, where nearly all Korean companies are headquartered and the economic ministries and other government offices are located.

**The Korea Exhibition Center (KOEX)** (159 Samsong-dong, Seoul; tel: 562-2161) stages trade fairs and exhibitions showing Korean manufactured goods. With over 32,000 square meters of exhibition space, KOEX is the largest such center in Asia; facilities include exposition halls and concrete and lawn areas. The conference hall offers simultaneous translation of six languages.

## OVERSEAS TRADE EXHIBITIONS

Korea promotes major trade exhibitions in the US and Western Europe where representatives can answer questions and initiate negotiations. Advance information on schedules is available from the commercial sections of Korean diplomatic missions and consulates throughout the world.

## BUSINESS NEWS

A good way to keep abreast of the latest trade developments is through *Business Korea* (monthly economics and trade review: Yoido, P.O. Box 273, Seoul, tel. 715-1461); and *Korea Business World* (monthly economic journal: 25-4 Yoido, Seoul, tel. 782-3648). Three informative newspapers are *The Asian Wall Street Journal* (published daily in Hong Kong, weekly in New York); the English-language daily *Korea Herald* (published in Seoul and reprinted in New York) and the *Korean Times* (published in Seoul). Additional publications and sources of information on the Korea market are listed in the Reading List for Korea Travelers (see Appendix).

## MAIN KOREAN COMPANIES BY INDUSTRY

**Trading**
Samsung
Hyundai
Daewoo
Lucky
Ssangyong
Sunkyong

**Textiles**
Sunkyong Fibres
Cheil Synthetic Tex.
Shin Young Textile

**Chemicals**
Hanyang Chem.

MAIN KOREAN COMPANIES

Lucky
Korea Plastic Ind.
Pacific Chem. Ind.
Hankook Cosmetics
Korea Explosives
Sam Chully Ind.
Sam Young Chem.
STC Inc.

**Steel**
Union Steel
Korea Iron & Steel Wks

**Construction**
Ssangyong
Dong Ah
Daelim Ind.
Namkwang
Hyundai Eng. & Constr.

**Machinery**
Ssangyong Hvy Ind.
Sunglee Machinery

**Electronics**
Samyoung
Shinyeong
Gold Star Elec.
Samsung
Anam Ind.
Korea Electronics

**Autos**
Kia Ind.
Hyundai Motors
Daewoo
Dong-A Motors

**Pharmacy**
Yuhan
Chong Kun Dang
Korea Green Cross

**Watches**
Orient Watch
Han Dok

**Cement**
Ssangyong
Hyundai
Sungshine

**Foods & Beverages**
Tai Han Sugar
Samyang Foods
Nhong Shim
Cheil Sugar
Crown Confec.
Seoul Miwon
Oriental Brewery
Lotte Chil-Sung
Bum Yang Foods

# FOREIGN-AFFILIATED BUSINESS FIRMS IN KOREA

## U.S.A.

**A & A Int'l., Korea Branch** 18. 1-ga, Namdaemun-ro, Chung-gu, Seoul (tel. 724-7933)

**A. C. Nielsen Co.—Korea Branch** 8-2 Samsong-dong, Kangnam-gu, Seoul (546-1181)

**AFIA Worldwide Insurance** 541 5-ga, Namdaemun-ro, Chung-gu, Seoul (779-0851)

**Agrico Int'l Far East Inc. (Korea Division)** 87, Sogong-dong, Chung-gu, Seoul (752-6797)

**Allied Stores Int'l, Inc.** 3–7 Chong-dong, Chung-gu, Seoul (313-0071)

**American Home Assurance Co., Korea** 65-228 3-ga, Hangang-ro, Yongsan-gu, Seoul (793-5051)

**American President Lines** 51 Sogong-dong, Chung-gu, Seoul (777-2811)

**Ameriko Insurance Agency** 47-3 4-ga, Namdaemun-ro, Chung-gu, Seoul (753-5966)

FOREIGN-AFFILIATED BUSINESS FIRMS

**Applied Magnetics Korea** 569-6, Kari-bong-dong, Guro-gu, Seoul (855-3341)

**ASOMA Corp., Korea** 1-1 1-ga, Chong-ro, Chongno-gu, Seoul (744-6666)

**Associated Merchandising Corp. Korea Branch** 45 Mugyo-dong, Chung-gu, Seoul (778-6541)

**AT&T Int'l Far East Ltd.** 1-1 1-ga, Chong-ro, Chongno-gu, Seoul (739-5225)

**Banff Int'l (F.E.) Ltd. Seoul Branch** 18 1-ga, Namdaemun-ro Chung-gu, Seoul (735-5291)

**Barclay & Co., Inc.** 118 2-ga, Namdaemun-ro, Chung-gu, Seoul (778-2361)

**Bechtel Int'l, Inc.** Rm. 1106, International Insurance Bldg., 120 5-ka, Namdaemun-ro, Chung-ku, Seoul (777-5581)

**Bristol-Meyers Overseas Corp. Korea Branch** 24/F, International Insurance Bldg., 120 5-ka, Namdaemun-ro, Chung-ku, Seoul (778-6522)

**Brochers Trading Corp., Seoul Liaison Office** 24-2 Mugyo-dong, Chung-gu, Seoul (776-1217)

**Chemstrand Inc. Korea Branch** 3-7 Chong-dong, Chung-gu, Seoul (722-7112)

**Connell Bros. Co., (Korea) Ltd.** Rm. 1708 International Insurance Bldg., 120 5-ka, Namdaemun-ro, Chung-gu, Seoul (777-7071)

**Corning Int'l Services, S.A. Korea Branch** 22/F, Kukje Center Bldg., 191 2-ka, Hangang-ro, Yongsan-ku, Seoul (796-9300)

**CP Overseas, Inc. Korea Branch** 118 5-ga, Namdaemun-ro, Chung-gu, Seoul (755-8745)

**Du Pont Far East Inc. Korea** Rm. 1214, Kyobo Bldg., 1 1-ka, Chong-ro, Chongro-ku, Seoul (734-3661)

**Eli Lilly Asia, Inc.** 50 Sogong-dong, Chung-gu, Seoul (753-7182)

**Everett Orient Line** 51 Sogong-dong, Chung-gu, Seoul (777-8681)

**Exxon Chemical Eastern Inc., Korea Branch** 1-1 1-ga, Chong-ro, Chongno-gu, Seoul (739-4201)

**Flour-Korea Corp., Ltd.** 188-3 1-ga, Ulchi-ro, Chung-gu, Seoul (753-8211)

**Freight Conference Services, Inc., Korea Branch** 70 Sogong-dong, Chung-gu, Seoul (757-1225)

**General Electric Korea Co.** 25 Taepyung-ro 1-ka, Chung-ku, Seoul (735-8651)

**Getz Trading & Engineering Co., Ltd.** 50-10 2-ga, Chungmu-ro, Chung-gu, Seoul (265-7192)

**IBM Korea, Inc.** 25-11 Yoido-dong, Youngpo-gu, Seoul (781-6114)

**IMS Korea** 53-1 Yoido-dong, Young-dungpo-gu, Seoul (784-5671)

**Ingersoll-Rand (Korea)** 119 1-ka, Jangchoong-dong, Chung-gu, Seoul (776-2541)

**ITT Asia Pacific, Inc., Korea Branch** 541 5-ga, Namdaemun-ro, Chung-gu, Seoul (776-6231)

**ITT World Communication Inc., Korea Liaison Office** 15-5 Chong-dong, Chung-gu, Seoul (752-4597)

# 220
## FOREIGN-AFFILIATED BUSINESS FIRMS

**Korag Co., Ltd.** 401-48 Hagik-dong, Nam-gu, Inchon (82-3521)

**Korea-Cargill Co., Ltd.** 101, 2-ga, Hangang-ro, Yongsan-gu, Seoul (793-6651)

**Korea Johnson Co.** 638-13 Shinsa-dong, Kangnam-ku, Seoul (544-2101)

**Korea Liquid Carbonic Co.** 298-2 Tok-san-dong, Guro-gu, Seoul (856-1061)

**Korea Silo Co., Ltd.** 3 1-ga, Puksong-dong, Puk-gu, Inchon (72-3211) Seoul Office (752-7621)

**Korea Upjohn Ltd.** 216 1-ga, Kwanghee-dong, Chung-gu, Seoul (265-9157)

**Korea Xerox Co.** 120-20 Sosomun-dong, Chung-gu, Seoul (754-7621)

**Korean American Oil Co., Inc.** 120 5-ga Namdaemun-ro, Chung-gu, Seoul (753-1913)

**Korean American Tobacco Co., Ltd.** 112-44 Sogong-dong, Chung-gu, Seoul (753-8128)

**Korean Sources** 284-1 Yonggang-dong, Mapo-gu, Seoul (715-8747)

**KORTEC, LTD. (Korea Tobacco Export Co.)** 250 2-ga, Taepyong-ro, Chung-gu, Seoul (753-8250)

**May Department Stores Int'l, Inc., Seoul Office** 21-1 2-ga, Sosomun-dong, Chung-gu, Seoul (778-0841)

**Merrill Lynch Int'l & Co., Seoul Branch** 1 1-ka, Chongro, Chongro-ku, Seoul (735-7651)

**Montgomery Ward & Co., Inc. Korea Office** 541 5-ga, Namdaemun-ro, Chung-gu, Seoul (755-1201)

**Motorola Korea Ltd.** 80-6, Soosong-dong, Chongro-ku, Seoul (733-3955)

**National Renderers Association, Inc. Seoul Office** 63 1-ga, Ulchi-ro, Chung-gu, Seoul (778-9116)

**NCR Corp., Seoul Office** 120 5-ga, Namdaemun-ro, Chung-gu, Seoul (752-8366)

**Nike Inc. Korea Office** 69 6-ga, Chungang-dong, Chung-gu, Pusan (462-8608)

**Northrop Int'l Seoul Office** 747-7 Hannam-dong, Yongsan-gu, Seoul (798-0141 Ext. 501)

**Purina Korea, Inc.** 120 5-ga, Namdaemun-ro, Chung-gu, Seoul (776-5167)

**Raychem Far East, Inc. Korea Branch** 831-45 Yoksam-dong, Kangnam-gu, Seoul (555-7752)

**RCA Global Communications, Inc. Seoul Office** 60 1-ga, Myong-dong, Chung-gu, Seoul (776-2868)

**Rohm & Haas Asia, Inc.** 823 Yeoksam-dong, Kangnam-ku, Seoul (555-7600)

**Sea-Land Service, Inc. Seoul Office** 118 2-ga, Namdaemun-ro, Chung-gu, Seoul (753-9241)

**Signetics-Korea Co., Ltd.** 272 Yeomchang-dong, Kangso-gu, Seoul (694-0876)

### FOREIGN-AFFILIATED BUSINESS FIRMS

**Sperry Ltd. Seoul Office** 23-4 Yoido-dong, Yongdungpo-gu, Seoul (811-0601)

**Telescopic Engineering, Inc.** 302-75 Tongbuichon-dong, Yongsan-gu, Seoul (792-6348)

**Texaco Korea Inc. Seoul Office** 60-1 3-ga, Chungmu-ro, Chung-gu, Seoul (261-1777)

**Texas Instruments Supply Co.** 678-39 Yoksam-dong, Kangnam-gu, Seoul (552-8000)

**3M Korea** 61 Youido-dong, Youngpo-gu, Seoul (785-4567)

**Union Carbide Eastern Inc.** 87 Sogong-dong, Chung-gu, Seoul (753-9251)

**United Technologies Int'l Operations Inc.** 17-1 Yoido-dong, Youngdungpo, Seoul (785-1930)

**Westinghouse Electric S.A.** 1 1-ka, Chongro, Chongro-ku, Seoul (733-2371)

**Weyerhaeuser Co.** 75, Sosomun-dong, Chung-gu, Seoul (753-2363)

**Woodward & Dickerson, Far East Co., Ltd.** 50 Sogong-dong, Chung-gu, Seoul (777-9551)

### JAPAN

**Chori Co., Ltd.** 21 Pukchang-dong, Chung-gu, Seoul (777-7861)

**C. Itoh & Co., Ltd. Seoul Branch** 250 2-ga, Taepyong-ro, Chung-gu, Seoul (753-0771)

**Gunze Sangyo Inc., Seoul Branch** 117 Ta-dong, Chung-gu, Seoul (777-4855)

**Japan External Trade Organization, Seoul Office** 360-1 2-ga, Taepyong-ro, Chung-gu, Seoul (752-8648)

**Kanematsu Gosho Ltd., Seoul Office** 50 1-ga, Ulchi-ro, Chung-gu, Seoul (777-5311)

**Kawatetsu Co., Ltd., Seoul Branch** 32-2 Mugyo-dong, Chung-gu, Seoul (777-5605)

**Kinsho-Mataichi Co., Ltd., Seoul Branch** 50 2-ga, Myong-dong, Chung-gu, Seoul (776-3571)

**Marubeni Corp., Seoul Branch** 1 Sogong-dong, Chung-gu, Seoul (779-0501)

**Mitsubishi Co. Seoul Branch** 1, Sogong-dong, Chung-gu, Seoul (754-8320)

**Mitsui & Co., Ltd. Seoul Office** 250 2-ga, Taepyong-ro, Chung-gu, Seoul (753-0651)

**Moritani & Co., Ltd. Seoul Branch** 32 1-ga, Ulchi-ro, Chung-gu, Seoul (778-0961)

**Nichmen Co., Ltd** 118 2-ga, Namdaemun-ro, Chung-gu, Seoul (777-8371)

**Nikko Securities Co., Ltd. Seoul Office** 1 Sogong-dong, Chung-gu, Seoul (778-1456)

**Nippon Koei Co., Ltd., Seoul Branch** 18 1-ga, Namdaemun-ro, Chung-gu, Seoul (723-0103)

**Nissei Sangyo Co., Ltd., Seoul Branch** 58-1 1-ga, Shinmun-ro, Chongno-gu, Seoul (722-5862)

FOREIGN-AFFILIATED BUSINESS FIRMS

**Nissho Iwai Corp. Seoul Branch** 1 Sogong-dong, Chung-gu, Seoul (778-0170)

**Nomura Securities Co., Ltd. Seoul Office** 1 Sogong-dong, Chung-gu, Seoul (752-0370)

**Overseas Economic Cooperation Fund** 118 2-ga, Namdaemun-ro, Chung-gu, Seoul (752-5964)

**Sumitomo Marine & Fire Insurance Co., Ltd. Seoul Office** 51 Sogong-dong, Chung-gu, Seoul (777-1712)

**Sumitomo Co., Seoul Branch** 51 Sogong-dong, Chung-gu, Seoul (777-1541)

**Taisho Marine & Fire Insurance Co. Seoul Office** 5-1 Namchang-dong, Chung-gu, Seoul (752-6279)

**Tokyo Marine & Fire Insurance Co., Ltd. Seoul Office** 118 2-ga, Namdaemun-ro, Chung-gu, Seoul (752-0858)

**Toshoku Ltd. Seoul Branch** 81 Sogong-dong, Chung-gu, Seoul (755-7201)

**Toyoda Tsusho Kaisha, Ltd., Seoul Branch** 51-1 Namchang-dong, Chung-gu, Seoul (753-3175)

**Yamaichi Securities Co., Ltd. Seoul Branch** 1 Sogong-dong, Chung-gu, Seoul (776-2230)


## GERMANY

**AEG-Telefunken** 135-3 Itaewon-dong, Yongsan-gu, Seoul (792-0221)

**BASF Korea Ltd., Seoul Office** 45 4-ka, Namdaemun-ro, Chung-gu, Seoul (778-4661)

**Bayer Vetchem (Korea)** 257-1 Kayang-dong, Kangso-gu, Seoul (662-2481)

**Birkart Far East Ltd. Korea Branch** 25-5 Chungmuro 1-ka, Chung-ku, Seoul (755-8186)

**Boehringer Ingelheim Korea Ltd.** 40-883 3-ga, Hanagang-ro, Yongsan-gu, Seoul (793-6355)

**German Engineering Co., Ltd.** San 77-7 Yoksam-dong, Kangnam-gu, Seoul (556-3350)

**Hertie Korea Branch** 34-145 Itaewon-dong, Yongsan-gu, Seoul (793-2735)

**Hoechst Korea Ltd., Seoul Office** 52 Chongdam-dong, Kangnam-gu, Seoul (541-3651)

**Miles (Hamburg) A.G.** 24-2 Yoido-dong, Youngdungpo-ku, Seoul (784-6671)

**Mondial Orient Ltd., Korea Branch** 15-5 Chong-dong, Chung-gu, Seoul (753-2121)

**Otto Versand (Hamburg)** 526 Namdaemunro 5-ka, Chung-ku, Seoul (757-3721)

**Pfizer Korea Ltd.** 191 2-ka Hangang-ro, Yongsan-ku, Seoul (797-4400)

**Pracht Int'l Ltd.,** 34-145 Itaewon-dong, Yongsan-gu, Seoul (792-7678)

**Quelle (Far East) & Co.** 28-11 Hannam-dong, Yongsan-gu, Seoul (792-7114)

**Rokenger Trading Co.** 26-5 Yoido-dong, Yongdungpo-gu, Seoul (783-5035)

## FOREIGN-AFFILIATED BUSINESS FIRMS

**Siemens Electrical Engineering Co., Ltd.** 31-7, Jangchung-dong 1-ka, Chung-gu, Seoul (275-6111)

**Siemssen & Co., Seoul Office** 44-6 Yoido-dong, Yongdungpo-gu, Seoul (782-9903)

## BRITAIN

**BP Far East Ltd.** 3-7 Chong-dong, Chung-gu, Seoul (739-5021)

**Dodwell Export Ltd.** 117 1-ga, Chang-chung-dong, Chung-gu, Seoul (269-6191)

**Edward T. Robertson & Son, Ltd. Seoul Office** 58-17 Sosomun-dong, Chung-gu, Seoul (776-8745)

**Ewkor Trading Co., Ltd. Seoul Office** 120 5-ga, Namdaemun-ro, Chung-gu, Seoul (778-3911)

**Far Eastern Freight Conference Seoul Office** 55-4 Sosomun-dong, Chung-gu, Seoul (777-2406)

**FOSECO Korea Ltd.** 235 Todang-dong, Puchon, Kyonggi Prov. (Seoul Office 662-2238)

**P & I Service of Korea** 58-17 Sosomun-dong, Chung-gu, Seoul (779-2831)

**Price Waterhouse** 5 Dangjoo-dong, Chongro-ku, Seoul (737-0151)

**P.S. Addision (Far East Ltd.)** 120 5-ga, Namdaemun-ro, Chung-gu, Seoul (755-1261)

**Spirax Sarco Korea Ltd.** 24-5 Youido-dong, Youngpo-gu, Seoul (782-6827)

**Swire (Korea) Ltd.** 51 Sogong-dong, Chung-gu, Seoul (752-9051)

## FRANCE

**C.G.E. Alstom Int'l, Seoul Office** 541 5-ga, Namdaemun-ro, Chung-gu, Seoul (753-7664)

**Framatome-Export (FRAMEX) Seoul Office** 56-85 1-ga, Changchung-dong, Chung-gu, Seoul (273-2681)

**French Trading Office** 112-5 Sogong-dong, Chung-gu, Seoul (776-0241)

**Pechiney Ugine Kuhlmann A.I.M. Korea Branch** 1-1 1-ga, Chong-ro, Chong-no-gu, Seoul (735-9311)

**Rhone-Poulenc** 368-2 3-ga, Chungjog-ro, Sodaemun-gu, Seoul (362-2388)

**Serem Int'l Co., Ltd., Seoul Office** 118 2-ga, Namdaemun-ro, Chung-gu, Seoul (778-2504)

## OTHERS

**ACOTEX Korea Co. Seoul Office** 15-5 Chong-dong, Chung-gu, Seoul (777-8927)

**Atomic Energy of Canada Ltd.** 3-7 Chong-dong, Chung-gu, Seoul (725-8439)

**BIMEREX Exports Seoul Office** 25-4, Yoido-dong, Yongdungpo-gu, Seoul (784-1795)

**COSA Liebemann Ltd.** 264-2 Hannam-dong, Yongsan-gu, Seoul (798-1981)

**Eisenburg and Co., Inc.** 24-1 2-ga, Cho-dong, Chung-gu, Seoul (266-7191)

FOREIGN-AFFILIATED BUSINESS FIRMS

**General Exports Ltd. Korea Branch** 62-10 2-ga, Chungmu-ro, Chung-gu, Seoul (777-8241)

**Italian State Trade Office** 70-1 Pukchang-dong, Chung-gu, Seoul (779-0811)

**Jacobson Van Den Berg Ltd.** 653-28 2-ga, Hannam-dong, Yongsan-gu, Seoul (792-7035)

**Jardine Matheson and Co. Seoul Office** 1-590 Yoido-dong, Yongdungpo-gu, Seoul (783-8811)

**Khemanico (Korea) Corp.** 24-23 1-ga, Chungmu-ro, Chung-gu, Seoul (776-1477)

**Novimex Fashion Ltd.** 729-74, Hannam-dong, Yongsan-gu, Seoul (797-7301)

**N.R.G. Co.** 907-4 Pangbae-dong, Kangnam-gu, Seoul (584-3169)

**Pacific Buying and Marketing Service** 34-145 Itaewon-dong, Yongsan-gu, Seoul (797-8721)

**Philips Electronics (Korea) Ltd.** 260-199 Itaewon-dong, Yongsan-gu, Seoul (794-5011)

**Tradeship Ltd.** 91-1, Sogong-dong, Chung-gu, Seoul (752-9117)

# KOREA TRADE CENTERS ABROAD

## NORTH AMERICA

**Chicago**
Korea Trade Center
111 East Wacker Dr., Suite 519
Chicago, Illinois 60601 U.S.A.
Tel: (312) 644-4323/4
Telex: 253005 KOTRA CGO

**Dallas**
Korea Trade Center
P.O. Box 58023
World Trade Center, Suite 147
2050 Stemmons Freeway, Dallas
Texas 75258-0023, U.S.A.
Tel: (214) 748-9341/2
Telex: 732343 KOTRA DAL

**Los Angeles**
Korea Trade Center
700 South Flower St.
Suite 3220, Los Angeles
CA 90017 U.S.A.
Tel: (213) 627-9426/9
Telex: 674639 LSA

**Miami**
Korea Trade Center
1 Biscayne Tower, Suite 3669
Miami, Fla. 33131, U.S.A.
Tel: (305) 374-4648
Telex: 515186 KTC UR MIA

**New York**
Korea Trade Center
460 Park Ave. Suite 402
New York, N.Y. 10022 U.S.A.
Tel: (212) 826-0900
Telex: 64904 KTC NYK

**Washington (Liaison Office)**
Korea Trade Center
1030 15th St. N.W., Suite 620
Washington, D.C. 20005
Tel: (202) 333-2040
Telex: 289608 KTCW UR

# 225
## KOREA TRADE CENTERS ABROAD

**Toronto**
Korea Trade Center
Suite 600, P.O. Box 9
Thomson Bldg.
65 Queen St. West
Toronto, Ontario
M5H 2M5
Canada
Tel: (416) 368-3399
Telex: 06-23426 MOOGONG TOR

**Vancouver**
Korea Trade Center
Suite 1710, One Bentall Center
505 Burrard St. Vancouver
B.C., Canada V7X 1M6
Tel: (604) 683-1820
     (604) 687-7322
Telex: 04-54276 MOOGONG VCR

## LATIN AMERICA
**Bogota**
Korea Trade Center
Carrera 7, No. 73-49
Seguros Colmena, Oficina 401
Bogota, D.E. Colombia
Tel: 211-2615, 211-2910, 211-2648
Telex: 43189 KOTRA CO

**Buenos Aires**
Korea Trade Center
Avenida Cordoba 462, Piso 19°
Departamento "C" Capital Federal
Buenos Aires, Argentina
Tel: 312-2203, 2206, 5218
Telex: 17230 KOTRA AR

**Caracas**
Korea Trade Center
P.O. Box 5368, Caracas 1010
Piso 4 Torre Banvenez, Av. Francisco
Solano Lopez Con Calle
Acueducto, Sabana Grande
Caracas, Venezuela
Tel: 729676, 729672, 729768
Telex: 21619 MUGNG VC

**Guatemala**
Korea Trade Office
Edificio Geminis 10
Oficina 513

12 Calle 1-25, Zone 10
Guatemala, Guatemala, C.A.
Cable: GONGKWAN
GUATEMALA
Tel: 311435, 311422

**Kingston**
Korea Trade Office
5th Fl., Imperial Life Bldg.
60 Knutsford Boulevard
New Kingston, Jamaica
P.O. Box 482, Kingston 6,
Jamaica W.I.
Tel: 92-92630/1
Telex: 2438 KOTRA JA

**Lima**
Korea Trade Center
Av. Rivera Navarrete 451, 40,
Piso-B San Isidro, Lima 27, Peru
P.O. Box L, 18-0337
Lima, Peru
Tel: 42-2834
Telex: 21182 PE KOTRA LM

**Mexico**
Korea Trade Center
Paseo de la Reforma
No. 250-207 Col. Juarez
06600-MEXICO, D.F.
Tel: 511-92-99, 514-54-57
Telex: 01774465 KTC ME

**Montevideo**
Korea Trade Office
Casilla de Correo 626,
Montevideo, Uruguay
Tel: 90-8504, 90-0636
Telex: 6987 KTMVD UY

**Panama**
Korea Trade Center
Edificio Banco Union 1 Piso
Local A, Ave. Samuel Lewis,
Campo Alegre Panama,
P.O. Box Aparado 8033,
Panama 7, Republic of Panama
Tel: 648105, 647970
Telex: 2199 MOOGONG

**Quito**
Korea Trade Center
P.O. Box 4752-A, Quito
Av. Amazonas 477 Y Robles Edif.
Banco de los Andes 3°,
Piso-Oficina 320, Quito, Ecuador
Tel: 230316, 525449
Telex: 2416 KOTRA ED

**San Jose**
Korea Trade Office
P.O. Box 151-100, San Jose
Edificio Centro Colon, Piso 4,
Apartado 10151-1000, San Jose,
Costa Rica
Tel: 334207, 331836
Telex: 3141 KOTRA CR

**Santiago**
Korea Trade Center
P.O. Box 1236
Fidel Oteiza 1956-Piso 16-B,
Providencia Santiago-Chile
Tel: 2515700, 2512521
Telex: 645207 MOOGONG CT

**Santo Domingo**
Korea Trade Office
Gustavo Mejia Ricart-Tiradentes
Apt. 201
Santo Domingo,
Dominican Republic
Tel: (809) 562-6282
Telex: (346) 0720 KOTRA DR

**Sao Paulo**
Korea Trade Center
Av. Paulista 1439, Conj. 132,
Bela Vista, Sao Paulo, SP, CEP
01311-Brazil
Tel: (011) 287-5726, 288-8521
Telex: 113418 ECOR BR

## EUROPE

**Amsterdam**
Korea Trade Center
Strawinskylaan 767
1077 XX Amsterdam,
The Netherlands
Tel: (020) 73055/6
Telex: 16368 KOTRA NL

**Athens**
Korea Trade Center
Sina & Vissarionos 9, 7th Floor
Athens 10672, Greece
Tel: 3626540, 3641567
Telex: 219596 KTCA GR

**Brussels**
Korea Trade Center
World Trade Center 1, 2 étage
Blvd. Emile Jacqmain 162
1210 Brussels, Belgium
Tel: (02) 218-5132, (02) 218-5499
Telex: 26256 KOTRA B

**Copenhagen**
Korea Trade Center
Holbengsgode 14-2 Sal 1057
Copenhagen K, Denmark
Tel: (01) 126658, 128039
Telex: 15291 KTC DK

**Frankfurt**
Korea Trade Center
Mainzer Landstr. 27-31
6000 Frankfurt am Main-1
Federal Republic of Germany
Tel: (690) 236895/7
Telex: 416357 KOTRA D

**Hamburg**
Korea Trade Center
Steindamm 71, 2000 Hamburg 1
Federal Republic of Germany
Tel: (040) 2803342/3
Telex: 2162400 KOTRA D

**Helsinki**
Korea Trade Center
Kalevankatu 4,00100
Helsinki 10, Finland
Tel: 641422
Telex: 122863 KOTRA SF

**Istanbul**
Korea Trade Center
Mete Cad. No. 24/1
Kat-2, Taksim, Istanbul, Turkey

Tel: 1435075, 1498223
Telex: 24490 KOTC TR

**Lisbon**
Korea Trade Office
Av. Eng. Duarte Pacheco Torre 2
10/F, Andar Sala 2
1000 Lisbon, Portugal
Tel: 690814/6
Telex: 62158 KOTRA

**London**
Korea Trade Center
Ground Fl., Vincent House
Vincent Square
London SW1P 2NB
United Kingdom
Tel: (01) 834-5082

**Madrid**
Korea Trade Center
José Lázaro Galdiano, 4-1°
28036 Madrid, Spain
Tel: 457-5929, 457-5955
Telex: 44093 KTP CE

**Milan**
Korea Trade Center
Via Large 31/2022 Milan, Italy
Tel: (02) 876-806, (02) 874-422
Telex: 312522 KOTRA I

**Oslo**
Korea Trade Center
Daeleneggata 20, 0567
Oslo 5, The Kingdom of Norway
Tel: (02) 382210, 382359
Telex: 77334 KOTRA N

**Paris**
Korea Trade Center
25/27 rue d-Astorg
75008 Paris, France
Tel: (01) 47.42.00.17
Telex: 281186 F MOOGONG

**Stockholm**
Korea Trade Center
Dobelnsgatan 95
P.O. Box 19052
104 32 Stockholm, Sweden

Tel: (08) 347343, 347353
Telex: 12384 KOTRA

**Vienna**
Korea Trade Center
Mariahilferstrasse 77-79, 1/5,
(Generali Center, 5th fl.)
A-1060, Vienna, Austria
Tel: (0222) 963073-4
Telex: 134945 KOTRA A

**Zurich**
Korea Trade Center
Leonhardshalde 21
8001 Zurich, Switzerland
Tel: (01) 252-3526, 3528, 3140
Telex: 816415 KTCZ

## ASIA AND OCEANIA

**Bangkok**
Korea Trade Center
G.P.O. Box 1896 Bangkok
8th Floor, Kong Boonma Bldg.
699 Silom Rd. (opp. Narai Hotel)
Bangkok, Thailand
Tel: 233-1322/3
Telex: 82335 MOOGONG TH

**Colombo**
Korea Trade Office
P.O. Box No. 965 Colombo
2nd Floor Unit No. 210,
Liberty Plaza, 250 Duplication
Road,
Colombo 3, Sri Lanka
Tel: 574441, 574442
Telex: 21513 KOTRA CE

**Dhaka**
Korea Trade Center
PMP Plaza, 2/F
14 Kemal Ataturk Ave.
Banani, Dhaka-1213
Bangladesh
Tel: 606984
Telex: 642696 PMPCO BJ

## KOREA TRADE CENTERS ABROAD

**Hong Kong**
Korea Trade Center
G.P.O. Box 5573
Korea Center Bldg., 2nd Fl.
119-121 Connaught Rd.
Central, Hong Kong
Tel: 5-459500, 5-459786, 5-459509
Telex: 73497 KOTRA HX

**Jakarta**
Korea Trade Center
P.O. Box 362/JKT
Jl. Gatot Subroto No. 57-58
Jakarta, Indonesia
Tel: 511408, 514523, 515524,
510296 (Ext. 52, 56)
Telex: 46188 MOOGONG IA

**Karachi**
Korea Trade Center
Bahria Complex Ground Fl.
24 Moulvi
Tamizuddin Khan Road
Karachi 2, Pakistan
Tel: 552190, 551659
Telex: 23687 KTC PK

**Kuala Lumpur**
Korea Trade Center
10/F, Mui Plaza
Jln P Ramlee 50250
Kuala Lumpur, Malaysia
Tel: (03) 2429939, 420756
Telex: 31191 KOTRA MA

**Manila**
Korea Trade Center
P.O. Box 1881 MCC, Makati
12th Fl., Citibank Center Bldg.
Paseo de Roxas, Makati
Metro Manila, Philippines
Tel: 873244, 871183, 8173369
Telex: 2512 KTM PH

**New Delhi**
Korea Trade Center
c/o Embassy of the Republic of
Korea
B-9/1-B, Vasant Vihar,

New Delhi, 110057 India
Tel: 674782, 675344
Telex: 65162 KTRA IN

**Osaka**
Korea Trade Center
10/F, Honmachi Meidai Bldg.,
1-3, 3-chome Azuchimachi
Higashi-ku, Osaka, Japan
Tel: (06) 262-3831
Telex: KOTRA J64880

**Tokyo**
Korea Trade Center
Yurakucho Bldg., No. 10-1,
1-Chome Yurakucho, Chiyoda-ku,
Tokyo, Japan
Tel: (03) 214-6951/3
Telex: J24393

**Rangoon**
Commercial Attaché
Embassy of the Republic of Korea
P.O. Box 445 Rangoon,
118, Boundary Road,
Shwegonding,
Rangoon, Burma
Tel: 32055
Telex: 21344 RGNKTC BM

**Singapore**
Korea Trade Center
P.O. Box 421, Singapore 9008
#15-07, Hong Leong Bldg.
16 Raffles Quay, Singapore 0104.
Tel: 2213055, 2213056
Telex: RS 23281 MOOGONG

**Taipei**
Korea Trade Center
P.O. Box 1555 Taipei,
Chien Hsin Bldg. 7th Fl.,
72, Nanking E. Rd. Sec. 2
Taipei, Taiwan, R.O.C.
Tel: (02) 5813030, 5813031
Telex: 21052 MOOGONG

**Auckland**
Korea Trade Center

C.P.O. Box 4007 Auckland
6th Floor, Sun Alliance House
40-44 Shortland St.
Auckland, New Zealand
Tel: 735-793, 735-792
Telex: 2818 MOOGONG NZ

**Melbourne**
Korea Trade Office
Suite No. EC 02C
World Trade Center Melbourne
Victoria 3005, Australia
Tel: (03) 6141733
Telex: AA 34085

**Sydney**
Korea Trade Center
P.O. Box H69, Australia Square,
Suite 3405, Australia Square,
George St.,
Sydney 2000, Australia
Tel: 27-3369, 27-2524, 27-5961
Telex: 25517 KOTRA AA


## MIDDLE EAST

**Amman**
Korea Trade Center
The Embassy of Republic of Korea
P.O. Box 3471, Amman, Jordan
Tel: 642182
Telex: 21993 KOTRA MJO

**Bagdad**
Korea Trade Office
P.O. Box 6097
Al Mansur Bagdad
915/22/278 Hay Aljame'a
Jadhriya Baghdad, Iraq
Tel: 7765496
Telex: 213271 KOR IK

**Cairo**
Korea Trade Center
Consulate General of the
Republic of Korea
P.O. Box 358 Dokki,
Cairo, Egypt
Tel: 715543, 3497690

Telex: 92317 KOTRA UN

**Casablanca**
Korea Trade Center
Tour Habous, Ave. des F.A.R.
8ème étage, Tour 14, Droite
Casablanca, Morocco
Tel: 314280, 314232
Telex: KOTRA 27636M

**Dubay**
Korea Trade Center
P.O. Box 12859 Dubay, U.A.E.
12/F, Arab Bank
for Investment and
Foreign Trade Bldg.
Bin Yas, Dubai, U.A.E.
Tel: 220643, 223285
Telex: 46294 KOTRA EM

**Jeddah**
Korea Trade Center
P.O. Box 4323 Jeddah, 21491,
Saudi Arabia
Tel: (02) 6690031, 6690073
Telex: 600066 KOTRA SJ

**Safat**
Korea Trade Office
Embassy of the Republic of Korea
P.O. Box 20771 Safat, Kuwait
Tel: 814004, 849143
Telex: 22606 MOOGONG KT

**Manama**
Korea Trade Center
P.O. Box 10254 Manama
Diplomat Tower Bldg., Rm 403,
Diplomatic Area, Manama,
Bahrain
Tel: 531018, 531019
Telex: 8507 KOTRA BN

**Muscat**
Korea Trade Office
P.O. Box 4887
Ruwi-Muscat, Sultanate of Oman
Tel: 706459
Telex: 3483 KOTRA ON

## KOREA TRADE CENTERS ABROAD

**Tehran**
Korea Trade Center
P.O. Box 11365-7877 Tehran
No. 190 Sepahbod Gharani Ave.
Assemi Bldg. 4th Fl. Tehran,
The Islamic Republic of Iran
Tel: 89-6694, 89-9789
Telex: 212395 MGTN IR

**Tripoli**
Commercial Attache
Embassy of the Republic of Korea
P.O. Box 987 Tripoli, Libya
9-4, Jamal Abdul Elnasser St.
Aburuquiba Bldg., 4th Fl.
Tripoli, Libya
Tel: 34138
Telex: 20894 KOTRA LY,
Attn KOTRA

**Tunis**
Korea Trade Office
71 Avenue Taieb Mehiri
1002 Tunis Belvedere
Tunisia
Tel: 780874, 781581
Telex: 15574 KOTRA TN

## AFRICA

**Abidjan**
Korea Trade Center
B.P. 3429 Abidjan 01
Avenue Jean Paul II,
Abidjan-Plateau, Ivory Coast 01
Tel: 324581
Telex: 22105 KOTRA CI

**Addis Ababa**
Korea Trade Center
P.O. Box 5978
Addis Ababa, Ethiopia
Tel: 151853, 154306
Telex: 21240 KOTRA ADDIS

**Dakar**
Korea Trade Center
1ère étage Imm. La Préférence
73 Ave. Peytavin

Dakar, Senegal
Tel: 21-00-74
Telex: 3163 KOTRABL SG

**Douala**
Korea Trade Office
B.P. 744 Douala, Cameroun
Centre Coreen
  du Commerce Exterieure
3ème étage, Immeuble Kitchner
(Annex de la Chambre
  du Commerce)
Rue de la Commerce
Bonanjo Douala
Tel: 42 79 58
Telex: KOTRADLA 5294 KN

**Kinshasa**
Korea Trade Office
Zone B, 16ème étage, C.C.I.Z. Bldg.
Bd. Col. Tshatshi Gomber. du Zaire
B.P. 14099 KIN 1
République de Zaire
Tel: 23687
Telex: 21407 KTC FIH ZR,
        21412 GK KIN ZR
        Attn KOTRA

**Lagos**
Office of the Commercial Attache
  of Embassy of the
  Republic of Korea
G.P.O. Box 1019 Lagos
Plot 1388A, Olosa St., Victoria
Island, Lagos, Nigeria
Tel: 611519, 614294
Telex: 22370 KECA NG

**Nairobi**
Korea Trade Center
P.O. Box 727789
Finance House 7th Fl.
Loita St., of Koinange St.
Nairobi, Kenya
Tel: 28928, 20458
Telex: 22360 MOOGONG

# MAJOR ECONOMIC ORGANIZATIONS & ASSOCIATIONS

**Korea Chamber of Commerce and Industry**
45 4-ka Namdaemun-ro, Chung-ku, Seoul, Korea
Tel.: 757-0757

**The Federation of Korean Industries**
28-1 Yoido-dong, Youngdeungpo-ku, Seoul, Korea
Tel.: 783-0821

**Korean Federation of Small Businesses**
16-2 Yoido-dong, Youngdungpo-ku, Seoul, Korea
Tel.: 783-0010

**Korean Traders Association**
(World Trade Center Building)
159 Samsung-dong, Kangnam-ku, Seoul, Korea
Tel.: 551-0114

**Korea Design & Package Center**
128-13 Yeonkun-dong, Chongro-ku, Seoul, Korea
Tel.: 762-9461/3

**Korea Trading Agent Association**
45-14 Yoido-dong, Youngdeungpo-ku, Seoul, Korea
Tel.: 782-2205/9

**Korean Commercial Arbitration Board**
(World Trade Center Building)
10-1 2-ka, Hoehyun-dong, Chung-ku, Seoul, Korea
Tel.: 778-2631/5

**Korea Federation of Textile Industry**
(World Trade Center Building)
10-1, 2-ka Hoehyun-dong, Chung-ku, Seoul, Korea
Tel.: 778-0821/3

**Korea Export Association of Textile**
33 1-ka Hoehyun-dong, Chung-ku, Seoul, Korea
Tel.: 752-8098

**Korea Garments and Knitwear Export Association**
(World Trade Center Building)
10-1 2-ka Hoehyun-dong, Chung-ku, Seoul, Korea
Tel.: 776-4121/3, 778-3591/2

**Electronic Industries Association of Korea**
648 Yeoksam-dong, Kangnam-ku, Seoul, Korea
Tel.: 553-0941

**Korea Auto Industries Coop. Association**
35-4 Yoido-dong, Youngdungpo-ku, Seoul, Korea
Tel.: 784-8261

**Korea Society for the Advancement of Machine Industry**

13-3 Yoido-dong, Yongdeungpo-ku, Seoul, Korea
Tel.: 782-5614, 5814

**Korea Machine Tool Industry Assn.**
35-4 Yoido-dong, Yongdeungpo-ku, Seoul, Korea
Tel.: 782-5330, 4187

**Korea Mould & Tool Industry Cooperative**
13-31 Yoido-dong, Yongdeungpo-ku, Seoul, Korea
Tel.: 783-1711/3

**Korea Foundry and Forging Industrial Association**
43-3 Yoido-dong, Yongdeungpo-ku, Seoul, Korea
Tel.: 782-6877, 782-6994

**Korean Association of Ships**
Machinery and Equipment Manufacturers
12-5 Yoido-dong, Yongdeungpo-ku, Seoul, Korea
Tel.: 783-6952/4

**Korea Footwear Exporters Association**
256-13 Gongduk-dong, Mapo-ku, Seoul, Korea
Tel.: 718-9531

**Korea Tire Industrial Association**
736-17 Yeoksam-dong, Kangnam-ku, Seoul, Korea
Tel.: 554-0174

**Korean Plastic Goods Exporters Association**
146-2 Ssangrim-dong, Chung-ku, Seoul, Korea
Tel.: 275-7991

**Korea Fishing Net Industrial Association**
(World Trade Center Building)
10-1 2-ka Hoehyun-dong, Chung-ku, Seoul, Korea
Tel.: 752-3837

**Korea Petrochemical Industrial Association**
1-1 Chongro 1-ka, Chongro-ku, Seoul, Korea
Tel.: 733-6724

**Korea Pharmaceutical Traders Association**
(World Trade Center Building)
10-1 2-ka Hoehyun-dong, Chung-ku, Seoul, Korea
Tel.: 752-8481; 753-2434

**Korea Foods Industry Association Inc.**
198-1 Kwan hoon-dong, Chongro-ku, Seoul, Korea
Tel: 732-1720

**Korea Canned Goods Export Association**
(World Trade Center Building)
10-1 2-ka Hoehyun-dong, Chung-ku, Seoul, Korea
Tel.: 752-0506, 755-6496

**Korean Living & Fresh Fish Export Association**
(World Trade Center Building)

10-1 2-ka Hoehyun-dong, Chung-ku, Seoul, Korea
Tel.: 755-1351, 752-3408

**Korea Frozen Seafoods Export Association**
(World Trade Center Building)
10-1 2-ka Hoehyun-dong, Chung-ku, Seoul, Korea
Tel.: 755-1744, 7427

**Korean Wall Paper Exporters Association**
120-3 4-ka, Chungmu-ro, Chung-ku, Seoul, Korea
Tel.: 267-5795

**Korea Leather & Fur Export Association**
(World Trade Center Building)
10-1 2-ka, Hoehyun-dong, Chung-ku, Seoul, Korea
Tel.: 778-3901/4

**Korea Hair Goods Export Association**
(World Trade Center Building)
10-1 2-ka, Hoehyun-dong, Chung-ku, Seoul, Korea
Tel.: 752-8487/9

**Korea Metal Flatware Exporters' Association**
6-1 Sunhwa-dong, Chung-ku, Seoul, Korea
Tel.: 752-9577, 776-5876

**Korea Toy Industry Cooperative**
2-361-1 Hangango-ro, Yongsan-ku, Seoul, Korea
Tel.: 792-9505, 9818

**Korea Optical Industry Cooperative**
125 4-ka Chungmu-ro, Chung-ku, Seoul, Korea
Tel.: 266-4565, 275-1587

**Korea Musical Instrument Industry Cooperative**
50-6 2-ka Chungmu-ro, Chung-ku, Seoul, Korea
Tel.: 272-8978/9

**Korea Sporting Goods Industry Coop**
1 7-ka Eulchi-ro, Chung-ku, Seoul, Korea
Tel.: 252-7154/5

**Korea Stationery Industry Cooperative**
36-3 5-ka Chungmu-ro, Chung-ku, Seoul, Korea
Tel.: 261-1207, 266-0417

**Korea Ceramic Industry Cooperative**
53-20 Daehyun-dong, Seodaemun-ku, Seoul, Korea
Tel.: 363-0361/3

**Korea Trading International Inc.**
(World Trade Center Building)
10-1 2-ka, Hoehyun-dong, Chung-ku, Seoul, Korea
CPO Box: 3667, 4020
Tel.: 755-9261, Tlx.: KOTII K27434, Fax: 753-5131

## 234

# FOREIGN BANKS IN KOREA

**Algemene Bank Nederland N.V. (Netherlands)** 146-1 Susong-dong, Chongno-gu, Seoul (tel. 733-2301)

**American Express Int'l Banking Corp. (U.S.)** 541 5-ga Namdaemun-ro, Chung-gu, Seoul (tel. 753-2763)

**Bank of America, NT & SA (U.S.)** 192-18, Kwanhoon-dong, Chongro-ku, Seoul (tel. 733-2455); 77-1 4-ga Chungang-dong, Chung-gu, Pusan (tel. 462-0621)

**Bank of California (U.S.)** 1-1 1-ga Chong-ro, Chongno-gu, Seoul (tel. 736-5431)

**Bank of Credit & Commerce Int'l (U.K.)** 150 2-ga Tapyong-ro, Chung-gu, Seoul (tel. 778-7168)

**Bank of Montreal (Canada)** 88 Suhrin-dong, Chongro-ku, Seoul (tel. 732-9206)

**Bank of Nova Scotia (Canada)** 45 4-ga Namdaemun-ro, Chung-gu, Seoul (tel. 757-7171)

**Bank of Tokyo (Japan)** 10-1 1-ga Ulchi-ro, Chung-gu, Seoul (tel. 777-6971), 89-1 4-ga Chungang-dong, Chung-gu, Pusan (tel. 463-0927)

**Bank of Yokohama (Japan)** 101-1 1-ga Ulchi-ro, Chung-gu, Seoul (tel. 753-8842)

**Bankers Trust Co. (U.S.)** 91-1 Sogongdong, Chung-gu, Seoul (tel. 778-9011)

**Banque Indosuez (France)** (630-1 2-ga Taepyong-ro, Chung-gu, Seoul (tel. 753-0355)

**Banque Nat. de Paris (France)** 250 2-ga Taepyong-ro, Chung-gu, Seoul (tel. 753-2594)

**Banque Paribas (France)** 1-ga Chong-ro, Chongno-gu, Seoul, (tel. 739-5151)

**Barclays Bank PLC (U.K.)** 541 5-ga Namdaemun-ro, Chung-gu, Seoul (tel. 754-3681)

**Chartered Bank (U.K.)** 9-1 2-ga Ulchi-ro, Chung-gu, Seoul (tel. 757-5131)

**Chase Manhattan Bank N.A. (U.S.)** 50 1-ga Ulchi-ro, Chung-gu, Seoul (tel. 758-5114), 44 2-ga Chungang-dong, Chung-gu, Pusan (tel. 22-8073)

**Chemical Bank (U.S.)** 250 2-ga Taepyong-ro, Chung-gu, Seoul (tel. 778-8941)

**Citibank N.A. (U.S.)** 89-29 2-ka, Shinmun-ro, Chongro-ku, Seoul (tel. 731-1114); 3-2 2-ga Tongwang-dong, Chung-gu, Pusan (tel. 23-1471)

**Continental Illinois (National Bank & Trust Co. of Chicago) (U.S.)** 541 5-ga Namdaemun-ro, Chung-gu, Seoul (tel. 778-0251)

**Credit Commercial de France (France)** 250 2-ga Taepyong-ro, Chung-gu, Seoul (tel. 756-5921)

### FOREIGN BANKS

**Credit Lyonnais Bank (France)** 541 5-ga Namdaemun-ro, Chung-gu, Seoul (tel. 778-3811)

**Crocker National Bank (U.S.)** 250 2-ga Taepyong-ro, Chung-gu, Seoul (tel. 776-9714)

**Dai-Ichi Kangyo Bank (Japan)** 9-1 Ulchi-ro, 2-ka, Chung-ku, Seoul (tel. 756-8181)

**Daiwa Bank (Japan)** 250 Taepyung-ro 2-ka, Chung-ku, Seoul (tel. 723-0831)

**Deutsche Bank (W. Germany)** 51-1 Namchang-dong, Chung-gu, Seoul (tel. 754-3071)

**Development Bank of Singapore (Singapore)** 1 1-ka, Chong-ro, Chongro-ku, Seoul (tel. 732-9311)

**Dresdner Bank A. G (W. Germany)** 150 2-ga Taepyong-ro, Chung-gu, Seoul (tel. 756-8917)

**First Interstate Bank of California (U.S.)** 1-1 1-ga Chong-ro, Chongno-gu, Seoul (tel. 733-0751)

**First National Bank of Boston (U.S.)** 17-7 4-ga, Namdaemun-ro, Chung-gu, Seoul (tel. 778-9211)

**First National Bank of Chicago (U.S.)** 50 Sogong-dong, Chung-gu, Seoul (tel. 753-8981)

**Fuji Bank (Japan)** 101-1 1-ga Ulchi-ro, Chung-gu, Seoul (tel. 755-1281)

**Grindlays Bank (U.K.)** 541 5-ga Namdaemun-ro, Chung-gu, Seoul (tel. 753-8411)

**Hokkaido Takushoku Bank (Japan)** 1-1 1-ga Chong-ro, Chongno-gu, Seoul (tel. 734-5274)

**Hongkong & Shanghai Banking Corp. (Hong Kong)** 146-1 Susong-dong, Chongno-gu, Seoul (tel. 739-4211)

**Indian Overseas Bank (India)** 25-5 1-ga Chungmu-ro, Chung-gu, Seoul (tel. 753-0741)

**Int'l Bank of Singapore (Singapore)** 1 1-ga Chong-ro, Chongno-gu, Seoul (tel. 739-3441)

**Kyowa Bank (Japan)** 250 2-ga Taepyong-ro, Chung-gu, Seoul (tel. 755-9305)

**Lloyds Bank International (U.K.)** 250 2-ga Taepyong-ro, Chung-gu, Seoul (tel. 754-2711)

**Manufacturers Hanover Trust Co. (U.S.)** 541 5-ga Namdaemun-ro, Chung-gu, Seoul (tel. 778-5411)

**Marine Midland Bank N.A. (U.S.)** 1-1 1-ga Chong-ro, Chongno-gu, Seoul (tel. 733-3501)

**Midland Bank** 250 2-ga Taepyong-ro, Chung-gu, Seoul (tel. 757-2561)

**Mitsubishi Bank (Japan)** 31-3 Taepyung-ro 1-ka, Chung-gu, Seoul (tel. 777-9561)

**Mitsui Bank (Japan)** 250 2-ga Taepyong-ro, Chung-gu, Seoul (tel. 778-4631)

**Nat. Bank of Pakistan (Pakistan)** 1-1 1-ga Chong-ro, Chongno-gu, Seoul (tel. 732-0277)

**Nat. Commercial Bank (Saudi Arabia)** 98-5 Unni-dong, Chongno-gu, Seoul (tel. 764-0018)

**Overseas Trust Bank (Hong Kong)** 1-1 1-ga Chong-ro, Chongno-gu, Seoul (tel. 732-5371)

**Rainier Nat. Bank (U.S.)** 1 1-ga Chong-ro, Chongno-gu, Seoul (tel. 739-4171)

**Republic Bank Dallas (U.S.)** 1-1 1-ga Chong-ro, Chongno-gu, Seoul (tel. 739-1316)

**Royal Bank of Canada (Canada)** 1-1 1-ga Chongno-gu, Seoul (tel. 730-7791)

**Saitama Bank (Japan)** 541 5-ga Namdaemun-ro, Chung-gu, Seoul (tel. 753-1241)

**Sanwa Bank (Japan)** 1 Sogong-dong, Chung-gu, Seoul (tel. 752-7321)

**Security Pacific Nat. Bank (U.S.)** 101-1 1-ka Ulchi-ro, Chung-gu, Seoul (tel. 757-6850)

**Societe Generale (France)** 101-1 1-ga Ulchi-ro, Chung-gu, Seoul (tel. 753-9400)

**Standard Chartered Bank (England)** 9-1 2-ga Ulchi-ro, Chung-gu, Seoul (tel. 757-5131)

**Swiss Air Transport Co., Ltd. (Switzerland)** 50 Sogong-dong, Chung-gu, Seoul (tel. 753-8271)

**Sumitomo Bank (Japan)** 1-1 1-ga Chong-ro, Chongno-gu, Seoul (tel. 739-0341)

**Taiyo Kobe Bank (Japan)** 188-3 1-ga Ulchi-ro, Chung-gu, Seoul (tel. 777-7092)

**Tokai Bank (Japan)** 1-1 1-ga Chong-ro, Chongno-gu, Seoul (tel. 744-9810)

**Union Bank (U.S.)** 9-1 Ulchi-ro, Chung-gu, Chung-gu, Seoul (tel. 28-3725)

**Union de Banques Arabes et Francaises (France, Arab)** 250 2-ga Taepyong-ro, Chung-gu, Seoul (tel. 778-8081)

**United Overseas Bank (Singapore)** 1-1 1-ga Chong-ro, Chongno-gu, Seoul (tel. 739-3918)

**Wells Fargo Bank (U.S.)** 1-1 1-ga Chong-ro, Chongno-gu, Seoul (tel. 739-3551)

**Westpac Banking Corp. (Australia)** 250 2-ka Taepyung-ro, Chung-ku, Seoul (tel. 732-7611)

# PERSONAL STRATEGIES FOR BUSINESS SUCCESS IN KOREA

*S. H. JANG*

## KOREA'S

## SKY-ROCKETING

## SUCCESS

### *THE MIRACLE OF THE HAN RIVER*

What the Nile is to Egypt, the Rhine is to Germany, the Mississippi is to the United States, the Amazon is to Brazil; the Han is to Korea. Along the banks of this ancient river, an economic miracle has been unfolding. In less than 30 years, South Korea has risen literally from ashes to affluence.

The whole world is taking notice of the economic avalanche which has swept over this little peninsula (more accurately its southern half, particularly). Underdeveloped countries look upon this miracle of the Han with envy and admiration; while the already industrialized countries looked upon this NIC (newly industrialized country) with apprehension and caution, referring to this economic tidal wave as one of the four tigers (or dragons) of Asia. The economic clout of this little nation is having worldwide repercussions.

The Republic of Korea, once dependent upon US aid, has become the seventh largest trading partner of the US, a good example of how US foreign aid bears fruit. At present, the US is Korea's second largest single trading partner, taking 38% of Korea's exports and supplying 21% of its foreign imports. Korean foreign trade has been heavily dependent on business with the US, but recently a dramatic change has taken place. The problems of protectionism, trade restrictions, and higher tariffs have motivated Korean businesses to expand their markets into such areas as the Middle East, China, South America, and Eastern Europe. Trade liaison offices have opened between South Korea and Hungary, business is blossoming with China, and approaches have been made to the Soviet Union.

South Korea achieved a trade surplus of more than US$1.6 billion in 1986 and $6.2 billion in 1987, for the first time since its

PERSONAL STRATEGIES FOR BUSINESS SUCCESS

birth as a Republic. The achievement of this trade surplus was due to the beneficial effects of:

- falling oil prices,
- a strong Japanese yen,
- lower international interest rates,
- a weak US dollar,
- the ceiling on imports of $32.5 billion.

The keys to Korea's rapid growth are:

- diligent work ethic,
- scrupulously executed planning,
- diverse and vigorous export drive ($47.2 billion in 1987),
- diversification from light industry to advanced high technology,
- joint ventures as the basis for acquiring knowledge for the next stage of industrial growth.

Sharp rises in domestic savings and investments have fueled the high growth of the nation's economy in the past quarter century. Owing to increased income, the national savings rate went up to 35.8% in 1987. Indeed, the Republic of Korea's approach to economic growth—development led by industrialization, and exports have proved to be very compatible with the tempo of economic development in the industrialized nations, particularly the US and Japan.

In South Korea there are over 5,000 manufacturers (export and import); nearly 300 foreign business firms from the US, Japan, West Germany, France and other friendly nations; and also 100 private trade associations for promoting exports. The Korean Trade Directory lists over 1,200 registered foreign trading companies.

Korea's export record has been nothing short of phenomenal. From a trifling export total of $835 million in 1970, the total for 1987 was $47.2 billion and the target for 1988 is $54.7 billion. The current account rose from a disastrous deficit of $5.32 billion in the red in 1962 to a whopping surplus of $6.2 billion in the black in 1987. Runaway inflation which hovered between 30% and 40% in the 1970s has been brought down to a steady 4% on both the wholesale and the consumer index.

The Korean economy, which ranked about 30th in the world in the 1980s, has moved up to 20th place and has become the world's tenth largest trading nation. Exports have doubled since 1982.

During the period from 1962 to 1984, the Korean economy grew at an annual average of 8.5% including negative growth of 5.6% in 1980 (caused by political turmoil, crop failure, and the second oil crisis).

In 1961, the per-capita GNP was a meager $82 and savings were

# KOREAN INTERNATIONAL TRADE AND MONETARY SURVEY, 1983–87

| | 1983 | 1984 | 1985 | 1986 | 1987 |
|---|---|---|---|---|---|
| GNP in US$ billion at current prices | 76.0 | 82.4 | 83.7 | 95.3 | 118.6 |
| Economic growth, real, % | 11.9 | 8.4 | 5.4 | 12.3 | 12.0 |
| Per capita GNP in current US$ | 1,914 | 2,044 | 2,047 | 2,300 | 2,826 |

| | Balance of Payments (Million US$) | | | Foreign Trade | | | | Exchange Rate | Budget Surplus | Money Supply M2 Average | | Consumer Prices Index | | Manufacturing Production Index | |
|---|---|---|---|---|---|---|---|---|---|---|---|---|---|---|---|
| | Current Account | Trade Account | Invisible Account | Exports Million US$ | %* Change | Imports Million US$ | %* Change | won/ dollar | won 10 billion | won 10 billion | %* Change | 1980= 100 | %* Change | 1980= 100 | %* Change |
| 1965 | 9 | -240 | 46 | 175 | 47 | 463 | 15 | 272 | 0 | 0 | 0 | 13 | 0 | 6 | 8 |
| 1970 | -623 | -922 | 119 | 835 | 34 | 1,984 | 9 | 317 | -51 | 777 | 0 | 22 | 16 | 16 | 12 |
| 1975 | 1,887 | -1,671 | 442 | 5,081 | 14 | 7,274 | 6 | 484 | -337 | 2,738 | 27 | 45 | 25 | 46 | 20 |
| 1976 | -314 | -591 | -72 | 7,715 | 52 | 8,774 | 21 | 484 | -158 | 3,537 | 29 | 52 | 15 | 61 | 32 |
| 1977 | 12 | -477 | 266 | 10,047 | 30 | 10,811 | 23 | 484 | -149 | 4,844 | 37 | 57 | 10 | 73 | 20 |
| 1978 | -1,085 | -1,781 | 224 | 12,711 | 26 | 14,972 | 38 | 484 | -50 | 6,747 | 39 | 66 | 14 | 91 | 24 |
| 1979 | -4,151 | -4,396 | -195 | 15,056 | 18 | 20,339 | 36 | 484 | 117 | 8,556 | 27 | 78 | 18 | 102 | 12 |
| 1980 | -5,321 | -4,384 | -1,386 | 17,505 | 16 | 22,292 | 10 | 660 | -584 | 10,764 | 26 | 100 | 29 | 100 | -2 |
| 1981 | -4,646 | -3,628 | -1,518 | 21,254 | 21 | 26,131 | 17 | 700 | -1,051 | 13,715 | 27 | 121 | 21 | 113 | 13 |
| 1982 | -2,650 | -2,594 | -554 | 21,853 | 3 | 24,251 | -7 | 749 | -713 | 17,575 | 28 | 130 | 7 | 119 | 5 |
| 1983 | -1,606 | -1,764 | -435 | 24,445 | 12 | 26,192 | 8 | 796 | 292 | 21,005 | 20 | 134 | 3 | 139 | 16 |
| 1984 | -1,373 | -1,036 | -878 | 29,245 | 20 | 30,631 | 17 | 827 | 663 | 23,261 | 11 | 138 | 2 | 161 | 16 |
| 1985 | -887 | -19 | -1,446 | 30,283 | 4 | 31,136 | 2 | 890 | 644 | 26,015 | 12 | 141 | 3 | 167 | 4 |
| 1986 | 4,617 | 4,206 | -628 | 34,715 | 15 | 31,584 | 1 | 861 | 959 | 30,396 | 17 | 144 | 2 | 199 | 22 |
| 1987 | 9,854 | 7,659 | 977 | 47,281 | 36 | 41,020 | 30 | 792 | 905 | 36,120 | 19 | 148 | 3 | 237 | 19 |

*Compared to the same period in the previous year.

Source: National Bureau of Statistics, Economic Planning Board; Statistical Department, Bank of Korea

negligible, with practically no exports, compared to a GNP per capita level of $3,000 now.

## FUTURE ECONOMIC STRATEGY

South Korea is capable of achieving one of the world's outstanding records of economic growth by the end of this century. In view of its past economic performance, and future growth potential, it is predicted that by the year 2000, Korea will emerge as the 10th largest trading nation in the world.

Free enterprise in Korea can be expected to change gradually. Although Korea's external debt was about $45 billion or less in 1986, the debt has steadily been reduced owing to its booming trade; by the 1990s it will be a creditor nation.

The Seoul 24th Olympiad in 1988 will be a springboard for the nation's economic growth and put Korea in the spotlight of world attention, offering an opportunity to promote the development of Korean trade in the 21st century.

A government thinktank is forecasting average economic growth of 8.6% per year until the early part of the next century when per capita GNP is expected to reach $10,000. The second consecutive year of double-digit GNP growth—12.2% in 1987 following 12.5% in 1986—was the highest in the world. The nation's economy is projected to grow 8% in 1988, for a per capita income of $3,300, a total of $140 billion.

Dr. Park Ungsuh, executive vice president of Samsung Co., Ltd., forecasts that Korea is the best suited country in the world to become an international manufacturing base up to the year 2000. He points out that the Korean government has designed various measures to attract foreign investment.

South Korea is keeping the door open to normalization with North Korea, the People's Republic of China, and the Soviet Union.

# GETTING DOWN TO
# BUSINESS IN KOREA

## GATHERING INFORMATION

A neophyte expatriate businessman must tap information and develop expertise on the way business is done in Korea, and on where to go for help.

# GUIDELINES OF THE ECONOMIC PLANNING BOARD FOR THE SIXTH ECONOMIC AND SOCIAL DEVELOPMENT PLAN

| | 1987 | 1988 | 1989 (proj.) | 1990 (proj.) | 1991 (proj.) |
|---|---|---|---|---|---|
| National income & prices | | | | | |
| Economic growth | 12.0% | 8.0% | 7.0% | 7.0% | 7.5% |
| GNP | 118.6 | 145.0 | 170.0 | 200.0 | 226.0 |
| Per capita GNP | 2,826 | 3,450 | 4,000 | 4,500 | 5,100 |
| Balance-of-payments | | | | | |
| Current account balance | 9.8 | 7.0 | 6.7 | 6.0 | 6.0 |
| Trade balance | 7.7 | 5.0 | 5.2 | 5.0 | 6.0 |
| Exports | 47.3 | 55.0 | 61.0 | 67.5 | 76.7 |
| Imports | 41.0 | 52.0 | 58.0 | 64.9 | 73.3 |
| Invisible trade balance | 0.9 | 1.0 | 0.5 | 0.7 | −0.5 |
| Unrequited transfer | 1.2 | 1.0 | 1.0 | 0.8 | 0.5 |
| Savings & investments | | | | | |
| Domestic savings rate | 35.6% | 35.5% | 35.0% | 34.3% | 34.0% |
| Gross investment rate | 29.8% | 32.0% | 32.0% | 31.8% | 31.7% |
| Overseas investment rate | −6.4% | −3.5% | −3.0% | −2.5% | −2.3% |
| Foreign debts | | | | | |
| Overall foreign debt | 35.6 | 31.0 | 27.0 | 24.5 | 23.0 |
| External assets | 13.2 | 15.5 | 17.5 | 20.0 | 23.0 |
| Net foreign debt | 22.4 | 15.5 | 9.5 | 4.5 | — |
| Population & unemployment rate | | | | | |
| Total population (1,000 persons) | 42,080 | 42,600 | 43,100 | 43,600 | 44,090 |
| Economically active (1,000 persons) | 16,870 | 17,350 | 17,750 | 18,130 | 18,500 |
| Jobholders (1,000 persons) | 16,350 | 16,710 | 17,070 | 17,430 | 17,820 |
| Unemployment rate | 3.3% | 3.7% | 3.8% | 3.8% | 3.7% |
| Industrial structure (% of GNP) | | | | | |
| Primary industry | 11.4 | 11.4 | 11.1 | 10.8 | 10.5 |
| Secondary industry | 31.5 | 32.0 | 32.3 | 32.7 | 32.9 |
| Manufacturing | 30.3 | 30.8 | 31.2 | 31.6 | 31.8 |
| Social overhead capital | 19.6 | 19.4 | 19.3 | 19.1 | 18.8 |
| Other services | 37.5 | 37.2 | 37.3 | 37.4 | 37.8 |

Source: *Bank of Korea* (Unit = $1 Billion)

In a rapidly changing environment, keeping up with the changes as well as developing the right expertise is a challenge for any businessman. Foreign executives in Korea also must deal with the fact that information is in Korean, since it is intended primarily for the benefit of the local business community. Very little is available for the foreign businessman to learn about local industry and business procedures.

Information is a perishable commodity anywhere, however it seems to be more so in Korea, where there is today an especially rapid and profound transition developing. Often the available information, particularly statistics published by various organizations, tends to be contradictory, to the dismay of foreign researchers. Moreover, Korean companies are reluctant to release information to outsiders, even if the data is not considered confidential in and of itself.

## TAPPING VARIOUS WELLS OF INFORMATION

While there are many organizations compiling information, securing this material is not an easy task. Library science is still in the developmental stage in Korea. It is a challenge even for Korean students to find titles and abstracts of master's theses on a national scale. Thus, to secure suitable information, a wide range of information and research sources must be tapped, including government, academic, and trade organizations. This is necessary because of scarcity and location, and also because of discrepancies in statistics, since different criteria are employed by these organizations.

Newspapers (two in English), economic dailies, and business journals are also an excellent source of information.

## CONDUCT CROSS-CHECKS

Since most available information is collected and processed for different purposes, a different set of criteria and definitions may be used. It is absolutely essential to compare and check information from different sources against each other. To get as accurate a picture as possible it is sometimes necessary to take an average of numbers on the same subject from differing sources.

## DRAW ON INSIDE PERSONNEL

The staff of business organizations are another valuable source of information. Often, one's closest associates are underestimated or ignored. Not only may they provide an extensive reservoir of information, but consulting them will also help develop working relationships. If they do not have the needed information, they may have access to sources through personal ties.

## CONSULTING FIRMS

Market research firms and consultants are emerging to cater to the needs of international business. Undoubtedly using their services is more economical and accurate than ferreting out this information alone.

# PRINCIPAL BUSINESS INFORMATION SOURCES IN KOREA

| Information | Primary Source | Secondary Source | Source of Specific Information |
|---|---|---|---|
| General Information on Korean Economy, Industry, Etc. | EPB, MOF, MTI, MCI, Embassies | Banks, A/C Firms, Foreign Chambers | Publications |
| Industry-Specific Information | Trade/Industry Associations | KCCI, FKI, KTA | Professional Service (Consultants) |
| Trade/Investment Regulations | MOF, MTI, SMIPC, KTA (KOTRA), KCCI | Foreign Embassy & Chamber | Professional Service |
| Technology | KAIST, KDI, KIET, MOST | Trade/Industry Association | Professional Service |
| Distributor/Partner Company Background | KCGF, Banks | Trade/Industry Association | Professional Service |
| Marketing/Distribution | MKT Research Organizations | Advertisement Agencies | Professional Service |
| Factory Location | MTI, ISWRDC | Real Estate Agent | Professional Service |

# TEN COMMANDMENTS
# FOR DOING BUSINESS
# IN KOREA

*I. Always have a formal introduction.*

It is strongly advisable to have a formal introduction to any person or company with whom you want to do business. Meeting the right people in a company almost always depends on having the right introduction. Whenever possible, obtain introductions rather than make contacts directly or just pop in on a businessman.

Use of the proper intermediary or go-between is desirable in your business meetings. If the person whom you wish to meet has respect for your intermediary, chances are he will have equal respect for you as well.

## II. *Always carry business cards.*

In Korea, every person has a distinctive place in an organizational hierarchy. A businessman is confident only when he knows from what company and the position of the person he has just met. Therefore, the exchange of calling cards in Korea is a formal affair and plays a very important role in introductions.

Have calling cards made prior to visiting companies and keep plenty on hand at all occasions. After the exchange, you may place the cards on the table in front of you as you proceed with the meeting, using them for further reference.

## III. *Assume that your English is **not** completely understood.*

Remember that the real level of comprehension of many English-speaking businessmen may not be as good as their mastery of courtesy implies. Their comprehension may be, and often is, surprisingly less than what you think it is.

Make a special effort to emphasize and report your key points in the same words for their understanding. Exchanging notes after meetings is very helpful for this purpose.

## IV. *Be patient.*

Korean businessmen are good negotiators. Be prepared to be patient, and firm, at the negotiating table but do not try to push your position too hard. Sensitive issues and details may be delayed for future discussions, preferably by a go-between or by your staff. Use of go-betweens can be very valuable, especially in financial negotiations.

Allow sufficient time for your counterparts. Their decisions are usually made collectively and often require more time than you may expect.

## V. *Develop human relationships.*

Legal documents are not as important as human relationships. Koreans do not like detailed contracts. They prefer, and often insist, that contracts be left flexible enough that adjustments can be made to fit changing circumstances. Therefore, it is very important to develop relationships based on mutual trust and benefit, in addition to the business contract. To a Korean businessman, the important thing about a contract is not so much what is stipulated, but rather who signed it and the fact that it exists.

### VI. Offer praise, not confrontation.

Koreans are extremely sensitive to situations which may cause them to "lose face." Their state of good feelings or "Kiboon" can do wonders far beyond your expectations, and, of course, you benefit from the good mood created.

### VII. Entertain and be entertained.

Entertainment plays an important role in any business relationship. When offered, it should always be accepted, and in some way reciprocated in due time. Parties are often like drinking competitions. Your capacity of alcohol consumption may be one of the deciding factors that can lead to a successful business negotiation and relationship. The giving of small gifts is also an accepted practice and is recommended. Recently, golf has also become a popular form of recreation. Join the game as often as possible.

### VIII. Know your counterpart.

Try to personalize all business relationships. An informal agreement with a trusted party is considered more secure than any written document. Try to find out as much about your counterparts as possible: their family status, hobbies, philosophies, birthdays, etc.

### IX. When in Rome . . .

Apply Western logic sparingly and cautiously, and try instead to find "emotional common denominators." Feelings and "face" are often far more important in local business dealings.

### X. Know the Korean market.

Many changes are taking place at an unprecedented pace in

Korean society. With increasing affluence and the development of mass communications, the lifestyle of Korean consumers is changing rapidly. Changes in fashion, diet, housing, and mobility are so rapid and profound that accurate market research is essential.

## BUSINESS ETIQUETTE

**C**ertain ground rules in business protocol and etiquette must be observed for productive business relationships. The "bull-in-the-chinashop" approach to business is bound to create disaster and misunderstanding in Korea. A brief survey of local etiquette can make all the difference in fostering a strong business future.

### THE 'GAME OF THE NAME'

Confucian social structure is hierarchical: everyone has his recognized niche or position, and is referred to and called by his title. Business relationships are almost never on a first-name basis, and certainly never between Korean company personnel and executives and management.

In addressing a corporate executive, his title is always affixed to his family name, "President Kim" or "Kim Sa-Jang." Addressing him Korean-style will be greatly appreciated.

The executive's position also entitles him to his special regal throne, both in his office and in his car; at the head of the table in his office, and the right, rear position in his car. Great care must be exercised to avoid usurping the monarchical seating position in these circumstances and even in a bit more informal but protocol position at dinner functions.

### "THE MEANS JUSTIFIES THE END"

In Korean business activities, the "process" is more important than the "substance." *How* negotiations are conducted may determine the outcome. Protocol and procedures are of primary importance in conducting business in Korea.

The local executive feels more comfortable in a more relaxed, low-key level of business discussions. "Getting to know you" is a basic ingredient of business relations. If there is time, and the possibility exists for extended, multiple meetings, the first meeting

PERSONAL STRATEGIES FOR BUSINESS SUCCESS

might well be a courtesy call merely to get acquainted. Even if time is short, small talk should be regarded as an essential prerequisite to serious business negotiations. The Korean executive wants to gain some impression of his foreign associate's sincerity and reliability.

As discussions reach the stage of serious negotiation, it is not usual to expect the top executive to engage in initial discussions. Usually, you will meet with local management personnel familiar with the situation.

In any event, the expatriate business client will get best results by paying attention to the "means"; in Korean business consultations, "the means justifies the end."

The expatriate businessman will have a much more relaxed and successful experience if he learns to recognize these differences as cultural factors rather than aberrations of behavior.

First among these is the slower process of decision-making. Korean business approval usually goes through an endless chain of command that may seem to require all the time in the world. One needs "the patience of Job" at times to wait for a business decision.

Secondly, Korean-style practice avoids direct confrontation or blunt speech. The practice of responding by stating "we'll study it further," or "we'll ask the top executives about it" or the convenient "*Keul-seh*" (meaning "we'll see" or "we'll think about it") can be accepted as a "no" for practical purposes.

## "BREAKING THE LANGUAGE BARRIER"

Your counterpart is at a distinct language disadvantage in English. Keep the following in mind:
- Accommodate your client by speaking slowly;
- Use simple vocabulary;
- Speak distinctly;
- Repeat key points during consultations;
- Exchange notes at the conclusion of each meeting.

## "LET YOUR HAIR DOWN"

Perhaps as much business is transacted in the informal setting of a dinner party as in the company conference room. Such events can be great ice-breakers, and can serve to ease sensitive business negotiations.

Without doubt, your local counterpart will invite you for some informal entertainment; accept the offer and show that you enjoy it. Be sure to reciprocate. Western expatriate executives may be surprised at the degree to which a usually staid, conservative national executive unwinds in such informal settings. Although you may think that such informality is completely unrelated to business, form the standpoint of your host, it is all part of the business relationship.

During such informal entertainment, your local host is weighing your sincerity, your integrity, and social graces, which are of paramount importance to Koreans in business relations.

## TRY A LITTLE
## HUMBLE PIE

**T**he impression of the Western business image is self-confidence and self-assertiveness that may border on aggressiveness, an inflated sense of self-importance and a "know-it-all" attitude. To succeed in business in this country, this image must be subdued at all costs. A foreign businessman will gain little ground in dealings without having an adequate portion of "humble pie."

Remember, you are confronting a culture that is more than 4,000 years old, with well-established modes of social behavior and interpersonal patterns. Technical know-how may have developed late, but this country has risen from the ashes of war just a few years ago to a level of industrial and technological development that is nothing less than remarkable. Realizing the contrast to other countries that have experienced industrialization over many decades without the interruption of disastrous war, should in itself have a humbling effect on Western self-centeredness.

If you come with an inquiring, sharing, and open mind, your local counterpart will put out the "welcome mat" and treat you with respect, confidence, and generosity, motivated by the desire to learn and progress and catch up by becoming an equal partner on the world trade scene.

Be careful not to confuse cultural humility and apology with weakness and ignorance. This is a cultural etiquette pattern that by no means reflects his business skill or knowledge, but illustrates why the Western expert must indulge himself in a wholesome dessert of "humble pie."

Finally, sensitivity to your Korean counterpart's etiquette patterns is one way to achieve success.

# MARKET ENTRY
# PREPARATION

The Korean market is currently going through a stage of profound and rapid transformation. Increasing disposable income, the emergence of younger consumers (approximately 60% of the population is under 27), rapid urbanization, as well as the improving quality and expanding variety of available goods and services are contributing to a considerable change in consumer behavior.

## MUSHROOMING POTENTIAL

With a population consisting of nine million households and an average per-family GNP of $8,700 in 1987, the domestic market is growing rapidly. The present size of the domestic automobile market is 300,000 cars a year and is forecast to double by 1990. Including exports, automobile production is expected to pass one million units in 1988. The size of the pharmaceutical market is over $1 billion and is ranked among the top ten major markets in the world. Advertising billings of $1.13 billion in 1987 is second in size in Asia.

The Korean market is rich in opportunities and has not been overlooked by many multinational companies. However, tapping this seemingly lucrative market requires expertise and endurance, since cultural and other barriers present considerable obstacles to many aspiring Western enterprises. Foreign businessmen should concentrate on some of the unique aspects of the local market, particularly with regard to consumer-oriented products.

# THE MARKET

**Consumer Behavior.** The near saturation of the nation's households with television sets and the development of the local transportation system combine with an increasing disposable income to accelerate the rate of change in the lifestyle of Korean consumers. They have begun to show inclinations towards quality, diversity, and aesthetic values in their choice of consumer products. While

80% of the population lives on 55% of the nation's income, the majority of those surveyed (56%) regard themselves as members of the middle class. They sometimes show a propensity to consume disproportionate to their level of income.

Heightened interest in leisure and health are much in evidence among both urban and rural populations. The increase in sales of the Bongo van, a recreational vehicle, and outdoor camping equipment attest to this trend.

Rapid Westernization of the lifestyle is also evident and will be even more so among the younger generation. Western fashion, music, and fast-food chains are a major influence on urban life. Consumers have shown a strong preference for foreign-made brands.

## WAYS AND MEANS

**Market Research.** In this young and dynamic market, having a good grasp of consumer behavior, distribution patterns, and future trends, is of utmost importance. The short history of the consumer market can often make it seem inscrutable to expatriate managers. In-depth market research by reputable organizations is desirable prior to any decision to launch a new product. As there are only a handful of research organizations in Korea, using the services of university-affiliated institutes may be an alternative.

**Test Market.** In order to avoid a marketing catastrophe, it is advisable to test-market a new product or concept in a limited market prior to a major campaign. One can learn a great deal from such an effort regarding the general consumer, distribution and media as well as the regulatory climate concerning a particular product, especially if it is new and somewhat novel to the local market. Seoul and the greater metropolitan area, which usually represents 40 to 50% of the consumer market, is a good place for testing. However, a smaller city like Taegu may be more suitable for the test-market, as it, ideally, represents many characteristics of the nation's market with its own TV station and its own distribution structure. There is no shortcut to learning the Korean market, but this trial may help to level out an otherwise costly learning curve.

**Distributor.** For a new entrant in the market either with finished, imported goods or with locally-made products under license/joint-

## PERSONAL STRATEGIES FOR BUSINESS SUCCESS

venture, distribution is always a major task. Setting up a new structure is both costly and time-consuming, while using an already established channel entails various problems such as lack of control and poor market penetration. Finding a good distributor can "make or break" a product launch.

One may attempt to identify a candidate as a distributor who may not be strong in the market but has sufficient enthusiasm in the partnership. While going with such a distributor, one can also develop one's own capability for eventual independence in distribution in the future. In a joint-venture, the local partner-parent company usually distributes the products of their subsidiary.

**Korean Staff.** In view of the magnitude of cultural differences, it would be extremely difficult for an expatriate manager to have a full understanding of the market. Limited tenure and exposure to the local situation hamper them in making proper decisions in the area of marketing. The expertise and experience of the local staff should be tapped. Good marketing managers are in great demand, and are not readily available to foreign firms. Scouting from a competitive company is sometimes the only alternative. Another way is to employ junior staff members and develop them over a period of time.

Business practices in this country often require a great deal of flexibility. The ingenuity of the local staff is indispensable in finding ways to balance this with existing corporate policies and regulations. It should also be noted that highly motivated and entrepreneurial local managers often make invaluable contributions in exploiting new and additional opportunities for the company in the changing market.

**Advertising.** Appointing the right advertising agency in Korea is almost as difficult as choosing the right business partner, especially for a joint-venture company or wholly-owned subsidiary. Some of the things to watch out for are:
- Does the agency have any international experience?
- Is it associated with any of the major US/global agencies?
- How strong is the association?
- Do they have an on-going program of training and transfer of information, etc., or is it a "name-value-only" relationship?

Look at the work that they have done for other clients carefully, and be sure that the same "best" people who made the presentation also are working for your account. Remember, concepts and copies that you may think are clever and creative may go over like a "lead balloon" with your agency people, and *vice versa*. If your agency staff feels they are being forced to do it the "foreign way" without regard for traditional customs and culture, they will quickly lose interest and motivation to do quality work.

**Consultants/Advisors.** Most foreign businesses in Korea profit from good local advice. More than one headstrong expatriate manager, intent on "doing it himself," has found Korea a career-buster. Good advisors are not easy to find but can be found among professors, retired executives, and a few practicing business consultants.

# THE KOREAN VIEWPOINT

Foreign businesses should be aware of the general Korean attitude toward foreign products and businesses, and then make any adjustments necessary to counter possible stereotypes or prejudices.

## FEELINGS TOWARD FOREIGN DEPENDENCY

Foreign companies, especially those based in the major countries, are looked upon with mixed feelings in Korea. While high technology and advanced products are admired and coveted, they are at the same time somewhat feared by Korean businessmen who perceive the possibility of having to become dependent upon them.

In recent years, however, Korea has generally become more accommodating to foreign business, perhaps not by choice, but by necessity as its overseas trade and investment activities expand rapidly. This trend is evidenced by the relaxation of regulations on imports and foreign investments.

## LINGERING DEPENDENCY

In relations with major trading partners, Korea tends to have a "poor country mentality." Only two decades ago, it was regarded as one of the poorest countries in the world, requiring huge volumes of relief aid from advanced countries. Even after attaining their present prosperity, Koreans still regard themselves as poor, needing preferential treatment by trading partners. The United States has always been looked upon as a generous big brother with unlimited affluence and resources, while Japan is a country that should eternally compensate for its colonial exploitation of Korea. In dealing with the evergrowing trade frictions with these two major trading partners, Koreans have maintained these attitudes. The readjustment of past relationships seems to take a long time, to the detriment of cooperation.

## GROWING NATIONALISM

Another aspect in relation to foreign business is the growing sense of nationalism, especially among the younger generation. As the nation's economy becomes healthier and stronger, there is a growing sense of nationalism.

## CONSUMER-BRAND PREFERENCE

Korean consumers generally associate foreign-origin brands with quality and durability. That's why many manufacturers and marketers like to name their products with Western brand names or in Western writing, even though the products are exclusively for local consumers.

The general perception of foreign companies in this country among ordinary consumers is favorable, owing to a reputation for quality goods and services, as well as the impression that foreign firms provide better working conditions. Success stories of some foreign consumer conpanies' assimilation in the local market have contributed to this impression.

## EMPLOYEE ATTITUDES TOWARDS FOREIGN BUSINESSES

During the roller-coaster years of the 1970s, when the Korean economy was still in a developmental stage, foreign firms were highly regarded as prospective workplaces by bright young university graduates. They provided their employees with excellent opportunities for training and overseas travel. Foreign firms offered higher incomes and better working conditions than local firms could offer at that time.

Attitudes have changed, however. Many of those who joined foreign firms in the early 1970s were disappointed by limited upward mobility due to slow company growth or other factors. They lacked long-term job security since many businesses that could not turn an immediate profit simply closed their doors and went home. Often there was friction between foreign management and the local staff; this problem was aggravated by the frequent change of expatriate managers.

Today's bright young prospects look more to major local companies for employment. Workers who apply to foreign firms for employment expect a better package than is offered by domestic companies.

# GOVERNMENT
# CONNECTIONS

**Economic Role of the Government.** The Korean government remains the undisputed formulator of economic policy and the ultimate arbiter of who receives the benefits of economic growth. Businessmen who freely pursue economic profits in domestic and international markets do so under the permissive supervision of government authorities.

## CONTROL FROM THE EXECUTIVE BRANCH

There are many important state-run enterprises, and some prices are under strict regulation. The trade system is in fact a mixture of free enterprise and government control. While the president has the final say on all policies, the prime minister and deputy prime minister are quite influential. The executive branch of the government predominates, and economic decision-making is highly centralized. The deputy prime minister is concurrently chief of the Economic Planning Board, the most powerful economic agency in South Korea.

At the national level, cabinet ministers have portfolios in commerce and industry, finance, energy and resources, science and technology, construction, agriculture and fisheries, transportation, and labor. They have subordinate units at various levels of local administration.

The government has successfully relied on its own ability to formulate and implement policy in directing the course of the nation's economy. Institutions specializing in international marketing and technological innovation have been created in the push to make Korea an industrialized country as rapidly as possible.

The government's chief tools for economic control are the national budget, market regulation, control over corporate behavior, the supply of credit, and the establishment of state-run enterprises which have been so successful. Recently, because the economy has grown so large and complex, government bureaucrats are unable to respond quickly to economic opportunity. The system has been liberalized by encouraging free markets and reducing overt government interference.

## TRADE DIPLOMACY

The Republic of Korea has held a series of governmental and private conferences with the United States, Japan, European nations, Southeast Asian nations, Taiwan, and other nations in an effort to promote trade and economic cooperation. Furthermore, Korea has taken an active part in a number of conferences organized by international banking and economic institutions.

South Korea's foreign trade policy has been shaped by the nation's basic economic requirements. Official government measures have thus favored essential imports of raw materials and capital goods needed to produce items for both export and domestic consumption, and has restricted non-essential imports, promoted exports and diversification of export products, and encouraged foreign investment in South Korea.

The economy in South Korea is essentially characterized by private enterprise, and the government is an important partner in the growing ranks of Korean businessmen, even as the government itself spearheads many types of industrial activity. A system of government support for exports and imports linked to trading privileges sometimes amounts to firm-by-firm regulation.

# FOREIGN BUSINESS
# INDUCEMENTS

**D**irect foreign investment in South Korea has risen dramatically to more than $250 million a year. Of the 75 foreign investment projects, most are in machinery, electronics, petrochemicals, and other sophisticated technological industries.

Recently, foreign investment in tourist hotels and tourism projects has drastically increased, indicating that foreign firms expect growing numbers of tourists and business travelers, in the wake of the 1988 summer Olympics in Seoul and other large-scale international events.

In terms of the amount approved for investment in Korea, Japan leads the United States; $2 billion for 800 projects and $500,000 for 300 projects accounting for 50% and 30% of total investments respectively.

## FOREIGN INVESTMENT EXPANSION

Following the government's policy of opening up the national economy to further foreign investment, rapid influx of foreign capital is expected to take place in the near future. In addition to Japan and the US, European investors have joined the fray, diversifying the sources of DFI in Korea.

In order to cope with the increased national economic scale and ever-increasing demand for international economic cooperation, the Korean government has amended the Foreign Capital Inducement act, opening up all areas of Korean industry to foreign investment, except for a few sectors restricted by presidential decree. The government plans to successively reduce the areas restricted to foreign investments.

## ALLOWANCES

Of the 521 industry categories currently open to foreign investment, 65 are industrial sectors, where up to 100% foreign ownership is permitted, while in the remaining 456 sectors up to 50% foreign ownership is allowed. The former is composed of manufacturers of automatic data-processing equipment, electrical equipment for use in aircraft and biological products, natural gas, electronic medical equipment, casting and founding industries, projects to explore crude oil, crop-growing services and tourist hotels with over 500 rooms.

The latter includes 320 sectors of manufacturers in textiles, farm machines, construction, mining, rawhide, medicines, and finance, real estate, and insurance.

Benefits commensurate with those offered to domestic industries are given to foreign businessmen.

## NEGOTIATED BILATERAL AGREEMENTS

The Republic of Korea has recently concluded investment guarantee agreements with over 10 major industrial nations such as the United States, Japan, Federal Republic of Germany, the United Kingdom, France, Switzerland, the Netherlands, and Belgium. In addition, Korea is dispatching missions to them to encourage foreign capital investment.

## INVESTOR INCENTIVES

Foreign investors are welcomed and accorded various incentives and privileges, including tax holidays, subject to screening by the Foreign Capital Inducement Deliberation Committee. The government allows foreign investors to possess or lease land throughout

South Korea. They are subject to the regulations of the Alien Land Law, which requires that a foreign-invested firm that holds over 50% ownership of stock in a corporation obtain approval for land ownership from the Home Affairs Ministry. With the approval of the Customs Administration, bonded warehouses and factories may be established at any location in the industrial estates.

## MINIMUM EQUITY

The minimum amount or value of foreign investment is set at $100,000 per project to make foreign equity investment in the country easier, and thus help to introduce more investment.

Currently, the government is granting authorization but prefers joint ventures to 100% foreign ownership, although there is no legal limit on the share of foreign investment participation.

Foreign investment in South Korea is energetically solicited to
• improve the balance of payments,
• utilize domestic resources, and
• increase employment.

As a result of the Korean government's efforts to attract foreign investment and technology, many foreign enterprises have made capital investments in South Korea either independently or in joint ventures with Korean partners.

Since the Korean government has been lifting import quotas to allow greater trade with foreign nations, foreign trade has been very active and is rapidly growing.

## GRADUAL LIBERATION

Recently, other import restrictions have been eased, adding many commodities to the "automatic approval" list. Forty-five banks operating in the country enjoy a thriving business.

# FOREIGN BUSINESS
# REGULATIONS

## AUTOMATIC AUTHORIZATION

If the foreign investment project fulfills some of the following conditions, it is automatically authorized by the Minister of Finance without reference to the pertinent ministries nor review by the

Foreign Capital Project Review Committee. These conditions are:
- it is not on the negative list;
- the project ratio is below 50%;
- the project amount is below $3 million;
- a request is not made to receive tax exemption;
- the project involves the export of more than a specified portion of its project;
- it plans to produce items that can be freely imported and the tariff rates are below a specified level.

Foreign-invested firms are allowed to export only their own products, and import raw materials and equipment required for local operations. The policies are designed to attract more small and medium-sized enterprises from advanced nations, and sharpen the international competitiveness of domestic industries through technology and capital cooperation.

Although a project is allowed when its validity is recognized by examination on a case-by-case basis through discussion with the ministries concerned, the scope of project areas are adjusted annually.

## ENCOURAGEMENT OF PARTNERSHIPS

Under the current rules, the government allows 100% foreign investment in projects that introduce advanced foreign technology and ultimately contribute to strengthening international competitiveness; in projects which are needed for development, but cannot attract Korean investment due to the large capital requirement or excessive risk; in projects that increase exports and help improve the balance of payments; and in other specified projects.

## TAX HOLIDAYS

At present, foreign-invested enterprises or foreign investors are exempted from income tax, corporation tax, and property acquisition tax for the initial five years and reduced by 50% for the ensuing three years as an investment incentive. The government allows them to choose any single five-year period for exemption of corporation and dividend income taxes within 10 years from registration of the enterprise for the maximum tax exemption benefits.

Instead of direct tax exemption, foreign investors may choose a special depreciation, which could be more favorable for capital-intensive industries. The companies will continue to be exempt from customs duties on capital goods which are imported as needed for foreign-invested projects, as well as being exempt from the special consumer tax, value-added tax, capital gains tax, and the commodity tax on the purchase of locally-made automobiles.

## INVESTMENT RECOVERY

The current law allows all foreign investors to withdraw their money invested in South Korean firms at any time after the first two years of business at the rate of 20% of the principal investment every year. For business purposes, they are permitted to acquire real estate and land, and unlimited remittance of principal. Overseas Koreans are allowed to make direct investment in South Korea only if they have lived overseas for over 10 years.

## LICENSING AND REGISTRATION OF FOREIGN FIRMS

Foreign firms must register with and obtain a license from the Ministry of Commerce and Industry, with exceptions granted for government procurement involving foreign trade, for semi-finished imports entering for processing and re-export, and for imports with a foreign-investment project approved by the Economic Planning Board.

## FISCAL REQUIREMENTS

An applicant for a new license must have paid-up capital of $10 million with standing export orders; manufacturing and supply capacities for export goods; issued capital; or an association with a foreign investor under the Foreign Capital Inducement Law. A licensed foreign trader can import general commodities up to a value of $100,000; designation as a foreign trader may be withdrawn if a firm fails to generate $250,000 in exports within a six-month period.

## LICENSE APPROVALS

Import and export licenses are granted by the Ministry of Commerce and Industry, depending on the current foreign trade plan and the general availability of foreign exchange; any import permit issued by the ministry entitles the holder to buy the required foreign exchange. The ministry is concerned with imports financed from South Korea's own foreign exchange resources; imports financed by foreign grants and loans controlled by the Economic Planning Board in consultation with the ministry.

The government maintains advance deposit requirements on most categories of imports by the private sector; a 200% deposit is required for imports that are subject to custom duties in excess of 50% or are categorized as non-essential or luxury items. There is no legal restraint on the proportion of foreign participation in investment in joint ventures with domestic partners, but they must hold at least 50% of foreign equity. The business projects eligible for foreign investment incentives are large-scale complex industries such as electronics and machinery.

## RESTRICTIONS

The government set up the Foreign Capital Project Consultation Center, which gives information about specific projects in an attempt to induce more foreign investment. Among those areas that are declared prohibited to foreign investment are:
- projects considered harmful to the country's health;
- projects that are contrary to good morals;
- public projects run by the government or public institutions;
- other business barred from foreign investment by future presidential decrees.

Currently, projects barred or restricted from foreign investment include red ginseng manufacturing, cigarette manufacturing, domestic airline service, railway service, power distribution-transmission, and water supply systems projects.

# PROBLEM AREAS

**Foreign Trade Friction.** Korean-American trade relations which have transpired smoothly in the past, recently hit some serious snags, aggravated by the invocation of Section 301 of the US Trade Law, which demanded that the countries trading with the United States open their domestic markets wider for American goods and services. Korea was also requested to strengthen protection of intellectual property rights and open its insurance market. The results of these negotiations between the two countries have great ramifications for the Korean economy, in particular exports.

Both sides are seeking ways to reach agreement on these issues relating to exports. The problems involved have at times reached a formidable impasse, but both sides have made concessions to defuse some of the obstacles. The American side pushed for the settlement of the insurance market issue first, but the Korean side insisted on an overall settlement including intellectual property rights, and the US side relented.

Some matters still need to be solved, including a retroactive clause regarding patent rights, protection periods, the number of insurance firms permitted to enter Korea, and the distribution of the fire insurance pool in Korea.

A separate and independent body was proposed to deal with trade frictions between Korea and the United States. There have been discussions on the results of the invocation of section 301. Korea and Taiwan were singled out as areas showing better results, while Brazil and Japan have shown no improvement at all.

The fact that Korea has cooperated to such a great extent has won substantial goodwill on Capitol Hill.

*Seoul Asia Games (1986)*

# Chapter VI
# FOR TRAVELERS WITH SPECIAL INTERESTS

# Education
# in Korea

While Korea has always been a land of scholars, in the past, little provision was made for imparting practical knowledge. Until modern times, education in Korea consisted of local day schools (*sudang*) in the cities and villages where boys were taught Confucian doctrines extensively, with a view to taking the government examinations (*kwaku*) and with the ultimate goal of becoming public servants. Successful candidates were awarded the degree of doctor and other special honors. Korea adopted a system of public education, and the government had a cabinet minister of education for many centuries. Reading and writing of Korean and Chinese and instruction in Confucian ethics were standard fare in the public schools.

Learning was by rote. The most important book was *The Thousand Characters* (*Chunja Mun*), a manual for teaching Chinese characters and the Korean *Hangul* alphabet as the basis of literacy. Before the arrival of Western civilization, Korean scholars were steeped in classical Chinese and other philosophies and literatures. Early education centered in the study of Confucianism and the Confucian principles: will power, fortitude, self-control, moderation, righteousness, humility, aspiration, and prudence. For a more advanced course, a "*hyangkyo*," or public school (*suwon*), was established in every major district; advanced work in Chinese literature (*sasu samkyung*) and teaching of the Korean language were the principal subjects. During the Choson (Yi) dynasty the highest institution was the Confucian College (Sung-kyun-kwan), a scholastic honorary society at Seoul. The curricula of these schools did not include the natural sciences.

In 1883 the first English-language school for interpreters was opened by the crown; three Americans were appointed to teach about 30 sons of noblemen, and Methodist missionaries established Ewha Haktang, now Ewha Woman's University, in Seoul. In the early twentieth century Pyongyang Union Christian College and Chosun Christian College at Seoul were founded by American Presbyterian missionaries. Western education was encouraged in Korea until the Japanese occupation, when Japanese language and history became the principal subjects and Korean language and history were banned. Proficiency in the Japanese language became the door to preferment, and because it was the official language of the government and the courts, Koreans who spoke no Japanese could obtain little justice. Education was severely limited, and native culture was suppressed. Only a small percentage of students were able to acquire a college education.

Since the liberation of 1945, Korea has accomplished much in modernizing education. Primary school enrollment, the number of secondary schools, and the number and variety of college-level institutions have increased, and an adult education program has been established. The proportion of the adult population unable to read the Korean alphabet has been reduced to 2 percent. Western and Japanese books have been replaced by newly written Korean books. On-the-job technical training programs, in place in most industries and government bureaus, have produced greater efficiency. Modern education has been one of the most successful fruits of the liberation.

Korean boys and girls enter primary school at the age of seven. Attendance is required by law. Tuition in the high schools, although moderate, drains the financial resources of many. The schooling offered is organized as follows: first through sixth year, primary school; seventh through ninth year, middle school; 10th through 12th year, high school; 13th through 16th year, college and university. In addition, there are graduate schools that bestow a doctoral degree. The primary and middle-school language curricula concentrate, as in Western schools, on instruction in speaking, reading, and writing of the native tongue. In the middle schools, Western languages are taught. The teaching of English in South Korea (and Russian in North Korea) comprises reading, writing, and speaking.

Coeducation has returned to the colleges and universities. Tuition rates remain beyond the reach of the poor, although some scholarships are provided. Higher education is more or less evenly divided between public and private institutions. South Korea has more than 90 universities, 130 two-year junior colleges, and 150 graduate schools, including law, medical, teachers', commercial, and engineering colleges.

More than 11 million children and young adults attend schools, colleges, and universities in South Korea, and there are over 300,000 teachers in these schools and colleges. The progress of education in South Korea is guided by the National Institute of Education, responsible for developing educational theories in the socio-cultural context of Korea; the Korean Educational Development Institute, responsible for planning and implementing educational reform; provincial and county institutes, which research

*Kyunghee University, Seoul suburbs*

subjects of local concern; and many other institutes both private and public, many related to institutions of higher learning.

Recently, the entrance examinations for middle school and high school were abolished, in preparation for the time when free compulsory education was extended through middle school during the Fifth Five-Year Economic and Social Development Plan, and to relieve the considerable pressure on middle school students preparing for examinations, which resulted in a great financial burden to pay for tutors as well as an emotional burden for students.

The number of students in each college and university in Korea is regulated by the government. There are more than half a million students attending four-year colleges and universities, over 50,000 in graduate schools, about 10,000 in two-year teachers' colleges and nearly 200,000 in junior colleges and vocational schools across the country. Faculty members total over 25,000. There is a Radio Correspondence College offering two-year junior college and five-year college courses largely to working youths. The government, in adjusting the ceiling of students to be enrolled in colleges and universities, assigns priority to fields of greatest national concern, such as engineering, medicine, electronics, and aeronautics.

South Korea's better known institutions of higher education are located in the capital city: Seoul National, Korea, Yonsei, Hanyang, Chunang, Sogang, Sungkyunkwan, Konkuk, Kyunghee,

Hankuk, Sejong, Dankook, Hongik, Sookmyung, Kookmin, and Ewha Woman's universities, the latter the largest women's university in the world. Now increasing enrollment at provincial colleges and universities is reducing the percentage of students going to Seoul to study.

More than 20,000 Korean students are studying at higher learning institutions in other countries (almost 15,000 are in the United States). Nearly 300 foreign professors are teaching in Korea, and about 250 Korean professors are on overseas study tours for one year. Overseas students who have a special interest in Korean studies are encouraged to study in Korea under government scholarships. There are more than 1,000 foreign students enrolled in Korea's colleges and universities. They usually receive a year's language training before taking up their major studies.

In South Korea, 98 percent of primary school-age children now attend school. For older students, the government provides a wide range of nonformal educational programs in addition to the formal system. The community education movement includes evening youth classes and women's classes. As part of the life-long education program, one channel, KBS-TV, is used exclusively for education; also, Education Television (ETV) and Instructional Radio are operated by the Korean Educational Development Institute. The government gives scholarships to deserving students for continuing study. Financial aid consists of government loans, scholarships provided by private individuals, and exemptions from or reductions of tuition.

The Korean people have been developing an independent spirit and self-governing abilities by the democratic operation of educational institutions. Recognizing that industrial progress and an informed electorate depend upon the widespread acquisition of knowledge, a thorough educational program is being provided.

# Korea's
# Health Care
# Facilities

Overseas visitors notice that Koreans are a vigorous and healthy people. Improvements in health are due to the fundamental social changes that have taken place in Korea since the Korean War.

Not only have adequate health care and medical services been provided, but also the quality of life has been enhanced by an improvement in the quality of diet, clothing, shelter, sanitation, and safe water supplies. South Korea has many medical schools and health-care facilities and a sufficient number of medical doctors and nurses. Modern pharmaceutical companies have accelerated the advances in health care. Furthermore, Korea's New Community Movement has brought health care, including many para-medical "barefoot doctors," to rural areas. Many Korean doctors and nurses are now working in various other countries.

There are excellent hospitals and medical specialists in Seoul, and the deluxe hotels offer convenient medical services to their guests.

In addition to doctors of modern Western medicine, there are also many Korean practitioners of the traditional Korean and Chinese medical techniques of acupuncture, moxibustion, and herbal medicine. Herbal treatments are often preferred to alternative Western-type medications because herbal formulations are cheaper and usually have no side effects. Kyunghee University is known for its Eastern medical school, which teaches Korean and Chinese techniques and herbal healing treatments.

For the traveler facing changes in diet and water, it is always a good idea to bring some medical supplies in a first-aid kit. An anti-dysentery medication, a stomach pacifier, a laxative, and charcoal tablets may be useful for immediate treatment, although most modern drugs are available in Korea.

# Religion
# in Korea

Koreans are a religious people with deeply rooted convictions. Every religion that has crossed their borders has been put to the pragmatic test. Though they are persistent in their quest for an adequate religion, no one faith has dominated the loyalty of the people as a whole.

Korea's religions have always reflected foreign influences. They were likened to a three-legged stool based on shamanism, Buddhism, and Confucianism, until the introduction of Christianity in the nineteenth century. The general belief was in shamanism, a form of animistic nature worship based on the veneration of spirits.

This religion is still practiced in rural areas by medicine men and women. Many centuries ago Buddhism reached the peninsula from China; at one time it was the state religion, but its devotees today are largely aged women. Though Confucianism is rarely practiced formally, Confucian ethics are deeply embedded in the Korean personality and culture as a philosophy and way of life. Many Confucian concepts still flourish. Founded in 1859, Chundokyo (Eastern Sect) is a comparatively new eclectic religion. A composite of the other religions, its nationalistic emphasis has won it some followers.

The first organized Christian missionary activities in Korea began in the nineteenth century, bringing Western influences to the Hermit Kingdom. Today, the only organized religions in South Korea are Buddhism and Christianity, the vital religion propagated by missionaries of various denominations. Notwithstanding the influence of Christianity, some Koreans still perform Confucian rites to the dead, offer prayers as Mahayana Buddhists, and worship at the shrines of mountain demons. It can be said that they follow three or more different religions at the same time. The religious belief of the majority of Koreans is a mixture of Christianity, Confucianism, Buddhism, local shamanism and perhaps one or two other faiths.

*Animist "grandfather" statuary, Chejudo Island*

# 270
## RELIGION

Islam was first introduced to Korea by Turkish soldiers stationed in Korea during the Korean War; in 1955 an *imam*, a Muslim prayer leader, came to Korea to work with the Turkish troops and began missionary work in Seoul. Inauguration of the Korean Muslim Federation in 1960 and South Korea's economic ties to the Middle East have produced an increasing number of Korean Muslims.

## SHAMANISM

Shamanism, or animism (Shinkyo), is the most ancient religion known to Korea, its origins having been lost in the mists of antiquity. Shamanism has no great edifices. Not many decades ago "devil posts" alongside the roads leading into the villages bore witness to the universal prevalence of demon worship and its plethora of superstitions. Small shrines may still be seen on the hilltops and near villages. They contain primitive yellow pictures and wooden tables. No regular meetings are held. Fetishes guard ridgepoles, doorposts, and granaries. Rituals for driving evil spirits from the sick and for determining the proper location for cemeteries, homes, and public buildings form the major part of its ceremony. The principal animistic festival is the post-harvest ceremony of paying tribute to these spirits. A primitive type of shaman, especially among the peasantry, is the "*mudang*," a female medium who makes contact with spirits by means of charms, secret rites, and hypnotism.

A thousand years after the deaths of Buddha and Confucius, Korean shamanism assimilated the doctrines of these great religious leaders. In animism it is believed that the heavens are living spirits, sometimes beneficent but usually maleficent. According to shamanism, the sun is one god, "Heaven Lord" (Hanunim), which embraces the idea of one supreme mind. A strong view of personal sin and punishment is held. The basis of the shamanists' ethic is: "Don't fight with your neighbor's children; love your neighbor; fighting is a sin." The fearful conception of personal sin and punishment tended to give Koreans a love of truth and encouraged them to fight for it as a principle.

In teaching Christianity, Western missionaries use the term Hanunim for "God." Thus this ancient religion of the past has made a positive contribution to the religion of the present. Korean forms of shamanism have been rooted in the Korean mind for so many centuries that its concepts remain a potent force in daily life. Though Buddhism and Confucianism swept over the country with great vigor, neither predominates today.

## BUDDHISM

In the fifth century B.C. a young Indian prince, Gautama Siddhartha, seeing that the world was filled with sadness and misery, came to believe that life is a continuous process of death and rebirth. He taught that salvation could only be worked out by the individual alone, through a cycle of continuous rebirths. Gautama became an object of worship to the people of Asia, and he was given the name "Buddha."

In 369 the first Buddhist missionary arrived in Korea from China. He was a practitioner of "Northern Buddhism," which had developed from scriptures written in Sanskrit, the language of ancient India. Buddhism reached Korea in the form called Mahayana, or the Great Vehicle. This religion spread rapidly through Paekje, Silla, and Koguryo and passed on to Japan before the close of the sixth century. Korean Buddhism reached its peak during the Koryo period (918–1392) and remained the dominant religion for four centuries. Korean Buddhists were a potent influence in national affairs, at times virtually overruling decrees of the king. Many social and political revolutions were led by Buddhist priests, who were well educated and thus able to act as scribes, lawmakers, counselors, and secretaries. There were nearly 1,000 temples, immense libraries, and a priesthood of over 10,000 during the height of Buddhist development. With the Choson (Yi) dynasty (1392–1910), Buddhism fell into a disfavor from which it has never recovered. The number of its professed adherents today is compara-

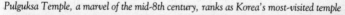

*Pulguksa Temple, a marvel of the mid-8th century, ranks as Korea's most-visited temple*

*Sŏkkuram Grotto Shrine; the Buddha Image in the grotto of Sŏkkuram, at Kyŏngju, is regarded as the most beautiful statue extant in Korea*

tively small, and many of its most famous temples have fallen into decay. Figures of the Milyak Buddha are found in all parts of the country, and the remains of great Buddhist temples can still be seen in high mountain villages.

Korean Buddhists believe in individual immortal souls, in a vicarious salvation through Amida Buddha, in reincarnation, in the confessional, in hell, and in a heaven, or "Western Paradise," achieved through faith. They believe that the six virtues—charity, morality, patience, energy, contemplation, and wisdom—must be perfected in order to pass from this world of misery to the shore of holiness of the Buddhist heaven. They believe in a host of gods and Buddhas, represented by idols or images, and practice many forms of sacrifice to or recognition of these spirits.

Buddhism brought rare beauty to Korea, including stately old temples, richly stained, gilded, and carved; exquisite rituals; and an ecclesiastical pageantry that endeared itself to Koreans, particularly to the women. Korean Buddhists excelled in architecture, graven images, stone sculpture, wood carving, and painting. Every temple and monastery is virtually an art gallery containing frescoes, murals, and enormous scroll paintings of Buddha, usually executed in bright colors and in exquisite detail, a delight to tourists. Korean Buddhism is a religion of light and illumination.

## CONFUCIANISM

Confucianism became dominant in Korea with the birth of the Choson (Yi) dynasty in 1392. Buddhism, condemned as a negative influence by the previous Koryo government, was cast out and the Confucian doctrine was established as the state religion.

Confucius (550–478 B.C.), a Chinese scholar and a statesman, taught his disciples that society is a series of social relationships consisting of five-fold loyalties: between ruler and subject, between father and son, between husband and wife, between elder and younger brother, and between friends, a belief formulated to promote the organization of the family unit and reverence for elders. The cardinal virtue of filial piety is a combination of loyalty and reverence. Confucius taught that, in order to gain a well-ordered society, five virtues must be applied to interpersonal relationships: love of humanity; consideration for another's feelings and emotions; justice, assigning each person to his particular duties and to his place in society; reverence, acknowledging another's rights; and sincerity and truthfulness of purpose.

On the subject of death and immortality, Confucius said, "Bones and flesh return to earth as is appointed, but the soul in its energy can go everywhere." His disciple, Mencius, taught that man is good by nature. This concept gave Koreans a high ethical standard. These moral rules of conduct, man to man, are quite similar to Christian ideals. However, the basic attitude is one of justice and loyalty rather than of love. Whereas Buddhism is mystical, Confucianism is realistic. The two religions blended with the indigenous spirit worship to form the religion finally adhered to by most Koreans. Many women favored Buddhism because it placed them in a higher social position than Confucianism did.

Confucianism became the religion and culture of the learned and official classes, thus creating a strong national influence. Ancestor worship is at the heart of Confucianism, and it has remained a national practice in Korea through the centuries. Another influence inherited from Confucianism is fatalism, a predominant trait of the people and a philosophical tenet congruent with the agrarian and bureaucratic character of this people.

Once Confucianism became the state religion, its schools became the centers of learning. Only the Confucian classics were studied, as their mastery was the main requirement for civil appointments. The scholars chosen by examinations were prepared to lead ceremonial rites as well as to hold political office. This system served to give Confucianism social, political, and financial stability as well as prestige. Not until 1895, as a result of the influence of Western education working inexorably against the old practices, was the examination system as the avenue to public office abolished.

Until the Japanese occupation, Korean society was governed rigidly by the ultraconservative Confucian doctrines, which were extremely stringent concerning sex segregation, ancestor worship, and the complete subservience of son to elder. Though Confucius did not create a priesthood or any monastic order such as is found among the Buddhists, and though he was not deified, some of the finest buildings were devoted to Confucian practices. The temple in Seoul was a kind of national hall of fame.

Confucianism, which is based on rational ethics, is a philosophy rather than a religion. There is no strong sense of worship of a divine power, but rather a code of morals which was responsible for shaping Korean life for more than 500 years, which still constitutes the moral law of Korea, and which is the source of cherished ideals and noble traditions. Since the beginning of the twentieth century, the study of Confucianism and the Chinese classics has declined with the spread of Christianity in Korea.

After the complete subjugation of Korea by Japan, there was an attempt to impose Shintoism on Korea, but it did not become popular. Since it was presented as a symbol of loyalty to Japan rather than as a religion, Koreans who were forced to accept Shintoism did so unwillingly, with a natural resentment toward the oppressor. Since the liberation from Japanese rule in 1945, Shintoism has become a negligible factor in Korea, and many of the shrines have been destroyed.

## CHRISTIANITY

Just as Buddhism and Confucianism came to Korea with the combined philosophical prestige of India and China, so Christianity brought modern influences, together with Western culture. Two thousand years after the death of Christ, animism, shamanism, Buddhism, and Confucianism in Korea made room for Christianity. The success with which the new doctrine was accepted may be attributed

*Yongnak Protestant Church, Seoul*

not only to the religious nature of the Koreans, but also to the fact that Christian ethics placed great emphasis on love, justice, and personal freedom. Missionary practice supplied the gifts of modern Western education and medical care to all, irrespective of age or position. This furthered a better understanding of the West by imparting a knowledge of modern natural science and technology. The healing techniques and general education of the missionaries made an impression on the practical Koreans. Christian missionaries completed a pure Korean grammar and translated the Bible, hymns, and other Christian literature into Korean.

The Christian religion was introduced into Korea in the fourteenth century. The first Christian to enter the Hermit Kingdom in modern times was a Jesuit priest who accompanied the Japanese invasion of 1592 to minister to Christians in the Japanese army. Catholic influence was brought from China in 1832, with the appointment of an apostolic vicar for Korea. During most of this time, Christians in Korea were subjected to persecution. In the nineteenth century, Roman Catholicism came to Korea through books.

In 1832 the Reverend K.F.A. Gutzlaff, a Protestant missionary, visited Korea; in 1835, Father Pierre Philibert Maubant, a French Catholic priest, became the first resident Christian missionary in Korea. It was difficult for the Christian religion to enter Korea in the days of the country's complete isolation, but after the country was opened up, missionary efforts were incessant, especially on the part of the Catholics, Presbyterians, and Methodists.

Christianity was accepted quite readily in the animistic north. In the south there was opposition from the Buddhists and Confucianists, but the missionaries carried on their work despite many obstacles and hardships. The principle of complete religious tolerance was finally established in Korea in 1882. After the opening of Korea by treaty with the United States, the first Protestant missionary to take up regular work there was an American physician, Horace H. Allen, who arrived in September 1884. He was soon followed by Dr. Horace G. Underwood, whose family is now in its third generation of devoted service to the Korean people. The Methodists began work at almost the same time; H.D. Appenzeller arrived in Seoul in the summer of 1885. James E. Adams came to Korea in 1895 and began educational mission work in Taegu. The Episcopalians, Seventh Day Adventists, Salvation Army, and YMCA are other principal Christian missionary groups that remain active in Korea.

Christianity underwent severe difficulties after Japan seized political control of Korea. Many Christian leaders were imprisoned. Japan had long suspected Korean religious groups of being involved in the leadership of independence movements, and it harassed Christian associations with missionaries from foreign countries. Most Christian converts, however, remained true to their faith. Christianity continues to exert great influence on the life of the people, and many Korean leaders were educated in Christian missionary institutions such as Yensei University, Sukang University, and Ewha University. Under the influence of American religious and medical missionaries, Christianity has a large and growing following. Now Korea is rich in houses of worship, and religion is one of Korea's strongest ties with the West. There are more than 25,000 churches spread throughout South Korea, and Seoul is often called the "city of churches"—crosses can be seen from every vantage point. There are more than six million Christians in South Korea, or 15 percent of the population (five million are Protestants, one million Catholics).

# Korea's

# Arts and

# Handicrafts

Since modern art paintings, scenic landscapes, and bird-and-flower still life studies are often painted in the style of the old masters, the overseas visitor's enjoyment of Korea's art, new and old, is enhanced by having a basic knowledge of how Korean art evolved.

**Painting and Calligraphy.** Painting has a long history in Korea, dating back to the colorful wall frescoes in the royal tombs of the Three Kingdoms period. During the Silla and Koryo periods, Buddhism dominated the cultural life of Korea, and sculpture became the predominant art form. Painting was largely of a religious character, portraits of the great patriarchs, for example. With the ascendancy of Confucianism in the Choson (Yi) dynasty, the form of literati painting associated with the scholar-gentry class was favored by the *yangban* aristocracy. Choson dynasty painting developed technically and stylistically. It is noted for dramatic landscapes, elegant portraits of great scholars, and genre painting, which sought to capture the common folk of Korea in their daily lives at work and play. Colorful and vivid, the unsigned folk art paintings of the period reflect religious beliefs (shamanism, Taoism, Buddhism) and real-life themes, whether the purpose was memorial, religious, record-keeping, or decorative. The style often seems impressionistic. On the whole, however, it was Confucian learning that became the key to the development of Choson dynasty arts, just as Buddhism nurtured the arts of Koryo.

In the Confucian tradition, calligraphy was regarded as a more noble skill than painting. During the 500-year period of Confucian dominance under the Choson dynasty, this art form exerted a strong influence on the cultural and social life of the Korean people. Calligraphy was a major adjunct of both scholarship and statesmanship. One who wrote good poetry in graceful calligraphy had greatly enhanced chances for promotion in the ranks of government.

## HANDICRAFTS

Korea has many richly creative and varied handicrafts inherited from the past. Most distinctive among these relics are gold items,

*Handcrafted drums are widely used in Korean traditional folk festivals, e.g., the Drum Dance and Farmer's Dance*

bronzes, pottery, and daily utensils of the time, which have been excavated from ancient tombs. Also preserved are sculpture, ceramics, wood crafts, and wood-block prints, all of which flourished during the Koryo and Choson periods and continue to this day.

**Ceramics.** Korea is justly famous for its long history of excellent ceramics—Silla earthenware, Koryo celadon, Choson blue-and-white porcelain—which are uniquely Korean. Koryo celadon, which dates to 993 and is universally praised, has never been matched for its color, inlaid patterns, and simple elegance of shape. The quiet hue of Koryo celadon and the subtle white tones of Choson porcelain reflect the Korean people's traditional love of plainness and sincerity. Korean artisans now are turning out excellent modern copies of world-famous Koryo celadons and Choson porcelains.

**Wood Crafts.** During the Choson dynasty, Korean wood crafts achieved remarkable development. Furniture reflected the Confucian influence on life in the Korean home and the creativity of the Korean people. Distinguishing features of Choson crafts are simple and sensitive design, practicality, and compact forms. Antique furniture is recognized as a folk art, and good pieces are becoming sought-after collector's items. Trays, boxes, mats, fans, and other novelties made of wood or bamboo by dedicated craftsmen also are popular souvenirs.

**Lacquerware and Brassware.** These centuries-old traditional Korean specialties are still flourishing handicrafts. Black (and more rarely white) lacquerware inlaid with stunning mother-of-pearl designs is made in many forms—boxes for candy, jewelry, and cigarettes; small and large tables; chests; and huge free-standing wardrobe closets. Brassware is heavy and decorative and ranges from rice and soup bowls to brass beds; Korea does a lively export trade in brassware.

**Pottery.** Korean earthenware evolved from the purely decorative into functional and utilitarian styles, keeping pace with social development. Silla urns are especially prized. They are of many shapes—box, jar, long-necked bottle, pot-with-tripod, cylinder, high-stemmed goblet. Some have lids in the shape of a ball with the top suggesting a flame, a pagoda, or a small bottle; most are glazed in green or golden-brown. Extraordinary examples include pottery vessels in the form of a mounted warrior, cups in the shape of horns, oil cups for lamps, and vehicle-shaped pots.

**Metalcrafts.** Fine artwork in metal is represented by the gold crowns, other golden ornaments, and jewelry excavated from ancient tombs and by the bells and statues found in ancient temples. A recently excavated sixth-century Paekje tomb yielded two gold crowns, necklaces, earrings, belts, and personal ornaments of the king and queen. The Gold Crown Tomb and Gold Bell Tomb of the Silla period also have been excavated with rich reward. The cylinder, a device to regulate the tone of a bell, is unique to Silla bells. The best and largest bell in Asia, cast in 771, is preserved in the bell pavilion at Kyongju National Museum. Other fine examples of temple art, in the gentle style and expression charac-

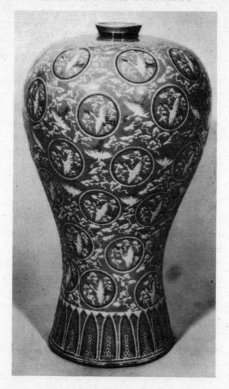

*Inlaid Celadon Porcelain: the Koryŏ Celadon is unique for its nephrite color and delicate form*

---

teristic of Buddhist sculpture, are a gilt-bronze Maitreya crafted during the Three Kingdoms period and a Paekje gilt-bronze trinity.

**Roof Tiles.** The size of roof tiles corresponds to the scale of the edifice; the decorative patterns and aesthetic intent varies according to the purpose of the building they grace. Roof tiles are made in "male" (round) and "female" (flat) forms; they may be demon-faced or falcon-headed. Silla period roof tiles are unsurpassed for diversity, elaborateness, and refinement of patterns. Among roof tile patterns, the most common are variations of the Buddhist lotus flower. Buddhist temple roof tiles venerated Buddha; their designs were intended to expel vicious spirits and to atrract auspicious influences. Royal palace roof tiles enhanced the dignity of the monarch, symbolized the kingdom, and sought to bring prosperity while eliminating evil fortune.

# SPECIAL INTEREST TOURS

Now that overseas visitors are going to Korea in increasing numbers, there is a greater variety of group tours and independent tours available to those who want to pursue a special interest. Among them are cultural tours (to museums, historic sites, and famous temples), industry tours (to the Ulsan Industrial Complex, Pohang Iron and Steel Mill, and Hyundai Shipyard, as well as ancient sites in Kyongju), family tours (to national parks or Cheju Island), shopping tours (to textile and handicraft manufacturers and shops), sports tours (playing golf, hiking, skiing, mountain-climbing, swimming), and highway tours (driving to scenic and historic sites, often staying at low-cost Korean inns or hotels). Now South Korea is rapidly gaining international recognition as a site for major international events because of its modern facilities, hospitality, culture, and natural beauty.

## INDUSTRIAL GUIDED TOUR

The industrial guided tour provides an opportunity to examine the Korean "economic miracle" in the Ulsan Industrial Complex, the Pohang Iron and Steel Mill, and the massive Hyundai Shipyard. It also lets the visitor enjoy the ancient treasures of the Silla capital, Kyongju. These sites are all in the Southeast Region, around Pusan. The itinerary is: first day—Seoul/Kimpo Domestic Airport/Pusan/Kyongju/Hotel (Lunch)/Pohang Iron and Steel Mill/ Hotel; second day—Pulguk Temple/Ulsan Industrial Complex/Diamond Hotel (Lunch)/Hyundai Shipyard and Motor Company/Ulsan Domestic Airport/Seoul. The price per person is $250 double occupancy or $280 single. The cost of the package includes American breakfast, guide service, air-conditioned coach travel, air transportation, accommodations at deluxe hotels, and miscellaneous fees. Requirements are: a minimum of 10 persons, reservations made a week in advance, payment two days prior to the tour date in U.S. dollars or traveler's checks. Reservations and payment can be made with: Korea National Tourism Corporation, C.P.O. Box 903, Seoul, Korea; Telex: KOTOUR K 28555; Cable: KOTOURSERV.

# TEMPLES TO VISIT IN KOREA

Korea once had 7,000 temples; now 2,000 remain. They are important elements of both the scenic landscape and Korean culture. Buddhist art enjoyed a golden age in the eighth century; then, after Silla succumbed to Koryo in 936, Buddhism became a powerful influence in the royal court for the next several centuries. During the Yi dynasty (1392-1910), Buddhism fell from favor with the rising power of Confucianism, and many temples were destroyed. Others decayed or were ruined during various foreign invasions. The most ancient temples, dating from the sixth century, are found in the central and southern part of the peninsula, where the repressing hand of the Yi dynasty in Seoul was less powerful. During the 1,000 years of Buddhist cultural dominance, the Korean elite patronized its arts—sculptural masterpieces, incense burners and temple bells, wood-block carvings, and paintings. Over 1,200 granite pagodas still mark the sites of now-vanished temples.

*Popchu-sa Temple; Korea's largest Buddha image is the 17-meter Maitreya next to Korea's oldest and best wooden pagoda, surrounded by a cedar pine forest*

Temple architecture is colorful and reflects a folk religion, uniquely combining nature worship in the form of Shaman images, such as the Mountain Spirit and the Sea Dragon King, with Buddhism. Temples represent both the work of scholars and the playfulness of the Korean people. The beams were painted with mineral colors that resist fading; huge wooden columns support unbelievably heavy tile roofs, with demonhead tiles to frighten away evil spirits; a complex system of brackets supports the eaves. Brightly colored and fanciful designs relieve the heaviness of the structure. The Korean tiger, a favorite folk symbol, often decorates doorway panels, and dragons writhe around interior columns or stretch over high altars. Many of the best paintings are on the ceilings. No two temples are alike, although the basic themes animating their construction all flow from the single impetus of the Great Buddha.

Most temples charge about 50 cents admission and permit photographs except of certain special objects. Thus temple visiting is a fascinating and inexpensive experience for visitors to Korea. Within the temple, the visitor passes through a gate called *Sachonwang* (Four Heavenly Kings) representing mythical rulers of kingdoms in the four corners of the universe. The main halls of the temple are the *Taeung-jon*, containing the Sokkamoni or Historic Buddha, and the *Kuknak-jon*, where the Amitabul, Buddha of the Western Paradise, resides. The Sokkamoni and Amita are the two most popular Buddha deities in Korea today. Attendants on each side are not Buddhas but Bodhisattvas attending the central Buddha. The Goddess of Mercy is the most popular Bodhisattva in Korea. In the *Myongbu-jon* (Judgment Hall) is the Bodhisattva who has the keys to paradise. Beautiful temples are found in Seoul, in other Korean cities, and nestled amid gorgeous mountain scenery throughout the countryside.

**Buddha's Birthday.** This national holiday falls in late April or early May, according to the lunar calendar. In Seoul at dusk a seven-kilometer-long parade begins at Yoi-do Plaza and ends downtown (newspapers give the parade route). A huge holiday crowd joins with hundreds of thousands of faithful carrying lighted lanterns along the parade route. All of the country's 2,000 temples are decorated with special paper lanterns of various shapes. Devotees purchase or make their own lanterns, inscribe them with their own or relatives names, and light them for good fortune during the coming year.

**List of Temples.** Eighteen of Korea's most beautiful and interesting temples are listed here. Each has its particular charm;

*Popchusa Temple: In Mt. Songnisan National Park, Popchusa Temple is famous for its Palsangjŏn Pavilion, a five-story wooden pagoda, and its statue of Buddha which stands 33 meters high*

most are open seven days a week from dawn to after dusk. Seoul and vicinity (*sa* is Korean for temple): Chogye-sa, Pongwon-sa, Yongju-sa; Pusan and Kyongju: Pomo-sa, Pulguk-sa, Sokkuram, Tongdo-sa; Central Region and Taegu vicinity: Haein-sa, Popchu-sa, Chikji-sa; Southwest Region: Kumsan-sa, Songgwang-sa; East Coast and Sorak area: Shinhung-sa, Woljong-sa; other sites: Pusok-sa, Naksan-sa, Hwaom-sa, Miruk-saji.

## MUSEUMS TO VISIT IN KOREA

Government-supported archeological excavations have produced vast quantities of artifacts, which can be enjoyed in various national, municipal, and private museums throughout Korea. Preservation of Korea's historic treasures and cultural legacy is a paramount national concern; ancient art, archeology, and folk culture are principal objects of research and display. The government-sponsored National Museum of Korea maintains the largest museum in Seoul and has branches in Kyongju, Kwangju, Puyo, Kongju, Chinju, Pusan, and Inchon. In addition to the national museums, there are municipal museums, over 30 university museums, and several important private collections. (See Interesting Sites section for each city.)

# MAJOR MUSEUMS OF KOREA

**National Museums**

| | |
|---|---|
| National Museum | (02) 720-2536 |
| National Folklore Museum | (02) 720-3137 |
| Modern Art Museum | (02) 503-7744 |
| Kyongju Museum | (0561) 2-5193 |
| Kwangju Museum | (062) 55-7111 |
| Chinju Museum | (0591) 42-5950 |
| Puyo Museum | (0463) 2-2011 |
| Kongju Museum | (0416) 2-2205 |

**Other Museums in Seoul**

| | |
|---|---|
| Gangsong Art Museum | (02) 762-0442 |
| Sungam Archives of Classical Literature | (02) 736-5151 |
| Korean Christian Museum | (02) 814-4491 |
| Suk Joo-sun Memorial Museum of Korean Folk Art | (02) 797-0581 |
| Museum of Korean Embroidery | (02) 269-7441 |
| Handok Medico-Pharma Museum | (02) 433-0151 |

| | |
|---|---|
| Korea Univ. Museum | (02) 94-4381 |
| Seoul Nat'l Univ. Museum | (02) 877-5693 |
| Ewha Woman's Univ. Museum | (02) 362-6151 |
| Sejong Univ. Museum | (02) 467-1701 |
| Yonsei Univ. Museum | (02) 392-0131 |
| Dongguk Univ. Museum | (02) 267-8131 |
| Sungkyunkwan Univ. Museum | (02) 762-5021 |

**Museums Outside of Seoul**

| | |
|---|---|
| Hoam Museum | (02) 234-6171 |
| Emileh Museum | (0433) 2-2955 |
| Onyang Folk Museum | (0418) 42-6001 |
| Cheju Folklore Museum | (0641) 22-1976 |
| Cheju Folklore and Natural History Museum | (064) 22-2465 |
| Pusan Municipal Museum | (051) 624-6341 |

*Seoul Olympics Complex*

# OTHER INTERESTING TOURS IN KOREA

**Resorts.** In order to encourage visitors to stay longer than the average five to six days, the Korea National Tourism Corporation has been creating resort facilities in many areas. It has promoted the construction of deluxe complexes for recreation, pursued conservation projects to preserve areas of great natural beauty, and developed international interest in Korea as a tourism destination. The KNTC has developed the Kyongju Pomun Tourist Resort Complex and Cheju Island, especially Chungmun, as international resort centers; other famous places are Hallyosudo Marine Resort and the Honam Resort Complex (Puyo area).

**National Parks.** There are 17 national parks in magnificent mountain regions all over the country; within their boundaries are many temples set in beautiful surroundings. The parks are managed by the government, and facilities, such as hotels, spas, and restaurants, are run on a concession basis. The most famous parks are Mt. Sorak, Mt. Pukhan, Mt. Songni, Mt. Kaya, Mt. Halla (Cheju Island), and Hallyo Waterway National Park. The Korean people especially enjoy the outdoors, with a spiritual relationship with many forms of nature—hence the special attention given to protecting places of natural beauty.

**Hot Springs.** Frequently used as health and recuperation resorts, there are 16 hot springs in Korea. Famous hot springs resorts are Paekam, Togo, Yusong, Onyang, Tongnae, Suanbo, and Pugok. Suanbo and Pugok are renowned as family swimming and entertainment complexes as well as for their hot springs facilities.

**Beaches.** The west coast is best for salt-water swimming, but the south and east coasts also have excellent beaches. West coast beaches are: Mallipo, at the western tip of Chungchong South Pronvince; Taechon, on the highway west of Puyo; and Pyonsan, northwest of Chongju. South coast beaches include: Haeundae, northeast of Pusan and probably the best-developed beach-resort area in Korea; and Namildae, on Namhae Island at the western end of the Hallyo Waterway. East coast beaches of note are: Pohang, a protected harbor; Kyongpo-dae, north of Kangnung; and Naksan, south of Sokcho.

**Winter Sports.** New ski resorts developed in the northeastern region of Korea provide excellent ski slopes, chair lifts, instructors, and equipment rental services. The best known is Dragon Valley Ski Resort, which lies just off the Suwon-Kangnung Expressway on the way to the Mt. Odae-Mt. Sorak area, an express bus route.

There is an excellent ski resort in the Seoul area, at Yongin Familyland, and another north of Seoul off the highway to Lake Chungpyung. Ice skating is very popular, but there are few indoor rinks. In winter, outdoor skating facilities are available all over the country.

# INTERNATIONAL CONVENTIONS

In addition to hosting the 1986 Asian Games and the 1988 Olympics, Korea has been selected as the site of several major international conventions in the late 1980s. In 1987, the 13th conference of the World Peace Through World Law Center met in Seoul, with 5,000 lawyers from 150 countries, including Eastern Bloc states, in attendance. The 50th annual congress of International P.E.N. (poets, playwriters, essayists, editors and novelists) convened in Seoul in 1988, with some 10,000 worldwide members in attendance.

In 1991, the Boy Scouts of Korea will host the 17th World Scout Jamboree. More than 35,000 scouts from over 100 countries are expected to participate in the nine-day festival of scouting. The jamboree will be held at an ideal location between famous Mt. Sorak and the eastern seacoast. Korea is actively inviting many groups to plan meetings in its cities and resort areas, offering the comforts of modern facilities and the delights of a unique traditional culture.

*Kimpo International Airport, Seoul*

# Korea Travel for
# Overseas Koreans

The Republic of Korea is seeking to strengthen bonds that link it with the more than a half million Koreans living overseas. Persons of Korean origin who reside abroad are accorded a special status and welcome as visitors to Korea. The government encourages their contacts with relatives in Korea. Recently, growing numbers of overseas Koreans have been establishing commercial relationships in Korea. Overseas Koreans may participate in any tour program, but there are special travel options available to them. Longterm visas will be granted to individuals or small family groups wishing to visit relatives in Korea. Within the country, overseas Koreans are usually accommodated at hotels that are excellent but somewhat simpler than the tourist hotels and charge much lower rates; they also offer "authentic" Korean cuisine. Travel agencies in the United States and throughout the world offer tour packages for overseas Koreans; assistance is also offered by the Korea National Tourism Corporation (KNTC), the Korea Trading Promotion Corporation, Korean embassies, and Korean consulates.

**Visiting Relatives in Korea.** For the overseas Korean, the reunion with long unseen relatives is a most joyous experience. It is exciting, also, for the visitor to travel to his or her birthplace or ancestral home. In order to take advantage of the brief time, many visitors arrange for relatives to accompany them on tours to places

*Yuch-nori, New Year's Day four-stick game*

of special interest to both parties, enhancing the enjoyment of all concerned.

**Gifts for Relatives.** Although Korea manufactures many Western goods now, there are still many items that are rare and expensive in Korea that make welcome gifts; among these are Western cosmetics, coffee, liquor, and household items. Books and other learning materials are especially appreciated by students and teachers.

# U.S. MILITARY SERVICE MEMBERS IN KOREA

Since the end of World War II, millions of Americans have served with the U.S. armed services in Korea. Today a strong bond of friendship exists between Korea and the United States, and a posting to Korea can be the beginning of a fascinating experience for those members of the U.S. military service who are adventurous enough to explore this exciting country and partake of its rich and historic culture. Korea has all the ingredients for a most interesting overseas tour: ancient cultural treasures, breathtaking natural beauty, the delights of a modern city, and a warm atmosphere of friendship with American service members stationed far from home.

The majority of the 40,000 military personnel of all services stationed with the U.S. Forces in Korea are on one-year individually sponsored tours known as remote or "hardship" tours. However, this is a misnomer: those who can appreciate the exotic will enjoy the differences and have an unforgettable experience. There also are some 3,500 civilian and military jobs in Korea that are designated as command-sponsored, two-year tours. These service members are authorized to bring their families to Korea at American government expense, and they are eligible for shipment of some household goods, for schooling for their children, for medical care, and for use of exchanges and commissaries.

Lifestyles and accommodations vary within and among Seoul, Osan, Taegu, Pusan, and Chinhae, where command-sponsored families make their homes. Yongsan in Seoul has the largest concentration of command-sponsored families and the most extensive facilities and activities. This busy post is headquarters for the United Nations Command, the Combined Forces Command, the U.S. Forces Korea, and the Eighth U.S. Army. It also is a high visibility area, with a steady stream of visiting VIPs from Washington. Department of Defense schools are located on the post, and medical care, including dependent dental care, is provided at the U.S. Army Community Hospital. The commissary, with some 4,000 items, and the Korea Area Exchange, with the usual concessions, are well-stocked. Volunteer, religious, and recreational activities (18-hole golf course along with other activities) at Yongsan are extensive.

Seoul beckons service members to explore ancient palaces and gardens that sit in the shadows of tall downtown office buildings, to browse in tiny shops or in the mammoth markets of East Gate and South Gate, to dine on *pulgogi* (charcoal-grilled marinated beef slices) in a traditional Korean-style restaurant or lunch in a luxurious Western-style hotel overlooking the city and surrounding mountains. For daytime excursions, there are museums filled with Korean art and historic treasures. After dark, nightclubs, discos, and casinos offer their own brand of excitement.

Outside of Seoul, too, lie wonders—from the sobering reality of Panmunjom to Kyongju, the "museum without walls." From Pusan it is an easy flight or cruise to Cheju Island, a semitropical paradise of waterfalls, exotic lava formations, and lovely beaches. Golf and mountain-climbing are popular activities on the island. Many of the 2,000 Buddhist temples in Korea dot the scenic mountainous areas of the country's 15 national parks, and others are conveniently located in the cities.

Another "silver lining" is Korea's position as a travel hub to the Orient. It is only two hours to Tokyo, and Hong Kong is just four hours away. The People's Republic of China, the Philippines, and other interesting destinations are also accessible. Community Family, Soldier Support Command–Korea (CFSSCK) Tour and Travel Centers offers tours to a variety of exotic places at reasonable prices.

There are many interracial marriages in Korea, with 3,000 new unions annually. In Hannam Village, a U.S. military housing area in Seoul for enlisted personnel and junior officers, 80 percent of the marriages are interracial, predominantly Korean-American. Interracial dating and marriages occur throughout the ranks, including field grade officers. In addition to the approximately 30,000 service members and families stationed in Seoul, there are about 5,000 at the headquarters of the 19th Support Command in Taegu; Osan is headquarters for the 314th Air Division, with 3,600 military personnel and 800 command-sponsored dependents; in Pusan,

Korea's second-largest city and largest seaport, there are 425 command-sponsored dependents in 116 family quarters at Hialeah Compound; and there are 32 enlisted families and nine officer families at Chinhae, famous for its springtime cherry blossoms.

Shopping is one of the treats of living in Korea. One of the best areas is Itaewon, convenient to the Eighth Army's Yongsan Compound in Seoul and worth a trip to Seoul from other locales. Also delightful for service families is the possibility of having a maid for around $10 a day, and for about twice that a Korean "sew lady" will make outfits from silks and other Korean fabrics at bargain prices. The U.S. military's Naija Hotel, Hamilton Hotel, and Seoul Garden Hotel have plenty of live music, dancers, and reputable restaurants (tel. 7904-8033).

The Confucian- and Buddhist-based Korean society has unique customs and ways of doing things that can be bewildering for overseas visitors. What the visitor takes for granted in his own country as being the right way is really just one of many ways to live and act. Although South Korea has clearly progressed into the modern and Western era, it still has not adapted to do-it-right-now promptness in many aspects. Since patience is a virtue, the visitor, to avoid frustration, should take time to enjoy the slow pace.

In Korea, using titles—Mr., Mrs., or Miss—is a tradition showing respect; first names are used only among very close friends. In public, men and women do not touch, but it is common for two young women to hold hands. Bear in mind that Koreans do mind having their pictures taken by outsiders.

When a new Korean friend invites you to his home, it is proper to arrive promptly, shake hands with the host, and bow slightly to the hostess. Upon entering just about any Korean dwelling (including temples, and dining areas of restaurants with the Korean-style floor, *ondol*), the visitor is expected to remove his shoes. The visitor brings a small gift that is wrapped; a host does not open it until after the guest's departure. It is impolite to cross one's legs on a sofa or chair if an elder is present.

Koreans are generally neat and meticulous in their dress; the visitor should dress comfortably, but neatly—touring off base in tattered blue jeans, tank tops, cutoffs, shorts, sundresses or skimpy clothes may offend Koreans.

While dining with a Korean, start eating after the host begins, and leave one piece of food on the serving plate. When served, grasp a cup or glass with both hands and pass and refill glasses using the right hand, supported at the wrist by the left. Tipping is not traditional.

The "Reunion in Korea" program, offered by the Korea National Tourism Corporation in gratitude for U.S. Forces in Korea whose support has helped ensure the security of Korea, is a wonderful opportunity for active-duty military personnel and Department of Defense civilian employees to bring family members to Korea at low cost. The program includes round-trip airfare and all costs for first-class hotels, regular meals, tours, and transportation within Korea for four nights and five days. After the five-day program of tours, dinner parties, entertainment, and a visit to Panmunjom, the visitors can remain up to 58 days at their own expense. Detailed information can be obtained at the tourism offices in U.S. military recreation centers in Korea or at Moyer Recreation Center at Yongsan in Seoul (7904-7959).

Long ago, Korea's strict isolation from the rest of the world earned it the name of "The Hermit Kingdom." Times have changed, however, and Korea now welcomes overseas visitors. There are many organizations that provide assistance to not only overseas tourists but also American service men and women. One should take advantage of the organizations that help visitors understand Korean culture better and make them feel more at home. Detailed information can be obtained at the CFSSCK Tour and Travel Centers (TTC) throughout Korea. The Yongsan TTC, in Seoul, is located on main post in building #2259 just inside the Main Gate (#5). The Reunion telephone number at Yongsan TTC is 7913-3474 when dialed from a Korean telephone located off-post. For further information on TTC programs call 7913-4130/1 or write to Yongsan TTC, CFSSA-III, CRD, APO San Francisco 96301-0074.

For those who come to Korea expecting it to be excitingly different, their tour of duty will be the opportunity of a lifetime, for them and for members of their families as well.

# Chapter VII
# THE KOREA TOUR: CITIES AND SITES

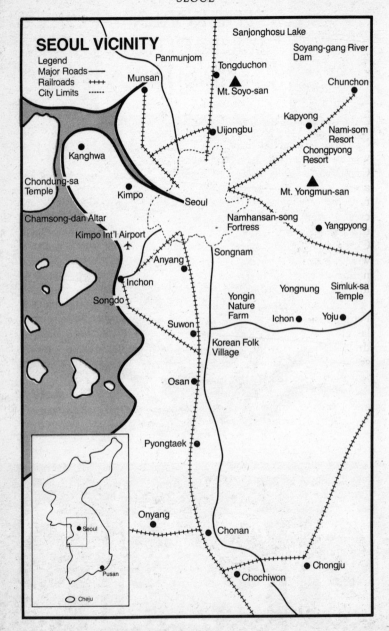

# SEOUL VICINITY

**Legend**
Major Roads ———
Railroads ++++
City Limits ·······

Sanjonghosu Lake

Soyang-gang River Dam

Panmunjom

Munsan

Tongduchon

Mt. Soyo-san

Chunchon

Kapyong

Uijongbu

Nami-som Resort

Kanghwa

Chongpyong Resort

Chondung-sa Temple

Kimpo

Seoul

Mt. Yongmun-san

Chamsong-dan Altar

Namhansan-song Fortress

Yangpyong

Kimpo Int'l Airport

Anyang

Songnam

Inchon

Yongnung

Simluk-sa Temple

Songdo

Yongin Nature Farm

Ichon

Yoju

Suwon

Korean Folk Village

Osan

Pyongtaek

Onyang

Chonan

Seoul

Pusan

Chongju

Chochiwon

Cheju

# 서울
# **Seoul**

## CENTRAL REGION

SEOUL, the capital of the rapidly developing Republic of Korea, was an apt site for the 10th Asian Games in 1986 and the 24th Olympiad in 1988. Like the Olympics, Seoul is both an ancient and a modern phenomenon, steeped in tradition and at the same time full of vitality. With its proud past and ambitious future, the capital offers the visitor some startling and wonderful contrasts of the ancient and the modern. Within living memory, the "Phoenix City of the Orient" has literally risen from its own ashes. Seoul, which means "the capital" in Korean, was first chosen as the nation's capital in the fourteenth century; for five centuries now it has been the center of national life.

Seoul is situated approximately at the center of the Korean Peninsula, near the western coast, in the Han River Valley. The largest city in Korea, it is endowed with great natural beauty, with the lofty peaks of the Bukhan Mountains to the north and the green slopes of Nam-san to the south. The old city of Seoul lies within this natural basin; the modern city spills out far beyond the valley. The Han River winds through the city, spanned by many bridges, including a modern steel bridge over which pass trains, electric trolleys, and a constant procession of automobiles.

Seoul is a world in itself. Many joys of discovery await the visitor. In places, the city sparkles with the glass, steel, and polished stone of the modern high rise. Elsewhere, it retains the quaintness and charm of another era. One of Seoul's most interesting aspects for tourists is this contrast of old and new. Men and women in traditional dress mix with those in the latest Western styles. Ancient royal palaces sit serenely next to bustling luxury tourist hotels and elegant new office buildings. Ancient gates to the city remind commuters of their history. Within Seoul are myriad tiny lanes lined with high stone walls, behind which traditional Korean houses with tilted-tip tiled roofs are situated. Above and beyond the ancient capital are broad avenues jammed with Korean-made cars, smart shops and stores, new subway lines and expressways, huge skyscrapers, the Capitol and National Assembly buildings—all proclaiming that Seoul is the center of a modern republic. For

*Statuary guarding Kwaenung Tomb*

Seoul is not only the political, administrative, financial and cultural heart of the Republic of Korea; it also is Korea's greatest repository of monuments and treasures of the Choson (Yi) dynasty era.

The downtown core is broadly demarcated by the course of the old city wall. Proud of their heritage, Koreans have carefully preserved Seoul's architectural masterpieces and landmarks. Sections of the wall and the gates that remain have been restored to their original magnificence. Most famous and visible are South Gate and East Gate, both officially designated national treasures. Within this boundary are the great palaces and gardens, with their splendid throne halls and exquisite pavilions set in lovely lotus ponds. While honoring its legacy, Seoul is nevertheless in a constant state of change, booming with the construction of offices and housing, extending transportation facilities, and creating recreational facilities. The city's newest and busiest area of development is south of the Han River, where most of the venues of the Asian and Olympic Games are located.

The major gateway to Korea, Seoul is a good starting point for the tourist. An extensive network of urban trains, subways, buses, and taxi services crisscrosses the city, and Seoul is the hub of the nationwide transportation system.

*Night View of Seoul: Namdaemun (South Gate), Korea's foremost national treasure*

Seoul boasts a large number of international luxury hotels which meet U.S. and European standards; budget watchers may enjoy the homey hospitality of a *yogwan*, the traditional Korean inn.

All of Seoul's deluxe hotels have quality restaurants; some have pure Korean, Japanese, and Chinese restaurants. Authentic international cuisines are also available.

The tourist can enjoy music and dancing to local and foreign bands at nightclubs in most of Seoul's major hotels. A more elegant and expensive evening can be had in a theater restaurant where, for a fixed price, one can have dinner and drinks while enjoying an elaborate musical show.

Seoul after dark is transformed by colorful neon lights. The visitor can enjoy native drinks, *makkolly* or Korean beer, and modern revues and discotheques. Museums and art galleries are scattered around the city, and there are innumerable entertainment facilities. Shopping is a delight: Seoul has many duty-free shops offering tax-free luxury items from foreign countries. Indeed, Seoul has something for everyone.

## CLIMATE

Seoul's weather reflects the fact that it lies along the Han River in an irregularly shaped valley encircled by mountains to the north, east, and west, plus Nam-san, a high, wooded hill, to the south. There are four distinct seasons, of about equal length. Except for a rainy season of approximately a month beginning sometime around the end of June or beginning of July, the weather is generally clear with lots of sunshine.

The annual range of temperature is quite wide in Seoul. The coldest month, January, has a mean temperature of 23°F (−5°C), and the warmest month, August, has a mean of 78°F (25°C). Annual precipitation is about 50 inches, mainly in summer. Seoul's winters are normally quite mild, with some cold spells. Temperatures moderate in March and April, and in May and June the trees and gardens burst into full bloom. Despite summer rains, frequent winds, and the wide range of temperatures, Seoul enjoys blue skies during much of the year. Colorful and comfortable, spring and autumn are ideal times to visit.

## SEOUL'S POPULATION

The industrialization that has made Seoul a city full of energy and surprises, the showcase of Korea's economic development, has attracted so many people that the population now exceeds 10 million, which makes Seoul the world's fourth largest city, after Tokyo, Shanghai, and Mexico City. Within its 650 square kilometers (102 square miles) are 21.5 million households, 20 domestic and 70 foreign banks, 270 kindergartens, 300 primary schools, 200 high schools, and 80 colleges and universities. In addition to 300,000 private cars and taxis, there are nearly 20,000 buses and 10,000 trucks registered with the municipal government, and subway lines run for 200 kilometers. The combination of economic progress and expanding rapid transit facilities has contributed to the high degree of concentration of population in Seoul, one of the world's fastest-growing capitals.

Many facets of life in Seoul still reflect traditional influences. In clothing, in furnishings, and in the celebrations on festive occasions, the past is revived and enjoyed. Various annual events promote the revival of folk games and traditional sports. The people of Seoul today look back fondly to the life of their ancestors and appreciate the wisdom and vitality of their forebears.

The citizens of Seoul are hardworking, but they also know how to enjoy life. To earn a living and to participate in leisure activities, the residents of Seoul work in thousands of factories, government and business offices, educational institutions, stores, hotels, medical centers, and transportation systems. The children, too, work hard in school and play hard at sports. Families often are seen enjoying outings together on weekends.

An increasing number of people are moving to Kangnam-ku, Kangdong-ku, Kangso-ku, and Kuro-ku, which are located in the part of Seoul south of the Han River.

*Shopping at It'aewon, just minutes from downtown Seoul*

## LIVING STANDARDS

Living standards of Seoul residents have risen dramatically in the 1980s, with yearly improvements in housing, transportation, clothing, food distribution, and consumer products. Seoul now has one of the highest standards of living in Asia.

Pollution is a problem, as it is in most large cities, mainly owing to coal residues from home heating and to emissions from cars, buses, and trucks. Many modern factories have been built in the southern suburbs to avoid adding industrial fumes to the prevailing dust-bearing northwesterly winds. The visitor will be impressed by the cleanliness of the city.

Once the seat of kings, Seoul now is the hub of the entire nation. Historically, the capital has been the center for educational opportunities and professional advancement, and living in Seoul still engenders personal prestige. For centuries, Seoul has attracted Koreans from all over the country.

The visitor will also be fascinated by the city's vitality. As a center of commerce, industry, and business as well as government, Seoul has come to symbolize the progressive outlook of a people determined to build a better life and a harmonious urban community. The strength of this determination is reflected in the vigorous building activity going on all over town. It is evident, too, in the long hours the people work. Even today the typical office worker labors from 8:00 a.m. until whenever the boss goes home, perhaps

7:00 p.m., and a half day on Saturday. But whereas it used to require such effort just to survive, now it is rewarded with an ever rising standard of living. Success is visible in the faces of the people on the streets of Seoul. More than ever, they are open, frank, earthy, assertive, and always friendly to visitors.

Departing tourists will want to say with the poet:

"The city where dreams overflow into every street,
Oh, beautiful city of Seoul, I will love thee forever."

## HISTORY

The advantageous position of Seoul at the crossroads of main trade routes contributed to its early development as a trading center. It also became a fortress for the kings of the Yi dynasty because the fertile valley of the Han River was protected by surrounding mountains. Seoul has a rich historical heritage, which is evidenced by the palaces, shrines, and monuments still standing all over the city.

Seoul was made the capital of Korea in 1394 by King Taejo, founder of the Yi dynasty, and it remained the capital of the kingdom for over five centuries. South Gate and the principal palace buildings were built during the first 200 years of the Yi dynasty. The starkness and strength suggested by the setting of the city, protected by a series of soaring granite hills, seem reflected in the harshness of its history, a story of survival against foreign encroachments. In 1592 Seoul was devastated by a Japanese invasion. It was twice occupied by Manchu armies, in 1627 and 1636.

In modern times, too, Seoul has been the target of foreign powers' efforts to dominate Korea. With the arrival of the Western powers in East Asia in the late nineteenth century, the Japanese hastened to penetrate the Yi dynasty's isolation. In Seoul, the king signed treaties opening the Hermit Kingdom to the United States, Britain, Russia, Italy, and other countries. When Queen Min was assassinated by the Japanese in 1895, the Korean court in Seoul invited China to dispatch troops to quell the Tongkak Rebellion; this gave Japan a pretext to dispatch troops to Korea, which became a major point of contention in the Sino-Japanese War of 1894-95. After the Japanese victory over China, the strategic rivalry between Japan and Russia in Korea exploded in the Russo-Japanese War of 1904–05. The war ended in Japanese victory and the establishment of a protectorate over Korea, which in turn led to Japanese annexation in 1910.

Seoul underwent many changes after the opening of Korea to the West in the 1870s and during the period of Japanese occupation from 1910 to 1945. When U.S. forces landed in Korea following the surrender of Japan at the end of World War II, the city became their headquarters. In 1948 Seoul became the capital of the newly proclaimed Republic of Korea, although national unity had not been achieved. After the Second World War, a joint U.S.-Soviet commission met in Seoul to organize a single Korean provisional democratic government under a trusteeship proposal, but their intermittent meetings during 1946-47 did not produce an agreement.

Seoul was severely damaged during the Korean War of 1950-53, changing hands four times. The tragic fratricidal conflict wreaked untold damage on both zones of the nation and separated many families and friends. But as the capital of the Republic of Korea, Seoul regained its position as a political, economic, and cultural center and has now become one of the world's fastest growing cities.

Aware that Korea still can be considered a pawn of the superpowers and appalled at the extent of psychological damage inflicted by an ideologically divided world, the government and people in Seoul press forward with modernization and look toward the restoration of national unity. The 1950s were marked by war, destruction, and terrible human suffering; the 1960s call to mind the student uprisings toppling dictator Syngman Rhee and the military coup ushering in General Park Chunghee's 18-year rule. During the 1970s and 1980s, however, Seoul has become a major business and tourism destination and the site of increasing foreign investment. Truly it deserves the title of "Phoenix City of the Orient."

## ECONOMY AND CULTURE

Rising from total devastation after the war, Seoul has undergone two decades of staggering development to become a stunning example of resurrection after destruction. Tall buildings mark the skyline, and busy downtown areas overflow with life. Despite its size and rapid rate of growth, Seoul conveys the impression of being a manageable and safe city.

Sparkling in places like a modern architectural jewel, Seoul retains quaint charm in others. Noisy peddlers hawking their wares and porters struggling under enormous burdens along a maze of alleyways are giving way to urban workers staffing factories and offices. Old buildings are constantly being razed to make way for glass and concrete modernity. Many shops and department stores supply everything from the latest electronic inventions to daily

*Old and new Seoul: South Gate juxtaposed to Tongbang Insurance Co. Building*

necessities. Nightclubs and theaters provide a variety of entertainment; restaurants of all kinds serve foods from the exotic to the ordinary. Business flourishes, schools ring with the sounds of children, construction goes on day and night in this ever-changing, ever-active city. High-rise buildings, broad avenues, and busy traffic attest to Seoul's cosmopolitanism, but there are many carefully preserved reminders of a stately and glorious past.

The urban dwellers of Seoul and of other bustling Korean cities, along with the agricultural population, are the backbone of national growth. The hurrying pedestrians who overflow the sidewalks on their way to work embody dedication to hard work for the sake of the nation, but above all for the bright smiles of the children. For Korea is a country where strong bonds between youngsters and parents are the greatest source of happiness.

Seoul, an expression of national hopes, is blossoming in every direction. The towering 63-story Daehan Life Insurance Building, new subway lines, and the development of recreational park space along the Han River are among the most impressive projects in Seoul's modernization. On Yoi-do, a man-made island in the Han

*Sejong Cultural Center*

River often referred to as the "Manhattan of Seoul," office buildings and huge apartment complexes are springing up. Now known as a prestigious business address and an exclusive residential area, it is fast taking on a new role by night as a center of chic nightclubs and dining establishments. Kangnam and Yongdong are rapidly growing business-residential areas south of the Han River, not far from the principal venues of the Asian and Olympic Games.

This ancient Phoenix City, reborn from its ashes as a modern metropolis, was proud to host the 1988 Summer Olympic games. A new Olympic village to house the athletes, officials, and press during the games was erected in one corner of the city. Sports facilities all over the city were prepared for the Asian Games and the Olympics.

As the cultural center of the nation, Seoul offers a variety of symphony concerts, operas, and recitals by local and visiting musicians in its many theaters. A city of universities, it is the country's intellectual center, with some 80 universities, colleges, and institutes. Perhaps 80 percent of Korea's working writers, painters, and musicians are concentrated in the capital city. With more than 20,000 students, Ewha Women's University, founded by American missionaries at the turn of the century, is a favorite with tourists, many of whom purchase excellent replicas of ancient pottery from the ceramics department.

The Sejong Cultural Center along Sejong Boulevard, named

for the king who introduced the Korean alphabet, accommodates 4,000 people. With fine acoustics and a huge pipe organ, it is used mainly for musical performances. Private art galleries in the districts of Insa-dong and Chunghak-dong are constantly exhibiting modern and traditional works. The old Capitol reopened as the main National Museum in July 1986, and the new Seoul Art Center, showcasing 5,000 years of history and culture, opened in 1987. 1987.

With thousands of foreign residents now working in embassies, commercial offices, and news agencies, Seoul inevitably is becoming internationalized. Since the very survival of South Korea depends on a mutual defense treaty with the United States, more than 30,000 American combat troops are stationed in Seoul as well as along the demilitarized zone to ensure national security. American soldiers and diplomats, American and Japanese businessmen and students are a common sight in Seoul, and English and Japanese are widely spoken. In fact, English is spoken in many shops, bars, theaters, and restaurants, as well as by group tour guides. Increasing numbers of residents of Seoul, always willing to help a visitor from overseas, are learning English. Thousands of students who spoke Japanese or English served as volunteers during the Olympic Games.

Since 15 percent of the 42 million South Koreans are Christians, Seoul is dotted with churches of many denominations. Every Sunday the Full Gospel Church, located south of the Han River, attracts tens of thousands who overflow the massive concrete building. The balcony for foreigners features simultaneous translation. Other churches favored by tourists are the Anglican Cathedral, a lovely Italianate structure located on Taepyong-ro near Toksu Palace, and the Catholic Cathedral, an 1890s steepled red brick building located in Myong-dong.

## HIGHLIGHTS
## FOR TRAVELERS

Seoul today is the vibrant modern capital of a developing, industrializing and tourism-oriented country that combines the fascination of the ancient Orient with the luxuries of the late twentieth century. The city skillfully blends the new—national museums, art galleries, high-rises, golf courses, sports stadiums, cinemas, con-

*City Hall Plaza*

cert halls, world-class hotels—with the old—well-preserved ancient palaces and gates, royal tombs, shrines, gardens, pavilions, and fortresses.

Proud of their heritage, the Koreans have restored and preserved Seoul's major architectural treasures and landmarks. The downtown core is broadly demarcated by the old city gates, which have been restored to their original magnificence. Within the area of the old city walls are the major royal palaces and temples; their enclosures provide a temporary haven of peace away from the din and bustle of the capital city. Most of these major sites lie within 30 minutes' walk of the city center. Toksu Palace is just across the street from City Hall; originally a royal villa, it served as the seat of government during the last years of the Yi dynasty. Kyongbok Palace, just behind the Western-style Capitol building at the end of the boulevard leading north from Seoul City Hall Plaza, is the best preserved and most illustrious monument of the Yi dynasty. Adding to Changdok Palace's grandeur is Secret Garden, a 78-acre tree-shaded park filled with ancient pleasure pavilions. On weekends Koreans in colorful national costumes stroll the palace grounds. Nearby are Changgyong Palace Park and Chong-myo Shrine.

Seoul is a relatively compact and attractively situated city. Central Seoul is located in a lowland surrounded by small mountains of about 1,000 feet; the old city was circled by a wall along the ridges of these hills. Main streets and major shopping areas occupy the lower part of the valley. With the growth of the city, construction has spilled out in all directions: toward Yongsan and Yongdung-po to the south, Mia-dong and Suyu-dong to the north, Mapo and Hongje-dong to the west, and Chongnyangni to the east. The present area of Seoul is 613 square kilometers.

Between the mountains and the gates, in the central city, beats the heart of the nation's government, education, business, entertainment, art, industry, transit, and finance. Street patterns in the city center are basically rectangular, but toward the foot of the surrounding hills, topographic irregularities influence the pattern. Outside the basin area, there are 10 radiating streets and three circular ones, connecting the radiating streets. Seoul is divided into districts (ku), which are subdivided into sections (dong); signs mark these areas. The capitol and other government offices are concentrated along Sejong-ro; banks, department stores, insurance companies, other business offices, and hotels along Namdaemun-ro and Taephyong-ro. The area of Chong-ro, Myong-dong, and Ulji-ro constitutes the central business district. Scientific and educational institutions are concentrated in the northeast section, but several—including Seoul National University—are located elsewhere. The southern and eastern sections are composed mainly of residential blocks, where the new and the old intermingle. Many new apartment buildings are in the Kangnam district on the outskirts of the city. Subway construction has followed the city's expansion, making the Seoul subway the seventh longest in the world.

New road signs with pictorial symbols make it easier for visitors to find their way. There are several romanizations of the Korean alphabet, with such slight differences between the sounds represented by K and G, P and B, T and D that they are often interchangeable. The same is true of ro and no indicating street, and of Lee and Yi as spellings of the name of the last dynasty. Owners of major buildings are being urged to post building names in English as well as Korean. Thus, Seoul is no longer a confusing city to newcomers; getting around just requires a map and a good guidebook.

As visitors appreciate the comfort and cleanliness of the hotels, the courteous efficiency of service personnel, the delicious meals and fine beverages of the excellent restaurants, the easy informality of people in the streets, they will want to see and learn more about the city. Indeed, Seoul is not only simultaneously exotic, clean, and safe, but also in constant motion, ceaselessly stimulating visitors from abroad to move about, see, buy, eat, and enjoy.

## SIGHTSEEING

Visitors can choose from among many well-planned guided tours of Seoul and its environs, or sightsee on their own. The tours are best for those who wish to see as many of the major attractions as possible in a limited time, who prefer to have explanations in their own language, and who appreciate having all the details of transportation and entry fees taken care of for them. The more adventurous may prefer the freedom to choose their itinerary and pace, allowing time to enjoy the unexpected pleasures which arise, instead of following a fixed schedule. Excellent maps are available, streets and subways are clearly marked and diagrammed, and Koreans are always ready to give directions or other help to a foreign guest.

**Guided Tours.** Below is a list of the sightseeing bus tours operated by Global Tours and the Korea Travel Bureau (KTB). They maintain information booths in major hotel lobbies or can be reached by telephone (Global Tours: 777-9921; KTB: 585-1191). Similar tours are available through other travel agencies, whose addresses and telephone numbers can be obtained from the Korea Tourist Association by writing or telephoning (12th floor, KNTC Building, 10 Ta-dong, Chung-ku, Seoul; tel. 757-0086). Tour fees are reasonable and subject, of course, to slight change over time or with variations in itinerary.

**Seoul Morning Tours**
■ Changdok Palace — Piwon — Tongdae-mun Market — Mt. Namsan (KTB, 10-1)
■ Kyongbok Palace — National Museum/Folklore Museum — Pugak Skyway — Tongdae-mun Market (Global, 9:30-1)

**Seoul Afternoon Tours**
■ Kyongbok Palace — National Museum/Folklore Museum — Chogye Temple — Pugak Skyway (KTB, 2-5)
■ Nam-san — Tongdae-mun Market — Changdok Palace — Piwon (Global, 2-5)

**Seoul Night Tours**
■ Nam-san/Seoul Tower — Korea House (Korean dinner, folk dance and music) (KTB, 6-10; Global, 5:30-10)
■ Riverside Motorway — Casino-Kayakum Theater Restaurant (KTB, 6-10; Global, 6:30-10:30)
■ Namsan — *yangban* entertainment with dinner (KTB, 6-10)

**Folk Village Tours**
- Seoul-Suwonsong — Folk Village — Itaewon — Seoul (KTB, 10:30-4:30)
- Seoul — Folk Village — Seoul (Global, 1:30-6)

**Panmunjom Tours**
- Seoul — Panmunjom (lunch and briefing) — Seoul (KTB, 9-5:30)
- Seoul — Imjin-gak — Seoul (Global, 10-1)

**Seoul City Tour Buses.** Six tours, designed for foreign visitors as well as Koreans, leave from Pagoda Park on regular schedules. For information, call 313-4331/3.

**Half-day Tours**
- Pagoda Park — Kwanghwa Gate — Changdok Palace — Toksu Palace — Namdae-mun — Seoul Tower — Pagoda Park (9 a.m. and 2 p.m.)
- Pagoda Park — National Assembly — Korean Broadcasting System (KBS) — Tongnim-mun — Kyongbok Palace — Pugak Skyway — Pagoda Park (9 a.m. and 2 p.m.)

**Full-day Tours**
- Pagoda Park — National Assembly — KBS — National Cemetery — Seoul Grand Park — Yangjae-dong — Tunnel No. 1 — Pagoda Park (9:30 a.m.)
- Pagoda Park — Pigak — Chonggak — Tongdae-mun — Chamshil — Songnam — Namhansan Fortress — Ichon Ceramic Kilns — Olympic Complex — Seoul Tower — Namdae-mun — Pagoda Park (10 a.m.)
- Pagoda Park — Toksu Palace — Namdae-mun — Seoul Station — Tongdae-mun — Chong-myo — Changdok Palace — Kyongbok Palace — Pagoda Park (9:30 a.m.)
- Pagoda Park — National Assembly — KBS — Chondung-sa — Chojijin (Kanghwa Island) — Pung-mun — Haengjusan Fortress — Songsandae Bridge — Pagoda Park (10 a.m.)

# TOURING SEOUL WITHOUT AN ESCORT

**M**ore adventurous travelers, not content with seeing the city through sealed bus windows and rapid walks around major landmarks, can easily and safely tour Seoul on their own. Much of the city's charm is found in quiet neighborhoods and narrow back streets where tour buses do not usually go, and some will want to linger over treasures in a museum or spend time visualizing palace life in a bygone era. To enhance the enjoyment of Seoul, the visitor, with a city map and the Guidebook in hand, can go exploring. Since the palaces and many museums lie within a compact area around Seoul City Hall and the Capitol Building, it is easy to see them on foot, allowing as much time for browsing as is needed. With the Guidebook, the tourist can work out comfortable daily itineraries and choose whether to walk or to go by public bus, tourist bus, subway, taxi, or rented car. Bicycling along Seoul's more crowded thoroughfares is not recommended.

**Arrival in Seoul.** Most travelers enter Korea at Seoul's Kimpo International Airport. Taxis are available, and buses wait in a stand just outside the airport to take tourists arriving by air to any of the large hotels in Seoul. From the big hotels, the traveler can walk or take a taxi to less expensive ones. It is best to select a hotel in advance and give the name to the bus driver, although it is usually possible to find accommodations in reasonably priced hotels and youth hostels without prior reservations (the peak April-May and September-October seasons being the exceptions).

The airport buses follow one of three routes: (1) Garden Hotel — City Hall — Chong-ro — Children's Park — Sheraton Walker Hill Hotel; (2) Garden Hotel — City Hall — Koreana Hotel — Sejong Cultural Center — Chong-ro — Sheraton Walker Hill Hotel; or (3) Garden Hotel — Seoul Railway Station — Hotel Shilla — Sheraton Walker Hill Hotel. Some hotels run their own buses to and from the airport.

Tourists arriving via Kimhae International Airport in Pusan, or who have taken the Pukwan Ferry from Shimonoseki, Japan, can travel from Pusan to Seoul by express bus or by train, a trip of about 4½ hours. From the Express Bus Terminal in Panpo in southern Seoul or from the Seoul Railway Station just southwest of downtown, the traveler can take a taxi, city bus, or subway to a hotel or other destination.

**Major Attractions.** High on anyone's list are the palaces that housed Yi dynasty royalty for 500 years, for they are truly impressive relics of Seoul's rich cultural heritage. The tourist with limited budget and time can choose among many such interesting places in Seoul.

The palaces (*kung* in Korean) Kyongbok-kung, Changdok-kung, and Toksu-kung, are all well-preserved and are within walking distance of City Hall. The new National Museum in the magnificent former Capitol Building and the National Folklore Museum

Cultural Property Maintenance Office

Folk Museum

Samchong Park

Secret Gardens

Changdok-kung Palace

Kyŏngbok-kung Palace

Hankook Hospital  Hyundai Bldg.

National Museum

French Cultural Center  Japanese

Kwanghwa-mun Gate  New Zealand  Arabic Cultural Center

Sajik Park

New Naija Hotel

Korea Times  Mary's Alley

Japan

Chogye-sa Temple

Sejong Cultural Center  U.S.A.

Italy

Saudi Arabia

Salvation Army Center

Australia

City Bank

Finland

Kyobo Bldg.

Seoul Tourist Hotel

Whashin Dept. Store  YMCA

Paoda Park

Changno St.

Sejong-ro St.

Kwanghwamun Post Office

Seoulin Hotel

Switzerland

Korea General Hospoital

Sweden

MBC

Seoul Red Cross Hospital

Korea Tourist Association

Chŏngdong Methodist Church

Seoul Immigration Office

Koreana Hotel

United Kingdom

Toksu-kung Palace

Supreme Court

New Seoul Hotel

Press Center  KNTC

Canada

Bank of Tokyo

Tourist Information Center

City Hall  Lotte Hotel

President Hotel

Brazil  Chosun Hotel

Seoul Plaza Hotel

KCCI

Midopa Dept. Store

KAL Bldg.

Bank of Korea

Saerona Dept. Store

Germany

South Gate Market

Austria

Samil Bldg.

Chase Manhattan Bank

American Cultural Center

Korea Exchange Bank

YWCA

Seoul Royal Hotel

Lotte Shopping Center

UNESCO  St. Mary's Hospit

Myongdong Catholic Cathed

Cheil Dept. Store

King Sejong Hot

Savoy Hotel

Central Post Office

Shinsegae Dept. Store  Korea Herald  Astoria Ho

Pacific Hotel

France

Tongbang Bldg.

Bank of America

Namdae-mun Gate (Great South Gate)

ICSK

Korea Red Cross

Namsan Tunnel #3

Seoul Hilton Int'l.

Daewoo Center

Seoul Station

Cable Car

Namsan Pa (Seoul Towe

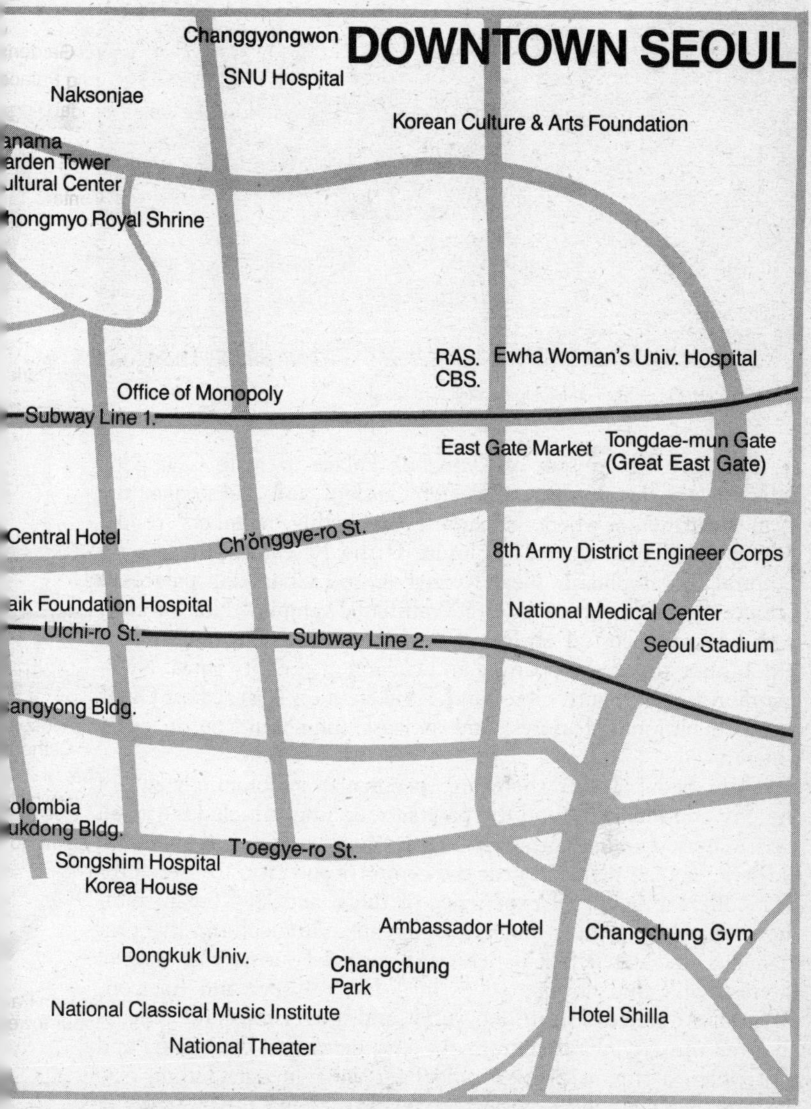

**DOWNTOWN SEOUL**

Changgyongwon

SNU Hospital

Naksonjae

Korean Culture & Arts Foundation

anama
arden Tower
ultural Center

hongmyo Royal Shrine

RAS.    Ewha Woman's Univ. Hospital
CBS.

Office of Monopoly

Subway Line 1.

East Gate Market    Tongdae-mun Gate
(Great East Gate)

Central Hotel

Ch'önggye-ro St.

8th Army District Engineer Corps

aik Foundation Hospital

National Medical Center

Ulchi-ro St.

Subway Line 2.

Seoul Stadium

angyong Bldg.

olombia
ukdong Bldg.

T'oegye-ro St.

Songshim Hospital
Korea House

Ambassador Hotel    Changchung Gym

Dongkuk Univ.

Changchung
Park

National Classical Music Institute

Hotel Shilla

National Theater

*Piwŏn (Secret Garden), Chuhabnu Pavilion, in Seoul*

are both on the grounds of Kyongbok Palace. Within Changdok Palace is the lovely 78-acre Secret Garden, and Naksonjae, the royal apartments where remaining Yi family members reside. Within the Toksu Palace enclosure is the Research Institute for Cultural Development. Near Kyongbok and Changdok palaces is Chogye-sa, headquarters for 1,500 affiliated temples. Not far away is the great ancestral shrine, Chong-myo, and the Great Bell, which once tolled the opening and closing of the city gates. Namdae-mun (Great South Gate) and Tongdae-mun (Great East Gate) are both national treasures, and at least one should be on every itinerary.

From Seoul Tower there are spectacular panoramic views of the city and environs, and the park surrounding it includes a small zoo, a museum, and other points of interest. Korea House, an old-style Korean mansion near the center of the city, to the southwest, offers a delightful experience of the beauty of Korean traditions; an evening there includes a Korean-style meal and live programs of traditional folk dances and music. Tourists with special interests will find antique shops in "Mary's Alley" and Itaewon, Oriental art galleries near Chogye-sa, and universities and colleges all over the city. Farther from the city center to the south, and well worth a trip, is Seoul Grand Park with an outstanding new zoo and Seoul Land (Korea's Disneyland). Many other places of interest are detailed elsewhere in this Guidebook.

**Transportation.** In Seoul, transportation is convenient and inexpensive, whether by subway, bus, or hired car. Traffic is heavy, but much has been done to alleviate congestion. Pedestrian flow is channelled through overpasses and underpasses. Overpasses and elevated expressways make fast arteries from the Han River to the northeastern and eastern parts of the city. These link up with a circumferential highway, which includes the riverside expressways in the south and the skyline drive in the north. Tunnels under Nam-san expedite crosstown traffic.

**Subway.** Seoul has an excellent mass-transit system, with efficient and clean subways and electric trains, which run every five minutes and cost only ₩200 to ₩300 (about 25 to 35 cents), according to distance. They cross and circle the heart of Seoul and run out into the countryside. Signs are diagrammed in color and printed in both *Hangul* and Roman letters.

*Line 1:* Kupabal — downtown — Yangjae
*Line 2:* (circle): Passing through Ulchi-ro to Children's Park, Chamsil (Olympic Sport Complex), Kangnam, Seoul National University, Yongdungpo, Shinchon, and returning to downtown
*Line 3:* Changdon — Chong-ro — Seoul Railway Station — Yongsan
*Line 4:* Changdon — Tongdae-mun — Chungmu-ro — Seoul Railway Station — Sadong
*Surface Electric Train:* Changdong — Songbuk — Chongyangri—downtown—Suwon/Inchon

**Buses.** City buses run from 4 a.m. to midnight, and the fare is ₩130 (about 15 cents), paid in the token box on the bus; there is no transfer ticket system. During rush hour the buses are extremely crowded, as the majority of Seoul's commuters still ride buses; the new subways are relieving the crowding somewhat, but the rush hour should be avoided by the tourist if at all possible. All buses are marked with numbers and signs showing their routes and stops; bus maps are available and helpful. Other passengers, if asked, will invariably assist a visitor from overseas. Six new articulated buses built in Sweden are being placed in service. Each carrying up to 217 passengers, they are expected to further ease the city transportation burden.

**Taxis.** Many people use taxis in Seoul — so many, in fact, which makes it difficult to even catch a cab. Riders must wait for long periods in the street or share the taxi with someone else going in the same direction. Street addresses are not used; rather the traveler tells the driver what area of the city and what prominent intersection or landmark is near the desired destination. Hotel taxi drivers and some others understand English and can be helpful guides. Principal taxi companies are: Daeji (tel. 832-8001); Hansong (tel. 613-7771); and Tongjin (tel. 634-0722). Like all big cities, some taxi drivers are honest, but unfortunately, there are enough crooked ones in Seoul now that tourists must beware. For a complete listing of types of taxis and fares, see section on "Getting Around in Korean Cities." Outlying hotels provide free shuttle services.

**Rent-A-Car.** An international driver's license is required to rent a car; otherwise the procedure is simple. Unless the tourist is a skilled and assertive driver, however, it might be wise to rent a car and driver. Rental fees run from $45 to $60 for 24 hours and an additional $20 per day. Limousine service rates are very reasonable, including a driver and full costs. Hertz has a rental office in the lobby of the Hotel Lotte (752-1851) and the Hotel Shilla (255-4490), and Avis is also in the Lotte (795-0801). Additional offices may be found at the airport and other hotels. Some have self-drive rental cars at $30–$50 for a 12-hour day.

**Travel Away from Seoul.** There are several points of interest for tourists in the vicinity of Seoul. In particular, to the south is the ancient Paldal Castle Gate and the Korean Folk Village near Suwon; to the north, the Panmunjom Armistice Conference Site. These can be reached by regular express buses or sightseeing bus tours. Modern and comfortable express buses also travel between Seoul and other cities, resorts, and tourist areas. Most lines leave from the Yongdong Terminal south of the Han River, about 15 minutes from downtown across the Chamsu Bridge. Departure times are frequent and no reservations are necessary; schedules can be obtained in hotels and from tourist agencies.

Seoul is the hub of six railway lines connecting it with provincial cities and ports, including Inchon and Pusan. Railways are used to transport goods and materials and are also important for passenger travel. Seoul Station (tel. 028-7788), near South Gate, handles 200,000 embarking and disembarking passengers a day. Fast express trains run between Seoul and Pusan, and between Seoul and Kwangju.

Kimpo International Airport, in the western part of Seoul, is also the center of the national airline network. A newly instituted shuttle flight commutes between Seoul and Pusan every hour from 8 a.m. to 7 p.m.; flight time is about one hour, the fare about $35. Korean Air offers regularly scheduled flights between all major cities in South Korea.

# ROYAL PALACES AND CITY GATES

S eoul is a city of royal palaces and historic gates. These major attractions provide glimpses into the traditional Korean culture and the 500-year history of the Yi dynasty. They are Korea's most imposing architectual masterpieces.

## CITY GATES

The old city of Seoul was protected by walls winding along the mountains that surround it; vestiges of the stonework can still be seen in several places. Four massive gates once provided access to the walled city. Most famous of these architectural classics and designated National Treasure No. 1 is Namdae-mun (Great South Gate), which stands near Seoul Station. High in the center of a busy traffic rotary close to Seoul Stadium is Tongdae-mun (Great East Gate). In the vicinity of both of these monuments are Seoul's huge public markets. A beautiful smaller gate can be found near the Chosun Hotel. Called "Ninth Gate," also the name of the hotel's French restaurant, it stands now as the focal point of a charming garden.

**The Great Bell.** For centuries the gates of the city were opened at sunrise and closed at sundown to the tolling of an enormous bell. Dating from 1468, the 12-foot-high Great Bell can be seen in Poshin Pavilion on Chong-ro (Bell Avenue), near Hwashin Department Store.

## ROYAL PALACES

Four of the five magnificent palaces that graced the city during the Yi dynasty remain and are open to visitors. Just west of City Hall Plaza is Toksu-kung (Toksu Palace), celebrated for its traditional architecture and the National Museum of Modern Art. To the north is Kyongbok-kung (Kyongbok Palace); within its grounds are the magnificent Western-style Capitol Building, the National Museum, and the National Folklore Museum. Directly to the east

*Outdoor Mask Dance performance, Toksu Palace, Seoul*

is Changdok-kung (Changdok Palace), with its exquisitely landscaped Secret Garden (Piwon) and royal apartments. Adjoining the palace wall on the east is Changgyong-won (Changgyong Palace Park), the entrance to which is opposite Seoul National University Hospital on Changgyong-ro.

Korean palaces were built near the center of the capital city, protected and beautifully framed by the semicircle of mountains on the north side of Seoul. They face south, the direction believed to be the source of the strongest *yang* or positive power. Palace design reflected the king's position as the Son of Heaven, ruling by Heaven's mandate and responsible to the whole Earth. The primary purpose of the king's palace, therefore, was to provide an appropriately splendid center for his transmission of the will of Heaven to the people. Residential structures in the palace grounds were elegant but subsidiary parts of the royal compound.

The great throne hall at the center of each palace faces a large courtyard. A wide walkway crosses the courtyard to an ornately carved stairway leading up the balustraded terraces to the throne hall. On each side of the walk, rows of stones mark the positions where high civil and military officials stood for royal audiences. In the name of the main gate of each palace is the character *hwa*, which means "transformation" and suggests the transmission of

*Seoul's National Museum, situated behind Kyongbok Palace, contains exhibitions dating back more than 5,000 years*

Heaven's mandate through the king to the people. The high central arch of the gate was reserved for the king; the raised centers of palace roadways and ceremonial stairways over which the king was carried also indicate his exalted position.

In Korean palaces the walls, courtyards, and gardens are integral parts of the architectural whole. The principle of complementary forms is found throughout Korean culture: order and harmony are created from opposites—vertical and horizontal, rough and smooth, rocks and water, mountain and plain. Rooflines with furrowed tiles and gracefully upward-curving ends link rectangular buildings with their natural surroundings. Many walls are preserved, their beautiful decoration and horizontal lines creating a peaceful ambience throughout the palaces. A lovely pattern of pastel bricks in a gable is repeated in a wall; harmonized design and repetition of patterns reflect the balance and moderation of the good life.

Symbols of longevity and abundance are popular decorative motifs. In addition to using characters for long life, blessings, and good luck, Korea has 10 symbols of longevity: two plants—pine tree and pullocho fungus; three animals—turtle from the water, deer from the land, crane from the sky; and five landscape elements—sun, rock, water, mountains, clouds. The cosmology of wall art in Korean palaces also includes the Buddhist lotus, grapes, ducks, other birds, and butterflies. Elegant designs of bamboo and plum give palace walls a poetic grace. The compositions seem free, almost impressionistic.

Pavilions are an important element of the landscaping. Built for enjoying the gardens, the sites were chosen as best for watching the dawn or moonlight on water, for spectacular scenes of spring flowers or autumn foliage, or where the wind seemed most musical. The reflection of the pavilions in ponds under the blue Korean sky imparts a feeling of infinity to the finite space of the gardens.

## 경복궁     KYONGBOK PALACE

Kyongbok Palace, known as Seoul's main palace and an abiding symbol of traditional Korea, is located at the north end of Sejong Street in the heart of the capital city. Built in 1392 by King Taejo, founder of the Yi dynasty, it was occupied by the royal family for nearly 200 years, until it was burned down during the Japanese invasion of Hideyoshi. The palace was left in ruins for 275 years; in 1867 Prince Regent Taewon-gun had it rebuilt as a residence for his son, King Kojong. Unfortunately, "shining happiness" (which is what Kyongbok meant) ended when Queen Min was murdered in her private quarters in 1895. The king and the crown prince took refuge in the Russian Legation while Toksu Palace was rebuilt for their use. Visitors can enter the palace, which never again served as an official residence, through East Gate.

광화문

**Kwanghwa-mun.** The main gate of the palace is Kwanghwa-mun (Gate of Transformation by Light). With its double-roofed pavilion above three ceremonial arches, it is the most magnificent palace gate in the city. In 1926, when the Japanese built the Government-General (Capitol) Building at the southern end of the palace grounds, Kwanghwa-mun was moved to the east wall, but in 1969 it was returned to its original location in the south wall, in front of the Capitol Building. Today the name board is written in *Hangul* instead of Chinese characters. Two stone *hae tae*, mythical animals believed to prevent fire, guarded the palace and still stand by Kwanghwa-mun as ancient symbols of justice.

**Other Palace Gates.** The names of other Kyongbok Palace gates reflect symbols of Korean cosmology, which assigns to each of the four directions an element, a virtue, a season, and a divinity.

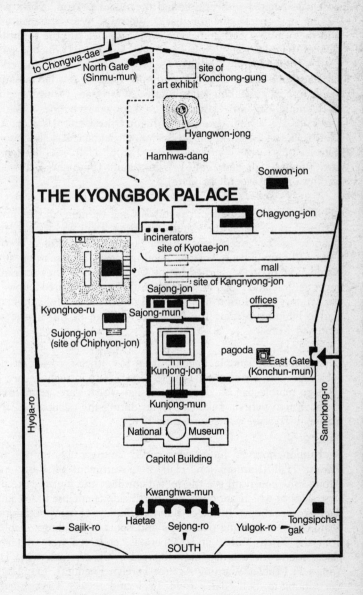

to Chongwa-dae

North Gate
(Sinmu-mun)

site of
Konchong-gung

art exhibit

Hyangwon-jong

Hamhwa-dang

Sonwon-jon

# THE KYONGBOK PALACE

Chagyong-jon

incinerators

site of Kyotae-jon

mall

site of Kangnyong-jon

Sajong-jon

offices

Kyonghoe-ru

Sajong-mun

Sujong-jon
(site of Chiphyon-jon)

pagoda

East Gate
(Konchun-mun)

Kunjong-jon

Hyoja-ro

Kunjong-mun

Samchong-ro

National ⬤ Museum

Capitol Building

Kwanghwa-mun

Haetae

Tongsipcha-gak

Sajik-ro

Sejong-ro

Yulgok-ro

SOUTH

East is associated with Spring and the Azure Dragon, North with Winter and the Divine (or Black) Warriors, West with Autumn and the White Tiger, and South with Summer and the Red Bird. Two of the other gates are still standing: East Gate (Konchun-mun, Gate of Establishing Spring), used by royal relatives and court officials; and North Gate (Sinmu-mun, Gate of the Divine Warriors), used by the king. The fourth, West Gate (Yongchu-mun, Welcoming Autumn Gate), was used for court business. Within the walls are several lesser gates. Behind the Capitol is Kunjong-mun (Gate of Government by Restraint), a graceful double-roofed gate leading to the courtyard of the Throne Hall; it is flanked by two smaller half-gates called Ulhwa-mun (Sunlight Gate) and Wolhwa-mun (Moonlight Gate).

중앙청

**The Capitol Building.** Beyond Kwanghwa-mun and in front of the Throne Hall is the Capitol Building. Built and used by the Japanese as the government-general building, it was used by the U.S. Military Government as administrative headquarters after World War II. It was burned by the Communists as they retreated north in 1950 and remained unused until it was renovated following the Military Revolution in 1961. In 1986 this beautiful stone and marble building became the National Museum of Korea, the art center of Korea.

경천사탑

**Kyongchon Temple Pagoda.** In the southeast corner of the palace grounds, Kyongchon Temple Pagoda is an intricately carved, 13-story marble pagoda of Indian design which dates from 1348, in the Koryo period. Taken to Japan during the occupation, this National Treasure was returned in 1948.

근정전

**Kunjong-jon.** A huge stone-paved courtyard surrounds the Throne Hall (Kunjong-jon, Hall of Government by Restraint). Around the courtyard is a tile-roofed corridor, the south, east, and west sides of which are open; the north side is enclosed for equipment-storage rooms. In the corridor are displays of name and notice boards that once hung over gates and doors of buildings. Tablets from the Koryo, Silla, and Yi periods, collected from different places round the country, are exhibited in the west corridor. The Yang-i Pi (Tablet Warning Against Foreign Enemies), found near the Chong-ro Bell, dates from 1871 and recalls Taewon-gun's hatred of foreign intervention, including Catholic missionary activities. A number of medium-size stone and iron Buddhas from Koryo and one from Silla are displayed on the upper level of the west corridor.

Lining the path from Kunjong-mun to the Throne Hall platform are stone tablets, set at intervals and marked with a number to indicate where officials of each rank should stand during royal audiences. There were nine ranks; when the country was at peace, the military stood on the king's right and the civilians on the left; in time of war, the arrangement was reversed. Iron rings set in the stone paving once tethered ceremonial awnings. Beautiful carved balustrades surround each of the two terraces of the stone platform of the Throne Hall. In the center section of each of the triple flights of steps is a stone medallion carved in the form of a phoenix, over which the king's sedan chair was carried. Many Yi kings were crowned in this great hall, and official audiences for important persons, Korean and foreign, were held here.

Kunjong-jon is a magnificent building, offering handsome views of all parts of the palace area. A massive, double-tiered roof is supported by 12 huge posts, and the beautifully carved ceiling is painted red and blue. Toward the rear a flight of five steps leads up to the throne platform, which is painted a dull red. A dull red lacquer screen stands behind the throne itself, and a red carved-wood canopy covers it. A golden dragon, symbol of royalty, is in the ceiling.

### 사정전
**Sajong-jon.** Through Sajong-mun in the rear corridor of Kunjong-jon, the visitor enters the courtyard of Sajong-jon (Hall of Pondering Government), where the kings once held private audiences and conducted routine government business. Formerly, Sajong-jon was flanked by two other buildings: on the east side was Manchun-jon (Hall of Ten Thousand Springs); on the west, Chonchu-jon (Hall of a Thousand Autumns), where kings discussed literature with the court scholars.

### 수정전
**Sujong-jon.** Passing through the western gate of the Sajong-jon courtyard, visitors come to Sujong-jon (Hall of Cultivating Government), which is now a small museum of Korean folk articles. Popular with Korean as well as foreign sightseers are the models of a man's room and a woman's room in a traditional Korean home and displays of kitchen and farming utensils, shoes and dress ornaments, books, and ink-brush paraphernalia from the old days. Even the most ordinary items are often beautifully carved and decorated. The present building stands on the site of the former Chiphyon-jon

(Wisdom Hall), King Sejong's royal library, and of Yehwa-gwan (Courtesy Hall), King Sejong's royal protocol office. King Sejong and his court scholars worked out the Korean alphabet, *Hangul*, in the original library building.

경회루

**Kyonghoe-ru.** A beautiful banquet hall, aptly named Kyonghoe-ru (Hall of Happy Meetings), stands on a rectangular stone island, reflected in a lotus lake. The lower story is open, and 48 huge stone pillars support the upper story. In dynastic times, up to 100 guests climbed the steep wooden stairway for royal banquets. Kyonghoe-ru is still used by the government for entertaining important guests on special occasions. Across the lake is a small hexagonal pavilion called Hyangwon-jong, and two small islands enhance the tranquil scene. Originally constructed by King Taejo as a small pleasure house, Kyonghoe-ru was enlarged and the lotus lake was created in the fifteenth century. Three graceful stone bridges connect the hall to the shore.

향원정

**Hyangwon-jong.** In a less formal setting than the classic perfection of Kyonghoe-ru is a hexagonal pavilion called Hyangwon-jong (Lotus Pavilion). It stands on an island in the center of a lovely natural-style lotus lake and is connected to the shore by an arched wooden bridge. Both of these graceful structures are painted a dull red, creating a delightful, peaceful scene. The modern building to the north of the pavilion is used for art exhibitions, and it stands approximately on the site where Queen Min was murdered.

터

**The Mall.** The Mall is a wide walk through a tree-shaded lawn to the east of the Kyonghoe-ru. The Kangnyong-jon (king's private apartment) and the Kyotae-jon (queen's private apartment), which originally occupied the Mall, were moved in 1919 to Changdok Palace. At the north side of the lawn are four incinerators, built of brick and carved with mythical figures, for the proper disposal of official papers in the Confucian tradition. Pagodas and other treasures line the walk.

At the north end of the palace grounds is Chagyong-jon, now used for offices, and in the northeast corner is Sonwon-jon, connected with the royal ancestral temple. Near another lotus pond is Hamhwa-dang, a small building that was King Kojong's private audience hall.

*Injŏngjŏn Hall, the main hall of Ch'angdŏk-kung*

# CHANGDOK PALACE 창덕궁

**B**uilt under King Taejo in 1394, Changdok-kung (Palace of Illustrious Virtue) is the best preserved among the palaces of Seoul. Burned in 1592, it was rebuilt in 1611, and it served as the royal residence until 1867, when Kyongbok Palace was reconstructed. The throne hall was burned in 1803 and restored in 1804. In 1907, the palace was occupied by the last king of Korea, Sunjong; today a few remaining members of the Yi dynasty still live in one of the palace buildings. At the north end of the grounds is Piwon, the 78-acre Secret Garden.

돈화문

**Tonhwa-mun.** The entrance gate, Tonhwa-mun (Gate of Mighty Transformation) was built in 1404 and is the oldest original gate in Seoul. Just beyond Tonhwa-mun is a small building in which there is an information office. Across the lawn is a building with vault-like doors, which holds rare and precious ancient books and important genealogical records.

인정전

**Injong-jon.** Injong-jon (Hall of Benevolent Government), or Throne Hall, is a large tiled building on the north side of the entrance road. Typically, it faces a large courtyard surrounded by a roofed corridor. Rooms along the side contain displays of porcelain, armor, official seals, royal sedan chairs, and other artifacts of palace life in centuries past. The double roof is supported by 40 wooden pillars. Behind the throne is a famous painted screen depicting the sun, moon, and five mountain peaks. In the twentieth century, Western-style electric chandeliers were added. Injong-jon is reached by three sets of ceremonial stairways which rise from the paved courtyard to the first and second terraces and to the hall. Mythical stone animals frame the stairs, and the center panel, over which the king was carried, is carved. The visitor will notice the stone tablets along the walkway which marked the places where officials of various ranks stood for audiences with the king.

선정전

**Sonjong-jon.** Sonjong-jon (Hall of the Dissemination of Government) is a smaller throne hall where the kings held private audiences. The building is noted for its brilliant blue glazed tile roof, which can be seen from the courtyard of the Injong-jon. Regrettably, the manufacture of these beautiful royal tiles has become a lost art.

왕실

**The Royal Apartments.** In 1919, the Kyotae-jon (queen's private apartment) and the Kangnyong-jon (king's private apartment) were moved from Kyongbok Palace to a site near Sonjong-jon, where Huijong-dang (Hall of Bright Government) and Taejo-jon (Hall of Great Accomplishments) had once stood. Those buildings had been destroyed by fire and were not rebuilt; the foundations were used for royal apartments. An unusual roof was added—constructed with no ridgepole, the roof tiles run up one side, curve over the top, and run down the other side. Thus nothing might roost above or fall upon a royal head. The apartments are well preserved and furnished to show visitors how the royal family lived at the turn of the twentieth century.

낙선재

**Nakson-jae.** The lilting roof of Nakson-jae (Retreat of Taking Pleasure in Goodness) rises above a beautiful wall carved in geometric designs. Built in 1847, Nakson-jae served as the private residence of Queen Yun, consort of the last king, Sunjong, who died in 1926. Located in the southwest part of the palace grounds, the villa has been occupied by Yi Pangja, widow of Korea's last crown prince, Yi Un, who died here in 1970, and other descendants of the royal family. After living for many years in Japan the crown prince and princess returned to Korea in 1964 and devoted themselves to charity work for the Korean people.

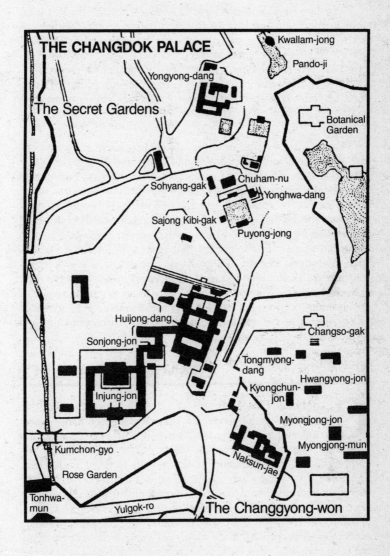

# THE CHANGDOK PALACE

Kwallam-jong

Pando-ji

Yongyong-dang

## The Secret Gardens

Botanical Garden

Chuham-nu

Sohyang-gak

Yonghwa-dang

Sajong Kibi-gak

Puyong-jong

Huijong-dang

Changso-gak

Sonjong-jon

Tongmyong-dang

Hwangyong-jon

Kyongchun-jon

Injung-jon

Myongjong-jon

Kumchon-gyo

Myongjong-mun

Naksun-jae

Rose Garden

Tonhwa-mun

Yulgok-ro

# The Changgyong-won

## 금천교

**Kumchon-gyo.** Kumchon-gyo (Forbidden Stream Bridge) is famous as the site where conspirators hid during an incident known as the Riot of 1884, a short-lived coup by a progressive faction in the court. At the center of the controversy was a new Western-style post office, a modern innovation advocated by progressives and bitterly opposed by conservatives as representing foreign influences. Nearby is a shed where visitors can see early automobiles and a horse-drawn royal coach used by the last king.

## 비원

**Piwon.** An exquisite example of Korean gardens is Secret Garden, Piwon, beyond Changdok Palace. Covering 78 acres of woodland, this tranquil retreat was reserved for royalty and women of the court during the Yi dynasty. Its 44 pleasure pavilions set among myriad ponds, bridges, and streams now delight the public, who may visit the garden on guided tours. The visitor will understand that Koreans have intended their garden not for displays of wealth and magnificence, but to delight the senses with a refined appreciation of natural beauty. To them, nature itself is a garden. In contrast to the architectural gardens of Western palaces with their insistence on physical control of the environment, traditional Korean gardens, of which Piwon is a prime example, were intended to enhance the natural landscape. Graceful entertainments and royal revels took place here.

# 창경궁 CHANGGYONG PALACE

Changgyong Palace (Palace of Glorious Blessings), built in the Koryo period, was the first residence of King Taejo, founder of the Yi dynasty, when he came to Seoul. After King Taejo moved to Kyongbok Palace, Changgyong Palace was allowed to fall into disrepair. It was rebuilt in 1484 under King Songjong. Like Changdok, Changgyong is a detached palace. The two were combined into one royal compound in the seventeenth century. The palace was damaged during an episode of factional fighting, all too typical of the Yi court, in 1761. After Taejo's residence, Changgyong Palace was never again occupied by a reigning king, but was used by several queens. The visitor will notice that the palace faces east rather than south, which is typical of Koryo as opposed to Yi palaces. At the north end of the grounds is a beautiful botanical garden.

궁문, 궁전

**Palace Gates and Halls.** Opposite Seoul National University Hospital on Changgyong-ro (Street) is Honghwa-mun (Gate of Vast Transformation), the elegant and impressive double-roofed main entrance to Changgyong Palace. Within the enclosure, across a road, is Myongjong-mun (Gate of Government by Intelligence), beyond which is the main throne hall, Myongjong-jon (Hall of Government by Intelligence), the oldest in the city. Behind Myongjong-jon are three other halls: Hwangyong-jon (Hall of Happiness), Kyongchun-jon (Hall of Spring), and Tongmyong-dang (Hall of Clear Thinking). In the latter, and in the corridors of the throne hall, are displays of royal sedan chairs, spears, parade lanterns, and other court relics. On a hill north of the main palace buildings is a modern structure, Changsogak, which contains a library of old books and records of the Yi dynasty.

식물원

**The Botanical Garden.** Since 1907 the area around Okchong-gyo (Jewel Stream Bridge), which crosses the O-gu (Royal Stream), has been developed as a botanical garden and zoo. Now called Changgyong Park, it is a popular place for cherry blossom viewing in the spring; the park offers a cool welcome in summer and is spectacular in autumn. In 1984 the zoo was moved to Seoul Grand Park, south of the Han River. On a knoll near the lake is Kwandok-jong, an ancient archery range that has recently been restored. Colorful rowboats often nearly cover the lake.

# TOKSU PALACE                          덕수궁

On the west side of Taepyong-ro (Avenue) opposite City Hall Plaza is Toksu Palace (Palace of Virtuous Longevity). It has undergone a number of changes since it was built for Prince Wolsan in the fifteenth century. Because the other palaces were destroyed during the Japanese invasion of 1592, King Sonjo, who had fled to the north, used this palace on his return to Seoul. In the seventeenth century its name was changed to Kyong-un Palace. In 1896 the palace was restored for King Kojong, who had left Kyongbok Palace after the murder of Queen Min and stayed in the Russian Legation until the renovation was completed. Gates were added, leading to the Russian, British, and American legations, in case another need for escape should arise. Kojong named himself Emperor of Tae Han (Great Korea) in 1897, and

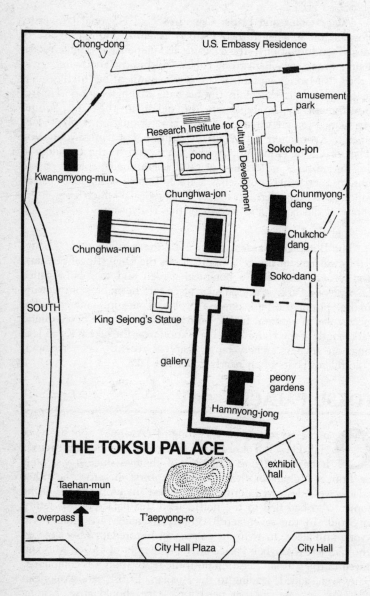

Chong-dong

U.S. Embassy Residence

amusement park

Research Institute for Cultural Development

pond

Sokcho-jon

Kwangmyong-mun

Chunghwa-jon

Chunmyong-dang

Chukcho-dang

Chunghwa-mun

Soko-dang

SOUTH

King Sejong's Statue

gallery

peony gardens

Hamnyong-jong

# THE TOKSU PALACE

exhibit hall

Taehan-mun

overpass

T'aepyong-ro

City Hall Plaza

City Hall

the palace became the center of activities involving the Independence Club and representatives of the neighboring great powers. In 1907 Kojong was forced to abdicate in favor of his son Sunjong. Sunjong restored the name "Toksu" (Virtuous Longevity) in honor of his father, who lived there until his death in 1919.

### 대한문

**Taehan-mun.** Some visitors may notice that the character "hwa" (transformation) does not appear in the name of the main gate of Toksu Palace. This is because Taehan-mun is not the original main gate. Before being destroyed by fire in 1904, it was called Tae-an Mun (Gate of Great Peace). The character *han* refers to the Han River.

### 중화젼

**Chunghwa-jon.** The throne hall of Toksu Palace is Chunghwa-jon (Hall of Central Harmony). Facing south in traditional fashion, it is approached through a free-standing gate, Chunghwa-mun. The large stone-paved courtyard in front of the hall has the familiar stone markers showing where the various ranks of civil and military officials stood for royal audiences. Ten huge wooden pillars support the roof in the classic architectural style, and great bronze braziers stand at the corners. The raised throne platform is covered by a wooden canopy, and a pierced screen stands behind the throne.

### 광명문

**Kwangmyong-mun.** Kwangmyong-mun (Bright Light Gate) in the southwest corner of the palace grounds contains a large bronze bell and a water clock. Made in 1536, the water clock is one of the oldest in the world. Water falling into three successive containers floated a tortoise arrow to indicate the time.

### 안채

**Residences.** Behind Chunghwa-jon throne hall are three smaller residential buildings. The western one, Chunmyong-dang (Deep Bright Hall), was used occasionally by King Kojong for receptions for foreign envoys. In the middle is Chukcho-dang (Ascension Hall), in which Lady Om, mother of the last crown prince (Li Un) lived until her death in 1911. On the east is Soko-dang (Old Royal Hall), to which the crown prince moved when he and his father left the Russian Legation in 1897. Until his death in 1919, King Kojong lived in the L-shaped building to the east, Hamnyong-jon (All Peaceful Hall), where he maintained contacts with foreign envoys.

*Gilt-bronzed seated Buddha, an exhibit in the National Museum, Kyŏngbokkung Palace, Seoul*

문화연구소

**Cultural Research Center.** Two Western-style buildings on the palace grounds were used as museums. One is Sokcho-jon (Stone Hall), which was designed by an English architect and built of Korean stone from a quarry near East Gate. It was the first building of Western design and modern motifs in Seoul. In the period following World War II, Stone Hall (or Stone Palace) was used by the American-Soviet Joint Commission on Korea for meetings on the future status of Korea and reunification of North and South Korea. It served also as the headquarters of the United Nations Commission on Korea with the outbreak of the Korean War. Sokcho-jon was used as the National Museum of Modern Art until the latter was recently moved to a new spacious museum building in the grounds of the Seoul Grand Park in Kwachon,

Kyongki-do Province, south of Seoul. Another building, which originally housed the Yi Household Museum, was the Toksu Palace Museum of Fine Arts, an annex of the National Museum. In 1987, the Research Institute for Cultural Development (Academy of Culture, Data and Film Center, and a Music Hall repository with some 7,000 tapes) was opened in these buildings.

세종대왕 동상

**King Sejong's Statue.** In 1968 a large bronze seated statue of King Sejong was placed in the Toksu Palace grounds, facing the mall and City Hall Plaza. The Sejong Tae-wang Sang (Statue of Great King Sejong) honors the fifteenth-century king for his invention of *Hangul*, the Korean phonetic alphabet, which made it possible for most of the population to become literate. Despite the opposition of many older scholars who had spent their lifetimes studying the Chinese characters, the king persuaded a group of younger scholars to work on the project. Their achievement was the *Hun-min Jong-um*, which introduced the new alphabet, matching sounds with very simple letters which could be grouped in syllables. King Sejong made the official presentation of *Hangul* to his people on the ninth day of the tenth lunar month, 1446. Since the Liberation from Japan in 1945, October 9 has been celebrated as Hangul Day, a national holiday.

마당

**The Grounds.** Less elaborate than Kyongbok and Changdok Palaces, the more modest scale of the Toksu Palace permits busy visitors to enjoy a quick taste of Korea's magnificent culture. Annual exhibits of chrysanthemums in October and the peony gardens in May are special attractions. In the spring, too, cherry blossoms frame views of the palace buildings and views of the city from the palace grounds. Koreans often dress in traditional clothes as they stroll in the parklike grounds, adding to the beauty and interest of the scene for foreign visitors. The tiled roofs of the palaces are dramatic in the snow of winter and strikingly lovely amid the colors of spring, summer, and especially autumn. Hidden paths, picturesque pavilions, intricate clay designs in brick walls—the beauty of Choson (Yi) dynasty architecture delights the sightseer.

# KYONGHUI PALACE 경희궁

Kyonghui Palace (Palace of Blissful Brilliance) no longer exists, but parts of it may be seen in various places in Seoul. The prestigious Seoul Boys' Middle School and Seoul

*The National Museum, Seoul*

High School once occupied this site, now a public park. The stone steps and foundations of Sungjong-jon (Hall of Honorable Government), the throne hall, now form the foundation of the Seoul High School gymnasium, while the hall has been moved to the Buddhist Tongguk University. Two other buildings were moved to Chogye Temple, north of Chong-ro Bell, and one gate is now the entrance to the Confucian Songkyun-kwan University. The main gate of the palace, Hunghwa-mun (Gate of Growing Transformation), now stands in Changchung-dan Park near the small stadium. Built in 1616, Kyonghui Palace became famous in the late nineteenth century as Mulberry Palace because of the grove of mulberry trees planted on the grounds for silk culture. The king's business venture was not successful, but the mulberry trees have survived.

# OTHER SIGNIFICANT SITES IN SEOUL

## MUSEUMS

Korea has long been called a "Treasure Land" for the rich cultural heritage of one of the oldest civilizations in the world. Thanks to the Koreans of ancient times who developed a unique system of recording the history of the nation, much of this cultural legacy has survived. The old Royal Library, Kyu Chang Kak, and all the palace libraries are filled with interesting relics. Many modern national museums, over 30 university museums, and some excellent private collections contain ancient documents, records, and historic treasures as well as items of folk culture and modern art exhibits. Included in the National Archives are innumerable Buddhist shrines, temples, and monasteries. These lovely archaic structures, like the royal palaces, show how Koreans have made original adaptations of Oriental styles that influenced all of Asia. The National Science Museum and the Korean War Museum have contemporary themes.

국립박물관

**The National Museum** (1 Sejongno, Chongno-ku; tel.: 720-2536). The National Museum has many branches. Before 1986, the main one was a magnificent three-tiered Korean-style building on the grounds of Kyongbok Palace. Today the National Museum of Korea occupies the beautiful Capitol Building. New provincial branches of the National Museum have been constructed at Chinju, Kongju, Kwangju, Kyongju, and Puyo. Artifacts and relics representing 5,000 years of Korean history are housed in the museum, which also incorporates modern replicas of national treasures, such as the five-storied pagoda of Palsang-jon. The visitor will delight in the world's finest collections of famed Koryo celadon (twelfth century), beautiful Yi Punchong pottery (fifteenth century), glittering gold crowns of the Silla period, blue and white porcelains, fabulous jewelry, many statues of Buddha in bronze and granite, ancient frescoes, and Yi scrolls annd paintings in the old tradition.

국립 민속박물관

**The National Folklore Museum** (1 Sejongno, Chongno-ku; tel.: 720-3137). Also located within the grounds of Kyongbok Palace, the National Folklore Museum displays artifacts of Korean folk culture in authentic traditional settings. Nine large rooms exhibit more than 5,000 articles of daily use: farming, cooking, hunting, and weaving tools; games, cards, and toys; musical instruments and costumes for mask-dance dramas; Shaman, Buddhist, and Confucian ceremonial and religious ritual artifacts; and other relics illustrating education, medicine, and commerce. A small but important display is the metal movable type invented in Korea in the thirteenth century. Visitors who have a particular interest in Korean folklore may wish to take a two-hour drive from Seoul to see the fine folk art collection in the Onyang Folk Museum, or a three-hour drive to the Emille Museum near the temple Popchu-sa. Throughout their history, Koreans have enjoyed elegant and graceful styles in everyday things, rarely missing an opportunity to carve or embroider a decorative design.

국립 현대미술 박물관

**The National Museum of Modern Art** (San 58-1, Makkye-dong, Kuadion, Kyonggi-doi tel.: 503-.7744). This museum has a permanent exhibition of over 200 works by contemporary artists and also offers special exhibits throughout the year. It was recently resituated at Kwach'on, near Seoul Grand Park.

세종대학 박물관

**King Sejong University Museum** (San 98, Kunja-dong, Songdong-ku; tel.: 467-1701). Located near Grand Children's Park, this museum contains beautiful displays of traditional dress, ornaments, furniture, and paintings. There is no admission fee, but it is necessary to make an appointment to view the collection.

세종대왕 기념관

**Great King Sejong Memorial Hall** (tel.: 966-2571). This museum, dedicated to King Sejong, fourth sovereign of the Yi dynasty, and to his invention of the Korean phonetic alphabet, *Hangul*, is located on the outskirts of Seoul, near Hongnung.

한국 기독교 박물관

**Korean Christian Museum** (1-1-1, Sangdo-dong, Tongjak-ku; tel.: 814-4491). Located on the Seoul campus of Soongjun University, the Korean Christian Museum contains historical items and materials related to Christian missionary work in Korea, which celebrated its bicentennial in 1984. An appointment is necessary to view the collection.

호암 박물관

**Ho-am Museum** (204 Kashil-ri, Pogok-myon, Yongin-kun, Kyonggi-do; tel. 234-6171). Ho-am Museum houses one of the finest private collections in Korea. This contribution to Korean culture by Yi Byongchul, chairman of the Samsung Group, is located on the southern outskirts of Seoul, in the compound of Yong-in Familyland. It can be reached via the Seoul-Pusan Expressway, one exit to the left before the Korean Folk Village.

석주선 기념 박물관

**Suk Joo-sun Memorial Museum of Korean Folk Art** San 8-3, Hannam-dong, Yongsan-ku; tel.: 797-0581). This museum on the Seoul campus of Tankuk University is devoted mainly to Korean traditional clothing, shoes, and accessories. There is no entrance fee, but an appointment is required.

대학(교) 박물관

**University Museums.** There are over 30 excellent university museums that can be enjoyed by making an appointment.

Outstanding are the collections at Seoul National University (tel. 877-5693), Korea University (tel. 94-4381), Yonsei University (tel. 392-0131), Tongguk University (tel. 267-8131), and Ewha Women's University (tel. 362-6151). No entrance fees are charged.

## 국립 과학 박물관

**National Science Museum.** This museum is located near the northeast corner of the Changgyong Palace grounds. A nominal entrance fee is charged. Each display offers buttons to push, switches to throw, and connections to be made. Exhibits include demonstrations of magnets and solar power, refineries, closed-circuit television, engine components, steering mechanisms, power plants, warplanes, and many more. Stuffed animals and birds also are displayed. A small movie theater on the ground floor has continuous showings of science films.

## 한국전쟁 박물관

**Korean War Museum.** This is actually an open-air display of military airplanes and tanks, located at the former military airport and landing strip on Yoido. The giant B-29 near the entrance can be boarded. Around the field are Russian MIG fighters and tanks captured during the Korean War. There is a small indoor display with photographs and other mementos of the Korean War. Benches and a refreshment stand are provided for the weary sightseer.

## 육·삼 빌딩

**Golden Tower ("DLI 63" Building)** (tel.: 784-6363). Rising 860 feet on Yoido Island in the Han River stands the 63-story Golden Tower (three floors underground), the symbol of the Republic of Korea's emergence as an economic, cultural, and tourism center of the Orient. The tower is a major tourist attraction, which many travelers from overseas as well as Korea visit.

On a clear day visitors to the Tower's top attraction, the observation deck on the 60th floor, which is reached by using either a high-speed elevator (₩900 per person) or a glass exterior elevator (₩1,300), enjoy an excellent view of the city of Seoul. They are able to see beyond the port city of Inchon out into the Yellow Sea, and even into North Korea. The view from the transparent elevator and the top deck is truly breathtaking; for national security reasons taking pictures from there is prohibited.

One of the few IMAX Theaters in the world is located just to the right of the main entrance of the Tower on the shopping ground floor. IMAX projects films on a screen 10 times larger than the normal 35 millimeter movie screen, giving the viewer the feeling that they are a part of the action taking place on the screen.

*Puchae-chum, a folk-ritual fan dance*

"Beautiful Korea," a 30-minute film in Korean, with English, French, and Japanese translation (with headphones) is shown every other day from 10:50 a.m. through 8:50 p.m. (₩1,200 per person).

Seaworld 63, the second most popular attraction in the Tower, is an aquarium where 20,000 marine creatures, representing a variety of freshwater and saltwater fish and 400 species from all over the world, are on display. Every 30 minutes divers enter the largest tank to cavort in dolphin shows and a fish circus featuring sharks, stingrays, the Pacific octopus, and other species (₩1,700 per visitor).

A huge American-style shopping mall occupies most of the ground floor of the Tower and is open daily from 10:30 a.m. to 7:30 p.m. The dining offered in the Tower runs the gamut from Korean, American, and Japanese fast food chains in the shopping mall to an affordable but elegant lunch and dinner buffet in the plush restaurants on the upper floors with spectacular views of Seoul. The Fountain Plaza Restaurant serves lunch and dinner buffets with 100 different dishes of Korean, Chinese, Japanese, and Western food and entertains with live and recorded music. In the center of the spacious and elegant main dining room is a state-of-the-art musical fountain that is synchronized by computer with each individual piece of music played. To get to the Golden Tower by taxi simply say, "Yoido Dae-han Saeng-myong" (Great Korea Insurance building on Yoi Island).

## CULTURAL AND EXHIBITION CENTERS

한국의 집

**Korea House** (80-2, Pil-dong, 2-ka, Chung-ku; tel.: 266-9101). In this beautiful and spacious Korean-style house, operated by the Foundation for the Preservation of Korean Cultural Properties, Korean food, beverages, and Korean-style buffets are served at reasonable prices. At 8:30 p.m., except on holidays, Korean folk dances and music are performed in the Korea House Theater. Booking two or three days in advance is necessary. Occasionally, visitors may glimpse a wedding party arriving for a ceremony to be performed in this lovely traditional setting. The high-quality handicrafts and Korean books on display are for sale at very moderate cost. Also exhibited are nearly 100 traditional musical instruments.

세종 문화회관

**Sejong Cultural Center** (81-3 Sejongho, Chongno-ku; tel.: 736-2721). The Sejong Cultural Center, centrally located on Sejong-ro across from the American Embassy, is among the most impressive of the city's centers for the performing arts. The center was named for King Sejong (1418—50), inventor of the Korean alphabet.

The main auditorium of the complex, with a seating capacity of 4,000, boasts one of the most modern acoustical and lighting facilities in Asia. The staging complex includes a rotating stage (17 m. in diameter), a movable proscenium ($10 \times 22$ m.) joined to the main proscenium ($12 \times 26$ m.), four sliding stages, a drop-screen, and an orchestra pit for as many as 100 musicians.

This magnificent building, with the most up-to-date accoutrements, even has a pipe organ shaped like a traditional Korean instrument and equipped with 8,096 pipes, 40 French bells, and 32 Korean Buddhist bells.

The Sejong cultural complex includes a main conference hall with facilities for the simultaneous translation of six languages, a hall with a seating capacity of 500 and a cinema, a small conference hall, and an underground exhibition hall.

The center is home for six major performing groups: the Seoul Philharmonic Orchestra, the Seoul City Choir, the Seoul City Dance Theater, the Seoul Musical Theater, the Seoul Traditional Music Orchestra, and the Seoul City Children's Choir. The center has also hosted many performances by major groups from throughout the world, including the New York Philharmonic, the Royal Ballet, and the Vienna Opera Company, together with famous artists. In addition to offering musical performances by both Korean and foreign artists, it also hosts major conferences and extravaganzas, such as the Miss Universe Pageant.

국립극장                                        국립 고전음악원

**National Theater** (San 14-67, 2-ka, Changchung-dong, Chung-ku; tel.: 274-1171) and **National Classical Music Institute** (tel: 274-1179). The National Theater is located near the Hotel Shilla on the slopes of Nam-san. As the center for Korean culture and arts, it has six affiliated groups: the National Drama Company, the National Changguk Company, the National Dance Company, the National Ballet Company, the National Opera Company, and the National Chorus. Performances of these traditional arts are held regularly in the small theater (3:30 p.m. every Fri. and Sat., March–June and September–November). On Fridays, performances of Korean music and dance are given by the National Classical Music Institute, which is devoted to the preservation and cultivation of the ancient musical traditions of Korea.

예지원

**Yejiwon.** (Tel. 333-2221) The Yejiwon Cultural Institute offers programs featuring traditional activities of Korean life, such as the wedding ceremony, the tea ceremony, flower arrangement, calligraphy, preparation of *kimchi*, and others. Special programs can be arranged by request for group tours.

한국 전람회관

**Korea Exhibition Center (KOEX).** (Tel. 562-2161) The Korea Exhibition Center in southern Seoul is the largest of its kind in Asia. Year-round displays of both Korean and foreign industrial products are accommodated in its excellent facilities.

리틀 엔젤스 공연관

**The Little Angels Performing Arts Center** (25 Nong-dong, Songdong-ku; tel.: 444-8221) is located in the Children's Grand Park in Sung-dong and is much like a European jewel-box opera house with a complex of schools and training centers known as the Little Angels Performing Arts School. Its impressive red and gold auditorium seats 1,500, with boxes, mezzanine, and two balconies. Its spacious lobby is French baroque in gilt travertine and ornamental plaster, all brilliantly illuminated by crystal chandeliers and wall sconces. The center has hosted a number of internationally-known concert artists in music and dance, including its home company and the Universal Ballet.

호암 미술관

**The Ho-am Art Hall** (Sunhwa-dong, Chung-ku; tel.: 7515-562) is located off the lobby of the handsome Joon-ang Daily News Building in the heart of downtown Seoul and is equipped to accommodate even the most demanding of theatrical productions. The Ho-am's stage

339
SEOUL

facilities, with a seating capacity of 1,000, are large enough to accommodate major dance productions. The Ho-am Theater presents many smaller modern dance groups, drama groups, and concert artists from around the world, as well as Korean artists.

문예극장

**The Munye Theatre** (1-130 Tongsung-dong, Chongno-ku; tel.: 762-5231) is located in the Dong-soong district of Seoul as an integral part of the complex known as the Korean Culture and Arts Foundation. The Munye has two theaters, each with characteristics and equipment suited to its performances. The main one is a proscenium-type theater with 700 seats, a revolving stage, an orchestra pit, and a five-step pre-set lighting system, and it is in constant use for modern dance recitals. The other theater has 200 seats and a variable and movable stage for experimental dance and theater.

Specific cultural events are listed in "The Monthly Guide to Metropolitan Cultural Programs," an insert in the *Korea Herald* and *Korea Times*.

화랑관광

**Art Gallery Tours.** Most of Seoul's galleries and antique shops are located within walking distance of major downtown hotels and the National Museum of Korea in the old Capitol Building. Among the well-known galleries are the Yon and Yedang in Insa-dong where Gold House, Tongin Store, and Du Choi's Antique Shop are located. Major galleries in Seoul include the Dongdok Art Gallery in Kwanhun-dong; the Dongsanbang Gallery near Chogye-sa; the Space Art Gallery near Secret Garden; the Sun, Mi, and Won galleries near Pagoda Park; Hankuk Gallery near the Saudi Embassy; Galéries de Seoul in Kugi-dong; and Hyundai and Jean's Art, both near the National Museum. Lotte and Shinsegae department stores and the Westin Chosun and Hotel Shilla all have art galleries.

대학 캠퍼스 관광

**University Campus Tours.** Visiting major universities in Seoul is a memorable experience. Most are within 30 minutes by taxi ride from downtown hotels. Among the 26 universities in Seoul, Seoul National University in Sillim-dong, southern Seoul at the foot of Mt. Kwanak, is outstanding for sheer scale and beauty. Ewha Woman's University, the largest women's school in the world, stands in a lovely wooded area in Shinchon, the western part of Seoul, surrounded by pear trees and magnolias. Ewha literally means pear flowers, and the school was founded by an American Methodist missionary in 1886 as the first public educational institution in Korea. Yonsei University is located not far from

Ewha and was founded by an American Presbyterian missionary in 1885. Korea University in the eastern part of Seoul is also worth visiting, and the university museum is well known. One of the nation's most prestigious institutions of higher learning, it was established in 1905 by Yi Yongik, a cabinet minister of the Choson (Yi) dynasty. After Yi, the school was headed by Sohn Pyonghee, one of the 33 signers of the famous Declaration of Independence of 1919, and then by Kim Songsu, an educational leader.

## MAIN PERFORMANCE HALLS IN SEOUL

| NAME | TEL. | NAME | TEL. |
|---|---|---|---|
| Art Space 3 & 5 Theater | (02) 653-3555 | Minye Theater | (02) 744-0686 |
| Theater Blue | (02) 313-7151 | Mun-Ye Theater | (02) 762-5231 |
| Changmu Chum Theater | (02) 312-7571 | National Theater | (02) 274-1151 |
| Shimin Theater | (02) 392-2601 | Parangsae Theater | (02) 763-8969 |
| Drama Center | (02) 778-0261 | Ryu Kwan-Soon Theater | (02) 752-0543 |
| Elcanto Living Theater | (02) 776-8035 | Sejong Cultural Center | (02) 736-2721 |
| Ho-am Art Hall | (02) 751-5557 | Sil-Hum Theater | (02) 765-4981 |
| Little Angels Performing | | Soong Eui Concert Hall | (02) 752-8924 |
| Arts Center | (02) 444-8221 | Space Theater | (02) 763-0771 |
| Madang Cecil Theater | (02) 737-5773 | Woori Madang Theater | (02) 313-7169 |
| Minjung Small Theater | (02) 312-9416 | | |

## GALLERIES IN SEOUL

| NAME | TEL. | NAME | TEL. |
|---|---|---|---|
| Art Cosmos Center | (02) 795-0246 | Mun-Ye Art Center | (02) 762-5231 |
| Paek-Sang Gallery | (02) 733-6673 | Park Ryu-Sook Art Gallery | (02) 544-7393 |
| Dongdok Gallery | (02) 734-8123 | Saemteo Gallery | (02) 742-0339 |
| Dongsanbang Gallery | (02) 733-6945 | Sejong Cultural Center | |
| Hangang Gallery | (02) 322-1077 | Exhibition Hall | (02) 736-2721 |
| Ho-am Gallery | (02) 751-5132 | Seoul Gallery | (02) 735-7711 |
| Hu Gallery | (02) 393-9714 | Shinsegae Gallery | (02) 754-1234 |
| Hyundai Gallery | (02) 734-8215 | Space Art Gallery | (02) 763-0771 |
| Korea Design & Packaging | | The 3rd Art Gallery | (02) 735-4151 |
| Center | (02) 744-0227 | Ye Chong Gallery | (02) 744-7874 |
| Kwan-Hun Gallery | (02) 733-6469 | Yeh Gallery | (02) 542-3624 |

# GOVERNMENT BUILDINGS

*CAPITOL BUILDING: NATIONAL MUSEUM OF KOREA*

Originally the headquarters of the government-general of Chosun under the Japanese colonial regime, this magnificent white stone building is one of the largest government edifices in Asia. Beautifully situated on the Kyongbok Palace grounds, it took nearly 10 years (1916-25) to build at a cost of almost $4 million. It is built of granite and marble with ferro-concrete reinforcement, and the interior decorations are of richly grained Korean marble. The Throne Hall is most impressive with its exquisite decorations, including dazzling chandeliers and artistic tapestries. The Grand Hall is noted for the bold designs of its mosaic marble floor. In 1986 this splendid building became the main National Museum of Korea.

An historic ceremony took place in the Throne Hall of the Capitol on September 15, 1945, following the Liberation of South Korea by U.S. Armed Forces. Japanese Governor-General Abe signed the surrender instrument in the presence of Lt. General John R. Hodge, U.S. commanding general. The Capitol Building was used by the Military Government until August 1948 when the new Republic of Korea formally assumed government functions there. Before the outbreak of the Korean War on June 25, 1950, the Legislative Assembly of the Interim Government met in the Throne Hall, and the ROK National Assembly convened in the Grand Hall. The building was gutted during the Korean War, but under the Third Republic it was restored to its original state of grandeur, with additional modern facilities, for use by various government ministries, including the prime minister's office. Under the Fifth Republic, it was opened to the public as the central jewel of the National Museum of Korea complex, exhibiting 7,400 Korean national treasures among 100,000 cultural objects displayed on a rotation basis. The museum provides a unique setting of elegance and historic significance, and includes foreign art works in 20 separate exhibition halls with a total floor space of 13,000 square meters. This magnificent museum is the third largest in the world, surpassed only by the British Museum in London and the Musée du Louvre in Paris.

On the ground floor, two special exhibition halls display Korean national treasures as well as objects from foreign countries—including China, Japan, Egypt, and Italy. The exhibits on this floor include a replica of a prehistoric Korean dwelling site and a reconstruction of the Buddhist temple Hwang-ryong-sa, the ruins of which were found in Kyongju and date from the Old Silla Kingdom (57 B.C.–668 A.D.).

The second floor features cultural properties dating from prehistoric periods, from the Karak League (first century–562 A.D.), and from the Silla (57 B.C.–935 A.D.), the Koguryo (37 B.C.–668 A.D.), and the Paekje (18 B.C.–660 A.D.) kingdoms, including many Buddhist sculptures that date to the later years of the Three Kingdoms period.

On the third floor, ceramics of the Koryo (918–1392) and the Choson (Yi) (1392–1910) and metalwork objects are displayed together with other cultural relics donated to the museum by individuals or organizations.

The fourth floor exhibits mostly paintings, including those on Buddhist themes, and items derived from the cultural heritage of Asian nations—especially Korea's closest neighbors, China and Japan. Among the Chinese artifacts displayed are the remains of a sunken mid-twelfth or early thirteenth-century Chinese trading ship, recently recovered from the waters off Mokpo, South Korea.

The new facilities enhance the clarity and simplicity of the exposition of this wide-ranging collection of Korean and foreign artworks and the ability of visitors to understand its many exhibits. In addition, short, informative films are shown on a video system installed in specially designated resting places between exhibition halls.

## THE BLUE HOUSE
### (CHANGWADAE: THE PRESIDENT'S RESIDENCE)

Set on a hill among evergreens at the foot of the lofty pyramid-shaped mountain, Pugak-san, north of Kyongbok Palace and the Capitol Building, is the president's residence. Named for its spectacular blue tile roof, the Blue House has a grand audience hall and a beautiful banquet hall, which are used for state occasions. The grounds include a lovely garden of cherry trees and a conservatory with various flowers and plants. In the spring when the cherry blossoms are in their full glory, the garden is open to the public.

## THE NATIONAL ASSEMBLY BUILDING

The Republic of Korea National Assembly occupies a huge granite building on Yoi Island in the Han River southwest of the city center. Considered the most outstanding of its kind in Asia, the building has seven stories aboveground and two underground. The central dome is 35 meters high; the floor space totals over 81,500 square meters, and the site covers 330,000 square meters. There are seating accommodations for 300 members of the House of Representatives and 100 members of the Senate, in anticipation of the day when legislators of united Korea will sit there. The building was completed in 1975 after five years of construction at a cost of $30 million. A colossal colonnade provides a magnificent entrance facade; inside, the impressive decor reflects traditional Korean designs.

# 탑, 성지, 묘　　TEMPLES, SHRINES, AND TOMBS

## *TEMPLES*

Seoul is a city of colorful temples (*sa* in Korean); 76 temples and monasteries can be found in the city and its immediate vicinity. Many are magnificent national treasures that have survived invasions and other vicissitudes of history.

조계사
**Chogye-sa.** (Tel. 725-5864) A temple of great significance, Chogye-sa, is located in Anguk-dong in the heart of Seoul. Chogye-sa serves as headquarters for over 1,500 affiliated Buddhist temples throughout Korea and is the site of the annual lantern parade held on the birthday of Buddha in May.

보문사
**Pomun-sa.** (Tel. 093-3576) Located on the eastern edge of Seoul, Pomun-sa is Korea's largest nunnery. The grotto behind the temple, similar to the Sokkuram Grotto near Pulguk-sa in Kyongju, invites a moment of silent meditation.

경국사
**Kyongguk-sa.** (Tel. 914-5447) North of Seoul, near Chongnung Valley and close to the eastern entrance to Pugak Skyway, is Kyongguk-sa. With possibly the most beautiful and picturesque grounds of any temple in Korea, the calm beauty of this isolated spot shields the visitor from the bustle of the capital city and presents a true image of the meditative atmosphere of Buddhist temples.

도선사
**Toson-sa.** (Tel. 993-3161) This temple is visited by more pilgrims than any other in the Seoul region. Located on the way to Uidong, a tourist resort popular for its scenic mountain beauty, Toson-sa is well worth the trip. The Miruk statue at the rear of

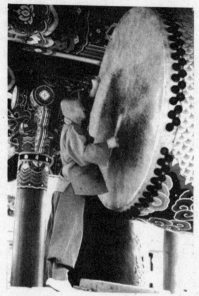

*Buddhist temple drumming*

---

the temple is said to possess miraculous healing powers. On Buddha's birthday, the temple glows with the light of thousands of lanterns.

봉은사

**Pongun-sa.** (Tel. 567-1448) Another large and ancient temple is Pongun-sa, located in Yong-dong, on the southern outskirts of Seoul. Most impressive are the four temple gate guards (*sachonwang*).

봉원사

**Pongwon-sa.** (Tel. 392-3008) Pongwon-sa is headquarters for the Taego sect of Buddhism. Located on a hill overlooking the Kumhwa Tunnel, the temple compound is frequently the setting for weddings and funerals.

## SHRINES

종묘

**Chong-myo (Royal Ancestral Tablet House).** An interesting complex of royal buildings is Chong-myo (The Royal Ancestral Tablet House). Begun by King Taejo in December 1392 and completed in 1393, Chong-myo contains the ancestral tablets of all Yi dynasty rulers and their queens. The buildings escaped burning during the Japanese invasion of 1592 because the enclosure was used as a military camp by the invaders.

Located south of the Changdok and Changgyong palaces, this royal shrine is secluded within a wooded garden area enclosed by a wall. A bridge across Yulgok-ro connects Chong-myo with the Changdok Palace grounds near Nakson-jae House. Entrance to Chong-myo is through Changyop Gate in the southern side of the enclosure, at the end of a short street running north from Chong-ro (Bell Avenue) between Waryong-ro and Changgyong-ro. The large gate has three sections and a single tile roof. The road leading into the shrine from the gate is paved with heavy stones and is higher in the center, over which the king was carried.

Angling off to the right is a stone-paved path leading to a walled, tiled building, which, as the king's ceremonial robing hall, was where he changed to appropriate robes before offering sacrifices to the spirits of the royal ancestors. Beyond this hall is another building where the sacrificial animals were prepared for the king's inspection and selection; now it is a small museum of ceremonial articles. Three other auxiliary buildings around a courtyard contain additional exhibits of official seals, small sedan chairs in which the ancestral tablets were carried, censers, lamps, and other paraphernalia. A model shows how the sacrificial foods were arranged: animals (cows, goats, and pigs—one for each day of sacrifice) on one side; and offerings of the first fruits of grain, fruits, and honey produced by the people on the other side. The sacrifices were not burned, but were placed on the altar and offered to Heaven; after the ceremony they were distributed by the king to favored officials.

To the west are two long halls that contain the royal ancestral tablets. The buildings look alike, except that the tiled roof of Chong-jon (Main Hall) is straight across, while that of Yongnyong-jon (Hall of Eternal Peace) has a raised section in the center. Both buildings stand on stone-paved terraces about six feet above the courtyard and are reached by three ceremonial stairways. Inside are small rooms of one *kan* (about six square feet) for each king. During ceremonies, the king's tablet was placed on a table in front of this room; he was attended by nobles who took their places in the courtyard. Only one room remains vacant.

Within each king's room are three sections: the central section for the ancestral tablet; the east section for his personal seal; the west section for his favorite books. Also placed in the king's room were tablets for his queen and other members of his immediate family. The tablets and the tables were carved in chestnut wood. The royal ancestral tablets were made in whatever length was necessary to hold the one long descriptive phrase listing the achievements and glories of the particular king, ending with his name. Holes through the tablets from top to bottom, front to back, and side to side represented all points of Heaven and Earth. They were useful, too, for stringing the tablets together for convenience in carrying them to safety in the event of war.

In Chong-jon, in addition to the rooms for the tablets of kings who died with direct heirs to the throne, there are rooms for 82 tablets honoring important ministers of state and individuals who supported Taejo in the founding of the Choson (Yi) dynasty. In Yongnyong-jon are the tablets of kings who died without heirs or who were posthumously honored as kings by being given reign titles. Under the raised section of the roof are four rooms containing the tablets of four direct antecedents of the founder of the Yi dynasty.

Ancient ceremonies, with authentic ceremonial clothing and instruments, are performed every spring (first Saturday in May) for the general public to keep alive the traditions of the last 600 years.

성균관

**Confucian Shrine (Sung-kyun-kwan).** Ten minutes' drive from central Seoul brings the visitor to the Confucian Shrine in a grove of ancient trees, including gingkos which make a wall of gold in the autumn. The tablets of Confucius and other famous sages are kept in this shrine. In spring and autumn the Confucius Festival is observed by leading Confucian scholars who hold a solemn and splendid ceremony, including a memorial address, the burning of incense, and the offerings of freshly harvested food and wine. The celebration of Confucius' birthday on August 27 of the lunar calendar features colorful classical dances to the accompaniment of ancient court music.

To teach Confucianism, the first Sung-kyun-kwan University was founded in the fourteenth century, during the Koryo period, but with the rise of Buddhism it fell into disrepute. With the founding of the Yi dynasty, King Taejo reestablished Confucianism, making it the national religion and moral foundation of society, so that it came to dominate government, education, and the code of daily life for 500 years. Filial piety and royal loyalty were the supreme virtues. King Taejo established the Sung-kyun-kwan as the highest seat of learning, and graduates were given positions in the government after passing the high civil service examinations in the King's presence. A modern Sung-kyun-kwan University has been founded near the Confucian Shrine to educate Korean youths with the moral discipline of Confucian ethics as well as in twentieth-century arts and sciences.

절두산 순교 성지

**Choltusan Martyrs' Shrine.** (Tel. 323-1950) Choltusan Martyrs' Shrine, on Taegonno Street near the second Han River Bridge, has become a tourist attraction since Pope John Paul II's visit to Korea in May 1984. Enshrined here are 25 native and foreign martyrs as well as some of the founding fathers of Korean Catholicism.

## TOMBS

왕능

**Royal Tombs.** Since there were 27 Choson (Yi) Dynasty rulers over 500 years, there are many royal tombs to be found in the rolling hills around Seoul. They provide a fascinating study in architectural design. Two of the most popular sites are the scenic tomb regions of Kumgok and Tonggu northeast of the city. Other tomb parks are Son-nung, Chong-nung, In-nung, Hon-nung, and also Tae-nung east of Seoul near the Korea Military Academy. In the royal tomb areas, spacious grassy areas among evergreen forests are delightful spots for picnics on holiday weekends from spring to autumn.

사육신묘

**Tombs of Six Loyalists.** The tombs of King Tanjong's six loyal courtiers who were killed by a usurper in 1456 are situated opposite the National Cemetery, across the Seoul-Inchon Highway, overlooking the Han River on an evergreen hill with a tall stone monument on its crest. Poems of the six martyrs are carved on the monument.

국군묘지

**Korea Military Cemetery.** A modern footbridge over the Han River leads to the Tomb of the Unknown Soldier in the Korea National Cemetery. Here lie 140,000 Korean War heroes, who fought valiantly to defend their homes and freedom. Syngman Rhee, first president of the Republic of Korea, is also buried here, on the Hill of the Phoenix.

# PARKS

For citizens of Seoul a day at one of the many parks in the city is a favorite form of recreation. Landscaped in the Korean manner, with a balance of nature and artifice, these green spaces become ever more appealing with the advance of industriali-

zation and the growth of the city with its modern buildings of
concrete, steel, and glass.

## 파고다공원
### PAGODA PARK

Pagoda Park in the center of the city is named for its lovely 10-story
pagoda, which is representative of the finest techniques of Yi
dynasty artisans. Originally constructed at Wongak-sa, it was modeled on the Kyongchon Temple pagoda, now in Kyongbok Palace.
Reading of the Korean Declaration of Independence in this park
marks the beginning of the 1919 Independence Movement against
Japanese colonial rule. Poignant scenes of that struggle are
memorialized on a series of bronze plaques. Seoul city tour buses
begin and end their sightseeing routes at Pagoda Park.

## 사직공원
### SAJIK PARK

In northwest Seoul, at the base of Mt. Inwang, is Sajik Park. In
the park is Sajik Altar, a sacred site where the king made sacrifices
on behalf of the nation to the spirits of Earth and the Harvest.
Next to Sajik Park is the entrance to Pugak Skyway, which offers
a picturesque drive over the ridges of Inwang-san and Pugak-san
north of the city. A tearoom on the crest welcomes travelers. The
skyway ends at Chongnung, a park and resort valley east of Seoul
below Pohyon Peak, which is part of the North Fortress.

## 비원
### SECRET GARDEN (PIWON)

Extending north from Changdok Palace to the base of the mountains on the northern perimeter of the city is the Secret Garden,
78 acres of secluded royal pleasure garden, and one of the most
charming outdoor spots in Seoul. First laid out in Taejo's time,
the garden was landscaped in 1623 and has been improved many
times over the centuries. Piwon is open to the public with hourly
guided tours conducted in English and Japanese.

Entrance to the Secret Garden is through a gate just north of
Nakson-jae in the grounds of Changdok Palace and follows a path
between the walls of Changdok and Changgyong palaces. At a jog
in the west wall there is a postern gate, through which Chongjo,
the "Coffin King," went each morning to bow to his queen mother
in her apartments. Farther along on the right is a short path leading
to an underground passage; this basement retreat of the king is
now hung with photographs of famous places in Korea.

Nearby is a lovely square stone-lined lotus pond. On the south side of the pond is a unique 20-sided pavilion built partly over the water and supported by stone pillars. It is called Puyong-jong after the special variety of Asian lotus that grows in the spring-fed pond. On the west side of the pond is Sajong Kibi Gak (Four-Well Memorial Shrine) housing a tablet that tells of the discovery of four springs by two young princes. On the east side stands Yonghwa-dang (Flower Viewing Hall), where kings once came to admire the flowers and to write and recite poetry. In the nineteenth century, military and civil service examinations on the Chinese classics were taken here under direct royal supervision. A path on the north side of the pond leads through Osu-mun (Fish Water Gate), noted for a heavy tiled roof supported by very slender posts. Up steep steps is Chuham-nu, a two-story building: the lower floor was a royal library, the upper hall the scene of theatricals and feasts. To the west is a smaller building that once housed Queen Min's silk culture projects; crates and other paraphernalia can be seen through the paper of a rear door.

### 용영당
**Yongyong-dang.** In the next valley, beside a pond, is Yong-yong-dang (House of Happy Events), where the royal family escaped from court ceremony to lead a more normal life. It was also used for entertainment; shortly before her death, Queen Min gave a banquet for 6,000 in this bucolic setting. Beyond the villa is Pando-ji (Peninsula Pond), a quiet fishing hideaway for the king, built in the shape of ancient Korea. The six-sided pavilion at the north end has a dragon painted on the ceiling; this royal symbol indicates that the king used it.

### 옥류천
**Okryu-chon.** This crystal stream (Jade Flowering Stream) flows through a tranquil wooded glen, enhanced by small waterfalls and clear pools. Many small pavilions decorate this lovely area, delicately integrating architectural forms into the natural setting. Beyond is the northern boundary wall, part of which adjoins the Sung-kyun-kwan University campus. South of Okryu-chon is a small shrine where the donor of the land occupied by the Secret Garden is still honored. To the west is a closed area, Sonwon-jon. Returning toward the entrance, the visitor can climb a path leading to the highest point in the garden to enjoy a breathtaking view of the mountains to the north and the city to the south. Throughout the changing seasons, the luxuriant foliage framing picturesque pavilions and reflected in the peaceful ponds delights visitors.

*Tumuli Park, comprising Silla Dynasty tombs*

## 남산공원
## *NAM-SAN PARK AND MOUNTAIN PLAZA*

Called the "Roof Garden" of Seoul, Nam-san Park surrounds the 236.7-meter Seoul Tower on top of Nam-san (South Mountain). Visitors who take the Nam-san Park cable car up the mountain and ascend the tower enjoy a 360-degree panoramic view of the entire capital and the surrounding countryside. On the top and sides of the mountain are ruins of 500-year-old fortress walls. Beautifully landscaped with pine and cherry trees, forsythia and azalea bushes, and many other plants, Nam-san Park beckons the stroller. Its modern facilities include two major libraries, a greenhouse and botanical garden, and a music amphitheater. Along its slopes stand the Ambassador, Hilton, Hyatt, Shilla and Tower hotels.

### 서울 타워
**Seoul Tower.** Seoul Tower, one of the city's major tourist attractions, can be reached by road or by cable car; both are scenic rides. The tower faces a large plaza and pavilion. Inside are elevators that carry visitors up and down between observation levels, eating places, and souvenir shops. From the tearoom in the Tower the view is spectacular. To the west is the red-brick Seoul Railway Station and Namdae-mun (Great South Gate). On a clear day the

visitor can see Seoul's urban area stretching far to the west, merging into Inchon on the Yellow Sea. A short distance north from Namdae-mun is Toksu Palace, and farther north, nestled at the foot of the northern mountains, are the great palaces of Kyongbok, Changdok, and Changgyong. Samillo Elevated Road can be traced from downtown to the eastern edge of the city and then southward to one of three tunnels under Nam-san. From the tower's southern windows the newest part of the city, south of the Han River, comes into view. Immediately to the west is the huge dome of the National Assembly Building on Yoi Island in the Han River; high-rise office and apartment buildings cover much of Yoi-do. Sixteen bridges cross the river, connecting busy traffic arteries. Seoul Sports Complex and the new Olympic facilities are visible to the east.

남산식물원, 동물원

**Nam-san Botanical Garden and Zoo.** Behind the Nam-san Public Library is a small zoo with ducks, owls, pheasants, monkeys, deer, and other wildlife. From the zoo, steps lead up to the hilltop Botanical Garden. Inside the large glass-domed structure are acres of ferns and cactus; outside are lovely walks and a fountain. The admission charge is reasonable. Downhill from the garden is a museum dedicated to the great Korean patriot, Ahn Chungkun. The Korean-style building contains papers and displays relating to Ahn's murder of a Japanese general in 1909, an event that kindled Korean nationalism and hope at a time of national despair over the impending annexation of the country by Japan.

장충단공원

## CHANGCHUNGDAN PARK

Changchungdan Park is adjacent to Nam-san Park on the east; it is south of Seoul Stadium and Tongdaemun (Great East Gate) and near the Changchung Gymnasium and the Shilla Hotel. The park takes its name from an altar in its center, the Altar of Encouragement of Loyalty, dedicated to the grand chamberlain and others who died defending the palace during the tragic murder of Queen Min by the Japanese in 1895.

어린이 대공원     어린이회관

## CHILDREN'S GRAND PARK
## AND CHILDREN'S CENTER

This famous park, located in the eastern part of Seoul not far from Walker Hill, offers amusements for the young at heart of all ages. Rides, outdoor play areas, restaurants, and a small zoo provide outdoor fun for everyone. Next to the park is the Children's Center, a highly participatory museum of science and technology for young people. Entrance fees are less than $1 for adults.

**Children's Grand Park.** Created on the site of the old Seoul Country Club, this lovely park has acres of lawns, wooded hills, and lakes. Small rock gardens cover the old sand traps; fountains and a botanical garden have been added. Along the paths are playgrounds with swings, slides, tunnels, seesaws, and climbing apparatus. Tables with sun shades, arbors with benches, flower gardens, a music shell, a swimming pool and a roller skating rink are among the many attractions. In the zoo are friendly goats, cows, monkeys, and birds; there are also lions, tigers, and two elephants. In the pony riding area, young riders can circle a pretty lake.

**Korean Children's Center.** The exhibits of the Children's Center demonstrate the basic scientific principles underlying much of today's technology. The first floor contains the Planetarium, the Fundamental Science Room, and the Applied Science Room. The Living Science Exhibition and the Space Science Exhibition are on the second floor. In the large section devoted to electronics, the young visitor can see friends on a TV phone, work an electric circuit, or learn how a calculator works. In the astronomy exhibit, planets can be moved in their orbits, and other models illustrate other aspects of the universe. The Planetarium offers regular showings. Additional participatory exhibits include volcanic eruptions and earthquakes, navigation locks, human and animal bodies, the environment, and the exploitation of natural resources. In the basement there is an amusement hall and a cafeteria where a variety of refreshments is available.

## SEOUL GRAND PARK

This large new park on the southern outskirts of the city has become a popular recreational area and a major attraction for tourists during and since the Olympic Games. Located off the Seoul-Pusan Expressway at the foot of Chonggye-san, the park covers more than 6.4 million square meters. Many city bus routes terminate at Seoul Grand Park, and there is parking for 4,500 cars. An entire day can easily be spent in the zoological garden. In addition to the zoo, the nation's largest integrated leisure park is being constructed here. The Modern Art Museum has reopened here; a botanical garden, Seoul Land (a Korean version of Disneyland), and other cultural facilities opened in time for Olympic visitors in 1988. The park is open daily from 9 a.m. to 6 p.m. Admission fees are reasonable.

### 서울 대공원 동물원
**Seoul Grand Park Zoo.** With more than 4,000 animals of about 450 species, Seoul Grand Park Zoo ranks fifth in size among world zoos. Many of the animals were moved from the old Changgyong-won Zoo; 1,870 animals of 187 species have been imported from abroad. For easy access to the zoo, electric cars called *kokiri* circle the park at frequent intervals. Dolphin shows throughout the day are popular with audiences of all ages.

### 식물원
**Botanical Garden.** In this garden are 14,000 plants of over 3,000 species arranged in two separate sections: a greenhouse, and a forest in which birds and other animals live.

### 청소년 문화회관
**Youth Culture Center.** Completed in mid-1988, the center illustrates Korea's culture and history. It is located just north of the playground.

### 서울 랜드
**Seoul Land.** The Korean version of Disneyland, Seoul Land covers 850,000 square meters of land near the Youth Culture Center. The first phase opened in time for the Asian Games in 1986; the second phase opened in May 1988. Four theme sections—Land of the Future, Land of Fantasy, Garden of Samcholli (referring to the Korean Peninsula), and Village of the World—offer a variety of educational and entertaining displays to visitors.

## 사직능
## SAJIK ALTAR

Sajik Altar, a sacred shrine of the Yi dynasty, is located in Sajik Park at the base of Inwang Mountain in the northwestern part of the old city. It is a short distance from the tunnel that runs under Inwang Mountain to Independence Arch. This beautifully landscaped park contains a playground and a statue of the great Yi dynasty philosopher Yi Yulgok. Actually, there are two altars: the eastern altar is dedicated to the god of Earth, the western altar to the god of Harvest.

The two great square altars stand on a large stone platform on a low stone terrace, surrounded by an iron fence. Ceremonial arrow gates once flanked the entrance steps on each of the four sides. At each corner is a small upright stone, and in the floor are heavy iron rings that were used to anchor ceremonial awnings. About 20 feet square, the altars are faced with cut stones and topped with earth; they stand open to the sky.

Sacrifices to the gods of Earth and Harvest were offered here each year, in spring and autumn, by the king on behalf of the nation. Sacrifices also took place on the twelfth day after the Tae Han (Great Cold of Winter), and special offerings were made from time to time for crops or for rain. In 1897, when the king took the title of emperor, ceremonies were transferred from Sajik Altar to the new Altar of Heaven.

## 독립문
## INDEPENDENCE ARCH

Independence Arch, a stone gate similar in design to the Arc de Triomphe in Paris, stands outside West Gate at the intersection of the Mun-san Highway and the road over Inwang Mountain, through the tunnel from Sajik Altar. Its name, Tongnip-mun (Independence Gate), is inscribed at the top, in Korean letters on the south side and in Chinese characters on the north. On each side a Korean flag is carved; during Japanese rule, this was the only place where the Korean flag could be displayed.

The arch was built by the Independence Club, founded in 1896 by a group of progressive-minded young men. Alarmed by Japan's victory in the Sino-Japanese War of 1894-95, the club sponsored debates and speeches on the subject of resistance to foreign domination. Their newspaper, *The Independent*, was printed in *Hangul* on one side and in English on the other. Independence Arch symbolized Korea's independence from China and the establishment of the Empire of Taehan (Great Han, as opposed to the Three Hans of antiquity); soon it became associated with the struggle for freedom from Japanese occupation.

## 팔각당　(팔각정)
## THE TEMPLE OF HEAVEN

All that remains of the Altar of Heaven is an outlying building, Hwanggung-u (Temple of the Imperial Firmament), which is commonly called the Temple of Heaven by foreigners and Palgak-tang (Eight Cornered Pavilion) by Koreans. Built to house a memorial tablet to the spirit of King Taejo, founder of the Yi dynasty, this three-storied building stands between the Chosun and Lotte hotels. The Altar of Heaven was built in 1897 on the site now occupied by the Chosun Hotel. When Japan annexed Korea in 1910, the Japanese tore down the altar and built the hotel (1914). The old building was replaced in 1967 by the new, modern Chosun.

Prior to 1897, when Korea declared her independence from China and King Kojong became Emperor Kwangmu, only the

Chinese emperor had been considered worthy to offer sacrifices directly to Heaven. The Korean king, who had accepted a position of subservience to the Chinese emperor, sacrificed instead to the spirits of Earth and Harvest, at Sajik Altar. With independence, the ceremonies of sacrifice were transferred to the new Altar of Heaven and the Korean emperor became entitled to offer sacrifices on behalf of his nation directly to Heaven.

The Altar of Heaven was built on a circular platform with three levels, hence the name Wongu-dan (Round Hill Altar). There were nine ceremonial steps leading from each terrace to the next, against the marble retaining walls. The number nine represented Heaven. The Altar was dedicated on October 11, and King Kojong officially assumed his new title of emperor on October 12, 1897, offering his first imperial sacrifice that morning. Also on that day Queen Min, who had been demoted to the rank of commoner at Japanese insistence following her murder, was posthumously raised to the rank of empress.

## 정동
### CHONG-DONG (LEGATION ROW)

Chong-dong (Benevolence Street) lies west of Toksu Palace and south of Sinmun-ro (Sinmun Avenue). The area took its name from the tomb of Taejo's Queen Kang; occupied by royalty in the sixteenth century, in the seventeenth century it became a residential area for aristocrats. When Korea was "opened" in 1876, an attempt was made to keep foreigners from living within the city. But in the 1880s, the king arranged for much of the land along Chong-dong to be sold to the foreigners who were coming in large numbers to staff the legations, do missionary work, and start commercial enterprises. King Kojong soon had reason to appreciate the presence of the foreign legations near the royal residences. He fled to the Russian Legation after the murder of Queen Min and at various times used the proximity of the American Legation to impress upon the Japanese that he had the sympathy of the American government.

By the turn of the century, the United States, Russia, Germany, Great Britain, and France had legations along Chong-dong; the Italians came in 1901. Gradually the Westerners replaced the existing houses with Western-style homes. Some of the churches and mission schools which were built near the legations are still standing. Ewha Girls' School, named "Pear Flower" by Queen Min, and Paejae Boys' School, named "Hall for Rearing Useful Men" by King Kojong, were built in the mid-1880s. The Chong-dong

Methodist Church dates from 1910, although the congregation began in 1887. Other remaining buildings include the compound of the American Embassy and ambassador's residence, the British Embassy and Anglican Cathedral, and the Russian Legation tower on top of the hill.

**American Embassy Residence.** The American Embassy building in Chong-dong has been in the possession of the U.S. government longer than any other embassy residence in the world. The Korean-style one-story structure has been remodeled and enlarged so many times that it bears little resemblance to the original, which had been the concubines' quarters, bought in 1884 from members of Queen Min's family by Lucius Foote, the first American minister to Korea.

**Seoul Club.** Several historic events took place at the Seoul Club, located beyond a wall to the west of the American Embassy residence. Originally built by King Kojong as a palace library, Chungmyong-jon (Hall of Double Brilliance), the king set it aside for the foreign community to use as a club. Kojong moved here during the Toksu Palace fire in 1904. On the night of November 18, 1905, in this building, Ito Hirobumi, first resident-general of Japan, forced the Korean court to sign a treaty making Korea a Japanese protectorate. It was here also that on July 24, 1907, King Kojong abdicated, another step toward the annexation of Korea by Japan in 1910. The building is still owned by the Yi family.

**British Embassy and Anglican Cathedral.** The British Embassy, built in 1890, is the only example of nineteenth century diplomatic architecture left in Seoul. Adjoining it is the Anglican Cathedral, built in 1926 and noted for its beautiful gardens.

**Former Russian Legation and Church of St. Nicholas.** The white tower is all that remains of the Russian Legation, which was built on the hill at the north end of Chong-dong in 1890. Since the Korean War, the property has been used as a housing area for refugees. But the ruins of the old legation, called Yangkwan, have been designated Community Cultural Relic No. 3 in memory of King Kojong's safe sojourn there after the Japanese murdered Queen Min. The Church of St. Nicholas was connected with the legation by a gate in the wall between them. The Orthodox congregation suffered much during the Russo-Japanese War of 1904-05 and, more recently, from the conflict of American and Soviet interests on the Korean Peninsula. With the presence of Greek and American soldiers since the Korean War, it has enjoyed a revival.

## 용인 자연농원
## *YONGIN FARM LAND*

This very spacious farm-park south of Seoul, reached via the Seoul-Pusan Expressway, offers performances by trained animals, a bus ride through Lion Country, an amusement park, picnic areas, formal gardens, and restaurants. A map can be obtained at the management office near the entrance gate. Cost of admission is about $3 (₩2,200) for adults and $1.50 (₩1,100) for children over five.

There are rocket rides, a roller coaster around the mountain, and a haunted castle in the amusement park. Paths in the zoo area are well laid out, and the cages are surrounded by low fences or moats. There is a small enclosed children's zoo where sheep, lambs, goats, and kids can be petted. For entertainment there is a pig and parrot show five times a day, and there is a peacock review every hour from 10:30 a.m. to 4:30 p.m. A bus takes visitors on the Lion Country Safari to see lions lazily lying in the sun or roaring and fighting each other for food tossed out by the gamekeepers. The museum at Yongin is in an impressive Korean-style building housing an extensive collection of native Korean arts and crafts. Cold drinks and ice cream are sold at refreshment stands in the park, and among several good restaurants are a Chinese restaurant and one offering Korean pork barbecue.

## 성
## *FORTRESSES*

In the vicinity of Seoul there are two major mountain fortresses, ancient barriers for the defense of the capital: Namhansan-song (South Fortress) and Pukhansan-song (North Fortress). Located 20 miles southeast of Seoul, South Fortress can be reached by either of two scenic routes, via Inchon or via Songnam City. North Fortress dates from the Paekje Kingdom, but the present five-mile wall and 17 gates were completed in 1626 to defend the city against the Manchus. On a clear day it is worth driving to the summit for a spectacular view of Seoul and the Han River Valley. North Fortress is reached by taking the Mun-san Highway past Sodae-mun intersection and turning right at the first checkpoint. The fortress wall encircles Samgak-san (Three Peak Mountain). Many hikers climb to these peaks for breathtaking views of Seoul.

## 한강 유람선
## *CRUISES ON THE HAN RIVER*

Seoul has recently inaugurated new cruises along its picturesque Han River. Pleasure boats start from Yoido, Seoul's affluent residential and business district, and Chamsil, site of the 1988 Olympic Games. Sailings connect Yoido and Chamsil, as well as Yoido and Tangsan Bridge. Fares for adults are ₩3000 round trip and ₩3,500 one-way; for children, ₩1,500 round trip and ₩1,900 one way.

# WALKING TOURS

**A**long the following walking routes are many of the most fascinating sightseeing spots in the colorful old city plus significant buildings of modern Seoul. Starting at the Lotte Hotel, a central location, the tours combine walking with taxi rides to compress maximum interest into a reasonable half-day walk. The historical sites on each route are explained below.

## TOUR I: KYONGBOK PALACE

Lotte Hotel — City Hall — "Newspaper Row" — Kojong Memorial — Yi Sunshin's statue — Sejong Cultural Center — Kwang-hwa-mun — Capitol Building (National Museum) — Kyongbok Palace

*Time:* 3 hours, plus browsing time
*Means:* Walk to Kyongbok Palace; taxi back to the Lotte Hotel

Walk west from the Lotte Hotel and enter the underpass on the corner; bear left, crossing under the street, and up the left-hand stairway at the end. A shopping arcade in the underpass sells a great variety of items. At the top of the steps is City Hall. Beyond City Hall and across the street, Taepyong-ro, is Toksu Palace. Down that street to the left is Great South Gate (Namdae-mun)— National Treasure No. 1, built in 1395. To the right is "Newspaper Row," beginning with the 20-story Korea Press Center Building. Across the street is the *Chosun Ilbo* newspaper building; at the next intersection, on Chong-ro, are the offices of *Tong-A Ilbo*, an influential daily.

At Kwanghwa-mun intersection there is an impressive view down Sejong-ro, a handsome boulevard with Pugak Mountain forming a background for the Capitol Building, Kwanghwa-mun, and Yi Sunshin's statue. Enter the underpass and bear right, using the stairway marked "To Monument Side." At the top of the steps is Kojong Memorial. Turn left and continue north on Sejong-ro. In the center is the statue of Admiral Yi Sunshin, the sixteenth-century naval hero who defeated the Japanese navy with his ironclad "turtle ships." Continue past the Ministry of Communications and the Overseas Telephone and Telegraph buildings. Across the street is the Sejong Cultural Center, a large building where cultural events take place almost every evening. On the right are two very similar buildings: the first is the American Embassy; the other is occupied by the Ministry of Culture and Information. The red brick building on the corner houses the Ministry of Construction; across the street is a new 20-story skyscraper housing government offices.

The main entrance to the Capitol Building enclosure is Kwanghwa-mun. Its arches are ancient, but the pavilion is a concrete replica built when the gate was replaced in this location in 1969. The *Hae Tae* seated in front guard against fire. Directly behind Kwanghwa-mun is the magnificent Capitol Building. Finished in 1926 by the Japanese, it was severely damaged during the Korean War and repaired in 1962. In July 1986 the Capitol was dedicated as the main Korean National Museum, housing the finest architectural and artistic treasures.

To enter Kyongbok Palace, go west on Yulgok-ro, named for Yi Yulgok, an outstanding Confucian scholar-philosopher of the Yi dynasty, and around the wall to East Gate. The tower in the intersection is Tongsipcha-gak, which originally was part of the palace wall. An inexpensive ticket admits visitors to the palace for an enchanting experience of traditional Korea.

From East Gate, proceed to the center of the grounds, to the huge courtyard of the throne hall, Kunjong-jon. There the visitor can pause and visualize rows of high military and civilian officials standing beside the stone tablets marking their places according to rank, awaiting a royal audience. Note the carved centers of the ceremonial stairways up to the balustraded terraces over which the king's sedan chair was carried. To the rear of the hall is the richly decorated throne chair, canopy, and screen. There are interesting displays in the courtyard corridors.

West of the throne hall is the "floating" banquet hall, Kyong-hoe-ru or Hall of Happy Meetings. Set on an island in a beautiful lotus lake, this pavilion was the scene of many royal banquets and it is still used by the government to entertain important guests on special occasions. This area is an excellent example of the most formal of Korean garden landscapes and is breathtaking in every season.

At the north end of the grounds is an exquisite smaller hexagonal pavilion, Hyangwon-jong, set in a natural-style lotus lake. Behind it is the National Folklore Museum, noted for its model man's room and woman's room from a traditional house. Utensils of everyday life show the Korean love of the decorative arts. The multi-level Korean-style building to the east is another national museum.

Returning to the center of the grounds, there is a hall containing the royal residential quarters, and through the center is a mall lined with pagodas and other national treasures. In the southeast corner is a unique 10-story intricately carved pagoda dating from 1348. Exit through East Gate and retrace the route along Sejong-ro and Taepyong-ro back to City Hall and turn left to the Lotte Hotel.

### TOUR II: TOKSU PALACE/SOUTH GATE

Lotte Hotel — Temple of Heaven — Lotte Arcade — Chosun Hotel — Toksu Palace — Museum — Taepyong-ro — Kim Yusin's Statue — South Gate

*Time:* 2 hours plus browsing time

*Means:* Walk to Toksu Palace, South Gate; walk or taxi back to the Lotte Hotel

Toksu Palace can be reached by following the first part of Tour I, but this tour leaves the Lotte Hotel through the courtyard. Here, between the huge Lotte and Chosun hotels, stands the triple-roofed Temple of Heaven. When Korea declared its self-reliance and independence from Chinese influence in 1897, King Kojong assumed the title of emperor and moved the sacred sacrifices from Sajik Altar to the Temple of Heaven. Enter the main floor of the towering Chosun Hotel for the view from the Ninth Gate restaurant in the Chosun. Walk west from the Chosun, past a number of shops, restaurants, and tearooms, to Taepyong-ro, a wide boulevard. Toksu Palace is across the street: go through the underpass to the opposite corner, then use the overpass; proceed north toward City Hall and cross a narrow street. The entrance gate, Taehan-mun, is at the southern end of the palace grounds, set back from the street. The price of admission is reasonable.

Take the broad walk past the ticket collector's booth to Chunghwa-jon, the throne hall. Walk leisurely through the beautiful grounds to the two Western-style buildings in the northwest part, now the National Museum of Modern Art annex. Follow the path back to the entrance gate and, exiting, turn right. Cross the

*Silk shop in Namdaemun Market*

street on the overpass and walk south on Taepyong-ro. On the right are the Samsung Main Building and the Tong Bang Life Insurance Company headquarters. Around South Gate are many street vendors; to the east is the huge Namdae-mun Market. Approaching South Gate, cross two alleys and pass two underpass entrances; continuing to a point just beyond the Gate, the red brick Seoul Railway Station is visible a long block away. Look at Namdae-mun, National Treasure No. 1, from this angle; then return to the underpass to cross Taepyong-ro. Walk, or take a taxi, north to City Hall Plaza and turn right to the Lotte Hotel.

## TOUR III: PAGODA PARK

Lotte Hotel — Pagoda Park — Pagoda Shopping Arcade — Insadong and "Mary's Alley" — Min Yong-hwan's Statue — Chogye-sa — Chong-ro Bell

*Time:* 2 hours plus browsing time
*Means:* Taxi to Pagoda Park; walk back to Lotte Hotel

Take a taxi from the Lotte Hotel to the entrance gate, Samil-mun, of Pagoda Park on Chong-ro just east of Samil-ro. This lovely small park in the center of Seoul is a popular spot for relaxing and remembering the Independence Movement of 1919. Among the sights is a statue of Son Pyonghui, leader of the Chondo-gyo and of the Independence Movement. Against the east wall is the

Independence Memorial, noted for its symbolic statuary and 10 bas-reliefs depicting episodes in the independence struggle. At the rear of the park is the famous Wongak-sa Pagoda, from which the park takes its name. A large stone turtle stands nearby; the tablet on its back once told the story of Wongak Temple.

Leaving the park through the main gate, turn right to the two-story Pagoda Shopping Arcade, a complete and modern shopping center. West of the arcade, across Samil-ro, is Insa-dong, a district famous for its curio shops. Sometimes called "Mary's Alley," the area no longer abounds with bargains as it once did, but the shopper who is willing to haggle can buy genuine antiques, paintings, old coins, brassware, books in many languages, and other artifacts at reasonable prices. Many of the shopkeepers speak English.

At the north end of the street is Anguk-dong intersection. In the rotary stands a statue of Min Yonghwan, a military aide-de-camp of the Yi dynasty who struggled valiantly against court acceptance of Japanese domination at the turn of the century; he failed and committed suicide in protest. Staying on the south side of Anguk-dong intersection, turn left across tree-lined Namdaemun-ro and again left. About a block to the south is a small alley with a metal arch and a sign in English marking the entrance to Chogye Temple. Around the courtyard are interesting stone carvings, lanterns, and a small pagoda. The large main temple is open to the public; the entrance door is on the east. Inside, Chogye-sa is classical and beautiful; it has been modernized with electric lights, a piano, and a public address system. One of the auxiliary buildings houses the temple bell.

Leaving the temple, turn right and walk south to Chong-ro, the old main street of Seoul. On the left is Hwashin Department Store, a multi-storied yellow-brown brick building. Across Chong-ro, on the southeast corner, set back from the sidewalk, is the Chong-ro Bell in Posingak Pavilion. This is the great bell that was rung at sunrise and sundown to signal the opening and closing of the city gates. One of the largest bells in the world, it is still rung on Samil Day in honor of the Independence Movement and on a few other special occasions.

Continuing south across Chonggye-ro, you'll see the Choheung Bank skyscraper. You will pass through the banking and tailoring district to the next main intersection, which is Ulchi Avenue; turn right to the Lotte Hotel.

## TOUR IV: CHANGDOK PALACE

Lotte Hotel — Tonhwa-mun — Changdok Palace Buildings — Secret Garden — Chong-myo

*Time:* 3 hours plus browsing time

*Means:* Taxi to Changdok Palace; walk or taxi from Chong-myo to Lotte Hotel

Take a taxi from the stand in front of the Lotte Hotel to Tonhwa-mun, the main gate of Changdok Palace. Buy a ticket at the window and enter the palace through this gate. Take the time to read the sign on the left, which explains the palace in English and Korean. To the right is the Bridge of the Conspirators. Cross the bridge and on the left is the complex of palace buildings surrounding the throne hall, Injong-jon.

인정전

**Injong-jon.** The palace office offers its own walking tour through the complex. To follow it, pay another small fee at the ticket booth in front of the throne hall entrance and go in. The route leads through the corridor museum, which displays royal costumes and artworks. From the courtyard of the throne hall the visitor can view its splendid interior. Passing through Sonjong-jon, Huijong-dang, and Taejo-jon, a complex of royal apartments, one gets a feeling for the lifestyle of Yi dynasty royalty from the displays of original furniture and implements. Many fixtures date from the reign of the last king, Sunjong (r. 1907–1910). In an exit corridor are exhibits of beautiful artwork on screens and scrolls that further illustrate palace life at the height of its glory. The Injong-jon tour ends across from Nakson-jae, the villa where surviving members of the royal family still live. Visitors who have previously obtained a permit and made a reservation can visit Nakson-jae.

비원

**Secret Garden.** To the left and over a rise are two gates: one leads down into Changgyong-won (Changgyong Park); the other leads up into the Secret Garden. Admission to the Garden is included in the palace entrance fee. Inside the gate and over a rise is the entrance to an underground passage, a hidden resting room for the king that is now hung with historical photographs. A small admission fee buys a brochure-ticket with a map and explanation of the Secret Garden.

Both the main path and the underground passage lead to a refreshment stand overlooking a large pond surrounded by buildings. On the far side of the pond, climb the hill and go through Osu-mun (Fish Water Gate) to Chuham-nu Pavilion. Behind

Chuham-nu small gates lead to a valley where there are several buildings, gates, refreshment stands, and a pond. Down a steep path and around the pond to the left is the elaborate Yongyong-dang, the house of 99 *kan* (the largest house a commoner could have), to which the king escaped in time of war or where the royal family retreated to avoid court formality and enjoy a more normal life. Over the ridge behind the house is Pando-ji (Pando Pond), a small lake in the shape of ancient Korea. Across the bridge over Pando-ji is a refreshment stand; go left up a broad path, over the next hill, and down to the Okryu-chon area. The highlight of this sylvan spot is the spring, which feeds water into a channel carved in rock. Kings used to set cups of wine floating down the channel, simultaneously beginning a poem and challenging officials to finish the poem before the wine spilled over the falls, or else be forced to drink it.

Roaming the garden on small side paths is permitted, but do keep oriented to the main path. Returning from Okryu-chon to Pando-ji, continue on the main path down into the central area of the garden. Skirt the hill of Chuham-nu and pass through a simple stone arch called Pullo-mun (Not Aging Gate) to ensure a long life. Next is a larger gate, Kumma-mun (Gold Horse Gate) and two small buildings on the hillside where the king once entertained guests. Gates on the east side of the enclosure lead into Changgyong Park. The visitor with time and energy may wish to see the botanical garden and the remains of Changgyong Palace.

종묘
**Chong-myo.** Enjoy the exquisite landscape views along the main path back to Nakson-jae in Changdok Palace and take the wide path to the left. It leads to a bridge across Yulgok-ro and into Chong-myo, the park of the Royal Ancestral Tablet Houses. Two huge buildings contain the royal tablets. The first is Yongnyong-jon, distinguished from the other by a raised portion in the center of the roof, which contains tablets of kings who died without direct heirs to the throne. The second hall, with a straight roof, is Chong-jin, containing tablets of kings whose sons succeeded them.

Near Chong-jin is a small enclosure containing the Chong-myo Museum, which displays utensils used in the sacrifices that were offered to ancestors on ceremonial days. Beyond the gate on the east is a large house where the king changed into his ceremonial robes. He used the raised center part of the path; others walked on the sides. Continue on the path to the gate and down to

Chong-ro (Bell Avenue). Taxis are available there or across the street at the Se-un Arcade shopping center. A short ride brings the visitor back to the Lotte Hotel.

# MAIN STREETS OF SEOUL

The suffixes *ro*, *lo*, and *no* mean avenue or road; *dong* means street. North-south streets in the old city have numbers, but are marked with their historic names as well. Forms used on printed city maps are given here.

### NORTH–SOUTH STREETS

Beginning on the eastern side of the city and moving to the west:

TAEPYONG-RO (Great Peace Avenue) runs from South Gate, Namdae-mun, north to the intersection with Chong-ro. On the western side is Taehan Gate to the Toksu Palace grounds; on the eastern side are the Seoul Plaza Hotel and City Hall.

NAMDAEMUN-RO (South Gate Avenue) angles northeast from South Gate and turns north toward the Great Bell at Chong-ro.

SEJONG-RO (named for King Sejong, who invented the *Hangul* alphabet in 1446) is the continuation of Taepyong-ro north to the famous Capitol Building. At the southern end is the statue of Admiral Yi Sunshin; opposite the northern end is Kwanghwa Gate and the southern wall of the Kyongbok Palace compound. Korean government office buildings, Sejong Cultural Center, and the American Embassy are located along this wide boulevard.

ANGUK-DONG (Peaceful Country Street) is the continuation of Namdaemun-ro north from the Chong-ro Bell intersection to Yulgok-ro. Chogye-sa (Chogye Temple) and Buddhist and Oriental art galleries are found at the northern end (First Street).

SAMIL-RO (March 1 Avenue, named for the date of the 1919 Independence Movement) angles south from the Anguk Dong rotary through "Mary's Alley," across Chong-ro, to Taegye-ro. Pagoda Park is located on the northeast corner of the intersection of Samil-ro and Chong-ro (Second Street).

TONHWAMUN-NO (formerly Tonhwa-ro) runs south from Tonhwa Gate at the southwest corner of the Changdok Palace grounds, south to Toegye-ro. Several theaters are located along this thoroughfare (Third Street).

CHANGGYONG-RO (Glorious Blessings Avenue) runs between the eastern side of the Changyong Palace enclosure and the western edge of the Seoul National University campus (dental college), south across Chong-ro and Ulchi-ro to Toegye-ro (Fourth Street).

## EAST–WEST STREETS

Beginning with the northern part of the city and moving southward:

YULGOK-RO (named for Yi Yulgok, a great Choson [Yi] dynasty scholar) runs east from the National Museum, along the southern boundary of the Kyongbok Palace grounds, eastward past Tonhwa Gate at the southeastern corner of the Changdok Palace grounds, between the Changgyong Palace compound on the north and Chongmyo Royal Shrine on the south, past Korea National University (dental college), and into Ihwa-ro, which goes to East Gate (Tongdae-mun). West of the National Museum, Yulgok-ro becomes Sajik-ro, which runs past Sajik Park where Sajik Altar is located.

CHONG-RO (Bell Avenue) runs from the intersection with Sejong-ro (north) to Taepyong-ro (south) eastward to Tongdae-mun and beyond. The Great Bell is located in a pavilion across from the Hwasin Department Store at the intersection with Namdaemun-ro. The continuation of Chong-ro to the west is called Sinmun-ro (New Gate Avenue); it in turn becomes Chungjong-ro.

CHONGGYE-RO (Clear Stream Avenue) runs from Taepyong-ro on the west to a point just south of Tongdae-mun and beyond. The Samil Expressway (elevated road) runs most of the length of Chonggye-ro.

ULCHI-RO (named for General Ulchi Mundok of the Kingdom of Koguryo who defeated a Chinese army in 612) runs between City Hall at Taepyong-ro on the west to the eastern edge of the city. Many tall modern office buildings, the Lotte Hotel, and Lotte Department Store line this busy avenue.

CHUNGMU-RO (named for the honorary title of Admiral Yi Sunshin who invented the ironclad "turtle boats" that helped defeat the Japanese Invasions of 1592-98) runs from the Central Post Office on Namdaemun-ro on the west, eastward to Samil-ro, after which it jogs to the north and continues eastward until it runs into Toegye-ro.

TOEGYE-RO (named for a great Korean philosopher of the sixteenth century) runs from Seoul Railway Station on the west to a junction with Ulchi-ro just beyond Seoul Stadium on the eastern side of the city. Nam-san rises along the south side of Toegye-ro.

MYONG-DONG (Bright Street) runs between Taepyong-ro, through a major commercial and shopping district, to the intersection with Samil-ro, and eastward to Seoul Stadium. Myong-dong is unparalleled as Seoul's top shopping and entertainment center. Along the broad new avenue and adjacent alleys crowd many shops for both tailor-made and ready-made clothes. On the fringes are such major department stores as Lotte, Shinsegae, and Midopa, and long underground arcades add further to the bewildering variety of shopping experiences available in this downtown area. Myong-dong is also known for its many restaurants, coffee shops, clubs, stand-up bars, and other entertainment spots. The old Myong-dong Catholic Cathedral, constructed in 1890s, the new Hotel Lotte, and Chosun Hotel are landmarks along Myong-dong.

ITAEWON-RO runs 1.5 kilometers from the main U.S. Army base at Yongsan to the Hannam-dong Rotary, just on the other side of the Third Nam-san Tunnel. Its proximity to the base has made Itaewon a shopping and entertainment district particularly appealing to American military personnel, foreign residents, and overseas visitors to Seoul. English is spoken widely, and American dollars are welcome. Itaewon offers affordable entertainment, with many places that especially accommodate tourists: fast-food restaurants, coffee shops, small bars, discos, and cafés offering jazz, country and western, or the latest pop music. The street is lined on both sides with many tailors, eelskin stores, and shops selling sporting goods, shoes, handbags, ready-to-wear clothing, jewelry, antiques, paintings, and calligraphy. There are many shopping bargains, including those of the world-famous Jindo Fur, where visitors can buy top quality furs at half the American price.

YONG-DONG is a part of the growing area of southern and eastern Seoul across the Han River, just over the Hannam Bridge. This huge section is new Seoul and has many high-rise apartments, hotels, fashionable shops, and elegant restaurants, as well as recreational facilities, parks, and gardens along the Han River. The Korea Exhibition Center (KOEX), also located in Yong-dong, is home to outdoor exhibitions and trade fairs for Korean and foreign companies. Most of the hotels are located in Chamshil, one of the southern suburbs across the Han River, and the site of the 545,000-square-meter Seoul Sports Complex, which was the center of the Olympic Games—five major facilities including the Main Stadium and the Olympic Villages—and will serve as the chief venue for international games of all sorts for years to come.

*YOIDO* 여의도

YOIDO (YOI ISLAND), a small island in the middle of the Han River just across a short bridge from Mapo-dong, is a major hub of the metropolitan area. The bridge connecting this island to the city to the north leads directly to Yoido Plaza, which is the site of military reviews and other huge outdoor gatherings; Pope John Paul II came here in 1984 and a million people flocked to the plaza to greet him. The island is the new home of a large number of government buildings such as the National Assembly, huge corporate office buildings, the headquarters of Korean Broadcasting System (radio and television), Munhwa Broadcasting Corporation (television), the Korean Stock Exchange, and the Daehan Life Insurance Building (the "Golden Tower"), which, at 63 stories, is the tallest in Korea. There are many tourist attractions in this building—an observation deck, an aquarium (Sea World), a roof garden, and the IMAX Theater ("eye maximum and maximum image"). Yoi Island is not only a commercial center, but also has high-rise apartment buildings, shopping centers, supermarkets, and small shops to accommodate the expanding populace in this burgeoning city of Seoul.

## HOTEL

## ACCOMMODATIONS

As of April 1989, Seoul had 76 Western-style hotels with a total of 16,000 rooms. Of the hotel total, 25 were in the deluxe category, 18 were first class, 16 second class, and 17 third class; there were also two youth hostels with 193 rooms. Seoul also has hundreds of Korean inns (*yogwan*). Many of the large hotels are located downtown, while others are located near Namsan, in Kangnam, and in other scenic areas farther from, but convenient to, the city center. A large number offer deluxe accommodations and attentive, English-speaking staff. Spacious rooms and suites are climate-controlled and typically have large beds, color TV, music, large desks, multiple phones, built-in refrigerators, and stocked bars. The many hotel restaurants offer a cosmopolitan array of cuisines and 24-hour room service. While the quality of room service offerings may vary, service staff are generally courteous and helpful to the extent language limitations permit. Music for dining is provided by Western-style ensembles and garish discotheques are common attachments.

*Hotel Lotte*

Seoul hotels focus their services on business travelers, with meeting rooms, convention facilities, and services including 24-hour telex, facsimile transmission, and multilingual secretaries. Over 30 airline offices, including numerous outlets of Korean Air, are located within the major hotels. A connoisseur's selection of antiques, fashions, jewelry, and gifts is found in the shops of hotel lobbies and arcades. With underground garages and valet parking, a car or taxi can usually be summoned at a moment's notice.

On the whole, the western-style hotels are more expensive than the Korean inns. Price ranges for deluxe hotels are ₩90,000-125,000 (suites ₩150,000 and up); first class, ₩57,600-72,000; second and third class, ₩25,200-36,000. Korean inns can range between ₩18,000 and 21,600. These prices do not include the 10 percent value added tax, which does not apply to overseas visitors (as an incentive to international travel). At tourist hotels, a 10 percent service charge for room, meals, and other services is added to the bill; tips are therefore not required. During the spring and fall, and when international conventions and other major events are taking place in Seoul, reservations are necessary. Hotel brochures can be obtained through hotels, travel agencies, or the Korea National Tourism Corporation (10 Ta-dong, Chung-gu, Seoul). All can be booked at Kimpo International Airport.

As a group, Seoul hotels are superb. A few rank with the world's finest. The top-rated luxury hotels as of November 1988 were: the *Lotte*,

*Lotte World, Shilla, Westin Chosun, Sheraton, Hilton, Hyatt, Sofitel Ambassador, Plaza, President, Palace, Koreana, Royal, King Sejong, Riverside, Seoul Garden, Ramada Renaissance, Ramada Olympia, Swiss Grande, Inter-continental, Tower, Nam Seoul Washington, New World, Riviera,* and *Capital.* Most were built with foreign participation and belong to international chains.

For their proximity to government offices, business and financial institutions, and the royal palaces, many business travelers, diplomats and tourists prefer the *Lotte, Westin Chosun, Plaza, Koreana,* and *President;* all are near City Hall Plaza. Located in the adjacent shopping area of Myong-dong are the *King Sejong* and *Royal.* The *Hilton* is located just south of the city center between the Daewoo Center and the western edge of Namsan (south mountain). Located along the northern and eastern edge of Namsan are the *Sofitel Ambassador, Shilla,* and *Tower.* Along the southern edge of Namsan is the *Hyatt,* which is also located just above the Itaewon shopping and entertainment area. Located just south of Itaewon is the *Capital Hotel.* Crossing the Panpo Bridge into the southern part of Seoul, known as Kangnam (south of the river), there are eight hotels arranged roughly west to east and running near to Olympic Park. They are the *Riverside, Palace, Nam Seoul Washington, Ramada Renaissance, New World, Riviera, Inter-continental,* and *Lotte World.* These hotels are convenient to the Korea World Trade Center and the Olympic sports facilities.

Four other hotels situated by themselves but within easy access to the downtown and Kangnam areas are the *Sheraton,* located along the north bank of the Han River in a resort-like setting on the eastern edge of Seoul; the *Ramada Olympia,* located at the foot of Mt. Pukhan National Park (10 minutes north of downtown); the *Swiss Grand,* located at the foot of Mt. Paenghyon (only 10 minutes northeast of downtown); and the *Seoul Garden,* located just before crossing the Mapo Bridge into Yoido from downtown.

More modest hotels are also available in the main areas of Seoul. Downtown are the *New Naija, New Seoul, New Kukje,* and *Seoulin.* In the Itaewon area are the *Crown, Hamilton,* and *Itaewon Holiday.* In Kangnam are the *Samjung, Young Dong, Hilltop, Prima,* and *Clover.* And in Yoido are the *Manhattan* and *Yoido.*

Seoul's hotels are social institutions for Koreans as well as centers for international business. Interviews of news sources, silent first dinners of young couples just introduced by their parents and a marriage broker, and lunchtime or after-work get-togethers take place in the great downtown hotels.

**Yogwan (Korean-style Inns) and Youth Hostels.** There are
hundreds of traditional style inns called *yogwan* throughout the
country. They range from large buildings with private bathrooms
and shower facilities to small traditional-style Korean homes. A
comfortable *yogwan* in Seoul can be found for ₩18,000-21,600
and in the countryside they are even less expensive. You remove
your shoes before entering the room. Korean-style bedding includes
a small mattress called a *yo* and a quilt called an *ibul*. A chain of
20 youth hostels has been established throughout most of Korea's
provinces, with rooms that accommodate two to eight persons at
very reasonable rates.

## SUPERIOR HOTELS

### NEAR CITY HALL
롯데 호텔

**Hotel Lotte** (Deluxe—1,282 rooms for some 2,000 guests).
With 38 stories in its main wing, this is the most prestigious
address for overseas visitors to the capital. Located in the heart of
downtown, this busy showcase offers spectacular views in all directions of the bustling city, palaces and monuments, and the surrounding hills. The hotel is part of the Lotte Center Complex, a
Seoul landmark and a veritable city within a city.

In early 1988, the Lotte completed a new 34-story wing featuring 307 guest rooms, a "sky" restaurant, and a Chinese restaurant
with floor shows. A notable adjunct to the new wing is an auto-
mated parking lot for 849 cars.

Chefs at the Hotel Lotte contribute much to the new international charisma of Seoul: La Coquilla serves fine seafood and Italian
specialties; Prince Eugene recaptures eighteenth century
Vienna; La Seine offers a magnificent international buffet and
windows overlooking the city; excellent Korean food is served at
Mugung-hwa and the Po-suk-jung Dinner Theater; the Benkay and
Momoyama offer Japanese delicacies; the Sky Cafeteria can be
reached by Korea's only high-rise exterior glass elevator; fish 'n'
chips and a game of darts can be enjoyed at the Bobby London
Pub; the Windsor Bar is an entertaining piano bar; the Cafe Gar-
denia is a delightful sidewalk restaurant on the Lotte Plaza; and
the Cafe Peninsula offers generous servings of Oriental, American,
and European fare. At night, the Bistro is a lively discotheque,
and the Lobby Lounge serves both cocktails and teas from around
the Orient against a spectacular backdrop inspired by Korea's famous waterfall at Mt. Sorak.

The Businessman's Corner provides every kind of secretarial and communication service. Convention facilities include 21 private banquet and meeting rooms, a completely equipped international conference center with modern audio-visual systems including wireless interpretation, exhibit facilities, underground parking for 1,100 cars, and the Crystal Ballroom, which can be converted into a huge restaurant, nightclub, or reception hall accommodating more than 1,400 persons.

Shops in the Lotte feature the best of everything that Korea has to offer: from Korean handicraft items to an exquisitely tailored wardrobe, and more than a dozen specialty restaurants and food shops. The duty-free shop on the eighth floor offers the widest selection of duty-free items in Korea. An efficient airport delivery system lets the visitor collect purchases at the time of departure.

*Address:* 1 Sokong-dong
*Telephone:* 771-10
*Cable:* HOTELOTTE
*Telex:* LOTTEHO K2353315

조선 호텔

**The Westin Chosun** (Deluxe—471 rooms for 900 guests). The Chosun is Seoul's first joint-venture hotel with participation by the Korean government and a foreign investment group. It is a notably serene and elegant hotel, located one block from City Hall. The Ninth Gate restaurant and bar on the ground floor of the Westin Chosun is famous for its fine French cuisine and for the lovely view of an ancient gate and the Temple of Heaven, landmarks of Korea's regal past. It is a favorite meeting place for international and Korean business people. The hotel provides four other excellent restaurants, several bars, the popular Xanadu nightclub, an indoor pool, and complete convention facilities. A huge underground shopping arcade includes a drug store, nightclub, sauna, barbershop, beauty salon, photo shop, packing center, and flower shop. The Chosun is popular with Americans in Séoul.

*Address:* 87 Sokong-dong
*Telephone:* 771-05
*Cable:* WESTCHOSUN
*Telex:* K24256

서울 플라자 호텔

**Seoul Plaza Hotel** (Deluxe—542 rooms for 1,050 guests). Located just opposite City Hall, some rooms in the Seoul Plaza offer a glimpse of Toksu Palace. All rooms are spacious and tastefully decorated. The Sky Lounge is very comfortable, and for dining

*Seoul Plaza Hotel*

there is a German-style pub as well as Chinese, Japanese, French, and Korean (highly regarded) restaurants. For shopping, the hotel has a modest basement arcade, and the Sogong Arcade is close by. A business center, telex rooms, an airline counter, tour information desk, bakery, laundry, and other amenities serve the needs of business travelers and tourists. The decor features appealing pastel marbles and carpeting. Despite its location, the *Plaza* succeeds as the most peaceful of the City Hall hotels.

*Address:* 23 2-ka Taepyong-ro
*Telephone:* 771-22
*Cable:* PLAZAHL SEOUL
*Telex:* K26215

프레시던트 호텔

**Hotel President** (Deluxe—303 rooms for 550 guests). Conveniently located on the eastern side of City Hall Plaza, the Hotel President commands a panoramic view of Toksu Palace. Its fine selection of dining facilities includes Western and Japanese restaurants and bars.

*Address:* 188-3 1-ka Ulchi-ro
*Telephone:* 753-3131
*Cable:* HOTEL PRESIDENT
*Telex:* PRETEL K27521

## 코리아나 호텔

**Koreana Hotel** (Deluxe—280 rooms for 560 guests). Within two blocks of the Capitol Building, which is home to the main National Museum, the Koreana also is within easy walking distance of Toksu Palace, City Hall, and Kyongbok Palace. Rooms are spacious and have all the amenities, including room service, laundry and valet service, telex and telephone, secretarial services, and free morning newspaper. Excellent restaurants include Japanese cuisine at the Saka-e on the 10th floor, an international menu in the Rendezvous main dining room, and light meals in the Danube on the second floor as well as the Sunrise coffee shop, serving tasty breads and pastries baked on the premises. The Koreana has five banquet halls that cater to gatherings of all sizes. The Lipo Bar off the main lobby is a popular meeting place.

*Address:* 61 1-ka Taepyong-ro, Chung-ku
*Telephone:* 720-9911
*Cable:*HOTELKOREANA
*Telex:* KOTEL K26241

## 서린 호텔

**Seoulin Hotel** (First class—207 rooms for 380 guests). The Seoulin is about a five-minute walk to the Capitol Building and about a 10-minute walk to leading businesses, the palaces, foreign banks, and entertainment. Accommodations are comfortable.

*Address:* 149 Sorin-dong, Chongno-ku
*Telephone:* 735-9115
*Cable:* HOTEL SEOULIN
*Telex:* SEOULIN K28510

## 스위스 그랜드 호텔

**Swiss Grand Hotel** (Deluxe—512 rooms). Seoul's first major hotel to be connected with a European chain, the Swiss Grand is a deluxe facility with a combined epicurean and health focus. L'Arbalete is Korea's first Swiss restaurant. The hotel also features an elaborate health club, tennis courts, swimming pool, and a 2-km. jogging course. Furnished two- to five-bedroom suites located in an adjacent hotel building are also offered at attractive rates for longterm guests.

*Address:* 201-1 Hong-un dong, Sodaemun-ku
*Telephone:* 356-5656
*Telex:* K34322

## AROUND NAM-SAN

신라 호텔

**Hotel Shilla** (Deluxe—672 rooms for 1,286 guests). The Shilla is an exciting combination of traditional Korean and Western architecture and offers a beautiful view of Nam-san and the city. Its Korean restaurant is expensive but excellent, and there are several other fine restaurants. Rooms are large and tastefully appointed; all have central air-conditioning and heating with individual controls, telephone, television, refrigerator, and music. The hotel has a shopping arcade, health club, nightclub, bar, sauna, swimming pool, massage, jogging course, and buses to the airport and the city.

*Address:* 202 2-ka Changchung-dong
*Telephone:* 233-3131
*Cable:* HOTEL SHILLA
*Telex:* SHILLA K24160, K24257

앰바사도 호텔

**Hotel Ambassador** (Deluxe—450 rooms for 906 guests). The Ambassador is near Changchung Park and Field House and adjacent to the National Theater, at the foot of Nam-san's eastern slope. An excellent commercial hotel, it is about 10 minutes' drive to downtown. The Ambassador has seven fine restaurants, five bars and a nightclub; convention facilities, sauna, beauty salon and barbershop, secretarial services, a hotel doctor, and a large shopping arcade. Car rental and tour agencies are located in the lobby.

*Address:* 186-54 2-ka Changchung-dong
*Telephone:* 275-1101
*Cable:* AMBASSADOR SEOUL
*Telex:* K23269

서울 힐튼 호텔

**Seoul Hilton International** (Deluxe—712 rooms for 1,424 guests). Opened in 1984, the Seoul Hilton occupies a four-acre site near Great South Gate. It is adjacent to the Daewoo business group center and only a short walk from Seoul Railway Station, Namdae-mun Market, and the subway. A business center offers full services and the convention hall and meeting rooms are the largest such facilities in Seoul. Six restaurants include the beautiful Garden Café, L'Orangerie (alongside a glass-roofed pool)—offering the best international buffet in the city—Juliana's of London club/disco, and an accomplished yet reasonably priced Italian restaurant. There is a health club, beauty parlor, barbershop,

*Hyatt Regency Seoul*

drugstore, gift shop, florist, bakery, music lounge, sauna, and gymnasium. Rooms are not overly large but are smartly decorated.

*Address:* 395 5-ka Namdaemun-ro
*Telephone:* 753-7788
*Cable:* HILTELS SEOUL
*Telex:* K26695 KHILTON

### 타워 호텔

**Tower Hotel** (First class—209 rooms for 400 guests). On Namsan's east slope, the Tower has a panoramic view of Seoul. It offers a nightclub, swimming pool, golf course, health club, sauna, barber and beauty shop, souvenir shop, and other amenities in addition to very comfortable rooms. The lobby has a spartan, metallic look.

*Address:* San 5-5 2-ka Changchung-dong
*Telephone:* 236-2121
*Cable:* TOWERTEL
*Telex:* TOWER K28246
*Fax:* 235-0276

### *ITAEWON*

### 하이얏트 호텔

**Hyatt Regency Seoul** (Deluxe—604 rooms for 1,136 guests). Located on the southwest slope of Nam-san, the Hyatt Regency has a spectacular view of the Han River and southern Seoul. Rooms are tastefully decorated and have all the amenities. The hotel offers simultaneous translation facilities for international meetings. A shuttle runs to downtown Seoul. Services include a tennis court, bar, nightclub, airline office, barber and beauty shops, indoor/outdoor pool, sauna, clinic, laundry, coffee shop, and shopping arcade.

One of Seoul's more social hotels, the lobby is a grand spot for people-watching, especially at night.

*Address:* 747-7 Hannam-dong
*Telephone:* 798-0061
*Cable:* HYATT SEOUL
*Telex:* K24136

### 해밀턴 호텔

**Hamilton Hotel** (First class—139 rooms for 278 guests). Near the mosque at the end of Itaewon, the Hamilton has a lively nightclub and Seoul's best Indian restaurant. Other services include a coffee shop, barber and beauty shops, and florist shop. The rooms are comfortable and there is shopping nearby (the Hamilton recently underwent renovation).

*Address:* 119-25 Itaewon-dong
*Telephone:* 794-0171

### 크라운 호텔

**Hotel Crown** (First class—157 rooms for 314 guests). In Itaewon, the Crown is close to shopping and to the U.S. Eighth Army post. It offers both Korean and Western restaurants, bar, nightclub, beauty salon, barber shop, and coffee shop. The Crown is a popular meeting place for high-ranking Korean and U.S. military personnel.

*Address:* 34-69 Itaewon-dong
*Telephone:* 797-4111

### 캐피탈 호텔

**Capital Hotel.** Completed in 1988, the first-class Capital has 288 guest rooms arrayed in 18 floors (plus 5 below ground). Accommodations include twins, suites, and Korea-style heated *ondol.* For active guests, the Capital offers swimming, sauna, and bowling, and convention seating for 800.

*Address:* 22-76 Itaewon-dong, Yongsan-ku
*Telephone:* 794-0778
*Telex:* K23502

## TOEGYE-RO

### 세종 호텔

**King Sejong Hotel** (Deluxe—250 rooms for 300 guests). Owned and operated by Sejong University, the hotel is located in the business district and adjacent to the downtown shopping area, facing beautiful Nam-san. The Sejong is noted for a delicious Korean buffet and a small museum of Korean artifacts. It has a beauty salon, barber shop, shopping arcade, game room, gift shop, coffee shop, nightclub, sauna, travel counter, health club, and secretarial services.

*Address:* 61-3 2-ka Chungmu-ro
*Telephone:* 776-1811
*Cable:* HOTESEJONG
*Telex:* SEJONTE K27265

### 퍼시픽 호텔

**Pacific Hotel** (First class—103 rooms for 220 guests). Conveniently located on Toegye-ro at the foot of Nam-san, the Pacific Hotel is noted for its lively theater restaurant with stage shows nightly. It also has Chinese and Japanese restaurants, a coffee shop, grill, nightclub, and shopping arcade.

*Address:* 31-1 2-ka Namsan-dong
*Telephone:* 777-7811.

## MYONG-DONG

### 서울 로얄 호텔

**Seoul Royal Hotel** (Deluxe—309 Rooms for 533 guests). Standing in the heart of the downtown area, the Seoul Royal is near major office buildings, embassies, shopping centers, and the Korea World Trade Center. Nearby, too, is the Myong-dong Cathedral. Services provided include restaurant, coffee shop, grill, snack corner, cocktail lounge, discotheque, nightclub, souvenir shop, barbershop, beauty salon, game room, tailor, and shopping arcade.

*Address:* 6 1-ka Myong-dong
*Telephone:* 756-1112
*Cable:* ROYALHOTEL
*Telex:* SLROYAL K27239

### 사보이 호텔

**Savoy Hotel** (Second class—105 rooms for 191 guests) is located in the middle of Myong-dong, in the center of shopping, restaurant, and entertainment areas. There is a Japanese restaurant as well as a steak house, coffee shop, and lobby bar.

*Address:* 23-1 1-ka Chungmu-ro
*Telephone:* 776-2641

### EASTERN SEOUL

쉐라톤 워커힐

**Sheraton Walker Hill** (Deluxe—770 rooms for 1,540 guests). In southeastern Seoul, the Sheraton stands amid 139 beautifully landscaped acres that overlook sweeping views of the Han River and surrounding hills. The Kayagum Theater Restaurant is a Korean showplace; the Casino and Disco nightclubs also are very popular. Rooms and facilities are elegant. Outside facilities include a golf driving range, tennis courts, and swimming pool; there is also an indoor pool. All amenities are available, including barber and beauty shops, health center, snack corner, and large shopping arcade.

*Address:* San 21 Kwangjang-dong Songdong-ku
*Telephone:* 453-0121
*Cable:* WALKERHILL SEOUL
*Telex:* WALKHTL K28517

맘모스 호텔

**Mammoth Hotel** (First class—219 rooms for 423 guests). Adjacent to Chongyangri Railway Station in eastern Seoul, the Mammoth offers easy access to the subway and downtown, as well as the Mammoth Shopping Center. For dining there is a theater restaurant and a buffet restaurant; there is a lobby lounge, bar, and nightclub; also provided are beauty and barber shops, a sauna, and a department store for shopping.

*Address:* 620-69 Chonnong-dong, Tongdaemun-ku
*Telephone:* 962-5611
*Cable:* MAMMOTH SEOUL
*Telex:* 32482

### NORTH OF SEOUL

서울 올림피아 호텔

**Ramada Olympia Hotel**      (Deluxe—310 rooms for 760 guests). The Olympia is located on the way to the scenic Pugak Skyway in Seoul's northern valley. It offers a coffee shop, buffet restaurant, banquet hall, Japanese restaurant, and barbecue garden; a lobby lounge and nightclub; barber and beauty shops; health club, sauna, and souvenir shop.

*Address:* 108-2 Pyongchang-dong, Chongno-ku
*Telephone:* 353-5121
*Telex:* SELOLYM K23171

*Hotel Inter-Continental Seoul*

## YOIDO

맨하탄 호텔

**Hotel Manhattan** (First class—182 rooms for 380 guests). Located on Yoido in the Han River, the Manhattan is close to the National Assembly Building and many business and government offices. The hotel offers Korean and Japanese restaurants and a Western-style grill and coffee shop. Facilities include a ballroom, night club, bar, barber and beauty shops, and a sauna.

*Address:* 13-3, Yoido-dong
*Telephone:* 782-8001
*Telex:* K24767

### 여의도 호텔

**Yoido Hotel** (Second class—120 rooms for 210 guests). The Yoido Hotel is located across from the May 16 Plaza and the Lucky Goldstar Twin Building. It has well-appointed rooms.

*Address:* 10-3 Yoido-dong
*Telephone:* 782-0121

## SOUTH OF THE HAN RIVER AND SEOUL SUBURBS

### 서울 팔래스 호텔

**Seoul Palace Hotel** (Deluxe —298 rooms for 600 guests). Located across from the Kangnum Express Bus Terminal, the Seoul Palace offers attractive accommodations, Western restaurants, a coffee shop, barber and beauty shops, sauna, health club, game room, souvenir shop, and shopping arcade.

*Telephone:* 532-0101
*Cable:* SELPALACEHTL
*Telex:* PALACHL K22657
*Address:* 135, 63-1 Panpo-dong, Kangnam-ku

### 라마다 르네상스

**Ramada Renaissance.** A deluxe 501-room hotel boasting a swimming pool and indoor tennis court, the Renaissance has Korean, Japanese, Chinese, and Continental restaurants, as well as a full range of athletic facilities. There is a complete business center on the premises.

*Address:* 676 Yoksam-dong, Kangnam-ku
*Telephone:* 555-0501
*Telex:* K34392     *Fax:* (02)553-8118

### 남서울 호텔

**Nam Seoul Washington.** (First class—179 rooms for 390 guests). Convenient to the new area of southern Seoul, across the Han River, the hotel is only half an hour from Kimpo International Airport and a short trip into the downtown area. It has a coffee shop and buffet restaurant, barber and beauty shops, game room, nightclub, bar, and other amenities.

*Address:* 602-4 Yoksam-dong, Kangnam-ku
*Telephone:* 552-7111

*Cable:* NASOTEL
*Telex:* NASOTEL K25019

리버사이드 호텔

**Hotel Riverside** (Deluxe—203 rooms for 450 guests). About 20 minutes from downtown by taxi, the Riverside is another popular hotel in the southern new development area. Its facilities include a buffet and a Japanese restaurant, grill, bar, nightclub, beauty salon and barbershop, and arcade.

*Address:* 6-1 Chamwon-dong, Kangnam-ku
*Telephone:* 543-1001

뉴월드 호텔

**New World Hotel.** The deluxe New World Hotel, completed in late 1987, has 250 rooms and is well situated for business people who need to be near KOEX or the Korea World Trade Center.

*Address:* 112-5 Samsong-dong, Kangnam-ku
*Telephone:* 557-0111
*Telex:* 23226

리비에라

**Riviera.** Opened in early 1988, the Riviera is a luxury-class hotel set conspicuously on the banks of the Han River. Although among the smaller of the Olympic-year hotels, the 15-story Riviera offers no less than seven banquet rooms, an art gallery, a waterfall lounge, and convention seating for 1,000. It also boasts a complete business center.

*Address:* 53-7 Chong-dam-dong, Kangnam-ku
*Telephone:* 540-0178

인터콘티넨탈 호텔

**Hotel Inter-Continental.** A large 33-story facility with 604 rooms, Seoul's first entry in the Inter-Continental chain opened in 1988. Deluxe accommodations include 222 large suites. Its huge convention room can seat 2,500. The hotel is situated in the Korea World Trade Center complex.

*Address:* 159-1 Samsung-dong
*Telephone:* 553-8181
*Telex:* K34254     *Fax:* 552-6422

롯데 잠실 호텔

**Hotel Lotte World.** This hotel is part of a huge entertainment and shopping complex located along Sokchon Lake. The complex features an amusement park, an indoor folk village, a sports center, and a shopping mall that includes two huge department stores. The amusement park extends out into Sokchon Lake, which is also the site of the Seoul Nori Madang, an outdoor performance arena for traditional Korean folklore presentations. With 35 stories and 511 guest rooms, the hotel opened in 1988. Facilities include a 5,000-seat banquet hall — one of the largest in Seoul — and the Viking buffet restaurant, shaped like an ancient Scandinavian pirate vessel.

*Address:* 40-1 Chamshil-dong
*Telephone:* 419-7000
*Telex:* K33728    *Fax:* 417-3655

## ECONOMY CLASS HOTELS

### 아스토리아 호텔
**Astoria Hotel.** On Toegye-ro at the foot of Nam-san, the Astoria is close to Korea House.
*Address:* 13-2 Namhak-dong
*Telephone:* 267-7111

### 그린파크 호텔
**Green Park Hotel.** In beautiful surroundings on the slopes of Pukhan-san in northeastern Seoul, the Green Park features a large outdoor swimming pool.
*Address:* San 14 Ui-dong
*Telephone:* 993-2171

### 서울 가든 호텔

**Seoul Garden Hotel.** The hotel is near the Mapodaegyo Bridge and has recently opened a Middle Eastern restaurant.
*Address:* 169-1 Tohwa-dong, Mapo-ku
*Telephone:* 717-9441

### 서울 호텔
**Seoul Hotel.** Located a short distance from the Capitol Building and the American Embassy, the Seoul offers Western and Japanese restaurants.
*Address:* 92-Chongjin-dong, Chongno-ku
*Telephone:* 735-9001

### 영동 호텔
**Yong Dong Hotel.** South of the Han River, across the Third Han River Bridge, this is a small but busy hotel.
*Address:* 6 Nonhyun-dong, Kangnam-ku
*Telephone:* 542-0112

## YMCA 호텔

**YMCA Hotel.** Conveniently located in downtown Seoul, the "Y" takes both male and female guests. Its facilities include indoor swimming pool and gymnasium; it also has a Western-style restaurant, barber and beauty shops. Language courses are offered.

*Address:* 9 2-ka Chong-ro, Chongno-ku
*Telephone:* 732-8291

## YOGWAN (KOREAN INNS)

There are many Korean-style inns in Seoul. The costs range from moderate to economy. On the bare *ondon* floor (heated underneath in cold weather) a mattress (*yo*), a quilt (*ibol*), and a hard pillow are provided. If ordered in advance, Korean breakfast and dinner are served. Washing and toilet facilities are shared, but a hot bath in the evening is private. For additional information on Korean yogwans, please call the Korea Hotel Central Association (KCHA) in Seoul at 783-9866.

### 은당 여관

**Undang Yogwan.** This inn provides a traditional garden setting in the midst of the city; rooms vary from large to small.

*Telephone:* 765-4194

### 대원여관, 대지여관

**Daiwon and Daeji Inns.** Both of these *yogwan* are conveniently located west of Kwanghwa-mun intersection in the second alley north from Sinmun-no, and are favorites with young travelers.

*Telephones:* Daiwon, 725-7891; Daeji, 723-4659

## YOUTH HOSTELS

### 반도 유스 호스텔

**Bando Youth Hostel.** In Yoksam-dong on the south side of the river, the Bando accepts only groups for a six-bunk room.

*Address:* 679-3 Yoksam-dong, Kangnam-ku
*Telephone:* 567-3111

### 아카데미하우스 유스 호스텔

**Academy House Youth Hostel.** A coffee shop and bar are provided for overseas guests.

*Address:* San 76 Su Yu-dong
*Telephone:* 993-6181

한국 아카데미 재단 하우스

**Korea Academic Foundation House.** In Dongsung-dong (former Seoul National University), this hostel accepts only foreign students. Rooms and meals are very reasonable; reservations are necessary.

*Address:* 199-1 Dongsung-dong
*Telephone:* 741-4630

Hospitality is a tradition in Korea. Whether the visitor goes to a hotel or an inn, an atmosphere of friendliness, warmth, and unlimited service prevails, and at rates that are very reasonable compared to costs in other world capitals. Further information can be obtained by calling the Korea Tourist Association (757-2345), the Korea Youth Hostel Association (266-2896), or, regarding *yog-wan*, 783-9866. See also the more comprehensive hotel listing in the Tourist Directory at the end of this book.

## CUISINE

### SEOUL CUISINE

Seoul offers many excellent restaurants with reasonable prices and attentive service. A wide variety of cuisines, from delicious traditional Korean meals to excellent American, French, Italian, Continental, Chinese, Japanese, and other ethnic dishes, are served at all major hotels and hundreds of restaurants in Seoul. A good restaurant listing is also available in *Sports and Dining*, published by KNTC (Korea National Tourism Corporation). The telephone number of the KNTC Tourist Information Center is 757-0086.

Despite the impact of the West on Korea, traditional cuisine has changed little. Most Koreans enjoy three hearty Korean meals every day. Especially popular with visitors are the famed barbeque beef dishes and the fiery cabbage *kimchi*, which stimulates the appetite.

## RESTAURANTS

Hotel restaurants usually specialize in Western, Chinese, and Japanese as well as Korean cooking. Their prices are somewhat higher than in smaller restaurants. Some of the best kept secrets of Korea are the small, privately owned restaurants now numerous throughout the city. Another is the *kisaeng* houses; they are expensive, but the food and entertainment are superb.

*Hanjongsik, a traditional array of Korean dishes*

All of Seoul's deluxe hotels have excellent restaurants and probably are the best in Seoul for Western cuisine. Lotte and Shilla have pure Korean restaurants; the others offer Korean fare at their buffet or cafe restaurants. All offer superb Continental, Chinese, and Japanese cuisine. Many small restaurants offer *yang sik* (Western food), such as breaded pork cutlet, spaghetti, Mexican salad (cabbage and mayonnaise), and steak with or without a fried egg on top. The food is good for the reasonable price.

Fast food has found its way to Korea: Burger King, Wendy's, Denny's, Dunkin' Donuts, and Kentucky Fried Chicken are located near Pagoda Park, and MacDonald's has several outlets in Seoul. Pizza Hut and Pizza Inn also have chains in Korea. The basement of the Daewoo building opposite the Seoul Railway Station has several Korean specialty food shops—noodles, vegetables, and rice; Chinese, Japanese, and Western-style restaurants; a "sandwich" cafeteria; and a small pizzeria.

## KOREAN CUISINE

용수산

**Yongsusan (Dragon Water Mountain).** Each party of guests is seated in a private room and treated to a highly stylized and refined meal of Korean royal court dishes. Connoisseurs will find the quality worth the rather high price.

*Address:* Samchung-dong (at the front of Kimyung Training Center)
*Telephone:* 732-3019

남문

**Nammoon (South Gate).** Authentic royal court dishes are served in private rooms for parties of several guests; expensive but excellent.

*Address:* 25-6 Samchung-dong
*Telephone:* 722-3423

**Changwon (Great Garden).** Excellent Korean food served in private rooms; expensive.

*Address:* 235 Chongjin-dong
*Telephone:* 072-1807

포석정

**Posukjung.** Located on the lower level of the Lotte Hotel, this dinner theater serves authentic Korean cuisine and features live traditional Korean folk music and dance performances; expensive.

*Address:* 1 Sokong-dong
*Telephone:* 771-0010, ext. 152

한국의 집

**Korea House.** Every dish served here is a delicacy. After dinner guests go to the theater on the premises for an excellent show of traditional Korean performing arts (8:30 to 9:30 p.m.). Reservations are necessary.

*Address:* 80-2 2-ka Pil-dong
*Telephone:* 266-9101

대원각 식당

**Taewongak Restaurant.** Diners are served in small thatched-roofed pavilions scattered over a hillside. All the popular traditional dishes are served with a wide array of side dishes. Reservations are necessary; prices are moderate.

*Address:* 323 Songpuk-dong
*Telephone:* 762-0034

**Samwon Gardens.** Located in Kangnam, Samwon Gardens has long been a favorite in Seoul. It is a traditional Korean restaurant, beautifully decorated with landscaped grounds that feature waterfalls, swings, a pond with goldfish, etc. It has a great atmosphere and is popular with foreign visitors.

*Address:* 623-5 Shinsa-dong, Kangnam-gu
*Telephone:* 544-5351

파인 힐
**Pine Hill.** A moderate-price chain restaurant serving good Korean food, especially "Genghis Khan" barbecue.
*Address:* 88-5 2-ka Cho-dong
*Telephone:* 266-4486

## CHINESE CUISINE

아리산
**Arisan.** Directly across from the entrance to the Hyatt Regency Hotel, the Arisan serves excellent Chinese food at rather expensive prices.
*Address:* 258-6 Itaewon-dong
*Telephone:* 794-0022

희래등
**Hee Lae Dung.** Located in Namsan Village Apartments, the Hee Lae Dung is popular with families on weekends and holidays.
*Address:* San 10, Hannam-dong
*Telephone:* 795-6633

동보성
**Tongbosung.** This is a huge place, popular for its many small specialized eating places. Prices are moderate.
*Address:* 50-8 Namsan-dong, 2-ka
*Telephone:* 755-2727

## JAPANESE CUISINE

Most fine Japanese restaurants are located in the major tourist hotels—Lotte, Seoul Plaza, Pacific, Royal, Hyatt—and they are quite expensive. Many small Japanese-style places offer excellent food, such as fried fish, tempura, *sashimi* (sliced raw fish), at very reasonable prices. A popular Japanese-style restaurant in the city is the Misori.

미조리
**Misori.** Located in the alley to the right of the entrance to the Chosun Hotel, toward Taepyong-ro, the Misori serves authentic Japanese dishes.
*Address:* 14-5 Pukchang-dong
*Telephone:* 771-05

## WESTERN CUISINES

나인스 게이트
**Ninth Gate.** This superb French/Continental restaurant is in the Chosun Hotel. It offers a charming view of a colorful traditional

Korean gate set in a lovely garden. Food and service are excellent; expensive; reservations required.

*Address:* 87 Sogong-dong
*Telephone:* 771-05

### 메트로폴리탄 클럽

**Metropolitan Club.** This is a private, members-only club located at the top of the Lotte Hotel (38th floor). It serves the best Western dishes in Seoul, with fine European wines; very expensive.

*Address:* 1 Sokong-dong
*Telephone:* 771-10, ext. 245

### 프린스 유진

**The Prince Eugene.** Located in the lower level of the Hotel Lotte, this Austrian-inspired restaurant serves superb continental cuisine and rotisserie in an eighteenth-century Imperial Vienna atmosphere.

*Address:* 1 Sokong-dong
*Telephone:* 771-10, ext. 156

### 라 세느

**La Seine.** With panoramic views from the 37th floor of the Lotte Hotel, La Seine serves an international buffet with 70 delicacies from which to choose. Expensive but excellent; charming musical ensemble plays during dinner.

*Address:* 1 Sokong-dong
*Telephone:* 771-10, ext. 047

### 곰의 집

**Bear House.** Located at the east end of the Pugak Skyway Drive, with a sweeping view of the city, the Bear House features steak and abalone.

*Address:* San 5-1, Songpuk-dong
*Telephone:* 762-1448

### 반줄

**Banjul.** Two stories of good food and live entertainment, the Banjul is centrally located and elegant.

*Address:* 12-16 Kwanchol-dong
*Telephone:* 733-4432

### 교보 빌딩 지하

**Kyobo Building Basement.** Located at Kwanghwa-mun intersection, the several small specialty restaurants and cafeteria with Western dishes are very popular at lunchtime; prices are moderate.

외교구락부

**Diplomatic Club.** Located at the foot of Nam-san, the Club serves excellent American food for a party of two or more in a private dining room; expensive.

*Address:* 26-8 Namsan-dong, 2-ka
*Telephone:* 752-5629

하이앗트 식당

**Top of the Hyatt.** The excellent buffet is popular with both Koreans and Westerners.

*Address:* 747-7 Hannam-dong
*Telephone:* 797-1234

사계절

**Four Seasons.** Located behind the Chosun Hotel, the Four Seasons serves good, moderately priced Western food; also has Chinese and Japanese menus.

*Address:* 70 Sokong-dong
*Telephone:* 752-5881

스카이 파아크

**Sky Park.** This deluxe restaurant is not expensive and provides a dazzling view of Seoul from the top of the UNESCO Building; orchestra and floor show nightly.

*Address:* 2-50 Myong-dong
*Telephone:* 776-2955

## *ITALIAN CUISINE*

세종 레스토랑

**Sejong Restaurant.** Located in the basement of the Sejong Cultural Center, the Sejong serves good Italian cuisine in a quiet atmosphere; expensive.

*Address:* 81-3 Sejongno, Chongno-ku
*Telephone:* 737-7863

오페라

**The Opera.** This deluxe Italian restaurant, located on the first floor of the Sejong Cultural Center, serves an excellent luncheon buffet.

*Address:* 81-3 Sejongno, Chongno-ku
*Telephone:* 723-7863

라 칸티나

**La Cantina.** In the basement of the Samsung Main Building, La Cantina serves outstanding pasta dishes, steak, and espresso.

*Address:* 50 Ulchi-ro, 1-ka, Chung-ku
*Telephone:* 777-2579

**Mama Mia.** Located across the river in South Seoul, this restaurant offers charming decor and good food at moderate prices.
*Address:* 58-4 Socho-dong
*Telephone:* 555-8028

## POPULAR RESTAURANTS

**Neul Bom Kong-Won.** This popular spot offers indoor/outdoor dining in several traditional-style buildings.
*Address:* 92-12 Nonhyun-dong, Kangnam-ku
*Telephone:* 543-8804

**Hanilkwan.** This is a chain of popular restaurants serving standard Korean dishes of reliable quality.
*Address:* 50-1 2-ka Myong-dong, Chung-ku
*Telephone:* 776-3388

**The Casa Mexico.** This restaurant is a nice place for Mexican food and atmosphere. It has Mexican decorations and a guitar player on many nights who often leads sing-alongs or plays while guests sing.
*Address:* 751-9 Pangbaepon-dong, Socho-gu
*Telephone:* 593-8136

**Chalet Swiss.** A great restaurant with superb decorations, atmosphere, and authentic entertainment is the Chalet Swiss. It is owned by "Yodeler" Kim who dresses Swiss-style and performs on TV in Korea. Chalet Swiss is located between the Hyatt and Itaewon.
*Address:* 104-4 Itaewon-dong, Yongsan-gu
*Telephone:* 795-1723

## SEOUL RESTAURANTS

### KOREAN STYLE SOPHISTICATED

| | | |
|---|---|---|
| Chjinam | 765-4306 | 34-6 Ikson-dong, Chongro-ku |
| Chongpung | 765-0101 | 99 Iksan-dong, Chongro-ku |
| Chongwungak | 723-3551 | 53-26 Chongun-dong, Chongro-ku |
| Chunyanggak | 725-2444 | 9 Muak-dong, Chongro-ku |
| Koryowon | 723-7266 | 32-43 Songw'ol-dong, Chongro-ku |
| Myongwol | 765-3991 | 34 Ikson-dong, Chongro-ku |
| Punggrimgak | 724-6601 | 11-2 Kyopuk-dong, Chongro-ku |
| Pyolchonji | 725-1828 | 179 Kwanchol-dong, Chongro-ku |
| Samchonggak | 762-0151 | 330-115 Songpuk-dong, Songpuk-ku |
| Shillagak | 725-9861 | 54 Chongwun-dong, Chongro-ku |
| Sonwungak | 765-3138 | 260-6 Wu-i-dong, Tobong-ku |
| Taeha | 765-1151 | 56 Ikson-dong, Chongro-ku |
| Taewongak | 762-0034 | 323 Songpuk-dong, Songpuk-ku |
| Tasong | 723-7900 | 85-18 Kyonji-dong, Chongro-ku |

## WESTERN STYLE

| | | |
|---|---|---|
| Banjul | 733-4432 | 12-16 Kwanchol-dong, Chongno-ku |
| Bear House | 762-1448 | San 5-1, Songpuk-dong, Songpuk-ku |
| Celadon | 445-0121 | Sheraton Walker Hill Hotel |
| Diplomatic Club | 752-5629 | 26-8 Namsan-dong, 2-ka Chung-ku |
| Elysée | 771-22 | Plaza Hotel |
| Four Seasons | 22-5881 | 15th Fl. Samku bldg. 70, Sokong-dong, Chung-ku |
| King's Buffet | 261-1101 | Ambassador Hotel |
| La Cantina | 777-2579 | Samsung bldg. 50 Ulchi-ro, 1-ka, Chung-ku |
| Mama Mia | 555-8028 (Ext. 142) | 58-4 Socho-dong, Kang-nam-ku |
| Ninth Gate | 771-05 | Chosun Hotel |
| Peninsula | 782-8001 | Lotte Hotel |
| Round Table | 776-2641 | Savoy Hotel, 1-ka Chungmu-ro, Chung-ku |
| Ristorante Opera | 723-7863 | Sejong Cultural Center |
| Scandinavian Club | 265-9279 | National Medical Center |
| Sky Park | 776-2955 | 11th Fl. UNESCO Bldg. 2-50 Myong-dong, Chung-ku |
| Steak House | 23-3131 (Ext. 274) | 188-3 1-ka, Ulchi-ro, Chung-ku |
| Tiger House | 22-7706 | 112-9 Sokong-dong, Chung-ku |

## KOREAN STYLE

| | | |
|---|---|---|
| Eunhasu | 776-1811 | Sejong Hotel |
| Kumsujang | 261-1102 | Ambassador Hotel |
| Myongwolkwan | 445-0181 | Sheraton Walker Hill Hotel |
| Poeokjong | 771-10 | Lotte Hotel |
| Flamenco | 776-3378 | 53-6 3-ka Myong-dong, Chung-ku |
| Gourmet | 724-3618 | 39 Insa-dong, Chongro-ku |
| Naksanjang | 763-2374 | 129 Tongsung-dong, Chung-ku |
| Pine Hill | 266-4486 | 88-5 Cho-dong, 2-ka Chung-ku |
| Shinjong | 776-1464 | 21 2-ka, Myong-dong, Chung-ku |
| Hanilkwan | 776-3388 | 50-1 2-ka, Myong-dong, Chung-ku |
| Dokcho | 724-1678 | 49 Insa-dong, Chongro-ku |
| Korea House | 266-9101 | 80-2 2-ka, Pil-dong, Chung-ku |

### CHINESE STYLE

| | | |
|---|---|---|
| Chungkukkwan | 445-0181 | Sheraton Walker Hill Hotel |
| Hongbokak | 260-4446 | Ambassador Hotel |
| Moon Palace | 771-05 | Chosun Hotel Fl. 20 |
| Tao-Yuen | 771-22 | Plaza Hotel Fl. 3 |
| Asowon | 266-1191 | 4-130 Ulchi-ro, Chung-ku |
| Hee Lae Dung | 795-6633 | San 10, Hannam-dong, Yongsan-ku |
| Kosang | 794-8001 | 319 Tongbu-i-ch'on-dong, Yongsan-ku |
| Kukildaepanjom | 777-9523 | 355 Chungrim-dong, Chung-ku |
| Tongbosung | 755-2727 | 50-8 Namsan-dong, 2-ka, Chung-ku |
| Arisan | 794-0022 | 258-6 Itaewon-dong, Yongsan-ku |

### JAPANESE STYLE

| | | |
|---|---|---|
| Akasaka | 798-0061 | Hyatt Hotel |
| Kotobuki | 771-22 | Plaza Hotel |
| Zakuro | 776-2641 | Savoy Hotel |
| Daebon | 776-9917 | 66-4 2-ka Chungmu-ro, Chung-ku |
| Kilcho | 267-7111 | 13-2 Namhak-dong, Chung-ku |
| Misori | 22-3966 | 14-5 Pukchang-dong, Chung-ku |

► ◄
# NIGHTLIFE AND
► ◄
# ENTERTAINMENT
► ◄

Seoul is not dull after dark, and the number of entertainment establishments is steadily growing. Korean nightlife includes *kisaeng* houses (like geisha in Japan) for well-to-do businessmen and visitors; *makkolli* houses (neighborhood pubs) for workers and ordinary folk; casinos for gamblers; cinemas, restaurants, bars, salons, discotheques, nightclubs, and theaters for everyone. For the classical taste, Seoul offers a variety of symphony concerts, operas, and recitals.

**Tours.** Night tours are recommended for the visitor who wishes to sample Seoul nightlife economically. Several major tourist agencies offer excellent packages. Two of the best are *Seoul Night Tour* (Global Tours, tel. 322-0171: $55), a dinner and floor show at the Kayakum Theater Restaurant in the Sheraton Walker Hill Hotel, a visit to the hotel's casino, and a drive along the Han River; and *Seoul Golden Night Tour* (Korea Tourist Bureau, tel. 585-1191), beginning with a trip to Namsan Lookout and a sunset bus drive, then a choice of dinner with a stage show at one of three places—Korea House ($50), Kayakum Theater Restaurant in the Sheraton Walker Hill Hotel ($58), or the Yangban Restaurant ($77).

**Theater-Restaurants.** Elegant entertainment lavishly presented, following an excellent meal, is found at several dinner theaters in Seoul. Outstanding is the *Kayakum Theater Restaurant* in the Sheraton Walker Hill Hotel (tel. 453-0121). Other popular theater-restaurants are *Holiday in Seoul* at the Pacific Hotel (tel. 777-7811; *Sofitel Ambassador Hotel* with a very nice traditional folklore show; *Sanchon*, a Buddhist Vegetarian Restaurant in Insa-dong, offers a small ensemble floor show of authentic Korean singing, dancing, and music; and *Pan Korea* (tel. 267-6105).

**The Po-suk-jung Theater-Restaurant.** This Korean dinner theater in the Lotte Hotel (tel. 771-10) serves delicious lunches from 12 to 3 p.m. and dinners from 6:30 to 9 p.m. to the accompaniment of excellent performances of traditional Korean folk songs and colorful dances. There seems to be no language barrier as beautiful Korean women perform the following programs:

*Shillanggaksi (Bride and Bridegroom)*—a dance recalling the child marriages of the Yi dynasty and celebrating the innocent display of affection between the child bride and groom as they get acquainted.

*Chunhyang Jun (Love Story)*—a dance based on a famous Korean folktale about a noble's son who falls in love with a common girl; they live happily ever after.

*Korean Folk Songs*—sung by ensembles, the songs come from various regions and usually have a tragic quality reflecting the sufferings of the people.

*Pansori (Korean Folk Opera)*—a singer relates a long dramatic story to the accompaniment of a drummer who establishes a basic tempo and varies the drum patterns according to the mood and progress of the story.

*Kayagum Byongchang*—a modern singing style based on folk songs, *pansori*, or long narrative poems, sung to the accompaniment of the *kayagum*.

*Alsong Dalsong (Puzzling)*—a nontraditional Korean dance that pokes fun at sexual identity as four dancers alternately tease and confuse one another through the playful reversal of their masks, which have a man's face on one side and a woman's on the other.

*Salpuri (Exorcist Dance)*—a solo dance telling the story of a widow who longs for her husband, sees his apparition, and then is painfully separated again.

*Farmers Dance*—widely performed at rural festivals as a dance celebrating abundance and thanksgiving, it has its origins in pre-Buddhist tribal rituals.

*Drum Dance*—expresses the feelings of a monk striving against temptation by beating a large drum and eventually achieving Nirvana.

*Angel Dance*—also known as "Heron Dance," it depicts a mystical Korean tale of angels dancing around a magical heron in the clouds with dancers in ethereal costumes moving to inspiring and complex rhythms.

*Nun's Dance*—follows a Buddhist nun's progress from the anguish of pain and hardship to the achievement of Nirvana.

*Fan Dance*—a dazzling array of color and movement in a dance derived from a folk dance form and fan rituals.

*Flower Crown Dance*—a royal court ritual dance by a troupe wearing beautiful flower crowns that were worn only at court ceremonies and moving to the slow tempo associated with court dances.

**Korea House.** This house was a former government guest house that has been turned into a repository for the best in Korean food and traditional entertainment. It is unquestionably the best and most authentic dinner-theater of its kind in Korea. The entertainers include numbered national treasures. President Regan was entertained by this group when he visited Korea in 1983. The entertainers are true artists at dance, music, mime, and play. Reservations are highly recommended. These Korean traditional dances with classical music can be enjoyed at the theater of Korea House (tel. 266-9101), a lovely old mansion located near Taegye-ro at the foot of Nam-san (South Mountain). Excellent performances of the traditional dances are presented, with an admission charge, at 8:30 every evening except Sunday.

**Nightclubs.** Most of the major hotels have nightclubs and discotheques, many with live bands that perform continuously for dancing and listening. *Club Copacabana* (tel. 777-2497) has two floors for dancing. Cabarets include *Pan Korea* (101-2 2-ka Eulji-ro, tel. 267-6105), the *Mammos Cabaret* (620-29 Chunnong-dong, tel. 962-0777), and the *Tower Cabaret* (san 5-5 Changchung-dong, tel. 253-3595). Among the hotel clubs, *Annabelle's* at the Lotte Hotel is quite good for dancing and a small Australian-imported floorshow, and *Holiday in Seoul* at the Pacific and *Xanadu* at the Chosun (tel.

753-9949) are always lively. Lately, the biggest and most popular hotel nightspot in Korea is *J.J. Mahoney's* at the Seoul Hyatt. It just celebrated its first anniversary, and it is where the U.S. Olympic swimmers got into trouble for stealing a vase.

**Casinos.** The one gambling casino in Seoul is at the Sheraton Walker Hill Hotel. The visitor will find posh facilities for roulette, blackjack, poker, and other games. Most of the major tourist hotels have game rooms with slot machines. Casinos in other Korean cities are the Olympos in Inchon, Sorak Park in Sokcho, Paradise Beach in Pusan, Songnisan in Poun, Cheju KAL and Hyatt Regency Sogwipo, both on Cheju Island, and Kolon in Kyongju.

**Discos.** The *Reflections Disco* at the Sheraton Walker Hill and the *Rainforest* at the Hilton are popular disco nightspots for foreigners.

**Cocktail Houses.** A recent phenomenon in Korea, these tend to be expensive. Most have bars and "private rooms" in which patrons willing to spend the money may have the services of hostesses. A tip for a hostess might be ₩10,000 (about $12) just for an evening of chatter. Premium label Western drinks are very high priced. Going with someone who knows his way around can be fun.

**Beer Halls.** Beer halls are relatively inexpensive and can offer a lively evening. Beer can be ordered by draft or by the bottle; those usually available are OB, Crown, and Heineken. The local wine (Majuwang) is inexpensive and quite good. Patrons are expected to order a side dish. Many beer halls present stage shows featuring well-known talent. Among the most popular are the *Empire* (30 Da-dong, tel. 777-3952) and the *Palace* (96 Da-dong, tel. 777-4969).

**Makkolli Houses.** These traditional common-man's drinking houses are found everywhere in Korea. The drink is a native rice brew; milky white in color, mild but quite potent. *Soju*, a stronger drink, can also be ordered. Literally it means burned liquor, that is, distilled and very potent. Interesting side dishes are served with either drink. *Pindaeduk* is a pancake with vegetables and meats mixed into egg batter. With *soju*, pork dishes with vegetables, such as green onions, garlic, and sesame leaves, are recommended. The houses tend to be crowded and rather noisy, but an evening spent in one gives a lot of local color for a reasonable cost.

*Korean classical ensemble performs at Korea House, Seoul*

**Tearooms.** In Korea, the *tabang*, or tearoom, is unique. Providing excellent stereo music as a background to light beverages and snacks, they serve as social and business meeting places. The usual cost for tea or coffee is about 75 cents, although the fashionable coffee houses in hotels charge $1. Barley tea is the most popular drink; extraordinarily delicious is *hodocha*, a thick, sweet walnut tea with pine nuts, into which an egg is dropped just before serving. During the summer months, cool drinks such as the juice of strawberries, watermelons, peaches, and apples are served. Ginger tea and ginseng tea are always available. Upon entering a *tabang*, something must be ordered, but there is no restriction on lingering. Seoul has over 5,000 tearooms, each with its own personality, decor, and clientele. The music varies from classical to hard rock, and the clientele tends to vary accordingly.

**Movies.** Both Korean and foreign films are very popular in Seoul. Korean films tend to be historical dramas or family melodramas. Foreign films stay for weeks at a time at one theater. First-run movie theaters cluster around Chong-ro 3-ka (*Picadilly* and *Dangsosa*), the Pagoda Arcade (*Hollywood Theater*), and Toegye-ro (*Daehan Theater*). Foreign films have Korean subtitles; the original language is retained on the soundtrack. Tickets are $2.50–$3.

**Concerts and Theater.** Western classical music is very popular with Korean audiences, and many concerts, with both Korean and foreign artists, are scheduled during the spring and fall seasons.

The *National Theater*, with two auditoriums, is the home of the National Drama Company, National Ballet, the National Dance Company, the National Opera Company, the National Chorus, the National Symphony Orchestra, the Seoul Philharmonic Orchestra, the National Changguk Company, and several other companies. The National Classical Music Institute, a combined school and research center that preserves Korea's traditional classical music, also sponsors performances. *Sejong Cultural Center* on the west side of Sejong-ro has an impressive dual theater for the performing arts, where both musical and dramatic performances are staged. Two excellent smaller theaters are the *Minye Theater* near Garden Tower, across from the entrance to Changdok Palace, and the *Munye Theater* at Chong-ro 5-ka. "Small Theater" flourishes in Seoul, presenting works by Korean playwrights and translations of popular foreign writers. The *Space Theater* near Changdok Palace specializes in jazz and presentations of traditional Korean performing arts. Daily information is printed in the *Korea Times*, *Korea Herald*, and *This Week in Seoul*.

**Kisaeng Houses.** An invitation to a *kisaeng* house is certain to provide a fascinating evening. Served by a bevy of attractive young women, one is almost overwhelmed by the flood of feminine attention. It is also very expensive. The *kisaeng* is the lovely product of an ancient tradition, initiated by the court during the Koryo Kingdom. Although changed since the turn of the century, much traditional excitement still pervades the *kisaeng* house. *Kisaeng* were chosen for their charm, beauty, and talent and trained from childhood to sing, dance, paint, write, and play many Korean traditional musical instruments. The *kisaeng* became the most highly educated women in the country, the companions of kings, scholars, artists, and high officials. They were not prostitutes, but formed a highly restrictive society. The Korean *kisaeng* culture passed to Japan as the *geisha*, likewise meaning talented and accomplished entertainer. Among the leading *kisaeng* houses are: *Han Lim* (142-2 Rakwon-dong, tel. 765-1144), *Sun Wan Kak* (260-6 Ui-dong, tel. 993-3986), *Dae Ha* (56 Iksun-dong, tel. 765-1151), *Shilla Kak* (Iksun-dong, tel. 725-9861), *Myungwol* (34 Iksun-dong, tel. 765-3991), *Ojin Am* (34-6 Iksun-dong, tel. 765-4306), *Pungrim Kak* (11-2 Kyojo-dong, tel. 724-6601), *Chungpung* (99 Iksun-dong, tel. 765-0101), *Daesung* (Kyongji-dong, tel. 723-6979), and the most famous and most expensive, *Sam Chung Kak* (330-115 Sungbuk-dong, tel. 762-0151). Most Seoul *kisaeng* houses are located in a section of Iksun-dong behind Pagoda Park, and reservations are required.

*Hotel souvenir shop, Seoul*

# SHOPPING

### Special Report
### by
### Nancy Griffin

Visitors to Korea will find that Seoul has some of the best shopping in Asia. Prices are very good and the careful shopper will find that many items are of high quality. The key to successful shopping in Korea is knowing where to look and what to look for. With the exception of the more modern shopping establishments (such as department stores), bargaining is still widely practiced.

## SHOPPING TIPS

## FOR KOREA

Within Asia, Korea ranks close to Hong Kong as a shopper's paradise. These days, more foreign and higher quality domestic products are appearing on the local market. Unfortunately, the shopper must have a keen eye to spot the huge array of counterfeit products that also abound.

1. *Counterfeit products are widespread in Seoul; some bear a striking resemblance to the real product.* This market of imitations ranges from phony Louis Vuitton bags and Ralph Lauren polo shirts to college textbooks and Apple Computer software, all at absurdly low prices. The heyday of counterfeit products may be coming to a close due to Korea's new copyright law (mid-1987) and to increased enforcement of existing trademark laws (both within Korea and by importing countries such as the United States).

2. *Shoppers are likely to encounter both overfriendly shopkeepers and rude store clerks in the course of a shopping spree.* But you must remember where you are. While English is being studied and practiced country-wide, Koreans' vocabulary and comprehension are still limited. This can bring out some insecurity on the part of the Koreans as they actually put their knowledge of the English language to practical use.

3. *If you've got the time, shop around and compare prices before making any purchases, especially major outlays.* Don't allow the clerk to pressure you into a sale. There's a good chance a similar outlet is within walking distance. Hawkers, particularly in the Itaewon district, will also try to pressure you to visit certain shops. Be careful and always compare prices.

4. *If at all possible, try not to look like a "tourist."* The tourist look will be especially counterproductive where haggling is practiced. Keep the "oohs" and "ahhs" to yourself. This is a dead giveaway that you are new to Korea, where a mask of disinterest is the mark of an experienced shopper.

5. *Familiarize yourself with Korean currency.* It is possible for shopkeepers to make honest mistakes and quote you a price of ₩20,000 when ₩2,000 was meant. This could result in an inadvertant loss of over $20.

6. *Major credit cards and travelers' checks are accepted almost anywhere*, except for the markets and arcades where you must pay in cash—Korean won. Don't be surprised if 4% is added to your purchase when you choose to pay with a credit card. This mark-up ostensibly covers the handling fee.

Cash is always the preferred method of payment. Shoppers should therefore be familiar with daily exchange rates. It is best to pay with Korean won (payment by foreign currency—especially US dollars—is sometimes requested by street venders, but the exchange rate will almost certainly be unfavorable). As a rule, you can leave your personal checkbook at home, although some merchants in Itaewon will accept a personal check for certain large purchases.

7. To Koreans, as in many countries in Asia, answering a question with a yes and a nod can actually mean no. Ask the question and listen carefully.

8. If you need a suggestion as to where to shop to find a particular item not included in this chapter, ask a friend living in Seoul or another foreigner on holiday. Locals, from the travel agents to waiters are, more likely than not, receiving a commission for suggesting a particular shop. Thus, this approach does not necessarily result in the best quality or price. Beware of the shop located outside a sightseeing bus stop that is pushed strongly by a tour guide.

9. Returning unused purchases is possible in the department stores and usually in shops with fixed prices. Keep the receipt for proof of sale. It may be difficult to return an item to one of the markets or even in Itaewon for that matter. You'll find that a once fluent English-speaking shopkeeper is suddenly deaf or totally confused when you attempt to communicate.

There is much more involved here than a simple return of an $8 soiled pair of jeans. The Korean shopkeeper could lose "face" and will go to great lengths to avoid a return. To steer clear of this confrontation, inspect your purchase carefully before buying. Many garments are seconds or rejects and there are no Korean laws forbidding their sale.

10. As mentioned above, to haggle or bargain over the price of an item is a practice acceptable in the traditional markets, some underground arcade shops and with street vendors. Prices in department stores, shopping centers, and hotel shops are not negotiable.

Despite the recent enforcement of "fixed-price stickers" on items, Itaewon prices are still somewhat flexible, depending on the shop and the particular purchase. If in doubt, give it a try. But don't push if the clerk is insistent on the fixed price.

11. On major purchases it is wise to consult and deal with the manager. He can often reduce the price when the employee cannot.

12. Try on clothing whenever possible. Do not rely on the marked size and inspect the garment carefully.

13. An "introduction" or "referral" to a shopkeeper by a local or foreign resident is the beginning of a good relationship with the shopkeeper.

# SHOPPING VENUES

Shopping in Korea will satisfy every type of potential buyer. The open air markets will excite the shopper looking for a taste of the traditional culture. The modern day convenience shopper will find his share of department stores, shopping centers, hotel shops, and arcades.

**Department Stores/Shopping Centers.** Seoul's department stores offer shoppers a convenient way to shop. Typically, groceries and food counters are located in the basement; clothing stores on the ground and lower floors; and housewares and electronics on upper floors. Prices are relatively high, but the selection and quality at department stores are also better. Downtown Seoul is the home of four of the most popular department stores. With the daily modernization of the city, suburban department stores, with adjacent parking lots, are becoming increasingly popular.

Purchases from department stores are generally more reliable and usually can be returned or exchanged without much difficulty. Prices are fixed and both Korean and foreign goods can be found. Seconds, counterfeits, and "knock-offs" are not available here. English and Japanese speaking clerks are on hand in most stores. Department stores accept credit cards and also provide money changing facilities.

Shopping hours are usually 10:30 AM–8:00 PM, but vary between stores.

**Hotel Shops/Above Ground Arcades.** These shops are found within, below, and near most of the major hotels. Prices are often 2–3 times what you would pay by spending a little time exploring the city and comparing prices at less expensively located shops. The quality of merchandise here tends to be high. Shopping hours vary among the hotel shops.

**Open Air Markets.** These old-style markets are best suited for the adventurous shopper. These colorful bazaars sell everything from strings of garlic to chinaware. Bargaining is a common rule and is even expected of foreigners. Prices will probably be cheaper here than anywhere else, but high quality items are harder to find.

Merchants in these markets generally do not speak English. Thus, communication can be something of a problem. Any purchases must be paid for in Korean won, as credit cards and checks are very rarely accepted. Some markets open as early as 4 AM and conduct business well into the evening hours. Most open-air markets are open every day except major holidays. Some shops close early on the first and third Sundays of the month.

If you don't mind being pushed and shoved about in these often crowded, traditional Korean markets, you will be rewarded with many insights into the Korean lifestyle. Indeed the congestion is decidedly friendly, since most people seem to be enjoying the commotion, banter, and jostling about.

**Underground Arcades.** Underground shopping arcades are most prevalent in the heavily populated areas of the city but can be found branching out beneath the major hotels and subway stations. A wide selection of goods is sold here, mainly through small, specialized shops. Prices are generally less than those in department stores. Arcade shopkeepers usually don't respond well to haggling, especially if prices on the items are marked.

► WHAT TO BUY ◄

## TRADITIONAL ITEMS

**Antiques/Reproduction.** Korean antiques are becoming increasingly scarce, but if you have time to look for the right piece, the reward is well worth the search.

Antique wooden blanket and coin chests, wedding boxes, and medicine chests are most abundant in the Itaewon and Insadong areas. One can also find antique ceramics, celadon, and other Korean artifacts dating back to the Silla, Koryo, and Choson dynasties. One must be cautious, though, since there are many cheap reproductions and "instant antiques" on the market. Do not automatically take the shopkeeper's word that an item is an antique; do your homework first to prevent disappointment later.

Any antique dating back more than 50 years must have an accompanying certificate for legal export. This should be provided by the shopkeeper.

*Where to buy:* Itaewon, Insadong, Changan Dong Antique Market.

**Celadon.** The Koryo Celadon Factory sells celadon at discount prices and offers tours of its facilities. This Korean ceramic was developed during the Koryo Dynasty, and is noted for its

*Traditional Korean ceramics*

pleasant grey-green color and its simple but elegant lines. The rarer blue-green shade is highly prized by some collectors.

**Cloisonné.** While the Westerner is typically more familiar with Chinese cloisonné, visitors to Korea will find the local cloisonné both unique and appealing. Korean cloisonné is used in a variety of items, including jewelry, mirrors, hair ornaments, and pottery.
*Where to buy:* Insadong, Itaewon, Changan Dong.

**Lacquerware.** A wide range of items such as tables, chests, vases inlaid with mother-of-pearl, and oxhorn are produced.
*Where to buy:* Itaewon, souvenir shops, traditional chinaware shops, department stores.

**Ginseng.** The "cure-all" natural medicinal herb of Asia is used not only to treat a vast variety of diseases and complaints, but is considered a powerful tonic, taken, for example, by the top weight-lifters of China to enhance their performance. Korean ginseng is considered to be the finest in the world. There are two types of ginseng—red (said to be of higher quality) and white. This elixir is produced in many forms. Ginseng tea is one of the most popular forms for foreigners.
*Where to buy:* Pharmacies, department stores, hotel arcades, souvenir and duty-free shops.

**Korean Dolls.** Usually dressed in the brightly colored traditional *hanbok* (see below), Korean dolls serve as lasting souvenirs for both adults and children and are reasonably priced.
*Where to buy*: Itaewon, department stores.

**Korean Costumes.** The *hanbok* is Korea's traditional attire for women and is comprised of the long skirt (*chima*) and short jacket (*chogori*). Usually made of strikingly colorful silks, the *hanbok* is most often worn during the holidays and at formal functions.
*Where to buy*: Downtown, Tongdaemun.

**Korean Masks, Ducks, Kites, Fans.** Korean masks of wood and paper-mâché have traditionally been used in folk dances. Carved wooden ducks make unique wedding gifts: they are said to bring happiness, wealth, and fertility to the recipients.
*Where to buy*: Insadong, Itaewon, handicraft stores.

**Korean Folk Painting.** Korean vendors practice the traditional art of writing by using colorful pictures to represent letters in a name or saying. You can purchase these banners custom-drawn with your own surname (in English or rendered into Korean).
*Where to buy*: Itaewon (there's an artist set up inside the Eastern Brass shop), Korean Folk Village.

**Bambooware.** Bamboo is popular in Korean homes since it provides good ventilation during the long, hot Korean summers. Trays, baskets, mats, lampshades, and boxes are all popular bamboo products.
*Where to buy*: Namdaemun, Tongdaemun, Itaewon.

## BRASSWARE

Brass items are available in every shape and size imaginable. The prices are cheap and the quality is usually quite good. Brass beds can be bought at one-third of prices in the US. Picture frames and fireplace sets are other popular items.
*Where to buy*: Itaewon has the best prices.

## SILK

Korea is a leading producer of silk fabric and clothing. Silk brocades and hand-printed silk fabrics are excellent values, and come in a broad range of colors.
*Where to buy*: Fabric: Tongdaemun has silk specialty shops. Dresses, blouses: Itaewon.

## CUSTOM-MADE CLOTHING AND SHOES

**Custom Clothing.** Because of cheap labor costs, clothing can be custom-made cheaply and quickly in Korea. The key to quality is the tailor's choice of thread and fabric. Most skillful tailors can copy a picture you bring in or duplicate a favorite article of clothing. Be sure to allow time for at least two fittings. Suits, shirts, blouses, and dresses can be completed in 3–5 days. Sportswear (ski suits, jogging suits) is a great Itaewon bargain.

Tailors within the hotels and department stores tend to produce finer garments due to the higher quality of material available in their shops. But you'll also pay substantially more for these enhancements.

**Shoes:** Eelskin and leather shoes are another popular made-to-order item, since most ready-made shoes are made to fit Korean feet.

*Where to buy:* Tailors, dressmakers, shoes: Itaewon, hotels, department stores. Ski Wear, running suits: Itaewon.

## SEMI-PRECIOUS STONES

Korea is an excellent place to purchase amethyst, smokey topaz, and pale green jadeite. These items can be set into custom-made jewelry at good prices; labor costs are low and workmanship high. However, the cost of gold and silver is expensive due to high import duties.

*Where to buy:* Itaewon, department stores, arcades.

## LEATHER GOODS

Seoul is an excellent place to purchase leather products. The quality of skins and workmanship is currently good and is becoming better. But it is still difficult to find leather of the highest quality. Be careful when purchasing name-brand products, since they could be counterfeit and might be impounded by US customs inspectors.

Custom-made leatherware is an excellent investment and can be made as quickly as 48 hours. Recommended products included coats, shoes, pants, pocketbooks, dresses, and skirts.

*Where to buy:* Itaewon, Myongdong.

## COMPARATIVE CLOTHING SIZE CHART

**LADIES**

| | | | | | | | |
|---|---|---|---|---|---|---|---|
| USA | 4 | 6 | 8 | 12 | 10 | 14 | 16 |
| UK | 6 | 8 | 10 | 12 | 14 | 16 | 18 |
| Italy | | 38 | 40 | 42 | 44 | 46 | |
| France | 34 | 36 | 38 | 30 | 42 | 44 | |
| Germany | 32 | 34 | 36 | 38 | 40 | 42 | |
| Australia | 8 | 10 | 12 | 14 | 16 | 18 | |
| Japan | | 7 | 9 | 11 | 13 | | |

**MEN**

**Shirts**

| | | | | | | | | |
|---|---|---|---|---|---|---|---|---|
| USA, UK, Italy | 14 | 14½ | 15 | 15½ | 16 | 16 | 17 | (in) |
| France, Germany, Australia, Japan | 36 | 37 | 38 | 39 | 40 | 41 | 42 | (cm) |

**Sweaters/T-Shirts**

| | | | | |
|---|---|---|---|---|
| USA, Germany, Australia | S | M | L | XL |
| UK | 34 | 36-38 | 40 | 42-44 |
| Italy | 44 | 46-48 | 50 | 52 |
| France | 1 | 2-3 | 4 | 5 |
| Japan | | S-M | L | XL |

**Suits/Coats**

| | | | | | |
|---|---|---|---|---|---|
| USA, UK | 36 | 38 | 40 | 42 | 44 |
| Italy, France Germany, Australia | 46 | 48 | 50 | 52 | 54 |
| Japan | S | M | L | XL | |

## EELSKIN

Eelskin leather can be found in abundance in Seoul. The particular eel species from which the skin is derived can be found in the coastal waters of Korea. Itaewon is where you will find the best prices. Eelskin products are available in many forms: belts, handbags, cosmetic bags, briefcases, shoes, and wallets. Unfortunately, prices continue to rise as eelskin becomes more scarce and labor costs rise.

*Where to buy*: Itaewon, Myongdong, department stores, arcades.

## STUFFED TOYS AND ANIMALS

Korean manufacturers are world leaders in the production of plush toys. Sidewalk vendors and shops sell a stuffed version of nearly every animal imaginable. Many of the products bear the

label of famous foreign companies such as Gund; here, too, beware of many counterfeits. A smart toy shopper can spot an authentic item by noting the quality of the fabric and the doll's glass eyes. Many times the label of the foreign company has been cut off or obliterated. Also be sure the product is well sewn and without adornments that can be easily removed or swallowed by children.
*Where to buy:* Itaewon.

## CASSETTES, RECORDS

Korean cassette-tape and record companies have for many years been licensed for local production by foreign companies, and prices for cassette tapes and records are very reasonable. Some shops offer a range of cassette tapes recorded by the shop-owner from another tape. The quality of these tapes is generally good, but is not the same as a tape produced from a master recording. Compact disks have only recently become available and the selection is limited.
*Where to buy:* Itaewon, sidewalk vendors, department stores, arcades.

## WIGS

Korea has for many years been a leading producer of women's wigs. The wigs are of high quality and can be purchased at substantial savings.
*Where to buy:* Tongdaemun.

## CASUAL WEAR

Korea has been a major textile producer for many years. Much of Korea's production is for export only, but some products filter out into the local markets. A wide range of casual wear bearing famous labels can be found. In addition, generic jeans, knits, and sweatshirts can be purchased, particularly in Itaewon.
*Where to buy:* Itaewon, Namdaemun, Tongdaemun.

## FURS

Over a relatively short period, Korea has become a world leader in the production of fur garments, and thus a wide range of styles and furs is available. Jindo was the first company to sell furs in Korea on a wide scale, but other companies such as Diana and

Woodan have entered the market. Furs should be purchased on a duty-free basis.
*Where to buy:* Itaewon.

## SPORTING GOODS

Korean manufacturers produce a substantial proportion of the world's sporting goods. Name-brand sports balls of all types (football, rugby, basketball, volleyball, etc.) are excellent values and pack well if deflated. Gloves of all types are a good buy, especially baseball, golf, skiing, and cycling gloves. Fishing rods and reels, camping gear, and sport racquets are also manufactured here.
*Where to buy:* Itaewon, Tongdaemun, Namdaemun.

## SPORTSWEAR

A wide range of custom and off-the-shelf sporting wear is sold in Korea. Running suits made of Goretex and other new fabrics are widely available. Ski parkas, ski jump suits, and cycling clothes made of spandex fabric can be found in sporting goods stores.
*Where to buy:* Itaewon, Namdaemun, Tongdaemun.

## SPORTS SHOES

Factories located in the city of Pusan produce an enormous variety and quantity of sporting shoes. Nearly every major sporting shoe company produces shoes in Korea for export. These companies include Reebok, Nike, Converse, LA Gear, Kangaroo, and Adidas. Nike, Reebok, Puma, and Adidas have entered into joint ventures and licensing agreements to sell shoes on the domestic market.

Korea's many shoe shops are filled to capacity with a wide range of sports shoes, some of which are genuine and some counterfeit. In general, the more well-known the brand, the more likely that the product is not genuine. Remember that shoes bearing trademarks may be confiscated by customs inspectors when you return home.
*Where to buy:* Itaewon, Myongdong.

## SUNGLASSES

Korea is a major exporter of frames for prescription eyeglasses and sunglasses. Most factories are located in the city of Taegu.

Sidewalk vendors and opticians offer a wide variety of products. Some are seconds and overruns while others may be counterfeits. Names which can be found include Ray Ban and Carerra. The majority of sunglasses offered for sale do not bear a trademark but closely resemble foreign brands. Most products are sold more for their fashion appeal than for optical purposes.

*Where to buy:* Itaewon, sidewalk vendors.


## KITCHENWARE

Many varieties of foreign and domestic kitchenware are available. For imported brands, the shopper should visit a specialty shop, otherwise, it is often difficult to find a complete set. The major categories of kitchenware available include flatware, copperware, chinaware, and cookware.

*Where to buy:* Namdaemun, Tongdaemun.


## OLYMPIC SOUVENIRS

A wide range of Olympic souvenirs is now being sold in Korea. Items available include pins, glasses, key chains, plaques, T-shirts, dolls, figurines, and posters. The Seoul Olympic Merchandise Exhibition (732-8886) is a treasurehouse of souvenirs and Olympic information.

*Where to buy:* Souvenir shops, Itaewon, department stores.


## ELECTRONICS AND COMPUTERS

Unless purchased duty free, electronic products are considerably more expensive than you might expect in a country so well-known for these products. High taxes on electronic and computer products as well as transportation charges discourage this type of purchase. Compact and micro radios, cassette recorders, and head phones that fit easily into your luggage can be good buys.

*Where to buy:* Saeunsanga Arcade, Itaewon (for computers).


## COMPUTER SOFTWARE

Korea recently enacted laws protecting developers of computer software. As a result, it is unclear what will happen to the many shops selling unauthorized copies of computer software for a few dollars more than the cost of a floppy disk. Chances are, as is the case in Hong Kong, that these stores will continue to exist in

out-of-the-way locations. If you buy, be sure to boot the program to make sure it runs.
*Where to buy:* Saeunsanga Arcade, Itaewon.

## FOREIGN BOOKS

A wide range of reprints of foreign books is available from local bookstores. Prior to October 1987, when Korea joined the Universal Copyright Convention, these reprints were very inexpensive. Korean publishers are now beginning to pay royalties to foreign copyright holders. It is not clear yet how these royalty agreements will effect prices.
*Where to buy:* Kyobo Book Store and Chongno Book Store in downtown Seoul, Wise Old Owl in Itaewon, hotel shops for foreign paperbacks and magazines.

## LOCAL FASHION/LOCAL DESIGNERS

**Clothing.** A substantial number of local designers manufacture and sell nearly every type of fashion product. Leading local designers include Andre Kim, Lee Kwang Hee, Nina Lee, and Nora Noh, along with the popular local brand names of Bando Fashion and Buckingham. Take care to try things on before purchasing as Korean garments tend not to fit Western body types. In particular, arm and hem lengths are special problems, since they cannot be remedied through alterations.
*Where to buy:* Designer Shops: Individual shops, Myongdong.
Chains: Department stores (Fashion Street Floor) and shopping centers.

**Shoes:** If your feet are larger than average or you have oddly sized or shaped feet, you'd do well to have your shoes custommade. For ready-made brands, try one of the boutiques in Myongdong or Itaewon. Local-name brands include Milano and Kumkang.

**Children:** Bambino and Mode Carina are local brands available for children.
*Where to buy:* In addition to Itaewon, the open markets are the cheapest. Chains: Department stores and shopping centers.

## JEWELRY

Other than the semi-precious stones discussed above (amethyst, smokey topaz, pale green jadeite), you'll want to save your jewelry purchases for Hong Kong. However, there are many shops which do excellent custom-made work. Turtle Hong Jewelry in Itaewon is a favorite among Seoul's foreign residents.

Costume jewelry and trinkets are great bargains at Namdaemun and Tongdaemun markets.

## FABRICS

Fabrics (or "piece goods") are sold in great quantities at the open markets to both foreign and local residents at remarkable savings. Be sure to check your pieces carefully for flaws and stains. Sewing notions are a bargain here, too. The largest selection can be found in Tongdaemun.
*Where to buy.* Tongdaemun, Namdaemun, individual tailors, Itaewon.

## EMBROIDERY

Embroidery is stitched by hand on items ranging from screens to casual clothing. Embroidery on jackets, hats, t-shirts, patches, and bags is popular. Embroidered linens and scarves are beautifully made and are a good buy.
*Where to buy.* Open markets, Itaewon.

## CRYSTAL

Parks Crystal is Korea's leading brand. This crystal is manufactured in forms ranging from stemware to wall ornaments and lamps. Well-known stores in the US such as Tiffany's, Saks, and Bullocks import this brand of fine crystal from Korea.
*Where to buy.* Insadong, department stores, arcades, and factory outlets (Doosan Industrial in Kwangju, tel.: 03472-4101/4; Seoul: 635-0151).

# WHAT NOT TO BUY

Unless they are purchased duty free, foreign products are not a good value in Korea due to high import duties. Electronics and computers are heavily taxed even if locally produced. Foreign liquor is particularly expensive and therefore visitors may want to bring their own supplies to Korea.

Except for the gems mined in Korea (see above), jewelry is not a good buy. You're better advised to buy your pearls, diamonds, gold, and silver in Hong Kong.

Limit the number of purchases of items which are imitations. Refer to US Customs Regulations, Section VIII B, for information regarding the allowable number of reproductions of brand names permitted to be brought back into the US.

# WHERE TO SHOP

## SHOPPING DISTRICTS

The following is an introduction to Seoul's principal shopping districts. Seoul's diversified shopping can be found primarily in the areas described below. You will notice the shortage of street names in defining these locations. This is because most streets in Seoul have never been named. Instead, addresses are identified by a "dong" (a Korean neighborhood) or a landmark. As a result, good street maps are essential for finding one's way through Seoul's neighborhoods.

시내
**Downtown.** The downtown shopping district is located in the center of the city. Downtown Seoul is made up of the city's major department stores, underground arcades, and Myongdong.

명동
**Myongdong.** This area in downtown Seoul is located between Taepyong-ro and the intersection of Samil-ro, and then eastward to Seoul Stadium. It is lined with boutiques and local designers' shops, and is a trendy hangout for university students. Myongdong has traditionally been the major shopping district for high fashion. The area is very cosmopolitan and has scores of exclusive boutiques. The attraction of Myongdong for shoppers has diminished in recent years due to the increasing number of department stores. The Korea National Tourism Corporation has begun a campaign to increase the popularity of Myongdong among foreign visitors. However, while Myongdong is a great place to see local fashion, Western buyers should proceed cautiously because of sizing problems as discussed above. Cars and buses are not permitted on the narrow streets here.

*The main shopping street of Itaewan*

## 이태원

**Itaewon.** The shopping district best known to foreigners, Itaewon extends primarily along one long main street ("the strip") on the southern side of Namsan Mountain near the US Eighth Army Youngsan Compound. Also called Foreigners' Village, Itaewon is one of Korea's most famous and busiest shopping areas. Its reputation for racy nightlife has been well overtaken in recent years by its image as a bargain center. Owing to its location, Itaewon shopkeepers have for years stocked Western sizes and have learned English. Also adding to its attraction is the fact that the merchants will accept US dollars in addition to Korean *won*. Most shops will add around 4% to the cost of any item purchased with a credit card. Checks will generally not be accepted.

The main street, known as "the strip," extends for over a mile and is lined on both sides with all types of shops. Restaurants and entertainment spots also draw shoppers to this area. Most shops are open seven days a week (including many holidays), from 10 a.m. to 10 p.m. The street is lined with sidewalk vendors, many of whom are deaf; they communicate prices by using a written card.
*Bargains:* Antiques/reproductions, clothing, athletic shoes, luggage, and bags.

## 인사동

**Insadong.** Known also to foreigners as "Mary's Alley," Insadong can be found between the Hankook Ilbo Building and

Pagoda Park in northern downtown Seoul. Shopping in Insadong is for foreign visitors interested in traditional and modern Korean art, crafts, and antiques. Numerous galleries, workshops, and antique stores line the streets of this shopping district. This is a good place to shop for carved wooden items, calligraphy brushes, and antiques. Numerous shops will custom-make seals of wood or stone, bearing initials or surnames. The prices in Insadong tend to be higher, but the quality of products is excellent.

동대문
**Tongdaemun.** Tongdaemun is one of Seoul's largest open-air markets. The name means "East Gate Market" because of its location in eastern downtown Seoul near the easternmost gate of the old walled city. The market area is located between Chongno and Chonggyechon streets at approximately the 6-ka block.

남대문
**Namdaemun.** Namdaemun is the second largest open-air market in Seoul. This market is situated southwest of downtown Seoul, south of the Shinsegae Department store, north of Namsan, and east of the South Gate. Namdaemun is within walking distance from many of the downtown hotels.

강남
**South of the Han River.** This shopping district actually includes many suburbs situated south of the Han River. Youngdong, Kangnam, and Chamsil are a few of the more populous areas. Since most residents of Seoul now live south of the Han River, numerous shopping districts have been developed to meet their needs. The stores are new, clean, and modern in appearance. Prices are higher, but the selection is good. Although parking is considerably better than in the downtown area, you may have to walk from store to store. Kangnam and Chamsil are two of the major shopping districts.

Major shops include the Socho Dong Plant and Flower Market, New Core Department Store, Yongdong Department Store and Hanyang Department Store and Supermarket.

여의도
**Yoido.** Yoido is an island located in the middle of the Han River in southwest Seoul. The striking, golden-hued DLI 63 Building, the tallest building in Korea, is located on Yoido and makes a good landmark when trying to locate this shopping area. The DLI 63 Building contains many shops, restaurants and other forms of entertainment (including an aquarium). Several department stores, including

Yoido Department Store, Life Shopping Center, DLI 63 Building, and Yoido Shopping Center, are located in Yoido, as well as a wide range of shops.

## 게이트 19

**Gate 19.** "Gate 19," consisting mainly of clothing stores, runs for several blocks outside the Gate 19 entrance of the US Eighth Army Base. This area is approximately a 10-minute drive from Itaewon. Gate 19 is frequented primarily by the foreign women residing in Seoul. Since this shopping area ia a well-kep secret, the selection is often quite good, particularly for wool garments and overcoats. In fact, some garments are exclusive to Gate 19.

There is usually a good selection of US and European designer labels, as well as women's suits. The selection in the shops changes rapidly and it is typical for there to be dozens of a single item. Once the item is sold, it is not restocked since supply is dictated not by the demand, but by what is currently available. Therefore, new items appear daily.

# ► SEOUL SHOPPING ◄
# ► DIRECTORY ◄

## *DEPARTMENT STORES/SHOPPING CENTERS*

Most of the department stores and shopping centers are open during the hours listed below; if not, the time variance is minimal. Some stores are open seven days a week. Most close one day a week, but usually not on the weekends. All of these stores are closed on national holidays.

HOURS: 10:30 a.m.–8 p.m.

| NAME/ADDRESS/PHONE | CLOSED ON |
|---|---|
| *Downtown:* | |
| Lotte Shopping Center<br>1, Sogong-dong, Chung-ku<br>(02) 771–25 | Tuesdays |

Shinsegae Department Store
52-5, 1-ka, Chungmu-ro, Chung-ku
(02) 754–1234

Mondays

Midopa Department Store
123, 2-ka, Namdaemunno, Chung-ku
(02) 754–2222

Wednesdays

Cheil Department Store
31-1, 2-ka, Myongdong, Chung-ku
(02) 776–2741

First/Third Mondays
of the month

Dongbang Plaza
150, 2-ka, Taepyongno, Chung-ku
(02) 757–1212

First/Third Tuesdays
of the month

Saerona Department Store
1-2, Namchang-dong, Chung-ku
(02) 778–8171

Thursdays

*South of the Han River:*

Hanyang Shopping Center
San 2, Apkujong-dong, Kangnam-ku
(02) 542–1161

First/Third Mondays
of the month

Hyundai Department Store
224-11, Apkujong-dong, Kangnam-ku
(02) 547–2233

First/Third Wednesdays
of the month

New Core Shopping Center
257-3, 3-dong, Panp'o-dong, Kangnam-ku
(02) 533–2121

Second/Fourth Tuesdays
of the month

New Town Shopping Center
200-1, Panp'o-dong, Kangnam-ku
(02) 532–3311

First/Third Tuesdays
of the month

Yongdong Department Store
119, Nonhyon-dong, Kangnam-ku
(02) 544–3000

First/Third Mondays
of the month

*Others:*

Crystal Department Store
57-1, Nogosan-dong, Map'o-gu
(02) 332–2300

First/Third Tuesdays
of the month

Yoido Department Store
(02) 783–7081

## UNDERGROUND ARCADES

롯데 일번가

**Lotte First Avenue.** Located between the Lotte and Midopa Department Stores; runs into Sogong Arcade. Favorite shops of foreign residents and visitors include Nine Lee Fashions and Charles Jourdan Shoes (776-9649). Packing/gift-wrapping services are available here.

반도 조선 아케이드

**Bando Chosun Arcade.** Located in front of the Chosun Hotel. Shops worth patronizing include Koryo Silk, Shin Wha Silk (757-6888), and Hallim Hand Weavers (755-3845) for hand-woven sweaters.

회현동 아케이드 (상가)

**Hoehyun-dong Arcade.** Near Namdaemun.

소공동 아케이드 (상가)

**Sogong-dong Arcade.** Between Plaza and Chosun Hotels.

## ABOVE-GROUND ARCADES

낙원 상가

**Nagwon Arcade.** This arcade is located between Insadong and Pagoda Park in the same building as the Hollywood Theatre. Groceries are in the basement and musical instruments are on the second floor.

세운 상가

**Sae Woon Arcade.** This arcade has shops selling nearly every type of electronic or computer product at wholesale prices.

강남 상가

**Kangnam Arcade.** Located near the Express Bus Terminal.

## OPEN-AIR MARKETS

남대문

**Namdaemun (South Gate).** This market is a favorite of visitors to Korea since it is convenient to downtown hotels and is not over-whelmingly large. Namdaemun glitters with local color and offers nearly every type of product imaginable. There are extensive produce and fish stalls, as well as hundreds of clothing vendors. The upper floors of the major buildings contain a variety of shops usually selling the same type of product: one floor might consist only of flower shops and another only of stores selling chinaware. After dark, many shops close and a large number of sidewalk vendors and street restaurants take their place.

## 동대문

**Tongdaemun (East Gate).** Tongdaemun is the largest of Seoul's markets. It has the best selection, but it is so large that it can take up to an hour just to traverse the area. An entire city block may contain only yarns and sewing supplies or tools. Prices are excellent and the diligent shopper can find real treasures if he or she is persistent.

## 평화시장

**P'yonghwa Market.** This market is located adjacent to Tongdaemun and is good for clothing bargains, particularly for children. Plan on sorting thorugh a lot of rubbish to find the gems.

## 장안동 시장

**Changan Dong Market.** This antique market located in the eastern outskirts of Seoul has only recently become popular among non-local shoppers. Nearly 200 stores selling a complete range of Korean antiques can be found in this area. Potential purchases include all types of Korean wooden chests, stone carvings, scrolls, ceramics, and metal utensils.

## 청계천 전자제품 시장

**Chunggyechon Electronics Market.** This market is located at the 4-ka block between Chrongro and Chunggyechon. For many years this area has been the principal place for purchasing electronic parts and wholesale electronic items such as televisions and stereos. Nearly every imaginable domestic and foreign part and product is available.

## 노량진 수산 시장

**Noryangjin Fish Market.** This market, located south of the Han River, is the central fish market for Seoul where myriad varieties of fish are sold. The early morning auction at this market is fascinating and is a great place for photographs.

## *DUTY-FREE SHOPS*

Duty-free shops are located throughout Seoul and other cities, as well as being situated at the major air and sea ports. Items purchased at a duty-free shop are picked up by the purchaser at the air or sea port immediately before departure. Luxury goods at tax-free prices draw shoppers to this type of store. Imported items and many domestically produced luxury items (such as furs) will be considerably cheaper when purchased in duty-free shops.

The goods available in such stores are typical of those found in duty-free shops around the world, and include such well known brands as Chanel, Dunhill, Yves Saint Laurent, and Cartier. A full selection of foreign-brand liquor is available, but only from duty-free shops operated in international ports by the Korea National Tourism Corporation.

Various credit cards and foreign currencies are accepted in these shops. Business hours and days vary among the shops.

## DUTY FREE SHOPS IN KOREA

| NAME | ADDRESS/PHONE |
| --- | --- |
| Donghwa Arcade | 1–41, Sajik-dong, Chongno-gu, Seoul (02) 738-1205 |
| Hotel Shilla Duty Free Shop | 202, 2-ga, Jangchung-dong Chung-gu, Seoul (02) 244-3131 |
| Lotte Duty Free Shop | 1, Sogong-dong Chung-gu, Seoul (02) 776-3940 |
| Korea Diamond Duty Free Shop | B1F, Hyundai Bldg., 77, Mukyo-dong, Chung-gu, Seoul (02) 757-7101 |
| Nammoon Duty Free Shop | 168–1, Kamjon-dong, Puk-gu, Pusan (051) 92-8926 |
| Pagoda Duty Free Shop | 15, Insadong, Chongno-gu, Seoul (02) 732-2511-4 |
| Paradise Duty Free Shop | 86-210, 2-ga, Changch'ung-dong, Chung-gu, Seoul |
| Han Ah Jewelry Co., Ltd. | 87, Sogong-dong, Chung-gu, Seoul (02) 757-6751 |

Diana Fur                          119–25, Itaewon-dong,
                                   Yongsan-gu, Seoul
                                   (02) 796-0051

Poong Jun                          73–1 2-ga, Inhyon-dong,
                                   Chung-gu, Seoul
                                   (02) 266-6108

Woodan                             176-2, Itaewon-dong
                                   Yongsan-gu, Seoul
                                   (02) 796-1981

Jindo Duty Free Shops              128-5, Itaewon-dong,
                                   Yongsan-ku, Seoul
                                   (02) 797-5601/3
                                   and
                                   371–62 Karibong-dong
                                   Kuro-gu, Seoul
                                   (02) 862-0051

Jindo Fur Salon                    Kukje-Hoekwan Bldg.
                                   69, Jungang-dong, 6-ka,
                                   Jung-ku, Pusan
                                   (051) 463-1444/7

KNTC Airport                       Kimpo Airport (Seoul)/(02) 665-2133
Duty Free Shops                    Kimhae Airport (Pusan)/(051) 98-1101
                                   Pukwan Ferry Terminal/(051) 462-2501
                                   Cheju Airport/(064) 42-0030

Hanjin Duty Free Shop              304-22 Yongdong
                                   Cheju, Cheju-do
                                   (064) 27-7217

## Handicraft Stores

These shops, for the most part, were developed to promote the sale of traditional Korean folk arts and crafts particularly in preparation for the 1986 Asian Games and the 1988 Summer Olympics. There are a number of handicrafts shops scattered around Seoul, with some selling more than 1,000 handicraft items. The quality of the items sold in these shops ranges from excellent to fair. Some of the better handicraft stores include:

**Chonsu Gongbang.** Located near the Korean Exhibition Center south of the Han River, this store offers a wide selection of handicraft items. Prices are reasonable and the quality is good.

Here you can watch master craftsman at work as they train their apprentices in traditional skills.

**Folk Handicraft Center** (130-17, Chamwon-dong, Kangnam-ku; tel.: 532-9161). Located near the Express Bus Terminal.

**Human Cultural Assets Handicraft Gallery** (Hongik Blg., 198-1 Kwanhun-dong, Chongno-ku; tel.: 732-8178). Located near Insadong.

**Korea Folk Handicrafts Center** (tel.: 557-3880). Adjacent to the Express Bus Terminal south of the Han River, near the Folk Handicraft Center (noted above).

**Korea House** (tel.: 267-8752). Located at the northern foot of Namsan near Taegye-ro.

**Korean Handicrafts Department Store** (5-21 Namdoemun-no, 5-ka, Chung-ku; tel.: 753-9341/20). Located on street level of the Nammun Building opposite Namdaemun (next to the Hilton Hotel).

**Living Arts** (732-9766). Located in Insadong.

**Yongsan Hanshin Kimchi Jars** (794-3687) and **The Kimchi Museum** sell traditional kimchi jars and more.

Many wood-carvers operate workshops and sales outlets in the Insadong area. Products include masks, paintbrush holders, carved signs, and sculpture.

**Silent Craft** (902-2097). This workshop is run by Sister Caritas to benefit the deaf.

**Tong In Gallery** (733-4867). Located in Insadong.

**Wood Craft.** Located in the Lotte First Avenue Arcade.

**Young Bo Crafts.** Located in Insadong.

### Souvenir Shops

Souvenir shops offer a wide assortment of folk art and crafts. Many items incorporate the theme of the 1988 Summer Olympic Games. In addition to the shops named below, souvenir sections can be found in department stores and hotels. For more information, see sections on Handicraft Stores and Olympic Souvenirs.

Olympic Merchandise Exhibition Hall
Hongik Building, 198-1
Kwanhun-dong, Chongro-ku
732-8886

Dongho-Plaza, 4FL 183–1,
Itaewon-doing, Yongsan-ku
796–1988/9

Korea National Tourism Corporation
10 Tadong, Chong-gu
757–5930

Arirang Souvenir Shop
269-0411

Bando Gift, Inc.
725–5215

Etoile Souvenir Shop (Chosun Hotel)
23–3084

Samsong Souvenir Shop
73–3948

Yuch'ang Souvenir Shop
266–0728

These shops carry a wide range of Korean traditional and modern souvenirs, as well as '88 Olympic souvenirs. Pins, dolls, traditional products, clothing, coins, posters, videotapes, calendars, and cards are some of the many items carried.

### Foreign Designer Clothing

Many designers throughout the world bring their own material to Korea and manufacture clothing here. These items are technically barred from sale within the country, and are earmarked for export only. It is from these factories that overruns and seconds evolve and make their way to the local market. These items tend to be bought quickly since they are mainly purchased by foreign residents of Korea.

There are also a number of foreign designer shops in Seoul that sell authentic, high-quality products made under license or by a joint venture. Prices reflect this higher quality.

The following designer shops are located in many of the suburbs and some department stores: Nike, Adidas, Reebok, Laura Ashley, Izod La Coste, Jordache, Levis, and Givenchy. The Ralph Lauren Factory is located at Shinhan International Ltd., 15-5 Jeong-Dong, Chung-ku, and both Royal Doulton and O'Neill/Bodrac are located at Kangnam-dong.

*Clothing bargains include Western fashions produced for export, often at half price or less*

## "Black Market" Stalls/Foreign Commissaries/Supermarkets

The following types of shopping are more for foreign residents of Seoul, but can be useful and interesting to tourists as well.

**"Black Market" Stalls.** You will probably come across tiny stalls or carts along the roads and in underground arcades offering a small array of strictly foreign products such as razors, shaving cream, cosmetics, peanut butter, soap, and liquor. These stalls are regarded as life savers for foreign residents who may come to crave familiar products not locally available. Some small shops also maintain a supply of foreign products; these goods, however, are usually acquired "under the table" from the US Army Commissary and Exchange. Whatever their origin, the buyer will pay at least three times the retail value of the product.

**Foreign Commissaries.** Foreign Commissaries are a type of supermarket supplied with only a limited variety of imported goods. These shops cater to foreign residents and travelers, and accept US dollars and American Express and Visa credit cards. Prices can be as much as two to five times the ordinary retail price.

**Supermarkets.** Although the typical tourist will probably not have an interest in doing any food shoping while in Korea, the supermarkets are still an interesting place to visit. The larger supermarkets are mostly found in department store basements. Prices for foreign brands of food and for any out-of-season fresh fruit and vegetables run high, as do foreign product types (e.g., corn flakes, cheese) which are, in fact, produced locally.

### Tax Refund Shops

Foreign visitors may obtain a tax refund when goods are purchased at authorized shops. The purchase price must exceed ₩50,000 and the goods must leave Korea within three months following the date of purchase. When purchasing an item at such a shop, the shopper must present a passport or other identification and a Tax Refund Form. When departing Korea, two copies of a Certificate of Selling Goods, a return envelope, and the goods themselves must be shown to a customs officer. A refund less a service and handling charge will be sent to you by mail about 20 days following your departure.

## TAX REFUND SHOPS IN SEOUL

| NAME | ADDRESS | TEL. |
|---|---|---|
| SEOUL | | |
| Dongbang Plaza | 250, 2-ga, T'aep'yongno, Chung-gu | 757-1212 |
| Hotel Shilla Arcade | 202, 2-ga, Changch'ung-dong, Chung-gu | 233-3131 |
| Lotte Dept. Store | 1, Sogong-dong, Chung-gu | 771-25 |
| Midopa Dept. Store | 123, 2-ga, Namdaemunno Chung-gu | 719-8105 |
| New Core Dept. Store | 398-2, Panp'o-dong Kangnam-gu | 532-3300 |
| Samick Musical Dept. Store | 66-9, 2-ga, Ch'ungmuro, Chung-gu | 778-5588 |
| Shinsegae Dept. Store | 52-5, 1-ga, Ch'ungmuro, Chung-gu | 754-1234 |
| | 434-5, Yongdŭngp'o-dong, Yongdŭngp'o-gu | 676-1234 |
| Yongdong Dept. Store | 119, Nonhyon-dong, Kangnam-gu | 544-3000 |
| Kolon Sports Co., Ltd. | 24-38, 1-ga, Ch'ungmuro, Chung-gu | 776-7475 |
| Esquire Co., Ltd. | 33-8, 2-ga, Myong-dong, Chung-gu | 776-4683 |
| | 51-3, 2-ga, Myong-dong, Chung-gu | 776-7368 |
| Elcanto Co., Ltd. | 32-5, 2-ga, Myong-dong, Chung-gu | 778-3371 |
| Kumkang Shoes Co., Ltd. | 33-14, 2-ga, Myong-dong, Chung-gu | 753-9411 |

# USEFUL INFORMATION

## FOR SHOPPERS

## US Customs

Visitors to Korea should keep in mind that all purchases will be subject to a customs inspection when they return to their own country. For US citizens who have visited Korea, customs inspectors may examine their purchases for possible violations of trademark and copyright laws. Counterfeit or pirated merchandise can be confiscated.

The following is a list of trademarks which have been counterfeited in the past:

a. Adidas
b. Alligator Symbol Chemise Lacoste
c. Apple Computers
d. Apple II System Monitor
e. Audamars Plugec Division
f. Britannia
g. Cabbage Patch Dolls
h. Cartier
i. Christian Dior Items
j. Converse
k. Disney Items
l. Donkey Kong Video Games
m. ECI (Members Only Jackets)
n. Esaikor
o. E. T. Items
p. Fila Items
q. Gucci Purses
r. Gremlins
s. Hasbro Robot Toys
t. Heavenly Kids
u. Ice Cream Dolls (Freckles)
v. IBM

w. Izod Shirts
x. Jordache
y. Calvin Klein
z. Lacoste Shirts
aa. Ralph Lauren Items (Jeana-Pol)
bb. Levi Strauss
cc. Mattel Inc.
dd. Nike
ee. Ocean Pacific
ff. Mr. Do Video Game
gg. Pac Man
hh. Pacek-Phillippe Watches
ii. Piaget
jj. Rolex
kk. Samsonite
ll. Sergio Valentini (Steerhead Design & "SV" Design)
mm. Smurf Items
nn. Velention Jeans
oo. Gloria Vanderbilt (Swan Design)
pp. Louis Vuitton Handbags & Items
qq. Reebok

There are three types of items sold in Korea: 1) authentic authorized; 2) authentic unauthorized; 3) "fake." Authentic authorized items are manufactured with the authorization of the company owner of the trademark rights. Authentic unauthorized items are those items produced by the real manufacturer without the consent of the trademark owner. "Fake" or pirated items are counterfeits or copies of the real item.

Authentic items will always be allowed into the United States and other countries unless they fall under a quota restriction (e.g., some types of clothing and shoes), or if you bring in a commercial quantity (more than three). Brass and eelskin are not quota items.

US customs can prohibit the importation of fake items, and can seize any item which they feel violates a trademark. The trademark owners and manufacturers tell the customs officials what to look for in distinguishing between a real and counterfeit product.

## Korean Export Regulations

In order to export cultural property, approval is required from the Minister of Culture and Information. The Cultural Property Preservation Bureau, located near the Capitol Building in Seoul (735-3053), also has a branch at Kimpo Airport (662-0106).

Approval from the Director of the Office of Forestry Administration is required to export wildlife, eggs, meat, and stuffed specimens.

Limitations on the amount of ginseng—the medicinal herb—which can be exported are: red ginseng, 600g.; white ginseng, 600g.; red ginseng products/extract, 900g.; ginseng products/sliced ginseng, 3kg.; extract powder, 450g.; extract, 900g.; powder, 1,800g.; tea, 3,000g.; capsules, 1,800g.; and tablets, 1,800g.

## Packaging Services

You may need the assistance of a packaging service for mailing purchases which are too bulky, heavy, or awkward to hand carry or pack with your luggage. Many shops will refer you to a packaging outlet if they cannot assist you themselves. Many of the antique stores will be able to handle packaging and mailing as they are quite familiar with the necessary regulations. Both the Chosun Hotel Shopping Arcade and the Lotte First Avenue Arcade have a packaging shop. Itaewon is also equipped with packaging services.

# DAY TRIPS OUTSIDE OF SEOUL

**A**s lively as Seoul is, the visitor who has the time will find it exciting to venture out of the capital city for a day or two for a change of perspective. The surrounding area, too, is replete with the splendors of earlier times mixed with the pleasures of today. Most tourist agencies offer tours to the best-known places: Panmunjom, the Korean Folk Village, Suwon, Inchon, and other historical sites and towns.

Guided tours around Seoul and the vicinity, as well as the Korean countryside, are offered by travel agents. There is a variety of tours especially designed for tourists from overseas. The Seoul City Tour Corporation operates sightseeing tours utilizing tourist buses, subways, and railways. Organized tour information booths are located in the major hotel lobbies. There are nearly 100 member travel agents of the Korea Tourist Association (10, Tadong, KNTC Building, (02) 757-0086 and a leading travel agent, Global Tours, provides further information and bookings (tel. (02) 333–0066).

## 판문점
### PANMUNJOM

The Allied victory over Japan in 1945 freed Korea from 35 years of Japanese colonial domination. But when World War II ended, Korea was divided at the 38th parallel to expedite the surrender of the Japanese troops: to United States forces in the south, and to Soviet forces in the north. Soon the two superpowers sponsored their own governments in the two Koreas, each gaining a permanent foothold on the Korean peninsula. On June 25, 1950, the Korean War broke out. It continued for three years, with 2.5 million military and civilian casualties, including 50,000 American deaths and 100,000 wounded. After two years and 17 days, 575 major meetings, and 18 million recorded words, the Korean Armistice Agreement was signed at Panmunjom on July 27, 1953. No peace treaty was signed; no political accord was reached. The battle was simply stopped in place by the Armistice Agreement. A demilitarized zone (DMZ) was created where the war's front line had been. There has ensued the longest cease-fire in modern military history.

The DMZ is 4,000 meters wide and winds for 151 miles across the middle of the Korean peninsula, from the Han River estuary in the west to a point just below the 39th parallel on the east coast, separating the northern and southern halves of the nation.

*Truce Village of Panmunjom, situated 10 km north of Seoul*

Situated within the DMZ, about an hour and a half's drive from Seoul, is Panmunjom. What once had been an obscure little village suddenly became the focus of world attention. More than three decades have passed since the Armistice, and the situation is still a tenuous and potentially volatile stand-off with a million armed men facing each other across the DMZ.

An important and poignant event occurred in the summer of 1985: a North Korean Red Cross delegation and a South Korean Red Cross delegation crossed the "Bridge of No Return" to visit Seoul and Pyongyang, respectively. Inter-Korea Red Cross conferences at Panmunjom had paved the way for this exchange and to the subsequent visits reuniting families that had been split by the division of their homeland.

Panmunjom straddles the Military Demarcation Line (MDL), which bisects the DMZ. It marks the end of the Korean War, but it is still a tense arena occupied by the United Nations Military Armistice Commission and the North Korean and Chinese representatives for discussions of alleged violations of the truce and other matters. At the same time, Panmunjom is a symbol of peace and a focal point of hopes for the reunification of the Land of the

Morning Calm. It is the pivot for on-going talks, a point for peaceful North-South contacts, and the guardian of the longest truce.

A visit to Panmunjom is an exciting and educational trip. It also is a sobering experience, as the visitor realizes its importance for world peace.

A Panmunjom Tour departs at 9 a.m., Monday through Friday, from the Korea Tourist Bureau office at the Lotte Hotel entrance driveway; guests at the Chosun Hotel are picked up there. Reservations must be made 48 hours in advance, and each person must give name, nationality, and passport number. A passport must be carried on tour day. The guided tour takes about six hours and includes an American lunch at the Advance Camp, which houses the United Nations Command Support Group. The group is briefed by an American noncommissioned officer. The cost is ₩24,400 (about $28). In case military or other official considerations prevent entry into the Joint Security Area, the tour cost is reduced to $23. Jeans, tennis shoes, sandals, and unkempt hair are not permitted in the military area. Tourists are cautioned not to make any gesture toward or in any way approach or respond to personnel from the other side. Equipment, microphones, or flags belonging to the communist side in the conference room are not to be touched. A United Nations Command security guard protects the flags of both the United Nations and of North Korea to ensure that they, too, are not touched.

The visitor may be surprised to see that even the green felt-covered conference table is divided down the middle. Visitors can cross the ever-present line only inside the Armistice Commission building. While expressionless soldiers stand guard outside the windows, most tourists take turns snapping pictures of each other "inside North Korea." At Freedom House, a pagoda-style observation tower, the visitor can view the entire Joint Security Area and the flags of the 16 nations that have served in the United Nations Command. Buildings on both sides are guarded by troops from neutral nations—Poland, Czechoslovakia, Switzerland, and Sweden.

## 한국 민속촌
### KOREAN FOLK VILLAGE

This traditional Korean village, located about an hour's ride by bus on the expressway south of Seoul, daily reenacts Korea's enchanting rural life of centuries ago. Designed to preserve and reconstruct what is fast vanishing as urbanization changes the Korean

*Tourists at the Korean Folk Village*

countryside, the restored village is a living, functioning community whose residents work in the manner of their forebears. It takes a full day, or more, to tour the 240 homes, visit ceramic and bamboo shops, and drink some rice wine in a wayside tavern in this authentic Yi dynasty village.

People in the Folk Village follow time-honored customs and wear traditional costumes. Artists and artisans ply their trades in an atmosphere of timelessness. Rustic houses of simple farmers nestle near ornate estates of country gentlemen; calligraphers are found alongside silk weavers; a potter's shop is next to a rice miller. The temples, pavilions, farmhouses, and aristocrats' (*yangban*) mansions are furnished with authentic antiques—chests, pots and pans, farm implements—and are lived in by the traditional artisans who populate the village. Altogether, this sizeable village provides a fascinating insight into the Korea of yesterday.

Tourists can wander freely through the village, looking into the door of any apparently private home. On a wood-floored porch a woman irons by beating the clothes with two sticks, while in the next courtyard another housewife is spinning silk thread from a small white cocoon simmering in a pot of boiling water. The fortune-teller, the calligrapher, the seamstress making gorgeous *hanbok* (Korean native clothing), the basket weaver, the charcoal maker, the papermaker, the blacksmith, the furniture carpenter, the potter, and the instrument maker can all be seen at work in their shops. A young man with his hair in one long braid is single; the hair is cut prior to the wedding day; a top-knot is then made, which will fit comfortably under a new horsehair hat, a symbol of married life. An elderly scholar with a slender bamboo pipe in hand and wearing a wide-brimmed horsehair hat strolls under the low eaves of straw-thatched homes, his flowing *turumagi* (overcoat) complementing the serene surroundings.

The Folk Village is a photographer's delight. In addition to seeing the sights, visitors can also participate in the wedding procession of a traditionally costumed bride and groom, transported via palanquin and trailed by a colorful, whirling farmers' dance band. Outdoor entertainment features the farmers' dance, acrobatics, a traditional funeral service, and kite-flying contests. One day is hardly adequate to see the wealth of fascinating exhibits and activities of this living, open-air museum.

The privately funded village is open from 10 a.m. to 5 p.m. seven days a week. Regularly scheduled tours leave from major hotels in Seoul every day; as an example, a KTB-operated tour leaves from the Chosun Hotel at 9:50 a.m. and returns at 5:30 p.m. The trip costs $42 and includes a brief visit to Suwon (see below), a Korean lunch, and admission to the village. It is much less expensive to go by express bus (₩1,100) and pay the admission fee when you get there.

## 수원
## SUWON

Suwon, the capital of Kyonggi-do Province, is located just 30 miles south of Seoul. It is easily reached by train, bus, or car. The fortress walls and gates are abiding relics of Korea's traditional walled cities. Like other Korean cities, Suwon is rapidly industrializing, but in the midst of modernization it carefully preserves landmarks of its proud heritage.

The city is surrounded by walls several meters high, in which there are four ancient gates: South Gate, East Gate, North Gate, and the towered West Gate. Also interesting are Hwahong-mun (Rainbow Gate) and the picturesque Water Gate along Hwa-chon (Flower Stream). The beautiful pavilion tower on top is built on seven arches at a point where the city wall crosses the stream. The seven cataracts flowing through the quaint archways are lovely. Lakes and streams among hilly slopes covered with forests of pine, oak, and willow create a dramatic setting and give the town its name—Suwon, Water Town.

*Suwon-song Fortress, on the way to the Folk Village*

A few miles south of Suwon is Yongju-sa (Dragon Jewel Temple), a spacious complex with the walls of the buildings painted with Confucian scenes (although it is a Buddhist temple) designed to reinforce the virtues of filial piety. An amusing scene shows a folk tiger smoking a long Korean pipe in the company of some unusual rabbits. Other attractions include a seven-story stone pagoda, a Koryo-era brass bell, and superb Buddhist paintings. Buses for Yongju-sa leave from Suwon's South Gate.

West of the town is the Government Agricultural Experiment Station, a large model farm on the bank of Soho (West Lake, a reservoir created by a dam) at the foot of Yogi-san (Pretty Dancing Girl Mountain). Established to aid the agricultural industry, the station conducts experimental research in all kinds of farming, such as rice cultivation, cotton growing, horse and sheep breeding, and other stock-breeding. It cooperates with the Agricultural College and the Sericultural Experimental Institution of Seoul National University.

The visitor to Suwon finds a more diversified collection of the most interesting forms of old Korean architecture within a smaller area than in any other town. Every gateway and wall turret is unique, each a little architectural masterpiece.

## 인천
## INCHON

One hour to the west of Seoul is its principal port, Inchon, the terminus of a Seoul subway line. Inchon was the site of General MacArthur's momentous surprise landing which led to the recapture of Seoul from the North Koreans 12 days after the assault in September 1950. Chayu (Freedom) Park has a monument to the general, facing the Yellow Sea. This coast is famous for the magnitude of the tidal rise and fall.

The harbor city of Inchon was the historic point-of-entry when the great powers in the late 19th century introduced the "Hermit Kingdom" of Korea to the international stage as an open trading port. One Chinese and two Russian ships were sunk in the outer port during the Sino-Japanese War and the Russo-Japanese War at the turn of the century. Today, Inchon is a booming harbor and is Korea's fourth largest city. The new canal of Inchon Port, 60 feet wide with a 25-acre dock, is able to accommodate five 5,000–6,000 ton vessels and can handle ships up to 10,000 tons.

The Hotel Casino Olympos (200 rooms) is situated on a small hill commanding a panoramic view of the harbor. It attracts high-rollers to the Lido night club and gambling casino, the grill and the swimming pool. There are several smaller resort hotels in the area, particularly near Songdo Beach south of the city. Inchon boasts a thriving Chinatown, an active nightlife, and the Songdo Recreation Area.

Popular nearby diversions include seafood dining on a land-linked island, Wolmi-do (Moon Tail Island), made of reclaimed land and famous for gourmet dishes of raw fish and other deep sea delicacies. The traveler will also enjoy visiting the big public seafood market on the southern side of Inchon's tidal basin. During the summer, ferryboats carry passengers to various off-shore islands, which are favorite Korean resort and fishing-trip destinations.

## 강화도
## KANGHWA-DO (KANGHWA ISLAND)

Fifty-six kilometers west of Seoul, in the mouth of the Han River as it flows into the Yellow Sea, is Kanghwa-do, Korea's fifth largest island and an area rich in history and natural beauty. The island boasts ancient burial dolmens, an altar to Tangun, the mythical founder of the Korean nation, fire-signal towers, and pagodas. Chondung-sa (Chondung Temple), located within a one-mile walled fortress with four gates, is the major attraction.

The historical importance of Kanghwa-do down through the centuries derives from its location near both Kaesong (Songdo) and Seoul. It was used as a place of refuge by kings fleeing from Mongol and Manchurian invasions in the thirteenth and seventeenth centuries, respectively, during the Koryo and Yi periods. Situated in the Han River estuary, it dominates the sea approach to Seoul. Several clashes with foreign naval forces took place here in the last years of the "Hermit Kingdom" just prior to the beginning of Korea's contacts with the outside world in 1876.

The famous Kanghwa reed mats, decorated with floral designs and used on floors in the summer to make houses cooler, are favorite purchases by tourists on Kanghwa Island.

## 여주
### YOJU

Yoju, about 50 miles south of Seoul, is easily reached via the Yongdong Expressway; intercity buses connect Seoul and Yoju on a frequent schedule. Of the many treasures in Yoju, Sejong's Tomb (Yong-nung) is the most important. Just inside the entrance gate is an imposing marble monument, on which is carved the royal proclamation of *Hangul*, the Korean writing system. King Sejong's reign, 1418–1450, was a high point in Korea's cultural history, with many advances occurring: scientific inventions, the restoration of ancient musical instruments and music notation, significant literary works. Such achievements are recorded and displayed in a small museum at the tomb site. Every fall on the anniversary of Sejong's death, Confucian rituals are performed in his honor.

Another attraction in Yoju is Silluk-sa (Silluk Temple), dating from 580 A.D. Situated on a high bluff, it offers a panoramic view of the curving Han River. Among the treasures on the temple grounds are an ancient brick pagoda, a nine-story pagoda, a marble lantern, important carved stone tablets, and a 370-year-old gingko tree. On the return to Seoul, many visitors stop to visit the pottery shops, which make excellent Koryo and Yi reproductions, along the Kwangju-Inchon Highway, where one can purchase beautiful vases and pottery goods.

## RESORTS

### 안양 유원지
**Anyang Resort.** Located just 24 kilometers south of the capital, Anyang Resort is famous for its swimming pools of natural river-water flowing from mountain ravines. Well-known since the Yi

dynasty, the area is recognized today as one of the best summer resorts near Seoul. Its accommodations include: hotels, bungalows, inns, a youth hostel, swimming pools, archery ranges, boat harbors, a children's playground, rest houses, and a tourist information center. With its beautiful background of dense forests, the resort is developing rapidly as a popular tourist destination.

### 송도 유원지

**Songdo Resort.** The Songdo Beach Resort, on the west coast just south of Inchon, boasts a huge artificial swimming beach, created by using a watergate to overcome the 10-meter difference between high and low tide. As the tide ebbs and flows twice a day, fresh seawater is always available for beach-goers. The resort's facilities include bungalows, cabarets, restaurants, a children's amusement center, teahouses, an outdoor amphitheater, campgrounds, lodges, and public houses. Additional accommodations are available nearby in Inchon.

### 청평 유원지

**Chongpyong Lake.** This beautiful artificial lake is known for its clear water and wooded hillsides. It was created by a dam constructed for a power plant on the Pukhan River. Since its designation as a national tourist area, 30,000 cherry tree seedlings and a variety of roses have been planted. Facilities include three hotels, 30 bungalows, villas, swimming pools, waterskiing, a boat harbor, a children's merry-go-round, restaurants, table tennis, stores, parking lots, observation bridges, and rope-ways for sightseers.

### 용문산

**Yongmun Mountain.** Situated in Kyonggi-do Province, southeast of Seoul, this grand and scenic mountain is noted for the colorful seasonal changes of the foliage on its slopes and for the many ancient temples built there. Mt. Yongmun is part of the Kwangju mountain range. Tourist attractions include Yongmun-sa (Yongmun Temple), founded in the Silla period (57 B.C.–935 A.D.), Sangwon-sa, and Sana-sa; the ruins of the Hamwang Mountain fortress wall built in the Three Kingdoms era amid giant rocks on the strategic natural precipice; a huge gingko tree over 1,000 years old; a mineral water fountain; Jungwon falls, and Bonghwang bower. Accommodations for visitors are adequate: a tourist hotel, Korean-style inns, recreational facilities, and souvenir shops are available.

### 팔당 댐

**Paldang Reservoir.** Sailboats are a special attraction on this reservoir located at the juncture of the north and south portions of the Han River near Seoul. Not far away is Yongmun-sa and the world's largest ginko tree.

남이섬

**Namisom.** This small island in the upper portion of the Han River is becoming increasingly popular for water sports such as swimming, boating, and waterskiing. It is more isolated and thus less crowded than Chongpyong.

춘천

**Chunchon.** Chunchon is the very attractive rebuilt capital of Kangwon-do Province, the most ruggedly spectacular of Korea's provinces. Surrounded by man-made lakes, Chunchon is appreciated for its clean air, clear water, and excellent fishing. It is popular as a quiet getaway from Seoul.

## SEOUL DIRECTORY

| | |
|---|---|
| **HEALTH AND EMERGENCY SERVICES** | **Telephone** |
| Catholic Medical Center (St. Mary's Hospital, Yoido-dong) | 794-7191 |
| Police–Emergency | 112 |
| Ambulance or Fire | 119 |

| | |
|---|---|
| **TELEPHONE AND TELEGRAM SERVICES** | |
| Information (Local and Domestic Long-Distance) | 114 |
| International Long-Distance | 1035/1037 |
| Domestic and International Telegraph Information | 115 |
| Overseas Operator | 117 |
| Telex Number Information | 104 |

| | |
|---|---|
| **TOURIST INFORMATION SERVICES** | |
| Korea National Tourism Corporation (KNTC) | 757-6030 |
| KNTC Tourist Information Center | 757-0086 |
| KNTC Kimpo Airport Information | 665-0086 |
| Seoul Tourist Information Center | 731-6337 |
| Seoul Railway Station | 392-7811 |
| Seoul Tourist Information Counters, Citywide Locations | |
| Seoul Express Bus Terminal | 598-3246 |
| Chongno | 732-0088 |
| Kwanghwamun | 735-0088 |
| Myong-dong | 757-0088 |
| Namdaemun | 779-3644 |
| Tongdaemun | 272-0348 |
| Civil Aviation Bureau, Ministry of Transportation, 21-168, 2-ga Pongnae-dong | 392-9801/2 |
| Tourist Complaint Center | 735-0101 |

| | |
|---|---|
| **BANKS** | |
| **Main Foreign Banks** | |
| Bank of America | 754-4445 |
| Chase Manhattan Bank | 752-1105 |
| Citibank | 733-3625 |
| Bank of Tokyo | 752-0111 |
| Mitsui Bank | 757-4631 |
| Royal Bank of Canada | 730-7791 |
| Hong Kong & Shanghai Banking Co. | 739-4211 |

**Main Korean Banks**

| | |
|---|---|
| Bank of Korea | 777-5611 |
| Korea Exchange Bank | 771-0046 |
| Export-Import Bank | 778-3951 |

## USEFUL TELEPHONE NUMBERS

| | |
|---|---|
| Antique Clearance Certificate Office | 735-3053 |
| Arirang Taxi Service | YS-5113 792-7348 |
| Emergency (U.S. Embassy) | YS-110 |
| Seoul Immigration Office | 734-4178 |
| SOFA | YS-6771 792-0460 |
| Towing | YS-5572 792-8132 |
| Weather | 733-0365 |
| Commercial Line to Yongsan Line | prefix. 0011 |
| Yongsan Line to Commercial Line | prefix. 9 |

## FOREIGN MISSIONS
### Embassies

Argentina: 135-53 Itaewon-dong, Yongsan-ku, Seoul (02) 793-4062

Australia: 5th, 6th & 7th Floors, Salvation Army Bldg., 58-1, 1-ka, Shinmunno, Chongno-ku, Seoul (02) 730-6490

Austria: Rm. 1913, Kyobo Bldg., 1-1, 1-ka, Chongno-ku, Seoul (02) 732-9071

Belgium: 1-65 Tongbinggo-dong, Yongsan-ku, Seoul (02) 793-9611

Bolivia: Rm. 1501, Garden Tower Bldg., 98-78 Unnidong, Chongno-ku, Seoul (02) 742-7170

Brazil: Rm. 301/306, New Korea Bldg., 192-11, 1-ka, Ulchiro, Chung-ku, Seoul (02) 720-4769

Canada: 10th Floor, Kolon Bldg., 45, Mugyo-dong, Chung-ku, Seoul (02) 776-4062

Chile: Youngpoong Bldg., 142 Nonhyon-dong, Kangnam-ku, Seoul (02) 549-1654

Republic of China: 83 2-ka, Myong-dong, Chung-ku, Seoul (02) 776-2721

Colombia: House No. 125 Namsan Village, Itaewon-dong, Yongsan-ku, Seoul (02) 793-1369

Costa Rica: 1105 Garden Tower Bldg., 98-75 Unni-dong, Chongno-ku, Seoul (02) 745-6163

Denmark: Suite 701, Namsong Bldg., 260-199 Itaewon-dong, Yongsan-ku, Seoul (02) 792-4187

Dominican Republic: A-908 Namsan Village Apt., Itaewon-dong, Yongsan-ku, Seoul (02) 744-1803

Ecuador: 133-20 Itaewon-dong, Yongsan-ku, Seoul (02) 795-1278

Finland: Office Suite 604, Kyobo Bldg., 1-ka, Chongno, Chongno-ku, Seoul (02) 732-6223

France: 30 Hap-dong, Sodaemun-ku, Seoul (02) 362-5547

Gabon: Rm. 701, Kunchang Bldg., 238-5 Nonhyong-dong, Kangnam-ku, Seoul (02) 548-9912

Germany: 4th Floor, Daehan Fire & Marine
  Insurance Bldg., 51-1, Namchang-dong,
  Chung-ku, Seoul  (02) 779-3272
Guatemala: B-116 Namsan Village Apt.,
  Itaewon-dong, Yongsan-ku, Seoul  (02) 793-1319
Haiti: 34-1, Tongbinggo-dong, Yongsan-ku, Seoul  (02) 797-9372
Holy See: 2 Kungjong-dong, Chongno-ku, Seoul  (02) 736-5725
India: 37-3 Hannam-dong, Yongsan-ku, Seoul  (02) 798-4257
Indonesia: 55 Yoido-dong, Yongdungpo-ku, Seoul  (02) 782-5116
Iran: 726-126 Hannam-dong, Yongsan-ku, Seoul  (02) 793-7751
Italy: 1-169, 2-ka, Shinmunno, Chongno-ku, Seoul  (02) 796-0491
Japan: 18-11 Chunghak-dong, Chongno-ku, Seoul  (02) 733-5626
Liberia: 657-42 Hannam-dong, Yongsan-ku, Seoul  (02) 793-6704
Libya: 4-5 Hannam-dong, Yongsan-ku, Seoul  (02) 797-6001
Malaysia: 4-1 Hannam-dong, Yongsan-ku, Seoul  (02) 795-9203
Mexico: 901, Garden Tower Bldg., 98-78 Unni-dong,
  Chongno-ku, Seoul  (02) 741-4060
Netherlands: 1-48 Tongbinggo-dong,
  Yongsan-ku, Seoul  (02) 793-0651
New Zealand: Korean Publishers Bldg.,
  105-2 Sagan-dong, Chongno-ku, Seoul  (02) 720-4255
Norway: 124-12 Itaewon-dong, Yongsan-ku, Seoul  (02) 795-6850
Oman: 1-35, 2-ka, Shinmunno, Chongno-ku, Seoul  (02) 736-2432
Pakistan: 58-1, 1-ka, Shinmunno, Chongno-ku, Seoul  (02) 739-4422
Panama: Rm. 101, Garden Tower, 98-78 Unni-dong,
  Chongno-ku, Seoul  (02) 720-4164
Paraguay: 1-68 Tongbinggo-dong, Yongsan-ku, Seoul  (02) 794-5553
Peru: House 129, Namsan Village, Itaewon-dong,
  Yongsan-ku, Seoul  (02) 797-3736
Philippines: 559-510 Yoksam-dong,
  Kangnam-ku, Seoul  (02) 568-9131
Saudi Arabia: 1-112, 2-ka, Shinmunno,
  Chongno-ku, Seoul  (02) 739-0631
Spain: 726-52 Hannam-dong, Yongsan-ku, Seoul  (02) 794-3581
Sweden: Boyung Bldg., 8F., 108-2 Pyong-dong,
  Chongno-ku, Seoul  (02) 720-4767
Switzerland: 32-10 Songwol-dong, Chongno-ku, Seoul  (02) 739-9511
Thailand: 653-7 Hannam-dong, Yongsan-ku, Seoul  (02) 795-3098
Turkey: 726-116 Hannam-dong, Yongsan-ku, Seoul  (02) 794-0255
United Kingdom: 4 Chong-dong, Chung-ku, Seoul  (02) 735-7341
U.S.A.: 82 Sejongno, Chongno-ku, Seoul  (02) 732-2601
Uruguay: Rm. 1802, Daewoo Center Bldg., 541 5-ka,
  Namdaemunno, Chung-ku, Seoul  (02) 753-7893
Venezuela: Garden Tower Bldg., 18th Fl.,
  98-78 Unni-dong, Chongno-ku, Seoul  (02) 741-0036

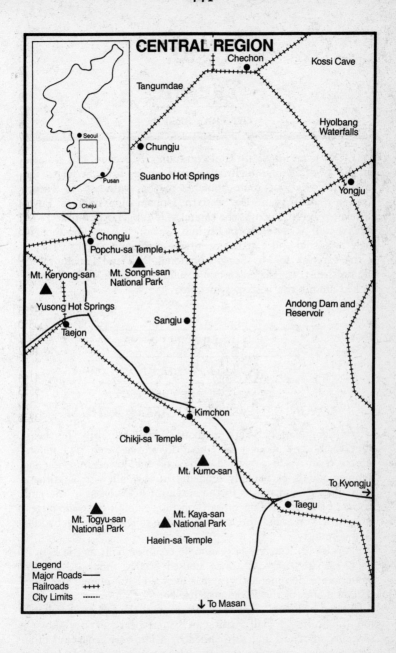

CENTRAL REGION

Chechon

Kossi Cave

Tangumdae

Hyolbang
Waterfalls

Seoul

Chungju

Yongju

Pusan

Suanbo Hot Springs

Cheju

Chongju

Popchu-sa Temple

Mt. Keryong-san

Mt. Songni-san
National Park

Andong Dam and
Reservoir

Yusong Hot Springs

Sangju

Taejon

Kimchon

Chikji-sa Temple

Mt. Kumo-san

To Kyongju

Mt. Togyu-san
National Park

Mt. Kaya-san
National Park

Taegu

Haein-sa Temple

Legend
Major Roads———
Railroads    ++++
City Limits  ------

↓ To Masan

# 大田
# Taejon

## CENTRAL REGION

TAEJON is an important transportation city because it is situated on the two rail and highway arterial routes from Seoul to the southern cities: one route branches to the southeast, to Taegu, Kyongju, and Pusan; the western Honam line goes to Puyo, Chongju, and Mokpo. As the capital of Chungchongnam-do Province as well as a transportation hub, Taejon is becoming increasingly industrial and a center of intense economic activity. Taejon is the gateway to Mt. Songni National Park and Popchu-sa, to the northeast. In Taejon's western suburbs is Yusong Hot Springs, ranked among the best spas in Korea.

## ► HIGHLIGHTS ◄
## ► FOR TRAVELERS ◄

### 속리산 국립공원 : 법주사
### SONGNI-SAN NATIONAL PARK: POPCHU-SA

Mt. Songni National Park is about a one-hour drive northeast from Taejon and about a three-hour drive from Seoul. The mountainous countryside is covered with pastel wildflowers in spring and summer and is particularly dramatic in the fall with a brilliant array of golds and russets in the autumn leaves. Deep in the pine woods of the park is Popchu-sa (Popchu Temple), once the largest temple in Korea and the location of the tallest statue of Buddha in the country.

Popchu-sa, a lovely large temple complex built at the base of Sogni-san in 553 A.D., once housed 30,000 monks. Now the grounds are dominated by a massive, modern, poured-concrete, 88-foot statue of the Buddha of the Future (Maitreya). The most celebrated historical treasure at Popchu-sa is the five-story Palsang-jon (Eight Image Hall), rising in symmetrical splendor above a spacious courtyard and surrounded by a forest of cedar and pine. The temple's structure suggests ancient Paekje pagodas and is echoed in Japan's Horyuji, which was built by Paekje workmen in the seventh century. In the courtyard is Korea's oldest and best wooden pagoda. Other registered National Treasures in the compound are the Twin Lions Stone Lantern, the Four Guardians Stone Lantern, the Stone Lotus water container, and the rock-hewn Ma-ae Buddha Image.

Inside the pagoda are "Life of Buddha" paintings and an unusual arrangement of 1,000 Buddhas along their base. On Buddha's birthday a huge painting is exhibited. The temple attracts large numbers of tourists as well as pilgrims. Impromptu performances of Korean folk music and dances by country people who picnic on the grounds around the temple add to the enjoyment of a visit. Across the road is Korea's leading folk art museum, the Emille.

## 직지사
### CHIKJI-SA (CHIKJI TEMPLE)

Located on Mt. Hwangak, 12 kilometers west of Kimchon City, Chikji Temple nestles beside a stream among pine-covered slopes, fantastically shaped rocks, dramatic waterfalls, and quiet pools. Azaleas bloom gloriously in the spring, and the leaves of autumn are equally splendid. Crowds of tourists come to enjoy the scene as groups of Buddhist believers visit the temple to worship. The monk Ado, who introduced Chinese Buddhism during the Silla period in 418, built Chikji-sa. Burned during the Japanese invasion of 1592, it was rebuilt in 1610. The ancient heritage of Chikji-sa can be seen in two Silla-period granite pagodas and a Koryo-period granite turtle, the best example of such stele bases. The bell in the temple is renowned: 1,700 pounds of copper and 150 pounds of gold were melted down to cast it.

Within the temple precincts are Buddhist structures and artifacts, including the main sermon hall, four Buddha guardians, Iljumun Gate, and a seated Yaksa-yorae Buddha image. Enshrined in the Main Hall (rather than in a separate shaman building, as might be expected) are some 7,000 paintings of shamanistic origin. A favorite is the Mountain Spirit and his Tiger-Messenger with hypnotic gold eyes. Chonbul-jon, or Thousand Buddha Images Hall, adjoins the Main Hall of the temple; it contains 1,000 small statues depicting Buddha as an infant, exquisitely carved on jade stones from Kyongju and lined up side by side. Devoted followers offer prayers for 1,000 days, believing that everyone can achieve enlightenment and become qualified to detect a Buddha, which is an image of himself.

Chikji-sa is also noted for the beautiful blue tiles on the walls of the main building and for the more than 1,000-year-old wooden pillars supporting the main gate. Located in the vicinity of Chikji-sa are the ruins of 26 other temples, including hermitages constructed during the height of Buddhist influence during the Silla Kingdom.

## 독립기념회관
## INDEPENDENCE MEMORIAL COMPLEX

The imposing Independence Memorial Complex, dedicated to the Korean independence movement, is located at the foot of Mt. Huksong in Chonwon County, Chungchon South Province. Its seven exhibition halls have over 43,000 relics which depict the history of the Korean fight for independence and convey a sense of national pride. At the entrance to the complex is the 51.3-meter-high Monument to the Nation and in the back is the Patriots Memorial, featuring sculptures which include the impressive Statue of Indomitable Koreans in the Grand Hall of the Nation. The $11 million complex, which is open from 10 a.m. to 5:30 p.m. Tuesday through Sunday, also contains an amphitheater.

## 안동, 영주
## ANDONG AND YONGJU

Andong City is just west of the vast Andong Lake Reservoir, which is being developed as a major recreational area for all types of water sports. Near the south end of the lake is the Andong Folk Village. Also of interest is the Tosansowon Confucian Institute, founded in 1560 by Yi Toekye, a famous Confucian scholar, as the first private school in Korea (it was reconstructed in 1575 by King Sonjo). The city of Yongju is a rail hub from which lines radiate in four directions. It also is a center of Confucian teaching.

## 단양, 충주호
## TANYANG, CHUNGJU LAKE, AND SUANBO

The Tanyang area is noted for its "eight natural beauty scenes," each created by the sculpturing effects of water erosion on the natural limestone formations. A favorite site is Hyolbang Waterfall. The city of Chongju is famous for the excellent grade of tobacco grown in the area, for Korea's only talc mine, and for Suanbo Hot Springs. This spa is noted for the high radium content of its water and for remarkable curative powers in treating skin disorders.

Taejon is a two-hour trip from Seoul Railway Station (tel. 392-7788), Seoul's Kangnam Bus Terminal (tel. 598-4151), and Seoul's Yongsan Bus Terminal (tel. 798-3355). Bus connections can be made to other cities and sites in the Central Region.

---

# HOTEL
# ACCOMMODATIONS

---

중앙 호텔

**Joong Ang Hotel** (Second class—59 rooms for 240 guests). Located in downtown Taejon.

*Address:* 318 Chung-dong  *Telephone:* (042) 253-8801/5

속리산 호텔

**Songni-San Hotel** (First class—145 rooms for 500 guests). Located at the entrance to Mt. Songni National Park.

*Address:* 198 Sanaeri  *Telephone:* (0433) 2091/8

대전 호텔

**Dae Jeon Hotel** (Second class—52 rooms for 130 guests). Downtown Taejon.

*Address:* 20-16 Won-dong  *Telephone:* (042) 253-8131

유성 호텔

**You Soung Hotel.** Taedok County (First class—108 rooms for 324 guests).

*Address:* 480 Pongmyon-dong, Chung-ku, Taejon
*Telephone:* 822-0611

만년장 호텔

**Mannyonjang Hotel** (Second class—62 rooms for 150 guests). Near Mt. Kyeryong National Park, Taejon.

*Address:* 478 Pongmyongri  *Telephone:* (042) 822-0061

**Suanbo Waikiki Tourist Hotel** (First class—90 rooms). A swimming and entertainment complex with hot springs and sauna, this hotel is very popular with families.

*Address:* 806-1 Onchon-ri  *Telephone:* (0441) 42-3333

**Suanbo Park Hotel** (First class—83 rooms).

*Telephone:* (0441) 42-2331/6

**Tanyang Park Hotel**

*Address:* 93 Tanyang-up  *Telephone:* (0444) 22-6000/3

The best shopping opportunities in the central region are in the town markets of each city, and in the hotel souvenir shops.

The Andong Folk Festival is held in spring each year. Popular with visitors, the festival features a Hahoe Mask Drama, a "Girls' Bridge-Crossing Game," and a strenuous competition called *chajon-nori*, in which two teams carry giant A-frames that they try to keep each other from toppling.

Golf courses are available at Osan, Yongin, Kwanak, Yoju, and Suwon.

# 大邱
# Taegu

## CENTRAL REGION

TAEGU, once called the apple capital of Korea, has a population of more than two million and is Korea's third largest city. Situated astride the railway and the superhighway linking Seoul and Pusan, Taegu forms the gateway to Kyongju from the west, and it is a regional center of importance in the upper Naktong Basin of southeast Korea. Completion of the new '88 Olympic Highway between Taegu and Kwangju has facilitated access to a number of well-known national parks and temples in the area. Taegu has become increasingly urbanized owing to rapid industrialization, and every year more people are flocking to this modernizing city.

Travelers from overseas will appreciate Taegu's modern hotels and its missionary colleges, hospitals, and churches. Taegu is a famous traditional market town and historic center of Korea's apple-growing and textile industries. When the Korean War broke out, the battle lines were only 12 kilometers north of Taegu, which was turned into a military town. It was headquarters for the Korean Army, the American Army, and the American Fifth Air Force until those units moved northward to the Seoul area.

## ECONOMY AND CULTURE OF TAEGU

Taegu is a primary collection and distribution center for a large producing area, which provides copper and tungsten as well as a variety of agricultural products. As an agricultural market center, So-mun Market (West Gate Market) in Taegu is one of the oldest and largest of the traditional Korean markets. Visitors will find a fascinating diversity of items for sale.

For many decades, Taegu has been famous for its delicious apples. At the turn of the century, James E. Adams, an American missionary, found that a native crabapple grew well in the Taegu basin; he grafted some cuttings imported from America onto the local crabapple trees. Thus he began raising apples to help the fast-growing Christian community. Soon Taegu became the center of a large apple industry, well known throughout Asia.

*Nŏlttwiki, New Year's Day "see-saw" game*

Originally Taegu's economy was based on textiles, and a significant modernization of textile manufacturing has taken place. In addition, diversified industrialization has been undertaken, based on Korea's national plan for economic development. During most of the Korean War, Taegu was outside the battle zones and therefore was at an advantage for postwar industrial growth. Now, except for Ulsan (near Kyongju), which was developed as a petrochemical center, Taegu is one of the most industrialized cities in southern Korea.

Taegu is still growing in terms of population, work force, and industrial products, but there has been concern over the movement of capital and brain power to the capital city, Seoul, the largest port city, Pusan, and the new industrial city of Pohang. Nevertheless, Taegu continues to expand production for international trade, with more diversification and increasingly advanced technology. It has a highly skilled labor force owing to excellent educational facilities.

The foundations of the educational system were established for Confucian scholars preparing to take the State Examination (*kwago*) during the Yi dynasty at private schools such as Sodang, Sowon, and Hyangkyo. Western education in Taegu began in 1897 when American Presbyterian missionaries James E. Adams and his wife, Nellie, established a missionary school. They also founded the Keisung Academy. Today the city has several universities and colleges. The university museums in Taegu provide excellent examples of the cultural and historical treasures that have been preserved from ancient times in the area. Outstanding is the Yongnam University Museum (tel. 82-7803).

# HIGHLIGHTS
# FOR TRAVELERS

## 해인사
## *HAEIN TEMPLE*

Haein Temple in the Mt. Kaya National Park, one of the most famous temples in Korea, is reached by passing through Taegu. A two-hour drive on a paved road brings the visitor to this extraordinary temple. This route, with its sheer mountain cliffs and cascading streams, provides some of the most spectacular scenery to be found anywhere in Korea. In spring, the temple's environs are alive with cherry blossoms and in autumn, with flaming maple leaves and golden oaks. The temple is large and includes a cluster of buildings that were built on several levels on the side of the mountain. The Haein Temple complex comprises 93 structures within a four-mile radius—shrines, hermitages, and small temples surrounding the main building. Buddhist believers study in the 12 hermitages, and their sutra-chanting echoes in the mountain silence day and night.

For almost 600 years the Haein Temple has been the repository of the most comprehensive compilation of Buddhist scriptures, the *Tripitaka Koreana*, which is a gem of Korean culture and a world treasure. The Sanskrit word *tripitaka* means "Three Baskets of Treasures" or categories of Buddhist works. It is divided into sections on (1) the disciplinary rules for monks and nuns; (2) the sutras or teachings, speeches and sayings attributed to Buddha and his disciples; (3) commentaries on the teachings and related literature.

Two ancient library buildings, which were built in 1488, house the 81,258 wood blocks on which the Buddhist canon is engraved in Chinese characters. The *Tripitaka* comprises 1,511 separate works; the wooden blocks (or plates) are 27 inches (90 cm.) wide, 9.5 inches (24 cm.) high, 1.5 inches (3.8 cm.) thick, and are carved on both sides, thereby making a total of 162,516 pages. The carving of the *Tripitaka* was completed in 1236 after 16 years of devoted work, representing the national aspiration to repel the Mongolian aggressors by virtue of Buddha. Thus these woodblocks were a religious expression of national defense and prestige.

The architecture of the buildings provides ventilation in all seasons, which has protected the treasure against dry rot, mold, and fire, and accounts for its preservation since 1392. The set is so perfectly preserved that it can still be printed; tourists can purchase samples of scriptures printed from these blocks at reasonable prices. A small admission fee is charged to enter the main temple and another at the entrance to the library.

Around Haein Temple and its vicinity are many historic sites and remains: Hyub Ju Chiin-ri Ma-Ae Buddha Image, Hwanggye waterfall, Hambyok Pavilion, Bansong bower, Bannya Temple, and a stone standing Amitabha are some of the treasures to be seen. Dense forests of old pine trees shade flowing brooks tumbling down mountains of strangely shaped rocks and stones, making excursions in the area very scenic. Oak trees provide fresh green in spring, deep shade in summer, and colorful red and yellow in the fall. The valley vistas around Haein-sa and majestic Mt. Kaya, 1,430 meters high, have been counted among the eight most scenic attractions of Korea since ancient times.

# HOW TO GET
# TO TAEGU

Taegu is on the Seoul-Pusan Expressway, 300 kilometers southeast of Seoul and 120 kilometers northwest of Pusan.

**From Seoul.** Korean Air flights leave daily, 7:40 a.m. and 6:05 p.m., and take 40 minutes. The deluxe express train, Saemaul-ho, takes about 3 hours and departs 12 times a day on the hour, with reservations required. Express buses depart several times each hour from Seoul's Kangnam Bus Terminal and take about four hours to Taegu. Reservations are needed during holiday periods.

**From Pusan.** KAL flights, train, and bus are available on frequent schedules.

To get to Haein Temple from Taegu, take the suburban bus leaving every half hour; the trip takes less than two hours.

---

# HOTEL

## ACCOMMODATIONS

---

There is a good selection of hotels to choose from in Taegu; they all are in the city and are in the $30 to $80 price range.

한일 관광 호텔

**Hanil Tourist Hotel** (First class—128 rooms for 190 guests). Located in downtown Taegu, with Korean and Western restaurants, nightclub, souvenir shop, bar, barber shop, coffee shop.

*Address:* 110 Namil-dong          *Telephone:* 423-5001

동인 호텔

**Dongin Hotel** (First class—92 rooms for 184 guests). Downtown location, with Korean, Japanese, and Western restaurants, nightclub, buffet restaurant, bar, souvenir shop, barber shop, coffee shop, game room.

*Address:* 5-2 1-ka Samdok-dong          *Telephone:* 46-7211

대구 수성 관광 호텔

**Taegu Soosung Tourist Hotel** (First class—86 rooms for 200 guests). Located downtown, with Korean, Japanese, and Western restaurants, nightclub, souvenir shop, game room, beauty salon.

*Address:* 888-2 Tusan-dong          *Telephone:* 763-7311

**Taegu Park Hotel.** This hotel is located just off the Kyongbu Expressway in a beautiful park-like setting with a large outdoor swimming pool.

**The Hotel Kumho** a deluxe facility with 128 rooms, opened in Taegu in June 1988.

*Address:* 28 Haso-dong          *Telephone:* 252-6001

Among the second class hotels, the following have moderate prices and are recommended: New-Young Nam (tel. 752-1001) and New Jong Ro Hotel (tel. 23-7111) (see also KNTC's *Hotel Guide* for more details).

---

## CUISINE

---

### KOREAN CUISINE

**Kugil Shikdang** (2 Namil-dong, tel. 023-7623); **Kammi Shikdang** (4 Talbong-dong, tel. 046-2829); **Haewon-dae Kalbi-jip** (2-50

Tongsong-ro, tel. 044-0556); **Myongmun-jang Shikdang** (42-2 l-ka; Chong-ro, tel. 023-6611); **Nampo-jip** (61 Kyo-dong, tel. 045-5338).

## JAPANESE CUISINE

**Kosong** (95-20 Kongpyong-dong, 044-2832); **Unjong Shikdang** (1-34 Tongsong-ro, tel. 246-1223).

## WESTERN CUISINE

The **Hanil, Dong In, Soosung Tourist Hotel**, and **Mido Department Store** serve Western-style food that is very good and only somewhat expensive; an excellent restaurant is the **Taegu Hoegwan** (45 Munhwa-dong, tel. 046-8766).

## KISAENG HOUSES

*Kisaeng-jip*, or *Kisaeng* house restaurants, serve excellent Korean food in full-course dinners, and accompanied by excellent *kisaeng* entertainment, for about $80 per person (more reasonable than in Seoul). The **Ilshim-Kwan** (27 1-ka Kyesan-dong, tel. 022-1394) and **Chongeng-Kak** (20-2 Sanso-dong, tel. 022-0810), located near the Kumho Hotel, have large dining rooms and many private party rooms and are popular both among Koreans and foreign visitors.

# ▶ SHOPPING ◀

Shopping for Korean products at the native markets is an interesting and delightful experience; many bargains can be found among the 60 markets in Taegu.

**So-mun Shijang (West Gate Market).** This is Taegu's major market and one of the three largest in the Republic of Korea. The market comprises several multi-story buildings and many outlying stalls and shops. It is particularly noted for fabrics, tailor shops, brassware, and the basement fish market. Near the fish market are excellent and reasonably priced Korean restaurants.

**Chilsong Shijang, Nam-mun Shijang, Kyodong Shijang**, and **Pongdok Shijang** are popular markets among local residents; the **Daegu Department Store** is best known to overseas visitors. In addition, there are **Dong-A, Daebo, Mido**, and **Mukunghwa** department stores; also Camp Walker and Camp Henry have stores for U.S. military personnel.

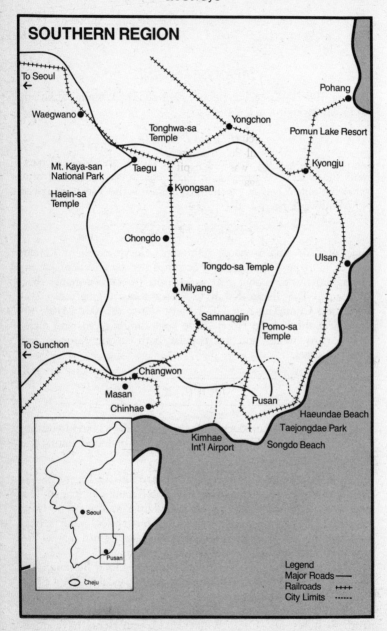

## SOUTHERN REGION

To Seoul

Waegwano

Tonghwa-sa
Temple

Yongchon

Pohang

Pomun Lake Resort

Mt. Kaya-san
National Park

Taegu

Kyongju

Haein-sa
Temple

Kyongsan

Chongdo

Tongdo-sa Temple

Ulsan

Milyang

Samnangjin

Pomo-sa
Temple

To Sunchon

Changwon

Masan

Chinhae

Pusan

Haeundae Beach

Taejongdae Park

Kimhae
Int'l Airport

Songdo Beach

Seoul

Pusan

Cheju

Legend
Major Roads ——
Railroads ＋＋＋＋
City Limits ------

# 慶州
# Kyongju

### SOUTHERN REGION

KYONGJU, Korea's "culture city," located between Taegu and Pusan just off the Seoul-Pusan Expressway on a fertile plain surrounded by mountains, was the capital of the Silla Kingdom (57 B.C.–935 A.D.). A legacy of beauty and mystery pervades the Kyongju Valley, where the kings and queens of ancient Silla reigned supreme for almost a millennium. Their devotion to Buddha is memorialized in myriad temples, statues, and other works of art in the city and on the encircling hillsides. Today Kyongju is a tourist city of royal tombs and ancient temples, attracting large numbers of visitors throughout the year.

Among the fascinating attractions of Kyongju are Tumuli Park, the burial place of Silla royalty; Chomsong-dae (Star Tower), a stone observatory; Posok Bower, a pleasure garden with a small pond shaped like an abalone shell; Panwol-song, the principal royal residence; and Anap Pond, which yielded a treasure of Silla artifacts when drained and which now is the center of a lovely recreation area. The Kyongju National Museum is known for magnificent gold crowns, gold jewelry, ceramics, and decorations from the great royal tombs. The Emille Bell, on the grounds of the museum, is one of the largest and most resonant of Asian bells. Pomun Lake Resort provides excellent tourist facilities and is a popular vacation spot. The two supreme treasures of Kyongju are Pulguk-sa (Korea's greatest Buddhist temple) and, high on Mt. Toham, Sokkuram Grotto, which contains many treasures of Buddhist art.

## KYONGJU IN HISTORY

Almost 2,000 years ago, when Caesar was ruler of Rome, three widely separated kingdoms emerged in Korea. In the northern part of the peninsula was Koguryo, whose vast territories sometimes extended far into Manchuria. The Kingdom of Paekje united peoples of the southwest, including the area where Seoul is located. In the southeast, one of the tribes created the Silla Kingdom. Originally the smallest and most isolated of the three, Silla grew to challenge its two rivals. Silla's advantages included shrewd dip-

*Pulguksa Temple, Kyongju*

lomacy, astute leadership, and internal cohesion, as well as help from Chinese armies. By 668, Silla had defeated both Koguryo and Paekje, and soon it also prevailed over its Chinese ally in the struggle for control of the peninsula. From the capital city of Kyongju, Silla ruled the country as a prosperous neighbor of Tang China until the tenth century, when a combination of dissension in the court and rebellion in the countryside caused its downfall.

Throughout the centuries, warfare among the Three Kingdoms led to contact with China; their search for military allies led to the importation of Chinese culture. The most important cultural import was Buddhism, which triumphed in Silla in the sixth century. Its influence is visible everywhere in the Kyongju Valley. Buddhism blended well with the native shamanistic practices and with Taoism. Some 60 temples were constructed in the capital city and hundreds more in the mountains surrounding Kyongju. Fire has destroyed all the wooden structures, but the stone temples, pagodas, and statues remain, providing eloquent testimony to the devotion of the people and the skill of the craftsmen during Silla's golden age. These qualities can be seen, too, in the many pre-Buddhist treasures that abound in the Kyongju area; excavations of royal tombs have produced a wealth of exquisite artifacts, including magnificent royal girdles and golden crowns decorated with comma-shaped pieces of jade. These early relics reflect the shamanistic tradition of northeast Asia.

All of the Three Kingdoms of ancient Korea achieved brilliant heights of culture and art, each with its own unique style. Koguryo, in the harsher northern region, tended toward massiveness in its works. Paekje was noted for fine, delicate designs. Silla artisans blended the two, creating works of boldness and refinement, splendor and subtlety, strength and softness. A sense of the harmony between humanity and nature dominates their art. The power of Silla monarchs is reflected in the size and magnificence of their palaces and pavilions.

In recognition of the significance of Kyongju, UNESCO undertook a major cultural survey of the area as part of its program of preserving the world's most important historic sites. The great Silla Kingdom, a continuum of 56 kings over a period of nearly 1,000 years, left innumerable valuable relics for research by modern scholars. The visitor to Kyongju discovers a veritable museum without walls—a vast array of temples, shrines, palaces, statues, and beautiful artifacts.

# HOW TO GET
# TO KYONGJU

On the Seoul-Pusan Expressway, Kyongju is 78 kilometers (49 miles) from Pusan and 363 kilometers (225 miles) from Seoul. Thus it is easily accessible by car. It is also served by express bus and by Korean Air via Taegu, then bus to Kyongju.

## FROM SEOUL

**Express Bus.** From Kangnam Express Bus Terminal, comfortable buses leave for Kyongju every 35 minutes from 7 a.m. to 6 p.m. The fare is about $5.50 and the trip takes about 4 hours 15 minutes. For information, call 598-4151 in Seoul.

**Train.** Fully equipped, super-express "Saemaul" trains leave for Kyongju from Seoul Railway Station beginning at 7 a.m. and leaving every 35 minutes until 6:10 p.m. The fare is about $14 (discounted on weekdays) for the 4-hour, 15-minute trip. For information, call 392-7811 in Seoul; 2-7788 in Kyongju.

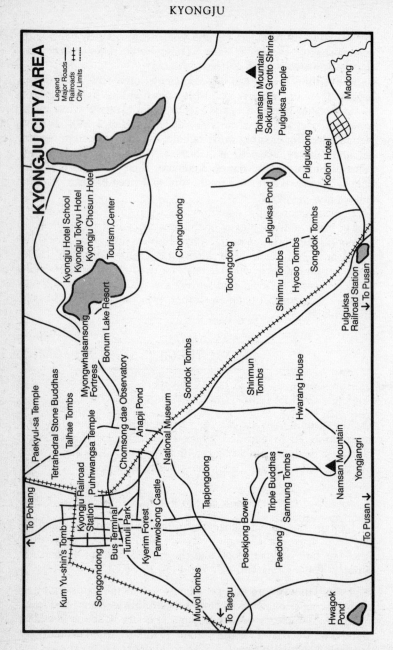

KYONGJU CITY/AREA

Legend
Major Roads
Railroads
City Limits

Tohamsan Mountain
Sokkuram Grotto Shrine
Pulguksa Temple

Madong

Pulgukdong

Kolon Hotel

Pulguksa Pond

Songdok Tombs

Kyongju Hotel School
Kyongju Tokyu Hotel
Kyongju Chosun Hotel
Tourism Center

Chongundong

Todongdong

Shinmu Tombs
Hyoso Tombs

Pulguksa
Railroad Station
To Pusan

Myongwhalsansong
Bonum Lake Resort

Myongwhalsansong
Fortress

Chomsong dae Observatory

Anapji Pond

National Museum

Sondok Tombs

Shinmun
Tombs

Hwarang House

Paekyul-sa Temple

Tetrahedral Stone Buddhas

Talhae Tombs

Puhhwangsa Temple

To Pohang

Kyongju Railroad
Station

Bus Terminal
Tumuli Park

Kyerim Forest

Panwolsong Castle

Tapjongdong

Posokjong Bower

Triple Buddhas

Samnung Tombs

Namsan Mountain

Yongjangri

To Pusan

Kum Yu-shin's Tomb

Songgondong

Muyol Tombs

Paedong

To Taegu

Hwagok
Pond

**Air/Bus.** Korean Air has daily flights to Taegu at 7:40 a.m. and 6:35 p.m. The fare is about $21, flight time about 40 minutes. From the main terminal at Taegu, the bus to Kyongju takes another hour. For information, call 664-7511 in Seoul; 423-4231 in Taegu.

## FROM PUSAN

**Express Bus.** Buses for Kyongju depart from Pusan Express Bus Terminal every half hour from 6 a.m. to 8 p.m. The trip takes about one hour and costs about $1.50. For information, call 53-5581/2 in Pusan.

**Shuttle Bus.** A shuttle bus operating between Kimhae Airport and the Kyongju Pomun Lake Resort leaves the airport every 1 1/2 hours from 12 noon to 6:30 p.m. The fare is about $2.50. For information, call 752-1974 in Seoul; 002-9716 in Kyongju.

## FROM CHEJU

**Air/Bus.** There are Korean Air flights to Taegu at 10:50 a.m. and 5 p.m. daily. The fare is about $25 and the flight takes 50 minutes. Another 50 minutes by bus takes the traveler to Kyongju. For information, call 22-6111 in Cheju.

**Car Ferry/Bus.** Car ferries leave Cheju for Pusan every day except Sunday at 7 and 7:30 p.m., and arrive at 6 and 6:30 a.m. the following morning. Fares range from $12-$86. Connections can then be made by express bus to Kyongju, a one-hour trip. For information, call 22-0291 in Cheju; 463-0605 in Pusan; 730-7788 in Seoul.

## EXCURSIONS

Information centers are located at the bus terminal (tel. 2-9289), Kyongju Railway Station (2-3843), Pulguk Temple (tel. 2-4747), and Kyongju Tourism Association (tel. 002-7198).

**Sokkuram Grotto Group Tour** (two hours). Pulgak-sa—Sokkuram Grotto.

**City Circling Group Tour** (five hours). Railroad Station — Pulgak-sa — Kyongju National Museum — Punhwang-sa — Tumuli Park — Chomsongdae — Panwol-song — Anap Pond — Posokjong — Onung Tombs — Muyol Tombs — Tomb of General Kim Yusin — Railroad Station.

**3-Hour Tour.** Pulguk-sa — Sokkuram Grotto.

**4-Hour Tour.** Tumuli Park — Kyongju National Museum — Pulguk-sa.

**6-Hour Tour.** Bus Terminal — Tumuli Park — Museum — Unification Hall — Pulguk-sa — Sokkuram Grotto — Pomun Lake Resort.

**One-Day Tour.** Bus Terminal — Tomb of General Kim Yusin — Muyol Tombs — Onung Tombs — Posok-jong — Tumuli Park — Chomsongdae — Panwol-song — Anap-ji — Punhwang-sa — Museum — Unification Hall — Pulguk-sa — Sokkuram Grotto — Pomun Lake Resort.

# HIGHLIGHTS
# FOR TRAVELERS

Ideally, the visitor would have several days to spend in Kyongju and vicinity. For the tourist with limited time, the following sites are recommended: Kyongju National Museum, Pulguk-sa and Sokkuram Grotto must be seen; other important and interesting sites to choose from are Tumuli Park, Chomsongdae, Punhwang-sa Pagoda, Tombs of Kim Yusin and King Muyol, Posok Bower, and Kwaenung.

경주 국립 박물관
### KYONGJU NATIONAL MUSEUM

In downtown Kyongju is the Kyongju National Museum, second only to the main National Museum in Seoul as a repository of Korea's finest treasures. It is most outstanding for cultural relics of the Silla period. Fabulous artifacts and art objects have been collected from temples and tombs all over the Kyongju Valley. In its picturesque grounds are many large stone pieces, including a gigantic stone lantern. The 10-foot-high, 23-ton Emille Bell, cast in 771, is one of the largest and most beautifully resonant bells in the world. According to legend, a child was thrown into the molten metal when the bell was cast and its cries for mommy ("emi, emi") are heard in the peal of the bell. It is said that the tolling of this bell is so resounding that it could be heard over a distance of 30 miles on a clear day. The surface of the bell is elaborately carved with lotus flowers, *apsaras* (Buddhist angels), and an inscription.

The displays inside the museum begin with prehistoric artifacts found in the Kyongju area. The simple pottery, stone knives, bronzeware, and swords were used by primitive early inhabitants. There are iron and bronze implements, unglazed pottery, and some relatively sophisticated objects from the Three Kingdoms period. Gold items from the pre-Buddhist era reflect the strong influence of native shamanism. Most famous are the winged golden crowns. These magnificent examples of Silla craftsmanship are striking for the elaborateness and delicacy of their design, which includes shamanistic flying horse, antler, and tree motifs, comma-shaped jade pendants, and dangling circles of thin gold. Silla's Buddhist heritage comes alive in rooms filled with sculpture; special temple roof tiles representing dragons, turtles, the mythical phoenix, and lotus petals; pagodas, and other relics. It seems incredible that these beautiful artworks were produced in the early centuries of this era, at a time when Europe was still in the Dark Ages.

The museum is open every day except Mondays and Korean national holidays, from 8:30 a.m. to 6:00 p.m.

# 불국사
# PULGUK-SA
# (NATIONAL BUDDHIST TEMPLE)

Pulguk-sa, built in 535 and extended in 751, is designated Historic Site No. 1. Recognized as Korea's greatest Buddhist temple, it is an architectural masterpiece and abiding symbol of traditional Korea. The magnificent temple buildings are characterized by simple lines and elegant decorations. Stone pagodas, terraces, bridges, stairways, and lanterns carved with Buddhist images demonstrate the balance and symmetry for which Silla works are noted. On the right are Blue Cloud Bridge and White Cloud Bridge; on the left, Lotus Bridge and Seven Treasure Bridge. The temple contains seven national treasures and many other unique and beautiful relics. Truly it is one of the most outstanding achievements of ancient Asia.

다보탑　석가탑
**Tabo-tap (Many Treasured Pagoda) and Sokka-tap (Buddha Pagoda).** These two great Silla pagodas stand in the terraced courtyard before the main hall. One is simple in design, the other is complex. Both are symbolic of Buddhism's attitude of contempla-

*Tapdori Ceremony, on the grounds of Pulguk-sa Temple*

tion and detachment from the world. The complexity of Tabo-tap is said to symbolize the manifestation of the Tabo Yorae (Buddha of Many Treasures) in a diverse universe. It is an elaborate three-story structure with pillars, stairways, and little balustrades. A small *haetae* (temple dog or lion) stands guard at the top of one stairway. This graceful monument was put together without mortar, a remarkable and very rare achievement. More typical of Korean pagodas is the simple Sokka-tap. Twenty-seven feet high, with stair-stepped eaves and low sloping roofs, this pagoda is without ornament or sculptured reliefs. During restoration a *sari* box, containing the cremated remains of a very high priest, was found in the second story. The outer box of gilt bronze in the pavilion style contained many other treasures. The box and its contents are among the oldest such items in the world.

The temple compound is surrounded by a wall and several buildings. Kukrak-chon (Hall of Heavenly Paradise) houses two seated buddhas of gold and bronze, outstanding examples of Silla sculpture which are designated National Treasures Nos. 26 and 27.

## 석굴암
## SOKKURAM GROTTO
## (STONE CAVE HERMITAGE SHRINE)

Sokkuram Grotto, National Treasure No. 24, is one of the most magnificent achievements of Oriental art. High on Mt. Toham behind Pulguk-sa, it was constructed by the Silla minister Kim Tae-song in the eighth century. Here, carved from the rock face and overlooking spectacular scenery, sits a towering Buddha gazing out toward the Eastern Sea and the morning sun.

Entry to the grotto is through an anteroom; a corridor connects it to the main hall. The anteroom is decorated with 10 standing figures cut in bas-relief on stone slabs. Three Deva Kings stand on the right and left walls; two other Deva Kings guard the sanctuary, on the wall opposite the entrance. On the walls of the corridor are Four Heavenly Kings, two on each side, facing each other. Two octagonal pillars flank the entrance to the round central hall.

Under the dome of the central hall is a softly illuminated statue of Sakyamuni, the historical Buddha, seated in the Pose of Enlightenment. The legs are folded in the lotus position, the left hand lies palm up in the lap, and the right hand rests, palm down, on the right knee. There seems to be a universal appeal in the massive, 11-foot Buddha, carved from a single piece of granite, sitting serenely in the rotunda of the Sokkuram to symbolize Buddhism's principles of peace, tranquility, and compassion for all life.

Although the Buddha seems to be in the center of the hall, it actually is slightly off center, so that when viewed from the anteroom it looks centered, revealing the Silla architects' ability to utilize optical illusion. The whole of Sokkuram is constructed with a refined sense of geometrical proportion and precision, representing the zenith of Korea's Buddhist architecture and sculpture. The main Buddha is surrounded, along the wall, by his 15 disciples; seated bodhisattvas are enshrined in 10 niches cut into the upper wall. The orderly arrangement of the various figures, and the contrasts of earthly and divine representations, are strikingly unique.

Sokkuram Grotto is impressive not only for its great size, but also for the subtler effects of the perfect natural setting, the sensitive and masterful artwork, and the awesome achievement of such a shrine being created in so remote a location. The grotto is now protected against the ocean winds by a glass enclosure. Visitors who obtain a permit can go into the grotto for more intensive viewing of the treasures.

왕능
## KINGS' TOMBS

오능
**Onung (Five Tombs).** This complex of five burial mounds contains the traditional tombs of Silla's first, second, third, and fifth kings, and of the first queen. It is said that the legendary

first king, Pak Hyok-ko-se, and his queen were inseparable in death as well as in life.

## 괴능

**Kwaenung (Tomb of King Wonsong).** King Wonsong ruled in the late eighth century, and his tomb is one of the largest, most accessible, and most elaborate of the Kyongju royal tombs. Twelve zodiac figures dressed in military uniform stand on a stone platform. Completely intact are four stone lions, military and civilian guards, and two nine-foot stone pillars that are said to represent filial yearning for the spirit of the deceased.

## 김유신 묘

**Tomb of Kim Yusin.** General Kim, the most famous military figure of the Silla Kingdom, is regarded as the architect of the victories over Paekje and Koguryo which brought about the unification of the country under Silla rule in 668. The tomb is located on Mt. Songhwa overlooking the city. Its most striking features are magnificent and well-preserved zodiac figures, animals dressed in Confucian attire, in relief on the retaining wall.

## 무열왕능

**Tomb of King Muyol.** The inscription on the tablet capstone resting on a traditional turtle base clearly identifies this tomb as that of the great Silla King Muyol. Designated Historical Site No. 20, the huge tomb, 380 feet in circumference, rests in beautifully kept grounds. King Muyol married the younger sister of Kim Yusin, his friend from childhood.

## 첨성대
### CHOMSONG-DAE (ASTRONOMICAL OBSERVATORY)

This unique bottle-shaped structure is the oldest existing observatory in the world and the oldest secular structure remaining in Korea. In modern times, Chomsong-dae has become a symbol of Korea and is often pictured on postcards, guidebooks, and postage stamps. It is designated National Treasure No. 31. Built in 634, the observatory is 29 feet high and is mounted on a 17-foot square foundation. It is constructed of exactly 365 stones, one for each day of the year; the tower's position, its angles, and the alignment of its corners with certain stars further show the importance that proper interpretation of heavenly signs held for Koreans in ancient times.

## 분황사 탑
### PUNHWANG-SA PAGODA

Contemporary with Chomsong-dae Observatory is Punhwang-sa-tap, the oldest datable pagoda of the Silla period. During restoration, the pagoda was found to contain a box holding scissors, needles, and other personal effects of Queen Sondok. The pagoda is noted for its superlative carvings and statuettes. On the four directions of the lower part of the tower, herculean wrestlers are carved in bold relief; on the four corners of the platform are carved stone lions. Although appearing to be built of brick, the pagoda actually is constructed of stones shaped to look like bricks. It is thought to have had nine stories, but only three remain.

## OTHER INTERESTING SITES

안압지, 임해정

**Anap Pond and Imhae Pavilion.** Anap-ji is a favorite recreation area for tourists. Developed in 674 during the reign of Silla's great King Munmu, the pond was part of the Panwol-song fortress complex. Surrounded by an exotic garden filled with rare trees, plants, animals, and birds, the beautiful grounds were a center for Silla diplomacy. The thousands of relics, including a perfectly preserved royal barge, that were dredged up from the pond are on display in the Kyongju National Museum: The Imhae Pavilion, part of Silla's royal villa, stands by the pond.

반월성

**Panwol-song (Half-Moon Fortress).** Now a popular park in the center of Kyongju, Panwol-song was once the site of the royal palace of the Silla kings. Flowing along the south side of the earthen fortress is Namchon Stream; the remains of two bridges, Iljong (Sun Spirit) and Woljong (Moon Spirit), can still be seen. Neither the palace nor the other splendid buildings that originally surrounded it have survived.

석빙고

**Sokping-go (Icehouse).** On the grounds of Panwol-song is a huge, stone icehouse, with an interior 56 feet long, 20 feet wide, and 18 feet high. Cave-like, it is covered with earth planted in grass. Visitors can peer in at the doorway.

포석정

**Posok Bower (Abalone Stone Pavilion).** The summer pavilion of Posok-jong was the most famous of the many such retreats in the Silla capital. This beautiful spot, where the royal family and courtiers once enjoyed sumptuous banquets with wine and poetry, became a scene of murder and rape in 926. King Kyonhwon of the Later Paekje Kingdom invaded Kyongju and found the court at Posok-jong. The attackers killed Silla king Kyongae, then assaulted and dragged off the queen and many palace women. All that can be seen now are the stone channels through which cool water flowed, water on which the courtiers floated wine cups as they composed poetry during banquets.

## 두문리 공원
**Tumuli Park.** In Tumuli Park, lovely landscaping covers burial mounds and tombs, many of which have been excavated, yielding a wealth of treasures from the early centuries of Korean history. Most famous is Tomb No. 155, the "Heavenly Horse Tomb," located in the northwest corner of the park. More than 10,000 items were found in this tomb, including golden jewelry, beads, girdles, a sword, earthenware vessels, and a magnificent gold crown. There is a small museum within the tomb, and many items are exhibited in the Kyongju National Museum. The tomb takes its name from a painting on birchbark of a galloping (or flying) white horse, a common motif among mounted tribal peoples in northeast Asia and a common theme in early shamanism.

## 남산
**Nam-san (South Mountain).** Within the more than 20 valleys of Nam-san are innumerable cultural remains, ruins of temples, and fragments of Buddhist images. Some are accessible only to the adventurous hiker; others can be reached with less difficulty. Worth a one-hour hike from Nam-san Village are the lovely stone relief carvings at Chilbur-am (Seven Buddha Hermitage). Easier to reach are the twin pagodas of Nam-san Village, on the eastern slope of the mountain. In Tap Valley is a treasure of relief carvings on a gigantic natural rock. On the western slope of Nam-san are many tombs of the Pak family and the site of the miraculous arrival of the legendary first king of Silla.

## 삼불상
**Buddhist Triad.** Only a half mile south of Posok-jong on the slopes of Nam-san stands the Buddhist Triad, three stone Buddhas dating probably from the sixth century. The central figure, over eight feet tall, is the Amita Buddha (Buddha of the Western Paradise); he welcomes to his paradise those believers who recite his name fervently. On either side are two Bodhisattvas. Designated National Treasure No. 63, the statues are carved from single blocks of granite and have round, smiling faces.

## 보문호 유원지
### POMUN LAKE RESORT

Pomun Lake is a 300 square kilometer planned recreation area five miles northeast of Kyongju city. During development by the Korea National Tourism Corporation, an ancient pond was enlarged into

*Pomun Lake Resort Complex*

a 1.6 million square meter lake. The complex includes several deluxe hotels, a marina, a large shopping center, and an 18-hole golf course and was developed at a cost of $60 million. A leisurely and tranquil atmosphere pervades the 2,570 acre resort, which is an excellent site for large-scale international conferences, exhibitions, and business conventions. Ideally located in southern Korea, near the rich historic relics of Korea's "golden age" and accessible from the large industrial cities, Pomun Lake Resort is rapidly gaining popularity as some two million foreign tourists and three million Korean tourists are now coming to Kyongju each year.

Scheduled for completion during 1989 are Doturak World, with camping sites, a dude ranch, and a zoo; Sorabol Green Park; Shilla Village, with 52 facilities evoking Shilla folk traditions; a botanical garden; and a 230-room youth hostel.

Respecting the cultural heritage of Kyongju, the buildings of the resort harmonize the traditional Silla architectural style with the demands of modern facilities. The roofs of the hotels, marina, and shopping center are all reminiscent of Silla Buddhist temples and royal pavilions. A large complex of Korean-style buildings overlooking the lake includes an excellent restaurant. Outdoor facilities include a meticulously kept golf course, swimming pool, tennis courts, and cycling and hiking trails. The lakeside restaurant offers traditional music and dance performances in the evening.

Guest accommodations at the resort include 845 rooms in three major hotels; Amenity Center with a 120-store shopping arcade, a 900-seat convention hall, a 1,000-seat open air theater, a health clinic, and administrative offices; a game center and a casino. Pomun is easily reached from downtown Kyongju by bus or taxi.

# HOTEL
# ACCOMMODATIONS

Kyongju consists of three principal areas: downtown, Pomun, and Pulguk-sa. Downtown centers on the main street running directly west from the railway station. To the south, toward Tumuli Park, are the majority of restaurants, coffee shops, gift shops, antique stores, and small drinking places. Pomun Lake is the heart of Kyongju's tourism and recreation area. Around the Pulguk Temple complex is an area of new hotels and *yogwan* (Korean inns), gift shops, and restaurants. Kyongju offers a variety of places for the tourist to stay, including Western-style hotels, Korean-style inns, and a youth hostel. Reservations are necessary, especially in spring and fall, the peak tourist seasons. The hotels and inns of Kyongju are about 1 1/2 hours by bus from Kimhae Airport, and from 10 to 30 minutes by taxi from the express bus terminal or the railway station.

## HOTELS

경주 조선 호텔

**Kyongju Chosun Hotel** (Deluxe—300 rooms for 600 guests). The Chosun is located near the lake shore and offers a high standard of accommodations and service. Facilities include Korean, French, and Japanese restaurants, a coffee shop, cocktail lounge, barber and beauty shops, golf course, swimming pool, and garden.

*Address:* 410 Sinpyong-dong
*Telephone:* 2-9601
*Telex:* CHOSUN K54467

코롱 호텔

**Kolon Hotel** (Deluxe—320 rooms for 573 guests). The Kolon is situated within easy walking distance of main attractions. Its facilities include a 500-seat dinner theater offering Western, Korean, and Japanese meals; coffee shop and pastry shop; barbershop and beauty salon; recreation room, game room, casino; indoor and outdoor Olympic-size swimming pools; souvenir shop; nightclub.

*Address:* 111-1 Ma-dong
*Telephone:* 42-9001
*Telex:* K54469
*Cable:* KOLHTL

### 경주 도큐 호텔

**Kyongju Tokyu Hotel** (Deluxe—303 rooms for 636 guests). The Tokyu is beautifully situated on Pomun Lake, about six kilometers from downtown. It offers Western, Japanese, and Korean restaurants, a discotheque, barber shop and beauty salon, lakeside restaurant, swimming pool, indoor golf, tennis courts, boating and fishing, and a shopping arcade.

*Address:* 410 Shinpyong-dong      *Telephone:* 2-9901
*Telex:* KJ TOKYU K54328    *Cable:* KYONGJU TOKYU

### 보문호 호텔

**Pomun Lake Hotel** (Third class—30 rooms for 60 guests). This hotel at Pomun Lake is an annex to the Korea National Tourism Corporation (KNTC) Hotel School, a training establishment for future hotel employees and managers. It offers a good location and low room rates.

*Address:* 645 Shinpyong-dong      *Telephone:* 43-4245

Other first-class hotels with Korean-style rooms include the moderately priced **Baekam Resort Hotel** (telephone: 82-3500), **Kyongju Hot Springs Tourist Hotel** with 89 rooms (address: 145-1 Kujong-dong, Kyongju-shi; telephone: (0561) 41-661/4); **Ulsan Koreana Hotel,** a deluxe hotel with 151 rooms (address: 255-3 Songnam-dong, Chung-gu, Ulsan-shi; telephone: (0522) 44-9911/20); and **Sung Ryu Park Hotel** (telephone: 82-3711). The Baekam and the Sung Ryu Park hotels are both located at Baekam Hot Springs Resort on the East Coast, quite a ways north of Kyongju.

## BUDGET ACCOMMODATIONS

Other recommended Western-style hotels in Kyongju, available at reasonable rates, include:

**Kyongju Youth Hostel** (Pulguk-sa), telephone: 2-9991/6
**Manhattan Hotel** (City Center), telephone: 2-3821/6
**Pulguksa Tourist Hotel** (Pulguk-sa), telephone: 2-1911

### KOREAN INNS (YOGWAN)

Slightly less opulent lodging is available at very reasonable prices in the numerous Korean-style inns in Kyongju. *Yogwan* guests sleep on the Korean-style *ondol* floor with traditional bedding—a mattress (*yo*) and a blanket (*ibul*)—which is put away during the day. Bathrooms are often shared. Meals can be ordered for an additional charge. Better class *yogwan* cost only $8–15 per night. A few recommended ones are:

**Sillajang** (near City Hall), telephone: 002-1004/6
**Kwibinjang** (Sobu-dong), telephone: 003-4681
**Yongbinjang** (near bus terminal), telephone: 002-6303
**Pulguksa Pyoljang** (near Pulguk-sa), telephone: 003-0111
**Wangnimjang** (near City Hall), telephone: 002-6602

Travel agencies to contact for additional information include: Andong (tel. 002-3668), Chon-woo (tel. 002-3694), Handong (tel. 002-2144), Kodo (tel. 002-3771), Kyongnam (tel. 002-2089), Hanyang (tel. 002-6201), and Havarang House Youth Hostel (tel. 002-3256). To accommodate the growing number of tourists, several new inns have been built near Pulguk-sa.

## CUISINE

### KYONGJU CUISINE

Kyongju offers a great variety of dining pleasures. The major hotels are best for Western meals; many restaurants in the city offer excellent Korean food. Meals accompanied by *kisaeng* entertainment are quite expensive, but usually it is possible to order the meal only at reasonable prices ($3–$5).

### WESTERN CUISINE

The three major hotels—Kolon, Tokyu, and Chosun—offer an international cuisine comparable to that found in Seoul. Delightful continental and American meals, as well as excellent Korean cuisine, are available. The dining room at the Pomun Lake Hotel School serves excellent Western food at rather expensive prices.

### KOREAN CUISINE

In Kyongju, Korean food tends to be somewhat less oily and hotter than northern food. The many Korean dishes that have gained popularity among international gourmets are available in Kyongju restaurants. The *hanjong-shik,* or meal of the day, served in Korean inns and popular restaurants consists of vegetables, egg, fish or meat, *kimchi* dishes, rice, and soup. Some of the most popular foods in the Kyongju region are listed below.

*Pulgogi*—marinated strips of beef charcoal-roasted over a brazier

*Pulkalbi* — short ribs prepared in the same manner

*Kimchi* — Korea's unique vegetable dish made with cabbage, or other vegetables such as turnip or radish, and always included in a meal

*Kungjung-chongol* — a rich variety of shellfish, fish, meat, and vegetables cooked in a broth—a court dish

*Mandu-kuk* — a soup with meatballs wrapped in dough

*Saengson jigye* — a tasty stew featuring vegetables and tender chunks of fish (the name of the *jigye* varies according to type of fish used)

*Maeuntang* — a hot fish soup with many vegetables

*Naengmyon* — a bowl of cold noodles served with vegetables, eggs, and pieces of meat (a summer favorite)

## RESTAURANTS

Korean, Japanese, and Chinese restaurants are found throughout the city, especially in the downtown area and the Pomun Lake *Resort Area.* Below are four better Korean restaurants and two popular restaurants that are enjoyed by both Koreans and overseas visitors.

**Yosok-kung.** A traditional-style Korean home converted into an excellent and picturesque restaurant; very popular with overseas tourists.

*Address:* 59 Kyo-dong          *Telephone:* 002-3347

**Songrim-jang.** Located in the downtown area, this restaurant serves excellent Korean *pulgogi jong-shik;* very popular with Koreans.

*Address:* 85-1 Nodong-dong          *Telephone:* 002-6102

**Kumho-Kak.** In the heart of the city, this restaurant serves excellent food in typical Korean fashion; some dishes are expensive, but the *pulgogi jong-shik* is reasonable.

*Address:* 236 Hwango-dong          *Telephone:* 002-7513

**Chungrim-jang.** *Kisaeng*-style entertainment is available, but a meal can be ordered without entertainment at a reasonable price.

*Address:* 165 Nodong-dong          *Telephone:* 002-2356

**Cheil-shiktang.** A popular restaurant with an attractive open dining room in a garden setting, serving excellent, moderately priced Korean meals.

*Address:* 203-17 Hwango-dong          *Telephone:* 002-7422

**Ilshim-shiktang.** Another good popular restaurant serving good food at reasonable prices.

*Address:* 120-7 Nodong-dong          *Telephone:* 002-3440

## CHINESE CUISINE

**Kyonghwa-Panjom.** The best Chinese restaurant in Kyongju.

*Address:* 133 Tonggu-dong          *Telephone:* 002-3875

# NIGHTCLUBS

The major nightclubs catering to overseas visitors are at the Kolon, Chosun, and Pulguksa Tourist Hotels; the Kyongju Tokyu has a discotheque. Downtown nightclubs popular with tourists include:

**Taebon Nightclub** (at Taegu rotary), telephone: 002-3404
**Hyopsong** (in Noso-dong), telephone: 003-7771/5
**Tomorrow** (in Hwango-dong), telephone: 002-2938

Kyongju's only casino is at the Kolon Hotel. Beer halls, drinking houses called *suljip*, and coffee shops are plentiful downtown and offer a chance to meet and mix with ordinary Koreans enjoying a night out.

# SHOPPING

Many shops in the downtown area of Kyongju specialize in folkcraft items, especially pottery and other arts reminiscent of the Silla Kingdom. There are 120 shops in the Pomun Lake complex carrying everything imaginable: locally produced souvenirs, clothes, accessories, musical instruments, jewelry, and handicrafts are of particular interest. At Kimhae Airport, duty-free shops offer liquor, perfume, cigarettes, watches, and other luxury imports.

Some of the major gift shops in Kyongju are:

**Kyongdo Gift Shop** (526-7 Inwang-dong), telephone: 42-6429

**Kyongju Minye Department Store** (Nodong-dong), telephone: 2-0307

**Minsoggwan** (Chinhyon Arcade, Chinhyon-dong), telephone: 2-4976

**Donghiva Pomun Arcade** (375 Shinpyong-dong), telephone: 3-0407/9

In addition to these newer shops selling contemporary goods, there are a number of antique stores scattered throughout the city where old Silla pottery, traditional Korean chests, paintings, calligraphy, and other goods can be purchased. Permission to export the better antiques is required; reputable merchants can make the necessary arrangements; hotels and information centers also are helpful. Silla-style earthenware and other porcelains are still produced in a kiln located about eight kilometers from Pomun Lake Resort. It is interesting to observe the age-old methods, and excellent reproductions are for sale.

## RECREATION

Hiking is the most popular outdoor activity in Kyongju because the entire valley is a treasure trove of cultural relics. The valleys of Nam-san (South Mountain) are most rewarding. For golfers,

*Traditional farmer's dance*

the Kyongju Chosun Hotel at Ponmun Lake offers a championship golf course; the Kolon Hotel has a nine-hole course; and the Kyongju Tokyo has an indoor golf course. All three of the major hotels have swimming pools, tennis courts, and fishing facilities. Bicycles can be rented at hotels and in various shops in the city, and biking is quite safe and pleasurable around Kyongju. The marina at the Kyongju Tokyu Hotel has exquisite Korean-style buildings, including a large lakeside restaurant, and offers cruises on the yacht "Swan," rental paddleboats and rowboats, and waterskiing.

# FESTIVALS AND
# CEREMONIES

The major annual event in Kyongju is the Silla Festival, which usually falls in early October (the date varies according to the lunar calendar). Tourist information offices, hotels, or the Korean National Tourism Corporation can provide information on this and other ceremonies. Highlights of the year include the following events.

**Memorial Ceremony at the Confucian School** (February 5 and August 5): The traditional Confucian ritual honors Confucius and other scholars and is held at Hyang-kyo near Panwol-song.

**Samjon Ceremony** (spring equinox): Ceremonies are held at the three major shrines of the city—Sungdok-jon, honoring the first king and queen of the Silla Dynasty, at Onung; Sung-shin-jon and Sunghye-jon, honoring the first of the Kim clan and other kings, located near the tomb of Mi-chu.

**Kumsan Ceremony** (March 25 and September 25): This traditional Confucian ceremony honors General Kim Yusin, the unifier, at the tombkeeper's house near the tomb site.

**Memorial Ceremony for Priest Wonhyo** (March 29): This greatest of Korean priests is honored with Buddhist ceremonies at Punhwang-sa, where his portrait is enshrined.

**Buddha's Birthday** (April–May): A national holiday; pilgrims visit the temples during the day, and a lantern parade winds through the streets in the evening.

**Memorial Ceremony for Yi Chadon** (August 5): A Buddhist ceremony is held at Hungnyun-sa, the site of Silla's earliest temple near Onung, to honor this sixth century martyr.

**Ceremony for the Six Village Elders** (August 17): A memorial ceremony at a small shrine near Na-jong honors the six village chiefs who witnessed the strange appearance of Pak Hyokkose, who was chosen as Silla's first king in the first century B.C.

**Sam-nung (Three Tomb) Ceremony** (August 21): Ceremonies honor kings of the Pak clan at their tombs on the western slopes of Nam-san.

**Ceremony at Yulsan Sowon** (October 3): Held at Tamun-dong Kyongsan-gun near Taegu, this traditional Confucian rite honors Milsung Taegun and other descendants of the first king of Silla.

**Memorial Ceremony for Paegyol** (October 28): This rite, held at Hyang-gyo (the Confucian School near Panwol-song), honors a poor scholar and artist who played the *komungo*, a traditional Korean musical instrument.

**Silla Festival** (October, date varies, three days of celebration): The largest festival of the year and one of the most impressive in the country, this celebration features a gigantic parade with floats portraying the folk stories of Silla, traditional folk dances, and games of skill. Thousands of visitors flock to Kyongju each year to participate in and photograph the festivities.

*Traditional folk dance in a farming village*

# 釜山
# Pusan

## SOUTHERN REGION

PUSAN, Korea's second largest city and principal port, takes its name ("cauldron mountain") from its location in a "cauldron" or rounded depression in the surrounding hills. Within its 430 square kilometers lives a population of 3.5 million. The climate of Pusan is milder than any other place in Korea except Cheju Island, making it increasingly attractive to Korean and foreign tourists. A number of popular beach resorts have grown up in the suburbs, especially at Haeundae and Songdo, where the sand is clean, the water warm, and the currents mild. Nearby, Tongnae, one of Korea's best-known mineral hot springs, is reputed to have medicinal benefits. The Naktong River delta welcomes a variety of migratory birds, and the coastal waters provide good fishing.

Between Hansando Island south of Pusan and the small harbor of Yosu to the west lies Hallyosudo (Hallyo Waterway) Park, a

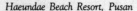
*Haeundae Beach Resort, Pusan*

maritime national park offering a scenic seascape dotted with picturesque islets, fantastic rock formations, quaint fishing boats, and traditional seaside villages. Hallyo Waterway is well-known for aquatic sports such as swimming, waterskiing, and boating.

Pusan is a center of industry and commerce. Like Seoul, it is a "special city" administered separately from a province. This thriving metropolis has grown to include major suburbs. Linked with the capital by the Seoul-Pusan Railway, the Seoul-Pusan Expressway, and Korean Air, Pusan offers the visitor international class hotels, fine cuisine, shopping, sightseeing, and beautiful beaches.

Pusan was the yacht race site for the Olympic Games. Construction for the events included a huge marine area accommodating 1,500 yachts, with an advanced mooring system and four racing courses, a modern village to house the participants, a press center, and a marina, as well as a large tourist center including a water park, a marine museum, hotels, and a shopping arcade. The site has become a new point of interest in Pusan.

## PUSAN IN HISTORY

Archeologists have determined that Pusan has been inhabited since the Neolithic period. Around the first century, a tribal group settling the area established a nation called Kochilsanguk. Later Pusan was called Tongnae. Throughout history, this port at the southern tip of the peninsula has been an important point of contact between Korea and Japan. A thriving maritime trade was developed in ancient times, even before the formation of the Three Kingdoms and Japan. At that time the area was called Kimhae ("metal sea") and was a primary source of precious iron ore for the peoples of northeast Asia.

The name Pusan was first used in the fifteenth century. During the Chosun period, the port became important both for trade with Japan and in defending the nation against Japan. In 1592, when Japan invaded Korea, the citizens of Pusan fought bravely against the invaders, and Admiral Yi Sunshin defeated the Japanese armada with his ironclad "Turtle Ships." The port of Pusan was first opened to other nations in 1876, when the government of the Chosun (Yi) dynasty was forced to abandon its isolationist policy and sign a treaty imposed on Korea by Japan.

During the Korean War (1950–53), Pusan served as the temporary capital of South Korea and as the home of many refugees. The United Nations Cemetery is a sobering reminder of that period.

## ECONOMY

Pusan, the historic seagate to Korea, is the nation's largest port and a major center of trade and industry. The port of Pusan is divided by Yong-do Bridge: on the east is the commercial port; to the south, a fishing port. A natural harbor equipped with modern facilities, Pusan handles half of Korea's total exports and imports and maintains commercial relations with many countries of the world.

South Korea's major heavy industry complex is located near Pusan, at Pohang and Ulsan. Its concentration of large enterprises includes petroleum refineries; concrete, steel, and automobile manufacturing; shipyards; and a power plant. At Jinju, also in the vicinity of Pusan, is a Korean naval base. Pusan is the southern terminus of a double-tracked main rail line from Seoul and other cities on the peninsula. As well as a vortex of Korea's great economic growth, Pusan has become a major cultural center. The city boasts over 25 colleges and universities and 39 theaters. The labor force is highly skilled, and many businesspeople have a modern higher education.

With the selection of Pusan as the site of yacht races for the Olympic Games, large construction projects have been undertaken. On schedule are both the maritime facilities for the races and the village to house participants and press during the Games. Also rapidly taking shape are tourist facilities at the Olympic site, and a full-scale tourist resort complex at Chungmu.

## HIGHLIGHTS
## FOR TRAVELERS

From the port of Pusan, ferry and excursion boats go to a variety of places. Pusan is the gateway to the Hallyo Waterway, through which hovercraft and regular excursion boats carry tourists on scenic trips to Koje Island, Chungmu, and Yosu. Regular ferry service links Pusan with Cheju Island; the Pukwan Ferry plies the route between Pusan and Shimonoseki, Japan; the Kukje Ferry connects Pusan with Osaka, Japan. Many international cruise ships stop at Pusan.

This port city has much to offer visitors. Formed of several fingers of land extending into the Korea Strait, the Pusan area has

*Yongdusan Tower, Pusan*

a long and diverse coastline. The visitor can watch big ships entering and leaving the harbor, go to one of several sandy beaches for sunning and swimming, or visit Korea's largest fish market. It is easy to walk around the downtown area; major hotels, large department stores, many restaurants, a variety of shops, the fish market, and Yongdusan Park are all accessible from the Pusan Railway Station plaza. There are many beautiful old temples in and around Pusan. Pomo-sa and Tongo-sa are in the city; Pomo, Naewon, Tongdo, Pyochung, and Unmum Temples are located along the expressway north of Pusan.

어시장

**Fish Market.** Sprawled along the fishing boat docks in Pusan, this huge market comes to life at 6:00 a.m. as fresh fish are sold by fishermen and hawkers to wholesalers and other buyers. The spectacle is colorful, the odors are pungent, and bargains in seafood abound.

광복동, 남포동

**Kwangbokdong and Nampodong.** This area offers Pusan's most interesting shopping, with many small shops crowded together along narrow side streets south of Yongdusan Park. Each of the open-front stores specializes in one item, such as textiles, foods, spices, sportswear, hardware, and gift items. Shopping centers and elegant shops are found along Chungmu, the main street where many hotels are also located.

태종대 공원

**Taejongdae Park.** Overlooking the sea at the tip of a peninsula on Yong Island, the park is named after King Muyol of the Silla Kingdom, who spent holidays there. The park features a lighthouse, picnic grounds, hiking trails, boating, and saltwater fishing.

용두산 공원

**Yongdusan Park.** This small hilltop park looks out over the city and the harbor. It contains several war memorials and a statue of Korea's great naval hero, Admiral Yi Sunshin. Pusan Tower accommodates both television transmission facilities and an observation dome offering spectacular views.

유엔 묘지

**United Nations Cemetery.** This impressive and solemn cemetery is on one of the spits jutting into the sea, and it is unique in the world. Flags of the 16 allied nations that participated in the Korean War are flown daily in tribute to the support and the sacrifice of those who are buried here. There is a grand central plaza and a beautiful small interdenominational chapel where memorial services are held.

시립 박물관

**Municipal Museum.** Cultural and historical treasures from prehistoric to modern times are housed in the Pusan Municipal Museum. It is open from 9 a.m. to 6 p.m. every day except Mondays and national holidays.

해운대 해수욕장

**Haeundae Beach.** Haeundae, the most popular bathing beach in the Pusan area, is located 11 miles northeast of downtown. Its long, curving, sandy beach is bounded on the west by Tongbaeksom, a rocky and wooded islet connected to the mainland by a narrow isthmus. This lovely spot is one of the most scenic in Korea. It is accessible by a 40-minute coastal ride from downtown; hotels and recreation facilities for tourists are excellent.

**Island Beaches.** Kujora Beach on the south shore of Koje Island near Choguri, Namildae Beach at the entrance to Namhae Island, and Sangju Beach on the south shore of Namhae Island are all popular with Pusan residents. Another fine beach is located on the Yochon Peninsula north of Yosu.

동래 온천

**Tongnae Hot Springs.** Nine miles north of the city center is this natural mineral hot springs, famous for the medicinal qualities of its waters for many centuries. Several tourist hotels and Korean inns (*yogwan*) offer comfortable visitor accommodations, and there is a variety of restaurants in the area.

금강 공원

**Kumgang Park.** Kumgang Park at Tongnae attracts visitors from all over the country to see the gorgeous cherry blossoms every spring. The park offers scenic wooded slopes, winding paths, meandering streams, and dramatic rock formations; an amusement park with rides for children; a cable car up to the ruins of an old fortress, several temples, and a lovely pagoda.

범어사

**Pomo-sa (Fish Temple).** North of Tongnae on the eastern slope of Mt. Kumjong is the important and lovely Buddhist temple Pomo-sa. One of the largest in Korea, it was founded in 678 A.D. The approach is via a graceful arched stone bridge over a mountain stream and through three handsome gates. A stone pagoda on the grounds dates from the time of the original founding of the temple.

The main hall, Taeung-jon (Hall of the Arhats), is reached by a steep flight of stone stairs, flanked at the bottom by an unusual pair of stone temple dogs, or *haetae*. The altar contains three seated gilt Buddha figures, surrounded by decorative wall paintings and an ornate wooden canopy with painted ceiling. The hall is designated National Treasure No. 434. To the left of the main hall is a seven-storied stone pagoda, and nearby are other typical temple structures, including a Sansin-gak, or Mountain Spirit House, and a Judgment Hall. There is a wooden structure that is divided into three sections: on the left is Palsang-jon, housing paintings of eight scenes from the life of Buddha; in the center is Toksong-jon, a worship hall; and on the right is Nahan-jon, containing 500 figures of *nahari*, or Arhats, disciples of Buddha.

한려 수도

**Hallyo Waterway Area.** Hallyo Waterway is a shimmering expanse of placid sea stretching from Koje Island past the fishing village of Chungmu to the refinery and petro-chemical industrial port of Yosu. This maritime national park is dotted with hundreds of picturesque islets of various shapes and sizes, displaying fantastic rock formations and deep evergreen groves. Fishing boats, freighters, and passenger ships come and go constantly through the clear waters. Grids of bamboo poles mark the location of nursery beds of oysters, a principal product of Pusan. The seaport village of Chungmu, named after the posthumous title of Admiral Yi Sunshin, is the resort center of the area. It can be reached in 90 minutes by hydrofoil through the Waterway from Pusan. A fine hotel, delicious seafood, and recreational activities including fishing, boating, and swimming await the visitor. At Yosu City there is a monument, designated National Treasure No. 324, honoring Admiral Yi's great victory over Japan in the sixteenth century. New tourist facilities are being developed on Odong Island. Other points of interest along the Waterway include the naval port of Chinhae, which has a cherry blossom festival in the spring; Masan, a pretty port at the head of Chinhae Bay with a superb view; temples and other historical and cultural relics.

충무 돈암 관광단지

**Chungmu Donam Tourist Complex.** Chungmu, located in Donam, was chosen for construction of a tourist complex because of its ideal location for a marina and coastal recreational facilities, its accessibility to neighboring cities, its many historical sites, and its central position along the Hallyo Waterway. The delightful, full-scale resort complex—completed in 1987 at a cost of $45 million—includes a marina, freshwater and saltwater swimming

*Traditional rice mortar*

pools, an oceanographic museum, tennis courts, a shopping center, a folk art training and exhibition center, world-class hotels and other lodgings.

**Cruises.** Aboard the Pusan-Yosu hydrofoil "Angel," tourists enjoy a scenic passage through the winding inside route of the Hallyo Waterway. The hydrofoil departs from Pusan six times a day on the 90-minute run to Chungmu; from there hydrofoils depart three times a day on two-hour trips to Yosu. One-way fare from Pusan to Yosu is $13. The Pusan-Cheju Island Car Ferry departs from Pusan every evening except Sunday for the 11-hour overnight trip to Cheju Island. Cars are charged from $54 to $134; passengers fares range from $12-$87.

**City Tours.** There are four daily tours of Pusan and environs (for information, call 44-2224). Excursions can be arranged with Global Tours (83-l 4-ka Chungang-dong—tel. 044-4561). One popular tour around the city visits the United Nations Cemetery, Yongdusan Park, and the fish market; it takes about four hours. Another tour, taking about five hours, includes the outskirts of the city and visits the two major temples, Pomo-sa and Tongdo-sa.

# HOTEL
# ACCOMMODATIONS

Second only to Seoul, Pusan offers a great variety of hotels. Among 21 Western-style hotels, four are deluxe. The majority of good hotels are located in the downtown areas—near the railway station, close to the port, in the heart of the city, or near Yongdusan Park—or in the Haeundae Beach area.

**Paradise Beach Hotel** (Deluxe—900 rooms for 1,700 guests). Located on Haeundae Beach, just 30 minutes from Pusan's Kimhae International Airport, the Paradise Beach Hotel provides its guests with a luxurious spa with saunas, a fitness center and natural indoor/outdoor hot springs and facilities for water-skiing, windsurfing, sailing, as well as tennis. The hotel has the Café Fontana coffee shop, the Western restaurant Pharos Grill, the Kaya Korean restaurant, a Japanese restaurant, the Crystal Garden lobby lounge, Cabin Pub a delicatessen, and the Morning Calm VIP Club. The Las Vegas-style Colonnade Casino is open year round, 24 hours. The room rate is over ₩90,000.

*Address:* 1408-5 Chung-dong, Haeundae-ku
*Telephone:* 742-2121
*Cable:* PARADISE BEACH HOTEL
*Telex:* PARABH K 52145

**Hyatt Regency Pusan** (Deluxe—363 rooms for 790 guests). Located beside the Paradise Beach Hotel, the hotel's facilities have been designed to serve both business travelers and tourists, providing excellent accommodations including many good restaurants, a fitness center, a casino, and a variety of entertainment. The top two floors are an exclusive hotel within the hotel, providing personalized concierge service. The average room rate is about ₩98,000.

*Address:* 1405-16 Chung-dong, Haeundae-ku
*Telephone:* 743-1234
*Cable:* HYATT PUSAN
*Telex:* K52668

**The Westin Chosun Beach Hotel** (Deluxe—333 rooms for 770 guests). Located in Haeundae Beach, this hotel's facilities include a coffee shop, disco nightclub, bar, outdoor swimming pool, sauna, delicatessen, shopping arcade, souvenir shop, barber and beauty shops, French, Japanese, and Italian restaurants, as well as excellent Korean food.

*Address:* 737 Uil-dong, Haeundae-ku
*Telephone:* 742-7411
*Cable:* WESTCHO
*Telex:* CHOSUNB K53718

코모도어 호텔

**Hotel Commodore** (Deluxe—325 rooms for 650 guests). In downtown Pusan, with magnificent views of the harbor; facilities include a coffee shop, cocktail bar, nightclub, banquet hall, game room, sauna, souvenir shop, convention hall, lobby lounge, Japanese, French, Western, Chinese, and Korean buffet restaurants.

*Address:* 743-80 Yongju-dong, Chung-ku
*Telephone:* 44-9101
*Cable:* COMMODORE
*Telex:* COMOTEL K53717

극동 호텔

**Hotel Kukdong** (First Class—105 rooms for 137 guests). Overlooks the shoreline of the Haeundae resort area; offers a nightclub, bar, coffee shop, grill, buffet restaurant, sauna, beach swimming in season.

*Address:* 1124 Chung-dong, Haendae-ku
*Telephone:* 72-0081
*Cable:* HOTEL KUKDONG
*Telex:* KUKDONG K53758

부산 관광 호텔

**Pusan Tourist Hotel** (First Class—274 rooms for 568 guests). Located in the center of the business and shopping district; offers a nightclub, coffee shop, sky lounge, sauna, barber and beauty shops, disco, bakery, Chinese, Japanese, and Korean restaurants.

*Address:* 12 2-ka Tongkwang-dong
*Telephone:* 23-4301
*Cable:* BUSANHOTEL
*Telex:* BSHOTEL K53657

Among hotels in the downtown area are: **Crown** (First class—tel. 69-1241), **Kukje** (First class—tel. 642-1330), **Sorabol** (Deluxe—tel. 463-3511), **Royal** (First class—tel. 23-1051), **Phoenix** (First class—tel. 22-8061), **Ferry** (First class—tel. 463-0881), and **Arirang** (Third class—tel. 463-5001—located adjacent to the Pusan Railroad Station). Also downtown is a youth hostel, the **Aerin** (tel. 27-2222). In the Tongnae hot springs area is the **Tongnae Hotel** (tel. 55-1121), which is rated second class.

There are many *yogwan*, or Korean-style inns, in Pusan and its vicinity. For these, reservations can be made through Seoul tour agencies or at tourist information centers in Pusan.

## THE ULSAN AREA

울산 코리아나 호텔

**Ulsan Koreana Hotel** (Deluxe—151 rooms for 350 guests). Facilities: coffee shop, steak house, sauna, bar, penthouse restaurant, Western, Japanese, and Chinese restaurants.

*Address:* 255-3 Songnam-dong          *Telephone:* 44-8611

다이아몬드 호텔

**Hotel Diamond** (Deluxe—290 rooms for 580 guests). The Diamond is located at the entrance of Hyundai Heavy Industrial Complex at Ulsan, not far from Kyongju. It serves Western, Japanese, and Korean foods. Facilities include: coffee shop, shopping arcade, indoor swimming pool, sauna, health center, tennis court, barber shop and beauty salon, jogging course, delicatessen, banquet room, and bar.

*Address:* 283 Chonha-dong, Ulsan
*Telephone:* (0522) 32-7171    *Telex:* DIAMNTL 52224

태화 호텔

**Tae Hwa Hotel** (Second class—103 rooms for 208 guests). Facilities: Western and Japanese as well as Korean restaurants, cocktail bar, coffee shop, sauna, barbershop, souvenir shop, night-club.

*Address:* 1406-6 Shinjong-dong, Nam-ku    *Telephone:* 73-8191

**Bugok Hawaii** (First class—185 rooms). Bugok Hawaii is Korea's original swimming and entertainment complex at a hot springs resort (Suanbo Waikiki was modeled after it). It is quite popular year-round wth families and tour groups. It has a giant indoor swimming pool along with a diving area and children's wading pools. There is also an outdoor amusement park, a small zoo, and an indoor entertainment show set amidst the swimming areas.

*Address:* 195-7 Komun-ri          *Telephone:* (0559) 36-6661/9

**Bugok Royal Hotel** (First deluxe class—158 rooms).
*Address:* 215-1 Komun-ri          *Telephone:* (0559) 63-6661/9

## THE MASAN AREA

부곡 호텔

**Bugok Tourist Hotel** (First class—186 rooms for 320 guests). Facilities: Western, Japanese, and Korean restaurants, sulfur-spring pool, beauty parlor, barber shop, game room, shopping arcade, bar, coffee shop, nightclub, banquet room, tennis court.

*Address:* 213-19 Komunri, Pugok-myon, Changnyong-kun
*Telephone:* (0559) 36-5181/3

롯데 크리스탈 호텔
**Lotte Crystal Hotel** (First class—121 rooms for 242 guests). Facilities: Western, Japanese, Korean restuarants, coffee shop, cocktail bar, banquet room, nightclub, game room, beer garden, barber shop, souvenir shop.

*Address: 3-6 4-ka Changkun-dong*     *Telephone:* (0551) 45-1112

**Changwon Tourist Hotel** (First class—166 rooms).
*Address:* 99-4 Chungang-dong     *Telephone:* (0551) 83-5551/60

# CUISINE

Pusan offers a wide variety of international cuisines. Excellent Western, Japanese, and Chinese restaurants are found in the major hotels. The French restaurants at the Chosun Beach and Commodore hotels and the Italian restaurant at the Sorabol are outstanding, but prices are high. Fresh fish is plentiful and excellent in Pusan.

Among the better Korean-style restaurants are **Kyomokjang** (Pumin-dong; tel. 244-1297); **Biwon** (Pumin-dong; tel. 244-1778); and **Chunhyangwon** (Choryang-dong; tel. 027-0221). Good, moderate-priced restaurants include: **Kayahoegwan** (15-4 Chungang-dong; tel. 463-3277); **Kokujang** (33 Kwangbok-dong; tel. 22-5858); and **Everspring Park** (178-7 Onchon-dong; tel. 53-1800).

Throughout the city there are Korean-style restaurants offering delicacies such as *pulgogi* and *kalbi*. The Haeundae Beach area offers many delightful restaurants along the shore; many of them offer freshly captured live fish prepared in a variety of delicious ways, from sliced raw fish (*hoe*) wrapped in lettuce and coated in hot pepper, to hearty, spicy fish chowders.

# ENTERTAINMENT

Nightclubs and bars are found in all the deluxe hotels and most of the Western-style hotels of all classes; they have English-speaking waiters and waitresses and cater to overseas visitors. There are some 53 nightclubs, 23 cabarets, and 18 go-go clubs in the city.

Dinner theaters offer lavish floor shows; among the best are the **White House** in Pujondong (tel. 806-7741), and the **Everspring (Nulbom)** in Onchondong (tel. 054-3529). Pusan offers numerous *suljip*—bars, wine shops, beer halls—and coffee shops where the visitor can enjoy inexpensive entertainment in the company of local Koreans. These are everywhere, but there is a concentration of them in the area south of Yongdusan Park. Near the Railway Station is an entertainment area catering to servicemen. For gamblers, the **Paradise Beach Hotel** (tel. 072-1461) at Haeundae offers a wide range of gaming facilities in Pusan's only casino.

**Hansan Victory Festival** (October). An annual event commemorating the great naval victory of Admiral Yi Sunshin over the Japanese fleet, held at Chungmu on Hansan Island. The ceremonies begin with the lighting of the sacred flame, then a cannon salute and a military parade. There is a victory dance and a sword dance by highly skilled performers.

**Kaechon Art Festival** (October—third day of 10th lunar month). The event celebrates local cultural activity, with competitions in Chinese poetry, calligraphy, music composition, artwork, and drama.

**Cherry Blossom Festival** (First two weeks of April). Thousands of cherry trees in beautiful bloom attract over a million visitors each year to Chindae. Events include naval celebrations.

# SHOPPING

Pusan has three major department stores: Mihwadang (tel. 23-7711), Yuna (tel. 023-6231), and Pusan Department Store (tel. 553-5383). Many smaller department stores are located downtown. All the deluxe hotels have souvenir shops, and Korean folkcraft items are featured in may small stores and shopping centers. Some of the best are: Kaya Native Arts (near the port; tel. 44-3526); Pusan Tower Shopping Center (Kwangbok-dong; tel. 22-2966); Shilla Native Arts (Kwangbok-dong; tel. 022-2828); Ilsung Native Arts (Kwangbok-dong; tel. 022-4994); and Hansung (downtown; tel. 462-5727). There are duty-free shops at Kimhae International Airport (tel. 98-1101), Pukwan Ferry Terminal (tel. 462-2501), and Nammun in Kamjon-dong (tel. 92-8926), where foreign visitors can find good bargains on imported luxury items. A good area for antique shops is Tongkwang-dong.

## SPORTS

Pusan boasts two golf courses, both north of the city: Tongnae Country Club (tel. 56-0101) and Pusan Country Club (tel. 56-0108). There are numerous tennis courts; hotels can supply information on making arrangements to play. Pusan offers many water activities. There are several good beaches in the area: Kwangalli and Haeundae are the closest, most famous, and most crowded. Boats can be rented for fishing trips, and surf casting also is popular. And there is the Pusan Yachting Center, built for the Asian and Olympic Games.

*Golf has become a major Korean pastime*

# 濟州島
# Cheju Island

### SOUTHERN REGION

CHEJU-DO, or Cheju Island, shimmers alluringly amid sparkling turquoise waters 60 miles off the southern coast of Korea. Called the Emerald Isle of Asia and the Island of the Gods, Cheju was chosen by *Newsweek* magazine as one of the world's ten most unspoiled tourist paradises. The largest of Korea's islands, it is a picturesque vacationer's retreat, with palm trees, tropical flowers, natural monuments, tumbling waterfalls, a snowcapped mountain, ancient temples and pavilions, broad bathing beaches, and a delightful subtropical climate. Still an uncrowded sanctuary of unique natural beauty, Cheju Island is well-known for its clean air and healthful sea breezes, which may explain why it is sometimes called the Hawaii of the Orient. All of Cheju-do's volcanoes are extinct. This great natural park covers some 1,800 square kilometers; the island is 73 kilometers from east to west and 41 kilometers from north to south. The population is about 500,000.

### CLIMATE

The average temperature on Cheju Island is 24 degrees Celsius (75°F); in winter the average is 6 degrees Celsius (43°F). Flora on the island includes 1,700 different plants, ranging from semitropical to frigid zone varieties. Oranges ripen in autumn. There is snow on the mountain peak in winter. In splendid isolation, subtropical Cheju-do is where the Koreans themselves escape from it all. It is an increasingly popular playground, a haven for sports and courting, a place to enjoy splendid landscapes and seascapes, a repository of colorful ancient legends and customs.

Although firmly rooted in its Korean identity, Cheju-do has always had a subtle ambiance all its own; the climate, landscape, dialect, and lifestyle are a bit different from those on the mainland. The modern Cheju Islander may live in the traditional way—in a quaint fishing village of thatched-roof, black basalt dwellings, their roofs weighted down with stones against the high winds. The women join teams of deep-sea divers bringing in edible seaweed

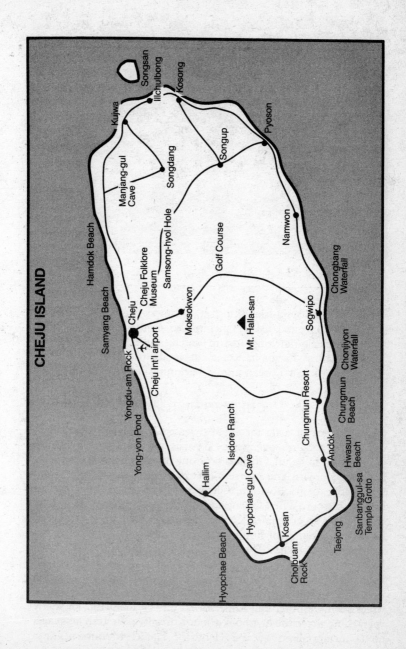

CHEJU ISLAND

CHEJU ISLAND

*Dragon Head Rock* (Yong-du-am), *Cheju Island*

and shellfish; Cheju Island, in fact, is famous for its women divers. Game hunting and cattle ranches also arouse interest. Cheju is the only cattle-ranching area in Korea, and it is the home, too, of the swiftest horses in Korea, descendants of those that were raised for ancient Korean armies beginning in Mongol times.

## CHEJU IN HISTORY

Once a place of exile for those defeated in political disputes at court, and a training center for officials appointed by the central government in Seoul, Cheju is now one of the prime tourist attractions for Koreans and overseas visitors alike.

In spite of its isolation, Cheju has played a distinct role in Korean history. When Ghengis Khan's Mongol hordes swept over central Asia and occupied Korea in the thirteenth century, military forces under Sambyolcho fortified the island for a heroic, but unsuccessful, last stand. The event is commemorated by the Anti-Mongol Monument at Hangpaduri Fortress, located between Hallim and Cheju City. Cheju Island was the first place in Korea visited by Westerners: in 1653, 36 Dutch sailors, survivors of a shipwreck, came ashore, and some stayed on the mainland for many years. One wrote the first book about Korea in a Western language; he is memorialized by the Hendrick Hamel Monument near

Hwasun Beach on the southern shore.

In 1946, the island became a province of the Republic of Korea. The trademark of Cheju Island is *Tolharubang* or "Stone Grandfather," sculptured in large and small likenesses from the porous lava stone of the area. The visitor will find him life-size and even larger in village squares and rural groves; he is a favorite at souvenir stands. Once a guardian deity, his persistence indicates that old beliefs have not entirely disappeared.

Cheju Island is rich in legends. It is known as the island of three manys: many women, many rocks, many winds. It is also the island of three no's: no thieves, no beggars, no gates. One popular legend purports to tell of the origin of the three largest families on the island. There is a hole on the northern slope of Mt. Halla, from which three divine figures called Ko, Bu, and Yang once emerged to spot a wooden box drifting ashore. Opening it, they discovered three beautiful women clad in elegant blue; they came with seeds of five grains, a cow and an ox, horses, and many servants. The divine figures married the women and all lived happily ever after. The Ko, Bu, and Yang families hold memorial services at the hole in the pine forest on the mountain each spring and fall.

## HOW TO GET THERE

Modern transport has brought the fabled island closer; it is now a unique paradise accessible to all. Located 220 miles off the southern coast port of Pusan, the island can be reached from any major Korean city and from Japan.

**From Abroad.** Korean Air flies to Cheju directly from Osaka, Japan, four times a week; flight time is 1 hour, 30 minutes (in Osaka, tel. 262-1110). The Pukwan Ferry links Shimonoseki, Japan, with Pusan; the crossing takes seven hours, and the fare ranges from $40 to $80. Another car ferry is being planned between Osaka and Pusan. From Pusan, the traveler can continue to Cheju by sea or air.

**From Mainland Cities.** Korean Air operates between Cheju and all major Korean cities (Cheju, tel. 22-6111). Car ferries serve Cheju on regular schedules leaving from Pusan, Mokpo, and Wando. For information, call Dong Yang Express (Cheju, tel. 22-0291).

## ON YOUR OWN IN CHEJU

**Tourist Services.** Tourist information is readily available at the KNTC head office, at information counters at Kimpo and Kimhae airports, and at Cheju Airport (tel. 42-0032).

**Tours.** Tours can be arranged through Cheju Tourist Service, which offers a wide variety of itineraries at costs ranging from $12 to $28 per person, per day. An all-day car rental is $35–$50; call Cheju Rent-a-Car (tel. 42-3301). A taxi with a driver who speaks some English can be rented for $40–$50 per day.

**Bus Service.** Local bus service crossing the island runs every 25 minutes from Cheju City to Sogwipo via Chungmun Resort. The trip takes 1 1/2 hours and costs $.90. There is also a bus that goes around the island and along the shore from Cheju City to Sogwipo in both east and west directions. The fare is $1.70, and it takes about 2 hours; a bus leaves every 20 minutes.

**Credit Cards.** VISA, American Express, Diners Club, Mastercard, and Carte Blanche are accepted at major hotels, department stores, and restaurants catering to an international clientele.

## EXCURSIONS

Although two days is considered the minimum stay for a proper appreciation of Cheju Island, some visitors see the highlights in a single day. Suggested itineraries for visits of one or two days are given below.

**One-Day Tour.** Cheju City (via West Halla Highway) to Yongdu-am (Dragon's Head Rock) — Halla Mountain — Waetolkwae — Sogwipo (fishing village) — Chonjeyon Waterfall — Chongbang Waterfall — lunch at Paradise Honeymoon House; return via East Halla Highway — Sangumburi — Songup Folk Village — Mokso-kwon (Wood Rock Park) — Cheju City.

**Two-Day Tour.** Visit the eastern part of the island the first day; stay overnight at Sogwipo on the south coast; tour the western part of the island the second day. *First Day Eastern Trip:* Coastal Highway east — Cheju Folk Museum — Samyang and Hamdok Beaches — inland to Manjanggul Cave — Ilchul-bong (Sunrise Peak) — Songup Folk Village — Haenyo (women divers) along the south coast — Chongbang Waterfall — Sogwipo City — spend night in resort hotel or Korean inn. *Second Day Western Trip:* Coast Highway to Chonjiyon Waterfall — Chungmun Beach and

Hwasun Beach — Sanbanggul-sa (Temple Grotto) — Cholbu-am (Fisherman's Wife Rock) — side trip inland to Hyopjaegul Cave — Hyopjae Beach — Hallim — Yongyon Pond — Yongdu-am (Dragon Head Rock) — Cheju City.

# HIGHLIGHTS
# FOR TRAVELERS

Exotic, semitropical Cheju Island is famous for its black basalt rock of volcanic origin, dynamic women divers, and dramatic Halla-san, one of the two highest mountains in South Korea. An unpolluted paradise, Cheju offers varied scenic splendors: plunging waterfalls — Chongbang, Chonjeyon, Chonjiyon; grotesque lava formations — Yongdu-am (Dragon Head Rock), Yongsir-am, Cholbu-am; lava tubes — Manjanggul, Kumnyongsagul Cave; and clean, sandy beaches — Hamdok, Hyopchae, Chungmun, Pyoson. Sports for all seasons include hunting, fishing, scuba diving, golf, and mountain climbing. In the Folk Museum near the Samsong-hyol shrine dedicated to the three legendary founders of the island, visitors can glimpse native beliefs and customs in the many artifacts. Modern hotels and highways that circle and crisscross the island have made Cheju a tourist's delight.

## 제주, 서귀포
## CHEJU AND SOGWIPO

The two principal cities on the island are Cheju City, the provincial capital, with a population of 200,000, and Sogwipo, the second-largest city, which is located on the south coast. Sogwipo is the distribution center for the island's exports to the mainland: oranges, kumquats, tangerines, pineapples, and bananas. In Cheju there is a beautiful shrine park called Samsong-hyol (Cave of Three Spirits), located near South Gate. In the center of the city is Kwandok-jong, a pavilion built in 1448 and designated a National Treasure. Remains of the ancient city are still visible.

### MUSEUMS
민속 자연사 박물관
**The Folklore and Natural History Museum** (996-1, 2-dong, 1-do; tel. 22-2465). Located near the Cheju KAL Hotel, the Folklore and Natural History Museum is open from 9 a.m. to 6

p.m. daily except Thursdays, the New Year's holidays, and Korean Thanskgiving Day. Admission fees are $.75 for individuals, $.50 for members of groups. The Museum is home to an interesting collection of folk tools and implements, as well as exhibits of plants, animals, and minerals indigenous to the island.

제주 민속 박물관

**Cheju Folklore Museum** (2505, Samyong 3-dong; tel. 22-1976). Located near Samyang Beach on the north shore, about 10 minutes by taxi from City Hall, Cheju Folklore Museum has a fine collection of artifacts and works illustrating native beliefs and folk customs. It is open from 9 a.m. to 6 p.m. daily except holidays. Admission is $.75

중문 휴양단지
## CHUNGMUN RESORT COMPLEX

Chungmun Resort is a world-class recreation center covering 2.2 square kilometers at a cost of $292 million. The first phase was scheduled to open in early 1988, with completion in 1991. Initial capacity is for 340 guests. Endowed with such natural attractions as a subtropical forest, fine sand beaches, waterfalls, and spectacular cliffs, the complex offers facilities for sailing and yachting on calm azure waters, parachute-sailing in the marina, scuba diving in crystal clear seas, and fishing in one of the world's best salt-water regions. Among entertainment opportunities are a playground, amusement park, marineland, folk arts performance center, botanic gardens, and shopping center.

한라산
## HALLA-SAN (MT. HALLA)

Mt. Halla, designated a national park, has one of Korea's three sacred peaks. In spring the slopes are covered with colorful azaleas; summer, fall, and winter each bring a different seasonal beauty. Rock formations and flora along the mountain trails are spectacular; the rock projections formed by turbulent lava flows often seem to take on human shapes. The climber who reaches the peak will find a lovely shallow lake, Paekrok-dam (White Deer Lake), and will enjoy a magnificent view. Sunrise and sunset viewed from Mt. Halla are breathtaking.

**Lava Rocks and Statues.** Cheju-do exudes an aura of mystery and legend. Yongdu-am, or Dragon Head Rock, on the coast near Cheju City is an uprearing crag of petrified lava that the islanders see as a mythical beast. The legend surrounding the west coast promontory known as Cholbu-am, or the Fisherman's Wife, is that the spirits of women who lost their husbands at sea keep eternal vigil there. There are many lava statues called *Tolharubang* (Stone Grandfather), which, with their bulging eyes, huge noses, and elongated ears, are a unique cultural artifact of the island and are regarded as protective guardians of the villages.

**Caves.** Three caves, which really are lava tubes formed when hot gases were forced through molten rock during the island's fiery volcanic birth millions of years ago, are accessible to visitors. Two of them are near the northeast coast; the other is close to Hyopchae Beach in the west. Kimnyong-sagul, or Snake Cave, in the north, is one of the largest lava tubes in the world. It is completely snake-free, but according to legend a monstrous snake—much like the dragons of medieval Europe—once lived in the cave and demanded the sacrifice of maidens in order to spare the nearby villages his wrath. A fearless young magistrate killed the beast but was bitten in the struggle and died of the venom.

**Waterfalls.** Within a few miles of the southern port of Sogwipo are three magnificent waterfalls. Just to the west of the harbor is the lovely Chonji-yon, which falls in a veil of foam to a placid lake. To the east is the exuberant 75-foot Chongbang Waterfall; it spurts over a lofty cliff jutting over the beach and plunges into the sea. Another scenic waterfall is Chonje-yon, nine miles west of Sogwipo.

**Tamna-moksogwon Park.** The heart of Cheju-do's mystery and uniqueness can be discovered in this pleasant park on the lower slopes of Mt. Halla, on the cross-island road between Cheju City and Sogwipo. Gathered in the park are strange specimens of "found art" in the form of storm-polished driftwood and weathered lumps of basalt, imaginatively arranged in combinations and given titles ranging from the whimsical to the satiric; some are even quite sinister. These strange tableaux reflect the visions of the simple island folk in their natural surroundings. The collection conveys a memorable impression of Cheju's mystical past and the people's love of legends and myths.

**Peaks and Valleys.** Near Yongshil, the visitor encounters an awe-inspiring network of wooded mountain valleys, gorges, and precipices. Picturesque in all seasons, but especially splendid in autumn, are the Obaeknahan, or 500 Generals, an impressive range of peaks, each representing one of the generals immortalized in an ancient tale. Inland is Kugugok or 99 Valleys, a tangled maze of crags and gorges adorned with unique island foliage. Not far from the airport west of Cheju City is Yong-yon or Dragon Pond, a forested enclave where ancient scholars gathered on moonlit nights to sip wine and improvise poems. Near Song-up Village is the Songumburi Crater, more than 140 meters deep and forested with over 420 species of plants and flowers. On the eastern side of the island are vast grasslands used for cattle grazing. A 200,000-acre ranch there is rated by foreign cattle experts as one of Asia's best stock farms.

**Song-up Village.** Song-up Village, located about 35 kilometers southeast of Cheju City, has been designated a folklore-preservation zone, where visitors can meet friendly island people still living in thatched-roof and rock homes, each with a high lava stone wall surrounding its courtyard.

**Sanbanggul-sa.** On the south coast is this lovely temple, with a serene seated Buddha gazing out over an ocean panorama. The picturesque spot was the dwelling place of a saintly hermit famed in Buddhist lore.

**Women Divers.** Cheju Island is famous for its *haenyo* or women divers, who dive in the deep sea for edible seaweed, shellfish, and octopus and are one of the island's unique attractions.

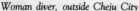

*Woman diver, outside Cheju City*

# HOTEL

# ACCOMMODATIONS

Modern hotel accommodations are becoming increasingly available on Cheju-do. Three large new hotels, including a Hyatt on the southern coast, were completed for the 1988 Summer Olympics. Thus the island boasts five deluxe hotels and some two dozen othe good Western-style hotels, plus Korean-style inns, or *yogwan*, and a condominium complex. The Western-style lodgings tend to be located in Cheju City and Sogwipo; the *yogwan* are scattered throughout the island. Reservations should be made in advance, especially during the spring and fall; travel agencies can handle both Western and Korean-style accommodations, and tourist information centers are particularly helpful for locating and reserving rooms at *yogwan*.

What Hawaii and Niagara are to the marriage industry in America, Cheju-do is in Korea. The island, with its mild weather, unique landscape, and idyllic beaches, is a famous honeymoon mecca. Every inn and lodging place on Cheju-do becomes a honeymoon hotel during the late fall wedding season.

### 제주 K A L 호텔

**Cheju KAL Hotel** (Deluxe—310 rooms for 760 guests). Conveniently located in Cheju City, the facilities include a nightclub, sky lounge, game room, sauna, outdoor swimming pool, beauty salon, Korean and Western restaurants, steak house, snack bar, casino, and golf course.

*Address:* 1691-9 2-do 1-dong
*Telephone:* 53-6151
*Cable:* CHEJUKALHTEL
*Telex:* JKALHTL K66744

### 제주 그랜드 호텔

**Cheju Grand Hotel** (Deluxe—522 rooms for 1,035 guests). Situated in the central downtown area of New Cheju; offers outdoor swimming pool, sky lounge, barber shop, beauty parlor, sauna, turkish bath, shopping arcade, nightclub, bar, tea and cocktail lounge, health center, tour counter and tour center, Korean, Western, and Japanese restaurants, and golf course, owned and operated by NIKKO Hotels International.

*Address:* 263-15 Yon-dong

*Telephone:* 42-3321
*Cable:* GRANHTL
*Telex:* GRANHTL K66712

**Sogwipo KAL Hotel** (Deluxe—221 rooms for 500 guests). Located in the heart of the Chungmun Resort overlooking the Pacific Ocean, the hotel's facilities include three restaurants, a swimming pool, a casino, and banquet halls.
*Address:* 486-3 Topyong-dong, Sogwipo
*Telephone* (164) 32-9851
*Telex:* SKALHTL K66717

### 제주 하이얏트 호텔
**Hyatt Regency Cheju** (Deluxe—224 rooms for 500 guests). Located in the heart of Chungmun Resort overlooking the Pacific Ocean, this new hotel offers three restaurants, nightclub, bars, casino, and extensive conference and banquet facilities. The atrium lobby gives one the impression of being in the tropics near a cascading waterfall.
*Address:* 3039-1, Sacktal-dong Chungmun Resort, Sogwipo
*Telephone:* 33-1234
*Cable:* HYATTCHEJU
*Telex:* K66749

### 서해 호텔
**Hotel Seohai** (First class—160 rooms for 340 guests). Located in the heart of New Cheju; facilities include nightclub, sauna, bar, coffee shop, barber shop, beauty salon, game room, Korea House, souvenir shop, tour counter, and sky lounge.
*Address:* 291-30 Yon-dong
*Telephone:* 27-4111
*Cable:* CHEJUHTL SEOHAI
*Telex:* SEOHAI K66783

Other Western-style hotels in Cheju are: **Cheju Royal** (first class, tel.: 27-4161); **Paradise Cheju** (second class, tel.: 23-0171); **New Plaza** (second class, tel.: (Seoul) 764-1134); **Cheju Washington Hotel** (first class, tel.: (064) 42-4111/9); **Cheju Oriental Hotel** (deluxe class, tel.: (064) 52-8222); **Mosu Tourist Hotel** (first class, tel.: (064) 42-1001); **Cheju Royal Hotel** (first class, tel.: (064) 27-4161); and in Sogwipo: **Prince** (deluxe class, tel.: 32-9911) and **Cheju Prince Hotel** (deluxe class, tel.: (064) 32-9911/32).

## CUISINE

The deluxe hotels have excellent restaurants serving Korean, Japanese, and Western food. Many Korean-style restaurants can be found in Cheju and Sogwipo; they offer *pulgogi* and other Korean delicacies. In Tapdong near the Ferry Terminal of Cheju City, there are several restaurants specializing in fresh seafood, such as the sliced raw fish called *hoe*, or the abalone-rice stew called *chonbokchuk*.

## ENTERTAINMENT

All of the deluxe hotels and most of the major Western-style hotels on Cheju-do offer either nightclubs or bars for nighttime entertainment. In downtown Cheju and Sogwipo there are several cabarets and go-go clubs. For less expensive evenings, there are many wine houses, or *suljip*, beer halls, bars, and coffee shops that are popular with local residents. Two casinos, one in the Cheju KAL Hotel and the other at the Hyatt Regency Cheju Hotel, offer a wide range of gaming facilities.

## FESTIVALS

The Halla Cultural Festival, held annually in September or October, is one of the largest and most impressive of Korean festivals. It features many cultural activities, exhibitions, and concerts; the events are held in Cheju Stadium. The Chilmori Shaman Ceremony, which is part of the larger Yongdong Festival, occurs on the first day of the second lunar month. It is a time of prayer for the safety of the fishermen and for an abundant harvest by the women divers.

## SPORTS

**Hiking and Biking.** Hiking, biking, backpacking, camping, and mountain climbing are favorite activities on mountainous Cheju-do.

**Water Sports.** Swimming, snorkeling, and scuba diving are popular at any of the dozen fine beaches encircling Cheju-do. A magnificent view of the sea life is offered in a glass-bottom boat available near Cheju City (see below).

**Golf.** The Cheju Ora Country Club, the finest on the island, is part of the Cheju Grand Hotel complex. The beautiful 36-hole course is laid out on the slopes of Halla-san, just five minutes by free shuttle service from the hotel. Major hotels prepare sports packages for guests planning to spend a day golfing, hunting, or fishing.

**Hunting.** Visitors are permitted to hunt on Cheju Island from November through February. Equipment, including rifles and dogs, can be rented. Duck and pheasant are the most popular game birds; wild pigeon and boar also are hunted. Procedures are handled by the Korea Hunting Association, and one should contact them 10 days in advance. The hunting preserve near Chungmun Resort is run by the Daeyu Hunting Club. Information can be obtained from either group: Korea Hunting Association (tel. (Seoul) 581-3275); Daeyu Hunting Club (tel. (Seoul) 552-6318).

**Fishing.** Surf and deep-sea fishing can be enjoyed year-round at various locations along the coast of Cheju-do. Travel agents offer organized fishing trips and should be contacted for precise information regarding seasons, locations, and tackle. One of the major fishing shops is in the Cheju Grand Hotel (tel. 42-3321).

**Scuba Diving.** The clear waters of Cheju-do are attracting growing numbers of diving enthusiasts; equipment can be rented at reasonable prices from the Scuba Diving Center at the Hotel Sogwipo Park (tel. 62-2161).

**Glass-Bottom Boat.** Run by the Cheju Royal Hotel, the glass-bottom boat offers a magnificent view of sea life near the port of Cheju City. The boat leaves every hour for the hour-long trip; the charge is $8 per person in a group. For information: in Seoul, tel. 733-2862; in Cheju, tel. 27-4161.

# SHOPPING

Shopping for souvenirs and gifts on Cheju-do is delightful. Everywhere on the island one encounters *Tolharubang*—Stone Grandfathers. These quaint statues of an old man with a warm smile have become symbols of Cheju. Carved of local basalt in a variety of sizes, from 15 centimeters to 3.5 meters tall, they are perfect mementos of Cheju. Also carved of basalt and popular with visitors are figures of women carrying water vases on their backs, and many products feature the women divers for which the island is famous. Tortoise-shaped stones, too, are valued as souvenirs. Pipes made from the local black coral make a unique gift. At the Cheju Folklore and Natural History Museum there are many craft items, including wooden bowls, purses made of wooden beads, water jars, and shell necklaces. Downtown antique shops offer an exciting variety of folk treasures from the past.

Among natural products, honey from the slopes of Mt. Halla and dried mushrooms are the most famous. Of special interest are the sweaters and other woolen goods made by the Hallim Hand Weavers, who have shops in the Cheju KAL Hotel (tel. 22-7221) and Chosun Hotel in Seoul (755-3845). The wool comes from 2,500 sheep on the Irish Catholic Mission Ranch.

Gift shops are plentiful along the main streets of Cheju City as well as in the hotels. Duty-free foreign goods are available at the Hanjin Duty Free Shop (tel. 27-7217) and at the KNTC Cheju Airport Duty Free Shop (tel. 42-0030). Brand-name watches, cosmetics, accessories, glasses, golf clubs, perfumes, and many other items are available at bargain prices; the shops also have Korean souvenir products such as ceramics, ginseng, and jewelry of amethyst and smoky topaz.

*Oedolgoe Rock, Cheju Island*

# 扶餘 公州
# Puyo and Kongju

### WESTERN REGION

THE HONAM (southwest) region, often called the ricebowl of
Korea, encompasses the major cities of Puyo, Kongju, Chonju,
Namwon, Kwangju, and Mokpo. The ancient alternate capitals of
Paekje (18 B.C.–660 A.D.) are worth a visit for their air of ancient
history. Puyo, located halfway between Pusan and Seoul, was the
center of splendid culture and arts, and many significant historical
relics and sites survive in the area. Kongju was the original capital
of the flourishing Paekje Kingdom, until it was replaced by Puyo.
On the way to Puyo and Kongju, at the town of Nonsan, is the
unusual Unjinmiruk Buddha Image at Kwanchok-sa. Two hours
northwest of Kongju is Onyang, a city famous for its hot springs.

In the center of Puyo is a branch of the National Museum of
Korea, a striking modern structure housing excellent displays of
Paekje art and artifacts, including fine ceramic pieces. The Kongju
Museum was built to exhibit the royal jewelry and ornaments
excavated from the tomb of King Muryong; it also has a fine
collection of other Paekje relics. At Kwangju is the third largest
branch of the National Museum. Its exhibits span the entire spectrum of Korean history from the paleolithic period to the Yi
dynasty. The Kwangju Museum also has the permanent display of
the Shinan relics—the cargo of ceramics and other artifacts discovered in a submerged 600-year-old Yuan dynasty Chinese ship.

## HIGHLIGHTS
## FOR TRAVELERS

### 고란사
### KORAN-SA (KORAN TEMPLE)

This ancient Buddhist temple is located on the banks of the
Paekma, or White Horse River, in the shadow of high cliffs. The
kings and queens of Paekje used to visit the temple and drink
mineral fountain water spiced with Koran-cho. Boats on the
Paekma River provide recreational activities in this beautiful area.

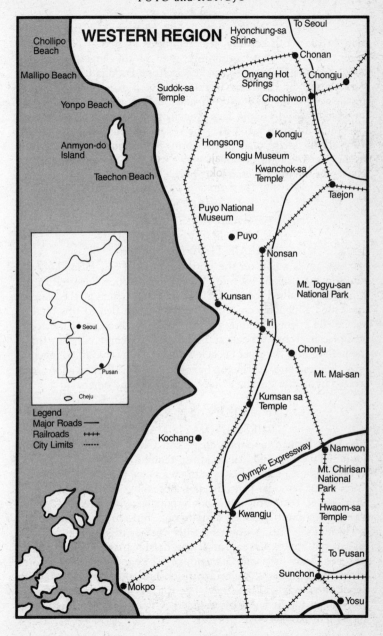

# WESTERN REGION

Chollipo
Beach

Mallipo Beach

Yonpo Beach

Anmyon-do
Island

Taechon Beach

Hyonchung-sa
Shrine

To Seoul

Chonan

Onyang Hot
Springs

Chongju

Sudok-sa
Temple

Chochiwon

Kongju

Hongsong

Kongju Museum

Kwanchok-sa
Temple

Taejon

Puyo National
Museum

Puyo

Nonsan

Mt. Togyu-san
National Park

Kunsan

Iri

Chonju

Mt. Mai-san

Kumsan sa
Temple

Kochang

Namwon

Olympic Expressway

Mt. Chirisan
National Park

Hwaom-sa
Temple

Kwangju

To Pusan

Sunchon

Mokpo

Yosu

Seoul

Pusan

Cheju

## Legend
Major Roads ——
Railroads ++++
City Limits ······

관촉사
## KWANCHOK-SA (KWANCHOK TEMPLE)

Built in the tenth century, this temple is located at Nonsan and is renowned for the Unjinmiruk, one of the largest images of Buddha in the Orient and the largest stone Buddha in Korea. The workmanship on the massive granite statue is exquisite. The towering figure is over 50 feet high and 30 feet around at the waist; the compassionate round face is eight feet from forehead to chin; the mouth is three feet wide; the seven-foot high hat is crowned with a lotus-inlaid diadem. In spring and autumn great festivals are held at the temple, which glows with the lanterns of pilgrims who come by the thousands to pray.

낙화암, 백화정
## NAKHWA-AM AND PAEKHWA-JONG
## (FALLING FLOWER CLIFF AND
## PAEKJE FLOWER BOWER)

Nakhwa-am is a cliff on the northern peak of Mt. Puso along the banks of the Paekma (White Horse) River. When Puyo fell to the attack of the allied forces of Silla and Tang China at the close of the Three Kingdoms era, 3,000 court women fled to this bluff to escape the enemy. Finding no way of escape because of the rocky precipice in front of them, and refusing to be captured, they threw themselves into the river far below. Falling Flower Cliff commemorates their sad fate. At the top hexagonal bower, Paekhwa-jong, was erected in memory of the loyalty of these court women.

지리산 국립공원
## CHIRI-SAN NATIONAL PARK

Like most Korean mountain areas, Mt. Chiri is well-known for its autumnal beauty and its Buddhist temples. Chiri-san is Korea's second-highest peak and covers an area twice the size of Sorak-san. Korea's first national park and now accessible by a good highway, Chiri-san is becoming increasingly popular with tourists. Among several important Buddhist temples on Chiri-san, the most famous is Hwaom-sa. Dating from the Silla period, this temple contains several national treasures and is the headquarters of the Buddhist sect that bears its name, Hwaom, or Flowery Splendor. The area is reached by way of Namwon, which has good connections with Seoul by railway and bus lines. The town is a favorite tourist spot, too, famed for its legendary maiden, Chunhyang, the heroine of an ancient Korean love story.

*Paekmakong River at Puyo*

## 덕유산 국립공원
## TOGYU-SAN NATIONAL PARK

Located on the border between Chollabuk-do and Kyongsangnam-do provinces, Mt. Togyu National Park is a favorite hiking and scenic area for tourists. It is easily accessible now by the '88 Olympic Highway linking Taegu and Kwangju. The mountain streams are stocked with rainbow trout, and there are both easy walking trails and unexplored wilderness slopes for seasoned hikers.

## 백제탑
## PAEKJE-TAP (PAEKJE PAGODA)

Paekje Pagoda, registered as National Treasure No. 9, is located in Chungchongnam-do province. Constructed at the end of the Paekje period, the granite pagoda stands 8.3 meters high, and its graceful craftsmanship has been praised as a high point of Paekje art. "Sunset at Paekje" is famous as one of the eight scenic wonders of the east coast.

## 대천 해수욕장
## TAECHON BATHING BEACH

On the west coast of Chungchongnam-do province is one of the best bathing beaches in Korea, Taechon, long noted for the clearness and warmth of its water. The curving beach stretches about three kilometers from north to south and is about 30 meters wide.

The sandy beach is mixed with granulated and powdered clam shells, which reflect the sunshine. In the distance the fantastic rocks of Tabo-do, or Abundant Treasure Islet, can be seen; to the south are woods and more spectacular rocks. Many Korean-style inns and several tourist hotels are available, and restaurants, a golf course, a boat pier, and other recreation facilities and amusement centers have been provided for visitors. Taechon can be reached by train from Seoul, by express highway buses, and by boat from Inchon.

## 온양 온천
## ONYANG SPA

Onyang Spa, celebrated for its hot springs, is located in Chungchongnam-do province where Mt. Kwangdok stretches southeastward with a number of scenic peaks. The temperature of the mineral water of the spa, which comes from an alkaline spring, is 50° C (122°F). It attracts tourists all year round. The town is an ideal resort area, with many top-class Korean-style inns and tourist hotels. In the vicinity are historical sites and relics such as Hyonchung Shrine, which commemorates the naval hero, Admiral Yi Sunshin, who used the first ironclad warships in the world to annihilate the invading Japanese fleet in the sixteenth century. Cabarets provide nighttime entertainment, and souvenir shops offer many appealing items.

## 전주시
## CHONJU CITY

Chonju is the 1,000-year-old capital of Hu-Paekje. Famous for its historical remains and scenic beauty, it is now a provincial capital and the seventh largest city in South Korea. It is a thriving area located along the main routes south from Kongju and Puyo to Namwon and the southern coast and from Seoul to Mokpo. To the west of the city is the huge Honam Plain, the largest in Korea and a principal rice-growing area. Chonju is the ancestral home of the family that founded the Yi dynasty and ruled Korea for more than five centuries. A point of interest in downtown Chonju is Pungnam-mun, a handsome Yi dynasty city gate, built in 1767 and a well-preserved example of the design and engineering of that period. Another significant site is the great Buddhist Kumsan-sa (Gold Mountain Temple), and there are other temples, pavilions, and parks to be enjoyed in the city.

## 남원
## NAMWON

Namwon is a popular tourist destination in southwestern Korea; it is accessible from Seoul via the Honam Expressway to Chonju and Route 17 to Namwon, or from Pusan via Taegu and the '88 Olympic Highway. This scenic region is dotted with statues of a pair of ill-fated lovers long known as the Romeo and Juliet of Korea. The ancient tale tells of Chunhyang, whose name means Spring Fragrance, the lovely daughter of a *kisaeng* who married a nobleman's son and was faithfully devoted to her lover through many hardships. Chunhyang Shrine contains a number of interesting buildings; a rabbit rides on a turtle's back over the entrance; and there is a famous portrait of the beautiful Chunhyang. Each year a festival is held in her honor.

**Namwon Tourist Complex.** A large tourist complex was completed in 1987 on over 100 acres in Namwon at a cost of $26 million. It provides excellent tourist accommodations, recreational facilities, and easy access for travelers to Chiri-san National Park in the Cholla area of southwestern Korea. The resort is notable for its cultural environment: it features a Korean classical music institute, a folk village, a folk game restaurant, and traditional Korean restaurants.

## 광주
## KWANGJU

Kwangju is a provincial capital and the fifth largest city in the Republic of Korea, with a population of 1.5 million. There are two universities in the city, which is a center for light industry, including textile mills, in southwestern Korea. It is accessible by expressway from both Seoul and Pusan.

## 목포
## MOKPO

Mokpo City, at Korea's "Land's End," is a busy port that is developing a large harbor to handle a growing volume of shipping. Processing plants prepare the products of the fishing industry and the oyster and shrimp beds for domestic and international markets. Excursion trips take the visitor to myriad offshore islands and south to Cheju Island.

## 여수
## YOSU

Yosu City, like Mokpo, a port, is the southernmost city in Korea. The huge Honam Oil Refinery is second in size only to that at Ulsan. Yosu is a major port for overseas trade and a center of tourism in the Hallyo Waterway, which welcomes visitors all year round. Spring comes early in the southern part of the country, and the beautiful beaches there offer relief from the hot summers. Fall is a delightful time for visiting historic sites on nearby spectacularly colorful mountainsides.

Puyo and Kongju are both about two and a half hours by express bus or train from Seoul; the more southerly cities take about five hours. Buses leave Seoul's Kangnam Bus Terminal for points south on hourly schedules, and trains leave from Seoul Railway Station frequently on the Seoul-Mokpo main line.

# HOTEL
# ACCOMMODATIONS

Deluxe and first-class hotels as well as many Korean inns (*yogwan*) are found in each city. Prices are quite reasonable, in the $35–$85 range for hotels, much less for *yogwan*.

### 내장산 호텔
**Naejangsan Hotel.** Chongju (First class—104 rooms for 260 guests). Naejangsan Tourist Hotel is located inside Mt. Naejang National Park. The park is renowned for its beautiful fall foliage from late October to early November. Rooms must be reserved months in advance for this period.
*Address:* 71-14 Naejang-dong, Chong ju
*Telephone:* 2-4131

### 신양 파아크 호텔
**Shin Yang Park Hotel.** Kwangju (First class—88 rooms for 200 guests).
*Address:* San 40 Chisan-dong
*Telephone:* 27-0671

### 제일 호텔
**Jeil Hotel.** Onyang (First class—93 rooms for 231 guests).
*Address:* 228-6 Onchon-dong
*Telephone:* 2-6111

**Core Hotel.** (Deluxe class—106 rooms).
*Address:* 627-3 Sonosong-dong, Chonju-shi, Chollapuk-do
*Telephone:* (0652) 85-1100

**Paradise Dogo Hotel.** (First class—214 rooms). Located in a
hot springs resort.
*Address:* 180-1 Kigok-ri, Togo-myon, Asan-gun,
Chunchangnam-do
*Telephone:* (0418) 42-6031/5

**Shinan Beach Hotel.** Mokpo City (First class—116 rooms).
*Address:* 440-4 Chukyo-dong, Mokpo-shi
*Telephone:* (0631) 43-3399

**Yosu Beach Hotel.** Collanam-do (First class—74 rooms).
*Address:* 346 Chungmu-dong, Yosu-shi
*Telephone:* (0662) 63-2011/5

For Western cuisine in this region, the hotel dining rooms are
best. Many Korean restaurants serve good Korean food at very
reasonable prices.

# ◆ ENTERTAINMENT

The deluxe hotels in the region have nightclubs, and there are
local wine houses and coffee shops in the downtown areas. The
southwestern cities are the scene of many national and regional
festivals. The four major ones are:

**Paekje Cultural Festival.** Held annually in the autumn in both
Puyo and Kongju, this festival features rituals honoring ancient
kings, loyal subjects, and court maidens.

**Village Ritual of Unsan.** Unsan is in the northern part of
the region; this festival is held over a five-day period each March
or April. Traditional events are performed at a shrine in the forest
outside Unsan to honor the mountain spirit and legendary generals
of the past. A procession is led by a band of farmer-musicians.

**Moyang Castle Festival.** Held in Kochang on the ninth day
of the ninth lunar month (mid-October), this is the only castle
festival in Korea. It celebrates the completion in 1453 of Moyangsa
Castle, built only with the labor of women.

**Chunhyang Festival.** The date varies according to the lunar
calendar for this festival in Namwon honoring Korea's Juliet, the
ancient heroine who is regarded as the embodiment of feminine
virtue. The festival features a traditional singing contest of *pansori*
(native folk songs) at a unique Yi dynasty wooden pavilion with
hand-carved dragons decorating the rafters; other regional folk
music and dances complete the entertainment.

## BEACHES

There are 12 major beaches in the area, as well as many small and delightful coastal spots—all offer excellent swimming. In the northern part of the region there are beaches in Sosan Sea National Park and two fine beaches near Taechon on the coast west of Puyo. In the central part is the beach in Peninsula Park northeast of Chonju; another good beach is located just west of Chonju. In the south around Mokpo there are several bathing beaches.

There are two spas in the southwest region: Yusong Hot Springs near Kongju, and Toksan Hot Springs just west of Onyang.

## SHOPPING

The city of Chonju is well-known as Korea's premier producer of traditional rice paper (*hanji*), a major export of the area. The Crafts Center in Chonju offers many local products for sale: paper fans, lanterns, umbrellas, and regional wood products. Renowned as the home of the faithful heroine Chunhyang, Namwon is famous for its woodcrafts. Kwangju is the handicraft center of Chollanamdo Province; there are more than 20 shops in Hwarang Street where antique chests, paintings, and world-famous Korean porcelain ware can be found.

Major shopping spots in the Honam region are: in Chonju, **Crafts Center** (31-3 2-ga Chungang-dong, tel. 2-5921); in Namwon, **Howansa** (84 Ssanggyo-dong, tel. 000-3354); in Kwangju, **Minsokkwan** (San 40 Chasan-dong, tel. 007-0671); and in Mokpo, **Haeng Nam Sa** (251-32 Sang-dong, tel. 005-2113).

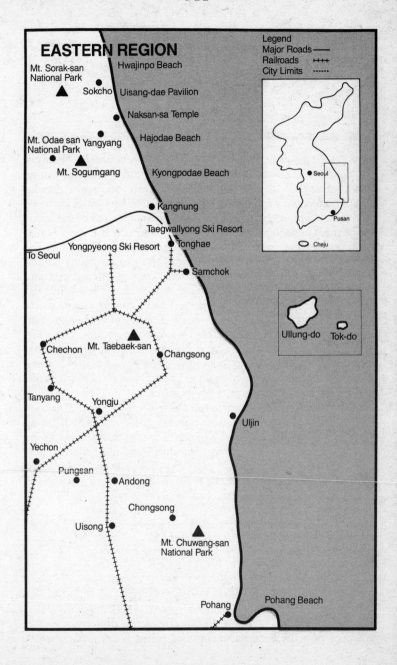

# EASTERN REGION

Mt. Sorak-san
National Park

Hwajinpo Beach

Sokcho    Uisang-dae Pavilion

Naksan-sa Temple

Mt. Odae san   Yangyang
National Park

Hajodae Beach

Mt. Sogumgang

Kyongpodae Beach

Kangnung

Taegwallyong Ski Resort

Yongpyeong Ski Resort   Tonghae

To Seoul

Samchok

Mt. Taebaek-san

Chechon                Changsong

Tanyang

Yongju

Uljin

Yechon

Pungsan

Andong

Chongsong

Uisong

Mt. Chuwang-san
National Park

Pohang        Pohang Beach

Legend
Major Roads —
Railroads   ++++
City Limits   ------

Seoul

Pusan

Cheju

Ullung-do    Tok-do

# 雪嶽山

# **Sorak-san**

## EASTERN REGION

KOREA'S east coast, particularly the portion between Sokcho in the north, the coastal metropolis of Kangnung, and the fishing port of Samchok to the south, has recently become a popular vacation area, with an abundance of recreational activities available year-round. The economy and tourism were stimulated by the opening of the Yongdong Expressway, which connects the main north-south expressway with Kangnung. The expressway crosses the Taebaek Mountain Range, which forms the eastern "spine" of the peninsula; toward its northern end are some of the steepest and most rugged peaks in East Asia. East of this barrier range is a flat plain facing the ocean. A paved road links coastal cities, quaint fishing villages, and long white sandy beaches. The combination of mountains and beaches makes the east coast an ideal all-season vacation spot for tourists with any number of interests—hiking, mountain-climbing, skiing, swimming, fishing, boating, or just enjoying the alpine scenery of dramatic peaks, spectacular waterfalls, and lovely lakes above soft sandy beaches.

Three national parks are found along the east coast: Sorak-san National Park in the north near Sokcho; Odae-san National Park with its famous Woljong-sa (Woljong Temple) and pagoda in the central region; and Chuwang-san National Park in the south. These lovely mountain parks provide excellent year-round resorts, offering the visitor deep forests, rushing streams, wild flowers, colorful autumn leaves, snow in winter, and ancient temples.

## ▶ HIGHLIGHTS ◀

## ▶ FOR TRAVELERS ◀

### 설악산 국립공원
### *SORAK-SAN NATIONAL PARK*

On the east coast of Korea just north of the 38th parallel is a group of ruggedly beautiful mountains called Sorak, which means

"Snow Hills." Although in the past they were somewhat over-shadowed by the world-famous Diamond Mountains which lie just to the north, in North Korea, and although Mt. Sorak is not as high as Mt. Halla (1,950 meters) on Cheju Island or Mt. Chiri (1,915 meters) in Kyongsangnam-do province, it is one of the most scenic areas in Korea because of its fantastic variety of rock formations, deep ravines, and lovely waterfalls. With giant ridges extending north and south from Daechong peak, Mt. Sorak is divided into two parts: east (Outer Sorak) and west (Inner Sorak). The heavily forested slopes are traversed by hiking trails that lead to the famous waterfalls of Taesung (Inner Mt. Sorak) and Piryong (Outer Mt. Sorak); to the stunning rock formations of Ulsanbawi, Wasondae, and Pisondae; and to the remote hermitages of Shinhung-sa (Outer Mt. Sorak) and Paektam-sa (Inner Mt. Sorak), which date back hundreds of years.

At the eastern entrance to this scenic area is Sorak-dong, a new tourist center with first-class hotels, motels, campgrounds, and a hot-spring spa. One of the highlights for visitors to Sorak-dong Tourist Village is a cable car that rises from the village to the peak, some 1,100 meters up. On the summit of the mountain is Kwongum-song (Kwongum Castle). There also is a new youth hostel offering accommodations and meals for tourists and climbers. All seasons are hospitable at Sorak-san National park: in April and May azaleas and dogwood decorate the slopes; in summer people enjoy the scenery and the nearby beaches; in late September, October, and early November, autumn leaves reach a crescendo of color; in winter, the Alps Ski Resort offers excellent facilities for skiers.

Scenic and historic points of interest include Hongnyon Hermitage; Uisang Pavilion; the statue of Sin Saimdang, mother of famous Confucian scholar Yi I; and Naksan Temple, one of the few Korean monasteries built in sight of the sea. The most prominent feature of the 1,300-year-old temple is a new 16-meter granite statue of the Goddess of Mercy; situated on a high bluff overlooking the sea, the goddess protects fishermen from storms and shipwreck.

**Climbs.** (1) Sorak-dong — Shinhung-sa — Kyejo Hermitage — Ulsanbawi Rock (time, 3 hours); (2) Sorak-dong — Yuktam Waterfall — Piryong Waterfall — Towangsong Waterfall (3 hours); and (3) Sorak-dong — Pisondae Plateau — Kwimyon Rock — Yangpok Waterfall — Sochongbong Peak — Taechong Peak (6 hours).

*Mt. Sorak*

**Skiing.** In Chinburyong Pass north of Sorak-san is the Alps Ski Resort. It is equipped with modern lifts and snow-making machines and offers excellent accommodations. Its three slopes range from 850 to 1,600 m., and from 20 to 40 degrees (in Seoul, call 546-6962 for information).

Dragon Valley also provides skiing — see following section entitled, "Youngpyeong."

**Getting to Mt. Sorak:** Korean Air has two flights daily to Sokcho from Seoul (in Seoul, tel.: 756-2000, 755-2221); express buses leave frequently from Kangnam Express Bus Terminal in Seoul (tel.: 591-3402, 598-4151) for Sokcho, Kangnung, Samchok, and Pohang; a shuttle shipping service runs daily from Soyang Dam to Inje (call Tongbu Travel Service in Seoul, tel.: 730-8311). From any of these points the traveler can take a bus or taxi to Sorak-san.

## 강릉
### KANGNUNG

Since the Yongdong Expressway opened the area for tourism, the busy coastal city of Kangnung has come to be known as the "Gateway to Sorak." The famous seaside resort of Kyongpo-dae offers excellent facilities for swimming and boating and modern waterfront hotels. Standing on a hill west of Kyongpo Lake is Kyongpo Pavilion, one of the "eight scenic wonders" of the east coast. Of historic interest is Ojukon, home of Yi I, a great statesman and Confucian scholar of the Yi dynasty. Express bus service is available from the Kangnam Express Bus Terminal in Seoul (tel. 598-4121); the fare is about $5 for the 4 1/2 hour trip.

## 삼척
## SAMCHOK

Samchok is a charming, unspoiled fishing village at the southern end of the east coast region. The excellent white sandy beaches are less crowded than those near Mt. Sorak. South of Samchok are Paegam Hot Springs and Songnyu Limestone Cave, which is 472 meters long. Three of the "eight scenic wonders" (*kwandong palgyong*) of the east coast are located in and around Samchok: Choksoru Pavilion stands on a rocky bluff overlooking a river and is reached by a suspension foot-bridge; Wolsong and Mangyang Pavilions provide panoramic views of the Sea of Japan. Sunrise and sunset are particularly lovely. Buses for Samchok leave from Seoul's Kangnam Express Bus Terminal (tel. 599-1865); the fare is $5 for the 5-hour trip.

## 속초
## SOKCHO AREA

Sokcho is a bustling port situated on the northern coastal road near the entrance to Sorak-san Resort. Originally a fishing town, Sokcho has benefited greatly in recent years from its ideal location for the development of new tourist sites. Famous beaches in the area are Songjiho in the north, and to the south Naksan, which takes its name from the nearby temple, Naksan-sa. This temple is noted for its dazzling views of the sea and a huge granite statue of the Goddess of Mercy; many visitors come to watch the sunrise as sea mists disperse over the ancient pine forest that surrounds the temple. Chonggan Pavilion, Choksan Hot Spring, and Hajodae Pavilion and Beach are other charming attractions in the area.

## 오대산 국립공원
## ODAE-SAN NATIONAL PARK

The park around Odae-san (Mountain of Five Terraces) encompasses nearly 300 square kilometers. The most famous spot within the park is Woljong-sa, one of the oldest temples of the Silla Kingdom. In the grounds is an octagonal nine-story stone pagoda, also dating from the Silla period. Midway to the summit of Odae-san is Sangwon-sa, a temple noted for its bronze bell cast in 725 and said to be the oldest and most beautiful in Korea.

## 용평
## YONGPYEONG

Dragon Valley Resort Complex, developed by Ssangyong Business Group, is located 205 kilometers east of Seoul. The year-round, world-class resort is a perennial sports center for national and international ski festivals. Facilities here include tennis courts, racketball courts, a swimming pool, a man-made lake, golf courses (a new golf course of world-class caliber, designed by a famous golf architect, opened recently), the Valley Sports center, a discotheque, and many other indoor-outdoor amenities. Its six ski-slopes range from 57 to 1,030 meters. There are snow-making machines on Dragon Valley's vast slopes, and its ten chair lifts facilitate 9,000 skiers per hour. Famed for its natural beauty, Dragon Valley attracts visitors not only in winter, but also in spring, summer, and fall. The resort, a three-hour drive from Seoul, offers a 191-room deluxe hotel, a 40-room youth hostel, and a 205-unit luxury condominium. (In Seoul, call 548-2251 for information).

## 울릉도
## ULLUNG-DO

Ullung-do, Korea's "lone island," lies 217 kilometers northeast of Pohang. This remote, peaceful island, with its rugged scenery, fine beaches, succulent seafood, and tranquil atmosphere, has been discovered by tourists who now flock to it for wonderful swimming, boating, fishing, and snorkeling. In the evenings, the squid-fishing fleet sets out to sea, each boat festooned with huge incandescent lights to attract the catch from the ocean depths. A cruise around the island takes two hours and offers beautiful seascapes, a mysteri-ous water-shrouded cave, tiny islets, and rugged rocks where flocks of seagulls nest. Small inns furnish food and comfortable lodging in a native atmosphere. Ullung-do is as green as the Emerald Isle in summer and also has been compared to Capri in Italy.

Comfortable ferryboats run between Pohang and the island; during the summer season, a hydrofoil leaves Pohang port daily at 2:30 p.m. and leaves Ullung-do at 7:30 p.m. The trip takes four hours, and the fare is $20 first class or $15 second class. For reservations, call 598-2101 in Seoul; 002-0711 in Pohang. Ullung-do is also now connected to the mainland by helicopter service from Korean Air.

## HOTEL ACCOMMODATIONS

The east coast area offers a variety of tourist accommodations, including Western-style hotels, Korean inns (*yogwan*), and a youth hostel for the adventurous. The two most modern hotels are the Sorak Park and the New Sorak at Sorak-dong Village. Sorak-dong Village has been developed for tourism and offers hotels, inns, stores, parking lots, and other public facilities; camping sites are also available. The four deluxe hotels in the region are:

설악 파아크 호텔
**Sorak Park Hotel** (Deluxe—121 rooms for 250 guests). Facilities include Western, Korean, and Japanese restaurants; a nightclub, gambling casino, beauty salon, and souvenir shop.
  *Address:* 74-3 Sorak-dong, Sokcho     *Telephone:* 753-2585

뉴 설악 호텔
**New Sorak Hotel** (Deluxe—120 rooms for 260 guests). Facilities include Western, Korean, Japanese, and Chinese restaurants; a beauty salon, barber shop, sky lounge, nightclub, game room, miniature golf, and souvenir shop.
  *Address:* 106-1 Sorak-dong, Sokcho     *Telephone:* 232-9385

낙산 비치 호텔
**Naksan Beach Hotel** (Deluxe—137 rooms for 250 guests). Facilities include Western, Korean, Japanese restaurants; banquet hall, souvenir shop, nightclub, bar, game room, coffee shop.
  *Address:* 32 Chonjin-ri, Yangyang     *Telephone:* 2-4000

용평 호텔
**Dragon Valley Hotel** (Deluxe—191 rooms for 280 guests). Facilities include Western and Korean restaurants, a ski resort, golf courses, a swimming pool, tennis courts, racquet ball courts, discotheque, game room, sauna, health club, and grass ski resort.
  *Address:* 130 Yongsan-ri Toammyon, Pyongchang-Kun
  *Telephone:* 32-5757

Western meals are served at the major hotels, and numerous restaurants in the coastal towns of Sokcho, Kangnung, and Samchok serve excellent Korean food. The New Sorak is especially famous for its pine mushroom dishes. In the beach areas freshly caught fish and spicy chowders are always delicious.

Major nightclubs catering to foreign guests are at the Sorak Park, New Sorak, and Naksan Beach hotels; Dragon Valley Hotel has a discotheque; the Sorak Park has a casino.

The Kangnung Tano Festival in June (fifth day of fifth lunar month) is an impressive event. Traditionally, *Tano* was a ritual day spent in prayer for good harvests, and it is a principal rural holiday. The festivities take place at a mountain shrine in Kangnung; a dance procession of shamans and a dramatic performance by actors wearing masks are highlights.

# APPENDIX

## The Korean Flag

The beautiful and richly symbolic emblems on the flag of the
Republic of Korea are among the oldest national symbols. The
Korean flag symbolically encourages the mind to observe and inter-
pret the varied meanings of the universe; its symbols are a key to
much of the thought, philosophy, and mysticism of the Orient.
The symbols, and the flag itself, are called "*Tae Kuk*."

The central thought in the *Tae Kuk* is that while there is
constant movement within the sphere of infinity, there are also
balance and harmony. The circle represents the Absolute, or the
essential unity of all being. The *yang* (positive) and *yin* (negative)
divisions within the circle represent eternal duality: heaven and
earth, fire and water, good and evil, male and female, night and
day, dark and light, life and death, being and not-being.

The four trigrams surrounding the *Tae Kuk* also carry the idea
of opposites and of balance. The three unbroken lines stand for
heaven; opposite this is the trigram for earth, three broken lines.
At the upper right-hand corner of the flag are two lines with an
unbroken line between, symbolizing fire. Opposite is the symbol
for water. The three aspects of a nation are the land, the people,
and the government. These are symbolized on the *Tae Kuk*: the
white ground represents the land, the circle represents the people,
and the four sets of bars represent the government.

# Korean
# National Songs

## AEGUKKA

### NATIONAL ANTHEM OF KOREA

동 해 물 과 백 두 산 이 마 르 고 닳 도 록,
Tong hae mul gwa Pack tu san i ma ru go tal to rok,

하 느 님 이 보 우 — 하 사 우 리 나 라 만 세.
ha nu nim i po u — ha sa u ri na ra man se.

무 — 궁 화 삼 — 천 리 화 려 강 — 산
Mu gung hwa sam chol li hwa ryo kang san,

대 한 사 람 대 한 — 으 로 길 이 보 전 하 세
Tae han sa ram Tae han, u ro kil i po jon ha se.

(Courtesy of Korea Annual 1986)

Until the East Sea is drained,
    And Paektu Mountain is eroded,
May God preserve this land as one,
    May it last ever more.
Land of rose-of-sharon,
    The fairest land!
May God preserve this folk as one,
    The people of Great Korea.

# KOREAN FOLK SONG

## (ARIRANG)

A - ri - rang, A - ri - rang, A - ra - ri - yo, ——
*A - ri - rang, A - ri - rang, A - ra - ri - yo,*

A - ri - rang, Pass is the long road you go.
*A - ri - rang Ko - ge - ro, Nŏ - mŏ - gan - da.*

If —— you leave and for- sake me, my own, ——
*Na - rŭl pŏ - ri - go, Ka - shi nŭn nim - ŭn,*

Ere three miles you go, lame you'll have grown.
*Shim - ni - do mot - ga - sŏ, Pal - byŏng - nan - da.*

*Puk-chum drum dance*

# An Annotated
# Reading List
# for Korea Travelers

The following bibliography is intended primarily as an acknowledgement of sources and as a guide to further study. Only English-language books published after 1961 are included. For publications on Korea before 1961, see the bibliographies in KOREA TOMORROW, NEW KOREA, and KOREA: THE THIRD REPUBLIC. Whenever the title does not clearly indicate the subject matter, a brief comment is provided.

## BACKGROUND

Chung, Kyung Cho. *Korea: The Third Republic*. New York: The Macmillan Company, 1971. An authoritative account of Korea's Third Republic, its history and government, and suggesting continuous dialogues between North and South Korea on reunification of Korea.

_____. *New Korea: New Land of the Morning Calm*. New York: The Macmillan Company, 1962. An examination of the First and Second Republics, the students' uprising, and the military coup; also a commentary on important problems of a divided Korea and recommendations for unification.

_____. *Korea Tomorrow: Land of the Morning Calm*. New York: The Macmillan Company, 1960, 3rd edition. A comprehensive survey of Korean history, geography, customs, religion, arts, language, culture, and economic and political structure, with commentary on vital problems facing a divided Korea.

Covell, Jon Carter. *Korea's Cultural Roots*. Salt Lake: Moth House Publications, 1981. An excellent study of Korea's culture with many fine prints and photographs; especially good description of shaman, Buddhist, and neo-Confucian roots in Korea.

Goulden, Joseph. *Korea, The Untold Story of the War*. New York: Times Books, 1982. The most complete account of the Korean War.

Han, Woo-keun. *The History of Korea*. Trans. Lee Kyung-shik. Honolulu: University of Hawaii Press, 1971. A general study of Korean history.

Hendrickson, Robin. *Land of the Morning Calm*. Seoul: Ladycom, October 1984. A concise view of South Korea.

Hinton, Harold. *Korea Under New Leadership*. New York: Praeger, 1983. A detailed survey of Korea's Fifth Republic under President Chun Doo Hwan.

Kim, Han-kyo. *Studies on Korea: A Scholar's Guide*. Honolulu: University of Hawaii Press, 1980. A comprehensive bibliography of Korean books.

Lee, Ki-baik. *A New History of Korea*. Trans. Edward W. Wagner. Cambridge, Mass.: Harvard University Press, 1985. A complete overview of the development of Korean history.

### ANNOTATED READING LIST

U.S. Department of the Army. *South Korea*. Washington: Dept. of Army, 1982. A country area study handbook on Korea.

Yang, Sung Chul. *Korea and Two Regimes, Kim Il Sung and Park Chung Hee*. Cambridge, Mass.: Schenkman Publishing Co., 1981. A study of two Korean political figures in North and South Korea.

## BUSINESS AND ECONOMY

Griffen, Trenholme J., *Korea: The Tiger Economy*. London: Euromoney, 1988.

Hasan, Parvez, and others. *Korea, Policy Issues for Long-Term Development*. Baltimore: Johns Hopkins University Press, 1979. World Bank economic report on Korea.

*Korea Business Directory*. Seoul: Korea Chamber of Commerce and Industry, 1988. Information on 5,000 major Korean trading enterprises and 2,000 economic organizations and service facilities in Korea.

*Trade Today of Korea, 1986-1987*. Seoul: Overseas Media Co., 1986. A directory of Korean trading companies.

Woronoff, Jon. *Korea's Economy: Man-Made Miracle*. Seoul: Sisa-yongo Co., 1983. The story of Korea's rapid economic progress.

## TRAVEL GUIDES

*All-Asia Guide*. Hong Kong: Far Eastern Economic Review, 1988. A brief description of South Korea with information for visitors including North Korea with maps.

*Asia & Pacific Review*, 1988. Essex, England. A brief guide to South and North Korea.

Crowther, Geoff. *Korea and Taiwan*. Victoria, Australia: Lonely Planet Publications, 1982. A travel survival kit with beautiful photographs and maps.

*Fodor's Korea*. New York: Fodor's Travel Guides, 1989. A concise guide for the intrepid budget traveler.

Hoefer, Hans J., Ed. *Korea, Insight Guides*. Hong Kong: APA Production, 1988. A comprehensive guide for tourists, with fine photographs.

## BOOKS FROM KOREA

Many English-language titles are published in Seoul. They are available from the Korea Branch, Royal Asiatic Society (C.P.O. Box 255, Seoul, Korea).

Adams, Edward B. *Korea Guide*. Seoul: International Tourist Publishing Co., 1988. An excellent compendium, especially on cultural aspects; numerous beautiful photographs.

_____. *Kyongju Guide*. Seoul: Samhwa Printing Co., 1979. Detailed information and well-illustrated guidebook on Kyongju.

ANNOTATED READING LIST

_____. *Seoul*. Seoul: International Tourist Publishing Co., 1984. A 58-page guide to Seoul with excellent maps.

_____. *Palaces of Seoul*. Seoul: Taewon Publishing Co., 1972. A colorful tour book with numerous photographs and ancestry of Yi dynasty.

_____. *Through Gates of Seoul*. Vols. I and II. Seoul: Sahambo Publishing Co., 1971, 1972. An absorbing account of historic buildings and ruins in Seoul, with excellent photographs.

Clark, Allen D., and Clark, Donald N. *Seoul: Past and Present*. Seoul: Royal Asiatic Society, 1969. Best detailed guide on historical sites in Seoul.

*Facts About Korea*. Seoul: Korea Overseas Information Service, 1983. A compact handbook on Korea; includes photographs.

Ha, Tae Hung. *A Trip Through Historic Korea*. Seoul: Yonsai University Press, 1972. A definitive account of historical sites of Korea.

Hyun, Peter. *Koreana*. Seoul: Korea Britannica Co., 1984. A compendium of all aspects of Korea; excellent photographs.

Kim, Il Hwan. *Beautiful Korea*. Seoul: Huimang Co., 1968. An excellent handbook of historical sites in each province, with photographs, in both Korean and English.

Kim, Young-kwon. *A Handbook of Korea*. Seoul: Korean Overseas Information Service, 1978. A large book of detailed information on Korea; photographs.

*Korea Annual*. Seoul: Yonhap New Agency, 1987. A comprehensive yearbook including Who's Who in Korea.

*Korea Kaleidoscope*. Seoul: U.S. Army Garrison, 1982. Information for U.S. service members in Korea.

*Korea, Past and Present*. Seoul: Kwangmyong Co., 1972. Detailed information, including Korean tourism.

*Korus*. Seoul: USFK/USA Public Affairs Office, 1984. General information on Korea for U.S. military personnel.

Kwak, Tae-hwan, Ed. *Korean Unification*. Seoul: Kyungnam University Press, 1984. A collection of 21 articles on problems of unification.

_____, and others. *The Two Koreas in World Politics*. Seoul: Kyungnam University Press, 1983. A collection of 19 articles on Korea in international politics.

_____, Ed. *U.S.—Korea Relations, 1882-1982*. Seoul: Kyungman University Press, 1982. A collection of 19 articles on a century of relations.

Middleton, William and Dorothy. *Some Korean Journeys*. Seoul: Royal Asiatic Society, 1976. A delightful travel book with numerous photographs of Korea's many scenic regions.

Nahm, Andrew C. *A Panorama of 5000 Years: Korean History*. Seoul: Hollym Co., 1983. A 121-page summary of Korea history, with pictures.

Rhee, Sang-woo. *Security and Unification of Korea*. Seoul: Sogan University Press, 1983. A study of the two antagonistic regimes in North and South Korea and problems of security and unification.

Rucci, R.B. *Living in Korea*. Seoul: American Chamber of Commerce in Korea, 1984. Excellent information for foreign residents.

ANNOTATED READING LIST

## KNTC TOUR BROCHURES

Korea National Tourism Corporation (KNTC) annually issues a great variety of brochures, maps, and posters published in English, Japanese, French, German, Chinese, Spanish, and Arabic. To obtain copies, contact any of the KNTC offices listed in this guidebook. Titles available include:

| | |
|---|---|
| *Korea* | *Korea's Buddhist Temples* |
| *Seoul, Korea* | *Shopping Guide* |
| *Kyongju and Pusan* | *Korea Hotel Guide* |
| *Cheju is Different* | *Travel Manual* |
| *East Coast, Korea* | *Tourist Map of Korea* |
| *Culture and Arts* | *Tourist Map of Seoul* |
| *Korea: Dining, Night Life, Sports, and Leisure* | |

Color posters depicting tourist attractions and sites are printed in two sizes: 60 x 42 cm and 60 x 90 cm.

## PERIODICALS

### PUBLISHED IN KOREA

*Business Korea.* Monthly. News and highlights of business in Korea.

*Business Korea Yearbook.* Annually. A comprehensive survey of the Korean economy.

*Korea Business World.* Monthly. Articles, news of Korean business and trade.

*Korea Herald.* Government English-language daily newspaper.

*Korea Newsreview.* Monthly. Important events in Korea; news photographs.

*Korea Times.* English-language daily newspaper published by the *Hankuk Daily News*, Korean paper.

*Korea Today.* Monthly. Brief articles on a wide range of subjects, with photos.

*Korea and World Affairs.* Quarterly. Research Center for Peace and Unification of Korea, CPO Box 6545, Seoul, Korea. Many scholarly essays on politics, international relations, and unification issues.

*Seoul.* Monthly. English-language pictorial magazine.

### PUBLISHED OUTSIDE KOREA

*Asian Survey.* Monthly. Institute of East Asian Studies, University of California, Berkeley, CA., U.S.A. Occasional scholarly essays on Korean politics and economics.

*Asian Wall Street Journal.* Weekly. Dow Jones, 22 Cortlandt St., New York, NY 10007. Comprehensive Asian economic news by Asia-based correspondents; often contains news of Korean developments.

*Off Duty. Welcome to Korea.* Annually. Hong Kong: Off Duty Publications, Ltd. General information on Korea for American military service members in South Korea.

## HOW THE KOREAN LANGUAGE WORKS

Since Korea's liberation from Japan by the United States armed forces, ever-increasing numbers of Koreans have been studying the English language. Today it is not only millions of school children and university students who are learning English, but also adults in every walk of life. An immensely popular English-language instruction program, covering fine points of pronunciation and colloquial usage as well as the basics of grammar and vocabulary, is broadcast every day from Seoul. Magazines and books in English are avidly bought and read.

It is much easier than it once was for the non-Korean-speaking tourist to visit Korea, but it is still necessary to have a tour guide or interpreter if the traveler is to learn much about the country and the people. Tour escorts and representatives of host organizations speak excellent English. The more experienced personnel can handle complex political and social issues with ease and will often have an amazing command of colloquial expressions. Younger guides may have some trouble with rapid-fire slang, but will enjoy learning the latest American idioms. The tourist who speaks slowly and simply, especially in the beginning, should have no difficulty being understood.

Uttering a few Korean expressions indicates the visitor's desire to meet the Koreans half-way. A pleasant "*An-nyong haseyo*" (How do you do?) is always appreciated and warmly returned.

Foreign publications usually adopt the McCune-Reischauer system of romanization of Korean words. (See the section on the Korean language in this guidebook.)

# Korean Phrases
# for Travelers

## GENERAL

| ENGLISH | KOREAN | |
|---|---|---|
| Good morning!<br>Good afternoon!<br>Good evening!<br>How are you? | annyong hasimnika? | 안녕하십니까。 |
| See you again. | to beopgetssumnida. | 또 뵙겠읍니다。 |
| Goodbye. | annyonghi kasipsiyo. | 안녕히 가십시오。 |
| Yes. | ye *or* ne. | 예, 네。 |
| No. | anio. | 아니오。 |
| Thank you. | kamsa hamnida. | 감사합니다。 |
| You are welcome. | chonmanneyo. | 천만예요。 |
| Excuse me. | silre hamnida. | 실례합니다。 |
| I am sorry. | mian hamnida. | 미안합니다。 |
| That is all right. | kwenchan sumnida. | 괜찮습니다。 |
| That is good (bad). | chossumnida (napumnida). | 좋습니다。 |
| Can you speak English? | Yongo halsu issumnika? | 영어할 수 있읍니까 ? |
| I can speak Korean. | hankukmal hamnida. | 한국말 합니다。 |
| Do you know? | aseyo? | 아세요。 |
| I understand. | ihaehajiyo. | 이해하지요。 |
| I beg your pardon. | tasi malsumhae chuseyo. | 다시 말씀해주세요。 |
| Just a moment, please. | chamkan kidariseyo. | 잠깐 기다리세요。 |
| Come this way. | iri osipsiyo. | 이리 오십시오。 |

| | | |
|---|---|---|
| *You* are pretty. | *tangsinun* yepumnida. | 당신은 예쁩니다。 |
| I like you. | tangsinul choahamnida. | 당신을 좋아합니다。 |
| May I have your name? | irumi muosimnika? | 이름이 무엇입니까 ? |
| My name is . . . . . . | jeirumi . . . . . . imnida. | 제이름은 ○○○입니다。 |
| *I* am an American. | *jonun* miguksaram imnida. | 저는 미국사람입니다。 |
| He *(she)* is my friend. | *kubunun* jechingu imnida. | 그분은 제 친구입니다。 |

## TRAVEL

| | | |
|---|---|---|
| Take me to the hotel. | hotelro kapsida. | 호텔로 갑시다。 |
|    Seoul railroad station | seoul chunggochang | 서울 정거장 |
|    Bus station | busu chungryuchang | 뻐스정류장 |
|    Kimpo Airport | kimpo konghang | 김포공항 |
| Keep right! | barunchokuro kaseyo. | 바른쪽으로 도르세요。 |
| Turn to left! | wonchokuro toruseyo. | 왼쪽으로 도르세요。 |
| Go straight! | kotchang baro kaseyo. | 곧장 바로 가세요。 |
| Stop here! | yokkiso naeryuchuseyo. | 여기서 내려주세요。 |
| How much is the fare? | yokumi olmaimnika? | 요금이 얼마입니까 ? |
| Please help me. | towachuseyo. | 도와주세요。 |
| How long does it take? | olmana kollimnika? | 얼마나 걸립니까 ? |
| Express-bus | kosokbusu | 고속뻐스 |
| Express-train | tukkupyolcha | 특급열차 |
| Subway | chihachol | 지하철 |
| Electric train | jonchol | 전철 |

| | | |
|---|---|---|
| Entrance | ipku | 입구 |
| Exit | Chulku | 출구 |
| Ticket | pyo | 표 |
| Luggage | jim | 짐 |
| Taxi | thakshi | 택시 |
| Customs | sekwan | 세관 |
| Police Box | pachulso | 파출소 |
| Post Office | uchekuk | 우체국 |
| Bank | unhaeng | 은행 |
| Embassy | taesakwan | 대사관 |
| Information Center | annaeso | 안내소 |

## AT THE HOTEL

| | | |
|---|---|---|
| Hotel | hotel, yogwan (Korean style) | 호텔, 여관 |
| Room | bang | 방 |
| Key | yulse | 열쇠 |
| Laundry | sethak | 세탁 |
| Telephone | junwha | 전화 |
| Toilet | whachangsil | 화장실 |
| Hello. | yoboseyo. | 여보세요。 |
| What is that? | chogosun muosimnika? | 저것은 무엇입니까 ? |
| Where is a KAL office? | kaal samusili odiissumnika? | 「카알」사무실이 어디있읍니까 ? |
| Would you show me the way? | odiro kamnika? | 어디로 갑니까 ? |
| Please call a taxi. | taxirul pullochuseyo. | 택시를 불러주세요。 |

| | | |
|---|---|---|
| Please bring me a bill. | kesanso katdachuseyo. | 계산서 갖다주세요。 |
| I will leave tomorrow. | naeil tonamnida. | 내일 떠납니다。 |

## SIGHTSEEING

| | | |
|---|---|---|
| I would like to visit. . . . | . . . .(l)ul kukyonghako sipumnida. | (○○○)을 구경하고 싶습니다。 |
| Capital Building | chungangchong | 중앙청 |
| National Museum | kukrip pakmulkwan | 국립박물관 |
| Toksu Palace | tokso kung | 덕수궁 |
| South Gate | namdaemun | 남대문 |
| Olympic Stadium | olimpic undongchang | 올림픽 운동장 |
| University | taehak | 대학(교) |
| Park | kongwon | 공원 |
| Department store | paekwhajom | 백화점 |
| Pulguk-sa (temple) | pulguksa (jol) | 불국사 |
| Take a picture. | sajinjikuseyo. | 사진 찍으세요。 |
| It is very beautiful. | aju arumdapsumnida. | 아주 아름답습니다。 |
| I am a tourist. | jonun kwangkwangkaek imnida. | 저는 관광객입니다。 |

## SHOPPING

| | | |
|---|---|---|
| Do you have a stamp? | upyoka issumnika? | 우표가 있읍니까 ? |
| How much is it? | olma imnika? | 얼마 입니까 ? |
| It is expensive. | pissamnida. | 비쌉니다。 |
| Show me another one. | tarungosul poyochuseyo. | 다른것을 보여주세요。 |
| I will take this. | igosul sagetssumnida. | 이것을 사겠읍니다。 |
| Book | chaek | 책 |
| Antique | koldongpum | 골동품 |
| Korean dress | hanbok | 한복 |

## AT THE RESTAURANT

| | | |
|---|---|---|
| I am hungry. | baegakopumnida. | 배가 고픕니다。 |
| I am thirsty. | mokimarumnida. | 목이 마릅니다。 |
| It is very delicious. | aju masisumnida. | 아주 맛있읍니다。 |
| It is a little hot. | jom maepsumnida. | 좀 매웁습니다。 |
| I will have tea. | chaul chusipsiyo. | 차를 주십시오。 |
| May I have more "kimchi"? | "kimchi" rul de chusipsiyo? | 김치를 더 주십시오。 |
| Traditional Korean food | hanjongshik | 한정식 |
| Barbecued beef | pulgogi | 불고기 |
| Broiled ribs | kalbi | 갈비 |
| Cold noodles | naengmyon | 냉면 |
| Korean salad | namul | 나물 |
| Soup & seaweed | kuk hako kim | 국 하고 김 |
| Fruit | kwasil (silkwa) | 과실(실과) |

## HEALTH CARE / MEDICINE

| | | |
|---|---|---|
| I have a cold. | kamgitulotsseyo. | 감기 들었어요。 |
| I don't feel well. | kibuni chochianayo. | 기분이 좋지않아요。 |
| I am ill. | byongi natsseyo. | 병이 났어요。 |
| Where can I find a doctor? | usaga odiitsseyo? | 의사가 어디있어요。 |
| May I use this telephone? | jonwharul ssodo toemnika? | 전화를 써도 됩니까 ? |
| Please call a doctor. | usarul pulrochuseyo. | 의사를 불러주세요。 |
| Medicine | yak | 약 |
| Pharmacy | yakkuk | 약국 |
| Hospital | pyongwon | 병원 |

KOREAN LANGUAGE GUIDE

## TIME/NUMBERS

| | | |
|---|---|---|
| What time is it? | myotssimnika? | 몇시입니까 ? |
| (number) o'clock | (. . . .)shi | (    )시 |
| a.m./p.m. | ojun/ohu | 오전, 오후 |
| Yesterday | oje | 어제 |
| Today | onul | 오늘 |
| Tomorrow | naeil | 내일 |
| Day/ Month/ Year | il/ wol/ nyun | 일, 월, 년 |
| One | il/hana | 일, 하나 |
| Two | i/tul | 이, 둘 |
| Three | sam/set | 삼, 셋 |
| Four | sa/net | 사, 넷 |
| Five | o/tasot | 오, 다섯 |
| Six | yuk/yusot | 육, 여섯 |
| Seven | chil/ilkop | 칠, 일곱 |
| Eight | pal/yodol | 팔, 여덟 |
| Nine | ku/ahop | 구, 아홉 |
| Ten | ship/yul | 십, 열 |
| Eleven | shipil/yulhana | 십일, 열하나 |
| Twenty | iship/sumul | 이십, 수물 |
| One hundred | paek | 백 |
| One thousand | chun | 천 |
| Ten thousand | man | 만 |

# Transliteration
# Glossary of
# Korean Place Names

## PROVINCES & REGIONS

| PROVINCES & REGIONS | CHINESE | KOREAN |
| --- | --- | --- |
| Kyungki-do/ Province | 京畿道 | 경기도 |
| Kangwon-do/ Province | 江原道 | 강원도 |
| Chungchong-pukdo/ North Province | 忠清北道 | 충청북도 |
| Chungchong-namdo/ South Province | 忠清南道 | 충청남도 |
| Kyongsang-pukdo/ North Province | 慶尚北道 | 경상북도 |
| Kyongsang-namdo/ South Province | 慶尚南道 | 경상남도 |
| Chulla-pukdo/ North Province | 全羅北道 | 전라북도 |
| Chulla-namdo/ South Province | 全羅南道 | 전라남도 |
| Cheju-do/ Island—Province | 濟州島 | 제주도 |
| Central Region | 中部地方 | 중부지방 |
| Eastern Region | 東部地方 | 동부지방 |
| Western Region | 西部地方 | 서부지방 |
| Southern Region | 南部地方 | 남부지방 |

# MAJOR CITIES AND OTHER LOCALITIES

| Cheju | 濟州 | 제주 |
|---|---|---|
| Inchon | 仁川 | 인천 |
| Jinhae | 鎭海 | 진해 |
| Kongju | 公州 | 공주 |
| Kwangju | 光州 | 광주 |
| Kyongju | 慶州 | 경주 |
| Panmunjom | 板門店 | 판문점 |
| Pohang | 浦項 | 포항 |
| Pusan | 釜山 | 부산 |
| Puyo | 扶餘 | 부여 |
| Seoul | 서울 | 서울 |
| Mt. Sorak | 雪嶽山 | 설악산 |
| Suwon | 水原 | 수원 |
| Taegu | 大邱 | 대구 |
| Taejon | 大田 | 대전 |
| Ulsan | 蔚山 | 울산 |

# TOURIST DIRECTORY

## HOTELS IN KOREA* (Unit: US$)

| | HOTEL NAME | ADDRESS | TELEPHONE TELEX | NO. RMS | RATES (Double) |
|---|---|---|---|---|---|
| **SEOUL** | | | | | |
| A | Ambassador | 186-54, 2ka, Chang-chung-dong, Chung-ku | (02) 275-1101 K23269 | 451 | 117-168 |
| | Hyatt Regency | 747-7, Hannam-dong, Yongsan-ku | (02) 798-0061 K24136 | 604 | 172 |
| | Inter-Continental | 159-1 Samsung dong | (02) 553-8181 K34254 | 604 | 157 |
| | King Sejong | 61-3, 2-ka, Ch'ung-muro, Chung-ku | (02) 776-1811 K27265 | 246 | 105-112 |
| | Koreana | 61, 1-ka, Taepyongno, Chung-ku | (02) 730-9911 K26241 | 280 | 105-112 |
| | Lotte | 1, Sogong-dong, Chung-ku | (02) 771-10 K23533 | 1,500 | 192-265 |
| | Lotte World | 40-C'hamshil-dong, Songpa-ku | (02) 419-7000 | 553 | 156-192 |
| | New World | 112-5, Samsong-dong, Kangnam-ku | 557-0111 K33226 | 250 | 115-415 |
| | President | 188-3, 1-ka, Ulchiro Chung-gu | (02) 753-3131 K27521 | 303 | 81-109 |
| | Ramada Inn Olympia | 108-2, Pyongchang-dong, Changno-Ku | (02) 353-5121 K23171 | 310 | 128 |
| | Ramada Renaissance | 676, Yokam-dong, Kangnam-ku | 556-0601 K28313 | 501 | 205 |
| | Riverside | 6-1, Chamwon-dong, Kangnam-ku | (02) 543-1001 K22063 | 203 | 120 |
| | Seoul Garden | 169-1, Tohwa-dong, Mapo-ku | (02) 717-9441 K24742 | 394 | 105-140 |
| | Seoul Hilton | 395, 5-ka, Namdae-munro, Chung-ku | (02) 753-7788 K26695 | 714 | 191-277 |
| | Seoul Olympia | 108-2, Pyongch'ang-dong, Chongno-ku | (02) 353-5521 K23171 | 310 | 80 |
| | Seoul Palace | 63-1, Panpo-dong, Kangnam-ku | (02) 532-0101 K22657 | 298 | 118 |
| | Seoul Plaza | 23, 2-ka, Taepyongno, Chung-ku | (02) 771-22 K26215 | 540 | 133-190 |
| | Seoul Royal | 6, 1-ka, Myong-dong, Chung-ku | (02) 756-1112 K27239 | 310 | 109-115 |
| | Sheraton Walker Hill | San 21, Kwangjang-dong, Songdong-ku | (02) 453-0121 K28517 | 770 | 150-155 |

*Ratings of hotels are as follows: A-Deluxe, B-First class, C-Second class, D-Third class, E-Undecided.

TOURIST DIRECTORY

| HOTEL NAME | ADDRESS | TELEPHONE TELEX | NO. RMS | RATES (Double) |
|---|---|---|---|---|
| Shilla | 202, 2-ka, Chang-ch'ung-dong, Chung-ku | (02) 233-3131 K24160, K24257 | 636 | 173 |
| Swiss Grand | 201, Hong-eundong, Suh Daimun-ku | 356-5656 K34333 | 512 | 135 |
| The Westin Chosun | 87, Sogong-dong, Chung-ku | (02) 771-05 K24256 | 471 | 173-213 |
| **B** Capital | 22-76, Itaewon-dong, Yongson-ku | (02) 794-0778 K23502 | 288 | 138 |
| Clover Hotel | 129-7, Chongdam-dong, Kangnam-ku | (02) 546-1411 | 52 | 47 |
| Crown | 34-69, Itaewon-dong, Yongsan-ku | (02) 797-4111 K25951 | 157 | 66-77 |
| Hamilton | 119-25, Itaewon-dong, Yongsan-ku | (02) 794-0171 K24481 | 139 | 50 |
| Han Kang | 188-2, Kwangjang-dong, Songdong-ku | (02) 453-5131 | 123 | 45-47 |
| Kyungnam-Tourist | 366-7, Changan-dong, Tongdaemun-ku | (02) 247-2500 K29389 | 108 | 75-90 |
| Mammoth | 620-69, Chonnong-dong, Tongdaemun-ku | (02) 962-5611 K32482 | 219 | 80-85 |
| Manhattan | 13-3, Youido-dong, Yongdungpo-ku | (02) 782-8001 K24767 | 182 | 84-102 |
| Nam Seoul | 602-4, Yoksam-dong, Kangnam-ku | (02) 552-7111 K25019 | 179 | 85 |
| New Kukje | 29-2, 1-ka, Taepyong-ro, Chung-ku | (02) 732-0161 K24760 | 149 | 76 |
| New Seoul | 29-1, 1-ka, Taepyong-no, Chung-ku | (02) 735-9071 K27220 | 141 | 71 |
| Pacific | 31-1, 2-ka, Namsan-dong, Chung-ku | (02) 777-7811 K26249 | 103 | 68-72 |
| Poong Jun | 73-1, 2-ka, Inhyon-dong, Chung-ku | (02) 266-2151 K25687 | 179 | 42 |
| Riviera | 53-7 Chongdam-dong, Kangnam-ku | (02) 540-0178 | 163 | 159-418 |
| Sam Jung | 604-11, Yoksam-dong, Kangnam-ku | (02) 557-1221 K26680 | 163 | 81 |
| Seokyo | 354-5, Sogyo-dong Mapo-ku | (02)393-7771 K26780 | 104 | 75 |
| Seoulin | 149, Sorin-dong, Chongno-ku | (02) 735-9115 K28510 | 211 | 59-77 |
| Tower | San 5-5, 2-ka, Chang-ch'ung-dong, Chung-ku | (02) 236-2121 K28246 | 205 | 66-94 |
| Universe Tourist | 56-1, Songnae-dong, Kangdong-ku | (02) 488-6011 | 100 | 85 |

*Ratings of hotels are as follows: A-Deluxe, B-First class, C-Second class, D-Third class, E-Undecided.

| | HOTEL NAME | ADDRESS | TELEPHONE TELEX | NO. RMS | RATES (Double) |
|---|---|---|---|---|---|
| C | Astoria | 13-2, Namhak-dong, Chung-ku | (02) 267-7111 K28740 | 80 | 45 |
| | Bukak Park | 113-1, Pyongchang-dong, Chongno-ku | (02) 352-7101 | 115 | 47 |
| | Green Park | San 14, Ui-dong, Tobong-ku | (02) 993-2171 K26486 | 92 | 45 |
| | Hilltop | 151-30, Nonhyon-dong, Kangnam-ku | (02) 54-3451 | 48 | 47 |
| | Metro | 199-33, 2-ka, Ulchiro, Chung-gu | (02) 776-6781 K26486 | 83 | 40-47 |
| | Savoy | 23-1, 1-ka, Chungmu-ro Chung-gu | (02) 776-2641 K23222 | 107 | 37-47 |
| | Seoul Prince | 1-1, 2-ka, Namsan-dong, Chung-ku | (02) 752-7111 K25918 | 86 | 37-42 |
| | Seoul Rex | 65, 1-ka, Hoehyon-dong, Chung-ku | (02) 752-3191 | 111 | 41 |
| | Seoul Transit | 92, Chongjin-dong, Chongno-ku | (02) 735-9001 | 102 | 45 |
| | Yoido | 10-3, youido-dong, Yongdungpo-ku | (02) 782-0121 | 116 | 44-47 |
| | Young Dong | 6, Nonhyon-dong Kangnam-ku | (02) 542-0112 K29310 | 160 | 47 |
| D | Boolim | 620-27, Chonnong 2-dong, Tongdaemun-ku | (02) 962-0061 | 60 | 37 |
| | Central | 227-1, Changsa-dong, Chongno-ku | (02) 265-4121 | 88 | 33 |
| | Chon Ji | 133-1, 5-ka, Ulchiro, Chung-ku | (02) 265-6131 | 70 | 28 |
| | Dae Hwa | 18-21, 6-ka, Ulchiro, Chung-ku | (02) 265-9181 | 99 | 37 |
| | Eastern | 444-14, Changshin-dong, Kangnam-ku | (02) 764-4101 | 51 | 27 |
| | Hye Jeon | 146-4, Samsong-dong, Kangnam-ku | (02) 552-5101 | 47 | 43 |
| | Korea Town Tourist | 90-3, Sangbong-dong, Tongdaemun-ku | (02) 496-6111 | 49 | 30 |
| | Mammoth | 620-69, Chonnong-dong, Tongdaemun-ku | (02) 962-5611 K27241 | 219 | 27 |
| | New Naija | 201-9, Naeja-dong, Chongno-ku | (02) 737-9011 | 68 | 38-41 |
| | New Oriental | 10,3-ka, Hoehyon-dong, Chong-ku | (02) 753-0701 | 84 | 38 |
| | New Yongsan | 737-32, Hannam-dong, Yongsan-ku | (02) 798-0051 K26358 | 56 | 34 |

*Ratings of hotels are as follows: A-Deluxe, B-First class, C-Second class, D-Third class, E-Undecided.

TOURIST DIRECTORY

| | HOTEL NAME | ADDRESS | TELEPHONE TELEX | NO. RMS | RATES (Double) |
|---|---|---|---|---|---|
| | Niagara | 259-1, Yomchang-dong, Kangso-ku | (02) 699-5611 | 51 | 33 |
| | Nostalgia | 1110, Hwagokpon-dong, Kangso-ku | (02) 691-0071 | 43 | 37 |
| | YMCA | 9, 2-ka, Chongno Chong-ku | (02) 732-8291 | 79 | 32 |
| **PUSAN** | | | | | |
| A | Commodore | 743-80, Yongju-dong, Chung-ku | (051) 44-9101 (02) 725-8931 K53717 | 325 | 58-65 |
| | Crown | 830-30, Pomil-dong, Tong-ku | (051) 69-1241 K53422 | 135 | 46-55 |
| | Haeundae-Hawaii | – | – | – | (opens 3/89) |
| | Hyatt | 1405-16, Chung-dong, Haeundae-ku | (051) 743-1234 | 363 | 164 |
| | Kuk Je | 830-62, Pomil 2-dong, Tong-ku | (051) 642-1330 K52096 | 139 | 49 |
| | Lotte | – | – | 545 | (Opens 4/89) |
| | Paradise Beach | 1408-5, Chung-dong, Haeundae-ku | (051) 742-2121 K52145 | 900 | 127 |
| | Sorabol | 37-1, 1-ka, Taechong, dong, Chung-ku | (051) 463-3511 (02) 776-3345 K53827 | 152 | 57-77 |
| | The Westin Chosun Beach | 737, Woo 1-dong, Haeundae-ku | (051) 742-7411 771-05 K53718 | 331 | 170-300 |
| B | Ferry | 37-16, 4-ka, Chung-ang-dong, Chung-ku | (051) 463-0881 K52282 | 122 | 37-45 |
| | Kuk-Dong | 1124, Chung-dong, Haeundae-ku | (051) 72-0081 K53758 | 105 | 39 |
| | Phoenix | 8-1, 5-ga, Nampo-dong, Chung-ku | (051) 22-8061 K53704 | 144 | 40 |
| | Pusan Arirang | 1204-1, Choryang-dong, Tong-ku | (051) 463-5001 K53707 | 121 | 34 |
| | Pusan Tourist | 12, 2-ka, Tongkwang-dong, Chung-ku | (051) 23-4301 K53657 | 274 | 50 |
| | Royal | 2-72, 2-ka, Kwangbok-dong, Chung-ku | (051) 23-1051 K53824 | 108 | 37-48 |
| C | Moon-Hwa | 517-65, Pujon-dong Pusanjin-ku | (051) 806-8001 | 77 | 30 |
| | Pusan Plaza | 1213-14, Choryang-dong, Tong-ku | (051) 463-5011 | 69 | 28 |

*Ratings of hotels are as follows: A-Deluxe, B-First class, C-Second class, D-Third class, E-Undecided.

## TOURIST DIRECTORY

| HOTEL NAME | ADDRESS | TELEPHONE TELEX | NO. RMS | RATES (Double) |
|---|---|---|---|---|
| Tong Nae | 212, Onchon-dong, Tongnae-ku | (051) 55-1121 | 80 | 34-81 |
| Tong Yang | 27, 1-ka, Kwangbok-dong, Chung-ku | (051] 22-1205 K53737 | 64 | 29 |
| D Bando | 36, 4-ka, Chung-ang-dong, Chung-ku | (051) 44-0561 K52286 | 60 | 30 |
| Dong Bang Tourist | 210-82, Onchon, 1-dong, Tongnae-ku | (051) 552-9511 | 44 | 27 |
| Green Beach | 1130, Chung 1-dong, Haeundae-ku | (051) 742-3211 | 65 | 31 |
| New Life Tourist | 830-174, Pom 2-dong, Tong-ku | (051) 67-3001 | 42 | 23 |
| Oscar Tourist | 522-40, Pujon 2-dong, Pusanjin-ku | (051) 807-3800 | 30 | 25 |
| Shin Shin | 263-11, Pujon-dong, Pusanjin-ku | (051) 88-0195 | 55 | 28 |
| Tae Yang | 1-62, Sujong-dong, Tong-ku | (051) 43-8801 | 80 | 33 |
| Tower | 20, 3-ka, Tongkwang-dong, Chung-ku | (051) 22-2527 K52046 | 108 | 20 |
| UN | 335-5, Amnam-dong, So-ku | (051) 26-5181 | 50 | 28 |
| **INCHON** | | | | |
| A Songdo Beach | 823, Tongchun-dong, Nam-ku | (032) 865-1311 | 180 | 58 |
| B Olympos | 3-2, 1-ka, Hang-dong, Chung-ku | (032) 762-5181 (02) 275-6644 K24894 | 176 | 44 |
| C Int'l Seamen's | 29-13, 3-ka, Shinhung-dong, Chung-ku | (032) 883-9841 | 75 | 27 |
| **TAEGU** | | | | |
| A Kumho | 28, Haso-dong, Chung-ku | (053) 252-6001 K54545 | 128 | 75 |
| B Dongin | 5-2, 1-ka, Samdok-dong, Chung-ku | (053) 46-7211 (02) 735-3626 K54325 | 92 | 43-60 |
| Hanil | 110-1, Namil-dong, Chung-ku | (053) 423-5001 K54428 | 94 | 48 |
| Taegu Park | San 98-1, Manchon-dong, Susong-ku | (053) 952-0088 K54446 | 60 | 50 |
| Taegu Soosung | 888-2, Tusan-dong, Chung-ku | (053) 763-7311 K54305 | 68 | 47 |
| Tongdaegu Tourist | 326-1, Shinchon-dong, Tong-ku | (053) 756-6601 | 60 | 48 |

*Ratings of hotels are as follows: A-Deluxe, B-First class, C-Second class, D-Third class, E-Undecided.

|   | HOTEL NAME | ADDRESS | TELEPHONE TELEX | NO. RMS | RATES (Double) |
|---|---|---|---|---|---|
| C | Kukje Tourist | 45-1, Kongpyong-dong, Chung-ku | (053) 422-3131 K54306 | 44 | 25 |
|   | New Jong Ro | 23, 2-ka, Chongno, Chung-ku | (053) 23-7111 | 48 | 24 |
|   | New Young Nam | 177-7, Pomo-dong, Susong-ku | (053) 752-1001 | 73 | 26 |
|   | Tongchon Tourist | 1006-34, Ipsok-dong, Tong-ku | (053) 952-1551 | 51 | 31 |
| D | Dongsan | 360, Tongsan-dong, Chung-ku | (053) 253-7711 | 54 | 24 |
|   | Kang Won Garden Tourist | 25-2, Pyongtaek-dong, Pyongtaek, Kyonggi-do | (0333) 52-2020 | 32 | 26 |
|   | Royal | 24-4, Namil-dong, Chung-ku | (053) 253-5546 | 50 | 26 |
|   | Suk San Tourist | 1-2, Kyo-dong, Suwon, Kyonggi-do | (0331) 46-0011 | 32 | 37 |

### KYONGGI-DO PROVINCE

|   | HOTEL NAME | ADDRESS | TELEPHONE TELEX | NO. RMS | RATES (Double) |
|---|---|---|---|---|---|
| B | New Korea | 674-251, Anyang-dong, Anyang | (0343) 3-5521 K27949 | 120 | 38 |
| C | Dong Suwon Tourist | 144-4, Uman-dong, Suwon, Kyonggi-do | (0331) 34-3411 | 68 | 37 |
|   | Song Tan | 274-190, Shinjang-dong, Songtan | (0333) 4-5101 | 97 | 40 |
|   | Grand | 199-3, Uijongbu-dong, Uijongbu | (0351) 42-3501 | 33 | 30-35 |
|   | Sung Nam Tourist | 4002, Sujin-dong, Songnam, Kyonggi-do | (0342) 48-6200 | 30 | 38 |
| D | Brown | 47, Kuchon-dong, Suwon | (0331) 7-4141 | 56 | 29 |
|   | Seol Bong | 313-5, Anhung-ri, Ichon-up, Ichon-kun | (0336) 2-5701 (02) 533-3941 | 81 | 72 |
|   | Yulim | 728, Saengyon-dong, Tongduchon | (0351) 52101 | 55 | 31 |

### KANGWON-DO PROVINCE

|   | HOTEL NAME | ADDRESS | TELEPHONE TELEX | NO. RMS | RATES (Double) |
|---|---|---|---|---|---|
| A | Naksan Beach | 3-2, Chonjin-ri, Kang-hyon-myon, Yang-yang-Kun | (0396) 2-4000 (02) 541-1214 | 137 | 49-78 |
|   | New Sorak | 106-1, Sorak-dong, Sokcho | (0392) 7-7131 (02) 232-9305 | 120 | 126-200 |
|   | Sorak Park | 74-3, Sorak-dong, Sokcho | (0392) 34-7711 (02) 753-2585 | 121 | 127-207 |
| B | Chuncheon Sejong | San 1, Pongui-dong, Chuncheon | (0361) 52-1191 | 68 | 42 |

*Ratings of hotels are as follows: A-Deluxe, B-First class, C-Second class, D-Third class, E-Undecided.

| HOTEL NAME | ADDRESS | TELEPHONE TELEX | NO. RMS | RATES (Double) |
|---|---|---|---|---|
| C Dragon Valley | 130, Yongsan-ri, Toam-myon, Pyong-chang-kun | (0374) 32-5757 (02) 273-9341 | 191 | 68 |
| Wonju | 63, Chungang-dong, Wonju | (0371) 43-1241 (02) 732-5600 | 75 | 26 |
| D Chunchon | 30-1, Nakwon-dong, Chunchon | (0361) 3-8285 | 50 | 28-34 |
| Dong Hae | 274-1, Kangmun-dong, Kangnung | (0391) 44-2181 (02) 737-0037 | 81 | 47 |
| Kyungpo Beach | 303-4, Kangmun-dong, Kangnung, Kang-won-do | (0391) 44-2277 | 60 | 41 |
| Kuk Dong | 255, Kangmun-dong, Kangnung | (0391) 3-2277 | 36 | 25 |
| Mt. Sorak | 170, Sorak-dong, Sokcho | (0392) 34-7101 | 59 | 49 |
| Tae Baek Tourist | 25-6, Hwangji 3-dong, Taebaek, Kang-won-do | (0395) 52-8181 | 60 | 27 |

## CHUNGCHONGBUK-DO PROVINCE

| | | | | |
|---|---|---|---|---|
| B Songnisan | 198, Sanae-ri, Naesong-ni-myon, Poun-kun | (0433) 2-2091 (02)777-0811 | 122 | 45 |
| Suanbo Park | 838-1, Onchon-ri, Sangmomyon, Chung-won-kun | (0441) 42-2331 (02) 276-1651 | 83 | 34 |
| Waikiki Suanbo Tourist | 806-1, Onchon-ri, Sangmo-myon, Chung-won-kun | (0441) 42-3333 | 89 | 37 |
| Suanbo Park | 838-1, Onchon-ri, Sangmomyon, Chung-won-kun | (0441) 42-2331 (02) 276-1651 | 83 | 34 |
| C Eun Sung Tourist | 844, Pongdae-dong, Chongju | (0431) 64-2181 | 66 | 37 |
| Suanbo Tourist | 291-1, Onchon-ri, Sangmomyon, Chung-won-kun | (0441) 44-2311 (02) 549-5511 | 50 | 41 |

## CHUNGCHONGNAM-DO PROVINCE

| | | | | |
|---|---|---|---|---|
| A Dogo Leisure Town | 180-1, Kigok-ri, Togo-myon, Asan-kun | (0418) 42-6031 (02) 267-0767 | 130 | 43 |
| B Jeil | 228-6, Onchon-dong, Onyang | (0418) 2-6111 (02) 598-2557 | 93 | 44-46 |
| Joong Ang | 318, Chung-dong, Tong-ku, Taejon | (042) 253-8801 (02) 778-8429 | 59 | 37 |
| You Soung | 480, Pongmyong-dong, Chung-ku, Taejon | (042) 822-0611 (02) 265-2396 | 140 | 47-68 |
| C Daejeon | 20-16, Won-dong, Tong-ku, Taejon | (042) 253-8131 | 52 | 26-35 |

*Ratings of hotels are as follows: A-Deluxe, B-First class, C-Second class, D-Third class, E-Undecided.

## TOURIST DIRECTORY

| | HOTEL NAME | ADDRESS | TELEPHONE TELEX | NO. RMS | RATES (Double) |
|---|---|---|---|---|---|
| | Man Nyon Jang | 478, Pongmyong-dong, Chung-ku, Taejon | (042) 822-0061 (02) 557-4737 | 75 | 26-35 |
| | Mu Gung Hwa Tourist | 213-1, Pongmyong-dong, Chung-ku, Taejon | (042) 822-1234 | 60 | 35-69 |
| D | Daelim Tourist | 230-6, Sonhwa 1-dong, Chung-ku, Taejon | (042) 255-2161 | 53 | 27-37 |
| | Hot Spring Tourist | 211-1, Pongmyong-dong, Chung-ku, Taejon | (042) 822-8220 | 64 | 25 |
| | On Yang | 242-10, Onchon-dong, Onyang | (0418) 2-2141 | 54 | 29 |
| | Royal Tourist | 202-5, Pongmyong-dong, Chung-ku, Taejon | (042) 822-0720 | 43 | 26 |

### CHOLLABUK-DO PROVINCE

| | HOTEL NAME | ADDRESS | TELEPHONE TELEX | NO. RMS | RATES (Double) |
|---|---|---|---|---|---|
| A | Core | 627-3, Sonosong-dong, Chonju | (0652) 85-1100 (02) 713-3814 | 110 | 45-62 |
| B | Naejangsan | 71-14, Naejang-dong, Chonju | (0681) 2-4131 (02) 777-3611 | 104 | 53 |
| C | Chonju | 28, 3-ka, Taga-dong, Chonju | (0652) 83-2811 (02) 277-1936 | 42 | 34-43 |
| | Kun San | 462-1, Kyongjang-dong, Kunsan | (0654) 3-4121 (02) 323-2483 | 113 | 38 |
| D | Victory | 21-1, Shinchang-dong, Kunsan | (0654) 2-6161 | 63 | 22 |

### CHOLLANAM-DO PROVINCE

| | HOTEL NAME | ADDRESS | TELEPHONE TELEX | NO. RMS | RATES (Double) |
|---|---|---|---|---|---|
| A | Shinyang Park | San 40, Chisan-dong, Tong-ku, Kwangju | (062) 27-0671 | 92 | 47-57 |
| B | Kwangju Grand | 121, Pullo-dong, Tong-ku, Kwangju | (062) 365-6111 | 65 | 37 |
| | Yosu Beach | 346, Chungmu-dong, Yosu | (0662) 63-2011 (02) 922-2421 | 74 | 30-37 |
| C | Kumkang | 22-20, Namnae-dong,, Sunchon | (0661) 52-8301 | 52 | 29-37 |
| | Kwang Ju Tourist | 20, 2-ka, Kumnamno, Tong-gu, Kwangju | (062) 232-6231 (02) 275-9062 | 58 | 28 |
| D | Baeg Je Tourist | 10-13, 1-ka, Sangnak-dong, Mokpo | (0631) 42-4411 | 36 | 25 |
| | Yosu Park | 979-1, Kwanmun-dong, Yosu | (0662) 63-2334 | 39 | 25 |
| | Yosu Tourist | 766, Konghwa-dong, Yosu | (0662) 62-3131 | 36 | 24 |

### KYONGSANGBUK-DO PROVINCE

| | HOTEL NAME | ADDRESS | TELEPHONE TELEX | NO. RMS | RATES (Double) |
|---|---|---|---|---|---|
| A | Kolon | 111-1, Madong, Kyongju | (0561) 42-9001 K54469 | 320 | 76-94 |

*Ratings of hotels are as follows: A-Deluxe, B-First class, C-Second class, D-Third class, E-Undecided.

| | HOTEL NAME | ADDRESS | TELEPHONE TELEX | NO. RMS | RATES (Double) |
|---|---|---|---|---|---|
| | Kyongju Chosun | 410, Shinpyong-dong, Kyongju | (0561) 2-9601 (02) 753-0300 K54467 | 304 | 76-89 |
| | Kyongju Tokyu | 410, Shinpyong-dong, Kyongju | (0561) 2-9901 (02) 753-2386 K54328 | 303 | 74-86 |
| | Liberty | – | – | 107 | (opens 4/89) |
| | President | – | – | 101 | (opens 4/89) |
| B | Keumosan | San 24-6, Namtong-dong, Kumi | (0546) 52-3151 (02) 756-1006 | 107 | 35 |
| | Baekam Resort | 964, Onjong-ri, Onjong-myon, Uljin-kun | (0565) 82-3500 (02) 276-1930 | 107 | 46 |
| C | Pohang Beach | 311-2, Songdo-dong, Pohang | (0562) 3-1401 K54507 | 53 | 27 |
| | Sungryu | 968-4, Onjong-ri, Onjong-myon, Uljin-kun | (0565) 82-3711 (02) 752-5572 | 158 | 35 |
| D | Kungjeon Tourist | 170-1, Noso-dong, Kyongju | (0561) 42-8804 | 32 | 27-29 |
| | Pul Guk Sa | 648-1, Chinhyon-dong, Kyongju | (0561) 2-1911 (02) 778-9241 | 83 | 33-40 |
| | Sang Dae Hot Springs | 590, Sangdae-dong, Namsan-myon | (053) 82-8001 | 48 | 24-30 |
| E | Hyupsung | 130-6, Noso-dong, Kyongju | (0561) 3-7771 | 30 | 23 |
| | Po Mun Ho | 645, Shinpyong-dong, Kyongju | (0561) 43-4245 | 30 | 37 |

### KYONGSANGNAM-DO PROVINCE

| | HOTEL NAME | ADDRESS | TELEPHONE TELEX | NO. RMS | RATES (Double) |
|---|---|---|---|---|---|
| A | Chang Won | 99-4, Chungang-dong, Changwon | (0559) 83-5551 (02) 542-4011 K52356 | 166 | 41 |
| | Diamond | 283, Chonha-dong, Ulsan | (0522) 32-7171 | 290 | 47-53 |
| | Pugok Royal | 215-1, Komun-ri, Pugok myon, Changnyong | (0559) 36-6661 (02) 756-4205 | 158 | 52-68 |
| | Ulsan Koreana | 255-3, Songnam-dong, Chung-ku, Ulsan | (0522) 44-9911 (02) 734-7234 | 151 | 50-62 |
| B | Chung Mu | 1, Tonam-dong, Chungmu | (0557) 2-2091 (02) 734-5636 K53850 | 50 | 55 |

*Ratings of hotels are as follows: A-Deluxe, B-First class, C-Second class, D-Third class, E-Undecided.

| | HOTEL NAME | ADDRESS | TELEPHONE TELEX | NO. RMS | RATES (Double) |
|---|---|---|---|---|---|
| | Hillside Tourist | San 34-1, Okpo-ri, Changsungpo-up, Koje-gun | (0558) 32-2932 | 96 | 42 |
| | Lotte Crystal | 3-6, 4-ka, Changgun-dong, Masan | (0551) 45-1112 K53822 | 121 | 55-68 |
| | Pugok Tourist | 213-19, Komun-ri, Pugok myon, Changnyong | (0559) 36-5181 (02) 738-8011 | 167 | 49-54 |
| | Pugok Hawaii | 197-5, Komun-ri, Pugok myon, Changnyong | (0559) 36-6331 (02) 234-6240 | 169 | 46 |
| C | Grand | 256-20, Songnam-dong, Ulsan | (0522) 44-1501 | 104 | 38 |
| | Masan Royal | 215, Sangnam-dong, Masan | (0551) 44-1150 | 56 | 32 |
| | Okpo | 330-4, Okpo-ri Changsungpo-up, Koje-kun | (0558) 34-3761 K52482 | 128 | 28 |
| | Pugok Garden Tourist | 221-1, Komun-ri, Pugok-myon, Changnyong-kun | (0559) 36-5771 | 86 | 37 |
| | Tae Hwa | 1406-6, Shinjong-dong, Nam-ku, Ulsan | (0522) 73-3301 | 103 | 41 |
| | Ulsan | 570-1, Yaum-myon, Ulsan | (0522) 72-7146 | 50 | 27-35 |
| **CHEJU-DO PROVINCE** | | | | | |
| A | Cheju Grand | 263-15, Yon-dong, Cheju | (0641) 42-3321 (02) 757-0035 K66712 | 522 | 99 |
| | Cheju KAL | 1691-9, Ido 1-dong, Cheju | (064) 53-6151 (02) 752-1234 K66739 | 310 | 103 |
| | Cheju Prince | 731-3, Sohong-dong, Sogwipo | (064) 32-9911 K66739 | 170 | 77-91 |
| | Hyatt Regency Cheju | 3039-1, Saektal-dong Sogwipo | (064) 32-2001 (02) 798-0061 K66749 | 224 | 164-300 |
| | Seogwipo KAL | 486-3, Topyong-dong, Sogwipo | (064) 322-9851 K66717 | 225 | 77-90 |
| B | Cheju Washington | 291-30, Yon-dong, Cheju | (064) 42-4111 (02) 735-4111 | 171 | 62-74 |
| | Cheju Royal | 272-34, Yon-dong, Cheju | (064) 27-4161 (02) 733-4567 | 115 | 65 |
| C | Cheju Marina Tourist | 300-8, Yon-dong, Cheju | (064) 27-6161 (02) 764-1134 | 80 | 53 |

*Ratings of hotels are as follows: A-Deluxe, B-First class, C-Second class, D-Third class, E-Undecided.

## TOURIST DIRECTORY

| | HOTEL NAME | ADDRESS | TELEPHONE TELEX | NO. RMS | RATES (Double) |
|---|---|---|---|---|---|
| | Cheju Palace | 1192-18, Samdo 2-dong, Cheju | (064) 53-8811 | 79 | 53 |
| | Paradise Cheju | 1315, Ido 1-dong, Cheju | (064) 23-0171 (02) 275-7751 | 57 | 53 |
| | Seogwipo Park | 674-1, Sogwi-dong, Sogwipo | (064) 62-2161 (02) 267-4664 | 66 | 53 |
| | Seogwipo Tourist | 314-1, Sogwi-dong, Sogwipo, Cheju | (064) 33-2121 | 89 | 53-64 |
| D | Seogwipo Lions | 803, Sogwi-dong, Sogwipo | (064) 62-4141 (02) 776-2232 | 60 | 43 |

*Ratings of hotels are as follows: A-Deluxe, B-First class, C-Second class, D-Third class, E-Undecided.

# KOREAN MISSIONS ABROAD

## EMBASSIES

Argentina: Av. del Libertador 2257, Cap. Fed., 1425 Buenos Aires, Argentina. Tel: 802-8865, 802-9665, 802-2737, 802-5499

Australia: 113 Empire Circuit, Yarralumla, Canberra, A. C. T. 2600, Australia. Tel: 733044, 733956, 733586

Austria: Kelsenstrasse 2, 1030, Vienna, Austria. Tel: 786318, 786164

Bahrain: P.O. Box 11700, Road no. 1901, Block no. 319, King Faisal Avenue, Manama, State of Bahrain. Tel: 291629

Bangladesh: NW (E) 17, Road 55, Gulshan Model Town, Dacca-12, Bangladesh. Tel: 604921

Barbados: 2nd floor, Mutual Bldg., Collymore Rock, St. Michael, Barbados, West Indies. Tel: 429-9650, 429-9651

Belgium: Avenue Hamoir 3, 1180 Brussels, Belgium. Tel: 375-39-80

Bolivia: Calle 15, –406, Obrajes, La Paz, Bolivia. Tel: 784262, 784263

Bourkina Faso: B.P. 618, Ouagadougou, Bourkina Faso. Tel: 33- 56-30

Brazil: Sen-Avenida das Naoes, Lote 14, 70436, Brasilia-DF, Brazil. Tel: 223-3466/3977

Brunei: 16 Simpang 427, Kg. Sg. Tilong, Jalan Muara, Brunei 3885, Negara Brunei Barussalam. Tel: 30383/4

Burma: 97 University Avenue, Rangoon, Burma. Tel: 30497, 30655, 32303

Cameroon: B.P. 301, Yaounde, Cameroon. Tel: 23-3223, 22-1725

Canada: 151 Slater Street, Fifth floor, Ottawa, Ontario, K1P 5H3, Canada. Tel: (613) 232-1715, 232-1716, 232-1717

Central Africa: B.P. 841, Avenue de France, Bangui, Rpublique Centrafricaine. Tel: 61-28-88

Chile: Av. Alcntara 74, Las Condes, Santiago, Chile. Tel: 2284214, 2284997, 2284791

Republic of China (Taiwan): 345 Chung Hsiao East Road, Section 4, Taipai, 10515, Taiwan. Tel: 761-9360

Colombia: Calle 94, no. 9-39, Bogot D.E., Colombia. Tel: 236- 1616, 236-2028, 236-3063

Costa Rica: Apartado 3150 Calle 28, Avenida 2, Barrio San Bosco, Paseo Colon, San Jose, Costa Rica. Tel: (506) 21-23-98, 33-19-29

Denmark: Dronningens Tvaergade 8, 1302 Copenhagen, Denmark. Tel: (01) 143123, 144705, 147907

Dominican Republic: Apartado Postal no. 20221, Avenida Sarasota no. 98, Santo Domingo, Dominican Republic. Tel: (809) 532-4314/5

Ecuador: Reina Victoria 1539 y Av. Colon, Edif. Banco de Guayaquil Ilavo Piso, Quito, Ecuador. Tel: 528-553, 524-991, 560-517

Ethiopia: P.O. Box 2047, Jimma Road, Old Airport Area, Addis Ababa, Ethiopia. Tel: 204490, 200117, 200882

Fiji: 8th floor, Vanua House, Victoria Parade Suva, Fiji. Tel: 311977, 311683

Finland: Mannerheimintie 76A7, 00250, Helsinki, Finland. Tel: 498955, 406446

France: 125 rue de Grenelle, 75007, Paris, France. Tel: 47-53-01-01

Gabon: B.P. 2620, Libreville, Gabon. Tel: 76-44-06, 72-36-44

Federal Republic of Germany: Adenauerallee 124, 5300 Bonn 1, Federal Republic of Germany. Tel: (0228) 218095/6

Ghana: P.O. Box 13700, no. 3 Abokobi Road, East Cantonments, Accra, Ghana. Tel: 776157, 777533

Greece: 1 Eratosthenous Str., 6th floor, GR-116 35 Athens, Greece. Tel: 7012122, 7016997, 7514382

TOURIST DIRECTORY

Guatemala: 16 Calle 3-38, Zona-10, Guatemala, C.A. Tel: 680302, 374041

Haiti: 46 rue Narcisse, Nerette Petionville, Port-au-Prince, Haiti. Tel: 7-6201, 7-1845

Holy See: Via della Mendola 109, 00135, Rome, Italy. Tel: (06) 3278120, 3273952

India: 9 Chandragupta Marg., Chanakyapuri Extension, New Delhi-110021, India. Tel: 601601, 604845, 604392

Indonesia: 57 Jalan Gatot Subroto, Jakarta Selatan, Indonesia. Tel: 512309, 516234

Iran: 37 Bukharest Ave., Tehran, Islamic Republic of Iran. Tel: 621125, 621389, 624127

Ireland: P.O. Box 2101, Dublin 4, Ireland.

Italy: Via Barnaba Oriani, 30, 00197, Rome, Italy. Tel: 805306, 805292, 878626

Ivory Coast: Bld. Botreau Roussel-Angle Ave., Nogus-Immeuble "Le Mans" 8me tage, Abidjan, Ivory Coast. Tel: (225) 32-22-90, 22-50-14

Jamaica: 2nd floor, Pan-Jamaican Bldg., 60 Knutsford Bd., Kingston 5, Jamaica, West Indies. Tel: 92-93035/36/37

Japan: 2-5, Minami-Azabu, 1-chome, Minato-ku, Tokyo, Japan. Tel: (03) 452-7611/9

Jordan: P.O. Box 3060, Amman, Jordan. Tel: 660745/6

Kenya: P.O. Box 30455, Nairobi, Kenya. Tel: 332839, 333581

Kuwait: Villa no. 12, Block 2, Division 42, Damascus St., Al Nezha, P.O. Box 4272 Safat, 13043 Safat, Kuwait. Tel: 2531816, 2513243

Lebanon: P.O. Box 114-5092, Beirut, Lebanon. Tel: 803157/8

Liberia: P.O. Box 2769, 10th Street, Payne Avenue, Sinkor, Monrovia, Liberia. Tel: 261532, 262407

Libya: A435 Trovato Partition, 6Km Gargaresh, Tripoli, Libya. Tel: 833503, 833484

Malawi: Old Mutual House, 2nd floor, Plot no. 28, Area 19, City Centre, Capital City, Lilongwe, Republic of Malawi. Tel: 733-250, 733-499

Malaysia: 422 Jalan Tun Razak, 50400 Kuala Lumpur, Malaysia. Tel: 2482177, 2482234

Mauritania: B.P. 324, Ilot O. 53, Nouakchott, Mauritania. Tel: 537-86, 537-88

Mauritius: Rainbow House, 23 Edith Cavell Street, Port-Louis, Mauritius. Tel: 08-3308, 08-2020

Mexico: Lope de Armendriz no. 110, Col. Lomas de Chapultepec, 11000 Mexico D.F. Tel: 596-7131, 596-7228

Morocco: 41 Avenue Bani Iznassen, Souissi, Rabat, Morocco. Tel: 517-67, 519-66

Nepal: Himshah, Tahachal, Kathmandu, Nepal. Tel: 211172, 211584, 212417

Netherlands: Rustenburgweg 1, 2517 KE, The Hague, Netherlands. Tel: 070-520621

New Zealand: 12th floor, Plimmer City Centre, Plimmer Steps, Wellington, New Zealand. Tel: (04) 739-073/074

Niger: B.P. 624 Niamey, Route de Ouallam Niamey, Niger. Tel: 72-22-31/2

Nigeria: Plot 934, Idejo Street, Victoria Island, Lagos, Nigeria. Tel: 615353, 617262

North Yemen: 42 Hadda Street, Sanaa, North Yemen. Tel: 204-522

Norway: Bjorn Farmanns gt. 1, Skillebekk, 0271 Oslo 2, Norway. Tel: (02) 552018/9, 436385

Oman: P.O. Box 5220, Ruwi, Muscat, Sultanate of Oman. Tel: 70-2322, 2458, 6250

Pakistan: No. 38, Street 86, Attaturk Avenue, G-6/3, Islamabad, Pakistan. Tel: (51) 824926

Panama: Edificio Torre Banco Union, Piso 12, Avenida Samuel Lewis, Apartado 8096, Panama 7. Tel: 64-8203, 64-8360

Papua New Guinea: P.O. Box 381, Port Moresby, National Capital District, Papua New Guinea. Tel: 25-4755, 25-4717

Paraguay: Rca. Dominicana 216 y Calle 160, Asuncin, Paraguay. Tel: 26-256, 202-651

Peru: Av. Principal 190, Piso 7, La Victoria, Lima, Peru. Tel: 70-4201, 70-4207, 70-4214

TOURIST DIRECTORY

Philippines: Alpap 1 Bldg., 140 Alfaro St., Salcedo Village, Makati, Metro Manila, Philippines. Tel: 817-5705/8

Portugal: Av. Antonio Jos de Almeida, Edificio Sao Joao de Deus, 6/F, 1000 Lisbon, Portugal. Pel: 777176, 774032

Qatar: Doha West Bay, Deplomatic Area, Doha, Qatar. Tel: 832238/9

Rwanda: 51 Kimihura, Kigali, Republic of Rwanda. Tel: 82024

Saudi Arabia: P.O. Box 94399, Riyadh 11693, Saudi Arabia. Tel: 4882211

Senegal: 66 Boulevard de la Rpublique, Dakar, Senegal. Tel: 22-58-22, 21-86-58

Sierra Leone: 22 Wilberforce Street, Freetown, Sierra Leone. Tel: 26404, 24269, 24041

Singapore: 101 Thomson Road, Goldhill Square, 10-02/04, 13-05, Singapore 1130. Tel: 2561188

Somalia: P.O. Box 4504, Mogadishu, Somalia. Tel: 80399

Spain: Miguel Angel 23, 28010, Madrid, Spain. Tel: (91) 4100053, 4100349, 4100352

Sri Lanka: No. 98, Dharmapala Mawatha, Colombo 7, Sri Lanka. Tel: 599-36/8

Sudan: House no. 2, Block 12, A, East, Street 1, New Extension, Khartoum, Sudan. Tel: 44028, 443689, 40358

Surinam: Malebatrumstr. 1, P.O. Box 1896, Paramaribo, Surinam; Tel: 76188, 77255

Swaziland: 4th floor, Dhlan'Ubeka House, Walker Street, Mbabane, P.O. Box 2704, Mbabane, Kingdom of Swaziland. Tel: 44055/6

Sweden: Sveavgen 90, 11359 Stockholm, Sweden. Tel: 08/16-04-80/4

Switzerland: Kacheggweg 38, 3006, Bern, Switzerland. Tel: (031) 431081/2

Thailand: Sathorn Thani Bldg., 12th floor, 90 North Sathorn Road, Bangkok 10500, Thailand. Tel: 234-0723/6 Trinidad

Tobago: 61 Dundonald Street, P.O. Box 1188, Port-of-Spain, Trinidad, West Indies. Tel: 627-6791/2/3

Tunisia: 16 rue Caracalla, Notre-Dame, 1002 Tunis, Tunisia. Tel: 893-060, 894-357

Turkey: Cinnah Caddesi, Alaam Sokak no. 9, 06690 ankaya, Ankara, Turkey. Tel: 1270074, 1264858, 1262590

Uganda: Baumann House, 1st floor, Parliament Avenue, Kampala, Uganda. Tel: 233653l, 233667

United Arab Emirates: P.O. Box 3270, Abu Dhabi, U.A.E. Tel: 338337

United Kingdom: 4 Palace Gate, London W8 5NF, United Kingdom. Tel: (01) 581-0247/9, 581-0240

United States of America: 2370 Massachusetts Avenue, N.W., Washington, D.C., 20008, U.S.A. Tel: (202) 939-5600

Uruguay: Jaime Zudez 2836, 100 Montevideo, Uruguay. Tel: 70-99-96, 70-95-34

Venezuela: Calle Alameda con Calle Andalucia, Qta. Mi Corry, Prados del Este, Caracas, Venezuela. Tel: 77-09-42, 77-05-26

Zaire: Galrie du Centenaire, Boulevard du 30 juin, Kinshasa 1, Zaire. Tel: 26132, 24345

## PERMANENT MISSIONS

Geneva: 20 route de Pl-Pois, 3me tage, CH-1215, Geneva 15, Switzerland. Tel: 91-01-11

United Nations: 866 United Nations Plaza, Ste. 300, New York, NY, 10017, U.S.A. Tel: (212) 371-1280

## CONSULATES

Naha: 9th fl., Kaei Sangyo Bldg., 15-3 Kumoji 2-chome, Naha, Okinawa, Japan. Tel: (0988) 67-6940/1

# 549

## CONSULATES GENERAL

Agana: 305 GCIC Bldg., Agana, Guam, 96910. Tel: 472-6488/8076

Anchorage: 101 Benson Blvd., Ste. 304, Anchorage, AK, 99503, U.S.A. Tel: (907) 561-5488

Atlanta: 229 Peachtree St., Cain Tower, Ste. 500, Atlanta, GA, 30303, U.S.A. Tel: (404) 522-1611

Baghdad: 915/22/278 Hay Al-Jame'a, Jadriya, Baghdad, Iraq. Tel: 7765496, 7760590, 7769103

Berlin: Ansbacher str. 5, 4th floor, 1000 Berlin 30, Federal Republic of Germany. Tel: 243079, 243070

Cairo: 6 El Hisn Street, Giza, Cairo, Arabic Republic of Egypt. Tel: 729011, 729273, 729162

Chicago: 500 North Michigan Avenue, Ste. 900, Chicago, IL, 60611, U.S.A. Tel: (312) 822-9485/8

Frankfort: Escherscheimer-Landstr. 327, 6000 Frankfurt/M 1, Federal Republic of Germany. Tel: (069) 563051/3

Fukuoka: 10-20, 1-chome, Akasaka, Chuoku, Fukuoka, Japan. Tel: (092) 771-0461/3

Hamburg: Hagedornstr. 53, 2 Hamburg 13, Federal Republic of Germany. Tel: (040) 4102031

Hong Kong: 5-6/F, Far East Finance Centre, 16 Harcourt Road, Central, Hong Kong. Tel: 5-294141

Honolulu: 2756 Pali Highway, Honolulu, HI, 96817, U.S.A. Tel: (808) 595-6109, 595-6274

Houston: 1990 Post Oak Blvd., Ste. 745, Houston, TX, 77056, U.S.A. Tel: (713) 961-0186/0798

Jeddah: P.O. Box 4322, Al-Sawaab Street 53, Hamraa District, Jeddah, Saudi Arabia. Tel: 6690050/70

Karachi: 51-C, Clifton, Karachi, Pakistan. Tel: 532955, 533955

Kobe: 2-21-5 Nakayamate Dori, Chuo-ku, Kobe, Japan. Tel: (078) 221-4853/5

Las Palmas: c/o Luis Doreste Silva no. 60-1, Las Palmas, Spain. Tel: (928) 23-0499, 23-0699

Los Angeles: 5545 Wilshire Blvd., Ste. 1100, Los Angeles, CA, 90036, U.S.A. Tel: (213) 931-1331/5

Montreal: 1000 Sherbrooke Street West, Ste. 1710, Montreal, Quebec, H3A 3G4, Canada. Tel: (514) 845-3243/4

Nagoya: 9-25 Higashi Ozone-cho, Higashi-ku, Nagoya, Japan. Tel: (052) 935-9221

New York: 460 Park Avenue at 57th Street, 5th floor, New York, NY, 10022, U.S.A. Tel: (212) 752-1700

Niigata: 3rd floor, Maruyama Bldg., 1-63, 3-chome, Yoneyama, Niigata, Japan. Tel: (025) 243-4771/2

Osaka: 12 Mitsudera-cho, Minami-ku, Osaka, Japan. Tel: (06) 213-1401

San Francisco: 3500 Clay Street, San Francisco, CA, 94118, U.S.A.. Tel: (415) 921-2251

Sao Paulo: Avenida Paulista 453, Andar-11, Cerqueira Csar CEP 01311 Sao Paulo, Brazil. Tel: 288-3455

Sapporo: Kita 3-cho Nisi 21-chome, Chuo-ku, Sapporo, Japan. Tel: 621-0288/9

Seattle: Ste. 1125, United Airlines Bldg., 2033 Sixth Avenue, Seattle, WA, 98121, U.S.A. Tel: (206) 441-1011/4

Sendai: 5-22, Kamisugi, 5-chome, Sendai, Japan. Tel: (022) 221-2751/4

Shimonoseki: 13-10, 2-chome, Higashi, Yamatomachi, Shimonoseki, Japan. Tel: (0832) 66-5341/4

Sydney: 12/F, 115 Pitt Street, Sydney, N.S.W., Australia. Tel: (02) 221-3866

## TOURIST DIRECTORY

Toronto: 439 University Ave., Ste. 700, Toronto, Ontario M5G 1Y8, Canada. Tel: (416) 598-4608/10

Vancouver: 830-1066 West Hastings Street, Vancouver, B.C. V6E 3X1 Canada. Tel: (604) 681-9581

Yokohama: 118 Yamatecho, Naka-ku, Yokohama, Japan. Tel: 001-8145, 621-4531/3

# Prominent Figures of
# the Republic of Korea

| NAME | POSITION |
| --- | --- |
| Cho Sangho | Minister of Sports |
| Choi Kwangsoo | Minister of Foreign Affairs |
| Chun Doohwan | Former President, Republic of Korea (ROK) |
| Chung Ilkwon | Former Prime Minister, Speaker of National Assembly, Chairman of Joint Chiefs of Staff, and Ambassador to United States |
| Chung Juyong | Honorary Chairman, Hyundai Business Group; President, Federation of Korean Industries |
| Chung Seyong | Chairman, Hyundai Business Group |
| Jeong Hanmo | Minister of Culture |
| Kim Daejung | President, Peace Democratic Party |
| Kim Jaesoon | Speaker, National Assembly |
| Kim Jongpil | President, New Democratic Republican Party |
| Kim Sanghong | Chairman, Samyang Business Group |
| Kim Sanghyup | Former Prime Minister; Honorary President, Korea University |
| Kim Sangman | Honorary Chairman, Dong-A Ilbo (Newspaper) |
| Kim Sangmoon | Chairman, Kia Business Group |
| Kim Seungyoun | Chairman, Korea Explosives Business Group |
| Kim Sukwon | Chairman, Ssangyong Business Group |
| Kim Woochoong | Chairman, Daewoo Business Group |
| Kim Youngsam | President, Reunification Democratic Party |
| Koo Chakyung | Chairman, Lucky-Gold Star Business Group |
| Lee Bumjun | Minister of Transportation |
| Lee Dongchan | Chairman, Kolon Business Group |
| Lee Hyunjae | Prime Minister |
| Lee Kunhee | Chairman, Samsung Business Group |
| Nam Duckwoo | Chairman, Korean Foreign Trade Association; Former Prime Minister |
| Park Dongjin | Ambassador to the United States |
| Park Sejik | Former President Seoul Olympic Organizing Committee (SLOOC) |
| Park Seongyang | Chairman, Kumho Business Group |
| Park Yongsung | Chairman, Doosan Business Group |
| Roh Taewoo | President, Republic of Korea; President, Democratic Justice Party; Former President, SLOOC |
| Shin Kyukho | Chairman, Lotte Business Group |

# CIVIC ORGANIZATIONS IN KOREA

| | | | |
|---|---|---|---|
| American Chamber of | | Korea Golf Association | 266-0487 |
| Commerce | 753-6471 | Korea House | 266-9101 |
| American Cultural Center | 722-2601 | Korea National Tourism | |
| American Legion Int'l Club | 51-1046 | Corp. | 261-7001 |
| American Red Cross | YS-3888 | Korea Social Communication | |
| Boy Scouts of America | YS-4890 | Research Institute | |
| Boy Scouts of Korea | 782-1867 | ("Korea Friend" | |
| Christian Literature Society | | Newsletter) | 722-2853 |
| of Korea | 724-1792 | Korea Tourist Association | 724-2702 |
| Christian Servicemen Center | YS-6445 | Korea Trade Promotion | |
| Clark Hatch's Physical | | Corp. (KOTRA) | 753-4181 |
| Fitness Center | 752-5269 | Korea Trade Service Center | 778-2151 |
| Cultural & Social Center | | Korea Trading Agencies | |
| for the Asian and | | Assoc. | 782-2205 |
| Pacific Region (ASPAC) | 633-7822 | Korean American Assoc. | 753-1876 |
| Eighth Army Golf Club | 7904-4340 | Korean American Business | |
| Eighth Army Officers Club | YS-5988 | Institute | 725-4181 |
| Family Sports Club | 793-5653 | Korean Classical Music | |
| Fulbright House | 752-0273 | Association | 724-7908 |
| Girl Scouts of America | YS-4890 | Korean National Red Cross | 777-9301 |
| Girl Scouts of Korea | 723-4347 | Korean Scuba Diving Club | 92-9065 |
| Hankang Bowling Center | 794-7041 | Korean Traders' | |
| Harvard Business Club | | Association | 268-8251 |
| of Korea | 753-7750 | Korea Veterans | |
| Hillside House | | Association | 269-5171 |
| (Servicemen's Center) | 794-6951 | Lions International | |
| International Cultural | | (Dist. 309-Korea) | 266-8566 |
| Society of Korea (ICSK) | 753-6461 | Lutheran Servicemen's | |
| Int'l Human | | Center | 794-6274 |
| Assistance Program | 723-0231 | Moyer Service Club | |
| International Pen Club | | (8th Army) | 7904-3921 |
| (Korea Chapter) | 725-9854 | Naija R & R Center | 753-5580 |
| International Press | | Namsan Athletic Club | 792-0131 |
| Institute | 724-6055 | Red Cross of Korea | 777-9301 |
| Int'l Society for Oriental | | Royal Asiatic Society (RAS) | |
| Medicine | 724-7388 | | 763-9483 |
| Journalists Association | | Sae Seoul Lions Club | 462-9093 |
| of Korea (JAK) | 725-6851 | Scandinavian Club | 265-9279 |
| Korea Amateur Sports Assoc. | 777-6081 | Seoul Club | 362-3129 |
| Korea America Friendship | | Seoul Jaycees | 244-6023 |
| Assoc. | 783-6137 | Seoul Union Club | |
| Korea Art & | | (inter-church) | 752-2871 |
| Culture Promotion | 762-5230 | UNESCO | 776-3950 |
| Korea Assoc. of | | UNICEF | 725-2315 |
| Registered Architects | 723-9491 | UNDP | 633-9451 |
| Korea Assoc. of | | Union Church | |
| Voluntary Agencies | 269-6973 | (Interdenominational) | 724-4772 |
| Korea Chamber of | | USO Club          YS-7301 | 793-3478 |
| Commerce | 777-8031 | YWCA | 777-5725 |
| Korea Foreign Counselling | | YMCA | 722-8291 |
| Service | 32-4647 | Yongsan Library | YS-3380 |

# THE FOREIGN CAPITAL INDUCEMENT ACT

## CHAPTER I. General Provisions

**Article 1. (Purpose)** The purpose of this Act shall be to effectively induce and protect foreign capital conductive to the sound development of the national economy and the improvement of the international balance of payments, and to properly manage such foreign capital.

**Article 2. (Definition)** As used in this Act, unless the context otherwise requires, the term:

1. "Foreign National" shall mean an individual who has a foreign nationality or a juridical person organized under the laws of a foreign country (hereinafter referred to as "Foreign Corporation") or an economic cooperative organization.

2. "National of the Republic of Korea" shall mean an individual who has the nationality of the Republic of Korea. Provided, however, that the provisions of this Act relevant to a foreign national shall also apply to an individual who has the nationality of the Republic of Korea and who has been a permanent resident of a foreign country.

3. "Juridical Person of the Republic of Korea" shall mean a juridical person organized under the laws of the Republic of Korea (including local autonomous entities).

4. "Foreign Investor" shall mean a foreign national who has subscribed for or owns stock or shares in accordance with this Act.

5. "Foreign Invested Enterprise" shall mean an enterprise in which a foreign investor has an equity interest and which is registered in compliance with Article 12.

6. "Subject Matter of Investment" shall mean any of the following items to be invested by a foreign investor for subscribing to or owning stock or shares in accordance with this Act.

   a. Foreign means of payment as prescribed by the Foreign Exchange Control Law or domestic means of payment arising in exchange therefor.

   b. Capital goods.

   c. Profit accruing from stock or shares acquired in accordance with this Act.

   d. Industrial property rights or any other technology equivalent thereto and any right to use it.

7. "Capital Goods" shall mean machinery, equipment, facilities, tools, parts, accessories, livestock, seeds, trees, fish and shell fish used as industrial facilities (including ships, vehicles, airplanes, etc.), as well as raw materials and spare parts which the competent Minister deems necessary for the initial test operation (including experimental projects) of the industrial facilities induced, including freight and insurance fees to be incurred by such inducement, and the technology or service to construct a facility or to provide advice.

8. "Raw Materials" shall mean primary materials, and other materials necessary for key industries or agriculture, forestry and fisheries, as well as freight and insurance fees to be incurred by such inducement.

9. "Foreign Capital" shall mean any of the following items, prior to a cancellation by the Minister of Finance of that nature of foreign capital.

   a. Subject matter of investment as prescribed in Item 6.

   b. Technology induced under a technology inducement agreement.

   c. Capital goods, raw materials, foreign means of payment induced in accordance with a loan contract or a public loan agreement, domestic means of payment, capital goods or raw materials acquired in exchange therefor.

10. "Loan Contract" shall mean a contract in which a national of the Republic of Korea or a juridical person of the Republic of Korea either borrows a foreign means of payment or induces capital goods or raw materials in the form of a long-term settlement from a foreign national (excluding an economic cooperation organization) and which falls within the scope of such agreement as prescribed by Presidential Decree.

11. "Public Loan Agreement" shall mean a contract or an agreement in which the government of the Republic of Korea either borrows a foreign means of payment or induces capital goods, raw materials, etc. under an export credit arrangement from a foreign government, economic cooperation organization, foreign juridical person or in which a juridical person of the Republic of Korea either borrows a foreign means of payment or induces capital goods, raw materials, etc. under an export credit arrangement from a foreign government or economic cooperation organization.

12. "Technology Inducement Contract" shall mean a contract in which a national of the Republic of Korea or a juridical person of the Republic of Korea purchases industrial property rights or any other technology from a foreign national, or induces the right to use thereof and which falls within the scope as prescribed by Presidential Decree.

13. "Borrower" shall mean the government of the the Republic of Korea, a national of the Republic of Korea, or a juridical person of the Republic of Korea who has an obligation (excluding a guarantee obligation) to a lender under a loan contract or a public loan agreement, or the one who assumes his obligation.

14. "Subborrower" shall mean one who subborrows all or part of a public loan in which the government of the Republic of Korea is a borrower and carries out the loan project concerned.

15. "Lender" shall mean a foreign government or a foreign national who has a claim against a borrower under a loan contract or a public loan agreement or the one to whom such claim is assigned.

### Article 3. (Criteria for the Inducement of Foreign Capital)

Paragraph 1. A national of the Republic of Korea, a juridical person of the Republic of Korea, or a foreign national may induce foreign capital in accordance with this Act, except any of the following items.

1. In case of causing trouble to the safety of the nation and the maintenance of public order.
2. In case of causing a negative effect upon the sound development of the national economy.
3. In case of violating the laws of the Republic of Korea.

Paragraph 2. The government shall not approve or accept a report concerning the inducement of foreign capital falling under any of the items in Paragraph 1.

### Article 4. (Guarantee of Overseas Remittance)
The overseas remittance of dividends of profit accruing from the stock or shares acquired by a foreign investor, sales proceeds of the stock or shares, principal, interest and fees to be paid under a loan contract or a public loan agreement, and royalties to be paid under a technology inducement contract shall be guaranteed in accordance with the contents of the approval, acceptance of the report or the agreement as of the r mittance.

### Article 5. (National Treatment)

Paragraph 1. A foreign investor and a foreign invested enterprise shall be treated equally as a national of the Republic of Korea or a juridical person of the Republic of Korea with regard to its business except where especially stipulated by laws.

Paragraph 2. Provisions of the laws relating to tax exemption or reduction applicable to a national of the Republic of Korea or a juridical person of the Republic of Korea shall also apply equally to a foreign investor, a foreign invested enterprise, a lender and a technology licensor under Article 23.

**Article 6. (Guarantee on Property Invested by Foreign Nationals)** Property right of a foreign investor and a foreign invested enterprise shall be guaranteed in accordance with the provisions of the laws.

## CHAPTER II. Investment by Foreign Nationals
**Article 7. (Approval of Investment by Foreign Nationals)**

Paragraph 1. In the event that a foreign national intends to subscribe for the stock or own the shares of a juridical person of the Republic of Korea (including a juridical person under incorporation) or an enterprise carried out by a national of the Republic of Korea (hereinafter referred to as "Foreign Investment"), an approval of the Minister of Finance shall be obtained in advance.

Paragraph 2. The Minister of Finance shall approve a foreign investment without delay unless it falls under any of the fllowing items. In this case, consultation with the competent Minister shall not be required notwithstanding the provision of Article 35.

1. In the event that the ratio of stock subscribed for or owned shares is fifty (50) percent or more; provided, except where a foreign invested enterprise exports self-manufactured products of a percentage as prescribed by Presidential Decree, or more, or imports of the self-manufactured products, the tariff rate of which is not more than a rate as prescribed by Presidential Decree, is liberalized.
2. In the event that the amount of stock subscribed for or owned shares exceeds the amount as prescribed by Presidential Decree.
3. In the event that the tax benefits under Paragraph 1, Article 14 are desired.
4. In the event that an investment is made in a project in which a foreign investment is restricted. In this case, the Minister of Finance shall select and give public notice of the project in which a foreign investment is restricted after consultation with the competent Minister in accordance with the criteria prescribed by Presidential Decree.

Paragraph 3. In the event that a foreign investment falls under any of the items in Paragraph 2, the Minister of Finance shall determine whether an approval of the foreign investment will be granted and whether the investment satisfies the criteria of tax exemption and reduction prescribed in Paragraph 1, Article 14 and shall so notify the applicant. In this case, the Minister of Finance shall consult with the competent Minister in advance.

Paragraph 4. When he deems it necessary, the Minister of Finance may attach conditions to an approval in accordance with the provisions of Paragraph 1.

Paragraph 5. In the event that a foreign investor intends to change the contents of approval, an approval of the Minister of Finance shall be obtained, provided, however, that an approval shall be replaced by a report to the Minister of Finance in the case of change in minor matters as prescribed by Presidential Decree.

**Article 8. (Report of Foreign Investment)** In the event that a foreign investor intends to acquire stock or shares falling under any of the following items, he shall report to the Minister of Finance notwithstanding the provision of Article 7.

1. In the event that a foreign investor acquires stock to be issued as a result of a transfer of reserved surplus or revaluation reserve into the capital of the foreign invested enterprise concerned.
2. In the event that a foreign investor acquires the stock or shares of a

remaining or newly-incorporated juridical person after a merger with another enterprise in exchange for his stock or shares of the foreign invested enterprise concerned at the time of such merger.

3. In the event that a foreign investor acquires the stock to be newly issued as a result of the division or consolidation of the stock owned by the foreign investor.

4. In the event that a foreign national acquires the stock or shares of a foreign invested enterprise from a foreign investor by means of purchase, inheritance, bequeath or gift.

5. In the event that a foreign investor intends to convert into stock convertible debentures which have received on approval of a loan contract in accordance with the provision of Paragraph 1, Article 19.

### Article 9 (Prohibition of Foreign Investment)

Paragraph 1. Projects, in which foreign investment is prohibited, shall be as follows:

1. Public projects to be carried out by the nation or public organizations.

2. Projects which cause harm to the health and sanitation of the nationals and maintenance of the environment.

3. Projects which are greatly in violation of public policy.

4. Any other project prescribed by Presidential Decree.

Paragraph 2. The contents of each of the items in Paragraph 1 shall be determined by Presidential Decree.

### Article 10. (Investment by Dividends)

Paragraph 1. A foreign investor may invest profit dividends accruing from the stock or shares acquired in accordance with this Act in a juridical person of the Republic of Korea or an enterprise operated by a national of the Republic of Korea.

Paragraph 2. A foreign investor shall report to the Minister of Finance in the event that he intends to invest dividends of profit in the foreign invested enterprise concerned in accordance with Paragraph 1, and shall obtain an approval in accordance with Article 7 in the event that he intends to invest in any other juridical person of the Republic of Korea orany other enterprise operated by a national of the Republic of Korea.

### Article 11. (Payment of the Subject Matter of Investment) A foreign investor shall complete the payment of the subject matters of investment within two years from the date of approval under Article 7. Provided, however, that this period may be extended with the approval of the Minister of Finance.

### Article 12. (Registration of Foreign Invested Enterprise) In the event that a foreign investor completes payment in accordance with Article 11, he shall register with the registry of foreign invested enterprises maintained by the Minister of Finance. The foregoing shall also apply to capital increases.

### Article 13. (Restriction on Disposition of Foreign Capital)

Paragraph 1. Anyone who intends to sell, assign or lease foreign capital induced by a foreign invested enterprise or to use it for purposes other than approved shall obtain in advance permission from the Minister of Finance. Provided, however, that permission shall be replaced by a prior report to the Minister of Finance in the case of minor matters prescribed by Presidential Decree.

Paragraph 1. Income tax, corporation tax, acquisition tax and property tax shall be exempt in accordance with Paragraphs 2 through 4 if a foreign investment, the purpose of which is to carry out any of the following items, meets the standards prescribed by Presidential Decree.

### Article 14. (Exemption of Income Tax, etc.)

Paragraph 1. Income tax, corporation tax, acquisition tax and property tax shall be exempt in accordance with Paragraphs 2 through 4 if a foreign investment, the purpose of which is to carry out any of the following items, meets the standards prescribed by Presidential Decree.

1. A project which makes a significant contribution to the improvement of the international balance of payments.
2. A project which is accompanied by advanced technology or large amounts of capital.
3. A project in which a non-resident Korean national invests in accordance with the Law concerning the Registration of Non-resident Korean Nationals.
4. A project which is located in a Free Export Zone in accordance with the Free Export Zone Establishment Law.
5. Any other project designated by Presidential Decree as a project for which tax reduction or exemption is essential in order to induce foreign investment.

Paragraph 2. Either of the following two alternative methods shall be applicable with regard to the exemption and reduction of income tax or corporation tax of a foreign invested enterprise.

1. Income tax or corporation tax on the foreign invested enterprise shall be exempt in proportion to the ratio of the stock or shares owned by foreign investors to the stock or shares of the enterprise concerned (hereinafter referred to as "foreign investment ratio") for five years after the tax year commencing first following the registration in accordance with the provisions of Article 12 only up to the income accruing from carrying out the business approved in accordance with Paragraph 1.
2. An amount equal to 100% of the ceiling of allowable depreciation, calculated in accordance with the provisions of Article 43 of the Income Tax Law or Item 12, Article 16 of the Corporation Tax Law, multiplied by the foreign investment ratio with regard to the fixed assets used in the approved project shall be incorporated into necessary expense or expense as special depreciation for calculating the taxable income for each tax year. In this case, if the sum of special depreciation for each year exceeds the amount invested by a foreign investor in the enterprise concerned, the excess amount shall not be incorporated into necessary expense or expense.

Paragraph 3. Income tax or corporation tax on the dividends accruing from the stock or shares acquired by a foreign investor shall be exempt up to the income accruing for five years after the tax year commencing first following the registration of the foreign invested enterprise.

Paragraph 4. Acquisition tax and property tax on the properties acquired and held by a foreign invested enterprise in order to carry out an approved project shall be exempt for five years from the date of registration in proportion to the foreign investment ratio of the enterprise concerned only in the situation where the properties were acquired and held after the registration of the enterprise concerned. Provided, however, that in the event that the enterprise, in which a foreign investor who has obtained an approval of foreign investment invests, has any property acquired before the registration for the original purpose of the project concerned, acquisition tax and property tax shall be exempt for five years from the date of acquisition of the properties in proportion to the foreign investment ratio of the enterprise concerned.

Paragraph 5. In accordance with the provisions of the Presidential Decree, the tax exemption or reduction period pursuant to Paragraph 2, Item 1 or Paragraph 3 may be selected, and applied for, from the tax year commencing first following the registration of the foreign invested enterprise to the tax year ending within ten years.

Paragraph 6. In the event a foreign investor or a foreign invested enterprise intends to submit an application for exemption or reduction in accordance with Paragraphs 2 through 4, such application shall be submitted concurrently with the application for approval in accordance with Article 7 and Article 10.

**Article 15. (Exemption and Reduction of Customs Duties, etc.)**

Paragraph 1. Customs duties, special consumption tax and value added tax on capital goods in each of the following items to be induced in compliance with the contents of approval in accordance with Article 7 and Article 10 shall be exempt or reduced in accordance with the provisions of the Presidential Decree, provided, however, that the foregoing shall not apply to capital goods designated by Presidential Decree.

1. Capital goods to be induced by a foreign investor as a subject matter of investment.
2. Capital goods induced by an enterprise in which a foreign investor invests, by means of dividends received by a foreign investor from a foreign invested enterprise or by means of foreign means of payment invested by a foreign investor.

Paragraph 2. The exemption or reduction in Paragraph 1 may be waived upon application.

**Article 16. (Tax Exemption or Reduction in Case of Capital Increase)**

Paragraph 1. In the event of an increase in the capital of a foreign invested enterprise, Article 14 and Article 15 shall apply, mutatis mutandis, to the tax exemption or reduction concerning the increased capital. In this case, the exemption or reduction period applicable to the increase in capital shall be from the beginning date of the tax year commencing first following the registration of the increase in capital to the tax year ending within five years, notwithstanding the provision of Paragraph 5, Article 14.

Paragraph 2. The tax exemptions or reductions relating to stock acquired by a foreign investor as a result of a transfer of reserved surplus or revaluation reserves into capital in accordance with Item 1, Article 8 shall follow the tax exemptions or reductions relating to the original stock which was the basis of such acquisition.

**Article 17. (Retroactive Collection of Tax)**

Paragraph 1. The director of a district tax office may collect retroactively income tax or corporation tax exempted in accordance with the provision of Item 1, Paragraph 2, Article 14 or may ignore the depreciation incorporated into necessary expense or expense for the calculation of the amount of income in accordance with Item 2, Paragraph 2, Article 14 in each of the following cases:

1. In the event that the approval is cancelled or the registration is deregistered in accordance with the provisions of Article 18.
2. In the event that the contents of the approval or the conditions attached to the approval are not complied with as prescribed by Presidential Decree.

Paragraph 2. The director of a district tax office or the director of a customs office may collect retroactively customs duties, special consumption tax and value added tax exempted or reduced in accordance with Article 15 in each of the following cases:

1. In the event that the approval is cancelled or the registration is deregistered in accordance with the provisions of Article 18.
2. In the event that foreign capital is used or disposed of for purposes other than as approved.
3. In the event that the contents of the approval or the conditions attached to the approval are not complied with as prescribed by Presidential Decree.

Paragraph 3. The chief of a local autonomous entity may collect retroactively acquisition tax and property tax exempted in accordance with the provision of Paragraph 4, Article 14, in each of the following cases. In the case of Item 2, when the changed ratio of stockholding or shareholding becomes less than the ratio of stockholding or shareholding as of the time of the exemption, a tax on the amount equivalent to the decrease in the ratio shall be collected retroactively.

1. In the event that an enterprise described in the proviso to Paragraph 4, Article 14, does not pay the subject matter of investment within the period prescribed in Article 11.
2. In the event that, as a result of a change of the stockholding or shareholding ratio of a foreign investor after the exemption of tax in accordance with the provision of the proviso to Paragraph 4, Article 14, the stockholding or shareholding ratio of a foreign investor becomes less than the stockholding or shareholding ratio as of the exemption.
3. In the event that the approval is cancelled or the registration is deregistered in accordance with the provisions of Article 18.
4. In the event that the contents of the approval or the conditions attached to the approval are not complied with as prescribed by Presidential Decree.

**Article 18. (Cancellation of Approval, etc.)** The Minister of Finance may cancel an approval or deregister a registration in the event that a foreign investor or a foreign invested enterprise falls under any of the following items:

1. In the event that a foreign investor does not pay the subject matter of investment within the period prescribed in Article 11.
2. In the event that a foreign invested enterprise does not conduct business activities continuously for two (2) years or longer.
3. In the event that an order for correction or necessary measure in accordance with Paragraph 3, Article 39 is not complied with.
4. In the event there occurs cause for dissolution of a foreign invested enterprise.
5. In the event that a foreign investor makes such a request.

## CHAPTER III. Loan Contract

**Article 19. (Approval of Loan Contract)**

Paragraph 1. When a national of the Republic of Korea or a juridical person of the Republic of Korea enters into a loan contract with a foreign national (excluding economic cooperation organizations), an approval of the Minister of Finance shall be obtained. This provision shall also apply when any change is made to the contract concerned.

Paragraph 2. If the Minister of Finance deems it necessary, he may attach conditions to the approval referred to in Paragraph 1.

Paragraph 3. The loan contract approved pursuant to Paragraph 1 must be enforced within six (6) months from the date of approval. This period, however, may be extended with the approval of the Minister of Finance.

**Article 20. (Restriction on Disposition of Foreign Capital, etc.)** Anyone who intends to sell, assign or lease foreign capital induced through a loan contact, or to use it for purposes other than approved shall obtain permission from the Minister of Finance in advance.

**Article 21. (Exemption and Reduction of Taxes with Respect to Interests on a Loan)**

Paragraph 1. Income tax or corporation tax shall not be assessed upon the interest accruing to a lender in accordance with the contents of a loan contract approved pursuant to the provision of Article 19 or other income derived directly in relation thereto.

Paragraph 2. Taxes referred to in Paragraph 1 may be assessed upon the request of the lender.

**Article 22. (Cancellation of Approval)** The Minister of Finance may, when a borrower of a loan contract has failed to enforce the contract concerned within the period prescribed in Paragraph 3 of Article 19, cancel the approval.

## CHAPTER IV. Technology Inducement Contract
### Article 23. (Report of Technology Inducement Contract)

Paragraph 1. In the event that a national of the Republic of Korea or a juridical person of the Republic of Korea executes a technology inducement contract with a foreign national, he shall report to the Minister of Finance. The foregoing shall also apply to a change of the contract concerned.

Paragraph 2. The Minister of Finance may request a supplement to or adjustment of, the contents of the report referred to in Paragraph 1 in accordance with the provisions of the Presidential Decree.

Paragraph 3. The report referred to in Paragraph 1 shall be deemed to be accepted at the date when twenty days have passed from the date of the report without a request for a supplement or an adjustment as provided for in Paragraph 2. Provided, however, that the Minister of Finance requests a supplement to, or an adjustment of the contents of the report, the report shall be accepted after the request has been complied with.

Paragraph 4. A technology inducement contract for which a report is accepted in accordance with Paragraph 1 shall become effective within six (6) months of the date of the acceptance of the report, provided, however, that the period may be extended with the approval of the Minister of Finance.

Paragraph 5. A report of a technology inducement contract which has not become effective within the period provided for in Paragraph 4 shall be deemed null and void.

### Article 24. (Tax Exemption or Reduction on Royalties)

Paragraph 1. Income tax or corporation tax shall be exempt for five (5) years from the date of acceptance of a report of the contract concerned with regard to the royalties to be acquired by the technology licensor in accordance with the contents of a technology inducement contract, the report of which has been accepted in accordance with Article 23.

Paragraph 2. The tax exemption provided for in Paragraph 1 may be waived upon the request of the technology licensor.

## CHAPTER V. Public Loan Agreement
### Article 25. (Public Loan Inducement Program)

Paragraph 1. A government agency or a juridical person of the Republic of Korea who intends to induce foreign capital through a public loan agreement (hereinafter referred to as a "Public Loan") in accordance with this Law shall submit an application therefor to the Minister of Finance.

Paragraph 2. In the case of receiving an application referred to in Paragraph 1, and deciding to promote the public loan project, the Minister of Finance shall establish a public loan inducement program specifying the contents of the projects, loan amounts, and expected lenders and terms and conditions and other necessary matters concerning each public loan project.

Paragraph 3. The Government shall obtain a resolution of the National Assembly in advance on the public loan inducement program referred to in Paragraph 2. If any of the following situations occur regarding the public loan inducement program with respect to which a resolution of the National Assembly has been obtained, a resolution of the National Assembly shall be obtained again thereon:

1. When the loan amount for a project exceeds that resolved by the National Assembly.

2. When the terms and conditions of a loan for a project deteriorate as compared with that resolved by the National Assembly.

3. When the content of a project is changed substantially as compared with that resolved by the National Assembly.

Paragraph 4. Without delay the Minister of Finance shall notify the applicants and related agencies of its decision as to whether to promote the public loan inducement concerned in accordance with the public loan inducement program, with respect to which a resolution of the National Assembly has been obtained.

**Article 26. (Conclusion of Public Loan Agreements)**

Paragraph 1. The Minister of Finance, on behalf of the Government, shall carry out the negotiation and coordination necessary for implementing the public loan inducement program referred to in Paragraph 2 of Article 25, and conclude public loan after obtaining a resolution of the National Assembly pursuant to the provision of Paragraph 3 of Article 25. Provided, however, that the borrower of a public loan is a juridical person of the Republic of Korea, such juridical person shall conclude the public loan agreement.

Paragraph 2. The public loan agreement concluded by a juridical person of the Republic of Korea pursuant of the proviso of Paragraph 1 and vairous contracts which are related thereto and which directly affect the conclusion of the agreement concerned, shall be approved in advance by the Minister of Finance. This provision shall also apply to any change thereto.

Paragraph 3. The Minister of Finance may, pursuant to the provisions of the Presidential Decree, relend a public loan, the borrower of which is the Government, in whole or in part to a government agency or a juridical person of the Republic of Korea which will carry out the project concerned.

Paragraph 4. Upon the conclusion of a public loan agreement pursuant to the provisions of Paragraph 1, the Minister of Finance shall give public notice regarding the same in the Official Gazette without delay.

**Article 27. (Restriction on Disposition of Foreign Capital, etc.)** Anyone who intends to sell, assign or lease foreign capital induced through a public loan agreement or to use it for purposes other than approved shall obtain in advance permission from the Minister of Finance.

**Article 28. (Exemption of Taxes, Public Charges, etc.)**

Paragraph 1. The taxes, public charges or the like to be imposed upon the lenders directly in connection with the inducement of a public loan shall be exempt or reduced, as provided for in the public loan agreement concerned.

Paragraph 2. Income tax or corporation tax to be imposed upon the remuneration paid to foreigners for the provision of technology or service in connection with the inducement of a public loan shall be exempt or reduced, as provided for in the public loan agreement concerned.

Paragraph 3. The exemption or reduction of taxes, public charges or the like referred to in Paragraphs 1 and 2 may be waived upon the request made by a lender or a person rendering such technology or service.

## CHAPTER VI. Payment Guarantee

**Article 29. (Payment Guarantee)**

Paragraph 1. A banking institution may issue payment guarantees for the obligations arising under a loan contract or a public loan agreement.

Paragraph 2. The Government may issue payment guarantees for the obligations arising under a public loan agreement for those projects for which it is deemed to be difficult for banking institutions to issue payment guarantees.

Paragraph 3. When the Government intends to issue a payment guarantee in accordance with the provision of Paragraph 2, it shall obtain a resoluton of the

National Assembly in advance. Provided, however, that matters regarding the issuance of payment guarantees by the Government are specified in the public loan inducement program with respect which a resolution of the National Assembly has been obtained pursuant to the provision of Paragraph 3 of Article 35, a resolution of the National Assembly shall be deemed to be adopted with respect to the issuance of payment guarantees by the Government for the projects concerned.

Paragraph 4. Any person intending to obtain a payment guarantee of the Government pursuant to the provision of Paragraph 2 shall apply to the Minister of Finance for an approval of the payment guarantee.

Paragraph 5. The Minister of Finance shall, when granting an approval referred to in Paragraph 4, obtain an approval of the President after deliberation of the State Council.

**Article 30. (Creation and Management of Security Interest)** The Minister of Finance shall acquire and safeguard security interests corresponding to the amount of payment guarantees to the Government approved pursuant to the provision of Paragraph 5 of Article 29 and the amount reloaned pursuant to the provision of Paragraph 3 of Article 26. Provided, however, that this provision shall not apply to local governments, government invested institutions and such persons as are provided in the Presidential Decree.

**Article 31. (Compulsory Disposition of Secured Property)**

Paragraph 1. When a juridical person which has obtained a payment guarantee of the Government to induce a public loan (hereinafter referred to as the "Government Guaranteed Juridical Person") has failed, in whole or in part, to perform its obligations for which the payment guarantee was issued, the Minister of Finance may dispose of the secured property acquired pursuant to the provisions of Article 30. This provision shall also apply to the relending provided for in Paragraph 3 of Article 26.

Paragraph 2. Notwithstanding the provisions of the Civil Code, the Code of Civil Procedure, and the Auction Act, the procedure for disposal of the secured property pursuant to Paragraph 1 may be effected pursuant to the procedures used in cases of delinquent tax payment under the National Tax Collection Law.

**Article 32. (Joint Liability of Executive Officers)**

Paragraph 1. Directors or executive officers of a government guaranteed juridical person or the borrower of relending (excluding government agencies) shall be jointly and severely liable for the compensation of all losses incurred by the Government due to the government payment guarantee or the relending of a public loan. In such a case, such director or executve officer, even if he is discharged from office, shall not be exempt from liability for losses incurred while he was in office.

Paragraph 2. The collection of compensation pursuant to the provisions of Paragraph 1 shall be carried out pursuant to the procedures used in cases of delinquent payment.

**Article 33. (Supervision of Government Guaranteed Juridical Persons, etc.)** The Minister of Finance or person designated by the Minister of Finance may, if it is deemed necessary for securing a claim upon subrogation in connection with a government payment guarantee or the relending of public loans and for attaining the purposes of the public loan projects, inspect the status of business operations and the property of the government guaranteed juridical person concerned or the borrower of the relending concerned and may take necessary measures including a demand for additional security.

## CHAPTER VII. Supplementary Provisions

**Article 34. (Report of Foreign Capital Inducement to the National Assembly)** Ninety days prior to the end of each fiscal year, the Minister of Finance shall prepare a report to the National Assembly concerning each of the following items.

1. Matters regarding the status of foreign capital inducement up to and including the previous year.
2. Matters regarding the result of the execution of the plan of public loan inducement which was resolved by the National Assembly in accordance with the provision of Paragraph 3, Article 25.

**Article 35. (Consultation)** The Minister of Finance shall consult in advance with the competent Ministers regarding those matters deemed important in granting on approval permission, authorization, or cancellation in accordance with the provisions of this Act.

**Article 36. (Review and Confirmation of Induced Foreign Capital)** The competent Minister may review and confirm the capital goods or raw materials to be induced under this Act and may not allow the inducement of the capital goods or raw materials concerned in accordance with the provisions of the Presidential Decree.

**Article 37. (Foreign Capital Inducement Deliberation Committee)**

Paragraph 1. A Foreign Capital Inducement Deliberation Committee (hereinafter referred to as the "Committee") shall be established under the Ministry of Finance in order to deliberate and render decisions on the following matters relevant to the inducement of foreign capital under this Act.

1. Important matters regarding the policy of foreign capital inducement.
2. Important matters regarding tax exemption or reduction.
3. Matters regarding foreign investment, loan contract, technology inducement contract or public loan agreements as prescribed by Presidential Decree.

Paragraph 2. Matters necessary for the composition, functions and any other operation of the Committee shall be prescribed by Presidential Decree.

Paragraph 3. The members of the Committee, who were not public officials, shall be deemed public officials in the application of the Criminal Code or the penal provisions of other laws applicable to a crime committee with regard to their duties.

**Article 38. (Report)**

Paragraph 1. Anyone who has induced foreign capital in accordance with this Act shall submit an inducement report to the Minister of Finance not later than one (1) month from the date of inducement or customs clearance of the foreign capital concerned.

Paragraph 2. The Minster of Finance and the competent Ministers may order a foreign investor, a foreign invested enterprise, borrower, subborrower, technology licensee, the governor of the Bank, the governor of the relevant financial institutions and any other interested person to report those matters deemed necessary with regard to the inducement and management of foreign capital in accordance with this Act.

**Article 39. (Investigation, Correction and Disposition)**

Paragraph 1. The Minister of Finance may cause his subordinate public officials or chiefs of the agencies relevant to the inducement of foreign capital to investigate the status of the inducement or use of foreign capital when he deems it necessary with regard to the operation of this Law.

Paragraph 2. The persons performing investigations in accordance with the provisions of Paragraph 1 shall have in their possession emblems showing such authority and shall present such emblems to the relevant persons.

Paragraph 3. The Minister of Finance may order correction or take necessary measures against such person who has induced or uses foreign capital concerned or any other interested person when illegal or unjust matters are found as a result of an investigation in accordance with Paragraph 1.

**Article 40. (Customs Clearance and Disposal of Foreign Capital)**

Paragraph 1. Any person importing foreign capital under this Act shall clear such foreign capital through customs and receive it within the storage period provided by the Customs Law.

Paragraph 2. When a person importing foreign capital fails to clear such foreign capital through customs and receive it within the period provided in Paragraph 1, the director of the customs office may sell such capital in the manner prescribed by Presidential Decree.

**Article 41. (Relationship with Other Laws)**

Paragraph 1. Except where otherwise specifically provided for in this Act, matters regarding foreign exchange and foreign transaction in this Act shall be subject to the provisions of the Foreign Exchange Control Law.

Paragraph 2. With regard to the inducement of foreign capital under this Act, an approval by the Minister of Finance or an acceptance of a report by the Minister of Finance in accordance with the provisions of Article 7, Article 10, Article 19 and Article 23 shall be deemed an import license under the Foreign Trade Transaction Law. In this case, with regard to a public loan agreement, a review and confirmatoin by the competent Minister in accordance with Article 36 shall be deemed an import license under the Foreign Trade Transaction law.

Paragraph 3. In the event that a foreign investor invests in accordance with the provisions of Article 11, a foreign investor may make a contribution in kind notwithstanding the provisions of Article 294 of the Commercial Code. In this case, a certificate of completion of the investment, by which the Director of the Customs Office confirms the making of the contribution in kind as well as the type, quantity, price and other subject matters, shall be deemed the inquiry report of an inspector in accordance with the provisions of Article 249 or the Non-Litigative Case Procedure Law, notwithstanding the provisions of Article 299 of the Commercial Code. The foregoing shall also apply to an increase in capital.

Paragraph 4. A national of the Republic of Korea or a juridical person of the Republic of Korea, who intends to pursue a project jointly with a foreign investor who obtained an approval in accordance with Article 7, may revaluate the subject matter of investment in accordance with the Assets Revaluation Law, having the first day of each month as the revaluation date, notwithstanding the provisions of Article 4 and Article 38 of the Assets Revaluation Law.

Paragraph 5. In the event that a national of the Republic of Korea or a juridical person of the Republic of Korea fails to pay the subject matter of investment revaluated in accordance with the provision of Paragraph 4 within the period specified in Article 11, such shall be deemed not revaluated under the Assets Revaluation Law.

Paragraph 6. The contents of a public loan agreement concluded in accordance with this law shall be complied with in accordance with the provisions of the contract concerned unless they are in violation of other laws.

**Article 42. (Relationship with International Treaties)** This Law shall not be construed as amending or restricting the provisions of the international treaties concluded and promulgated by the Republic of Korea.

**Article 43. (Fee Supply)** Inducement and management of assistant funds, etc. supplied freely to the Government from foreign government or international organizations, etc. shall be in accordance with the provisions of the Presidential Decree.

**Article 44. (Delegation of Authority)** The Minister of Finance or the competent Minister may delegate or entrust part of the authority provided for in this Act to the chiefs of the agencies relevant to the inducement of foreign capital in accordance with the provisions of the Presidential Decree.

## CHAPTER VIII. Penal Provisions

**Article 45. (Penal Provision)** Anyone who is in violation of the provision of

Article 13, Article 20 or Article 27 shall be subject to penal servitude of up to five (5) years or a criminal fine of up to fifty million (50,000,000) Won.

**Article 46. (Penal Provision)** Anyone who has refused or has rejected, obstructed or evaded an inspection or investigation under the provision of Article 33 or Paragraph 1, Article 39 (including a representative in the case of an enterprise) shall be subject to penal servitude of up to one (1) year or a criminal fine of up to ten million (10,000,000) Won.

**Article 47. (Penal Provision)** Anyone who has not complied with a necessary measure or order in accordance with the provision of Article 33 or Paragraph 3, Article 39 (including a representative in the case of an enterprise) shall be subject to penal servitude of up to one (1) year or a criminal fine of up to ten million (10,000,000) Won.

**Article 48. (Penal Provision)** Anyone who has submitted false documents with regard to an approval, permission or report under this Law or has made a false report provided for in Paragraph 1, Article 38 shall be subject to penal servitude of up to three (3) years or a criminal fine of up to thirty million (30,000,000) Won.

**Article 49. (Penal Provision)** Anyone (including a representative in the case of an enterprise) who has unlawfully transmitted foreign capital abroad with regard to an overseas remittance or the inducement of foreign capital under this act shall be subject to penal servitude not less than one (1) year or a criminal fine not less than two times, but not more than ten times the amount unlawfully transmitted. In this case, the foreign capital unlawfully transmitted shall be confiscated, and if confiscation is impossible, an amount equivalent thereto shall be collected.

**Article 50. (Administrative Fine)**

Paragraph 1. Anyone who has failed to submit an inducement report within the period provided for in Paragraph 1, Article 38 shall be subject to an administrative fine of up to two million (2,000,000) Won.

Paragraph 2. The administrative fine provided for in Paragraph 1 shall be imposed and collected by the Minister of Finance in accordance with the provisions of the Presidential Decree.

Paragraph 3. Anyone who objects to the imposition of an administrative fine provided for in Paragraph 2 may raise a rebuttal to the Minister of Finance not later than thirty days.

Paragraph 4. In the event that anyone, upon whom an administrative fine is imposed in accordance with Paragraph 2, raises a rebuttal in accordance with Paragraph 3, the Minister of Finance shall notify the court having jurisdiction of such fact without delay and the court having jurisdiction notified of such fact shall impose an administrative fine in accordance with the Non-Litigative Case Procedure Law.

Paragraph 5. In the event that a rebuttal is not submitted, nor is the administrative fine paid, not later than the period provided for in Paragraph 3, then such fine shall be collected in accordance with the national tax collection procedure.

**Article 51. (Concurrent Penal Provision)** If a representative of a juridical person or an agent, employee or any other worker of a juridical person or an individual has violated the provisions of Article 45 through Article 49 with regard to the business of such juridical person or such individual, such juridical person or such individual shall also be subject to the criminal fine prescribed in such Article in addition to the punishment of the actual offender.

**Article 52. (Penalty)**

Paragraph 1. In the event that a foreign invested enterprise, which falls within any of the following items, does not export all or part of the manufactured products in accordance with the conditions of approval under this Act, the Minister of Finance shall collect twenty percent of the amount of the products not exported as a penalty except the case prescribed by Presidential Decree.

1. In the event that a foreign invested enterprise has obtained an approval, the contents of which provide for the export of not less than a certain percentage of the manufactured products in accordance with the provision of the proviso to Item 1, Paragraph 2, Article 7.
2. In the event that a foreign invested enterprise has obtained an approval on the condition that not less than a certain percentage of the manufactured products be exported in accordance with the provision of Paragraph 45, Article 7.

Paragraph 2. The method of the calculation of, or the timing of the collection of, the amount of the products not exported under Paragraph 1 shall be determined by Presidential Decree.

Paragraph 3. The National Tax Collection Law shall apply, mutatis mutandis, with regard to the collection of the penalty prescribed in Paragraph 1.

**Article 53. (Prosecution)** Any crime specified in Article 45 through Article 49 shall not be prosecuted unless the Minister of Finance lodges an accusation.

**Addenda**
**Article 1. (Effective Date)** This act shall become effective on July 1, 1984.
**Article 2. (Abolition of Other Laws)** The laws in each of the following items shall be abolished:
1. The Law concerning inducement and Management of Public Loan
2. Foreign Capital Management Law

**Article 3. (Transitional Measures on Approval, etc.)** As approval, permission, authorization, filing, report, confirmation or registration, etc. (hereinafter referred to as "approval, etc.") received under the previous Law prior to the effective date of this Act shall be deemed an approval, etc. received, respectively, under this Act.

**Article 4. (Transitional Measures on Tax Exemption and Reduction)** Prior to the effective date of this Act, tax exemption and reduction and the retroactive collection thereof shall be subject to the previous provisions with regard to a foreign investment, loan contract, technology inducement contract or public loan agreement approved, reported or executed in accordance with the previous Act.

**Article 5. (Transitional Measures on Penal Provisions)** The application of penal provisions to acts committed prior to the effective date of this Act shall be subject to the provisions of the previous Act.

**Article 6. (Transitional Measures on the Management of the Assistant Funds)** Assistant funds supplied from a foreign government or international organization, etc. prior to the effective date of this Act shall be managed by the mutatis mutandis application of the provisions of Chapter V of this Act regarding public loans.

**Article 7. (Amendment of Other Laws and Relationship with Other Laws)**
Paragraph 1. The Export Free Zone Establishment Law shall be amended as follows:
"The Minister of the Economic Planning Board" of Paragraph 1, Article 11 shall be amended to "the Minister of Finance," and "Chapter V (Article 37 through Article 42) and Article 48 of the Foreign Capital Inducement Act" of Paragraph 2, Article 11 shall be amended to "Article 36 and Article 37 of the Foreign Capital Inducement Act."

Paragraph 2. The Temporary Special Law Concerning Labor Unions and the Labor Dispute Adjustment of the Foreign Invested Enterprise shall be amended as follows:
"Article 6 of the Foreign Capital Inducement Act" of Article 2 shall be amended to "Article 7 of the Foreign Capital Inducement Act."

Paragraph 3. The Technical Service Promotion Law shall be amended as follows:
"Foreign Capital Inducement Act or Law Concerning Inducement and Management of Public Loan" of Paragraph 4, Article 4 shall be amended to "Foreign Capital Inducement Act."

Paragraph 4. Citations by other laws, prior to the effective date of this Act, to the provisions of the previous Foreign Capital Inducement Act and the laws to be abolished under Article 2 of this Addenda shall be deemed a citation to the provisions concerned of this Act.

# INDEX

119–120; people's characteristics, 21; people's traditions, 21. *See also specific headings under* Korea

Special Economic Zones, 193–94

Special interest travel, 263–92; arts and handicrafts, 277–80; business, 216; education, 264–67; health care, 267–68; industry, 281; museums, 284–85; national parks, 285–86; overseas Koreans, 288–89; religion, 268–76; resorts, 285; temples, 282–84; tours, 281–86; visas, 124

Souvenirs, 410, 422–23

Sporting goods, 409

Sports, 117–19, 160; games, 161. *See also* sports *under* Cheju Island; Pusan

Stock corporations, 208–9

Stock market, 188–89

Subsidiaries, 206

Subway, Seoul, 141–42, 313

Suwon, 432–33

# T

Taegu, 446–51; cuisine, 450–51; economy and culture, 446–47; highlights, 448–49; hotels, 450; how to get to, 449; shopping 451

Taejon, 442–45; highlights, 442–45; hotels, 445

Tailoring, 406

Tangun, legendary ruler of Choson, 35

Tax refund shops, 425

Taxation, 181–84

Taxis, 140–41; Seoul, 313–14

Tearooms, 396–97

Technology, licenses, 209–11

Telecommunications, 147–49

Telegram service, 148

Telephone, 147–48

Television and radio, 161–62

Temple of Heaven (Seoul), 354–55

Temples, 282–84; Seoul, 343–44

Textile industry, 96–97

Theater-restaurants, 394–95

Theaters, 156–57, 338, 339, 340

Time zones, 149; conversion chart, 102

Tipping, 132

Toksu Palace (Seoul), 327–31; 360

Tombs (Seoul), 347

Tour groups: choosing, 109–10; costs, 112; itineraries, 110; special interest, 111, 263–92; visas, 125

Tourism, 103–4; arrivals by nationality, 104; domestic, 105; duration of stay, 105; earnings, 104; popular destinations, 104–5; resorts, 107

Tourist centers, 146, 202–4; 214–16

Trade: selling, 194–201. *See* Foreign Investment; Foreign Trade

Trade associations, 231–33

Trade centers abroad, 224–30

Trade fairs and exhibitions, 217

Trademarks, 192; counterfeit, 426–27

Trader's license, 194

Trading companies, 167

Translations, business proposals, 179

Transportation: airlines, 112–13, 126–28, 137–39; boat, 140; buses, 139–40; cruise ships, 128; rail, 139; Seoul, 313–14

Travel connections, domestic, 137–42; air, 137–39; buses, 139–40, 141; rail, 139; rent-a-car, 141; ships, 140; subways, 141–42, 313; taxis, 140–41

Travel connections, international, 126–28; airlines, 126–28; cruise ships, 128; ferry, 128

Travel guides, 523

Travel in Korea, behavior during, 131–33; business, 216; customs,

*Photo courtesy of Hon. Roh Taewoo*